EDUCATION IN A GLOBAL SOCIETY

A COMPARATIVE PERSPECTIVE

KAS MAZUREK

University of Lethbridge

MARGRET A. WINZER

University of Lethbridge

CZESLAW MAJOREK

Pedagogical University of Krakow

ALLYN AND BACON

Boston   London   Toronto   Sydney   Tokyo   Singapore

Executive Editor: Stephen D. Dragin
Editorial Assistant: Bridget McSweeney
Senior Editorial-Production Administrator: Joe Sweeney
Editorial-Production Service: Walsh & Associates, Inc.
Composition Buyer: Linda Cox
Manufacturing Buyer: Dave Repetto
Cover Administrator: Jenny Hart

Copyright © 2000 by Allyn & Bacon
A Pearson Education Company
160 Gould Street
Needham Heights, MA 02494
www.abacon.com

Library of Congress Cataloging-in-Publication Data

Education in a global society : a comparative perspective / [edited
   by] Kas Mazurek, Margret A. Winzer, Czeslaw Majorek.
       p.   cm.
   Includes bibliographical references and index.
   ISBN 0-205-26752-1
   1. Comparative education.   2. Education—Social aspects.
I. Mazurek, Kas.   II. Winzer, M. A. (Margret A.), 1940– .
III. Majorek, Czeslaw.
LB43.E385   1999
370′.9—dc21   99-41940
                                                                CIP

Printed in the United States of America

10 9 8 7 6 5   03

For Barb Krushel in deep appreciation of her dedication to this project, her patience and collegiality, and, especially, her unfailing good humor

Contents

About This Book: An Introduction, Overview, and Study Guide for Students

This introduction is written for you, the student. Please take the time to read it carefully; we have written it to help you get the most out of working with this textbook. We, the editors, will tell you why we compiled this book, why we went about things in the manner we did, why comparative studies courses are important for future teachers, what comparative education is, how this book is organized, what the main findings of the investigations are, and how you can read and study this book for your maximum benefit.

On behalf of our contributing authors, we also warmly invite you to an exciting and informative journey around the world. The teacher educators and scholars who contributed to this book want to share their worlds with you. Think of each chapter as a window allowing you a glimpse into their societies, to help you better understand the realities, successes, problems, and aspirations of teachers, students, parents, and citizens in countries and education systems that are sometimes strikingly different from, sometimes surprisingly similar to, your own experiences and to the future that awaits you as a member of the teaching profession.

COMPARATIVE STUDIES AS A COMPONENT OF TEACHER EDUCATION

Much of current education planning is focused on preparing students for the increasingly interdependent (economically, technologically, politically, ecologically, and so on) world and diverse (multicultural, multiracial, multinational, and so on) societies they will graduate into. This places an obligation on our profession. The need for teachers to have a sound awareness of other nations—their social milieus, cultures, customs, political and economic processes, education systems, and so on—is now well understood by professional educators, parents, and policy makers. Accordingly, teacher education programs in colleges and universities around the world have responded by introducing courses of study and program components to help meet this need.

TYPES OF COMPARATIVE STUDIES IN EDUCATION

Such courses and programs fall under the generic heading of *comparative education,* but may have different labels in different institutions. The most common designations are *comparative studies in education* and *development education.* While we do not wish to gloss over the differences in these varieties of comparative education, this book will not cover extended discussions on terminology. Suffice it to say that all courses in comparative education have at least two characteristics. First, they describe education systems in different nations. Second, the roles of education systems within societies are examined—that is, how they interact with other components of the social structure, the functions they serve, and so on.

These two components constitute the minimum content of all comparative education courses and the core knowledge of programs (i.e. majors, minors, specializations, and so on, in undergraduate and graduate teacher education degrees and diplomas). The editors prefer the term comparative studies in education, will treat it as synonymous with comparative education, and will use the two terms interchangeably.

THE VALUE AND UTILITY OF COMPARATIVE STUDIES IN EDUCATION

There are many specific reasons why a particular course in comparative studies may be offered and different programs may emphasize some elements over others. But a general rationale for all such courses is likely to include the following.

First, there is a sense that current events are such that all societies and their citizens must become very knowledgeable about the world beyond their national borders. Most commonly, this imperative is cast in economic terms. Business and political leaders constantly warn us that the world's economies and financial systems are incredibly interconnected and our material well-being is dependent upon professionals and workers who have a sophisticated knowledge of this new global economy.

But this perspective goes beyond a merely selfish desire to maintain a "competitive edge" in protecting one's standard of living. It is part of a more inclusive belief that the world is becoming infinitely more complex and that events in one nation or part of the world have global ramifications.

As we embark upon a third millennium, we simply cannot afford the luxury of parochialism. There is no place to hide; the world is such that our professional, political, economic, social, cultural, and moral decisions and actions are intimately tied into new global realities. We must possess the knowledge and skills to act wisely and prudently. Unless people are able to grasp issues and events well beyond their homes and national borders, they will not be able to anticipate, understand, and intelligently respond to such events. The new millennium demands sophisticated citizens who are competent to deal with rapidly changing realities.

A second major rationale for comparative studies switches our focus from the global to the local. That is, as teachers you will want to be the most competent professionals you possibly can be. To accomplish this, individual teachers and teachers' professional associations cannot limit themselves only to the knowledge and experience that local practitioners and education systems possess and generate.

Schooling in all its aspects—pedagogical strategies, curricular content, evaluation, classroom management, organization and administration, and so on—is conducted in fundamentally different ways around the world. Research into how children learn, what constitutes "best practices" in pedagogy, how schools serve social and class interests, and so on, is being conducted in many societies and in many different national and cultural contexts. All around the world teachers, departments of education, education research institutes, professors of education, and others are working conscientiously to produce pedagogy, curricula, and diagnostic tools to better serve students, parents, society, and the teaching profession.

Without drawing upon this collective wisdom, without benefiting from the experiences or our colleagues in other societies, without becoming informed of each other's experiments, successes, and failures, our individual professional practices are doomed to be parochial and myopic. We can only know how competent we are, how "good" our professional choices and practices are, if we know the full range of options available and have a fully documented story of the successes and failures of all the alternatives. Individual teachers, schools, and education systems can gain such insights only by consciously reflecting on their practices and theories in the light of information and experiences gathered from around the world and then testing these in the crucible of their own schools. In this sense, comparative studies are an essential strategy for the improvement of local practices.

The third major rationale complements the second, but is more expansive. Improving local practices is a concrete benefit that is the result of enhanced technical knowledge possessed by educators. The educator who is informed about education theory, practice, and research around the world gains more than technical knowledge; also gained are valuable insights that might be labeled "professional" knowledge. Comparative studies do more than merely provide educators with strategies for becoming more effective teachers.

Our earlier discussion emphasized that comparative education courses and programs always do more than merely describe the educational systems of different nations. They also provide analyses of the roles of education systems within societies and how education systems interact with other components of social structures. Such insights allow educators to appreciate the larger social context of the education enterprise. That is, we become aware of the pressing issues of our time, not just in our profession but in our society and around the world.

Such understanding is very important because it is a foundation for fulfilling our responsibility, as privileged members of society, to work toward a better world and to be proactive in public debates about the evolution of schools and societies in a positive direction. This is a great and sometimes ignored responsibility. However, we want you to know that we use the phrase "privileged members of society" very consciously in describing professional educators.

As future teachers, you will be just that. You will be members of a profession; you will have autonomy; you will have authority and control over your society's most cherished possession, its children; you will have the responsibility of evaluating and certifying your students, and your professional judgment will greatly influence their future lives. But you will have an even greater, more general responsibility.

You will be, by definition and by virtue of your credentials, a formulator of public opinion and a leader in the debate of public issues. Your years of advanced education, your position of trust, the power you exercise in your classroom, the respect you command in your community, and the political influence and moral authority your professional associations wield, make it inevitable that yours will be a respected voice in the public domain. It is a burden, responsibility, and privilege that comes with the career you have chosen.

There is a word for this role and responsibility; one that sadly has been out of vogue recently. Your education, social roles, and professional status make you a member of the *intelligentsia*. You, and the professional associations you will be a member of, will be expected to take a leadership role in the social debates—be they political, economic, cultural, or other—of your time. This is not an elitist concept. It is simply a recognition that you have had the benefit of considerable advanced education, that you occupy a position of trust and authority in your community, that you have accepted an inherent duty of continued professional development, and that your career is one of public service.

This is simply the fundamental difference between a job and a profession. A job demands technical competence. A profession demands technical competence and something more, a vocational element. Comparative studies serve our profession well here; they give us a global perspective on world issues and the choices that have to be made as we embark on a new millennium.

APPROACHES TO COMPARATIVE STUDIES IN EDUCATION

Courses in comparative education tend to fall into two general categories: survey courses and courses dealing with specific issues. Survey courses have three basic objectives. First, they seek to introduce students to the field of comparative studies in education. Students begin to learn about the nature of this interdisciplinary field, to appreciate its value, significance, and relevance, and to understand how comparative studies are pursued. Second, examinations of selected countries are undertaken as case studies. These case studies provide the database and substantive content for the third learning objective: comparing national systems of schooling; discerning common themes and trends; appreciating differences; understanding problems and controversies; and drawing conclusions, insights, and lessons.

A second category of courses focuses on specific issues in contemporary schooling, examined in an international context. In such courses, pressing issues in education are illuminated through an examination of how they are manifested in and grappled with in different societies and different national contexts. The scope of issues addressed by the current literature is quite remarkable; for example: equality of educational opportunity; educational achievement; evaluation and examinations; the treatment of minority groups; women in education; formal, nonformal, and informal education; delivery modes; teacher training, certification, and supply; citizenship education; politics, ideology, and schooling; language and literacy; schooling and the economy; education, modernization, and development; education reform; accountability; effective schooling; school administration and governance.

THE NEED FOR THIS TEXTBOOK

Almost all current textbooks in comparative education are tailored to the second category of courses. Many of the texts are excellent and are wholly appropriate for comparative education courses dealing with issues in education. However, they are not well suited for survey courses in comparative education. This is because books taking an "issues" approach assume students possess a great deal of background knowledge about individual countries and national systems of education. That is not always the case. As students, you know very well the difficulty of keeping abreast of local, let alone national and international, developments in education and society. Consequently, texts taking the issues approach cannot stand alone as assigned course texts in survey courses.

For approximately two decades, research in comparative education has exhibited a trend toward ever-increasing specialization. The consequences of this have been both positive and negative. On the positive side, specialization has brought remarkable progress in extending the depth of investigation in narrow and precisely defined subfields. Those subfields are the issues that have been noted in our discussion above. There are many suitable texts on the market that address, in detail, the plethora of issues that have been identified.

On the other hand, this concentration on in-depth studies of specific aspects of education in an international context has resulted in a marked lack of survey textbooks discussing school systems and societies around the world. For students in comparative education courses, the results have been unfortunate. In the absence of overview texts, students must access a wide variety of books, journals, encyclopedias, and government reports in order to piece together a coherent overview of both schooling around the world and the social context of the nations within which schooling is defined and practiced.

Now you understand the editors' motivation for compiling this textbook to provide you with a comprehensive overview of many countries around the world and their educational systems.

The nations and education systems represented in this book encompass a sizable percentage of the world's population: countries that are home to about 2.8 billion people. You will also notice a balance between "dominant" nations—for example, in terms of population, economic, and military power—and less prominent nations. But, above all, our one overriding consideration in the selection and organization of nations was to provide you, within the limited space a textbook can reasonably allow, with a sampling of the diversity and complexity of the world's nations and education systems. These nations have been grouped in five sections by regions. They could have been grouped in a number of ways, but our experience is that people tend to "think regionally," that is, to mentally group nations geographically. Therefore, we felt you would be more comfortable working with this structure.

Our goal is also to encourage you to look beyond the nations represented herein. While each chapter provides an overview of education structures, practices, and so on, as well as a clear picture of the social climate within which each national school system exists, that is not the full extent of the book or each chapter. *Education in a Global Society* presents even more important analytical thrusts: interpreting the cultural forces and social milieu that shape the nature and direction of schooling; understanding the major current debates on the objectives, practices, structures, and functions of education; and discerning the directions in which education around the world is evolving.

Thus *Education in a Global Society* is designed to serve as both an encyclopedic resource (describing national systems, curricula, and programs) and an analytical treatise (defining the social forces shaping national school systems, examining debates about education, projecting the futures of schools and societies). The analyses in this book are a beginning, a foundation, for your continued study of education systems worldwide.

To ensure that your journey begins with the best possible preparation, we invited extraordinarily talented and accomplished scholars and educators to contribute to this book of readings.

A NOTE ON CONTRIBUTING AUTHORS

Because our contributing authors literally speak for the nations represented, the question of who should have that voice was a central consideration. Our strategy was to invite scholars who are themselves residents of the nations they write about and are active professionals within the education systems of their nations. Only a few exceptions to this rule were made. However, even in those cases the contributors are scholars who have extensive professional experience in the nations they write about.

This is important. It allows the cultural uniqueness of the nations and their education systems to come through to readers because contributors are speaking as cultural and education "insiders" of the nations represented. Our quest was to obtain and convey a truly intimate knowledge of societies and schools, one that only an "insider" can adequately capture. The contributor, by definition, will not be observing and interpreting that culture and schooling system from the worldview of another cultural perspective.

We therefore consider any unevenness in tone

and expression between chapters to be a strength of this book. We have edited only for continuity of structure between chapters, length of manuscript, and, because English is a second or third language for many of our contributing scholars, clarity of expression. We always tried to avoid editorial changes that might affect cultural nuances. We did not want to homogenize the distinct voices of many nations into an even monotone.

THE STRUCTURE OF CHAPTERS

However, to assist you in comparing the societies and education systems presented, drawing out common themes, and identifying areas of difference, we felt it important that each of the contributing chapters have a specific and consistent format. Accordingly, authors were asked to write their chapters within the following framework.

The first section of each chapter begins with the heading "The Social Fabric." In this section, authors were first asked to describe and then to explain the major and most significant social realities that constitute the distinguishing features of their nations. Included are elements such as a basic demographic, economic, political, cultural, and religious profile; identification of the major forces and events that shape the contemporary social milieu of the nation; and insights into the unique cultural and social realities of the nation.

It is important to understand why we asked our contributors to begin with an opening focus on the social context for education objectives, practices, and structures. A basic premise of this textbook is that a nation's education system cannot be understood in isolation from the social milieu that defines and nurtures it. The demographic, economic, political, cultural, religious, and historical peculiarities of a nation determine the unique manifestations of schooling in that society. To understand schools requires that the social context that shapes education must be made clear first.

Authors then turn their attention to their nations' education systems, and the nature, contents, processes, and structures of schooling in each nation are described and explained. In this second section of each chapter, entitled "Schooling," guiding educational philosophies, educational objectives, formal legislation and policies, pedagogical practices, student characteristics, curricula, evaluation, teacher education programs, the professional responsibilities of practicing teachers, bureaucratic and administrative structures of education, the organization and governance of schooling are among the topics elaborated.

A primary objective of the second section is to provide a clear and comprehensive description of the education system in each nation. However, there is more to it than that. Accordingly, the authors take care to make the link between education system and social milieu to illustrate the degree to which their nations' education systems are a reflection of the broader social milieu outlined in "The Social Fabric" section.

By this point in each chapter, you will have a very good knowledge base of both the nation and its education system. However, you will develop something even more important; you will begin to have a good "sense" of why things are as they are in that nation. The social forces that have shaped and continue to shape the nation, the characteristics of the education system, why that system is as it is rather than having evolved in another direction, the professional preparation and working lives of teachers, and the contents and processes of schooling will be clearer to you. This is because you will have taken a critical step in trying to "get inside" the cultural and social reality of that nation. This is very important. It begins to allow you to see that society from the perspective of one who lives there. You begin to feel less of a clinical, detached, outside observer.

Of course, this is a very difficult task to accomplish without prolonged physical immersion in a culture. It is too much to ask that this be done through reading, thinking, and discussion alone. Certainly a claim is not being made that you are now able to empathize with and understand that society in a way that its citizens do, but you have gone some distance in that direction. That is important; in fact, very important, because you are now in a better position to appreciate the complexities brought out in the third section of each chapter.

"Major Issues, Controversies, and Problems" is the section where you will grapple with the pressing issues facing each nation represented in this text. First, authors document and discuss issues, controversies, and problems faced by their countries and education systems. Their analyses will make sense to you because, as we have emphasized above, the first two sections have provided you with the background knowledge to understand the issues presented. What are the major issues, controversies, and problems that are taking place in their societies? How are they impacting upon the nature and evolution of the social fabric defined and discussed in the opening sections of their chapters? How are these issues affecting the educational system that was outlined and discussed in the second sections? How are education debates connected to larger social debates? These are the sorts of questions that are addressed in the third section of each chapter.

It is at this point that you will most fully realize one of the important reasons why comparative education courses and programs are included in your professional training. You recall that, earlier, we highlighted the point that comparative studies courses offer educators a global perspective on the issues and choices education systems face as we embark on a new millennium, and they seek to provide educators with insights and analyses that will yield an awareness of the pressing issues of our time—not just in our profession but in our society and around the world.

In the third section of each chapter you will begin to develop this broader perspective. Some of the issues, debates, and problems will be alien to you—concerns of places and peoples unlike the society you live in and the education profession you recognize and plan to enter. But we promise you that is the exception. More often, much more often, the education and social issues, debates, and problems you read about will be eerily familiar, invoking a sense of *déjà vu*. You will be struck by how educators in distant nations and in remarkably different cultures are struggling with the same professional and social issues that concern you as a professional and a person. You will see how much you have in common with your fellow educators around the world. We are bonded more by similarities than alienated by differences.

So what then? The next and obvious step is go beyond understanding to action. But what is to be done? What are the best courses of action in the never-ending task of building a better education system and society? That is the focus of the concluding section of each chapter—"The Future of Society and Schooling." Building upon their discussions and analyses, authors briefly project and speculate upon the direction in which society and schooling will evolve in their nations. Please compare and consider your own analyses, speculations, and projections with theirs.

A BLUEPRINT TO ASSIST YOU

Each contributing chapter provides information and insights in the context of a specific nation and its education system. The cumulative effect of reading all the contributing chapters is a scope of understanding that will help you address the issues relevant to your professional life from a global knowledge base. But your role in this is far from passive. We stress that it is ultimately you, the reader and student, who will integrate for yourself the data, analyses, and lessons from the separate chapters into a coherent, meaningful whole. However, we would like to facilitate that process for you a bit. Indeed, we already have— by ensuring that there is structural consistency between each of the contributing author's chapters. You will not find it difficult to make comparisons and draw out similarities and differences between nations. We are sure that the structural continuity between chapters will allow you to discern thematic coherences and give you a basis for understanding both similarities and differences among the individual nations represented. Your own framework for comprehending these similarities and variations in schooling and society around the globe will emerge.

However, we do not want to put all the responsibility on you, so, to help prepare you for your reading of *Education in a Global Society,* we would like to share with you some of the major lessons and insights we have drawn from our reading of these chapters.

But, please understand that what follows is not intended to be a definitive summary of what this book is about. Rather, it is merely a general blueprint to assist you in reading and finding meaning in the chapters that follow. We only wish to summarize and share with you some of the themes that seemed most important and interesting to us. Our hope is that in sharing these with you we will prepare you to read the chapters and assist you in interpreting and integrating the material.

We therefore would like to list and briefly discuss seven major themes, elements common to virtually every chapter—factors, issues, problems, and so on, that virtually every author feels are important and are addressed in each chapter. You may be surprised by how many similar discussions took place. We encourage you to look for, and think about, these common themes as you read this book.

Finally, we will also provide you with a brief description of each of the five sections into which we have grouped our represented nations that will highlight the unique themes and anomalies found in that section.

MAJOR THEMES

We are struck by the fact that all contributing authors feel the following issues, forces, and developments are very significant. These constitute themes that are reflected in all chapters.

Change

One thing that all authors address, yet have perhaps the greatest difficulty in conveying precisely, is the notion that schools are caught in an era of incredibly rapid change. This change is not localized, it is ubiquitous.

The sense we get from the authors in this regard is almost a feeling of helplessness. It seems that change is so pervasive, so fundamental, and so rapid that education communities do not know how to cope with it. Indeed, looking at the chapter titles, you will be struck by how often the word "change," or a synonym for it, appears. When we break down the changes rocking education establishments around the world into specific components, we find the following addressed most frequently.

1. *Uncertainty on how to prepare students for the future.* This is quite unsettling. We are charged with inculcating the next generation with academic and cultural knowledge, instilling attitudes, habits, and skills that will serve students well in the world of work and prepare them to cope with their responsibilities as members of society. Yet, there is a crisis in the profession because the future is uncertain: What knowledge is of most value? What skills will the economy demand? What values will be appropriate in the new social order students will graduate into?

In other words, educators are in a dilemma because their job is to teach, but as a global professional community we are not confident of what we should be teaching. We are not sure how the content of schooling can keep up with the rapid changes around us. Very often, this crisis is framed in the language of vocational training; that is, what job skills are needed by today's students to succeed tomorrow in a rapidly changing economy. One institutional response to this has been an emphasis upon vocational education. Another is a proliferation of comprehensive schools.

2. *Curricular change.* The above noted uncertainties do not seem to be preventing wholesale innovations in the area of curriculum. Virtually all education systems are embarking upon almost wholesale revisions of their curricula. This is placing an enormous strain on the profession. Teachers are at a loss on how to keep pace.

3. *Pedagogical strategies.* School systems across the world are debating pedagogy, and experimentation in instructional strategies is rampant. Some nations are experimenting with what might be called "progressive" approaches, including ele-

ments such as student-centered teaching and individualized assessment and progress. Others are turning to "traditional" approaches rooted in teacher-centered instruction, uniform curricula, standardized evaluations, and so on. Between these poles, a myriad of alternative and hybrid approaches can be identified in specific nations.

The common theme, however, is that the nations of the world seem to be turning away from monolithic, system-wide, pedagogical strategies. To greater or lesser degrees, depending upon the individual nation, an increased diversity in pedagogical strategies is becoming manifested in schools.

4. *Technological changes.* The need to make teachers and students both aware of technological advances and competent in using new technologies is universally acknowledged. However, there is not a consensus on which technologies are most crucial or how to teach technological awareness. Thus, while coping with technological change is a demand made on both teachers and students, what needs to be done and how it should be done is far from clear.

5. *Administration policies and regulations.* For education systems, there is little bureaucratic or legislative stability in the world today. Fundamental revisions in the structures, rules, regulations, policies, and laws under which schooling is carried out seem to be the norm. Sometimes these changes constitute quite dramatic attempts to revamp virtually the entire education system of a nation. Other times we see incremental changes. Regardless of what the case is in any particular nation, the results—to greater or lesser degrees— are the same: administrative reconstitution of schools and redefinition of educators' duties. The usual justification is that social, economic, or technological changes make these administrative, policy, and legal changes necessary and desirable.

6. *Increased demands on the profession.* Whether this takes the form of more students per classroom, increased teaching hours, or extracurricular duties, the demand for teachers and administrators to do more seems to be universal. The justification for this is often an economic argument. Declining resources are said to dictate such necessities, and this leads into our next major theme.

However, before we leave the theme of change, we emphasize this list of six categories of change is far from exhaustive. Its function is only to illustrate a key point—that societies around the world are in a state of flux. The world is in an era of incredibly rapid social change, and national systems of education are undergoing changes as profound as any other component of society. We also encourage you to look deeply into each chapter to identify additional areas of change that seem to be prominent and significant.

Demographic Transformations

Although this theme could logically be placed under the preceding discussion on change, it warrants a separate category. Nations around the world are witnessing a redrawing of their population profiles. This has tremendous consequences not just for schools, but for the entire social system. Everything from the economy to social security is being affected. These demographic changes assume two major forms.

In some nations, the issue takes the form of an aging population. As ratios of youth to elderly and workers to retired increase, the social welfare systems of many nations are reaching a crisis point. Other nations have the exact opposite problem—a burgeoning population of children who require quite different services. The consequences for education are dramatic.

In societies with aging populations, the expansion of post-secondary education and nonformal education is redefining traditional notions of education and schooling as people become "lifelong learners." Societies with youthful populations worry about how increasing numbers of children can be accommodated in school systems that are already stretched to the limit in terms of resources. And, once these children graduate, will there be jobs for them in the volatile global economy?

But the global demographic landscape is changing in ways other than a redistribution on the basis of age. All nations are becoming increasingly diverse in terms of culture, race, ethnicity, religion, and social ideologies. Even traditionally homogenous national populations are feeling the impact of minority populations and alternative political, social, and cultural views. The result is that school systems around the world are grappling with how to accommodate the minority populations increasingly found in their classrooms and the increasingly diverse worldviews emerging within their societies.

Responses to the forces of pluralism range from embracing diversity to outright resistance in the form of assimilationist policies. However, regardless of dominant groups' attitudes and responses, a new reality is being forced upon all societies. As countries become increasingly diverse in terms of culture, race, and social ideas, their very character is becoming redefined.

Financial Constraints

If it is clear that the world's education systems are not sure of how to cope with the changes buffeting them, it is equally clear that they will not get adequate financial resources even if they agree on what should be done. A financial crisis has gripped the world's school systems; in some cases, it has crippled them. In virtually all nations, the financing of education is a very major concern and issue.

In all cases the underfunding of education was linked to broader economic concerns: the general state of the global economy and the particular state of the national economy. Needs are seen to be outstripping available resources, and there is little indication the situation will improve in the near future. In many countries, the situation has reached a crisis point.

This is an interesting phenomenon in view of our preceding discussion on change. The important roles assigned to schools to meet the challenges imposed on the next generation by a rapidly changing world, the increasing demands placed on the education community, and the number of structural, bureaucratic, legal, curricular, and program changes taking place in the world's education systems all point to the conclusion that education should receive financial priority. This is not the case. Within each chapter you will find documentation on how education is unable to meet its objectives because of a lack of adequate financial support.

As a consequence, difficult decisions have to be made about which education projects, programs, and initiatives should receive priority. This debate is consuming educators all over the world and causing much tension, dissent, and frustration. We encourage you to enter this debate, to evaluate how financial constraints are manifested in your nation and your education system, to compare your situation with that of other nations, and to project solutions and resolutions in light of the knowledge you gather from the experiences of other nations and other school systems.

Inequality of Educational Opportunity

In a world of rapid change and inadequate resources for education, perhaps it is to be expected that there will be winners and losers in the race for access to "better" schools, teachers, and programs. Indeed, that is the case. The most disturbing theme running through this book is the huge and depressing lack of equality of education opportunities for all children.

The particular forms assumed by inequality of opportunity vary. Sometimes there is outright discrimination on the basis of race, ethnicity, gender, or religion. Sometimes the problem takes the form of regional inequalities, as in the case of urban versus rural communities or prosperous jurisdictions versus impoverished areas. Then there are more subtle manifestations, such as bias on the basis of social class or cultural background. These become particularly evident as public education systems become increasingly replaced with private schools catering to selective clientele.

Different as these forms of inequality are, the general phenomenon is pervasive. All nations seem to be struggling with how to provide all chil-

dren equal access to, and services within, the educational arena. Unfortunately, solutions are more elusive than ever, and some societies have literally abandoned the ideal of equality of educational opportunity for all. Perhaps this is understandable in light of the preceding discussion on financial constraints.

Nevertheless, educators continue to resist this trend and work toward innovative, if partial, solutions. Carrying on the battle is becoming increasingly difficult, however. Schools are becoming institutions where, for some, forwarding specific agendas and gaining competitive advantages are the real goals.

Schools as Arenas of Social and Ideological Conflict

Even as changes accelerate and financial hardship grips societies and their schools, one constant remains. Schooling, in the form of credentials earned, continues to correlate significantly with economic success and social status. Indeed, the instability resulting from profound social and economic change has made this increasingly the case. The result is predictable. Dominant groups—identified by economic status, race, gender, and so on—consciously attempt to "use" schools for the advantage of their children.

This, of course, heightens inequalities in educational opportunities. The groups with the greatest resources secure access to the most prestigious institutions, their children enjoy greater academic success, and upon graduation the returns on their education are largest. However, education is a contested arena in more ways than a simple cost-benefit formula equating better schooling with getting a better job.

Some of the most bitter battles in education are being fought over issues that have little to do with economics. Because schools are value-transmitting and consciousness-shaping institutions, political, religious, cultural, and all manner of socioeconomic-ideological groups aspire to have their views legitimized and propagated through the sanction of public and private schools. In this quest some groups and their viewpoints prevail; others are subordinated.

Sometimes the dominant values are nationalistic or cultural, sometimes they are religious or secular, sometimes they reflect political values or social philosophies; usually they are a potent mixture of all these and more. In some places one set of values dominates, in others diverse orientations coexist. However, it is always the case that the situation is dynamic and fluid. Competing viewpoints emerge and education institutions are arenas in which they clash and vie for supremacy. This affects all aspects of schooling—curriculum, pedagogy, authority relations, and so on. To borrow a phrase, schools around the world are a microcosm of societies' culture wars.

Our authors recognize that the schools in their societies stand for something—they are not value-free institutions. Indeed, they are not meant to be. If you think about it, a value-free school system is an education system without a purpose, without a vision. But, with this acknowledged, a problem immediately emerges.

If schools were institutions somehow closed to external influences, then perhaps they might be able to implement a consistent vision or realize a particular ideology. But they are not. As has been repeatedly emphasized, schools are part of a larger social milieu. And, in today's world, no society is completely isolated from external influences.

That is why schools are necessarily arenas of social conflict. Inevitably, different groups in today's increasingly pluralistic world will hold different ideological visions. All want to build a better world through an enlightened education system, but sometimes their visions clash. When that happens, a contest between social factions begins as each wants the education system to recognize, respect, disseminate, and, ultimately, to legitimize its particular orientation.

In reading the case studies in this book, you may be struck by how the values promulgated by some schools systems challenge your own cultural, political, social, economic, and religious views.

We encourage you to wrestle with these issues. As individual teachers, you will bring your values into the classroom, and as an education system your schools have an identifiable value base. What values does your school system embrace and promote? Why do you hold the values you do? Should all viewpoints be explicitly included in schools or should some perspectives take precedence over others? On what bases can the acceptance of some values over others be justified? What are the responsibilities of teachers when it comes to shaping the values of students?

Teacher Training and Qualifications

In light of the themes discussed above, it is obvious that important social responsibilities weigh on teachers' shoulders. Therefore, it should not come as a surprise that all authors addressed the issue of teacher education and certification. Most nations have made substantive changes in both areas recently; those that have not are planning to do so.

Two things are clear: Training is becoming increasingly rigorous and the time of study for certification is increasing. As measured by certification requirements, there seems to be a rapid professionalization of teaching. There is also great diversity; teachers are educated and certified in a myriad of ways around the world. Much can be learned from this diversity as teacher training institutions continue to experiment and refine their programs and approaches.

An Enduring Faith in Schools

Our final theme provides an optimistic note. It is interesting that so much of the above focused on problems and areas of contention. One can be forgiven for coming to the conclusion that our contributing authors foresee a bleak future. That is not at all the case. In fact, quite the opposite is true. In spite of all the issues, dilemmas, and problems facing nations and schools around the globe, and in spite of the fact that education institutions and professional educators have been at best only partially successful in meeting these challenges, societies continue to have faith that their schools and the education community will make progress.

In a way, this validates the belief upon which today's schools are founded—the belief that a better society can be built if we succeed in providing an appropriate and enlightened education for the next and successive generations. That faith unites educators, parents, policymakers, and all citizens in a common cause. It is encouraging to see that optimism reflected in the following chapters.

PART I

The Americas: Struggles for Equality and Quality in a Diverse Hemisphere

It is not the purpose of this and all subsequent Part introductions to provide a comprehensive summary of the chapters in the section. These introductions also do not repeat the seven major themes that are detailed in the About This Book section—those major themes are reflected in every chapter of this book; we encourage you to review them before you start reading individual sections.

Each section introduction will provide general overviews of issues and developments that are of particular significance within the nations represented in that section, with a focus on common elements that emerge from contributing authors' analyses. Highlighting these elements serves to draw attention to education issues and developments that transcend national borders in the geographic regions we are using.

In focusing on common elements, we certainly must not forget that the five countries represented in this first section are diverse societies. We encourage you to look for the individual differences that make them unique and distinct national and cultural entities. Yet, the authors of the chapters on the United States of America, Brazil, Canada, Mexico, and Chile have independently identified several common and significant issues and developments in education. Prominent among these are education reform, economic rationalizations for undertaking reforms, accountability, concentration of authority, and decentralization of responsibility. These have implications for everything from teacher training to preschool education. However, in spite of fundamental reforms, social divisions remain and inequalities persist.

The fundamental reforms under way in all five nations are really quite amazing. Literally all aspects of the education enterprise—from preschool education to university teacher preparation programs; from administration to curriculum—are undergoing sometimes dramatic changes.

In the United States and Canada, some of the more immediate agents demanding these reforms include the media, interest groups, parents' organizations, and politicians. In Chile and Brazil, the impetus is a result of a return to democracy and therefore part of a general and national social/political reform movement. Reforms in Mexico are a response to a combination of political and social agitation.

Yet, these are only the obvious forces pressing reforms. A deeper impetus, economic in nature, underlies the demands for reform. Financial crises, perhaps most dramatically illustrated in the cases of Mexico and Brazil, have imposed an urgency on all education reform ideas. Reform, so it is argued by policy makers, the media, and many other segments of society, is something that goes beyond mere desirability; it is a necessity if wholesale economic and attendant social catastrophes are to be avoided.

The economic imperative is clearly the most significant force that has shaped the reform of education in all five countries. But it is difficult to separate the economic from the political here. Although the arguments advanced are economic in language, they are political in tone, practice, and consequences. Specifically, governments, public opinion shaping institutions, special interest groups, and the business communities have succeeded in making synonymous the ideas of reform in education, public accountability in education, and economic development.

This so-called accountability movement is particularly well articulated in the United States, Canada, and Brazil. The movement is also very pervasive. It involves more than a fiscal agenda and demands for "returns" on public money "invested" in schooling. It also includes education reforms in areas as diverse student evaluation, curriculum revision, pedagogy, and the professional status of teachers.

Ironically, the centralization of authority that the accountability movement requires is simultaneously accompanied by a process of administrative decentralization. Decision-making responsibilities have ostensibly been increased at the local levels. In reality, however, this is a red herring.

To preserve the illusion of not eroding democratic rights at the local level (indeed, the argument is that such rights are being increased), governments are granting regional authorities more power over their day-to-day affairs. However, because the criteria upon which educational institutions are increasingly being held accountable (such things as student achievement results, adherence to the curriculum, satisfaction of parents' organizations, and so on) are not set by local institutions or educators, real autonomy is severely curtailed. Local and regional educators and administrators implement education policies, deliver curricula, and evaluate students and teachers, but they may do so only within parameters and criteria that are determined by higher authorities.

The consequences of this accountability movement, wrapped in the disguise of "decentralizing" and "democratizing" education, are very far reaching. For example, teacher training has been influenced. On the one hand, teacher training is becoming increasingly "professionalized" in the sense that it is moving toward exclusively university-level certification requirements, and length of programs of study are increasing. Yet, the content of teacher training programs is becoming deintellectualized. The emphasis is increasingly on practical programs with a heavy focus on in-school practical experience, classroom management, mastery of curriculum, evaluation techniques, and teaching methods. Correspondingly, what may be labeled the liberal arts component of teacher training—courses dealing with issues, problems, and controversies in education; courses on the social, political, historical, economic, and ideological dimension of public schooling—is becoming deemphasized.

This is understandable in light of the primacy of economic considerations, political desires for control of education, and public demands for accountability in the teaching profession. After all, teachers are going into school environments where their tasks increasingly resemble those of workers rather than autonomous professionals.

The duties of these teacher workers are no longer seriously defined (although lip service is paid) in the liberal-democratic rhetoric of developing creativity, autonomy, analytic skills, and a critical social and political consciousness. Instead, the goal is to ensure that schools produce students with appropriate vocational skills, a sound work ethic, cooperative behaviors and attitudes, and a sense of civic pride and responsibility.

What this translates into is that schools are increasingly defined as institutional vehicles to provide a workforce that is educated in the sense that it will contribute to national economic productivity and technological progress and a citizenry that shares common values and attitudes. Other education objectives are those that complement this. For example, sound literacy and numeracy skills are necessary because they have been shown to correlate with higher national economic productivity and lower social welfare costs.

The drive to realize these goals, as has been emphasized, has affected all aspects of schooling. It is even extending beyond the current boundaries of formal public education. Because school systems are doing only marginally well in the tasks of increasing economic productivity and creating a sense of civic consciousness (as evidenced in alarmingly low levels of student literacy and numeracy, apathy and antisocial behavior among youth, inadequate skills upon entry in the labor force, and so on), further steps must be taken to adequately prepare students. One major problem, it is perceived, is that formal school begins too late in children's lives.

Increasing attention is therefore being paid to the idea of preschool reform. The argument here is that "school readiness" must be increased. That is, schools should take early preventive measures to reduce risks of future literacy, numeracy, and social/psychological adjustment problems in elementary schools, reduce dropout rates, and so on.

Such is the context within which a myriad of separate, and sometimes seemingly unrelated, education reforms may be understood. Yet, as reforms and innovations in everything from education technology to curriculum to pedagogy to evaluation proceed at a breathtaking pace, all five nations continue to be divided on bases as varied and fundamental as race, socioeconomic status, gender, ethnicity, geography, and politics. To date, schooling and educators have not succeeded in bridging these divisions. Nor have they succeeded in equalizing either educational opportunity or achievement.

Yet, schools across the Americas continue to hold out hope that such divisions will ultimately be healed and greater equality of opportunity may be achieved. Perhaps the hope is realistic; the progress documented by our authors has been great in all five countries.

CHAPTER 1

Social Cohesion or Individual Excellence?
Searching for Opportunity and Community
in the United States of America

GLENN SMITH
ROSITA LOPEZ MARCANO

Glenn Smith *grew up in West Texas and holds a Ph.D. in history and philosophy of education from the University of Oklahoma. He has been a full-time faculty member at Oklahoma Christian College, the University of Oklahoma, Iowa State University, the University of Houston, and Northern Illinois University. He is currently professor of educational leadership and policy studies at Northern Illinois University.*

Rosita Lopez Marcano *is a Puertoriquena. She grew up in Chicago on Division Street in the Humbolt Park area. After working her way through the University of Illinois as an adult, she became an elementary teacher. During and after earning her Ed.D. degree from Northern Illinois University, she spent several years as an administrator for the Chicago Public Schools. She is currently an assistant professor in and chair of the Faculty of Educational Administration and School Business Management, Northern Illinois University.*

The United States is a geographically and culturally diverse country. More than 98 percent of its current residents trace part of their family ancestry to other countries, many within the last three generations. Recently, a European professor was in a small, midwestern town to meet with colleagues about developing a "multicultural" exhibit to tour Germany. He arrived during a celebration that this historically rural community calls Cornfest. After eating boiled corn on the cob and wandering with camera at the ready for half an hour through milling crowds of celebrants, the guest said, "This

is all very interesting—but where are the American-looking people?" The faces surrounding him were black, Mexican, Puerto Rican, Korean, Native American, Vietnamese, caucasian, Arabic, Chinese, and east Indian. The host laughed and said, "You're lookin' at 'em. This is as American as it gets." Americans, writes one social commentator, "can now be said to come from everywhere." Calling the United States "the first universal nation," he adds that there "everyone is a minority of some kind" (Wattenberg, 1991, pp. 54, 57).

THE SOCIAL FABRIC

Two circumstances make generalizations about the United States difficult. The first is that nearly everyone on the planet has a mental picture of what life there must be like. And there are as many strongly held metaphorical views about what U.S. culture symbolizes as there are people holding them. Impressions of the United States come from numerous sources. Movies and television influence people's views around the globe. A majority of nation states receive Cable Network News (CNN); a staggering (and growing) number of people see the Academy Awards and the Super Bowl in real time. Ubiquitous U.S. films now make about half of their profits from distribution outside the country. It's a rare village around the world where someone doesn't have a family member, friend, or acquaintance who has visited the United States.

The second factor that makes general observations about the United States problematic is the extremes found there. Direct political jurisdiction extends from Pago Pago in American Samoa to San Juan, Puerto Rico, to Point Barrow, Alaska. It takes longer to fly from one of these three points to another than from the northernmost European capital to the tip of South Africa. Social and cultural distances can be nearly as extreme. The richest 2 percent of U.S. society controls ten times more resources than the poorest 20 percent. The children of the wealthy are twenty to thirty times more likely to earn a four-year college degree than are those from poor families. And, at least until recently, members of one of the multiple linguistic and ethnic cultures found in the country could live out their lives with little knowledge of the beliefs and practices of other citizens in the same geographic neighborhood.

No matter how intensely they may disapprove of some aspects of the country, many people around the world see the United States as a place of opportunity. Most U.S. citizens share this view.[1] Recently, 71 percent of those polled said they believed they had a good chance of improving their standard of living (fewer than half thought so in Holland, Hungary, Britain, West Germany, or Italy); 72 percent said freedom is more important than equality. Only 20 percent thought equality more important. Fewer U.S. citizens (28 percent) think the government should reduce income differences between people than hold this opinion in seven European countries polled, but 69 percent of those asked in the United States believe that opportunities for people to go to college should be increased. In Europe, those thinking college access should be expanded ranged from 55 percent in Britain to 19 percent in Austria (Wattenberg, 1991).

Demographics

Approximately 275 million people inhabit the United States. Current projections suggest that,

until around the year 2020, this number will grow by about 2.5 million per year. After that, annual increases may slow to under 2 million (U.S. Bureau of the Census, 1989, in Wattenberg, 1991). Since the early seventeenth century, immigrants have accounted for a significant portion of population growth. Though the rate is now lower than at many times in the past, emigres still make up about 800,000 of the annual additions. Until the 1950s, more than half of all immigrants came from Europe and Canada. In the late 1990s, only 10 percent of immigrants were from those sources, and the percentage was steadily decreasing. The largest numbers now arrive from Latin America and Asia, a trend likely to continue.

The Census Bureau classifies three-fourths of current U.S. residents as white, non-Hispanics.[2] Most of these have European roots, with Britain, Germany, and Ireland contributing the largest percentage. Most twentieth-century European immigrants came predominantly from southern, central, and eastern countries—despite the notorious 1924 immigration law designed to discourage people from these regions.

Resentment of new immigrants by those whose families arrived a generation or two earlier is a recurring theme in U.S. history. A 1982 Roper poll showed that a majority of people of white, European ancestry thought that English, Irish, Jewish, German, Italian, and Polish immigration had been a "good thing" for the United States. Less than half thought that Japanese, Black, Chinese, Mexican, Korean, Vietnamese, Puerto Rican, Haitian, and Cuban immigrants had been a "good thing." The level of approval diminished, in the order that groups are listed, from 66 percent for the English to 9 percent for the Cubans (Wattenberg, 1991). Some time in the twenty-first century, white non-Hispanics will constitute less than 50 percent of the population. Many optimists about the future of the United States think it will be a "good thing" when minorities become the majority.

It will also be a "good thing" when people admit that it is no longer feasible to officially classify people by race or ethnicity. Intermarriage, and more importantly informal social mixing, has been so extensive that many people who have African or Native American blood don't even know it. Official estimates of 12 percent African Americans or less than 2 percent Native Americans severely understate the actual number of people who have family connections within these "official" groups. Indigenous cultures of Africa and the Americas have penetrated most immigrants in ways that few people recognize (Weatherford, 1991).

Other demographic data of educational significance involve fertility phenomena. The United States, like most of the world, has experienced an overall decline in birth rates. The average fertility rate is less than two children per woman in the United States. However, Mexican Americans, Puerto Rican Americans, and African Americans have higher fertility rates. In large U.S. cities, most of the school-aged children are no longer white, non-Hispanic; most of their teachers still are.

Finally, the baby boomers have had—and are still having—a significant educational impact. In the first half of the 1940s, many people postponed having families because of the Second World War. Then they made up for lost time with a resulting boom that sent a bulge of students through the school systems and then the universities. The schooling industry flourished, then contracted as numbers shrank, then flourished again as the boomers themselves provided a "boomlet" that is currently moving through the schools. Now, as the boomers near retirement, they loom as a major factor in many aspects of U.S. life, including the economy. Will they bankrupt underfunded retirement systems, including federal social security? Accustomed to easy credit, they helped fuel a bull market in the 1990s by investing savings in mutual funds. Optimists say they will enjoy the most splendid retirements of any generation in history. Skeptics caution that a serious market "correction" could leave most with little on which to retire.

Finances

The United States is unquestionably a consumer society. For example, home ownership has re-mained at about 65 percent for the past thirty years. The size of houses has nearly doubled and their cost has increased, making ownership less frequent for people under age 40. More than two-thirds of householders enjoy air conditioning (compared to 12 percent in 1960); 90 percent have cars. Almost all households have color televisions, and a steadily growing majority of these are connected to cable. Nearly everyone has access to telephones; the level of personal computer ownership is increasing rapidly (Wattenberg, 1991). Credit card shopping by phone, television, and personal computer is now widespread.

In contrast to this upbeat picture is the 12 to 18 percent of the society (depending on who compiles the numbers and which indices they use) that social critic Michael Harrington called the "other" Americans. Even in times of optimum employment, every city has "homeless" people living on the streets. Some of them beg; others have jobs. They just don't have houses. While the homeless phenomenon is hardly unique to the United States, it is a feature of life that the press and most citizens ignore. Twenty million poor people in a society whose members think of their country as the world's cornucopia is both ironic and disturbing. The problem is especially severe for single, female heads of household. Census Bureau data show that there are now more than twice as many female-headed families with children under 18 as in the 1950s. They are more than six times as likely to be in poverty as families with two parents (Wattenberg, 1991).

For most of the twentieth century, U.S. citizens saw themselves as enjoying the world's highest standard of living. Until the early 1980s, United Statesians with ordinary jobs could afford food and hotels almost anywhere in the world. By contrast, most visitors to the United States struggled with unfavorable exchange rates and high prices. In the last twenty years, this picture has changed. Now middle-class travelers from several parts of the world vacation in the United States because it's a comparative bargain. And people from the United States must budget carefully if they travel in other industrialized countries. Government programs for the disadvantaged have increased two and a half times since the 1950s, and tax rates in the United States have grown steadily closer to those of comparable countries. Personal savings rates are among the lowest for industrial nations.

Increased taxation has gone partially for schools. Annual expenditure per pupil (in constant dollars) has increased 300 percent from 1960 to the 1990s (U.S. National Center for Educational Statistics, 1992). Only about 6 percent of school funds come from federal sources; the other 94 percent comes from state and local taxes. Despite "equalization" formulas in most states, the wealthiest districts spend from two to four times as much per child as the poorest districts. Increased local spending rates for schools often require direct voter approval, usually a two-thirds majority.

Religion and Philosophy

Many residents of the United States describe themselves as religious. Most religious affiliations are with Christian groups, of which there are many, but Islam and Judaism claim a significant number of adherents. Television ministries have enjoyed popularity in the last twenty years. Because no one sect commands a majority position, the government tries to maintain a neutral attitude toward all religious groups. For this reason, it has traditionally been easy to gain official recognition as a religious organization. For several decades, the courts have consistently insisted on rigorous separation of church and state in tax-supported schools, though school officials sometimes allow religious ceremonies in communities where there is strong public support for these and where a court ruling has not been specifically directed at their district.

Politics

Political arrangements in the United States reflect the consensus paradigm of pragmatism. The two major political parties, Democratic and Republican, are centrist and mainstream. Their rhetoric differs, especially at election time, but their funda-

mental views of the world are similar. Whatever nebulous terms like "liberal" and "conservative" actually mean, both parties try to appeal to the broadest possible spectrum of "stakeholders." One result of this approach is that other political parties (for example, Socialist, Communist, Libertarian) have rarely had any practical impact on what happens, no matter how many votes they may get, because there are no coalition mechanisms. Government at national, state, and local levels is almost always either Democratic, Republican, or a combination of the two. Critics say these are distinctions without differences.

History

Though 96 percent of those responding to a recent poll said that they are proud of the United States (blacks and whites were equally proud to say they were Americans), it is an unavoidable fact that aggression has been a major part of the country's history. All of the territory now under the U.S. flag once belonged to other people. Europeans did not stumble on empty land. They manipulated, negotiated, and waged brutal warfare to wrest it from people who already lived there. Even the "purchases" of Florida and almost everything west of the Mississippi were leveraged through military force. And Hawaii and Puerto Rico came to the United States by conquest, not plebescite. Perhaps this accounts for the extensive violence so often seen in Hollywood films. Maybe it also helps explain why in 1986 both Gallup and Harris polls found that the most trusted institution in the United States was not churches, courts, or schools, but the military (Wattenberg, 1991). This was after the disappointment of Vietnam and before the Gulf War.

SCHOOLING

Taxpayers spend more than three-quarters of a trillion dollars each year to school 45 million young people in the United States. They attend 85,000 schools in 15,000 local education authorities called school districts. The number of districts grows smaller each year as their average size grows larger because of ongoing consolidation. The public school system is so large that it employs nearly 5 million people, most of whom are extensively trained professional educators. These figures don't include several thousand more independent and parochial schools or their staffs and physical plants. Nor do they include a growing number of home schoolers—people who have opted out of regular teaching establishments. And the data do not reflect several hundred billion more dollars spent annually by corporations to offer "basic skills" and other training specific to each company or industry, much of which they believe should already have happened before their employees joined them. The figures also do not include the industries that manufacture the books, backpacks, clothing, busses, athletic, and musical equipment used in this vast enterprise—an undertaking that has for the past decade been under intense scrutiny and criticism by students, parents, the press, employers, and politicians for alleged failures of many kinds.

One-fourth of these 45 million students go to school in the 100 largest local districts in the country. The 7,754 least populated districts in 1992–1993 (53.2 percent of the total 15,030 districts reported that year) accounted for only 1.7 percent of the total student enrollment. The 10 largest districts had 7 percent of the students; 9 of these 10 reported minority students made up more than 50 percent of their pupils. Half of the hundred largest districts have more than 50 percent black, Hispanic, or Asian/Pacific Islander enrollments. Chicago reported that 88.4 percent of its pupils were from minority groups.

Governance and Its Development

Schooling patterns developed from the 1640s to the 1780s, a time when nearly all Europeans thought education the responsibility of church and family. By the late eighteenth century, when thirteen ex-colonies on the Atlantic coast of North America adopted a constitution, most communities had basic schools. These were nearly always in single-room structures, built by voluntary community labor on donated land, serving children from age 3 up to young adults as old as 21. Most pupils were 5 to 12 years old.

Teachers lived and ate with one or more families in the district. Parents usually paid a "head tax" for each pupil, so large schools were more lucrative to teach than small ones. The curriculum was reading, writing, and computation. Extras, like music, Latin, geometry, surveying, or elocution, cost more. In ungraded, multiage classrooms of 30 to 90 pupils, peer teaching was standard. Those who knew each skill best felt honored to help those who hadn't yet learned it—and of course reinforced their own mastery in the process.

By the 1820s, these kinds of schools were often called *common*. This was to distinguish them from *academies*. The strongest academies, like Exeter and Phillips in Massachusetts, were chartered (incorporated) by the state, had more than one teacher, taught more advanced subjects, and cost more. With the exception of a few charity schools for those who could not pay, this system was strongly existential. Those who used schools ran them and paid for them. Individuals and families decided how much and what kind of schooling was enough. The idea that the state should compel attendance, certify teachers, approve curriculum, inspect buildings, or force the childless and elderly to pay for schools was unheard of until the nineteenth century.

Change came in the thirty-year period just before the Civil War broke out in 1861. New Englanders feared loss of social and political control as people poured west to occupy new territories acquired through purchase and conquest. From 1830 to 1860, Henry Barnard of Connecticut, Horace Mann of Massachusetts, and other "friends of education" led a movement that completely redefined the common school. The new common public school would be organized around "townships"; be taught only by state-licensed teachers; have standardized curricula and methods; be supervised by full-time administrators (principals, superintendents) who were also to be licensed by the state; be graded by pupils' ages; be paid for by state and township taxes, not tuition; and be compulsory for all, with fines or jail for parents and guardians whose children did not attend.

The bureaucratized approach rapidly became the official model. One condition of the seceded Southern states' readmission to the Union after they lost the Civil War was that they explicitly adopt the new model in their rewritten constitutions. In 1867, Congress created the United States Department of Education to "promote the cause" of the what Commissioner Harris would soon call "the Anglo-Saxon frame of mind."

Governance in Contemporary Schools

To understand twentieth-century U.S. schooling, one must keep in mind the dynamic tension between those who believe that schools should be judged by how accountable they are to parents for teaching academic skills and those who believe that society will disintegrate unless professional agents of the state acculturate and socialize each generation into uniform civic values. Most of the 5 million professional educators in the United States have been trained to provide civic values, even if it isn't clear just which values should make up the pragmatically correct "frame of mind" for each generation. Many employers and not a few parents yearn for a shift in emphasis back to academic skills. But a technologically sophisticated consumer society wants willing shoppers more than millions of academic superstars. The tension is ongoing, with neither point of view gaining clear ascendancy in either of the two main political parties.

Today's 15,000 "independent" school districts are faint reflections of their historic roots. Unlike the trustees of existential and idealist communities of the early nineteenth century and earlier, today's board members derive their power not from the electorate but from the state constitutions that authorize their existence. Members of most local school boards deal not with schools but with superintendents. Most superintendents (90 percent) are males; 97 percent are white, non-Hispanic. Superintendents don't work with schools. They interact

with principals or, in large districts, with associate, district, or area superintendents and other central office administrators. And they work with school boards. The hallmark of a successful superintendent is his ability to keep a majority of the five, seven, or nine members of his board on his side. His job depends on this. Nearly three-fourths say they have "some" or a "great deal" of job security; 58 percent have been in their current jobs four years or longer (Saks, 1989, 1992).

Principals answer to superintendents but work with schools, and research suggests that the quality of the principal's leadership is usually the biggest single variable in how well a school runs. The majority have twenty or more years of service, work 50+ hour weeks, make 1.5 to 2.5 as much as the average teacher in their building, and feel underpaid. High school principals (88 percent male; 93 percent white) make 15 percent more than elementary principals (60 percent male; 87 percent white). Forty percent of elementary principals are female (Saks, 1992).

Teachers answer to principals and work with students. On average, teachers get paid for working six days more than the 180 days that children go to school. The act of teaching, of interacting with young people and "seeing the lights go on" is what teachers report liking best about their jobs. What teachers dislike most about their jobs are negotiations with school boards over salaries and teaching conditions, being unsympathetically supervised by administrators, and feeling unappreciated by pupils and parents. Gallup polls show that in 1969, 75 percent of parents said they would approve their children becoming teachers; in 1990, only 51 percent agreed that teaching could be a good choice. Another poll at about the same time asked a cross section of U.S. residents to rank eleven occupations. In terms of prestige/status, public school teachers ranked seventh, after physicians, clergy, bankers, judges, lawyers, and public school principals (in that order) but ahead of funeral directors, local political officials, advertising people, and realtors. But rated on "social value," teachers ranked third, after clergy and physicians (Elam, 1989, in Wattenberg, 1991).

Most teachers are white, non-Hispanic (over 90 percent). A majority of secondary teachers are men. At the elementary level, most are women; at preschool and first through third grades, almost all are female. A baccalaureate degree and a state-granted license are usually minimum requirements for regular employment. Some districts bend this rule by hiring "permanent substitutes" or by asking for exceptions in individual cases. About half of teachers, especially at the secondary level, have master's or higher degrees. College students majoring in education in the last few years have shown college admissions scores that are equal to or better than those of noneducation majors (Smith & Smith, 1994).

Structure and Attendance

By the 1950s, all states had adopted a de facto model of six years of elementary and six years of secondary schooling. Children in grades 1 to 3 tended to stay with the same teacher all day. In grades 4 through 6, one main teacher still taught most subjects but more specialized teachers (for example, music, art) took part of the day. Grades 1 through 6 usually exist in a common building. Typically, elementary schools have three to six classes or rooms of each grade. This means that most elementary schools have 350 to 800 pupils and twenty to forty full-time professional staff. In addition to the teachers, most elementary schools have a full-time janitor, secretary, principal, a full- or part-time nurse, and may have a social worker, a reading specialist, and several teachers' aides and parent volunteers. While principals often take over for teachers who are absent, they rarely have classes of their own. They see themselves and are seen by others as full-time administrators, not lead teachers with some added administrative duties.

The first two or three years of secondary school has traditionally been called junior high school. Pupils normally have five to seven subjects, each from a specialist. Teachers usually have a room assigned and pupils move every period (usually 45 to 55 minutes in duration) to the room of the teacher to whom they are assigned for that period.

A significant number of school systems have changed their junior highs to middle schools. Middle schools usually have fifth through seventh or eighth grades. In theory, middle schools should be more child-centered than the traditional subject-oriented junior high. In practice, they often look quite similar. Typically, junior highs or middle schools occupy a separate physical plant. In large enrollment districts, they tend to be two or three times as large as the elementary schools that feed them.

Senior high schools, usually simply called high schools, have separate physical facilities—often including extensive athletic fields—and include either grades 9 to 12 or 10 to 12. Larger high schools typically enroll 3,500 to 5,000 pupils and may have 200 to 300 teachers. They may have a dozen or more counselors and social workers. This group handles discipline, truancy, and student recordkeeping, usually under the supervision of an assistant or associate principal. They also help students choose appropriate courses.

To graduate from most high schools, students must successfully complete at least 16 Carnegie units. This means not less than two or three years of English, one or two years of math, two or three years of social studies, two years of science, three years of physical education, and five or six one-year electives. Each unit represents approximately 5 clock hours per week for an academic year. Graduation is based on accumulating the minimum number of required units in each mandatory category. Each teacher determines whether a student passes or fails each subject or unit. While most students take several standardized achievement tests before leaving high school, these do not substitute for teacher-made tests. Except for Advanced Placement tests and CLEP tests taken by a small number of academically talented eleventh and twelfth grade students (for freshman college credit), there is no equivalent in the United States of the British O and A levels or of the French baccalaureat exams or the other European versions of these.

Most of the fifty states now mandate attendance at school from ages 6 to 16 (or in some states through the completion of eighth grade). But practice exceeds the law. Nearly three-fourths of 3-year-olds are in preschool or day care. Nearly all 5-year-olds attend at least half a day of kindergarten. The growth of single parent families (marriage rates have dropped 45 percent since the 1950s and divorce rates have doubled) and two-income families means that most parents must arrange child care as soon as feasible after birth. And even families with a parent at home send children to preschool and kindergarten to ensure readiness skills by first grade. Except for a few parents who want home schooling (and have an approved adult available as teacher), nearly all 6-year-olds are in school. About 80 percent stay until high school graduation at 18. The finishing rate is higher for whites, a little lower for Asians, somewhat lower for blacks, and still lower for Hispanics and Native Americans. But many of those who dropout later finish General Equivalency Diplomas (GEDs) as adults.

Households with substantial incomes (2 to 5 percent of the population) can usually buy any kind of schooling they want for their children. The next most affluent 10 to 15 percent may have a choice of parochial or tax-funded schooling. Most of the rest must send their children to the public— that is, tax provided—school that their school district designates. This doesn't always mean the closest school to their residences. During the first sixty years of the twentieth century, many districts drew "attendance boundaries" to keep down excessive mixing of upper and lower social classes. In the last four decades, districts have either voluntarily redrawn attendance boundaries, or in some cases been forced by court order, to ensure racial, ethnic, and social class mixing. Many parents are not happy about this development.

Curriculum

Since 1918, tax-funded schools in the United States have generally followed the sentiments expressed in a U.S. Office of Education/National Education Association document called *Cardinal Principles of Secondary Education*. This was the foundation of comprehensive rather than specialized (academic, vocational) secondary schools. The seven principles are health, command of fundamental processes, worthy home membership, vocation, citizenship, worthy use of leisure, and ethical character (Cohen, 1974).

The *Cardinal Principles* sought to ensure "cooperation, social cohesion, and social solidarity" while providing for selective educational achievement. All pupils were to mix socially through music, drama, sports, dances, and extracurricular clubs. But there was no thought of everyone taking physics, advanced mathematics, or Latin. "While developing . . . distinctive and unique individual excellencies, the . . . school must be equally zealous to develop those common ideas, common ideals, and common modes of thought, feeling, and action whereby America, through a rich unified and common life, may render her truest service to a world seeking for democracy" (Cohen, 1974, p. 2278).

An elective system under careful supervision of guidance counselors used standardized tests to track students into one of three main streams: college preparatory, commercial, or general. College preparatory students who sat in the same algebra courses were also together in all or most of their other classes. Commercial track students had typing and bookkeeping together—and in the same English, social studies, and business arithmetic classes. General track students, by having home economics or shop classes in common, also saw each other in every other class they took. In theory, any student could elect any subject. In practice, counselors could usually persuade pupils toward "appropriate" courses. Of course, much of the tracking had already been in place since first or second grade on the basis of reading readiness tests and teacher recommendations. This remains the modus operandi of U.S. schooling.

Students

Most U.S. secondary school structures, policies, and procedures came into being between 1870 and 1920. It was a system predicated on the assumption that many students would drop out before graduation. In 1870, less than 3 percent of 17-year-olds were enrolled in high school; in 1920, about 15 percent were enrolled. By 1970, nearly 80 percent of students and parents had learned how to keep the schools from "cooling" them out before age 17. But the testing/tracking/grading system of earlier years continued an implicitly adversarial system between teachers and a majority of students.

Robert Rosenthal (1973) found that students who get the best teaching and most approval from teachers are those whom the teachers think *should* succeed. Those who get the least extensive attention and approval from teachers are, surprisingly, not those who do least well. Students who do well *despite teachers' believing they shouldn't* are the ones whom teachers most ignore and disapprove. It's no surprise that working class, black, Hispanic, and Native American students—taught by middle-class white, non-Hispanic teachers—drop out in the largest proportions.

College and University Attendance

The United States has about 1,500 four-year baccalaureate degree granting colleges and universities. The annual cost of books and tuition is from a few hundred dollars to more than the national average family income. Most provide some partial or full scholarships. Junior (now usually called community) colleges offer low-cost, often high-quality alternatives for gaining the first two years of four-year college degree programs in most metropolitan areas. They also offer vocational training. Community colleges developed rapidly in the second half of the twentieth century as democratic alternatives to expensive, elitist institutions. Anyone with a high school diploma (including a General Equivalency Diploma) can enter. Classes are scheduled to accommodate both working adults and full-time day students.

For the past 200 years, collegiate access has been greater in the United States than in most other countries. Two factors help explain this phenomenon. The first is that even before independence in the 1780s, colonists had established a number of colleges that did not answer to "mother country" supervision. The second is that when the new country officially got underway in the 1790s, all collegiate and university establishments had sectarian religious connections. Since no single denomination had a monopoly, most of the new states made chartering colleges easy and inexpensive so as not to favor one group over another.

This tradition has continued. It is still relatively simple in many states to incorporate a degree-granting university. One result is that some of the 1,500 colleges and universities are not well funded or academically strong. Another result is that somewhere in the United States a college seat exists for almost any high school graduate who really wants one.

From 1940 to 1980, the percentage of 25- to 29-year-olds with 4+ years of college and one or more degrees went from 6 percent to 22 percent. It remained at about 22 to 24 percent in the 1990s (Wattenberg, 1991). Half the entering college freshmen drop out each year. Around a third of these return later (Kowalski, 1977). The dropout rate is much lower for selective (usually expensive) colleges than for open admission institutions.

MAJOR ISSUES, CONTROVERSIES, AND PROBLEMS

As a new century and millennium open, U.S. schools and the citizens who use them appear to be more and more philosophically incongruent. Professional educators—trained almost exclusively in pragmatic and social reconstructionist views of reality, knowledge, and values—find themselves bravely trying to build a new social order through the schools. They agree with the *Cardinal Principles'* assertion that schools are "the one agency that may be controlled definitely and consciously by our democracy for the purpose of unifying its people" (Cohen, 1974, p. 2278).

Pragmatists think that ultimate reality is

unknowable, so they advocate basing everything on shared experience. Knowledge, beauty, and truth are always in process of being socially constructed and are therefore always subject to change; today's essential knowledge or skill may be tomorrow's discarded artifact. Curriculum must evolve with community consensus about what's most worthwhile at any given time. There is no power greater than human imagination; therefore, humans working together to make better communities is the ultimate good.

A significant number of twentieth-century U.S. citizens have never agreed with the assumptions on which pragmatism rests. Three other philosophical approaches—scientific realism, idealism, and existentialism—claim significant numbers of adherents.

Scientific realists, for example, believe that reality—how things really are and have to be—is knowable, is material in nature, and is independent of human perception or wish. Philosophical idealists share the realists' view that how things really are is knowable and not socially constructed. They see the "ground of our being" as ultimately spiritual, not material. Existentialists believe that reality is subjective and individually constructed. Choice and responsibility are the watchwords and any attempt to force individuals to conform to group norms is to be resisted, even if the costs of doing so are high.

Of course, most citizens don't think or talk in terms of philosophical categories. The dissatisfactions they feel about their school systems are specific, but the specifics tend to fit into each person's overall philosophical orientation. And there are enough specifics so that it is clear that many people are not pleased.

The "unity" envisioned by the *Cardinal Principles* authors has not fully occurred, partly because it was a unity envisioned by professional educators (90+ percent white, non-Hispanic) and violates the cultural norms of numerous minority groups. In fact, the disjuncture was so obvious by the 1970s that the American Association for Colleges of Teacher Education (AACTE)—made up of administrators of teacher training programs in colleges and universities who were themselves overwhelmingly white, non-Hispanic—felt compelled to declare "that there is no one model American." Educators were encouraged to recognize and promote the diversity in schools and society as a positive aspect of American life (AACTE, 1972).

There are many specific issues in contemporary U.S. schools. We've grouped the more pressing ones into five categories: purpose, approach, restructuring schools, gangs, and choice. Each is briefly discussed.

Purpose

In the 1950s and 1960s, one could have reasonably assumed that the pragmatic agenda of moving all U.S. people to common ideas, ideals, and modes of thought, feeling, and action was well on the way to fulfillment. In fact, much of this happened across the twentieth century. If it had not, 90 percent of black and white respondents would not say they are proud to be Americans. But as the new millennium begins, the question is open as to whether schools can foster enough individual choice, social unity, spiritual transcendence, and traditional academic excellence to keep all factions satisfied.

So far the professional education bureaucracy, including the two main teachers' unions (the American Federation of Teachers and the National Education Association), has been able to block moves to create vouchers—certificates entitling parents to their children's share of per capita tax funds to be used in buying whatever kind of education parents and students want. The education establishment has offered instead the possibility of school choice. While this appears to offer some advantages, it means parents must shop on a first-come, first-served basis among existing tax-funded schools, usually only in their own local district. They must then get their children to school and back home at their own expense. What shows plainly in these transactions is that the professional education bureaucracy has a vested interest in maintaining the status quo.

Approach

Researchers, mainly in the scientific realist tradition, have found promising results in their quest for approaches that will allow anyone to learn any subject at a high level of proficiency. We mention four separate streams of this research, involving learning styles, multiple intelligences, the pygmalion effect, and bilingual instruction.

Learning Styles   It appears that people have four primary modes or preferences in how they encounter and process information. Some of us are random or global; others of us see reality sequentially. Some of us experience the world abstractly while others need concrete, hands-on experience; they want to learn specific skills or accomplish tasks by doing the things concretely.

To approach learning styles, many educators advocate cooperative learning or peer coaching. These were standard approaches in one-room, district schools but fell out of favor with the advance of organized age-specific grading. Now researchers are showing that most people learn better in a cooperative rather than competitive atmosphere. Some cultural groups—for example, Native Americans—have strong preferences for and do much better when sharing responsibilities for teaching and learning (Locust, 1988; Thilde & Shriberg, 1990).

Multiple Intelligences   For most of this century, professional educators have put students into treatment groups by assessing their intelligence through standardized achievement tests. These tests have been strongly oriented to spatial relationships, linguistic rules/English vocabulary, and logical/mathematical principles. These are three of seven intelligences that Harvard cognitive scientist Howard Gardner has exhaustively researched. The other four are musical, bodily kinesthetic, interpersonal knowing, and intrapersonal knowing (Gardner, 1983, 1993). Each person has all seven, according to Gardner, but each of us tends to have greater natural facility in one or two than in the others. Although schools address all seven, typical tax-funded schools favor the three stressed by achievement tests.

Pygmalion Effect   To go with the idea that almost everyone is more intelligent than we ordinarily suppose, consider the work of Harvard psychologist Robert Rosenthal and California teacher Lenore Jacobson. In *Pygmalion in the Classroom* (1968) they described an experiment in a working-class elementary school. They administered a standard IQ test to all eighteen rooms (grades 1 to 6) of the school. Without looking at how anyone actually scored, they randomly selected 20 percent of the names from each classroom and told the teachers of each room that their test had predicted that those children were about to start performing much better than they had been doing, whatever that was. Eight months later they retested with the same IQ test. Both experimental and control groups gained IQ points, but on average the 20 percent randomly selected group gained 4 more IQ points from pre- to posttest than did the 80 percent not so designated.

Bilingual Instruction   In 1974 the United States Supreme Court said that non-English-speaking students of Chinese ancestry in San Francisco were entitled to instruction in their first language. The court did not accept the district's argument that such an arrangement would be too expensive (*Lau v. Nichols,* 1974). The same year, another court gave a similar ruling about students from Spanish-speaking homes in Portales, New Mexico (*Serna v. Portales Municipal Schools,* 1974). Based on these decisions, many districts provide some instruction in languages other than English for students of limited English proficiency (LEP). While some schools teach all students in two languages, most programs are transitional; they seek only to offer a bridge so students won't fall behind while learning English.

Bilingual education has strong opposition, although efforts to declare English the official language of the United States, either by federal law or by constitutional amendment, have so far failed to generate enough support to be enacted. However, the courts have softened their early stand (*Guadalupe Organization, Inc. v. Tempe Elementary School Dist.,* 1978; *Keyes v. School Dist. No. 1,* 1975). And parents cannot keep their children out of school if instruction in the parents' heritage and culture is not offered (*Matter of Baum,* 1978; *Matter of McMillan,* 1976).

Restructuring Schools

Every U.S. president since Lyndon Johnson in the 1960s has addressed school issues and called for change. Some states and some large cities have undertaken massive reform campaigns. Still, problems persist.

When Abraham Maslow (1970) postulated five basic human needs, he ranked safety second from the most basic. Safe is what students, teachers, and administrators want to feel but often don't, especially in the country's large, urban secondary schools. In fact, a significant number of schools fail to provide for the highest four of Maslow's five basic needs (physiological, safety, social, esteem, and self-actualization).

The problem with schools, says John Maguire, a California university president, is to be found in relationships. Good relationships are hard to have in top-down bureaucracies. Asymmetrical power comes from the state to the school board to the superintendent to the principal to the teachers and is exercised on (sometimes against) the students. Information flows the same way. Directives can be issued, offices reorganized, strategic plans redone, but little dialogue occurs. Boards evaluate superintendents who evaluate principals who evaluate teachers who evaluate students. Boards can fire superintendents who can fire principals who can reassign teachers who can fail students. None of this can happen in the opposite direction. The flow is unidirectional. Communication is a two-way process that can't happen because the structure doesn't allow for it.

Add to this the fact that the entire system is conceptually built on the notion of the standard curve. The grading scale—only invented in the twentieth century—assumes a few As, some Bs, two-thirds Cs, some Ds, and a few Fs. So the student–teacher relationship is adversarial from the beginning. To get a grade lower than B is to be out of grace in a system that evaluates, sorts, tracks, and rewards on grades. It's hard for 100 percent of the students to be in the top 20 percent for grades. Someone must lose in this zero sum game. What kind of relationship should a prisoner have with his jailer, a slave with her master?

Thirty years ago, Jerry Farber, a California college English teacher, wrote an essay entitled "The Student as Nigger." It circulated widely, though mostly underground (Smith & Kniker, 1975). Farber cited separate restrooms, lunch rooms, lounges, for teachers and students as a parallel of Southern "separate but equal" laws for whites and blacks. He pictured young women kneeling before male principals (many schools required women's skirt hems to be knee length, so kneeling was a standard way of verifying this) in what he called rituals of mock fallatio. Most teachers and administrators didn't like the book. Many students identified with it.

The rituals may have changed since the 1960s, but the relationships appear to be the same. A group of Claremont University researchers recently concluded, after collecting and analyzing 24,000 pages of information, that it is accurate to consider the serious problems facing students, teachers, and schools as consequences of more deeply rooted societal problems (Institute for Education and Transformation, 1992). Among the other Claremont findings: Students want both rigor and fun, and they want schools that are orderly, spacious, and beautiful—and that reflect the cultures from which they come. The schools they attend often don't have these qualities. Students see little relevance to their lives in most of what they study; teachers say they are bored by much of what they are must teach. Many students, especially those of color, say they experience schools as racially and ethnically prejudiced. Fear, name calling, threats, violence, and hopelessness too often characterize urban schools. Students, teachers, and others who work in the schools sometimes fear physical violence. Drugs, gangs, and random violence threaten some students, especially in inner city schools. They usually feel physically safer in classrooms than in hallways between classes and traveling to or from school.

Delinquent Behaviors and Gangs

Since 1970, 18 percent to 26 percent of citizens polled by Gallup on the issue of "the biggest problem with which the schools must deal" cited discipline. This was the number one worry until 1986. That year, drugs took first place (28 percent). Since then about one-third of U.S. adults list this as the biggest problem schools face. Other polls show that drug use among students went up steadily until 1981 and has been slowly and steadily declining since (Wattenberg, 1991).

In general, schools have followed U.S. society in expanding the categories of delinquent behaviors and then amplifying social interventions aimed at controlling the new crimes. The country has built more prisons. The result: 3.5 times as many prisoners in 1990 as there were in 1955. Schools use a variety of methods to ensure orderly operations: security (police) in the buildings, metal detectors, video surveillance, and strict background checks of all school personnel. Locked doors and electronic equipment often greet visitors as they try to enter schools. Children have been seriously hurt and some have even lost their lives over expensive gym shoes and jackets that depict their favorite sports team. Many districts advise parents against buying these items for their children, and many schools have implemented strict dress codes that prohibit logos of any kind on clothing, notebooks, or backpacks. Schools often send students home if they do not comply; some schools require uniforms instead of street clothes, but this is not yet a widespread practice. A number of school districts have adopted what they call the zero tolerance approach. Of doubtful legality, this "police-state" orientation guarantees automatic expulsion from school of any student engaging in any activity that might pose harm for anyone in the school. Despite (some critics say because of) these stringent precautions,

school violence and crime do not seem to be declining.

Related to, but hardly synonymous with drugs, violence, and discipline problems in schools is the phenomenon of street gangs. Associated in popular imagination with movie parts played by actors like Marlon Brando and James Dean, many white, non-Hispanic adults in the United States suppose that gangs are a fringe element in which a few teenaged boys go through macho rituals as part of growing up. There is an assumption that if "regular people" stay out of "bad" neighborhoods and "hard core" urban schools in especially tough areas, gangs will have no effect on most citizen's lives.

This is a major misconception. Ernest Gonzalez, Assistant Principal of Elgin High School just outside of Chicago, is one of the country's foremost authorities on gangs. He estimates that more than 90 percent of all students in every major U.S. city's schools are affiliated with one of the 200 or more gangs that operate independently or are under the auspices of either the Bloods or Crypts on the west coast or the Folks or Disciples on the east coast or in the midwest. Most suburban and even many small town schools have a gang presence.

Affiliation can be at one of several levels. At the center are adults, often in the burgeoning prisons where virtually all prisoners are now affiliated. Ultimate command decisions are made here. At the second level are young adults not in prison who oversee day-to-day operations. At the third level are minors, many in middle school or junior high, who do the dirty work if any must be done. They are eager to prove themselves and incur smaller penalties if caught carrying a weapon than is the case for older members. At the next level are girlfriends, and at the next close family members and friends who aren't active participants but who know and understand what's happening and who have the gang's protection. At still a more remote level are "crew," young people who show affiliation by wearing the colors (with permission) and playing the music associated with the gang—even though they aren't officially members. Finally, there are people from the neighborhood and the school who don't display the gang's symbols and who are also not official members but who have allegiance to the gang and receive protection.

Some teachers are gang affiliates, as are some police officers, some lawyers, and others. While the organizations deal in drugs and weapons, two lucrative sources of income, they also invest legitimately in neighborhood retail businesses. Gang leaders quickly develop the leadership skills required to head major corporations. They have become a kind of unofficial nobility, much like soldiers of fortune who fought and negotiated their way to dukedoms and earldoms in Europe prior to the emergence of nation states. And as offensive as drive-by shootings may be, gangs don't do anything that citizens haven't watched footage of their government's agents doing on the 6:00 o'clock news.

Recently a white, non-Hispanic teacher petitioned officials to suspend a Hispanic student for insubordination—meaning that the student tried (politely) to explain something about his assignment. The same student's gang leaders petitioned school officials for another chance for the young man. In return, they guaranteed that he would do all his future homework on time and to the letter of the teacher's requirements, that he would attend all classes, never appear disrespectful toward the teacher, and be well prepared for all examinations. They kept their pledge. Gangs now want their members to succeed in school. Many urban and suburban administrators who respect students and, in return, have students' respect, can tell these kinds of stories.

Choice

If the professional school lobby and their pragmatic supporters continue to insist on the seven cardinal principles as the central purpose of schools, critics of that belief system say several things must happen. One is that the normal-curve-based grading system designed to cool out a substantial proportion of students must be replaced by an evaluation system genuinely grounded in helping each student realize all, or at least most, of her

or his potential. This means that all minorities must be treated as if they are the wonderful addition to the society that they, in fact, are. To do this, far more black, Spanish-speaking, Asian, and Native American teachers and administrators must be licensed. This will mean significant changes in current admissions practices in nearly all professional education programs. Official nondiscrimination rhetoric will not suffice. Real people will have to be admitted and graduated. And more real choices will have to be allowed: dual language academies, alternative and specialty schools, home schooling, vouchers—whatever it takes to provide meaningful access to the education that pupils and their parents want.

THE FUTURE OF SOCIETY AND SCHOOLING

Forecasting is, to put it mildly, an inexact enterprise. Guessing what will likely happen depends on what's assumed. Will the future be an elaboration of the current paradigm? Or will fundamentally different assumptions about how things are (ought to be, must be) shape a future that is dramatically different from the past and present?

To put this concretely in the context of twentieth-century U.S. schooling, will the twenty-first century see mass marketing, mass democracy, mass entertainment, massive cities, and mass schooling continue—with appropriate reforms and adjustments? If so, the main outlines of the future are reasonably clear. Minorities will win more concessions but will inexplicably stay a little behind the curve set by white, non-Hispanic leaders. Schools will look pretty much as they do now, but will have more computers. Schools in poor neighborhoods will be more crowded and less attractive than those in wealthy areas. Teachers will have more and better training, will be members of a strong union, and will enjoy about the same social status as they now have. The United States will dominate the world militarily, economically, linguistically, and culturally. People everywhere will play U.S.-style basketball, football, and hockey. Hollywood will be synonymous with entertainment, and no one anywhere in the world will be farther than a half hour's drive from a bucket of Kentucky Fried Chicken. The reader can continue this extrapolation with ease.

This picture, or a close variant of it, is what the twentieth-century pragmatic paradigm promises. It is what optimistic proponents of that way of understanding reality see coming. The problem with seeing things from inside the dominant paradigm is that all other ways of understanding are either absurd or invisible. So the forecasting question seems to come down to whether the pragmatic paradigm will prevail. If the answer is yes, we need not linger on the deliberation. If the answer is no, even the near future may look dramatically different from the present.

Advocates of two philosophical paradigms that have long competed with pragmatism say change is already strongly underway. These are existentialistic and idealistic proponents whose basic views are mentioned earlier in the chapter. Existentialists believe in choice and individual responsibility, including the power for each person to make a life world that is whatever she or he wants and is willing to be responsible for. Idealists think the phenomenal world of sensation is a misleading curtain, hiding an existence of peace, love, balance, and spiritual insight. Sincere believers in both these approaches think pragmatism's dominance is ending. Pragmatists fear that existentialists and idealists are dangerously delusional. These beliefs have energized disagreements throughout the twentieth century, and the battle seems to be intensifying.

The existential critique and forecast is elaborated by James Davidson, an American of early colonial lineage, and Lord William Rees-Mogg, English peer of the realm. They divide the world's social history into four stages of economic life: hunting-and-gathering, agricultural, industrial, and information (Davidson & Rees-Mogg, 1997). In their estimation, the fifteenth-century change from agriculturally based economies to industrial ones was traumatic but less so than the current switch from an industrial to an information-based economy. They draw a parallel between the dominant role of organized religion in the fifteenth

century and that of government at present. They see the collapse of the Soviet Union as an indicator of the future for all large industrially based entities, including nation-state governments. As national governments recede and downsize, so will schools become a shadow of their former selves. Instead of looking to governments to provide services, individuals and small groups will contract for these.

The information society, with its network economy, works on opposite assumptions from its industrial forerunner. As Kevin Kelly, executive editor of *Wired* magazine, points out,

> The technology we first invented to crunch spreadsheets has been hijacked to connect our isolated selves instead. Information's critical rearrangement is the widespread, relentless act of connecting everything to everything else. We are now engaged in a grand scheme to augment, amplify, enhance, and extend the relationships and communications between all beings and all objects. That is why the Network Economy is a big deal. (Kelly, 1997, p. 140)

There are too many implications of the changes at work to discuss all of them here, but six will illustrate. First, in the industrial age, value came from scarcity (oil, diamonds, carpets), but in the network economy value comes from abundance: Each fax machine increases in value (while decreasing in cost) as more machines join the network. Two, citizenship is obsolete. The network economy can work from any geographic location, so why not choose one with friendly tax laws and a pleasant climate. Three, communication is wireless, rapid, and getting cheaper. Friends and customers can live anywhere and stay connected. Fourth, seeking opportunities, which is about an unfolding future, is more important than solving problems, which is about our weaknesses from the past. Ideas will become a form of wealth. Five, encryption will be vital in the network economy, which will become larger than any nation state economy. And finally, large-scale organizations will "devolve" and careers will be replaced with "patchworks of vocations" (Kelly, 1997, p. 196).

Based on these and related projections, citizens give way to netizens who are, to use Davidson's and Rees-Mogg's term, "sovereign individuals." By implication, expensive, place-bound universities should be replaced by virtual universities operating mainly in cyberspace. Faculty members and students can live anywhere in the world. They can meet online. Actually, a number of traditional universities already offer degrees online. Any issue of the Sunday *New York Times* advertises a substantial number of such programs.

Even more indicative of the probable future of the effect of the Internet and World Wide Web on higher education are not so traditional institutions that have been operating for only a couple of decades—for example, the University of Phoenix, the Fielding Institute, the California Institute of Integral Studies (CIIS) all offer degrees in which the internet and the World Wide Web figures centrally. The differences between these and usual universities is more radical than the absence of athletic teams and mascots. These are not electronic correspondence schools. Their students interact with each other and with their teachers on profound levels. Elizabeth Kasl and Dean Elias note that a cohort of doctoral students at CIIS got to know each other faster and at a much deeper level when they did not meet face-to-face until several months after working together on the Internet (Kasl & Elias, 1997). The program's director, initially skeptical that online learning could be effective, ended up a strong advocate: "In some mysterious holographic sense, the whole person is present in the on-line script, and the quality of intimacy develops when participants disclose authentically and receive others compassionately" (Kasl & Elias, 1977, p. 27). Of course, anyone who has "cybered" could have told him that.

If virtual universities succeed, why not virtual high schools? Students could still meet in person for social and athletic events. At the same time, physical plants would shrink, as would administrative and ancillary jobs. Learners (or their parents) would buy whatever instruction they wanted. When Ivan Illich suggested such an idea (1970),

pragmatic educators dismissed the idea. If Davidson and Rees-Mogg (1997) and Kelly (1997) are right, these changes will come to pass whether today's educators approve or not: "To a greater degree than most would now be willing to concede, it will prove difficult or impossible to preserve many contemporary institutions in the new millennium. When information societies take shape they will be as different from industrial societies as the Greece of Aeschylus was from the world of the cave dwellers" (Davidson & Rees-Mogg, 1997, p. 14).

Some idealists and many existential idealists foresee a future that in many ways complements the existential analysis just described. They see a building energy force leading more and more people to turn inward in search of the path back to internal peace, centeredness, and "God-realization." While much of the language is compatible with that of churches and traditional religion, many people in this movement are not church members. They draw on classic idealist writers like Plato and Emerson, on mystic writers like Kabir and Osho, on self-help authors like Shakti Gwain, Depak Chopra, and Louise Hay, and on autobiographic accounts like those of Dannion Brinkley and Brian Weiss. They don't agree about everything but find common ground in an optimistic view that loving and purposeful spirit undergirds all of existence and that every life is part of each entity's search to reunite with cosmic harmony.

Neither idealism nor existentialism are new concepts, but both perspectives seem to have found renewed expression in the United States as the millennium closes. Their energies, which in many ways resonate in reinforcing patterns, present a challenge to the dominant paradigm. The result remains to be seen. In the midst of substantial disagreements there is some anxiety about the future—and a great deal of optimism.

ENDNOTES

1. Except in direct attribution to other sources, we avoid using the word "American" as a synonym for cit-

izens or residents of the United States for two reasons: (1) Canadians, Mexicans, Colombians, Guatamalans, Chilanos, and so on have as strong a claim to Amerigo Vespucci's name as do people in the United States; (2) some citizens of the United States—notably Hawaiians and Samoans—are not geographically part of the Americas. We generally employ the awkward usage of "U.S. citizens" or "U.S. residents," but in this chapter we sometimes follow the suggestion of our colleague Ernest Gonzalez and use the term "United Statesians." The linguistic logic is consistent with Germans, Mexicans, Canadians, and so forth.

2. We realize that many United Statesians of Spanish-speaking heritage do not appreciate being lumped together as Hispanics because of the European colonial baggage of that term. We use it in this chapter, despite its disrespectful undercurrent, because it is a U.S. Bureau of the Census official category for which no alternate term is available.

REFERENCES

American Association of Colleges for Teacher Education (AACTE). (1972). *No one model American: A statement of multicultural education.* Washington, DC: Author.

Cohen, S. (1974). *Education in the United States: A documentary history.* New York: Random House.

Davidson, J.D., & Rees-Mogg, L.W. (1997). *The sovereign individual: How to survive and thrive during the collapse of the welfare state.* New York: Simon & Schuster.

Gardner, H. (1983). *Frames of mind.* New York: Basic Books.

Gardner, H. (1993). *Multiple intelligences: The theory in practice.* New York: Basic Books.

Guadalupe Organization, Inc. v. Tempe Elementary School Dist. (1978). 587 F.2d 1002 (9 Cir.).

Illich, I. (1970). C*elebration of awareness: A call for institutional revolution.* Garden City, NY: Doubleday.

Institute for Education and Transformation. (1992). *Voices from the inside: A report on schooling from inside the classroom, part I—Naming the problem.* Claremont, CA: The Claremont Graduate School.

Kasl, E., & Elias, D. (1997). Transformative learning in action: A case study. *ReVision, 20,* 20–27.

Kelly, K. (1997, September). New rules for the new economy: Twelve dependable principles for thriving in a turbulent world. *Wired,* 140–144, 186–197.

Keyes v. School Dist. No. 1. (1975). Denver, Colorado, 521 F.2d 465 (10 Cir.).

Kowalski, C.J. (1977). *The impact of college on persisting and non-persisting students.* New York: Philosophical Library.

Lau v. Nichols (1974). 414 US 563, 94 S.Ct. 786, 39 L.Ed.2d 1.

Locust, C. (1988). Wounding the spirit: Discrimination and traditional American Indian belief systems. *Harvard Educational Review, 8,* 315–330.

Maslow, A.H. (1970). *Motivation and personality.* New York: Harper & Row.

Matter of Baum (1978). 61 A.D.2d. 123, 401 N.Y.S.2d. 514.

Matter of McMillan (1976). 30 N.C. App. 235, 226 S.E.2d. 693.

Rosenthal, R. (1973, September). The Pygmalion effect lives. *Psychology Today, 7* (4), 56–63.

Rosenthal, R., & Jacobson, L. (1968). *Pygmalion in the classroom.* New York: Holt, Rinehart & Winston.

Saks, J.B. (1989). You're overworked, underpaid, but reasonably happy anyway. *Executive Educator,* 11, 20–21.

Saks, J.B. (1992). Education vital signs. *American School Board Journal,* 179, 38–39.

Serna v. Portales Municipal Schools. (1974). 499 F.2d 1147 (10 Cir.).

Smith, J.K., & Smith, L.G. (1994). *Education today: The foundations of a profession.* New York: St. Martin's Press.

Smith, L.G., & Kniker, C. (1975). *Myth and reality: Readings in education.* Boston: Allyn & Bacon.

Thilde, H.M., & Shriberg, L.D. (1990). Effects of recurrent otitis media on language, speech, and educational achievement of Menominee Indian children. *Journal of American Indian Education,* 29, 25–43.

U.S. Bureau of Education. (1918). *Cardinal principles of secondary education: The report of the Commission on the Reorganization of Secondary Education, appointed by the National Education Association.* Washington, DC: Government Printing Office.

U.S. National Center for Educational Statistics. (1992). Washington, DC: Government Printing Office.

Wattenberg, B.J. (1991). *The first universal nation: Leading indicators and ideas about the surge of America in the 1990s.* New York: Free Press.

Weatherford, J. (1991). *Native roots: How the Indians enriched America.* New York: Fawcett Columbine.

CHAPTER 2

Brazil: Overcoming Five Centuries of Undereducation

CÂNDIDO GOMES
CLÉLIA CAPANEMA
JACIRA CÂMARA

Cândido Gomes is an advisor for educational affairs at the federal Senate of Brazil, professor of education at the Catholic University of Brasília, consultant to international organizations, and author of numerous books and articles published in Brazil and abroad.

Jacira Câmara has a Ph.D. in education (curriculum) from George Peabody College for Teachers of Vanderbilt University and studies towards a Post Doctorate at the Institute of Education of the University of London. She is a professor at the Catholic University of Brasília and a senior researcher at the University of Brasília. She has published a variety of works on different aspects of education, with a particular focus on curriculum.

Clélia F. Capanema is a professor of education at the Catholic University of Brasília, Brazil, and was previously a professor at the University of Brasília, from which she retired recently. She has a B.A. in pedagogy and her M.Sc. in educational administration and planning, as well as her Ph.D. in international and multicultural education, taken at the University of Southern California in the United States. From 1985 to 1986 she was in a post-doctoral program in comparative education at the Institute of Education, University of London. She was a visiting fellow at the same institution in 1996. Her main research interests include educational policies and management. She has published in books and in academic journals in Brazil and in the United States.

THE SOCIAL FABRIC

Brazil, a country of continental dimensions, with 8.512 million square kilometers (5,313 square miles), occupies the central-eastern part of South America. Its absolute GNP in 1995 was in the order of US$688,310 million. Its population was estimated in 155.8 million in the same year, with the projection of 184.2 million for the year 2010. This places Brazil among the nine developing countries of highest population in the world: Brazil, People's Republic of China, Mexico, India, Pakistan, Bangladesh, Egypt, Nigeria, and Indonesia. The per capita value, the division of the GNP by such a great population, in 1995 was US$3,720. Hence, the country is characterized by acute social and regional disparities.

Historical Developments

Brazil was one of the greatest jewels of the Portuguese colonial empire. Early Brazilian colonial society was elitist and ornamental. The rich cities of the time were marked by the flourishing baroque style adapted to Brazilian environment. However, society was based on slave labor. All the schools were religious, thanks to the association between the Portuguese Crown and the Catholic Church, but educational opportunities were in general scarce. Women of European origin did not receive any education, and education was nonexistent for the slaves.

Sugar was important until the seventeenth century, when the sugar economy declined in the Brazilian Northeast and the monopoly shared by the Portuguese and Dutch ended. The beginning of the eighteenth century saw the discovery of gold and diamonds in the central region, and the mining economy opened opportunities for free labor and an urban society. However, the decline of mining in the last quarter of the eighteenth century led to a disassociation of interests between the colony and its colonial power.

A political pact in 1822 brought separation from Portugal. Despite national integration (which took a little longer than one century), the country was marked by acute regional and social disparities, in great part, resulting from the tardy legal abolition of slavery (1888). As well, primary and teacher education was particularly neglected— precisely those levels that could have been of benefit to those of lower socioeconomic group status.

Modern Brazil

In the early 1800s Brazil's economy began to shift to the exportation of coffee, a product whose market had greatly expanded in the United States and Europe with the Industrial Revolution. The coffee economy was only displaced by the Great Depression of 1929. Not being able to generate foreign exchange credit, a vigorous process of industrialization to substitute for imported goods was undertaken in Brazil. As in other Latin-American countries, the industrialization era counted on the incentive of the State as a planner and investor.

This continued into the 1970s. But the country started facing problems of stagnation: It had a closed economy regulated by the state and was not competitive internationally. Therefore, a crisis of external debt that affected the developing countries in the 1980s found Brazil with an economy that was commercially introverted and financially extroverted. The fiscal crisis and the elevated inflation that followed made public services unstable, including education.

Brazil today discusses and implements the adoption of fiscal, administrative, and social security reforms, among others, and many plans of economic stabilization have been put into practice. For example, in 1994 the introduction of a

new currency, the Real, was successful. A new general law of education and new mechanisms for financing it (1996) are aimed at elevating the efficiency, the quality, and the equity of education, mainly in the historically neglected primary level.

Demographics

Despite already surpassing 155 million inhabitants, the country is characterized by rapid urbanization. An urban population of 31.2 percent in 1940 reached 77.5 percent in 1994. Population growth diminished from an annual 2.4 percent in 1970–1975 to 2.1 percent in 1980–1985, and 1.7 percent in 1989–1994. Hence, the youth population has diminished in relative terms: The population under 17 years of age corresponded in 1995 to 38.8 percent of the total, while the group of 60 years of age and older reached 8.4 percent. In 1984, these percentages reached, respectively, 43.3 and 6.8 percent, evidencing a progressive aging of the population.

In 1995, the economically active population corresponded to 61.3 percent of the population of 10 or more years of age; the rate of activity was 75.3 percent for men and 48.1 percent for women. From this contingent of workers, 26.1 percent still made a living from agriculture, 19.6 from industry, and 54.3 percent from commerce and service. As a consequence of economic adjustment after the fall of inflation, the rate of open unemployment reached 4.64 percent in 1995, an elevated rate for the Brazilian reality. In São Paulo, the biggest city of the country, the total rate of unemployment was 13.2 percent.

Concurrently with this profile, the rate of illiteracy was 14.8 percent in 1995 for the population of 14 years of age and above. In the Northeast it was 29.4 percent. As to the years of schooling of the population of 10 years of age and above in the same year, 72.1 percent did not conclude primary education; that is, they did not have up to seven complete years. Only 15.4 percent had concluded secondary education and/or had started higher education.

SCHOOLING

Education is seen as a duty of the government. However, while some gains have been made, the search for lost time is urgent. After 1950, the expansion of the system became faster, especially at the primary and secondary levels. In 1950, only 36.2 percent of the population between 7 and 14 years of age were enrolled; three decades later this number rose to 80.4 percent. Increased enrollment occurred despite the difficulties in reaching the rural habitat and despite internal migrations that today empty schools in certain areas and over-crowd them in others, mainly in the outskirts of the big cities. Nevertheless, in relation to other countries of the same level of development, Brazil presents a contrast between economic output and social conditions, particularly in education.

The most recent international estimates show that Brazil has the sixth highest rate of illiteracy of Latin America and the Caribbean, coming after countries of low income, such as Haiti, Guatemala, Honduras, El Salvador, and Bolivia. Furthermore, Brazil has the highest rate of grade retention on the continent and the greatest absolute number of grade-repeating students in the world (UNESCO, 1996). Due to the retention of students in the ele-mentary grades, Brazil has the fifth lowest rate of student registration in secondary education among the thirty-two countries of Latin America and the Caribbean. Moreover, international comparative research of twenty countries showed that the gain of Brazilian students in mathematics was next to last place and in last place in science. Such defi-ciencies point to serious problems of efficiency, quality, and equity, and to neglectful and nonef-fective social policies.

The challenges that education faces today are determined by the large territory, great population, and economic problems. Too, with a representa-tive democracy, Brazil is a federative republic with three levels of government—federal, state, and municipal. The articulation of what these three levels do in the area of education deserves more precise definitions as well as the creation of more daring mechanisms of financing to reduce inter- and intraregional inequalities. On the plus side, the deceleration of demographic growth opens perspectives for educational betterment as the country will finally be able to shift its priority from quantitative expansion to the betterment of quality and equity of life.

Educational Philosophies

The Brazilian Constitution, enacted in October 1988, is based, among other things, on the princi-ples of civil rights and the dignity of the individual. The major goals for the Republic involve the con-struction of a free, just, and mutually cooperative society; the guarantee of national development; the elimination of poverty and social exclusion; and a reduction in social and regional imbalances to pro-mote the welfare of all without discrimination by origin, race, sex, color, age, or any other form of prejudice.

Education is regarded in the Constitution as a "right that belongs to everybody, the duty of the State and of the families, promoted and stimulat-ed with the cooperation of society, with a view to the full development of the individual, preparation for the exercise of citizenship and preparation for work" (*Constituição*, 1988, Art. 205). The gener-al goals and objectives of national education are stated in the new Law of Guidelines and Basic Tenets for National Education (LDB) approved by the President of the Republic on December 20, 1996.

Basic Tenets for National Education (LDB)

The new law of 1996 includes some novel features and presents a variety of measures when com-pared to previous educational legislation. A few of the most innovative points are:

• *Decentralization and autonomy for educational systems.* The LDB states that the educational sys-tem must be organized as a system of collaboration among the union, the states, and the municipali-ties. It determines what part each administrative entity will play.

• *Enhancing the teaching profession.* For the teaching profession, the LDB establishes higher standards of training than those currently accepted, requiring "the association of theory with practice, including the possibility of on-the-job training" (Art. 61). It stresses the participation of teachers in the drafting and implementation of schools' teaching programs and also establishes some mechanisms to assist the enhancement of education professionals.

• *Decentralization and autonomy for schools.* Schools will be henceforth responsible for drafting and implementing their pedagogic proposals and managing their personnel, materials, and financial resources. This empowers primary and secondary educational institutions to exercise autonomy, not only in the presentation and execution of their pedagogic proposals, but also in the management of their personnel, materials, and financial resources. This also gives teachers the freedom to carry out their work plans, to make use of appropriate methods to help students, and to work more closely with families and communities.

• *Universities' decentralization and autonomy.* The LDB presents ideas for universities' rights to autonomy and decentralization. It does establish certain conditions for this—the authorization and the recognition of courses, as well as the certification of higher education institutions, shall be given only for specific periods of time. Periodic renewal will be contingent upon a regular evaluation process.

Organization and Structure of the Education System

In accordance with the LDB, the Brazilian educational system is organized into two levels: basic education, including preschool education, primary, and secondary education; and higher education. Basic education is compulsory for children 7 to 14 years of age. It seeks the development of the student to assure skills that are indispensable to the exercise of citizenship and offers a means to progress into the job market and higher studies. Basic education can be organized in diverse ways

depending on whatever the interest of the learning process recommends. These include annual grades, semester periods, cycles, alternating regular study periods, nongrade groups, or groups based on age, competence, or other criteria. However, basic education relating to the primary and secondary education levels must be organized in accordance with some common rules, such as:

• A minimum of 800 class-hours of activities per year is recommended and must be distributed in a minimum of 200 days of work, excluding those days earmarked for examinations, when they exist.

• Verification of educational performance must observe the following criteria: continuous and cumulative evaluation of the student's performance with special attention to qualitative over quantitative aspects, and of results throughout the period in addition to those of eventual final examinations. The possibility of acceleration of studies by advancing in courses and grades for students through verification of learning is also provided for. For cases of low educational performance, remedial studies are mandatory and preferably taken throughout the school year.

• Minimum attendance of 75 percent of the total school hours is required in order to be approved, the control of which is the schools' obligation.

• The curricula of primary and secondary education should have a national common basis, and a diversified basis according to regional and local characteristics of the society, its culture, economy, and clientele. Arts and physical education should be highlighted. Teaching of Brazilian history should take into account the contributions of the different cultures and ethnicities toward the formation of the Brazilian people, especially those indigenous, African, and European. At least one foreign language should be offered.

Preschool

Preschool education seeks integral development of children under the age of 6 and must be offered by day care and preprimary schools. Evaluation at this level is made through close observation and records of development, not aiming at promotion, not even for access to primary education.

Primary Education

Primary education is compulsory for children of 7 years of age and optional to those of 6 years of age. Its objective is the basic formation of a citizen through:

• The development of the capacity to learn shown in a full command of reading, writing, and arithmetic.

• Understanding of the natural and social environment of the political system, technology, the arts, and of the values upon which society is founded.

• The development of the capacity to learn, having in mind the acquisition of knowledge and abilities and the formation of attitudes and values.

• The strengthening of family ties, the ties of human solidarity and mutual tolerance.

• Regular primary education given in Portuguese, but still granting indigenous communities the utilization of their mother tongues and peculiar learning processes.

• Presupposing the presence of the educator and the student. Distance education is used as an aid to help learning or in emergency situations.

The minimum annual class hours as well as the number of school days has changed from 720 to 800 hours, and from 180 to 200 school days. There should be at least 4 daily hours of actual class work. Brazil is, however looking at a progressive increase of these 4 hours to a full-time period, associated with supplementary programs of alimentation, health assistance, didactic-school material, and transportation. The priorities for these measures are targeted at the metropolitan areas with a high incidence of poverty and low educational performance and to the first grades of primary education, expanding until they reach the last grade.

The teaching of religion, an optional subject, is given in the regular schedule of the public schools. To the students who do not opt for religious education, an alternative activity that develops ethical values and the feeling of justice, of human solidarity, respect for the law, and the love of liberty, is provided.

Secondary Education

Secondary education is the final stage of basic education, lasting three years. Its goals are the consolidation and deepening of the knowledge acquired in primary education, making the continuation of studies possible. It also seeks to provide basic preparation for work and citizenship and the refinement of the student as a person. This includes ethics formation, the development of intellectual autonomy, and critical thinking.

The secondary education curriculum should highlight basic technological education; an understanding of the meaning of science, of the letters, and of the arts; the historic process of the transformation of society and culture; the Portuguese language as a tool of communication and access to knowledge; and the exercise of citizenship. Besides the requirement of a foreign language, the inclusion of another optional language is suggested.

Secondary education has a flexible organization in order to respond to the different needs of the students. All the courses of secondary education have legal equivalence and qualify for a continuation of studies. The preparation for work and, optionally, the professional qualification, may be developed in the institutions of secondary education or in cooperation with institutions specialized in vocational education.

Higher Education

The objectives of higher education are to stimulate cultural creation and to develop a scientific spirit and analytical thought, to advance graduates in the different areas of knowledge, and to make them capable of participating in the development of Brazilian society. Higher education aims, as well, to stimulate research and scientific investigation; to promote the dissemination of cultural, scientific, and technical knowledge; to stimulate the knowledge of national, regional, and of present world issues; to render community service and establish a reciprocal relationship with it; and to continue the cultural and professional formation of citizens by promoting adequate forms of cultural extension.

Higher education embraces sequential courses by areas of different levels of application. Undergraduate courses are open to candidates who have finished secondary education. Graduate courses—master's and doctoral programs (*stricto sensu* and *lato sensu*)—include greater comprehension of a specialization, improvement courses, and extension courses.

The offer of undergraduate courses at night, maintaining the same standards of quality of those offered during the day, is mandatory in public institutions. The institutions of higher education may also offer regular courses in a serial regime of in a credit system.

The 200 days of effective academic work required in basic education is also required in higher education. The presence of students and professors is mandatory, except in programs of distance education. As they are autonomous, the universities are assured certain rights. These include the right to create, organize, and extinguish courses and programs, and establish their curricula as long as the general norms of the union or of the appropriate education system are respected; establish plans, programs, and projects of scientific research and artistic production; and create extension activities.

Youth and Adult Education

The LDB also sets norms for youth and adult education designed for those who have not attended or finished regular schooling at the appropriate age. The educational systems will have courses and supplemental exams on understanding the common national base in the curriculum, thus enabling the continuation of studies in a regular

manner. The exams will be done at different levels of schooling and for different age groups.

Professional Education

Professional education leads to the permanent development of the aptitude for a productive life. It is an education integrated to different forms of education, work, science, and technology. Professional education should be developed in articulation with regular education or through different strategies of continued education. It takes place in specialized institutions or in the work environment.

Vocational and professional schools, in addition to their regular courses, offer special courses open to the community. Enrollment for these courses is conditional on the capacity of an individual to benefit from the course, not necessarily the student's level of schooling.

Special Education

Special education, understood in the law as the modality of school education for the student with special needs, is offered preferably in the regular education system. It begins with the age group from zero to 6 years of age. The education systems assure specific assistance in modifying the curricula, methods, techniques, educational resources, and organization for students with special needs.

Nonformal Education

Illiteracy in Brazil today is a well described phenomenon, particularly in the Northeastern region. Therefore, the Brazilian government has encouraged companies to participate in the war against illiteracy and foster schooling in the workplace for their employees. The Ministry of Education and Sports (MEC) provides the educational supplies for the teachers and students. As part of this program, a project called *Education for Quality at Work* was created. It aims to increase efforts to eliminate illiteracy and also strengthens primary education in the public and in the private spheres.

Another program created by the government, *In Solidarity with Literacy,* is currently being implemented via a pilot project in thirty-two municipalities with illiteracy rates above 55 percent, all located in the Northeast. The basis of this project includes of partnerships between the MEC, companies, universities, the states, and the municipalities.

Management of the Educational System

The responsibilities of each educational level are defined by the Brazilian Constitution. These educational tasks are divided between the union, the states, the Federal District, and the municipalities. In a spirit of collaboration, each one organizes its respective educational systems and each one has specific responsibilities. The private sector is free to participate in all levels of education, depending on the approval and evaluation of the government.

The Constitution of 1988 gave the states, the Federal District, and the municipalities many responsibilities. For the first time, the municipalities became participants in the exercise of responsibilities involving education. At the municipal level, more and more secretariats and councils of education are being created.

At the federal level, political decisions are taken by the MEC, aided by the National Council of Education, a consultative and deliberative body. The Ministry of Labor and Education work together in defining the vocational training, which is carried out by vocational schools and agrovocational schools; the Federal Center for Technological Education (CEFET); the National Service for Industrial Training (SENAI); and corresponding agencies in the area of commerce, transportation, and activities in the rural area (SENAC, SENAT, and SENAR). The Ministry of Health also participates in educational programs through vaccination campaigns and by giving information about hygiene and the prevention of diseases. Other government and nongovernment organizations are also involved through specially signed agreements and through the articulation of activities with specific objectives.

The Ministry of Communications also con-

tributes to educational activities, sponsoring the transmission of educational programs via radio and television to the remotest corners of the country. These not only increase but perfect the knowledge of teachers and currently benefit 25 million students. Many other agreements have been signed between the MEC and other government agencies seeking to develop studies and projects in the areas of agriculture and animal husbandry.

Private schools, as long as authorized, enjoy the same rights granted the public schools, be they federal, state, or municipal. The military ministries have their own elementary schools (starting in the fifth grade) and secondary schools. These schools are open to the public in general and are projected to offer appropriate training to students who wish to pursue a military career. Military academies, at the level of higher education, are also maintained by the military ministries.

Changes and Innovations in Education

The MEC feels that if the proposed innovations are to be successful, the involvement of society as a whole, mobilization, and the search for partnerships are key elements. Certain actions are intended to encourage and foster partnership not only among levels of government, but also among them and different segments of civil society. The MEC considers these as crucial in the quest for quality and it expects that they will make Brazilian education more effective.

Recently, two major national education plans have been proposed.

• *Education for All Ten Year Plan.* The Brazilian MEC has made quality education the hub of National Policy on Basic Education and drafted the Education for All Ten Year Plan. The main goals are to promote equality and to correct educational disparities among different regions and social classes.

• *Pluriannual Education Plan.* The goal of this plan is to obtain better student results by means of quality management applied to all forms and levels of education. Primary education is a priority for the 1996–1999 period and mechanisms for the support of public state and/or municipal agencies involved in this segment will be provided. The active participation of the community as well as different segments of society are considered important aims to boost schools in their autonomy.

As well, eight discrete programs are being developed:

1. *Allocation of resources for the support of schools.* The purpose of this program is to give schools the autonomy to decide on pedagogic, administrative, and financial issues. The distribution of resources directly to the schools requires that the institution have a parent-teacher association, a school board, or a school treasury. It means each school will receive an amount proportional to the number of students, determined by the region it belongs to. In 1996, 30 million students and 180,000 institutions benefited from the direct allocation of US$260 million to the schools.

2. *Distance education.* The goals of the distance education policy are to contribute to the improvement of the quality of education, to create permanent nationwide training and preparation programs for public education network managers and teachers, to carry out cultural and vocational training programs for broader social sectors, and to organize the institutional field by coordinating an integrated and interactive distance education system. For these purposes, two activities are underway: school TV and the Program on Information Sciences and Technology in Education.

3. *National curricular parameters.* The National Curricular Parameters (NCPs) seek to improve the quality of education in all primary education so as to orient the educative actions in the schools. During the first stage, a core curriculum in Portuguese, language, mathematics, sciences, history, and geography is being defined for all four grades.

The NCPs present general principles for education and its operationalization. They include basic information about the function of the school, the teaching and learning process, pedagogic experiences, and areas of knowledge, defining, in

general lines, "what," "why," "when," and "how" to teach and evaluate.

The innovative aspect of NCPs is the systematic study of themes such as ethics, environment, sex education, economic studies, cultural plurality, and health, all grouped under the title *Social Harmony and Ethnic Relations*. These themes are integrated into the core subjects using the concept of tranversality, that is, trying to permeate the core subjects with new issues.

4. *Decentralizing and extending the School Meal Program.* The School Meal Program, already fully decentralized, reaches 34 million children. It provides funds to states and municipalities to permit them to provide one meal a day. These meals were served by schools on 170 days in 1996 as compared to 101 days in 1994.

5. *National textbook program.* The following aspects deserve to be highlighted in this program. First is the expansion of the coverage to benefit children from fifth to the eighth grades. Thus, all the first through eighth grade pupils in public primary school are being covered simultaneously for the very first time. In 1996, 110 million books were transferred, compared to 60 million in 1995. Second is the evaluation, by the teacher and specialists of the university, of textbooks of primary schools for the four core knowledge groups for the first through the fourth grades that are currently included in the Program. The final aspect is the operation established by the Student Aid Foundation (FAE) to ensure that all books reach every school in the country in the beginning of the school year.

6. *Evaluation.* Evaluation has been one of the great concerns of the MEC, which is making every effort to institutionalize an evaluation process of the educational system, seeking, above all, to improve the quality of the system.

7. *Mobilizing the public.* Mobilization of the public has become one of the characteristics of this government. The MEC believes that the participation of the society as a whole has great influence on the quality of public education, particularly in the case of primary education. The objective of the

Ministry is to encourage the community to get involved with the schools, stimulating direct inspection of the performance of institutions.

Two programs deserve special notice: The first is *Wake up, Brazil! It's time for school!,* a program created to mobilize the Brazilian public through a partnership system giving support to the efforts of the government or private institutions, to equip schools, renovate their facilities, and cooperate with the administration of the schools.

Speak up, Brazil is another program in which public service establishes partnership with the private sector, supporting a toll-free number that provides Brazilians with a direct channel of communication with MEC. An average of 2,000 phone calls a day, including requests, suggestions, and complaints about education are received by the *Speak up, Brazil!* program.

8. *Specific action for the Northeast.* The Northeast is a region characterized by low productivity in the public system of education. Thus, this region is especially targeted by the Project of Basic Education for the Northeast. The main goal is to improve the quality of primary education, particularly the first four grades.

Teacher Training

The 61st Article of the LDB establishes the basic fundamentals for the training of professionals in education. They are close association between theory and practice, including training in the workplace; the use of training and prior experiences in teaching institutions and other activities; and training, preferably at the higher education level. To teach in secondary education, a teacher must obtain qualifications from a course at the level of higher education corresponding to a teaching degree. This means mastery of knowledge in a specialized area in addition to mastery of teaching methodology and materials.

The training of teachers for specialized technical areas of instruction follows two schemes. Scheme I is for holders of diplomas from higher education related to the intended area of certification, subject to completing training in teaching

methodologies. Scheme II is for holders of technical diplomas from secondary education related to the intended area of certification. In addition to the completion of training in teaching methodologies required in scheme I, scheme II is subject to the completion of courses with contents related to the intended area.

In higher education, the training of professors and specialists in the different areas and the mastery of knowledge and practical skills is comprised of the following different levels. These are training through graduate programs (*lato sensu*) with a minimum duration of 360 class hours (specialization and improvement courses) and training in graduate programs (*strictu sensu*) (masters and doctoral programs).

MAJOR ISSUES, CONTROVERSIES, AND PROBLEMS

In Society

The major issues, controversies, and problems that are taking place in Brazilian society are challenges resulting from the country's profile as described above. This analysis is closely linked to the already mentioned economic difficulties from the 1980s onwards that have had obvious repercussions in social matters such as education. Of course, it is necessary to add the issue of Brazil's need to work on taking its place in a globalized world combined with the challenges of modernity that the country cannot avoid facing.

The fact of the matter is that after more than a decade of "redemocratization," a political process that started in the 1970s following two decades of military regime, Brazil has not yet solved its more serious problems. However, one can now identify a very positive feature in the Brazilian picture. This is an awareness of the seriousness of the situation and of the urgency to solve it on the part of policymakers, politicians, the academic community, the media, and society at large. Another important feature in the Brazilian scenario is the nation's determination to fight inflation.

Of no lesser importance, there is a national conviction that the pattern of income distribution in

Brazilian society must change drastically. The existing social inequalities are unacceptable for a nation that intends to be democratic. There are indications of some improvement in the figures of social exclusion, but they are still quite unsatisfactory for the Brazilian democratic consciousness.

Politically, Brazil has made remarkable progress and today enjoys a democratic state organization. However, the restoration of a democratic relationship between the state and Brazilian citizens has not occurred without much pain and tension, and the tide has turned very slowly.

As introductory measures for the political and juridical reorganization of the Brazilian state, the Congress enacted important laws such as the revival of direct elections for the President of the Republic and mayors of capital cities of the states and tourist cities, as well as reorganization of the political parties and legalization of those that were functioning on a clandestine basis, such as the Communist parties. Media censorship was abolished.

The 1998 Constitution, as mentioned above, represents an idealized profile of the new nation Brazil is striving to become. Labeled as *Citizen Constitution* or *Courage Constitution,* it was enacted in a mood of optimism, cheerfulness, and hope, close to utopia. It is said to address the main Brazilian problem, that is, the building of citizenship, and to include every Brazilian person, down to the illiterate, the jobless, and the homeless. It is intended to fight poverty, eliminate social exclusion, and reduce the social and regional imbalances that are quite visible in the Brazilian social scene.

Once more, Brazil has hope, this time placed on this set of rules and regulations dubbed *Magna Carta.* Yet Brazilians know quite clearly and by experience that the law itself will not make the difference for which the country is looking. Legislation alone does not promote change; a great deal of political will is necessary to enforce it. By itself, however, the Constitution represents the nation's eloquent response to the authoritarianism and to the lack of state legitimacy experienced during two decades of military government.

The degree of public participation during the debate on the Constitution is noteworthy. Different organized groups of society, forming rural and urban lobbies of opposite ideological orientations, all tried to influence the important decisions about the Brazilian future that were taking place at the Congress. The population's participation in political affairs had been increasing a great deal, even before the constitutional debate, the most outstanding being the national campaign for direct elections (*Diretas Já*) in 1984, followed by the national movement led by students, the *caras pintadas,* so called because they painted the national colors on their faces, to press the Congress to decide for the impeachment of a president, Fernando Collor. This was a memorable event in the early 1990s, unprecedented in the history of Latin America, and represented a strong popular reaction to corruption in political life.

Social movements have been playing a part in Brazilian day-to-day politics ever since; political representation does not suffice any more. Numerous and differentiated groups such as women, senior citizens, blacks, children, and homosexuals are demanding participation in the decisions, especially those that affect their lives and give them the right to have their distinctiveness respected by the state and by society at large. They are trying to create political alternative spaces other than the Parliament and thus are opening new fields of political participation. Instead of expecting the continuation of conventional instances of political representation, those groups go to the streets and cry out for their demands, concerns, and interests (Diniz & Boschi, 1989).

An eloquent example of a powerful social movement is that the *Sem Terra* (the landless), a large group of rural workers striving to own a piece of land to cultivate and to live on. This is a popular movement. So loud is its voice and so just are the requests that it shows the potential of pushing agrarian reform in Brazil. This movement is also gaining strong political support on the part of prestigious organizations such as the Catholic Church, political parties, and several civil organizations. Brazil is convinced of the urgent need to promote agrarian reform, but there is disagreement on the part of some segments of society with the methods used by the Movement of the Landless who have occupied farms all over the country so as to force the government to attend to their demands. Recently, when thousands of marchers in a demonstration for agrarian reform peacefully assembled in Brasilia, the capital city of Brazil, there was unanimous support from the government, the Congress, the media, various nongovernmental organizations, and the population in general.

Nevertheless, one still must be cautious about defining democracy in Brazil because, in order to fulfill the democratic principles of the Constitution, the Brazilian project of development must involve a global process including not only the economic targets but also the political and the psychosocial aspects of life. While on one hand Brazil is enjoying freedom and some political development, on the other hand the standard of living is very low for the majority of the population.

Resorting to Structural Reforms

In its struggle to recover from the effects of the economic crisis and to promote a balanced and sustainable development, Brazil is today looking for structural reforms considered to be indispensable in the solution of complex and combined problems. Among these problems, the most serious and urgent are the need to resume the process of sustainable development and the maintenance of a low rate of inflation. In order to achieve a lasting economic stability, the war on poverty, particularly by means of jobs creation, must continue and consequently diminish the social exclusion of a large part of the population.

As mentioned above, Brazil launched a monetary reform known as the *Real Plan* on July 1, 1994. This economic stabilization plan has been remarkably successful in fighting inflation. So encouraging have been the results that Brazilian economists now to talk about the "maintenance" of economic stability. For that purpose, there are a number of measures in political agenda, such as

the redefinition of the state's functions, the promotion of an administrative reform, and a social security reform of the fiscal and the public sector, particularly of the state's productive sector.

At the moment, the revision of the state's roles stresses the privatization of state enterprises with reduction of the state's size. This process of privatization, as should be expected, has generated different reactions from rival organized groups of society, especially the left-wing politicians and academics, as well as the ordinary people in the streets. Generally, there are the workers in the private sector and the civil servants on one side and liberal politicians and businessmen on the other side. While the former accuse the government of imposing a policy identified as having a neoliberal orientation harmful to the interests of the working class, the latter criticize the slowness of the process that they would like to see going faster and with a broader scope.

A number of companies have already been privatized, but by far the most important and controversial transaction to be carried out is the privatization of the *Companhia Vale do Rio Doce,* the third largest major iron mining company in the world. Its assets amount to over US$ 10 billion, out of which the government will sell US$ 3 billion. It will be the most valuable privatization auction ever to occur in Latin America (*Veja,* 1997).

In the middle of these controversies, the worldwide debate on the merits and evils of neoliberalism is an animated issue in Brazil—inside universities and other centers of academic studies, in the media, and in the Congress. It is open to question whether neoliberalism will face more resistance to its full implementation in Latin America than it will meet in Europe or in the former Soviet world, considering that it is a coherent, self-conscious doctrine in its structural ambition and its international extension (Anderson, 1995), with no concrete alternative presented so far. Yet, as a universal paradigm of modernity, the liberal state in Brazil faces the same well known difficulties and contradictions shown in the developed capitalist societies, with even more complexity due to Brazil's condition as a developing country.

As mentioned above, Brazil reveals striking social inequalities and insufficient investment in the social sectors such as education, health care, housing, and social security. All of this is aggravated by the huge external debt that requires a large amount of financial resources for the payment of high interest rates, of course to the detriment of vital social programs. It is indisputable that Brazil will enter the twenty-first century handicapped by three structural deficiencies: the lack of internal savings to finance the needed investment for the country's development, the incipient state of its technology, and the low level of schooling and work qualifications of a great part of the population.

In Education

The connection of the educational debates to the larger ones discussed above is quite apparent. Parallel to the challenge of poverty and social inequalities, and also as a way of minimizing them, is the task of providing effective basic education addressed to the building of citizenship and the ability to play a role in the process of the country's development. As discussed above, the per capita income in Brazil is reminiscent of colonial times when compared to the industrialized countries, a fact attributable to the low quality of jobs and the low qualifications of workers.

Education should help to narrow the wide gap between the country's economy and the low educational level of the population, a significant blockade to the technological advancement that the country badly needs. Above all, the future of democracy depends on the creation of a citizenship consciousness. Brazil faces a major problem: the promises that states have failed to keep over decades, one of them being the provision of education for citizenship.

It is undeniable that significant progress has been achieved in terms of school enrollment. In 1994, 31.2 million pupils were enrolled in the national primary education system, predominantly concentrated in the Southeast (39 percent) and Northeast (31 percent), followed by the South (14

percent), North (9 percent) and Midwest (7 percent). The absolute majority of pupils (88.4 percent) attended public schools in urban areas (82 percent) because of the urbanization process in Brazil.

The question of the education system's performance remains to be solved. The hope of educating for citizenship is hindered by the poor quality of primary schools, which should be the first place to provide education to the citizens. Studies have shown that retention rate is one of the most serious Brazilian education problems. It is noteworthy that a pupil spends an average of five years before dropping out and it takes him or her 11.2 years to finish the eight grades of compulsory primary education. It is a deplorable waste of material and human resources, has high social costs, and means great harm to the self-esteem of a significant number of Brazilian school children who do not succeed in finishing basic school.

This disastrous picture has multifarious causes. As education is dependent upon social, economic, and political background, most children from disadvantaged environments do not manage to complete even the first part of primary school. Data show that 25 percent of those aged 10 or older spent just one year in school; 34 percent had two years of schooling. Regional disparities are apparent as far as education is concerned; 37 percent of pupils aged 10 and over living in the Northeast of Brazil had either never been to school or had spent less than a year.

Speaking of *transition rates* (advancement, retention, and dropout rates), the Ministry of Education proclaims considerable improvement in the last decade. There has been a rising trend in advancement rates, which increased from 55 percent in 1984 to 62 percent in 1992, combined with a decrease in the average of retention and dropout rates, which reached 33 percent and 5 percent respectively in 1992. Despite the improvement in dropout rates, the figures of advancement and retention for the first grade of primary education are still very disappointing. Only 51 percent of the pupils enrolled pass to the next grade and 44 percent of them repeat the same grade. This retention rate is responsible for the dropout rates, since those pupils, pressed by socioeconomic forces, leave school discouraged and hopeless, enter the labor market prematurely, and lack a minimal qualification for work (Brazil Ministry, 1995b). Solutions are being tried, as mentioned before.

The issue of quality has been raised since a more careful analysis of the retention and dropout rates shows a large waste of financial resources besides significant social damage. The official statistics have been reexamined and errors of interpretation have been recognized, leading to the conclusion that the most serious problem of primary education planning in Brazil is the retention rates, calling for quality sustained by an efficient system of evaluation.

It is fair to say that the issue of quality is omnipresent in the educational debate at any level in Brazil at the moment, as it is in most parts of the world. Educators are supposed to always show concern for quality, no matter how unclear the concept of quality in education is. The state's declared concern with quality education seems to contain a message to the educational systems; it sounds like a pledge for correcting failures committed in the past. However, underlying the rhetoric about quality is the state's desire to make schools more publicly accountable.

As in the rest of the world, education in Brazil is expected to play a role in the preservation of the cultural heritage, as well as in the promotion of personal growth and self-fulfillment, besides helping the promotion of economic growth. That is why it should be emphasized that Brazilian society is aware of the reciprocal obligations by which it invests a considerable proportion of revenue to provide educational services to the whole population. That makes the government, in all instances, accountable to all citizens for delivering good educational services, in quantity as well as in quality.

The quest for quality has as one of its implications the building of a culture of evaluation at all levels of schooling. It is a requirement not only based on the Constitution but also on the complementary guidelines and basic tenets of 1996. The State's obligation to provide public schooling should be effective under the guarantee of the establishment of minimum learning standards that are defined as the indispensable means to develop the learning process.

The Place of Secondary Education

While in practice only primary school is compulsory and free, the target determined by the Constitution is to provide for the progressive extension of mandatory requirement of the secondary level of schooling. The integration of preschool, primary, and secondary education structures is called *basic education* in Brazil. The rationale for this school organization is the nation's conviction that primary education is no longer sufficient to prepare people for the technological world into which it is entering, though certainly as a latecomer. For budgetary reasons, this target will certainly not be reached shortly. However, despite not being compulsory yet, secondary schools are free of charge within the public school network.

Within the framework described above, it is relevant to renew the discussion about secondary education in Brazil, starting by noting that it does not differ from the debate that is taking place in other countries. The worldwide difficulty in clarifying the objectives of this level of education has a topographical denomination—that of being in the middle. As Gomes (1996) argues, this happens because secondary education plays a role in social mobility and it presents a complicated relationship between conclusiveness—with readiness to enter the labor market—and continuity—with preparedness to go to higher education.

From this ambiguous character of secondary education come a number of controversial questions about its goals and relations with the world of work. For example, should secondary school be comprehensive or should there be different options and roads for the students to choose? Would it not be more convenient to provide vocational education after a sound general education?

The problem of balancing general and vocational education is a classical one, beginning when

Western philosophical thought started speculating on the value of work and people's different paths to it according to some attributive criteria. For the modern educational systems the concern goes back to the first industrial revolution. So far, we do not have definite answers.

Another current issue relating to secondary school is the question of financing so that this level of schooling gains identity and stops being the ugly duckling of the educational system. This will require sufficient budget to install laboratories, workshops, better and modern libraries, and, above all, better qualified teachers for which state resources have proved so far to be insufficient. Perhaps the way is to establish partnerships with businesses, communities, and other social organizations interested in education. Of course, none of these initiatives will be effective without competent management.

Educational Management

In the context of the historical-social movement called post-modernity, the concepts of school education and its management have undergone significant mutations all over the world. It has been no different in Brazil. Democratic management and public schools' and universities' autonomy are the key words in the Brazilian education ideology, starting with the language of the Constitution and the complementary laws. It is a recurrent theme in the literature as well.

Within the atmosphere of political liberalization, the application of democratic principles to the educational set became a natural consequence right after the Constitution. Brazilian educators are able now to put into effect a long-cherished ideology that links together school effectiveness, school improvement, and school-based management. The Ministry of Education leads a program of allocation of resources for the support of public schools as a starting point to autonomy. This means autonomy to decide on pedagogic and administrative issues, which in turn calls for greater responsibility on the part of the schools' personnel, the parents' and teachers' associations,

and the communities within which the schools are located.

Democratic management all over the country as well as a reasonable amount of research indicates great optimism on the part of education professionals and many of the experiences and outcomes are, in fact, very positive and promising (Brazil MEC, 1995a, b; Wittman & Cardoso, 1993). However, in order to avoid more apparent than real consistency, scholars, researchers, and practitioners must delve deeper into the subject to improve democratic management in the public schools and in the educational system as a whole. Taking an international view of the problem should help. Countries like Australia, New Zealand, Canada, England and Wales, and the United States have much to contribute from a number of studies carried out in their search for a better understanding of the effects of school-based management. They provide a multinational perspective and a variety of models, all of them based on empirical research.

The most significant research question we should ask ourselves relates to the linkage of school-based management and the quality of the curriculum, teaching, and learning (Dimmock, 1993). As far as Brazil is concerned, numerous successful experiences of democratic management with a great deal of community school participation are under way. Democracy in school life is becoming widespread at all levels, and school autonomy becoming a most cherished principle among educators.

The Kaleidoscope of Higher Education

As far as higher education is concerned, it is opportune to raise two current issues. The first is the debate around quality that brings as a natural consequence the question of evaluation and the role of research as paramount for good quality higher education. The second is the problem of financing, interwoven with the matter of autonomy; both are thought of as indispensable instruments to promote quality.

Universities in general and public universities in particular have been asked to undertake research to generate knowledge, to stimulate creativity, and to promote innovation and change. The aim is be able to lead the development of the country by combining education, science, and technology and by being the origin of an intellectual elite. Besides demanding a highly qualified staff, those roles should be monitored by efficient evaluation.

Private universities, with some exceptions, such as those of community character or confessional denominations, are sharply criticized. They are seen as being much more interested in financial profits. That is, they are viewed as businesslike institutions offering only courses of low cost such as business administration, law, fine arts, and pedagogy, which demand no expensive premises and equipment such as laboratories. These universities, by and large, do not hire a better qualified staff (Demo, 1993). This situation is likely to improve since the new complementary law of guidelines and basic tenets prescribes an external evaluation every five years to renew the authorization for the functioning of each higher education course. Courses that do not meet the official requirement of minimal standards of effectiveness must be closed down.

The issue of evaluation has been controversial due to its complexity, but cannot be postponed. It is involved in the same type of questions posed to universities by post modernism from the status of knowledge in the post-industrial age to the social construction and legitimation of performance of the universities that are supposed to be productive and to deliver a certain kind of product, subject to quality control and carried out by managers other than academic leaders (Cowen, 1996).

It is true that over the last two decades higher education in Brazil has gone through a quantitative expansion and a qualitative development as well. The quest for quality is quite apparent. While evaluation is an omnipresent issue, the approaches to it are divergent. For the government, the cost-benefit argument prevails, while for academics evaluation should have an educational, critical, and emancipatory orientation. These rival views may meld some day (Figueiredo & Sobreira, 1996).

Evaluating higher education in Brazil means dealing with a multifarious set of institutions ranking from the top in excellence to the bottom of mediocrity. A great deal of criticism addressed to higher education is rooted in the fact that legislation and policies treat those heterogeneous entities as if they were homogeneous (Castro, 1994).

The second issue raised above is the funding of higher education. This is closely related to the issue of autonomy both as part of the university ideology and as a matter of necessity. The costs of higher education are elevated in both private and public institutions, making the expansion of the public higher education network difficult for the state to bring about. At the same time, the fees in the private sector are increasingly too high for the students, who paradoxically happen to belong to the less privileged segment of society because they only can attend night courses after a working day.

This ugly face of social injustice is very upsetting for policymakers, for academics, and, of course, for the university clientele. Every now and then it raises the question of transforming the public university, which has delivered free services since its foundation, into a fee-paying institution for those students supposed to be in a position to pay for their higher education. The debate on this subject has been sharp and often emotional, with a heavy ideological component.

An innovative idea to solve this difficult question was conceived by Castro (1994), consisting of the creation of a philanthropic association managed by the students with the participation of the university and community leaders to collect taxes from students who can afford them. The money collected would be destined to students from the working class and the low-middle class in order to make them able to attend good public universities on a full-time basis. The issue remains controversial, and it seems that it will be an open question for the years ahead.

At the moment, the Ministry of Education is considering the creation of *social quotas* in the public universities in order to minimize the sharp inequalities of educational opportunities in higher education. However, the measure does not seem to be able to solve the difficulty of access of the underprivileged students to higher education. A much more efficient mechanism would be the amelioration of the system of public primary and secondary schools to qualify the candidates to the entrance examination without any form of favoritism or special quotas. The measure might be accepted as provisional and carried out with close attention to the risk of being unjust and harmful to the quality standards of each institution. The most sensible posture, in the face of so many complex problems in Brazilian education, is not to discard any initiative.

THE FUTURE OF SOCIETY AND SCHOOLING

In the perception of social scientists and educators, Brazil has been criticized for the contradiction between the official and the real country. Resulting from exaggerated importance attached to academic degrees and the ornamental culture of the colony, such contradictions show up the existence of excellent norms but a low degree of efficiency. However, Brazil has a favorable historic opportunity for transformation. The high rate of inflation has been overcome and there is relative financial stability. It will be very difficult to be content with only these results. Reforms of the state and various sectors of economic activities and social policies are essential if we do not want to return to the nightmare of the inflationary syndrome.

So education becomes a significant concern and the priority of elementary education emerges as a coherent governmental option. Brazil is an undereducated country in relation to its economic development level and the way to boost development is by providing quality elementary education for the totality of the population.

If the present historic opportunity is seized, the deceleration of demographic growth, the development of elementary education, and the growth of its coverage in rural areas and the outskirts of big cities will contribute to Brazil's building a solid base for development. At the same time, Brazil can change from an introverted economy to an internationally competitive economy. Then it will be able to address the unfair picture of concentration of income, above all in rural areas, and build solid bases for a democratic regime. If, however, the economic difficulties are overcome, but the social policies are neglected and only a small layer of the population has access to the benefits of prosperity, as happened in the 1970s, then not only the educational system but the country as a whole could be compared to an idol with feet of clay, and the contradictions will become almost unbearable.

REFERENCES

Anderson, P. (1995). "Balanço do neoliberarismo." *Pós-neoliberalismo—as políticas sociais e o Estado democrático.* [Inventory of neo-liberalism. Postneoliberalism—social policies and the Democratic State] (pp. 9–23). Emir Sater (Org.). Rio de Janeiro: Paz e Terra.

Brazil, *Constituição.* (1988). República Federativa do Brasil. Brasília: Senado Federal, Centro Gráfico. [Brazil, Constitution. Federative Republic of Brazil. Brasilia: Federal Senate.]

Brazil, Ministry of Education and Sports, Secretariat for Primary Education. (1995a, December), *Parâmetros Curriculares Nacionais para o Ensino Fundamental.* [National curricula parameters for elementary education introductory document.] Brasilia: Author.

Brazil, Ministry of Education and Sports. (1995b). *Planejamento político-Estratégico (1995/1998).* [Strategic-political planning 1995/1998.] Brasilia: Author.

Castro, C. (1994). *Educação brasileira: consertos e remendos.* (Brazilian education: Repairs and mendings). Rio de Janeiro: Rocco.

Cowen, R. (1996). Performativity, post-modernity and the university. *Comparative Education, 32,* 245–258.

Demo, P. (1993). *Desafios modernos da educação.* [Modern challenges of education.] Petrópolis, RJ: Vozes.

Dimmock, C. (1993). School-based management and linkage with the curriculum. In C. Dimmock (ed.), *School-based management and school and school effectiveness* (pp. 1–21). London and New York: Routledge.

Diniz, E., & Boschi, R. (1989). *Modernização e consolidação democrática no Brasil: os temas da Nova República*. [Modernization and democratic consolidation in Brazil: The themes of the New Republic.] São Paulo: Vértice/Iuperj.

Figueiredo, M.C.M., & Sobreira, M.I.F. (1996). The evaluation of the higher education system in Brazil. In R. Cowen (Ed.), *The evaluation of higher education systems, World yearbook of education 1996* (pp. 34–50). Series Editors: David Coulby and Crispin Jones. London: Kogan Page.

Gomes, C.A. (1996, November). *Ensino Médio. Mudanças em que direções. MIMEO*. Paper written under the auspices of Brazilian Society of Comparative Education, the Ministry of Education, and UNESCO. Brasília.

UNESCO. (1996). *Educação—um tesouro a descobrir*. [Education—a treasury to be discovered: Report of the International Committee for education for XXI Century.] Rio Tinto, Portugal: Edições Asa.

Veja. (1997, 12 March). Year 30A (10), 110–111.

Wittmann, L.C., & Cardoso, J.J. (Orgs.). (1993). *Gestão compartilhada na escola pública: o especialista na construção do fazer saber fazer*. [Shared Management in the public school: The specialist in the construction of making and the knowledge of making] Florianópolis: AAESC:ANPAE/SUL.

CHAPTER 3

Northern Dreams: Schooling and Society in Canada

J.L. KACHUR

J.L. Kachur *is a historical sociologist, social theorist, and policy analyst in the Department of Educational Policy Studies at the University of Alberta, Canada. His recent research focuses on theories of the capitalist state; the effects of human capital and technology transfer models on development theory; the entrepreneurial marketing of human resource development services; and the emerging national, class, and professional conflicts over intellectual property rights.*

As the second largest country in the world, Canada's 9.9 million square kilometers are rich in natural resources. With a population of 29.9 million, there are only 2.9 residents per square kilometer. The average rate of population growth from 1991 to 1996 was 5.7 percent. In 1995 the urban population made up 77 percent of the total population. Most people reside along a southern strip of land within 400 kilometers of the U.S. border and two-thirds of the population live in the provinces of Quebec and Ontario. One-third of the population resides in the three largest cities: Toronto (4 million people), Montreal (3 million), and Vancouver (2 million) (Mitchell, 1997). The population is spread over three geopolitical regions that incorporate ten provinces and two territories from east to west: the Atlantic Region, the Central Region, and the West Region.[1]

THE SOCIAL FABRIC

As in other capitalist countries, the major means of production in Canada, such as industry, transportation, retail trade, and banking, are owned by private individuals as shareholders in corporations. Canada exemplifies state-facilitated capitalist development. In 1996, the United Nations Development Program Report ranked Canada as the best place to live in the world for the fourth time in a row (Knox, 1997).

While well off according to world standards, Canada is not without its own glaring inequalities of income and wealth. Substantial inequalities are increasing for regions, classes, genders, languages, races, and religions, and they set important limitations on what the school systems can accomplish without fundamentally challenging economic and political structures.

A low population density in combination with commodities (timber, mining, agriculture) production, long distances, and rugged terrain has meant that the country's development priorities have focused on financing transportation and communication networks to benefit trade in primary resources (see Conrad, Finkel, & Jaenen, 1993; Naylor, 1987). Since the seventeenth century, the economy has been organized around the extraction and export of natural resources. In the colonial period these staples were fur, fish, and timber. In the post-colonial period wheat and minerals were developed. Following the Second World War, new energy resources such as hydroelectricity, petroleum, and natural gas were added to complement the older resource base.

Canada's status, first as a colony of Britain and later as an economic dependency of the United States, has meant that the economy has been and still is dominated by a very high concentration of foreign interest, investment, and ownership. U.S.

transnational corporations control key sectors of the economy.

While Canadians must continually struggle with U.S. power and the influence of Wall Street, Hollywood, and Washington, the country is further weakened by strong regional identities created by a culturally diverse population and geographic barriers. Issues of race, religion, language, and foreign influence are interwoven with regional differences over power and governance, and these issues regularly flare up and destabilize the country's sovereign control. In spite of regional and provincial fragmentation, different levels of government work to create a relatively risk-free environment for investors to build and profit from the country's productive base.

SCHOOLING

Structure

Canadian schooling has developed to meet a diversity of needs and interests. Canadians have a federated system for education that has created a patchwork of jurisdictional authority, including a diversity of education structures, practices, and policies. In the post-war period, education authorities have been guided by a historical sense of social hierarchy, equalization of individual and group opportunities, and a pragmatic balance of interests while dealing with various economic forces and political movements.

No federal ministry of education exists in Canada. Because of historical precedents, especially the British North America (BNA) Act of 1867, the development of Canadian schooling has resulted in a highly differentiated set of education systems with varied jurisdictional authority residing with the provinces.

However, the federal government retains responsibilities for funding support for education programs of national priority such as bilingualism, multiculturalism, occupational and apprenticeship training, international development and postsecondary education; sectoral jurisdiction over education related to the armed forces and penitentiaries; funding for services in the two northern territories (Yukon, North West Territories), and the education of status Indian and Inuit children.

In addition to federally controlled schools, Canadian laws allow for private schools. These must meet provincial curriculum standards and are independent and fee-charging institutions. As a proportion of total school enrollment, about 5 percent of Canadian students go to private schools. Although insignificant in number, this proportion has doubled from 2.4 percent since 1971 (Peters, 1996). Another private alternative is home-schooling whereby parents offer off-campus study for their own children. Charter schools, first implemented in Alberta in 1995, also offer an alternative form of schooling. But unlike private schools, charter schools are public institutions that introduce quasi-market competition between diversified and specialized forms of education provision. Canada also has schools for special education, that is, for students who are physically handicapped, learning disabled, emotionally disturbed, or gifted. Increasingly, these schools are being phased out and special needs students are being integrated into mainstream programs.

Funding, Programs, Completion Rates

Despite moderate declines, investment in Canadian education is relatively high when compared to many countries. Canada has recorded the highest level of public investment in all levels of education relative to the economy among the G7 countries (CESC, 1996). In 1993, the Organization for Economic Cooperation and Development (OECD)[2] estimated expenditures on education for Canada to be roughly 7.3 percent of Gross Domestic Product (GDP), including 4.5 percent on secondary schooling and 2.6 percent on tertiary schooling (OECD, 1996). By 1993–1994, various levels of government were spending a total of $56 billion a year on education and training, second only to the amount spent on health care. Local and provincial educational expenditures accounted for 19.8 percent of this total spending. The education sector employs close to 1 million people, or 7 percent of the total workforce.

In 1993, approximately half a million students were at the preprimary level with 17 students and 0.4 teachers per thousand of population (OECD, 1996). Pre-grade 1 education is provided by a mix of public and private institutions with private institutions dominating prekindergarten. Most 5-year-olds attend kindergartens for half days as part of the public school system. Other forms of early childhood care, such as day-care centers and nursery schools, are licensed by the provinces and usually privately organized.

Formal and compulsory schooling begins for students at the age of 6. Although kindergarten is not mandatory, half-day programs are usually delivered in elementary schools as preparation for formal schooling. Compulsory education for most students includes grades 1 to 8, or elementary schooling, at the first level. Grades 9 to 10, or lower secondary, is the first stage of the second level, and grades 11 to 13, or high secondary, is the second stage of the second level. An average school year for students (age 13) is 185 to 200 days. The months of July and August provide a summer holiday and the year-end break. Public education is provided "free" for all Canadian citizens and permanent residents until the end of secondary school—usually at age 18.

Most secondary schools are differentiated according to subjects areas (e.g., algebra, biology, music), level of difficulty (e.g., basic, general, and advanced) and reflective of the segmented labor market (e.g., vocational versus academic). Secondary diplomas are granted to students who pass the compulsory and optional courses of their programs whereby students either enter the labor market or go on to further schooling.

While completion of a high school education is not mandatory, by the mid-1970s most Canadians considered a high school diploma the minimum credential to secure employment. School expansion, therefore, included increasing retention rates related to employability and potential post-secondary schooling. In 1952–1953, only 22 percent of students graduated from high school, and in 1976, 75 percent were doing so. By 1991, 82 percent of students had a high school diploma.

Post-secondary schooling in Canada can include either private or public vocational and technical institutions, a community college or technical institute, university, or, in Quebec, CEGEP (*College d'enseignement general et professionel*). Although some colleges allow for completion of two years of academic coursework, only universities have degree-granting status. CEGEPs offer both a general program that leads to university admission and a professional program that prepares students for the labor force.

Data for post-secondary education show high and increasing attainment levels. In fact, Canada is consistently ranked high when levels of post-secondary attainment are compared to other developed countries. In 1976, 8 percent had some college or university; 11 percent had a college diploma or certificate; and 8 percent had a university degree. By 1991 the numbers had changed: 24 percent had a college diploma or certificate and 13.3 percent had a university degree (CESC, 1996, p. 35; CMEC, 1995). By 1994, Canada had the highest proportion of adults with some university education (28%) and the fourth highest percentage of the population with some post-secondary education (30%) (Statistics Canada, 1996a, 1996b).

An increasing percentage of high school dropouts and graduates now consider important alternative forms of upgrading or post-secondary schooling. Adult learners who are not high school graduates can apply to enroll in six-month to three-year programs in colleges (such as technical and vocational institutes), community colleges, institutes of technology, and CEGEPs. Other programs for adult learners include schools for continuing education and careers in business, applied arts, technology, social services, and some health sciences. Enrollment in adult learning programs has more than doubled in the past two decades (CESC, 1996).

SOCIAL AND EDUCATION ISSUES

While school provision is varied across Canada, educators face similar economic and political forces. Six such forces and their effects on Canadian schooling are of particular interest and significance because of the fundamental issues they raise.

Women, Work, and Schooling

From 1941 to 1991, the Canadian population increased from 12 million to 29 million, a 2.4-fold increase that accounts for approximately 70 percent of the absolute increase of the labor force and 50 percent of the wage labor market over the five decades. A substantial portion of labor market expansion can also be attributed to the increasing percentage of women in the labor force. Male labor force participation peaked in 1941 at 85 percent and started a slow decline to 78 percent in 1961 and to 76 percent in 1991. The female participation rate doubled over four decades to 40 percent by 1971 and reached 60 percent in 1991.

Being married does not reduce the likelihood of women in the labor force; married women with children tend to have a higher participation rate than women in all ages combined. Young women can look forward to working more than young men. The labor participation rate of women aged 20 to 44 surpasses the total adult male participation rate of 78 percent. Since 1945, women have been more likely than men to be wage earners in the labor market (Li, 1996). While on average, women may expect to work more than men in the future, they should not expect the same income. In 1995, women earned on average 65 cents for every dollar earned by men. Because this figure is up from the 1981 figure of 54 cents, the gender-based wage-gap has narrowed over the decade— but the differences are still substantial.

The increasing number of women in the workforce and the existing inequities in income have created new demands on Canadian schools. Since one of the major economic functions of Canadian schools over the past three decades has been to provide equalization of opportunity, schools were treated as the primary vehicle to create economic parity between men and women. During that time, many disparities between males and females in education attainment were overcome. In 1991,

29.6 percent of men and 25.4 percent of women were university-educated; but the proportion of women aged 15 to 19 who attended schools marginally exceeded men: 80 percent to 79 percent.

In 1993, 27 percent of women and 21 percent of men were enrolled in university programs as part-time or full-time students. Women, though, continue to be underrepresented in engineering, mathematics, and science programs and overrepresented in the social sciences, humanities, education, and health programs (CMEC, 1995; Statistics Canada, 1996a, 1996b). So while differences between female and male school attainment still exist, they disproportionately affect older women, they are related to program choice, and they are not as great or as pervasive as inequities in income.

At least two feminist views exist on the issue of gender parity. Because women are still overrepresented in many education fields and lower-paying sectors, liberals argue that it is not only years of schooling but the kind of schooling that counts. The correlation between gender, kind of schooling, and segmented labor markets means that schools might still be used as a mechanism to further equalize gender opportunity. Equity would take the form of getting more women into male-dominated subject areas as prerequisites for higher-paying jobs. This approach requires the resocialization of girls so that more of them will go into engineering, mathematics, and science programs. The radical view suggests otherwise. It is not the right kind of schooling that women lack, but rather the power to set the rules of the reward system. The problem is the undervaluation of female labor, whatever that labor. The question is not merely one of socialization, skill deficits, differential school opportunities, or segmented labor markets, but gender oppression.

Work, Immigration, and Schooling

Along with population growth and the recruitment of women into the labor market, the Canadian state met the increased demand for wage labor through the recruitment of immigrant labor and capital. In the late nineteenth and early twentieth centuries, immigrants to Canada were required for agricultural settlement and industrial expansion. In the latter half of the twentieth century, the rising demand for skilled labor saw Canada shift its focus from farm and industrial workers to technical and professional workers. Immigration policy priorities are now motivated to satisfy the requirements of capital and to save on the cost of education and training. The changing demand for skilled labor and entrepreneurial capital has gone hand in hand with changes to immigration policy.

Entrepreneurs, self-employed persons, and investors who can invest at least $250,000 in Canada can qualify for landed immigrant status. Thus, the cultural origins of immigrants no longer play as important a role as they once did in selecting who will become a Canadian citizen. The shift toward technical skills and capital requirements means that immigrants who were once drawn only from the United States and Europe are no longer given top priority because of their affinities with Anglo-Saxon culture.

Many of these new immigrants created demands on Canadian schools related to the professions, assimilation, multiculturalism, and privatization. First, the increasing emphasis on professional and educational qualifications as well as competition with the United States for skilled labor—the so-called "brain-drain"—meant that graduates from Canadian colleges, technical institutes, and universities could not fill the demand. Canada had to supplement its domestically produced technical labor force with qualified immigrants. Since the late 1960s, Canada has been relying on Asian countries to supply over 20 percent of immigrants with professional and managerial skills. In 1981 and 1991 immigrants continued to account for 20 to 21 percent of the managerial, professional, and technical occupations in Canada. In certain professional fields—such as in natural sciences and engineering—immigrants account for a quarter of the jobs.

Second, changing patterns of immigration meant that assimilation practices based on Anglo- conformity would no longer work with racial differences playing an increasingly important part in cultural conflict. Since the 1980s, Canada could no longer follow the assimilation models and patterns established in countries with more homogeneous populations. Because governments now focus on the accumulation of capital for determining immigration policy, racial characteristics are less important in establishing selection criteria. As the cultural filters related to race and national origins were removed at the Canadian border, Canadian schools have had to take on a greater role in assimilating recent immigrants. The result has been increased cultural diversity and new stresses on school systems because of racial, language, and religious differences. The assimilation and credentialing functions of schooling thus became closely associated with the implementation of multiculturalism as government policy.

Third, the ideology of multiculturalism links immigration and school attainment and has become the site of conflict over equitable opportunities for minorities. While schooling in Canada grew and differentiated to meet the needs of industrialization, it also retained a significant level of diversity in response to constraints created by cultural traditions and political resistance. Multiculturalism provided a pragmatic solution to the conflicts between French, English, aboriginal, old immigrant, and new immigrant groups.

Although the number of immigrant children as a proportion of total population is small, new immigrants tend to settle in Canada's largest urban centers (Vancouver, Toronto, and Montreal). In 1995, approximately, two-thirds or about 32,200 of school-age immigrants spoke neither official language. Despite these small numbers, urban clustering creates special demands on schools to expand programs for English and French language instruction and other related cultural and counseling services in a few metropolitan areas (CESC, 1996).

School policymakers have responded by developing culturally sensitive or multicultural curricula, pedagogies, and teacher education to cope with the social conflicts exacerbated by cultural diversity and racial antagonism. Multiculturalism provides the primary ideology for accommodating pluralism and assimilating immigrants over a longer period of time without arousing the resistance created by models of assimilation based on Anglo-conformism (McAndrew, 1995).

The issue of barriers to attainment or the effects of racism for "visible" minorities is contradictory at best as is the colonial history of North American Indians, Africans, and Asians. The role that schools should play in overcoming inequities and dealing with the questions of race are usually guided by the assumption that European/whites share advantages that non-European/non-whites don't have. But this dichotomy does not account for the complexity of differential effects, contradictory facts, and limited strategies intended to overcome racial inequality. For example, in both 1981 and 1991, people born in Canada showed lower levels of educational attainment than persons immigrating to Canada. Furthermore, people from Asia, Africa, and South America showed higher levels of educational attainment than those from Europe, Oceania, and North America. Yet those whose mother tongue is other than English or French did show lower levels of education attainment. But in 1991 those whose mother tongue was other than English or French had a higher proportion of people with university degrees (15.1 percent) than those people whose mother tongue was English or French (13.6 percent). Furthermore, the designation "other" masks a number of differences between minority groups. For example, in 1991 more than 20 percent of all persons who had Chinese as a mother tongue had obtained a university degree, but fewer that 5 percent of those who had Portuguese had the same standing (CESC, 1996).

Evidently educational and economic advantages attained by different cultural, racial, and language groups do not follow any straightforward rules. Quite simply, being from a minority language, ethnic, or racial group is not necessarily a disadvantage in Canada, nor are the strategies intended to overcome such disadvantages so obviously going to equalize opportunity. Strategies based on simple dichotomies may in fact enhance already existing advantages for some racial minorities at the expense of others.

Socioeconomic Forces and the Demand for Schooling

Socioeconomic deprivation and organizational changes for Canadian families have been significant factors in creating new kinds of demands for schooling. Wealth in Canada is disproportionately skewed in favor of the richest people. In 1986, differentiations in wealth reveal that the bottom fifth owned less than one percent of the total. The next poorest fifth owned 2.4 percent; the middle fifth owned 9.3 percent; the second highest fifth owned 19.8 percent; and the richest fifth owned 68.5 percent. The wealth of the top 10 percent accounted for half of total wealth. The richest 20 percent of the population owned at least twice as many assets as the bottom 80 percent combined (Davies & Shorrocks, 1989).

Evidence furthermore suggests that there has been an upward distribution of wealth since 1984, that it is even greater in the 1990s, and that there has been a diminishing return in the growth of disposable income for the general population. According to Human Resource Development Canada's tracking of fifteen quality of life components, social inequality has increased and the social well-being of the average Canadian has been in relative decline when compared to GDP since 1977 (HRDC, 1997). Finally, although income differentials are less favorable to the rich than differences in wealth, economic policy over the past two decades has increasingly favored the very highest earners. Generally speaking, then, the wage-earning population has no longer been making relative or absolute gains from the expanding economy over the past two decades.

That is what the distribution of wealth in Canada looks like, but what about income? From 1973 to 1993, Statistics Canada data indicate that Canadian citizens enjoyed real income increases, with the 1970s registering the best years for all fifths of population. By the 1980s, though, only the bottom fifth continued to have real income increases. The use of government transfers—based mainly on welfare, unemployment insurance, old age securities, and pensions funded by taxation—did redistribute income, but this redistribution did not significantly close the gap between rich and poor. In the 1990s, however, policy changes marked the removal of this state support with huge consequences for the poor whose income came disproportionately from government transfers (Little, 1996a).

Canada's unemployment rate for the spring of 1997 has been stuck at around 9.4 percent, which places Canadians in the middle of the G7. The low was set by Japan at 3.2 percent and the high was set by France at 12.6 percent. This 1997 Canadian figure compares unfavorably to the 1968 figure of 4.5 percent. Furthermore, government policy differentially affects Canadian youth unemployment at twice the national average. In April 1997, youth unemployment (between ages 15–24) registered 17 percent (compared to 7.7 percent in 1968), and unemployment for those with a university degree or post-secondary certificate doubled to 26 percent from 13 percent in 1980 (Little, 1997c).

The increasing differentiation in age, credentials, and employment is often described as the "good-jobs/bad-jobs syndrome." The winners are those with solid school credentials or job skills who take the well-paying jobs and losers are those on the other end of the education-skills spectrum who are left with poor-paying jobs or no job at all. This trend reflects the reality of the 1990s with an increasing polarization in the income that people earn from their work based on the level of school attainment and age (Little, 1997b). Employment for those with a university degree or post-secondary diploma or certificate has increased by 26 percent from 1990 to 1995. For those who graduated from high school, there has been little change, and for those with less than a high-school diploma employment has dropped 25 percent (Little, 1996b).

On an individual basis, years of schooling has become an increasingly important factor for enhancing employment possibilities. In 1990, those with a post-secondary degree or diploma held 49 percent of all jobs, up from 41 percent in 1990; and those who dropped out before earning a high-school diploma have 19 percent of all jobs, down from 27 percent. Since 1990, the number of jobs for those with elementary-school education has fallen 30 percent, for those with a university degree it has risen by 30 percent, and unemployment rates are higher for persons with lower levels of education (Little, 1996b,1997a). Generally, those people who are older and/or more schooled tend to have more economic opportunity than those who are younger and/or have lower levels of educational attainment.

Declining Socioeconomic Status, Families, and Schooling

In the 1990s, the most significant factor that schools have had to deal with has been changes to Canadian families and the diversity of households that their students are coming from. Central to the fact of increasing demands on teachers is the growing number of student problems related to the organization and socioeconomic difficulties of their families who have had to come to terms with reduced incomes and reconstituted family arrangements.

The socioeconomic status of families and school success have been highly correlated for a long time (Lessard, 1995; Olson, 1995). Data continues to confirm that children who are better off financially do better in school. Canada's poorest children are three times as likely as the economically best off children to be in remedial classes, and the richest children are almost twice as likely to be in gifted classes as the poorest. Poor students are at greater risk of dropping out. Children from lower socioeconomic status families exhibit higher levels of physical aggression. Children from single-parent families have an increased risk of experiencing emotional, behavioral, social, or academic problems and tend to score lower on tests of verbal ability (HRDC, 1997).

School systems in Canada reproduce the social

system of inequality. In a 1996 study of individual mobility of fathers and sons from 1982 to 1993, Statistics Canada tracked 400,000 men aged 16 to 19. Young men were three times as likely to move from poverty to poverty than from poverty to riches, and the most likely event was to move from riches to riches. Just being born to a father in the top 10 percent gave a son the likelihood of making 40 percent more than a son born to a father in the bottom 10 percent. Even among the children of middle-income families, richer boys tended to rise higher in the rankings while poorer boys tended to fall. While there is a good deal of movement between adjacent levels on the income scale, the richest and poorest tended to inherit income levels from their fathers (Mitchell, 1996).

Increasing educational opportunity and improving the socioeconomic status of the less fortunate in society is the working assumption for most school reform initiatives. However, at the bottom end of status attainment, the link between poverty and schooling suggests that the Canadian school systems, in spite of being focused on amelioration strategies, have been unable to overcome the structural inequalities in Canadian society, much less dismiss the school's contribution to the reproduction of these same inequalities. Furthermore, recent cutbacks have increased the differentiation within the systems and created the potential for a return to lower rates of upward mobility and a more rigid class structure. So on issues of equity and equality, schools are lagging. In result, early and ongoing intervention strategies have once again become a hot topic for discussion.

But current debates about intervention have a different dynamic in the 1990s than in the 1960s. Calls for more compensatory programs must be justified in an environment where governments are restricting the amount of resources that will be available for social problems arising from the unequal effects of the market. Poverty-related hunger, violence, illness, domestic problems, and deprivation can only hint at the increasing resources required to retain the Canadian standard of civilized behavior while at the same time dealing with fiscal restraint.

The Scientific Management of Diversity and Learning

While assessment has been a cornerstone of educational practice, it is only recently that Canadians have moved toward national measures of student progress. In 1994, all provinces and territories (excluding Saskatchewan) participated in the School Achievement Indicators Program (SAIP). The initial testing showed that 60 percent of 16-year-olds demonstrated competency in mathematics knowledge and skills but only 24 percent were able to solve more complex mathematics problems. More than 70 percent could read and understand complex texts. About 80 percent of those tested demonstrated control over elements of writing, including style, grammar, and vocabulary. The first SAIP was intended to establish a baseline for longitudinal studies of literacy and to take part in the International Assessment of Educational Progress (IAEP) surveys that started in 1991. The IAEP assessed the mathematical abilities of 13-year-olds in twenty countries. In the mathematics and science components, Canadians scored in the mid- to above-mid range, exhibiting a consistent pattern with past studies of this nature (CMEC, 1995).

Along with SAIPs and IAEPs, many provinces are reintroducing compulsory provincial final examinations and moving away from using a combination of school-specific exams and cumulative performance assessments by teachers. Past systems of evaluation are thus undergoing reform. Governments are centralizing departments of education and introducing province-wide performance assessments on specific school outputs. For example, Ontario now administers a province-wide test of grade 9 students in reading and writing. Alberta expanded its assessment program in 1995, administering tests annually to all students in grades 3, 6, and 9. Alberta has also introduced a battery of evaluations, including attitudinal surveys of the population about the quality and goals of schooling. In Ontario, similar changes are underway.

Attempts to standardize testing continue to fly

in the face of an extensive body of literature that suggests that standardized measures of school performance are limited by many factors:

1. They sacrifice depth for breadth of coverage or validity.
2. They are based on outdated conceptions of knowledge.
3. They establish limited pedagogical and organizational patterns of learning.
4. They show, by definition, that some will score below the average while some will score above the average.
5. They exacerbate competition.
6. They assume that knowledge on objective standardized tests is neutral, but in fact it gives an advantage to some at the expense of others along cultural lines.
7. They either motivate for the wrong reasons or do not motivate at all, resulting in apathy or cheating.
8. They inevitably become the tool of policymakers and politicians.

While it is debatable whether the consequences of assessment reform and the multiplication of province-wide assessments will be effective tests for literacy or accurately measure the quality of public education, they have nevertheless become the focus for parent and business leaders (see, for example, Barlow & Robertson, 1994).

The Rise and Stall of the Teaching Profession

Standardized testing and performance indicators have become highly politicized and used to challenge the professional prerogatives of teachers to evaluate students and to determine classroom goals for students. Once schooling was linked to industrial productivity and credentials were treated as economic property for market exchange, economists came forward to assess the value of education, evaluate the organization of teacher labor, and anticipate the kinds of new jobs that would require new kinds of skill training. Throughout the 1980s economic demands increasingly were placed on schools. In addition, school suc-

cess and international competitiveness were pushed to the front of the business agenda. In the process, Canadian teachers have come under more public scrutiny for their economic role.

A closer look at teacher labor in Canada reveals an older, feminized, stressed, and politicized profession. First, following the expansion of mass schooling that peaked in the 1970s, the number of full-time educators reached a relative low point in 1984–1985. The number has increased consistently since then. In the period between 1984–1985 and 1991–1992, the educator work force increased by 13 percent, even though total enrollment increased only 5 percent, and, since 1991, there has been a moderate decline in the number of educators. From 1989 to 1994 the number of college teachers increased 10 percent and the number of university teachers increased only 0.2 percent. Throughout the 1990s there has been an increasing percentage of educators who work part-time (CESC, 1996).

Second, as part of a general demographic trend for all workers, educators are getting older. The average age of educators increased from 34 years in 1972–1973 to 42 years in 1992–1993, and more than 45 percent of the 1992–1993 cohort could be retiring in the first decade of the twenty-first century (CESC, 1996). Like elementary and secondary educators, the full-time university–teacher work force is also aging. In 1983, 16 percent of full-time faculty were 55 years and older; a decade later, the percentage rose to 25 percent (CESC, 1996).

Third, in addition to the teaching profession getting older, it is a profession where the majority is female. Teaching is a feminized occupation and thus shares the constraints of other feminized occupations in a patriarchal society. In terms of male/female composition, the number of male teachers has remained relatively stable for the past two decades while the number of female teachers has increased consistently in the last decade. In 1992–1993, women made up a 61 percent of educators employed in elementary and secondary education. About three in four elementary teachers are women and one in three secondary teachers is a woman. More women are becoming administrators. While women occupied 15 percent of administrative positions in 1981–1982, they held 29 percent in 1992–1993. Still, women face many difficulties in getting managerial equity (CESC, 1996; ECC, 1992).

Fourth, teachers live with greater demands and fewer rewards. Teachers have absorbed real static incomes and reduced spending on school infrastructure. They also work in an increasingly inhospitable work environment. Burnout continues to spur an exodus from teaching. The pull of retirement is marked by the push of increased pressures in schools related to discipline problems; an aging teacher population; student relations; unrealistic expectations by administrators, parents, and students; and an intensifying workload. Many of these problems are related to the harsh economic and social realities, such as single-parent families, increasing levels of child poverty, and dual income families. Students and teachers increasingly lack the community resources that were available during the halcyon days of the 1960s and 1970s. Also, because school systems offer limited opportunities for advancement, the incentive to stay after the maximum salary qualification has been reached is minimal (King & Peart, 1992).

A major Quebec survey found, though, that 77 percent of teachers would choose the same profession again if they had the opportunity. So teaching is a relatively attractive occupation, confirmed by the fact that Canadian universities contribute to a teacher surplus by training 2000 teachers per year. With 35,000 teachers available for full-time work, competition in the new market reality is intense. Demand, though, will vary regionally. The Atlantic provinces will require fewer new teachers and in Ontario the demands may be significant.

Given the rising stress on teacher labor and the dual threats to most working people of decreased real income and increased probability of unemployment, why would someone still want to become or to stay a teacher? According to King and Peart (1992), teacher satisfaction comes primarily from students and collegial relationships. But economic and social status might also be the answer. In a relative comparison to other countries, Canadian teacher salaries are among the highest in the world (relative to GDP per capita). And, in relation to the incomes of other professional occupations in Canada, teachers rank in the mid or lower-mid range for socioeconomic status (ECC, 1992).

Using income as an indicator of status, Canadian teachers rank higher in relation to teachers in the rest of the world but middle to low in relation to other professional occupations in Canada (ECC, 1992). Furthermore, if public attitudes about education indicate the public perception of teacher status, then educators have been consistently ranked higher than other professions (such as business, government, and medicine). Canadian teachers, however, have suffered a loss of public confidence in their performance over the last decade—as have many other professional and managerial occupations (Livingstone & Hart, 1995).

Finally, teachers are becoming politicized in response to challenges created by education reform. Teachers have been caught up in continuous rounds of provincial reform, which required changes to the administration of the schooling process. But teacher practice did not always conform to the interests of either parents, bureaucrats, politicians, or business spokespersons. In the politics of education, all claimed to speak for the good of children and society. Debates over what schools should do and what they were doing increased in the late 1980s. Central to the debate was the power of teacher organizations. The latest wave of intense education restructuring took hold in 1993 and has led to further changes in the rationalization of school governance and challenges to the teaching profession.

The scope of government reforms across the country include these commonalties:

1. The adoption and expansion of province-wide and national testing and student achievement exams

2. The tentative statement of national standards (with the exception of Quebec) for science and other subjects
3. The creation of partnerships between schools and corporations
4. The establishment of parent advisory councils for administrators
5. The formation of influential stakeholder commissions at the provincial and national levels
6. The centralization of control over funding and curriculum
7. The reduction or elimination of the power of local democratically elected school boards
8. The regionalization of curriculum development and evaluation
9. The end of thirty years of sustained growth in spending to education and the initiation of deep cuts in some provinces (Lewington, 1997)

In spite of the high levels of literacy in Canada and because of the differential and comparative effects of interventions, school reformers now demand that teachers "do more with less," which means that the country should increase the level of education service and meet the diverse needs of the public and business community while at the same time reducing the cost of government expenditures. Approximately four-fifths of the cost of education—as in other public service occupations—goes to labor. Because schooling is a teacher-intensive process, relative to other economic sectors, cost containment of education expenditures implicitly means lowering the real wages of teachers. To accomplish this task, governments have challenged the organizational power of teacher unions and their professional monopolies as service providers with new kinds of schooling relationships.

Major teacher-government conflicts have heated up in Canadian educational politics throughout the 1990s. Initial threats have come from government challenges to traditional forms of union organization and the increasing pressures on teachers to form self-regulating bodies or traditional professional associations to govern training, discipline, and certification. In British Columbia

and Ontario, where they now have regulatory colleges, and in Alberta and Manitoba, where colleges have only been suggested, teachers have strongly resisted the formation of these professional associations that could undermine union solidarity and power.

In Alberta and Ontario, teachers marked 1997 with mobilizations in marches, work to rule, and possible strikes, but for the most part teachers have acquiesced to government initiatives in the 1990s. The Canadian Teachers' Federation (CTF) and its member organizations began working on a priority campaign for the fall of 1997 to deal with eight focus issues:

1. The erosion of confidence in public schools
2. Less adequate and equitable education funding
3. Privatization, including charter schools, private schools, vouchers, and contracting out
4. The diminishing quality of life of children and young adults
5. The narrowing of curriculum and standardized testing
6. The diminishing quality of life of teachers
7. Agenda-driven governance such as increased parental control, site-based management, and the decline in the number and power of school boards
8. The declining social commitment to equity

THE FUTURE OF SOCIETY AND SCHOOLING

Political forces have shaped the rules and reward systems of Canadian society, and Canadian teachers are currently organizing to fight for their jobs and public education. But teacher politics is part of a larger dynamic. A new debate has emerged. It is about democratic pluralism and the rise of anti-democratic forms of capitalist governance. Along with the right of teachers to collectively organize and protect their own incomes, the discussion also includes questions about the role of technology, rule by experts, fiscal restraint, bureaucratic centralization, the effects of market-led decentralization, and the delivery and cost of education programs. Thrown into this mix is the rise of market-based models of educational delivery and the assimilation of higher education into the global knowledge-based economy. Looming ever larger is the specter of unemployment, underemployment, and poverty that threatens many people.

Within this milieu, Canadians exhibit a radical and contradictory will to change something. The public wants governments to pressure business to live up to some kind of social responsibility while at the same time expressing unease about deficit cutting timetables, tax cuts, pro-business agendas, and the diversity of claims on state expenditures. Into the ideological void have stepped the New Right politicians whose solutions also express contradictory interests.

Education reform and New Right politics marry neoliberal economics to residual forms of conservatism. Neoliberals (or technoeconomic liberals, as they are sometimes called) are the leading force within the New Right coalition. Their agenda places increased importance on the role of science and technology (especially the new information and knowledge-based technologies). They argue that the enhancement of human capital in conjunction with new information technologies provides a viable solution to productivity declines. They also believe schools should be modeled on the just-in-time organization of the most advanced transnational corporations.

While neoliberals privilege the power of large corporations, they must also secure popular support, so they have been forced to moderate the corporate agenda in a process of pluralist coalition building. Because many of the central policy issues in education relate to language and religion, the doctrine of conservative communitarianism has been highly influential in creating a basis of support across the country. The result is a contradictory set of reform packages that offer new possibilities as well as resurrect old inequities and attitudes. Radical democratic and socialist traditions have been influential in pressing the schools in the development of a democratic and egalitarian ethos, but for the most part radical democratic and socialist ideas on education have become indistinguishable from progressive liberal ideas

and all have been treated by the New Right as part of the problem.

In spite of ideological differences in degree, certain neoliberal similarities are evident—such as the reduction in the number of boards, the centralization of administration in the ministry, and the implementation of parent advisory councils for many schools—but many traditional differences remain. Different emphases are promoted by New Right and social democratic provincial governments.

A New Right restoration has included the politicization of the business community and major challenges to public education. Large corporations and small businesses have fundamental concerns about schooling. Economists have placed education institutions under considerable scrutiny and have been fervent promoters of economic liberalism and human capital theory. They argue that Canada's competitive position in the global marketplace has been compromised by poor educational performance. The corporate sector and its neoliberal representatives have mobilized public support through New Right organizations and defended the "little person" against the incursions of the state and "special interests." Populist resentment against the welfare state has been mobilized to free up state revenues for capital investments in the business sector and to eliminate or redefine the universality of social services that were the mainstay of support for all Canadians.

The corporate sector, in alliance with other movements, has influenced the reorganization of Canadian schools in four ways. First, it has shaped the fiscal, monetary, and industrial policy of the Canadian state. Second, it has provided an educational model for the internal reorganization of the bureaucratic relations of schooling according to the logic of the new transnational enterprise. Third, it has entered into partnerships with schools as steering agents. Fourth, it has directly subsumed parts of education systems through the privatization, marketization, and commodification of educational services.

School reformers led by big business expertise and driven by populist sentiment call for primary and secondary schooling to incorporate the assumptions of Human Resource Development (HRD) for the benefit of educational entrepreneurs and to return to the hierarchical values of social order. Post-secondary institutions are most sympathetic to the new HRD and are taking a hard look at the neoliberal strategies related to science and information-based technologies. These valuable assets in the new knowledge economy are potentially open to reorganization and marketization according to the science–city model or "information corporation." Thus the development of human capital for the labor market and applied research for the capital market is having a pervasive effect on Canadian schooling.

In accounting for economic globalization and postmodern industrialization, the current economic woes of the poor and unemployed have been attributed primarily to the personal failing of individuals to acquire the right skills through schooling. Furthermore, political and moral leadership has been left to the managers of transnational enterprises and Canadian institutions in alliance with small business promoters who want to lead Canadians out of the desert and back to the garden.

But who will be led back to this garden? In response to the challenges of workers, women, First Nations, some minority groups, and others, powerful agents talk a lot to each other and have succeeded in getting governments to protect the interests of the business community and institutional administrators at the risk of polarizing Canadian society as it has never been polarized before. Government policies since the late 1970s have accelerated the polarization between rich and poor, old and young, the employed and unemployed, the corporate elite and waged and salaried workers. Governments have changed the rules of the market in favor of corporations and their managers and lessened their commitment to those who are least able to protect themselves.

The failure of a critical intellectual community to provide a viable alternative to the neoliberal and neoconservative agenda leaves much to ponder. The hearts and minds of many Canadian citizens remain ambivalent, bewildered, or dis-tempered. Many are working harder for lower wages; some are not working at all. Some Canadians may not be able to compete in the knowledge-based economy. Many students may not find a better life at the end of their schooldays as did their parents. Not everyone will have the money to pay for schooling or a computer—but each will probably face a treadmill of new school programs that have less to do with enlightenment and more to do with getting that elusive job: lifelong learning and an eternal pilgrimage to credential heaven.

It was not so long ago that Canadians anticipated their future in a much friendlier country and contemplated an education for the leisure society. Today leisure has an unsavory appeal, redefined by the threat of unemployment, underemployment, or poverty, especially for a quarter of Canada's youth. For many, Canada is still a great place to live, but intolerance is on the rise and the benefits of growth are increasingly skewed in favor of the few. If anywhere in the world, it is in Canada where one should be able to feed, clothe, and shelter all children, to provide meaningful work for all youth, to create fulfilling lifestyles for all the elderly, to ensure a safe and secure work environment for all adults, and to provide a rich and rewarding education for all citizens. If not now, when will Canadians have the resources or the luxury to do such things? This question seems eternal. To live in a rich country like Canada is a great privilege. At its worst it is still a garden; at its best a northern dream. As Canadian society increasingly distances itself from the Old World, it is hesitating. It seems to share a dream with Mean Streets in a New World—yet there sleeps another vision, one that existed before the land was mapped by Europeans, a dream that things are going to happen.

ENDNOTES

1. I want to acknowledge the judicious editing and cogent insights provided by Deanna Williamson.

2. The Organization for Economic Cooperation and Development (OECD) is mentioned many times in this book. It was founded in Paris in 1960 as an organization for economic cooperation and development. The following countries are part of it: Belgium, Denmark, Germany, France, Greece, Ireland, Iceland, Italy, Canada, Luxembourg, the Netherlands, Norway, Austria, Portugal, Sweden, Switzerland, Spain, Turkey, United Kingdom, USA, Japan, Finland, Australia, New Zealand, Mexico, Czech Republic, Hungary. Although primarily a body for economic cooperation, the OECD is, thanks to its center for research and innovation of the education system (CERI), also an important international platform for educational questions.

REFERENCES

Barlow, M., & Robertson, H.J. (1991). *Class warfare: The assault on Canada's schools.* Toronto: Key Porter.

Canadian Education Statistics Council (CESC). (1996). *Education indicators in Canada: Pan-Canadian education indicators program.* Toronto: Author.

Conrad, M., Finkel, A., & Jaenen, C. (1993). *History of the Canadian peoples. Vol. 1.* Toronto: Copp Clark Pitman.

Council of Ministers of Education, Canada (CMEC). (1995). *Report on education in Canada.* Toronto: Author.

Davies, J.B., & Shorrocks, A.F. (1989). Optimal grouping of income and wealth data. *Journal of Econometrics, 42,* 97–108.

Economic Council of Canada (ECC). (1992). *A lot to learn: Education and training in Canada.* Ottawa: Author.

Human Resources Development Canada (HRDC). (1997, Winter-Spring). Social audit. *Applied Research Bulletin, 3*(1), 22.

King, A.J.C., & Peart, M.J. (1992). *Teachers in Canada: Their work and quality of life. A national study for the Canadian Teachers' Federation.* Queen's University at Kingston. Social Program Evaluation Group.

Knox, P. (1997, June 12). Canada still place to live, UN says. *The Globe and Mail,* p. A1.

Lessard, C. (1995). Equality and inequality in Canadian education. In R. Ghosh & D. Ray (Eds.), *Social change and education in Canada* (3rd ed.; pp. 178–195). Toronto: Harcourt Brace.

Lewington, J. (1997, September 3). Education takes on national flavour. *The Globe and Mail,* p. A4,

Li, P. (1996). *The making of post-war Canada.* Toronto: Oxford University.

Little, B. (1996a, February 12). How earnings of the poor have collapsed. *The Globe and Mail,* http://www.TheGlobeAndMail.com/docs/webextra/middle_kingdom/ama/MKamadex.html.

Little, B. (1996b, August 26). Why it pays to stay in school. *The Globe and Mail,* http://www.TheGlobeAndMail.com/docs/webextra/middle_kingdom/ama/MKamadex.html.

Little, B. (1997a, April 21). The industries that will define the decade. *The Globe and Mail,* http://www.TheGlobeAndMail.com/docs/webextra/middle_kingdom/ama/MKamadex.html.

Little, B. (1997b, May 19). Nineties take an income bite from the middle. *The Globe and Mail,* http://www.TheGlobeAndMail.com/docs/webextra/middle_kingdom/ama/MKamadex.html.

Little, B. (1997c, May 15). Youth left out, Canada warned. *The Globe and Mail,* p. A1.

Livingstone, D.W., & Hart, D. (1995). Popular beliefs about Canadian schools. In R. Ghosh & D. Ray (Eds.), *Social change and education in Canada* (3rd ed.). Toronto: Harcourt Brace.

McAndrew, M. (1995). Ethnicity, multiculturalism, and multicultural education in Canada. In R. Ghosh & D. Ray (Eds.), *Social change and education in Canada* (3rd ed.). Toronto: Harcourt Brace.

Mitchell, A. (1996, January 25). Like father, like son in incomes, Statscan finds. *The Globe and Mail,* p. A1.

Mitchell, A. (1997, April 16). It's official: Quebec less than 25% of population. *The Globe and Mail,* p. A1.

Naylor, R.T. (1987). *Canada in the European age 1453–1919.* Vancouver: New Star.

Olson, P. (1995). Poverty and education in Canada. In R. Ghosh & D. Ray (Eds.), *Social change and education in Canada* (3rd ed.; pp. 196–208). Toronto: Harcourt Brace.

Organization for Economic Cooperation and Development (OECD). (1996). *The OECD observer: OECD in figures, statistics on the member countries.* Paris: Author.

Peters, F. (1996, March). Perspectives on private schools. *First reading: Fundamentalisms—searching out the truth.* Vol. 14, No. 1. Edmonton: Edmonton Social Planning Council.

Statistics Canada. (1996a). *Catalogue 11-008-XPE.* Ottawa: Minister of Supply and Services.

Statistics Canada. (1996b) *Catalogue 11-008E.* Ottawa: Minister of Supply and Services.

CHAPTER 4

Education in Mexico: Sociopolitical Perspectives

CARLOS TORRES
OCTAVIO PESCADOR

Carlos Alberto Torres *is a professor in the Graduate School of Education and Information Studies and Director of the Latin American Center at the University of California, Los Angeles (UCLA). He has degrees in sociology, political science, and education from universities in Argentina, Mexico, and the United States, including a Ph.D. in International Development Education from Stanford University. He is the author or editor of three dozen books and more than 100 articles in English, Spanish, and Portuguese, in a number of different fields including educational policy, political sociology, nonformal education, and critical theory. He has for many years been a close collaborator of Paulo Freire, especially during Freire's term as Secretary of Education in Sao Paulo. He is currently President of the Comparative and International Education Society and Vice President of the Research Committee on Sociology of Education of the International Sociological Association.*

Octavio Pescador *is a doctoral candidate in the Graduate School of Education and Information Studies at the University of California, Los Angeles.*

Mexico constitutes one of the most diverse polities in the world; it is a land of stark contrasts. The Mexican republic is divided into 31 states and a federal district. With a population of 93 million and 2 million square kilometers of territory, Mexico is one of the largest countries in the region both demographically and geographically. While over 40 percent of its population lives in poverty, Mexico is the home of 24 of the richest 500 individuals on the globe.

This chapter, first, examines the extant conditions of Mexico's economic, political, and social realms. Second, it provides an overview of the most relevant administrative and pedagogic traits of the educational system. Finally, it identifies current educational problems and challenges for the future.

THE SOCIAL FABRIC

Economic

There are over 35 million people in the labor force—the vast majority employed in the service and industrial sectors. Of Mexico's $335 billion GDP, only 5.4 percent results from the agricultural sector. Today, in contrast to most of its postrevolutionary history, the Mexican economy can be characterized as outward-oriented and closely tied to the United States. Mexico has established trade agreements with the United States (NAFTA, 1994) and Chile (1995), and it is currently negotiating the establishment of commercial treaties with the European Community and other Latin American trade associations.

Changes in trade, fiscal, and exchange rate policies over the past decade have resulted in favorable trade balances in the recent past—particularly with respect to its northern trade partners. Over 80 percent of Mexico's $95.9 billion in exports in 1996 were sold to the United States. Likewise, over 75 percent of Mexico's $89.5 billion imports came from the United States.

In spite of the stability that the externally designed privatization and deregulation reforms of the past fifteen years were expected to produce, recurrent economic crises continue to strike the nation since the oil shocks and the default on debt service payments of the early 1980s.[1] The periods of instability have generated a staggering external debt, high inflation rates, negligible growth, an insulting income inequity, and considerable budget deficits. The combination of these factors, along with an exorbitant population growth, has resulted in a permanent employment deficit of over one million jobs annually and an enormous and rapidly growing informal economic sector.

Following the 1994 solvency crisis, the nation implemented a harsh stabilization plan financed by the Clinton administration along with international financial institutions. Over $50 billion were needed to keep the economy afloat; the largest portion of the funds actually used went to foreign investors cashing in their short-term bonds from the Mexican treasury. Mexican bankers were another main recipient of foreign currency during the last post-crisis adjustment process. In contrast to the 1982 expropriation of the banking industry, after the 1994 "solvency crisis" the state was extremely careful not to threaten domestic and foreign capital. Consequently, the bulk of the Mexican population has endured serious hardship throughout the macroeconomic stabilization phase: high inflation, exorbitant interest rates, and job cuts.

The meager salaries received by most people are insufficient even for subsistence purposes. Hence, they have resorted to procuring supplemental income via the informal sector and, in many cases, to defaulting on their debts. Street vendors have multiplied throughout the country and are taking over the streets of all urban centers in the country. Although official violent crime rates have dropped, the inhabitants of the largest cities in the country—especially those of Mexico City—experience greater threats to their patrimony and physical integrity. The discrepancy between what the public denounces privately and to the media and the official statistics stems from its distrust and, in some cases, fear of law enforcement institutions.

Political

The student movement of 1968 and its suppression by the military constituted the threshold of the political stability Mexico enjoyed since the formation in the early 1930s of the clientelist State apparatus articulated by the *Partido Revolucionario Institucional* (PRI).[2] That was the critical juncture from which the political debacle that currently affects the nation gained its initial momentum. During the mid-1980s, the Mexican corporatist state undertook a structural adjustment program as recommended by the International Monetary Fund and the World Bank. In essence, it renounced its role as a benefactor and began selling most of its assets, cutting social spending, and increasing taxes.

After more than twenty-five years of pervasive abuse of power, ideological intolerance, political repression, and grotesque mismanagement, and over half a century of single party rule, a natural disaster—the 1985 Mexico City earthquake—shook the core of the monolithic governance system forged by the heirs of the Revolution. Nature revealed the financial, political, and, most importantly, moral incapacity of the state to serve its constituents when they needed it most. Confronted by this vacuum of support, diverse social forces mobilized, initially, to face adversity; subsequently, in the 1988 presidential election, to claim the basic right for a responsive and freely elected government. Such an election was preceded by the first major break in the Revolutionary family when the initial massive political realignment in post-revolutionary history took place with the formation of the *Partido de la Revolución Democrática* (PRD).

After a highly questioned ascent to power, the last of the hegemonic PRI administrations tried to appease the initial popular clamor over fraud and failure through several strategies. Among those the most significant ones included co-opting businessmen, intellectuals, public opinion leaders, and even clergymen; replacing traditional corporatist hierarchies; injecting resources to rural and poor urban localities; crushing certain opposition political groups and pampering others; and devising a dexterous domestic and foreign public relations campaign. This strategy succeeded in so far as it temporarily stabilized the economy and created a short-lived mirage of growth.

The lack of access to traditional reward and co-optation resources and a bloodstained conquering of the presidency in 1994, in conjunction with the economic collapse of 1995 and the worsening of blatant corruption and impunity within governmental agencies, accelerated the demise of the ruling party's control over the state. Over 50 percent of Mexico's population is now governed by opposition-elected officials. The PRI has lost control over the most important cities in the nation, including Mexico City, and, for the first time since its creation, it no longer dominates Congress. While the right wing *Partido Acción Nacional* (PAN) gained positions during the early dismantling of the corporatist structure, the center-left PRD consolidated its presence during the midterm elections of 1997. Mexicans may enter the next millennium with a dramatic transfer of power that will certainly be considered the most significant accomplishment of the current administration.

Sociocultural

Cultural manifestations are the greatest asset of Mexico and its people. They link Mexicans' pre-Columbian, colonial, and modern experiences. Indigenous and southern European institutions, traditions, and beliefs have been fused through the ample interaction between natives, Creoles, *mestizos,* and Europeans, developing a peculiar and hybrid culture that Nestor García Candini (1989) so aptly discussed in his anthropological work. Long before post-modernism acquired its current prominence, Mexican popular and high art were appreciated in an equal standing both within the country and abroad. Distinguished Mexicans and their works have been featured in the most prestigious forums from the Vienna Opera House and

the Louvre to the Metropolitan Museum of Art and the Smithsonian.

Mexicans' cultural heritage covers approximately three thousand years and embodies a dichotomy of splendor and subjugation. The artistic and scientific talent of the peoples of *Mesoamerica* manifested themselves in their majestic and architecturally precise constructions and precious crafts that one can admire still, for instance, at Teotihuacan, Tula, and Yucatán, in the poetry of Nezahualcoyotl, or the mathematical sophistication of the Aztecs' sun stone or calendar. Yet there were some exploitative societies and key figures with a totalitarian drive, such as Tlacaelel, who instituted among the *Mexicas* a religious prerogative and need to conquer, enslave, and sacrifice other peoples. Likewise, the new Spain produced numerous virtuosos in all the arts and sciences from Sor Juana Inés de la Cruz to Bernal Díaz del Castillo. But the colonizers also willingly, and again in the name of religion, destroyed the knowledge and culture of pre-existing Mesoamerican societies and dispossessed all the indigenous peoples and the emerging group of *mestizos* from land and dignity.

Newly independent Mexico nourished great strategists and humanists who strove to develop a national Mexican identity and a unified nation, for example, José María Morelos y Pavón and Benito Juárez. Nonetheless, the emergent nation also produced ravenous and dictatorial persons such as Agustín de Iturbide and Porfirio Díaz, whose utilitarianism and servitude to foreign and domestic elites brought misery and hardship to the Mexican people. Similarly, post-revolutionary Mexico has offered the world numerous talented artists, scientists, and academics such as José Vasconcelos, Angela Peralta, Octavio Paz, and Mario Molina who have helped to consolidate the national identity. Mexico has also engendered murderous, dishonest, and insidious individuals who have maimed the moral character of the people, hampered the development efforts of the state and the productivity of the private sector and thus perpetuated and intensified economic inequity.

Needless to say, alongside this gallery of

prestigious intellectuals there is, particularly accentuated in the nineties, an underworld of Mafia bosses connected to drug trafficking and with powerful liaisons to the political and economic spheres whose social preponderance challenges the future of Mexico's democracy. Mexicans will no doubt receive the next century with an incipient democratic renaissance and an idiosyncrasy that is being formed amidst the turmoil of a collapsing status quo and an increasingly anarchic state of affairs.

SCHOOLING

Teachers have long been considered an important force in forging the nationalist character of the Mexican people. Even as the social standing of the teaching profession has been severely downgraded over the years, public schooling has been one of the main institutions sustaining the post-revolutionary state.[3] The philosophical tenets of the educational system, based on the notion of normalism (Ponton, 1989), have not varied greatly since the consolidation of the extant state. Nevertheless, the overwhelming authority of the presidential office over the public sector has impacted public education whenever a politician with a strong personality has conquered such office.

Since the Constitution establishes the general traits of public education, the current schooling system can be considered as a product of the pedagogical ideals emerging from the Revolution. Notwithstanding, critical public educators have actively participated in moving Mexican society away from acquiescence and docility—which public schools used to promote, according to some critics. While schools produced the governing elite controlling the status quo for many decades, they are currently forming many of the militants and leaders that will soon debunk the dominant political aristocracy.

Guiding Educational Philosophies

The guiding principles of schooling in Mexico are clearly expressed in Article 3 of the Constitution, which states that public education should be compulsory, secular, nationalist, humanist, integral, objective, and democratic. The state must provide educational services to the population. Mexicans are a highly devout people and public education is one of the most important civic rituals since the early 1920s. The heroes and memorable occasions of the nation's vast and eventful history were celebrated in the schools long before the consolidation of the post-revolutionary state. Yet only after the revolution were the masses inducted formally into civil society with the same ideological agenda as the governing military-bureaucratic elite. The ideology of Mexican post-revolutionary liberalism sought to integrate all social groups under one protecting and materially rewarding political-economic governmental apparatus.

Legislation and Governance

Due to the precarious economic condition of states and municipalities following the Revolution in 1917, the constitutional mandate for municipal provision of educational services was never fulfilled. The role of municipalities in schooling was reduced even further with the creation of the Ministry of Education (*Secretaría de Educación Pública* or SEP) in 1921 and the accompanying legislative mandate for public schooling expansion, curricular design, and normative enforcement by the federal government. By the early 1990s, central educational authorities controlled nearly three-fourths of the nation's schools as well as a massive administrative apparatus with bureaus in all states.

With the enactment of the new General Education Law in 1993, the Ministry of Education transferred administrative and operational control of basic education (preschool, primary, and secondary) and teacher training institutions to states' educational authorities. Central authorities maintained the normative control over the system, designing national curricula, producing and distributing the national free textbooks, approving materials for secondary and teacher training institutions and elaborating and conducting national evaluations. SEP also maintained control over adult education, in-service training, and compensatory programs.

Teachers are legally mandated to acquire union membership; thus, there are over one and one quarter million unionized basic education instructors. The economic, pedagogical, and particularly social-political might of the union makes it the most powerful actor in educational policy making next to the SEP. In addition to its rank and file, the teachers' union controls the inspectorate system for basic education and key positions within the ministry, the former via a tacit system of rewards and sanctions (promotions, paid licenses, red-tape in administrative affairs, manipulating fringe benefits and the like) and the latter via co-optation and political pressure.

Technical and post-secondary institutions lack a governing body coordinating curricula, academic and training programs, and administrative structures. Additionally, universities have administrative and programmatic autonomy both in Mexico City and the states. Only federal institutions are centrally controlled. In the early 1980s a general organizational plan for higher education was devised and implemented through various planning committees at the national, regional, and state level. By the early 1990s, the National Association of Higher Education Institutions (ANUIES) was created along with the national evaluation committee so that programs could be coordinated and educational policy and fund allocation decisions could be informed by the results obtained from institutional quality and performance assessments.

Educational Demographics

Since 1993, following a constitutional amendment, there are nine years of compulsory schooling and the school calendar has been extended to 200 days. The quality of services varies greatly across the nation—with southern states faring worse on all indicators contrary to Mexico City and some northern states. During the last two decades, the system has increased its coverage and efficiency in all basic education levels.

Overall educational enrollments have increased uninterruptedly from 1970 (11.5 million) to 1996 (26.4 million) (*Subsecretaria de Coordinacion Educativa,* 1993). During this time period, preschool coverage experienced the greatest increase of all educational levels: In 1976 only 14.3 percent of all 4- and 5-year-old children were enrolled in preschool; by 1993, 68.1 percent of all children in this age cohort received educational services. Likewise, the percent of incomplete primary schools considerably decreased: In 1976 it was 50.6 percent of all schools, by 1993 it was only 13.8 percent. Secondary absorption, moreover, increased up to 1981 (86.8 percent), decreased throughout the eighties (in 1991 it was 82.9 percent), and started recovering in 1992 (82.9 percent).

In terms of systemic efficiency during the last two decades, dropout levels in primary and secondary education have gone down steadily: In 1976 they were 8.7 percent and 11 percent of all primary and secondary students respectively; by 1993 they decreased to 4.1 percent and 8.4 percent. The number of repeaters in these educational levels has only slightly decreased: In 1976 primary and secondary school repeaters totaled 10.3 percent and 27.3 percent respectively, and in 1993 they amounted to 9.8 percent and 26.3 percent. Terminal efficiency in primary and secondary schooling has improved: In 1976 primary terminal efficiency was 42.6 percent and secondary terminal efficiency was 70.7 percent; by 1992 terminal efficiency was 61.1 percent at the primary level and 75.3 percent in secondary schools.

Educational Finance

The Ministry of Education apportions funds to the states through its central planning office. Traditionally, the central educational leadership determined most educational expenditures; thus, local educational authorities had exclusive managerial responsibilities. With the new General Education Law, states acquired discretionary faculties over some educational funds. Since most pecuniary resources are employed to pay teacher salaries and to build and maintain facilities, it is in the design and operation of regional content programs, in the acquisition of supplemental teaching materials and facilities, and in staff development where the states can allocate resources according to their perceived needs and preferences.

There have been fluctuating trends in the amount of resources devoted to education since the 1970s. From 1971 to 1982 there was a continuous growth of educational expenditures as a percent of total GNP. From then on, education's portion of GNP started dropping until 1989 when it reached the record low of 3.8 percent of GNP. During the 1990s increasing resources began to flow into education, and by 1992 education's share of GNP reached 5.1 percent and 5.8 percent in 1993. By 1994 educational spending reached nearly 6.0 percent of GNP—the highest level in this century (Office of the Secretary of Education, 1993, 1994; Pescador & Torres, 1985; *Subsecretaria de Coordinacion Educativa,* 1993). Yet due to the crisis of December 1994, governmental spending in education collapsed nearly 50 percent in real terms. In 1995 educational expenditures amounted to only 5.2 percent of the GNP and there was not a considerable increase in spending during 1996 and 1997. Official estimates suggest that spending will substantially increase over the following three years yet such growth will depend on the success of the crisis-adjusted economic program unveiled by the present administration over one year after its ascent to power.

Spending on education, as a share of total government expenditures, increased from 1970 (6.58 percent) until 1982 (12.8 percent), when a decreasing trend initiated (Pescador & Torres, 1985; *Subsecretaria de Coordinacion Educativa,* 1993). This downward pattern reached its lowest point in 1987 (8.3 percent). From the late 1980s to the mid-1990s there was a recovery in governmental spending in education as a share of total government expenditures. Such increased spending has severely deteriorated since the late 1994 economic crisis.

Nearly three-quarters of governmental expenditures in education are paid by federal funds. By 1991 states' and municipalities' contribution to education accounted for 16.3 percent of total educational expenditures. Even though their share of educational spending increased in successive years, since 1994 localities also reduced their educational budgets—in 1996 they provided only 10.1 percent of total public spending in education. Likewise the private sector's investment in education has been low, yet as the federal government increased spending in education, private contributions to education have grown at a substantially slower rate. In 1996 the government provided over 95 percent of total educational expenditures as opposed to the 90 percent it provided in 1986.

Teachers' Salaries

Mexican teachers are the most valuable asset of the educational system. The average educational attainment of the Mexican population is six years of schooling but, in spite of their severely low wages and precarious working and living conditions, public pedagogues have helped to increase by two grade levels the average educational attainment of the population during the last two decades. What makes their work admirable is the adverse economic and social contexts that teachers defied to accomplish it. During the 1980s teachers' salaries devalued approximately 70 percent, yet enrollment increased nearly 20 percent. Currently, teachers' salaries continue to be significantly lower than in 1979. There are three payment categories for teachers, depending on the region of the nation where they reside and the type of position (state or federal) they hold. High-paid teachers receive approximately $300 per month (including salary and fringe benefits) and their low remunerated colleagues are paid between 10 and 15 percent less per month.

Given that their salary does not suffice to cover even subsistence needs, the vast majority of teachers hold several teaching positions (teaching sometimes 10 hours a day) or they are employed in fields other than education in both the formal and informal sectors. Pay-related concerns have been the major source of disruptions in the educational system for nearly twenty years. In spite of ideological and political differences within the union, teachers have demanded, collectively in some instances, that the state remunerate fairly the growing working demands they face and for which they are accountable. Typically, however, only the insurgent factions of the union have belligerently fought for pay increases (unfortunately ceasing to impart lessons) even after the official union leadership and the apathetic yet professionally committed rank and file agree to the terms set by the state.

Teacher Training and *Carrera Magisterial*

Until the creation of the National Pedagogic University (UPN) in the mid-1980s, the teaching force had been educated in normal schools. As a result of a new law established in 1984, aspiring teachers possessing a higher education degree were required to pass an examination to obtain a teaching post. Also an open certification system for in-service teachers was created to provide them an opportunity to attain a higher education diploma.

Currently, the curriculum for teacher training institutions has a common core focusing on learning skills and classroom practice for the three levels of basic education. Several mechanisms are being used to train in-service teachers combining distance education and formal instruction.

With the new educational law and the approval of the union, a career system for teachers was established—the *Carrera Magisterial*. It is an innovative attempt to improve the quality of instruction and system efficiency by providing monetary incentives to teachers. It is a horizontal promotion system based on a direct evaluation of teachers' seniority, educational level, and participation in staff development courses, and on an indirect assessment through their pupils' performance. The system establishes five salary categories within a teaching position, with increases to teachers remuneration allotted as salary and not as fringe benefits.

Curriculum

The National Technical Council of Education, SEP's pedagogical core, designs and modifies curricular frameworks. To a certain extent curriculum development involves, in an advisory role, the different programmatic bodies at the state and site levels. The curriculum applies to all basic education, yet regional contents complement the national core program. Rural and indigenous schools utilize adaptations of the core curriculum so as to better satisfy the needs of their pupils. Moreover, after a selection of proposals, SEP produces and gratuitously distributes over ten million primary education textbooks for the subjects of mathematics, Spanish, history, civics education, geography, and natural sciences. A special series of textbooks is published in the most important indigenous languages spoken in the country.

Academic secondary schools offer college preparatory curricula; they also provide some technical training in several trades and industrial occupations. Vocational secondary schools emphasize technical instruction and laboratories and, given their terminal character, are more intensive than regular secondary institutions. SEP does not publish textbooks for secondary schools, yet it authorizes curriculum changes and designates the textbooks employed.

Evaluation

Evaluation of the Mexican educational system has been limited. It was not until the early 1970s that the first systematic data collection, analysis, and distribution was initiated. This focused on quantitative information ranging from enrollment rates to budget allocations. Until 1993 no national standardized examinations were administered; instructors used their discretion to grant or deny grade-level promotion. SEP provides completion certificates for basic education (primary and secondary schooling) through public schools or through officially recognized private institutions. Access to upper secondary education is not automatic. Each school establishes its entry tests and requirements and all private institutions must be accredited by a public institution—generally the National Autonomous University of Mexico (or UNAM).

CURRENT ISSUES AND FUTURE PROSPECTS

Schooling in Mexico is confronted by political-economic, pedagogical, and social challenges. Problems in the educational sector resemble the larger societal difficulties pervading the Mexican populace. The initially violent struggle for the democratization of hierarchical structures has created a sense of anxiety and uncertainty on the part of traditional actors (teachers, union officials, academics, and bureaucrats). Yet it has also strengthened the social presence and negotiating power of an emerging leadership (insurgent teachers, independent labor unions, and opposition leaders). Moreover, disparities in income distribution generated by corruption, mismanagement, and the neoliberal policies of structural adjustment have deeply affected the middle and working classes, multiplied the dispossessed and the informally employed, and enriched an elite (for example, union leaders).

A combination of political cynicism, economic disillusionment, and social perplexity are turning many Mexican youngsters from all social strata into apathetic, spiritless, self-interested spectators; in the worst cases, into criminals. Needless to say, Mexican youth has deteriorated in its readiness for learning and has turned more violent. In contrast to the student movements of the late 1960s which had long-term socially oriented objectives, the current student rallies have taken place due to immediate individual concerns. Within a decade, nihilism has flourished in the popular culture to a degree completely unexpected by social critics.

There are also strictly pedagogic problems afflicting the educational system. A simplistic diagnosis, based on *a priori* values of causality, would suggest that all educational illnesses are due to the scarcity of resources and that they could be changed with increased investment. Undoubt-edly there has been a severe educational deterioration due to the grim regression in the living and working conditions that teachers and the entire population experienced over the past two decades. Yet one cannot guarantee that corporatist decision making, mismanagement, and corruption would have been tamed with increased resources. Nor can one argue that greater economic resources would have reached the lowest strata in the educational hierarchy, be it in the form of better prepared teachers exclusively devoted to teaching; newer and sufficient facilities, instructional aides, and technology; or context-relevant curricula, pedagogic processes, and organizational structures generated by synchronous and goal-oriented educational research.

An increase in spending on education by both the public and private sectors is long overdue and the present administration has started moving in that direction. Nevertheless, there are some structural and operational problems that may deter the benefits accruing from a more robust educational budget. First, there is the prevailing extreme fiscal centralization that limits the decision-making authority and implementation capacity of municipalities and local governments. In spite of the mandated decentralization of authority, there continues to be concentration of authority in most aspects of schooling. Second, the politicization and shortsightedness of planning processes prevent policy enactment and implementation unfettered by sectarian interests. The collusion of some bureaucrats, particularly those supervising site operations and program design, with the teachers' union deprives the system of its accountability mechanism that is essential to guarantee continuity, stimulate productivity, and adjust programs to site-based special needs and characteristics. For example, the current shortage of preschool teachers and surplus of primary school teachers is partly due to a poor estimation of enrollment growth rates at the different educational levels.

The precarious qualifications of many middle- and low-ranking bureaucrats, especially in the educational sector, can be partly explained by the highly limited access to higher education, the low quality of many programs taught at public universities, and the lack of investment in strategic areas such as research and development.

Furthermore, the lack of a meaningful private involvement in education—from provision of services to participation in school councils—promotes the inefficiency of the public schools. Although the new education law mandated the creation and active site-based involvement of school councils, both the union and its allies in the official bureaucracy have derailed the implementation of this measure. In other words, the citizenry has no effective representation in or control over schooling.

A historic yet recently aggravated discordance between the statutory foundation of the state and its habitual behavior has disadvantaged the majority of the population, as the case of the new educational law exemplifies. A social treatise ceases to be effective when the guarantor of organized freedom neglects or cannot fulfill its basic obligations such as the provision of security and employment opportunities. Citizens emerging from educational systems in decadent states do not uphold the values conducive for the reproduction of pre-existing political and economic structures. On the contrary, since they have no risk of losing property or decent living standards, they are motivated to expedite the establishment of a new social contract.

Mexican schools appear to be forming citizens who are economically without hope yet are politically conscious and participatory. In January 1994, disenfranchised and landless indigenous peasants along with rural teachers organized an armed revolt that effectively defied the power of the state for the first time in over six decades. Their actions have encouraged other groups to take up arms and challenge the state.

A new social contract is gestating and the schooling system is at the core of this process. Educational debate will no doubt intensify in the years to come, since the social arrangement that will emerge from the collapse of the corporatist state will need the schooling system to succeed. The Mexican people have proven resilient to adversity throughout their history and they will certainly come out soundly from the current turmoil.

ENDNOTES

1. Relying on its increasing oil reserves and revenues, Mexico borrowed extensively from American and European financial institutions during the seventies. Yet the global collapse of the oil market during the early eighties along with the changes in fiscal and exchange rate policies of the Reagan and Thatcher administrations severely damaged the economic standing of the nation.

2. In an extremely broad generalization, Mexico's political history has had three defining moments: the war of independence at the turn of the nineteenth century, which transferred power from foreign monarchical elites to domestic landed aristocrats; the war of Reform by the mid-nineteenth century, where ecclesiastic and foreign-serving conservative elites were defeated by liberal republican forces, and the Revolution (1910–1920) in which landed aristocrats were crushed by the *caudillos* who commanded the support of the peasantry. After the Revolution there was a decade of turmoil and political violence that concluded with the formation of an all-inclusive political structure that distributed power and control over public resources among its members. That was the birth of the Mexican post-revolutionary state.

3. It is important to mention that education has been a public enterprise throughout the twentieth century. The role of private sector has been minuscule in the basic education system (currently less than 5 percent of schools are privately operated) and moderate in higher education.

REFERENCES

Candini, N.G. (1989). *Culturas híbridas: Estrategias para entrar y salir de la modernidad*. México, D.F.: Grijalvo, Consejo Nacional para la Cultura y las Artes.

Office of the Secretary of Education, Estados Unidos Mexicanos, miscellaneous.

Pescador, J.A., & Torres, C. A. (1985). *Poder politico y educacion en Mexico,* Mexico: UTHEA.

Ponton, B.C. (1989). *Educacion normal y control politico.* Mexico: Centro de Investigaciones y Estudios Superiores en Antropologia Social, Ediciones de la Casa Chata.

Subsecretaria de Coordinacion Educativa, Direccion General de Planeacion, Programacion y Presupuesto, Direccion de Analisis y Sistemas de Informacion (1993). *Compendio Estadistico del Sector Educativo.* Mexico City: Author.

CHAPTER 5

"Growth with Equity": Social Change and Challenges to Education in Chile

ANNETTE BARNARD

Annette Barnard is a lecturer in the Education Department, University of Newcastle upon Tyne, U.K., and an adviser on special educational needs to The British Council. She has most recently worked as a consultant in Europe, the Middle East, and Latin America. She worked in Chile from 1965 to 1973, remains a frequent visitor to that country, and maintains a professional interest in the development of its educational system. She is the author of an extensive report, commissioned by the Chilean Government, on the integration of children with special educational needs within Metropolitan Santiago.

THE SOCIAL FABRIC

Chile is located on the western seaboard of South America, stretching from its northern border with Perú to the South Pole, and reaching out into the Pacific to the island territories of Easter Island and the Juan Fernández group. Chile's Antarctic Territories comprise some 1,250,000 square kilometers, but the people of Chile are mostly to be found within the 756,626 square kilometers of mainland territory that runs between the Andes mountain range and the Pacific Ocean for some 4,345 kilometers, north to south.

Rarely more than 170 kilometers wide at any one point, mainland Chile offers a considerable range of geography and climate throughout its length. This, together with historical factors, has influenced patterns of human settlement. Thus, since colonial times, the majority of the population has lived within the 1,100-kilometers-long Central Valley, and this pattern continues today.

Chile has 14.4 million inhabitants (UNESCO, 1995) and approximately 57 percent of the total population of the country can be found in the Central Valley. Outside the Central Valley, regions and their provinces vary greatly in area and population density as well as in their economic and social development.

Historically, the diversity of Chile's geography and climate within the corridor between ocean and mountain has been the main determiner of Chile's financial health. Nitrates and copper in the northern desert have long been a source of wealth for Chile's economy and the motor force of its development. Even today, with Chile's successful efforts to penetrate international markets with agricultural products, copper accounts for 37 percent of export earnings (Barclay's Bank, 1996).

Chile is a land of immigrants, Europeans in particular, which has given a particular connotation to the racial uniformity of the country (Lavanchy, 1993). One-third of the population is directly descended from Spanish and European immigrants, and the other two-thirds are the *mestizos,* the descendants of colonial or other immigrant groups who intermingled with the indigenous population. Today, the relatively small indigenous population, to be found in the south (the *Araucanos*) and in the north (the *Atacameños*), constitute a neglected minority (Avalos, 1996).

However, it is from this rich and diverse mix that Chile draws its cherished customs, its literature, its music, and its art. The cultural heritage is a source of pride and there are few Chileans who cannot quote from the poetry of Chile's two Nobel Prize winners for literature, Pablo Neruda and Gabriela Mistral. Yet despite the many icons that signal a strong cultural unity, Chile is a divided country where rigid social divisions between distinct groups are ordained by wealth and breeding. Tironi (1990) wrote of two Chiles, co-existing but barely touching: one an affluent elite looking beyond national boundaries and the other an increasingly impoverished underclass struggling, and often failing, to establish itself within a free market culture.

Economic Aspects

Chile is the current "economic tiger" of all of Latin America, including South America, Central America, the Caribbean, and Mexico. GDP per capita was US$4,741 with a growth rate of 8.5 percent in 1995, the highest rate in Latin America (*World Factbook,* 1996). It is seen as a stable country with a robust and responsible fiscal policy and a government dedicated to social improvement. Behind the economic miracle is a country that has undergone profound economic, political, and social change.

To the foreign observer, Chile's performance on a number of international indicators signifies the efforts made by successive governments to improve the quality of life of its people. For example, life expectancy for women is 77.72 years and for men 71.26 years (*World Factbook,* 1996), and infant mortality rates are 17 per 1,000 live births, contrasted with an average of 45 for the rest of Latin America (UNESCO, 1995).

World funding institutions, such as the IMF and the World Bank, have identified the efforts of the Chilean government to improve the economy and to control inflation and have responded with appropriate funding. However, while the figures above can be taken as evidence of social investment during the last decades, it should be noted that these figures are presented as averages for the country as a whole and they cannot be assumed to reflect the wide range that, in reality, exists between the different regions. A gulf continues to exist between rich and poor that, despite the stable, high economic growth and the dynamism that it signals, is widening (ECLAC, 1995).

Political Aspects

Since independence in the early nineteenth century, successive Chilean governments, located in the capital city of Santiago, have had little difficulty in exercising their authority over the rest of the country, given good sea communications with much smaller regional population areas. The relatively tranquil history of Chile during much of that time and the concentration of influence and wealth in the Central Valley favored centralized government and, to better govern the more distant regions, the creation of an administrative bureaucracy that took to itself decision making at every level and in every area of activity.

Education was by no means immune from this development, and a complexity of regulations, governing each and every area of educational provision from the curriculum to the fabric of school buildings, required consultation with and the permission of Santiago. Bureaucracy grew increasingly irksome, but restructuring during the last thirty years has enabled regions outside the Central Valley to gain a greater say in the decision-making process and some mastery over the administration of their internal affairs.

Today Chile is divided into thirteen regions countrywide; Metropolitan Santiago is a separate administrative entity, housing national government ministries but independent of them. Government policy is decided centrally but each region, together with Metropolitan Santiago, is responsible for its own government and is linked to central government through the Ministry of the Interior.

The shift to a more decentralized bureaucracy, together with fundamental changes related to the introduction of the Market Economy Model, structural adjustment pressures, and the expectations of a people newly returned to democracy are just part of the essential background to understanding the complexities involved in current changes in education provision in Chile.

SCHOOLING

Chile has a history of educational achievement of which she is justifiably proud. Universities teaching theology, canon law, and philosophy were established by the Dominican and Jesuit orders in the early seventeenth century. In 1747, following a petition to the King of Spain by the Council of Santiago, a new university began to offer training in the disciplines of medicine, law, and mathematics in addition to the established studies of philosophy, law, and theology (Schiefelbein, 1991). Following independence and the return of a cultured elite from exile in Europe, enlightened ideas, especially relating to secular education, found fertile ground. The University of Chile was established in 1842 by Andrés Bello, whose interest in research, in addition to teaching, imprinted an academic tradition on the university sector that exists today. Concerning public education, the *Instituto Nacional* (offering free public education to selected children in the capital) was established in 1813 and still exists as the preeminent school within the publicly maintained sector.

The major educational reforms throughout this century have continued the trend toward greater access to basic education and secondary education for previously disadvantaged groups. The effect of this can be observed in the adult literacy rates for both men and women, 95 percent in 1995 (UNESCO, 1995). Today, access to free education in both primary and secondary is guaranteed through the political constitution of 1980 and the LOCE, the National Law for Education (*Ley Orgánica Constitucional de Enseñanza;* March 1990).

The provision of that education at preprimary, primary, secondary, and higher education levels is through a publicly funded educational system. However, alongside the public system is a substantial private system of primary and secondary schools, professional institutes, and universities.

Private education has always been an important part of educational provision in Chile, reflecting the interests and concerns of religious groups, immigrants, and the social elite. The two systems share commonalities of curriculum but differ widely in their client group and level of resourcing. The existence of this dual system is sanctioned by legislation passed to regulate the role of the private sector in education, identified in the same legislation as collaborating with the educational role of the state *"colaboradores de la función educativa del Estado"* (Ministry of Education, 1980).

Within the school system, both for public (free of charge) and private schooling, there are the eight years of compulsory primary education (*Educación Básica*) offering the same national curriculum. Primary education consists of two four-year cycles. Cycle I provides basic education in the core subjects of Spanish, mathematics, sciences, history, and geography. Cycle II provides the same core subjects but requires a foreign language, usually English, to be taught from Year 7 (the third year of the second cycle). Art, music, physical education, and religious education complement the core subjects in both cycles.

Secondary schooling (*Enseñanza Media*) begins at age 14. Two routes through secondary schooling are offered to students. The first is to enter a *liceo,* which offers a scientific-humanist, academically oriented education within a four-year cycle. Students selecting this option might be expected to proceed to higher education in a university or a professional institute. The second route is oriented toward training programs of a technical vocational nature offered in technical training schools. This is a five-year cycle, and students are expected to graduate with a middle-level qualification for industry, commerce, agriculture, or other technical-vocational occupations.

The Chilean educational system serves roughly 3 million students, 67 percent of whom are enrolled in primary education. Figures available for 1990 show a total of 739,015 students attending secondary school compared to an enrollment of 2,051,143 at the primary level (Ministry of Education, 1990). Presently 96.4 percent of children eligible to attend primary education are on roll, most of these remaining, on average, for 7.5 years out of the 8 years allotted to this phase of education (Milicic, 1996).

High enrollment during the primary cycles with a falling off in the secondary phase is a recognized pattern. Milicic (1996) ascribes the differences in enrollment between phases to elevated dropout rates among students of secondary age rather than to demographic factors. According to Téllez (1994), rural children and children living in urban poverty have the greatest problems of access to schooling, attending for only a few years. In their study on poverty and social exclusion in Chile, MacClure and Urmeneta (1996) found the familiar problem of family poverty as the main cause of failure to sustain school attendance. Thus, even though the overall years of schooling in 1992 stand at 9.24 compared to 4.33 years in 1970 (Téllez, 1994), global figures for primary and secondary school attendance in Chile should be viewed against the spread of family income and geographical location.

In the tertiary sector, two different university groupings can be identified—the traditional state universities (*estatales*) and those universities created by the private sector following the 1981 educational reform (*privadas*) (Fried & Abuhadba, 1991). In addition to universities, there are a range of professional institutes and technical training centers, some of which are eligible for state funding.

Traditional is the ascriptive given to the older, well-established, and academically respected universities existing prior to the 1981 reform. The private sector universities, often employing established lecturers from the traditional universities for additional contracted hours, offer a more limited concept of university life. Such universities are teaching universities with little or no access to research funds from the national commission for university research CONICYT (*Comisión Nacional de Investigación Científica y Tecnológica*). They have targeted those academic areas that are highly prized by students but where infrastructure and academic resourcing is less demanding of investment. Thus, there has been a considerable expansion in professional training for lawyers, economists, and educators (mainly at preschool and primary phase), but not in those areas such as medicine, dentistry, and engineering where specialist and more expensive facilities are required.

In both sectors, public and private, students pay fees for tuition, and these must reflect the real cost of tertiary education as agreed by the universities jointly (Fried & Abuhadba, 1991). The key features regarding the two university sectors for students relate to the greater prestige enjoyed by the traditional sector and the financial assistance available through *crédito fiscal,* a student loan system operated by the state but one not open to students within the private sector.

Access to the university is increasingly reserved for those who have benefited from uninterrupted progress through secondary schooling and who have the ability to pay or the confidence to take out loans. Brunner (1993) raises the issue of equity within the tertiary sector, pointing out that the enrollment figures for the higher-income group is around eight times that of the group with the lowest income. He reports that young adults from the poorest backgrounds represent one-fifth of the total 18-to-24 age group, but constitute less than 5 percent of enrollment in higher education. This is contrasted with young people in the upper-income group, representing just 13.5 percent of the total age population, but accounting for approximately one-third of total enrollment. Access to student loans also favors students from more affluent families.

Teacher training is the preserve of the university sector and has a strongly academic focus (Avalos, 1996). As with other university courses, students continuing education are self-financing. Trainee teachers, in whatever phase (preschool, primary, secondary, or special education), undertake five years of professional studies. They graduate as *Licenciado en Educación* and may then enter the public or private sector, where they are permitted to teach only in the phase for which they have been trained. Post-qualifying courses for teachers are few in number and mainly concentrated in the capital city. The Ministry of Education offers short courses within regional centers and distance courses. These are mainly concerned with changes, for example, in national curriculum content and pedagogy rather than with a wider professional development.

Until 1981, Chile, in common with many other countries in Latin America, had a centralized and overly bureaucratized educational administration. Following the 1981 reform, the Chilean education system was decentralized, with administration devolved through regional and provincial levels to schools and other educational units. To foreign observers, the present organization may seem intensely complex. For example, currently several kinds of intermediate authorities work at various levels between the central government and the schools to provide secondary and primary education. In total, the educational system has five levels of management: national, regional, provincial, municipal/corporation, and the school.

The national level has control over curricular and technical matters and is organized, after the office of the Minister and Deputy Minister, into General Education (responsible for specific phases including adult and technical education); Tertiary Education, Culture, Planning, and Finance; Legal, General Administration; and the National Center for Experimentation and Research in Education (which also develops and delivers the in-service provision for teachers nationally). There are several "functionally decentralized bodies" (*organismos funcionalmente decentralizados*), for example, the National Board of Tertiary Education, the National Board of Students' Grants, the National Board of Pre-School Education, the National Commission for Scientific and Technical Research, the Board of University Chancellors (chancellors of publicly funded universities), and the National Board of Libraries, Archives, and Museums (Ministry of Education, 1993).

The regional and provincial levels maintain an administrative structure similar to that existing at national level. The main administrative functions

of regions relate to "planning, regulating and supervising the educational process in schools under their jurisdiction" (Ministry of Education, 1993, p. 20). In the case of the provincial level, its functions relate to technical supervision (monitoring the quality of curriculum delivery), administration and supervision of the financial administration of schools (the collection of data relating to student attendance) and the accreditation of new and existing schools within both the public and private sectors, and the maintenance of the school fabric in public schools only (Espínola, 1995).

Municipalities have responsibility for the financial administration of public education at the local level. Each city has a municipality—larger cities have more than one—that has autonomy over its administration and resources and its own budget for education (Ministry of Education, 1993). The distinct role of municipalities in education relates to budget allocation and the selection and recruitment of teaching staff (including headteachers) within public schools for which they are responsible. The schools' budgets are managed centrally by the municipality and the sum allocated is based on the averaged attendance of pupils.

Difficulties arise where a municipality cannot cover school running costs on income devolving from the *subvención* alone and must allocate additional funds from its own budget. At some point, this became problematic. Where funding has been insufficient, teachers' wages and working conditions have been adversely affected. However, with the enactment of a Teachers Law (*Estatuto de los Profesionales de la Educación,* Ley 19.070, July, 1991), the central Ministry of Education assumed the function of "regulator of teachers' wages and their working conditions" (Espínola, 1995, p. 9).

The municipal school is just one of the ways in which students may receive an education through public funding. There exists also a semiprivate sector, *particular subvencionado,* a mixed market of privately owned schools that are also state subsidized. The present mix of schooling may perhaps best be understood through a consideration of the funding to schools. The present financing of the public education system overall is based on a central government subsidy per student (*unidad de subvención educacional*) that is adjusted annually (Ministry of Education, 1993). In the case of municipal schools, the *subvención* is paid directly to the municipality, which then funds the schools. In the semiprivate sector, the owners of the school receive the *subvención* directly from the central government and are financially accountable for monies received. Auditing is carried out at least once a term through the provincial supervisors who check student attendance against enrollment.

Entrance to the two publicly funded systems differs. Municipal schools may not select places but must be filled on a first-come, first-served basis. Schools in the semiprivate sector may exercise selection of student intake but may not demand additional fees from parents. Common practice within this state-subsidized private sector, however, is for parents to enter into financial arrangements (often by banker's order and thus legally enforceable) to pay additional fees while at the same time signing a document to attest to the voluntary nature of such an agreement. Municipal schools, which account for 60 percent of primary school pupils and just over 50 percent of secondary pupils (Ministry of Education, 1994), thus receive the same *subvención* per student as schools in the subsidized private sector, but manage with fewer resources.

Schools in the private sector are owned, administered, and financed independently of the central government. They account for 7.5 percent of primary-aged children and around 10 percent of secondary pupils (Ministry of Education, 1994). Such schools may be owned by individuals and/or the parents of students attending who buy shares in the school for the duration of their child's stay. Private schools are fee paying, even where parents own the qualifying shares for admission. There is no government limit to what fee may be charged nor are such schools accountable to government for their financial administration. Private schools exist at all levels of preschool, primary, and secondary education. They follow the National Curriculum but may offer additional subjects, in particular alternatives in modern foreign languages.

When taking into consideration all the levels of the education system, the public sector—schools that provide free education—constitute 56.7 percent of the whole system. The private system, however, increases alongside the natural progression of schooling, starting from 34.2 percent in preschool level to 74.1 percent at the tertiary level (Ministry of Education, 1993).

MAJOR ISSUES, CONTROVERSIES, AND PROBLEMS

During the past thirty years, major educational reforms have been undertaken within the Chilean system. A major reform came in the mid-1960s when the number of years of primary schooling was extended from six to eight years, a reform of the primary curriculum through pedagogical initiatives, teaching guides, and in-service training. It was at this time also that technical-vocational education was given recognition and became one of the choices for students entering the secondary phase, carrying with that choice the opportunity to continue to tertiary studies.

The government of the 1960s was concerned with improving access and modernizing the curriculum throughout the whole of Chile and, in particular, to extend and improve primary education in rural areas where poverty and illiteracy were most pronounced. During these years, public spending overall increased twofold, with education as a major cost to the government (Arellano, 1988). Later, the brief Popular Unity government of Salvador Allende Gossens planned rather than executed major reforms within primary and secondary phases. Its plan for the National Unified School, providing a common curriculum and social engagement with the community at large for both the public and the private sector, was cut short by the military coup. Indeed, this proposed reform (still at the discussion stage) generated such heated political debate that it became a factor in the process that led to the overthrow of the Allende (Farrell, 1986). However, one achievement of the government was within the tertiary sector. Access was provided to mature students, especially workers, through greater flexibility in admission criteria and the opportunity to study outside regular working hours.

The installation of the military Junta led by General Pinochet heralded unprecedented changes throughout Chile. Political repression and the suspension of democratic processes were the early precursors to the formulation and execution of social and political policies that changed the face of Chile. The engine for change within social policy was the philosophy of the free market and with it the concept of the unencumbered state embraced so fervently by the government of General Pinochet. Garreton (1986) describes this process precisely as nothing less than an "attempt at an overall reorganization of society directed from above" (p. 166).

The adoption of a neoliberal economic model in regard to social policy signaled an end to the state interventionist tradition that had held sway in Chile since the late 1930s. In education, as in other areas such as health, spending was reduced and services privatized and decentralized. Indeed, the spur for social policy reform within the neoliberal economic model adopted was the desire to cut monies available for social programs, including education, and to target the reduced fiscal resources to the very poorest sectors of society. The purpose of financial targeting was to assist those at the very margins of society to grasp opportunities to establish themselves in the market. Recent criticism of targeting has suggested that the most vulnerable groups of society lost more than they gained because of the drastic reduction in the government's social policy budget overall (Scott, 1996). Because the redirection of public monies was at the heart of the decentralization process, within education decentralization was achieved through the shifting of responsibility from the central Ministry of Education to regions and provinces and on down to the deliverers of educational services through the system of *subvenciones* already described.

The repercussions of this transition had enor-

mous social impact. The public school system was essentially placed in the hands of municipalities and private entrepreneurs. Prior to the reform, the activities of municipalities had been limited to the issuance of *patentes*—a system of licensing for a wide range of activities within the community such as vehicle licensing and the collection of the local land tax—and community services such as garbage collection and public gardens. Municipalities had no tradition of administering areas related to social provision. Their response in the main was to view the financial implication of the reform as the first major concern and to appoint business managers and accountants to direct the educational services they were now called upon to provide.

The conditions of teachers under the new reforms became critical as they ceased to be civil servants with rights to public pensions and social benefits, the traditional prerequisites of those working for the state, and became commodities in the free market. The profession itself was traumatized by its loss of professional standing. Its members lost their rights to unionization, which opened up the labor market in teaching to the manipulation of wages and teaching conditions by employers. The resulting tension added to that arising from the political repression that was particularly fierce against activists in the teaching profession throughout all three phases of education (Schiefelbein, 1991).

The application of the neoliberal model to schooling carried with it the rhetoric of the market. The introduction of a free market would ensure quality through competition, good schools would prosper, and poor schools would close. The debate about quality internationally centers on the efficiency of education, assessed on a number of variables (Hawes & Stephens, 1990); the Pinochet government chose to measure student outcomes. SIMCE, the System for Measuring the Quality of Education, was introduced in 1988. The results of national testing were published so that discerning parents could exercise their right to seek out the most successful schools in which to enroll their children. Parental right to open and free enrollment was seen as an important adjunct to the efficiency of the market model.

In 1990, democracy was restored to Chile. All political parties opposed to Pinochet joined together in the *Concertación* to present a realizable alternative, united by their opposition to Pinochet, if not by the unity of their political philosophy. The incoming government had the unenviable task of uniting the country after prolonged and repressive military government. The new government assumed, of necessity, the role of consensus and transition to democracy for a nation separated from this in all its forms for seventeen years.

One of the major dilemmas faced by the *Concertación* headed by Aylwin was the debate on the future of the education system restructured in the 1981 reform. In particular, concerns were concentrated on the poor levels of attainments by students enrolled in municipal schools. Test results published by SIMCE revealed marked differences in attainment between students in the public and private sectors. According to Garcia-Huidobro (1994): "Experts estimated that the scores of public schools trailed those of private ones by at least 25 points. In Spanish, the highest scores were registered in the private paid primary schools located in the high income neighborhoods of Santiago, while the lowest scores were recorded in rural municipal schools. This gap widened in the 1982–1989 period" (p. 8).

The new government, acknowledging the weaknesses within the system, expressed a desire to see an increase in parental, community, and teacher participation in decision-making processes in relation to teaching and learning at the local level. Garcia-Huidobro (1994) observed that the government's view was that education was now everyone's task and that the whole community had to be involved in solving educational problems.

The alleviation of the perceived inequalities within the educational system was a central issue in the political program of the new democratic government and generated a fierce debate in the polarized political arena. Parties to the right (parties supporting Pinochet) wished to retain the financial benefits of a decentralized educational

system, while groups to the left in the *Concertación* envisaged a return to a more centralized educational system and a restoration of the status of the teaching profession. In reality, however, the reforms of the Pinochet government had radically altered the structure of government, in particular in the area of social policy, and the new government found itself inevitably reliant on the social market mechanisms already in place.

Within education, the *Concertación* decided to maintain the decentralized education system and address the issues of quality and equity directly through policies targeted at the municipal schools. Here, rather than raising the level of the subsidy (the funding policy set in place by the military government), the new government decided to channel additional resources through major educational projects. The purpose of the additional funding was to improve the quality of teaching and learning in the public sector where teaching styles within classrooms were seen as too formal, too didactic, and too focused on the transmission of curriculum content (Avalos, 1996; Espínola, 1994; Milicic, 1996). In part, these problems were seen as stemming from the shortcomings within the teacher training system. Filp (1994) observed that: "Although teachers have been trained in universities or institutes, . . . [t]heir training to meet the challenges of teaching is too much based upon theoretical aspects of teaching and too little based on practice" (p.192, our translation).

The Aylwin government was not insensitive to the global challenges facing the country. These included equal access to education for the rural and urban poor, the low quality of attainment in the public sector, the destruction of the professionalism of the teaching force, the lack of diversity within secondary education, and the inability of that sector to provide a vocational and technical training both publicly acceptable and able to support the processes for economic growth. The government's priorities focused on two strands: emergency programs (the improvement of quality in basic education and the diversification of secondary education) and constitutional reforms to counter the worst effects of the military regime. A key concern within the remit of constitutional reform was the restoration of the professional status of teachers through the *Estatuto Docente* in 1991. This Teachers' Statute established minimum salaries and removed the local pay bargaining that had placed teachers at the mercy of employers under the military regime. It established a career structure incorporating increments for in-service training and a points system. Although not implemented in its entirety, the Statute was an attempt to protect teachers from the merciless buffeting of the market and ultimately to benefit the children attending schools by bringing greater stability and security to the profession (Undurraga, 1994).

The financial constraints faced by the new government were considerable. The government of Pinochet had cut public spending to the bone and the lack of allocated funding for education called into question the government's ability to act swiftly to implement reforms. Fortuitously, the ending of military rule coincided with the Jomtien Conference and its attendant focus on quality and equity in basic education and on access for marginalized groups. Thus the international cooperation that followed the return to democracy was marshaled in support of the new government's desire to act promptly on perceived weaknesses within public education. The first concrete steps toward improving quality and equity were taken by the Aylwin government in 1990 with the initiation of the P-900 program (*Programa de las 900 Escuelas*) directed towards the poorest achieving municipal primary schools and funded with support from the Swedish and Danish governments (Gajardo, 1992).

Using the test results of the SIMCE database for a purpose not envisaged by the military regime (Garcia-Huidobro & Jara, 1994), 969 urban, middle-sized schools enrolling students from low-income families were selected nationwide. In 1991, another 416 schools were incorporated into the program, now representing 15.1 percent of all municipal sector schools. The following year, a program was established to include schools in remote rural areas, which shared the features of low income and poor test results of the urban

schools, but were smaller in size. The program reached 1,456 municipal primary schools involving 235,183 pupils and 7,000 teachers (García-Huidobro, 1994). Its stated purpose was to raise levels of achievement in reading, writing, and mathematics of children in grades 1 to 4 in the worst performing schools in the municipal sector, to be achieved through improvement in the quality of school buildings, additional teaching resources, and workshops for teachers. An innovative aspect of the program was that it offered additional support to children out of school through learning workshops led by nonprofessional community members trained for that purpose.

Running parallel to the P-900 Program since its implementation in 1992 and continued by the second government of *Concertación* is MECE (Program for the Improvement of Quality and Equity in Education). MECE, with a budget of US$243 million (two-thirds of which was provided by a loan from the World Bank) was conceived as a six-year program running from 1992 to 1997. Unlike the P-900 program, MECE was ostensibly directed at all schools within the municipal sector (not just those with the poorest attainment levels) and the private subsidized schools. Its stated purpose of improving both the quality of education and the equal distribution of that quality was to be achieved by measures to improve teaching and learning within preschool and primary education; to improve the quality, relevance, and equity of secondary education; and to address the capacity of the Ministry of Education, much diminished during the years of the military government, to support change. At this time the P-900 was incorporated into the MECE program as a measure of political expediency.

As stated earlier, the P-900 was initiated as a direct result of aid from Scandinavian countries, which allowed the government of Aylwin to proceed immediately to substantial support to the poorest sector. When the World Bank loan leading to the establishment of MECE was affirmed, it was useful to place the P-900 under that umbrella. MECE was conceived as a major project within the Ministry of Education, dedicated to addressing the complex issues of school improvement; it had financial resources and was funded for a longer period of time. The differences pedagogically between the P-900 and the MECE programs were that the P-900 had told teachers what to do, while MECE was concerned more with the empowerment of teachers as professional agents of change.

The Ministry of Education also increased funding for the improvement of teaching and learning in the primary school, while MECE proposed a range of strategies to support teaching and learning channeled through identified projects. Two relating directly to school improvement are of interest here: the MECE-Media and the PMEs (Projects for the Improvement of Education).

The introduction of the five-year MECE-Media in 1995 reflected public and governmental concerns about the quality of secondary education in public sector schools. According to Avalos (1996), the MECE-Media project bases its actions on the assumptions that

- Teachers must be helped to improve the way they manage teaching and learning and be given the time and opportunity to do so
- School administrators must be helped to provide effective and supportive leadership
- Resourcing must increase and broaden to include access to information technology
- Schools should recognize the existence of a distinct youth culture and include, rather than exclude, that culture within the ethos of the school

In addition to direct support for improvement, secondary schools could also apply for funding under the PME.

The Projects for the Improvement of Education (PMEs) are directed toward all school phases and are a mechanism for distributing finite resources. A school may present a development project designed to improve the quality of its educational provision to MECE, which then selects those schools and projects worthy of funding under the program. There is a program allocation of 5,000 projects weighted toward applications from schools in the high and medium risk categories

identified through SIMCE and a combination of social factors. Despite the weighting, PME is a demand-led program rather than one based on priorities identified by the government. In the first three years of this five-year program, 4,785 schools applied for funding and 2,073 were successful (Ministry of Education, 1994). Of these, 1,711 were municipal schools and 362 fell in the private subsidized sectors (Téllez, 1994). P-900 schools are not excluded from applying for a PME but must withdraw from P-900 if their application is successful (Milicic, 1996).

Although initiated by the government of Frei Ruiz-Tagle, both the MECE-Media and the PMEs can be viewed as a continuance of the strategic thinking of the Aylwin administration. The present government, too, is committed to the view that education can lead to substantial improvements in productivity, economic growth, and equity and has signaled its intention to increase the funding of education from 4.4 percent of GNP to 7 percent within eight years (World Bank, 1997).

The decision of the post-dictatorship governments to link policies to improve educational quality and equity into broader strategies for greater global competitiveness raises two issues for discussion. First, the effectiveness of targeting as a strategy for improving school effectiveness, and second, the weight of the claim that education is the means by which the bulk of Chile's poor might enter into the competitive market.

There is little doubt that responses to the P-900 and the MECE-Media have been favorable among those who saw in these initiatives confirmation of post-dictatorship governments' desire to increase investment in education and to target those resources where they seemed most needed. There is evidence that teachers involved in the P-900 regarded the experience as positive for both themselves and pupils, in particular the introduction of a more culturally appropriate curriculum and in-service support (Undurraga, 1994).

However, the distance between the expectations of the P-900 and what it could realistically deliver opened the program up to criticism. Moreover, it was felt that the program, administered from Santiago, was too centralized and that an uncertain understanding of the purpose of the program and an inconsistency of response by school management diluted its impact (Undurraga, 1994). Of greatest concern was the fact that the results regarding attainment levels were not entirely as the government expected. By 1993, 41 percent of the schools in the program had increased their learning averages, 43 percent had maintained them, but in about 15 percent averages had actually fallen. The increased improvement averaged 18 percent in the P-900 schools as against an 11 percent in the private subventioned schools (which had not participated in the program) during the period 1990–1992 (Ministry of Education, 1993). These findings, of course, relate to the SIMCE testing, a narrowly conceived measure of educational outcome.

The more subtle effects of greater investment and greater autonomy for schools and teachers through projects like the P-900 and the PME are more difficult to quantify. Regional and provincial levels are staffed with regional supervisors whose main role is to visit schools to evaluate how effectively the curriculum is being delivered, yet a disparity between the number of regional and provincial supervisors and the 5,600 primary schools they are supposed to inspect would indicate that this is a sporadic exercise at best (Ministry of Education, 1993). Thus, attempts to measure improvement fall back on what can be easily demonstrated. But the essential question remains: If greater resourcing truly has made little measurable difference by outcome in addressing inequalities, where does the problem lie? It might be said that it is unrealistic to expect a program, even a well-designed one such as the P-900, to make and sustain significant differences when we understand that municipal schools are those that open their doors to the poorest in society. Improving teaching and learning in such schools by encouraging greater flexibility in teacher control over the curriculum and more decision making at the local level finds resonance with international debates about the effectiveness of schooling. However, implicit in this thinking is that the ulti-

mate responsibility for school improvement is placed firmly on teachers and on schools, the sector least resourced and least empowered to introduce and sustain innovative change. The PME, for example, assumes a sophisticated teaching force, able and willing and free to make the kinds of changes that are envisaged in schools able to take control of their own destiny. Even a brief glance at the extensive literature relating to effective change in school systems would indicate the difficulties involved in introducing self-reflective school improvement within an educational system inexperienced in making decisions at any level.

The government's own declaration that education is the task of all is underpinned by the view that individuals can effect change. It also assumes a confidence on the part of all teachers to engage in processes of this kind and an equal ability of all schools to respond. How realistic is this view given the predemocratic professional context and recent political experiences? Chilean teachers, whether under democratic or repressive governments, have had little involvement in decision making about content and teaching styles within the schooling system. Regarding community and parental participation, under the military regime no form of association was encouraged, leading to a diminution of community and parental activism in relation to children's education. Several points can be made here. First, Freire (1980) referred to a mindset of peoples living under military repression as a state of "domestication," suggesting that even when democratic processes are restored, if they are unaware of the phenomenon, such peoples will continue to be nonparticipating. Second, could a participatory desire in civil society be assumed as a consequence of the restoration of democratic processes? The effects of previous reforms might be said to prevail. For example, what of the school within its local community? The school representing its immediate community is a concept that is no longer widely valid in Chile given the process of selective enrollment exercised either by the school or by parents.

In addition to concerns about teachers' confidence to support change at the level required to achieve government policies, what of the municipalities themselves? Municipalities reflect the socioeconomic reality of their populations, and there is a wide variation in the quality of the social provision they are now expected to deliver. Thus, despite a standard *subvención,* a municipality's overall wealth largely determines the level of educational resources that schools under its administrative aegis receive. Moreover, under decentralization, some municipalities chose to accept responsibility for administering the twin areas of social provision (health and education) while others chose to be selective (choosing only education). In municipalities that chose to administer both services, education found itself the poor relative as municipalities trimmed the budget to meet the escalating costs of providing basic health care. Hojman (1993) presents evidence to suggest that in wealthy areas, spending per pupil in the public sector is twice that of schools in the poorer municipalities. Thus, not only are there resulting qualitative differences between schools of the same type, but teacher salaries, working conditions, and contracts will vary from one city to another and within larger cities such as Santiago, which has fifty-four municipalities, and from one municipality to another.

The market economy model is one of supply and demand. Teachers may move from school to school seeking better conditions, but so may pupils. Between 1980 and 1989, private subsidized schools increased their share of enrollment in primary education from 14 percent to 31.3 percent and in the secondary sector from 10 percent to 31.7 percent. Enrollments in the private nonsubsidized sector remained stationary (Schiefelbein, 1991).

The increase in enrollment during 1990 to 1993 was 3.3 percent in privately subsidized schools against 0.9 percent in municipal schools (CIDE, 1994). During this same period, additional resources were being pumped into municipal schools through targeting to improve the quality of education. Yet the slippage to the private subsidized sector continued. Lack of confidence in the municipal sector led, and still leads, parents to seek placement elsewhere wherever possible. Each year schools seek to attract new students by publicizing school achievement on a number of indicators, including attendance records and the numbers of students successfully transferring to secondary school or university. Submitted to the law of supply and demand, schools work to attract and, in the case of the private subsidized sector, select the best students they can in the knowledge that good students equate with good scores on the SIMCE. Within the neoliberal model, such competition can be seen as a valuable market mechanism; however, it can be argued that selectivity itself can be a brake on school improvement. Barnard (1992) in a report relating to the integration of children with disabilities into the public school system in Metropolitan Santiago, observes that where

> there is selectivity of intake, groups and programs within the school become increasingly circumscribed and the "good:" school becomes "good" because it has the best pupils not because of the quality of the education which it provides. . . . The more pressing issue, then, for many professionals and parents is not whether children with disabilities should be included in the system but how to stop children who fail to meet the school's requirements being marginalized. (p. 4)

The situation for municipal schools is critical. Municipal schools, which cannot select, must contend with a situation that for many schools is a self-defeating cycle of enrollment from among the poorest sectors of society, low scores on published testing, and a flight to the private subsidized sector wherever possible for those parents able to take advantage of the system. Thus municipal schools become the refuge of those who have no other choice. How does this situation match with the government's stand in identifying education as the means to help all Chileans to become stakeholders in the market? In addressing this question, we must face the most pressing issue in Chile today, which is that the inequalities existing within education are a mirror of the divisions that prevail in society at large.

The claim that education is the means by which the bulk of Chile's poor might enter into the competitive market is a central plank of post-democratic government thinking. The government's position is that the poor may work their way out of poverty through access to an educational system that offers quality and equity. The view that the modern state requires an educated workforce with the qualifications and skills to participate productively in society is not unique to Chile; it has international currency. Implemented as policy, such a view offers each citizen the opportunity to access to all levels of educational provision through ability and hard work (for example, the educational reforms in Britain following the ending of World War II). Inherent to such a view is that education is the means by which the individual can move between established social strata, overcoming the disadvantages that might have been theirs by birth and social class.

Two problems emerge within the Chilean context. First, Chile is not a meritocracy. Its history has imposed a colonial and then an immigrant elite upon a native and *mestizo* majority. Although it has a larger middle class than other Latin American countries, Chile remains a stratified society (Durston, Larrañaga, & Arriagada, 1995) where the assigned characteristics of family, race, and wealth assume greater importance than acquired characteristics such as education and skills. *Cuña* (social networking), with its attendant resources of information and influence, permeates Chilean society. While oiling the wheels of daily living, this social networking also prescribes the parameters within which the different strata in society function (MacClure & Urmeneta, 1996). As such, *cuña* presents a barrier to the social mobility implied within an egalitarian educational policy. This leads to the second problem: Those with the means to buy into the educational system of their choice, either through the private or the misnamed private subsidized sector, will do so. The result is a three-tiered educational service with municipal schools as no one's first choice and the poor's only option.

THE FUTURE

The slogan of the post-democratic governments has been "Growth with equity" with its implication, through "positive discrimination" policies, that education can be a level playing field. Through policies of positive discrimination, it has attempted to target the poorest sectors in society who are the worst served in the area of social provision. In doing so, both the governments of Aylwin and Frei Ruiz-Tagle have distanced themselves from the targeting policies of the military regime. The government of Pinochet provided minimal support to the very poorest sectors to aid their incorporation into a self-regulating market. The post-democratic governments have emphasized positive discrimination as an investment in human capital and in the belief that the market will not of itself regulate for the abolition of poverty. However, though both governments have emulated the social conscience of the Christian Democrat government of the 1960s, neither has turned its back on the rhetoric and the policies of neoliberalism. Nor have they been able to deal appropriately with the educational structure they have inherited from the years of military dictatorship.

The present government acknowledges the serious inequalities existing within the Chilean educational system today. It recognizes that the children from the poorest sectors of society are to be found in municipal and subsidized schools where resources are limited and learning outcomes are lowest. It has attempted to meet the challenges in innovative ways through programs such as the P-900 and the MECE. However, the ability of such programs to close the gap that exists between the poorest schools in the municipal sector and more affluent providers must be questioned at the present time. The overwhelming reason is that the central problem remains; the educational reforms of the democratic governments have failed to address the issue of the three-tiered schooling system set in place by the reforms of Pinochet. Municipal schools in rural and poor urban areas will continue to struggle with unequal resources, both human and financial, to confront the sea of human disadvantage that surrounds them. They are unequal participants in an unequal race. Where an educational system is still selective by ability (in the subsidized sector) and by income (in the private sector) how can quality and equity be achieved for all?

Radical measures are needed if the educational system is to create the technologically advanced society envisaged by the present government in its desire to place Chile surely within the world economy.

REFERENCES

Arellano, J. (1988). *Políticas Sociales y Desarrollo: Chile 1924 to 1984*. Santiago de Chile: CIEPLAN.

Avalos, B. (1996). Education for global/regional competitiveness: Chilean policies and reform in secondary education. *Compare, 26,* 215–231.

Barclay's Bank country report: Chile. (1996). London: Barclay's Economic Unit.

Barnard, A. (1992). *The integration of disabled children into mainstream schools in metropolitan Santiago.* Report to the Chilean Ministry of Education. Newcastle: University of Newcastle.

Brunner, J.J. (1993). Higher education in Chile from 1980 to 1990. *European Journal of Education, 28,* 71–84.

Centro de Investigación y Desarrollo de la Educación (CIDE). (1994). *La decentralización de la educación en Chile: Continuidad y cambio de un proceso de modernización.* Santiago de Chile: Author.

Durston J., Larrañaga, O., & Arriagada, I. (1995). *Educación y oportunidades de empleo e ingreso en Chile*. Santiago de Chile: Serie Políticas Sociales No. 10, ECLAC.

ECLAC (1995). *Panorama social de América Latina.* Santiago de Chile: Author.

Espínola, V. (1995). *El impacto de la decentralización sobre la educación gratuita en Chile.* Paper presented at International Seminar, La Construcción de Políticas Educativas Locales, Buenos Aires, Argentina.

Farrell, J.P. (1986). *The national unified school in Allende's Chile: The role of education in the destruction of a revolution.* Vancouver, Canada: University of British Columbia Press.

Filp, J. (1994). Todos los niños aprenden. Evaluaciones del P-900. In M. Gajardo (Ed.), *Cooperación internacional y desarrollo de la educación* (pp. 179–249). Chile: AGCCI.

Freire, P. (1980). Concientizar para liberar. In C.A. Torres (Ed.), *Educación y concientización* (pp. 73–84), Salamanca: Sigueme.

Fried, B., & Abuhadba, M. (1991). Reforms in higher education: The case of Chile in the 1980s. *Higher Education, 21,* 137–149.

Gajardo, M. (1994). (Ed.) *Cooperación internacional y desarrollo de la educación*. Chile: AGCCI.

Garcia-Huidobro, J.E. (1994). Positive discrimination in education: Its justification and a Chilean example, *International Review of Education, 40,* 209–221.

Garcia-Huidobro, J.E., & Jara, C. (1994). El programa de las 900 escuelas. In M. Gajardo (Ed.), *Cooperación internacional y desarrollo de la educación* (pp. 39–72). Chile: AGCCI.

Garreton, M. (1986). Political processes in an authoritarian regime: The dynamics of institutionalisation and opposition in Chile, 1973–1980. In J.S. & A.V. Valenzuela (Eds.), *Military rule in Chile: Dictatorship and oppositions* (pp. 161–178). Baltimore: Johns Hopkins University Press.

Hawes, H., & Stephens, D. (1990). *Questions of quality: Primary education and development.* Harlow, U.K.: Longman.

Hojman, D. (1993). *Chile: The political economy of development and democracy in the 1990s.* Hong Kong: Macmillan.

Lavanchy, S. (1993, Autumn). The development of early education in Chile: Lessons for the future. *International Journal of Early Years Education, 1,* 44–55.

MacClure, O., & Urmeneta, R. (1996). *Evaluacón de las políticas frente a la pobreza y la exclusión social en Chile.* Santiago de Chile: International Labour Organisation.

Milicic, N. (1996). Children with learning disabilities in Chile: Strategies to facilitate integration. In L. Artiles & D.P. Hallahan (Eds.), *Special education in Latin America* (pp. 169–188). Westport: Praeger.

Ministry of Education. (1980). *Decreto supremo de educacíon, No. 81433/215.09.80.* Santiago: Author.

Ministry of Education. (1990). *Cifras estatísticas.* División de Planificación y Presupuesto. Santiago de Chile: Ministerio de Educación.

Ministry of Education. (1993). *Políticas educacionales: Temas de gestión.* Santiago de Chile: Ministerio de Educación.

Ministry of Education. (1994). *Unidad de educación especial.* Chile: Ministerio de Educación.

Schiefelbein, E. (1991). Restructuring education through economic competition: The case of Chile. *Journal of Educational Administration, 29,* 17–28.

Scott, C. (1996). The distributive impact of the new economic model in Chile. In V. Bulmer-Thomas (Ed.), *The new economic model in Latin America and its impact on income distribution and poverty.* London: University of London, Institute of Latin American Studies.

Téllez, M.A. (1994). *Proyectos de mejoramiento educativo en el desarrollo de la educación básica Chilena.* Santiago de Chile: Ministry of Education.

Tironi, E. (1990). *Autoritarismo, modernización y marginalidad: El caso de Chile 1973–1989.* Santiago de Chile: Ediciones Sur.

Undurraga, C. (1994). Pedagogía y gestión. Informe de evaluación del programa de las 900 escuelas. In M. Gajardo (Ed.), *Cooperación internacional y desarrollo de la educación* (pp. 179–249). Santiago de Chile: AGCCI.

UNESCO. (1995). *Basic indicators: Latin America.* Paris: Author.

World Bank. (1997). *World Bank Annual Report.* New York: Author.

World Factbook. (1996). Internet at http://hplus.harvard.edu/alpha/CIAWEB.html.

PART II

Western Europe: Diversity and Unity in an Evolving Community

Well-embarked along a path that was almost unimaginable a generation ago, western Europe is entering a brave new world. The European Union is a reality, and an increasingly concrete one. Yet, most of the case studies in this section do not dwell on this important phenomenon. Perhaps this is because it is viewed as a *fait accompli*. The larger and more economically dominant nations are well advanced in the process of adapting to an increasingly integrated western Europe under the umbrella of the European Union. They have already implemented many of the reforms necessary for realizing more open borders, the free flow of commerce and labor, a common currency, consistency in social welfare systems, and so on.

However, other nations are still wrestling with the issues that a united western Europe presents. In reading the chapter on Greece, for example, one gains an appreciation for the profound controversies and challenges that a nation faces as it embraces the "new" Europe that is taking shape under the European Union.

It can be argued, however, that such a transformed western Europe already exists— with or without the formal framework of the European Union. Powerful forces transcending political boundaries are at work, profoundly affecting all societies in their path, as is illustrated by the case of Greenland.

One such force is the headlong drive toward "modernization" that is rocking education establishments. Technological development, invariably tied into economic productivity and the need for highly skilled labor forces, is a priority in all countries. Education has thus found itself with a new priority: a technology and business orientation at all levels.

The question of how to adequately prepare students for the work force is a theme running through all chapters. The most common response of national governments and their education bureaucracies takes the form of vocational education. But, this is not without controversy. Some nations, like Switzerland and Sweden, have strong vocational education elements in their schools. In others, like France and Spain, there is greater resistance to changing the traditional academic focus of schooling. And, at the post-secondary level, debates rage in all countries on what the proper focus of education should be.

However, about one priority there is no debate. All western European nations have a long and distinct cultural heritage of which they are fiercely proud, and a major potential consequence of greater integration is erosion of this cultural identity. This is particularly relevant for educators because, in all the nations represented, one of the primary objectives of schools is the preservation and transmission of national culture. It is instructive to read each chapter with an eye to the theme of education's cultural mission.

Fear of an erosion of cultural identity comes from several sources. First, in a more integrated Europe, it is difficult to keep out cultural influences from other nations. Second, the process of modernization is undermining traditional culture and values through technology, consumerism, and the free flow of ideas. However, the greatest threat is a demographic one. The complexion of western Europe is changing and society is changing with it.

Western European nations are becoming increasingly multicultural and multiracial, a result of the growth of minority groups. The relatively stable and homogenous cultures of many nations are now changing from within as the voices of minority groups and cultures grow. The challenge of a multicultural society, and a multicultural education system to serve that society, is an important theme in our case studies. It signals an issue that is fiercely debated in western European societies and among educators.

Discussions on minority group issues inevitably lead to another very prominent theme in this section: the issue of equality, which is still a somewhat distant goal in western Europe. Some contributing authors spend considerable time grappling with the matter. A variety of approaches to solving the problem have been implemented in different countries, and there is much to be learned in examining the strengths and limitations of those attempts.

The administration and governance of education is another open question. Some nations, like England, Ireland, France, Sweden, and Greece, have embraced centralized systems. The strengths and drawbacks of these are explored by our authors. In other instances, such as Switzerland and Spain, decentralization has produced its own benefits and limitations. As the matter goes to the heart of the important question of "Who should control education?" the issues raised are vital for all educators.

All these issues and debates have spawned a plethora of reforms in the education systems of western Europe. From the debates that led up to these reforms, the changes made, and the outcomes of these experiments, we may draw lessons and improve our school systems and education practices.

CHAPTER 6

Vision or Revision? Conflicting Ideologies in the English Education System

PHILIP GARNER

Philip Garner *has taught in English mainstream and special schools in Coventry, Lancashire, and London for over fifteen years. He is now Senior Lecturer in Special Education at Brunel University, Middlesex, where he is also the Director of the Center for Comparative Studies in Special Education. He teaches on both Masters and Doctoral programs in Special Education, and has been involved in a number of teacher education initiatives in Central and Eastern Europe funded by the European Union. His major research interests are in the field of comparative analyses of special education policy and practice and in the education of children with perceived emotional and/or behavioral difficulties. His major publications include* What Teachers Do *(Paul Chapman Publishers);* Advocacy, Self-Advocacy and Special Needs *(David Fulton), and* At the Crossroads: Teacher Education and Special Needs *(David Fulton). He is the co-editor of the* 1999 World Yearbook of Education, *which focuses on inclusivity.*

Briault in 1976 argued that the education system of England was characterized by a "triangle of tension" between central government, local government, and individual schools. Providing that there was a mutual dependence between the three constituent parts, any tension could be interpreted as constructive, enabling a balance to be retained and thus avoiding the dangers arising from the concentration of power in any given point of the triangle. Although this interpretation is now over twenty years old, it is still relevant given the most recent changes in educational provision in England. One possible redefinition of Briault's "triangle of tension" would be to view the three points as society, the state, and the providers of education.

In this chapter it is my intention to highlight, with reference to Briault's model and the variant I have suggested, some of the ongoing tensions that have resulted from a period of unprecedented change to the fabric of the education system in England in the period following the Education Act of 1988. In particular I want to focus on three aspects of sociopolitical and economic organization because of their unprecedented level of impact on the education system: centralization versus individual autonomy, levels of achievement and underachievement, and inequality and educational disadvantage. These themes constitute a highly personalized selection: however, the argument I present is that each subsumes a further range of structural and ideological issues that hallmark educational policy and practice.

THE SOCIAL FABRIC

Demographic

Geographically the British Isles stand apart from mainland Europe, albeit by a distance of only twenty miles at one point. It extends from the Scilly Isles in the southwest to the Shetland Islands in the northeast, a distance of some 900 miles. The United Kingdom of Great Britain and Northern Ireland is a constitutional monarchy, comprising England, Wales, Scotland, and Northern Ireland. Scotland and Northern Ireland have their own legal and educational systems, which largely function independently; that of Wales more closely follows the English pattern. Reference will be made, nevertheless, to the United Kingdom as a whole at various points throughout this chapter.

The population of England is approximately 46 million, the majority of whom live in urban settings. Greater London alone has over 7 million inhabitants. Almost 20 million people in England are under the age of 25, a factor that has important implications for educational policy, planning, and provision.

Economic

The economy of England has witnessed rapid transition in the post–1945 period. Regeneration after the Second World War helped to temporarily maintain the preeminence of heavy engineering industries, but the period from about 1970 onwards was characterized by a decline in this sector and a commensurate growth in high-technology industries and a broad-based service sector. Manufacturing industries retain some of their importance, helped by inward investment from the European Union and the Far East, while there has been a rapid growth in recreation/tourism-based industries. Natural gas and oil have taken over from coal as major sources of energy, with a corresponding effect on the industries involved in their production.

There are substantial employment variations from region to region in the United Kingdom, with unemployment being above the national average (9.8 percent of the work force in 1992, for example) in the north of England, the northwest of England, and the West Midlands. Substantially more men than women are economically active, and the latter tend to be employed on a part-time basis or in low-paid occupations.

Political

England is administered by a democratically elected Parliament comprising a House of Commons and a House of Lords. The former consists of regionally elected members. The two main political parties in the last fifty years have been the Conservative (Tory) party who enshrine large-

ly right-of-center politics, and the Labor party, whose approach has been of a more socialist, left-of-center nature. The period between 1945–1997 has witnessed the election of three successive Conservative governments (1951–1965) followed by a further four (1979–1997). The most recent General Election (1997) saw a dramatic shift in voting patterns, with a Labor government being elected with a huge majority. A third political grouping, Liberal Democrat, has begun to make some impression in the last ten years on what has largely been a two-party political system. While the monarch is recognized as the Head of State, and government is carried on in her name, she *reigns* rather than *rules,* having little constitutional power. Likewise the House of Lords is not an elected chamber.

Local government is provided for by a system of councils, each comprising elected members. While central government has, in the last twenty years or so, remained Conservative, local councils have increasingly become Labor or Liberal Democrat. Local councils are responsible for the direct provision of such things as social services, education, and welfare, while central government determines policy matters in each of these areas. Because of this difference in political affiliation, there has been considerable tension between the perceptions and policies at national and local levels.

Cultural

The cultural map of England, as elsewhere, is heavily influenced by historical factors. Among the most significant of these are class, race, and gender. Each has made, and continues to make, a significant impact on the social, economic, and educational patterns of the country.

The terms "working class" and "middle class" are in almost universal use in England. The most recent classification suggests that approximately 57 percent of the population is "middle class": in other words, they are mainly employed in the professions and are referred to as either "white-collar" or "blue-collar" workers. There are considerable regional differences: The southeast, in particular, has a major concentration of "middle-class" population; the north, northwest, and the Midlands have the greatest concentration of "working class."

The ethnic composition of England changed dramatically after 1945 when immigrants from the Caribbean were encouraged to fill the employment vacuum created by post–Second World War reconstruction. This was followed in the 1960s by immigrants from the Indian subcontinent and East Africa. Characteristic of their settlement in England is their concentration in specific locations and their adherence to their own cultural norms. The 1991 census indicates that 5.5 percent of the total population of the United Kingdom belongs to a minority ethnic grouping. These groups are located in particular areas of the country: Nearly two-thirds of the total minority group population live in the metropolitan areas; only a small percentage of ethnic minority groups are located in rural (or "country") areas.

Religious

The official religion is Christian Protestant, or Church of England. Substantial sections of the population are Roman Catholic, with Methodist, Baptist, and other religions also significant. In common with many other post-industrialized nations in recent years, there has been a perceptible increase in numbers subscribing to new, alternative, or culturally nonnormative religions. The growth of ethnic minority populations has been naturally accompanied by high levels of religious observation in Islamic, Sikh, and Hindi groups. Having said that, however, there has been a sharp decrease in regular service attendance over the last twenty years. While organized religions, particularly the Church of England and Roman Catholicism, retain some social importance, their influence over peoples lives has been sharply loosened and England is characterized more by "moral pluralism" in which secular morality is the dominant idiom.

Related Themes

Each of the above themes is characterized by a series of overarching ideological imperatives that continue to make their mark on the way in which contemporary society in England is shaped and that differentially condition the lives of individuals within it. Notably, they also contain sites of conflict, not least between those areas referred to earlier by Briault (1976). While their effects on educational policy and provision in England will be considered in some detail in the substance of this chapter, some of their societal manifestations are now briefly considered.

England has struggled to retain its place among the most economically prosperous group of nations. It has experienced considerable difficulty as the advantages of being among the first to encounter the Industrial Revolution in the eighteenth and nineteenth centuries have given way to the handicapping condition of having a largely entrenched preindustrial social structure (Barnett, 1986). Moreover, the twentieth century coincided with England's demise as a colonial and imperial power, with a commensurate diminution of export markets and reliable sources of cheap raw materials. The technological revolutions in post–Second World War Europe were only partly realized in England, and the traditional tension between socialism (represented particularly by the nationalized control of certain industries, public utilities, and transport) and capitalism (characterized by private ownership, self-help, and entrepreneurship) provided a negative backdrop to attempts at economic regeneration. Moreover, the preservation of a largely capitalist *status quo* preserved the traditional wealth and power of the "ruling class" (Lawton, 1989). The enterprise culture, as interpreted and applied by recent governments, has thus created a widening of the gap between rich and poor in England (Kumar, 1993). The tensions created by changing work patterns (particularly short-term contracting—now applied even to professions such as teaching, social care, and medicine) and unemployment have impacted on the social framework of peoples' lives and on individual attitudes concerning, for example, state welfare, membership of European social and economic institutions, and (ethnic) minority groups. The impact of these is particularly felt by those currently progressing, or about to progress, through the education system.

In England the dominant belief system, shared by a vast majority of the population, and particularly by those who function as social gatekeepers, is legitimated by three interconnected ideologies—*individualism, intelligence,* and *behavior.* Each is underscored by perceptions of what constitutes *normality.*

Individualism in contemporary English society is celebrated up to that point where it begins to threaten traditional values. Competition is largely the means by which this is facilitated, whether in respect of economic competition, educational success, sporting achievement, and so on. Emphasis on competition and individualism ultimately means that English society will retain its hierarchical profile, with economic, political, and ideological power remaining in the hands of the few, in spite of some evidence that the Thatcherite capitalism of the 1980s has enabled a small percentage of people to become wealthy with "new" money. Those who are unable to compete according to the "rules" of individualism will be the least successful in society.

Contemporary England is largely ambivalent about social behavior. Working as I do near a famous rugby football ground, I am particularly conscious that boisterous behavior by a group of "middle-class" rugby supporters is simply viewed as high spirits but rapidly becomes hooliganism when the participants are "working-class" supporters of an inner-city soccer team. Likewise, within the criminal justice system there is a differential attitude towards certain criminal acts. White-collar crime is therefore seen as more respectable than burglary (felony), even though it may involve the misappropriation of significantly more sums of money or property.

Perceptions about education in England have remained heavily influenced by the historical importance of the mental testing movement in the late nineteenth century. Even given the recognition during the 1960s of social disadvantage as a factor in explaining educational performance, decisions about educational placement (whether within schools or among schools) are frequently made in whole or in part on a pupil's intelligence as measured by IQ scores. Theories of intelligence, and both public and professional application of them, adopt some controversial conceptions: that intelligence can be measured (as an IQ score) across all the population in a uniform way; that intelligence is subject to very little change over time; that certain racial and cultural groups have a higher intelligence than others, and so on. Such beliefs have provided fruitful grounds for politicians and interest groups to promote their views. Moreover, as the public consensus appears to be that psychology is a science, and that IQ testing is a precise instrument, this is a *bona fide* device in educational assessment.

England is currently witnessing a debate about social and moral values. This is underscored by a traditional view of being "British" and by the fears expressed by Church and political leaders that, without official direction, individuals may assume the position of moral relativists in which morality is viewed simply as a matter of personal taste. These worries have been fueled by increases in juvenile delinquency, violent crime and street disorder, and unrest. As with other components of ideology, however, "values" within any society, while at one level remaining largely subjective, are invariably those that the significant gatekeepers in that society wish to maintain. In England there is a tension in this respect between the value norms of the individual, those of certain marginalized groups, and those of the dominant state apparatus.

Much of the foregoing is crystallized in the relationship between the individual and the state. In England, depending on one's cultural orientation, there are two interpretations. The state, on the one hand, can be viewed as an agent of control and of policing individuals. Alternatively, it can function in a protectionist mode, as a welfare agency for groups and individuals. The struggle between these contrasting interpretations is classically exemplified in the education system.

SCHOOLING

The United Kingdom as a whole has a total of 34,000 schools, with over half a million teachers and more than 9 million pupils. The education system of England has undergone far-reaching change in the last twenty years, and there is little evidence at the time of writing of any reduction in the rate of innovation. The changes, and the controversies that inevitably surround them, have affected all sectors of the system, from nursery schools to higher education. A major causal factor hereabouts has been the increasing concern about levels of achievement (particularly when compared to other countries). At the same time, there has been a significant preoccupation with vocational initiatives in order to provide a competitive and increasingly skilled work force; with providing value for money; with the assessment and monitoring quality and effectiveness; and with such ongoing concerns as pupil behavior and the mainstreaming of those with learning disabilities.

It is important to establish a historical context for the recent changes in the education system in England. I want to dwell upon just two aspects of this, as manifested in the recent past: the relationship between state and individual and the power structures that govern this and the underpinning philosophies of education that have sharply divided the community at large and the educational community in particular.

Education has been seen as an instrument of both control and entitlement. In Victorian times, for example, moves towards mass general education were regarded as the product of a "moral panic" induced by the prospect of civil disorder, rather than egalitarianism. In the 1960s, debates concerning the raising of the school leaving age from 15 to 16 years revolved around the (then) government's need to retain within education large groups of underqualified pupils who would otherwise flood a labor market that had become increasingly selective in its demand for skilled

workers. More recently, the initiatives taken by central government in connection with "pupils with problems" (Department for Education, 1994) have been prompted, according to some commentators, by the desire to segregate a section of the school population who are regarded as ineducable in the mainstream and thus become a source of political, social, and educational embarrassment.

I draw these historical parallels in order to define what is a deeply rooted tension concerning the nature and purpose of education and of society's expectations of it. This tension has been apparent in the way in which society at large, and educationists in particular, have polarized the service during the last twenty or so years according to two main philosophical orientations (Darling, 1994). On the one hand, there is a view that argues that the purpose of education is the pursuit of knowledge for its own sake, an activity that is fundamental to those proponents of so-called child-centered education. According to Darling (1994), child-centered teaching stemmed from a radical dissatisfaction with traditional practice, where mastery of factual information is emphasized at the expense of experiential learning. In contrast to this, much of the thinking in the last twenty years or so has viewed education as a technical device, stemming from a wish to have a sharply defined end product to the process of schooling, geared to meet the needs of a wider society, and industry in particular. Schooling, according to supporters of this ideology, had lost touch with the "real world" in which economic success allows for a viable system of state education.

Recent Legislation

Current educational provision in England has to be considered against the background of recent legislative changes resulting from the 1988 and 1993 Education Acts and in light of the economic difficulties faced by post-war England that paved the way for an ideological shift and its supporting legislation. A 1976 speech by the then Prime Minister marked something of a turning point in attitudes towards public education. He argued that schools were failing to equip pupils with a basic curriculum and appropriate academic or vocational skills suitable for the needs of industry.

From 1979, political decision making in England was dominated almost exclusively by Thatcherite neoconservativism. This reached its culmination in the passing of two Education Acts in 1988 and 1993 whose contents act as descriptors of right-wing thinking, both on the nature of society and on the function, organization, and control of education itself. Both acts sought to increase the power of central government on the pretext of providing more choice and diversity within the system.

The *1988 Education Act* contained 238 clauses and took more than 360 hours of parliamentary time to debate. Its enactment gave the Secretary of State 415 new powers across the spectrum of educational provision. None of these were without controversy, resistance being most notable at local levels.

The Act introduced a National Curriculum that, for the first time in England, established a formal, legally binding framework for what should be taught in schools. This included a set of foundation subjects (English, mathematics, science, technology, modern foreign language, history/geography, art/music/drama, and physical education). There were also a set of attainment targets in each of the core subjects that established what children should normally be expected to know and understand at the ages of 7, 11, 14, and 16 years. Each subject should have a "program of study" designed to reflect the attainment targets and set out the overall content of a given curriculum area. Children would be formally assessed at the ages of 7, 11, 14, and 16 years, and the results of these assessments were to be made public. All of these arrangements were to be supervised by a National Curriculum Council (NCC).

Subsequently, and largely because of local protest by teachers, associated professionals, and many parents, changes were introduced to modify both the rigorous and prescriptive nature of the National Curriculum (Dearing, 1993) and the way in which the various subjects were assessed. Within five years, the majority of the curriculum proposals contained within the 1988 Act had been amended in some form or other.

A system of open enrollment to schools was introduced by the 1988 Education Act, allowing schools more control over their recruitment of pupils (and parents more choice). This, combined with the promotion of local financial management where schools directed the way in which their budget was allocated, and the introduction of a new type of school, referred to as grant maintained, removed a considerable amount of power from the Local Education Authorities (LEAs), who in many areas were traditionally oppositional to the Conservative central government. As with the implementation of the National Curriculum itself, none of these measures was without dispute or controversy. Indeed, one of the major complaints about the Act as a whole was that little consultation had taken place with educationists and other regarding specific content. Lawrence (1994) noted that the Act was certainly not developed in a political consensus; rather the cabinet that introduction it explicitly drew attention to its 350 nonconsensual features.

It should be noted, therefore, that the paradox of granting more power to individual schools (decentralization) with the desire to assume a more centralized control of education was more apparent than real. In giving more schools day-to-day control over their own affairs, the government was, at the same time, stripping power from LEAs, thereby largely ridding itself of what had become, during the post-war period, a major source of dissent and criticism of central government action.

The *1993 Education Act* came after an influential white paper (a consultation document), entitled *Choice and Diversity,* sought to deal with the confusion and complexity created by the 1988 Act. In much the same way as the 1988 Act resembled a party political manifesto, so too *Choice and Diversity* set out a new framework for schools that was shaped largely by ideological prejudice and sectarian dogma. The white paper highlighted seven main changes in the way that schools would be controlled, notably the establishment of a new body with powers to take action on failing schools, streamlining of opting-out procedures, and the establishment of a School Curriculum and Assessment Authority (SCAA) to supervise the National Curriculum. The subsequent Act, which incorporated each of these strategies, also established new regulations regarding pupils excluded from school on account of their unacceptable behavior. These were reinforced in detail the following year (Department for Education, 1994). The Education Act of 1993, in sum, represented the culmination of almost fifteen years of reform by Conservative governments that sought to mold an education system on five themes: quality, diversity, increased parental choice, greater autonomy for schools, and greater accountability by schools.

Control and Administration

Education in England is jointly administered by local education authorities (LEAs) and central government. Since the Education Act of 1988, there has been a noticeable shift in the power relations between these, with LEAs gradually losing and central government gaining.

The Department for Education and Employment (DfEE), the government department responsible for education in England, functions on three levels: political, administrative, and inspectoral. Its political function is to set the policy and framework for the national education system. Its administrative role is to act as the body that introduces and disseminates the decisions of central government concerning all sectors of education according to the existing statutory frameworks. Much of this function is fulfilled by civil servants and an increasing number of quasi-autonomous nongovernment organizations (*quangos*). Finally, it fulfills an inspectoral and advisory function through the Office for Standards in Education (OfSTED), the Teacher Training Agency (TTA), the Further Education Funding Council (FEFC), and the Higher Education Funding Council (HEFC), among others. Prior to 1988, Her Majesty's Inspectors (HMI) had considerable powers concerning the monitoring of individual schools and colleges, together with an important advisory function; much of this power has been eroded since the Act, with OfSTED assuming far more importance.

LEAs were established as the local device for administering education by the 1944 Education Act. There are 109 LEAs, including 36 metropolitan districts and 33 Greater London boroughs. LEAs are part of local government and operate via local education committees comprising (mainly) elected representatives and a smaller number of permanent education officers. The specific responsibilities of LEAs include the employment and payment of teaching and nonteaching staff; the awarding of mandatory and other grants to students; the building of schools and colleges (subject to the approval of the DfEE); provision of support services for pupils, including medical and social services, transportation, careers services and recreational facilities; and curriculum support and professional development for teachers.

As indicated previously, however, the period post–1988 has seen a marked diminution of the power of these organizations. From that year individual schools, through their governing body, were able to have direct control over their own budgets, could appoint or dismiss staff without reference to the LEA, and could even opt out totally from even minimal LEA control by assuming "grant maintained status" (GMS).

Educational Institutions

Compulsory schooling is provided for all children between 5 and 16 years. Many LEAs are increasingly offering opportunities for children to begin school at 4 years of age. Nursery education is provided between 3 and 5 years, primary education between 5 and 11 years, secondary education between 11 and 16 years, and post-compulsory (further vocational or higher education) from the ages of 16 or 18. Schools are referred to as being either state-controlled, voluntary-controlled (usually church schools), or independent schools (frequently, and confusingly, referred to as public schools). Alongside these schools is a parallel system of special schools offering education for pupils with a range of learning difficulties according to their age level. The salient features of each of these are briefly outlined below.

• *Nursery schooling.* Preschool provision invariably comprises either separate day nurseries, often privately funded, playgroups, nursery classes within primary schools, or reception classes for children who are just under compulsory school age. Because of a shortage of places in these facilities there has been a significant growth in the use of registered childminders. It should be noted that nursery education is by no means universal, with some (frequently disadvantaged) locations having very little provision.

• *Primary schooling.* Three kinds of primary school meet the educational needs of 5- to 11-year-olds: infant schools cater to children ages 5 to 7 years; junior schools for those between 7 and 11 years old; and combined infant and junior schools for both age groups. The latter are the most common. All schools are required to provide the National Curriculum for all pupils.

• *Secondary schooling.* The secondary education system comprises a wide range of types of school. Most common are mixed ability comprehensive schools for children aged 11 to 16 or 11 to 18. These are either LEA-controlled, church-affiliated, or opted-out grant-maintained schools. Most are mixed, although some retain single sex status. They are referred to as state schools.

Selective grammar schools remain an important feature of the education system: They provide a mainly academic curriculum for pupils, often in single sex settings, between the ages of 11 and 18. As with the primary sector, secondary schools are required to implement the National Curriculum. The 1980s saw the growth of privately funded city technology colleges and other specialist secondary schools using the model of magnet schools from the United States. It also witnessed an increase in the number of assisted places in independent schools, whereby children from less economically advantaged backgrounds could acquire a grammar school education.

• *Special schooling.* Children who are regarded as having learning difficulties such that they cannot be satisfactorily educated in mainstream schools are provided for by a parallel system of special schools, usually smaller establishments catering for specific kinds of learning difficulties. Alongside these are a series of free-standing units or centers offering specialist support for certain kinds of learning difficulties. Each child attending a special school has a legally binding statement of special educational needs. Since the Education Act of 1981, there has been considerable movement towards mainstreaming this part of the school population; nevertheless, it retains an important function within the overall system. An important feature of special education provision in England is its interdisciplinary nature: Education, social work, and health professionals are involved in working collaboratively.

• *Post-16 (non-compulsory) schooling.* This sector of educational provision is optional and is provided for in further education colleges specializing in both vocational and academic qualifications, and sixth-form colleges that offer a somewhat more restricted range of opportunities.

• *Higher education.* Traditionally higher education in England has been provided by three kinds of institutions: universities (including specialist establishments, for example, medical schools); polytechnics; and institutes of higher education (IHEs). Since 1992 there have been moves to unite and simplify this system, with many polytechnics and IHEs assuming the status of university.

Guiding Educational Philosophy

The overarching philosophy that has guided recent governments in formulating educational legislation and subsequent policy in schools is arguably a combination of reconstructionism and bureaucratic-technicism. The former incorporates a belief that education should improve society by emphasizing the usefulness of knowledge and the importance of moral values and citizenship; the latter stresses utilitarianism and vocationalism, with a highly systematized control mechanism from the center. Indicative of this philosophy in recent years has been the desire on the part of central government to define precisely what is taught in schools and the emphasis upon assessment. Ultimately, however, the whole philosophical orientation of education has been predicated by the principle of marketization, which, according to central government, will lead to an increase in quality, diversity, and choice.

Pedagogical Theory and Practice

During the 1960s and 1970s there was a notable preoccupation with so-called progressive methods, such as individualized learning, team teaching, and open-plan schools. Subsequently, however, this was implicated (mainly by right-wing politicians and educationists) in the decline in levels of educational attainment among English children. As a result, the period from about 1980 onwards saw a return to a more traditional pedagogy: whole-class teaching, formal testing, and an emphasis upon didactic methods of learning. An example of this shift in orientation since 1988 has been the way in which judgments are now made about the effectiveness of teaching in schools. The body responsible for this is OfSTED, which now provides a series of statutory frameworks for the inspection of schools, emphasizing the importance of subject knowledge, sets of skills, and good classroom order and discipline.

Curricula

The National Curriculum asserted the need for a focus on citizenship education and vocationally relevant education (Department of Education and Science, 1987). It was initially viewed with considerable suspicion by teachers in particular, who had previously been subject to little direct control over what they taught (or how they taught it). Many argued that the initial proposals for the curriculum were far too prescriptive in respect of individual subject content; there were worries, too, expressed about the ability of children who had learning difficulties to access the new curricu-

lum. After initial resistance, however, a consensus view shared by most with an interest in education is now that a national curriculum has been a positive innovation. Many of the concerns about the prescriptive nature of the National Curriculum were assuaged by the introduction of more flexibility in 1993, while those working with children with learning difficulties have come to regard the common curriculum as a major device in ensuring the educational rights of their pupils.

Legislation and Politics

The educational innovations of the 1980s and 1990s were introduced by a central government whose ideological stance was, at the very least, right-of-center. As local councils were frequently dominated by the opposition parties, this has resulted in ongoing tension between the two groups. Much of this tension has arisen because the traditional power base of the principal opposition party (Labor) is the urban districts of England. Demographically these are dominated by low-income groups, where unemployment, poor housing, welfare, and other social problems are above the national average, Local councils in these areas have largely opposed central government intervention on both ideological and practical grounds. Most importantly, these locations traditionally have a far higher proportion of children who are underachieving, have learning difficulties, or are referred to as "children with problems" on account of their unacceptable behavior. The physical infrastructure of many schools is very poor and pressure on local budgets means that funds are unavailable to provide new facilities. Against this backdrop it is not surprising that local politicians, educationists, and parents view market-led government intervention with some cynicism.

Certainly, there can be little doubt that the 1980s saw a steady deterioration in the relationships between central and local government. Central government was of the view that there was an obvious need to emphasize that national political power overrides local power.

Organization and Governance of Schooling

It should be apparent from the foregoing that both in 1988 and the 1993 Education Acts had a huge impact upon the way in which schools were organized and governed. Subsequent to the Acts, schools were faced with a somewhat paradoxical situation. On the one hand, they were made more accountable for their implementation of a national curriculum and for the levels of performance of their pupils. Central government dictated the terms of both. Conversely, schools assumed responsibility for their budgetary arrangements and could, from 1988 onwards, recruit pupils from an unrestricted catchment area. School governors were also given much enhanced powers and more demanding duties.

Evaluation

Recent changes in the organization and control of education in England have been characterized by a more structured and heavily scrutinized system of evaluation—both of whole schools and of individual pupils and their teachers.

MAJOR ISSUES, CONTROVERSIES, AND PROBLEMS

In Society

England, in common with most other post-industrial countries in Western Europe, has encountered a series of problems that have resulted in a significant degree of controversy as to how best they might be resolved. Broadly speaking, these can be viewed as being political, economic, or social in origin. Of course, there is a high degree of interrelationship between each, and the problems and resulting controversies seldom function in isolation of each other. Equally important is the requirement not to generalize from what will inevitably be a very crude and brief analysis—and one that has been adumbrated in a highly personal manner. In reading this section—bear both of these points in mind.

Political.   The major political struggle during the last ten years or so has been conducted on two fronts. First, there has been increasing introspection and self-doubt concerning a role on the world stage. Accompanying the decline of Great Britain as an imperial power was a loss of influence in political decision making in the global arena. This has been fundamentally linked to the loss of the economic resources in the colonies, the failure to adjust to the demands for new technologies and streamlined work practices, and to the "moral failure" of certain groups to meet the challenges of living in a post-modern international community. There has been a tendency, on the part of Thatcherite Tories, to recall a "Golden Age" when Britain was in the ascendancy and was the preeminent political and economic force in the world. This notion, reinforced by cultural and social prejudice, is largely an illusion.

One arena in which England has had an opportunity to shape the political dimension is within the European Union. This has caused problems, particularly for the Tory governments of the last fifteen years. For the British, Europe has traditionally meant "the Continent"—somewhere to go on vacation rather than a political, economic, and social union as it is now seen by most mainland Europeans. Brussels represents, for many Conservatives, a challenge to British sovereignty—a threat that has been assiduously fueled by the Tory-controlled media. At best, the concept of Europe to many in Britain is a somewhat ambiguous one.

Economic.   While it is only a sense of national pride that may be damaged by no longer having significant political influence on the world stage, there can be little doubt that one of the most important structural effects of this relative decline has been on the economy. In the 1970s and early 1980s some 2.5 million jobs disappeared from manufacturing industry. These would be jobs, often unskilled or semi-skilled, that would never return and that have contributed to the creation of an economic underclass of adults who have never been employed, full-time or otherwise. Here there is a great deal of blame allocation. A legacy of Britain's imperial and colonial past is that there has been a highly visible increase in immigration of people from the old colonies, a process that was encouraged by post-war governments to meet the demand for labor during a period of reconstruction and industrial growth. While in times of economic prosperity this is viewed as acceptable (immigrants are normally employed in low-pay work and in jobs that, given alternatives, few others are prepared to do), during times of recession there is usually a complaint that "they are taking our jobs" and the accompanying advice that "they should be sent back to where they came from." It escapes the attention of many that such advice is usually reserved for particular minority groups (usually nonwhite) and that, in any event, there is far more immigration from the white Commonwealth (Australia, New Zealand, Canada, and so on) than from elsewhere.

Social.   Entwined with the above is the frequently deteriorating relationship between central and local governments. The tensions between the two are representative of sharp differences in ideology and of their contrasting interpretations of what constitutes social justice.

Large sections of the economic and social underclass predominate in spatially segregated urban locations. An economic and social map of London, for example, will reveal a schizophrenic city with high-income groups but a far larger population compressed within boroughs characterized by a withering list of social and economic problems, not least unemployment, poor housing, peripheral access to social welfare, and so on. Local councils in such boroughs have been strident in their opposition to many aspects of central government policy and, as a result, have been portrayed as belonging to the "loony left" because of their attempts to introduce radical solutions to the problems. Budget overspend was a common feature of many such councils, a state of affairs that, given the social and economic deprivation in such localities, was virtually inevitable. Central government's response was to penalize their local counterparts by introducing "rate-capping," a financial penalty that meant that many local ser-

vices in education, social welfare, and health had to be curtailed or abandoned. The ideological stance of the two adversaries in this struggle represents contrasting interpretations of what constitutes social justice and individual autonomy.

During the 1980s there has been a growing debate about "values" in society. This arose, like the question of nonwhite immigration, at a time not of economic prosperity but during the period of economic uncertainty in the late 1980s and early 1990s that followed the boom of the Thatcher years. As well, the debate surrounding "values" has been underpinned by widespread worries about the fragmentation of society. The common perception among a large section of the population, and particularly among those of right-wing persuasion, is that there has been a deterioration in standards and moral values. An apparently rising level of crime, juvenile delinquency, and the fragmentation of families is seen as indicative of some kind of moral decay in society, while such highly visible issues as child abuse and pornography assumed new notoriety.

The recent discussions in England concerning the nature of citizenship is one representation of the values debate. There was a view, promoted by the New Right, that by the mid-1980s there was too much of a preoccupation with individual rights. Thus, by 1988 a government minister was calling for moves toward "correcting the balance of the citizenship equation." In a free society, the equation that has "rights" on one side must have "responsibilities" on the other. For more than a quarter of a century public focus has been on the citizens' "rights" and it is now past time to redress the balance (Moore, 1988). A central component in the New Right's version of social responsibility is that the "dependency culture" should be curtailed. One way of doing this was to enforce an obligation to work, either by spurious forms of vocational training (which frequently come with no guarantee of future employment) or by restricting the levels of benefit claimed by unemployed people.

England has enjoyed the status of a welfare state in the period following the Second World

War. Indeed, the concept of universal education, social care, and medical provision had its origins in Britain (Gould, 1993). Until the mid-1970s, state welfare provision was characterized by expansion of services and improvements in benefit. The range of these was vast, relating, for example, to sickness, unemployment, housing, provision for free school meals, and allowances for school uniforms. By the early 1980s, however, a number of factors conspired to bring about a fundamental review of the welfare state. Not least among these were continuing economic difficulties, inflation, and rising unemployment. Welfare, in other words, had become too costly.

The 1980s and 1990s saw successive Conservative governments introduce legislation designed to dismantle the welfare state, driven by the rightist ideology of self-help and competition towards a post-Fordist mixed economy of welfare (Deacon, 1991). Evidence suggests that the governments of the last fifteen years have largely succeeded in this aim. Social expenditure has been reduced, many public services have either been drastically cut back or eliminated, and the private sector has become more prominent. Moreover, as in education, policy decisions regarding social welfare have tended to be taken by those most sympathetic to the ideological aims of the government. Importantly, welfare services have been most heavily curtailed in areas of most need, thereby maintaining a "cycle of disadvantage" (Rutter & Madge, 1976).

This brings us, not unnaturally, to the deep-seated problem of disadvantage and deprivation that, according to statistics, indicate that the gap between "rich" and "poor" had widened between 1981–1991, with more than 20 percent of the total population living at or below the poverty line (Frayman, 1991). This proportion, accounting for almost 12 million people, included over a quarter of all children in the United Kingdom. Poverty is synonymous with unemployment, ill-health, poor housing, family separation, and divorce, among other social ills. While this litany of the effects of deprivation is unexceptional in that they comprise a structural feature in the lives of all those living at or below the poverty line in all post-industrial societies, the trend during the last fifteen years provides a depressing summary of Conservative welfare policy. Given the debilitating effects of this policy on large sections of the population, the rhetoric of successive prime ministers on the subject verges on hypocrisy. John Major, for example, expressed a vision of a classless society in which a better quality of life would be provided for "all our citizens." Sharp ideological distinctions in popular attitudes about poverty have accompanied Conservative welfare changes, again suggestive of a deeply confused and divided society.

Social problems have also arisen subsequent to the rise in immigration from the New Commonwealth countries in the Caribbean, the Indian subcontinent, and Africa. England discovered in the period from the 1960s onwards that it was racist to an unexpected degree, with prejudice and discrimination being demonstrated in employment, housing, education, and the welfare services. Often these racist attitudes were institutional, subtle, and systematic. Black people in England are twice as likely to be unemployed than their white counterparts, and working class Afro-Caribbeans, Pakistanis, and Bangladeshis are predominantly relegated to the lowest-paid jobs with the most unsatisfactory work conditions. As ethnic minority groups have concentrated in particular urban locations where problems of disadvantage and deprivation are most apparent, there has been a tendency to identify such social problems as "black problems" (Gould, 1993). Typical of these negative associations is the public perception that ethnic minority groups are prone to idleness and dependence on state welfare, and that they are frequently the perpetrators of criminal acts.

Finally, then, some commentary is required on the public concern—vicariously and cynically exploited by government, interest groups, and the media alike—regarding levels of crime, juvenile delinquency, and associated problems of substance and alcohol abuse, together with concerns about the moral welfare of children at a time when the extent of child abuse first came to be widely publicized. The links between crime, social class, and poverty have long provided an explanatory synthesis, in spite of the counterindicator that the majority of members of the most disadvantaged groups in society were not identifiably criminal.

The 1980s and 1990s witnessed increased public concern with crime and violence, and the Conservative response was to adopt a get-tough approach. The 1982 Criminal Justice Bill was an early indication of a new draconian attitude to offenders. According to one Member of Parliament, it was a "reflection of public opinion which says that we are fed up with letting sentences be decided by social workers rather than the courts . . . encouraged by wet socialist intellectuals from all over the place" (quoted in Rutherford, 1986).

In Education

Given the scope and intensity of educational change in England over the last decade, it is too ambitious here to present anything other than a brief synopsis of current dilemmas facing teachers and others in the education service. What I have done is to isolate three issues that appear to underpin the current areas of debate.

Centralized Authority versus Local and Individual Autonomy.   My previous description of the educational provision and its underpinning legislation has made reference to the tension, brought a head during the last decade, between the conflicting ideology of the state and the providers and recipients of education. From 1988, successive governments sought to establish their authority over both LEAs and the teaching profession, which were both perceived as being oppositional to the prevailing wish of the ruling Conservatives to create an education service in which choice, competition, market forces, business methods, and systems of accountability should prevail (Heller, 1992).

It had been possible up until the early 1980s to sustain an uneasy partnership between LEAs and teachers and the central government. The legislation introduced in 1988 attacked the autonomy of both, making the term *partnership* appear unreal-

istic, even pejorative. While many professionals involved in the education service would probably agree that there was at least some wastage and mismanagement in certain LEAs, many were also aware that local councils represented an important interface between central government policy and the recipients of education. LEAs, for example, provided support services for children with learning difficulties, advisory services for schools' curricula, child protection schemes, and welfare services for children at risk. They also provided guidelines for, and were arbiters of, school enrollment. These facilities were decimated in the period following the 1988 Act by the shift of educational funding away from the LEAs to individual schools (NUT, 1993). Opponents of the legislation have argued that, in bringing the ruthlessness of the marketplace into education, the first groups of children to feel the effects have been the disadvantaged and those children who have learning difficulties.

The shift in power from local to central government has created a power vacuum. Increasingly, it has been the prerogative of nonelected committees and quangos who make the decisions. The paradox between the distribution of power and responsibility has not escaped the attention of the government's critics. LEAs still have the *responsibility* for those children who are excluded from school on account of their poor behavior yet have no *power* to influence decisions concerning this action; further, because of underfunding from the central government, they are frequently unable to meet the educational needs of these pupils.

Central government, during the last ten years, has also sought to control the teaching profession by a number of devices. It has assiduously cultivated a climate of antagonism toward teachers via a sustained series of attacks on the profession from the Chief Inspector of Schools, politicians, and other interest groups. These implicate teachers alone in the failure of English pupils to compete with the educational achievements of their foreign counterparts. This made the imposition of government will more straightforward. Teachers no longer have the power to enter into collective pay bargaining with government, and they have to work to a predetermined hourage per year. Moreover, their classroom practice now comes under regular, close scrutiny by inspectors from OfSTED. This has created both professional and personal tension. Teachers have argued that the process of inspection is superficial and that the privatization of school inspection has had a negative effect. Too, the results of inspections, however flawed, are now publicly available and, in the new market of education, schools are finding that a poor OfSTED evaluation means that fewer parents will elect to send their children to a school that is perceived to be failing. Another pressure on teachers.

Public scrutiny of schools and teachers has also intensified as a result of the government's insistence that performance tables of schools in England are published in the national press on the spurious grounds that it somehow increases parental choice. This has provoked huge amounts of criticism, which has largely fallen on deaf ears. For example, this has been seen as an open invitation to teachers to make the curriculum fit the test. It provides an example of how the National Curriculum has been used as a device to control not only on what teachers teach but also on how they teach it. The restrictive nature of the National Curriculum as it was conceived in its original form in 1988 was so controversial that, five years later, it was simplified and made more flexible as a result of the Dearing Report (1993). These amendments, although coming as something of a grudging afterthought, nevertheless confirmed a view that those operating at classroom level were right in protesting that the National Curriculum in its 1988 form was virtually unworkable.

Achievement Levels.   There has been a rising level of concern during the last fifteen years regarding the apparent failure of English children to reach the attainment levels of their counterparts elsewhere. The disparity in achievement levels among pupils remains a concern for politicians, professional educators, and the public alike. In spite of the progress made in recent years, there is a concern that the education service in England is still ineffective, illustrated by the extent to which pupils are falling behind their foreign counterparts. For instance, one study showed that English pupils were spending less than two-thirds of their time on number work, and that by the age of 10 they were often two years behind similar children in Germany or Switzerland. The Basic Skills Agency reported that as many as 15 percent of 21-year-olds have limited literacy skills and 20 percent have limited capability in mathematics.

Interestingly, the concerns expressed about apparently low educational performance have been expressed mainly by particular groups. These include right-wing politicians, certain sections of the media, and industrial enterprises and organizations. Education is viewed by these groups to be in service of the state—a means of ensuring industrial growth and economic wealth. What is equally apparent, however, is that recent surveys have indicated that parents are more inclined to choose schools that offer security and a welcoming environment and that make their children feel content and happy (Knight, 1992). The tension between the academic needs of pupils and their affective (that is, noncurriculum, developmental, and emotional) needs is currently a major topic of debate.

The controversy has been fueled by public attacks on the education service in general and on teachers in particular by politicians and pundits alike (e.g., Phillips, 1996). In consequence, there is a public perception, fueled by extravagant claims in the media, that a "crisis in education" is occurring (Barber, 1996), characterized, by declining standards of educational attainment and by a descent by pupils in many schools into misbehavior, indiscipline, and even anarchy.

Typical of contemporary concerns regarding supposedly falling standards is the debate concerning children's behavior. A climate of "moral panic" has developed in the 1990s, with a residual national anxiety about "problem behavior" reinforced by the highly publicized events of 1993 concerning the kidnap and murder of a 3-year-old child by two truant 11-year-olds. Later, when a

London headteacher was murdered outside his school, calls for a tougher stance on indiscipline and misbehavior reached a crescendo.

In 1994 the government published a set of instructions to schools concerning ways of improving the behavior of pupils (DfE, 1994). The following year, the national school inspection agency included within its new *Framework for the Inspection of Schools* details of pupil behavior that was to be a principal criterion of how schools would be judged (OfSTED, 1995). And currently, under a new Labor administration, there are widespread calls for the introduction of the teaching of morals and values in schools and for parents to be made more accountable for the behavior of their children.

What must be borne in mind in relation to the controversy regarding standards in educational achievement in England is that there exists little incontrovertible evidence to support the view that academic performance levels or standards of behavior are declining. In fact, it may be safer to argue that debates concerning the two issues represent a structural feature of the educational scene in England and that the interpretation of data relating to them depends inevitably on the ideological stance of the individual.

Inequality and Disadvantage.   The debate concerning educational achievement is closely linked to that of inequality and disadvantage. According to Learmonth (1993), educational disadvantage

> *results from the interaction between the educational system and its clients, whether pupils or their parents. It occurs when the use of inappropriate educational processes and practice, often in combination with personal, social or environmental circumstances, significantly reduces the capacity of an individual or group fully to accept, participate in or profit from educational provision. (p. 148)*

In England there has been evidence throughout the last ten years that certain groups perform less well in the education system than others. The problem needs to be examined on two levels: the level of educational achievement of individual

children from disadvantaged social groups and the overall levels of educational performance of schools situated in areas of disadvantage.

The failure of individual pupils from certain backgrounds to perform as well as their peers has been highlighted by Kumar (1993). Among the groups most at risk in this respect are children from low-income families where unemployment and poor housing and social environment are endemic. Recent research has indicated that social class remains one of the key factors in determining whether a child does well or badly at school. This finding is nothing new, of course, as illustrated by the findings of the Plowden Report (1967). What worries educators in England is that, in spite of thirty years of supposed affirmative action, notably by the introduction of comprehensive (that is, all-ability) schools, little appears to have changed in the educational lives of such children.

Research findings help to illuminate the seriousness of the problem. Mortimore and Blackstone (1982), following a quantitative survey of educational attainment of primary school children, concluded that "there is a strong and persistent relationship between social class and attainment in primary school and, in particular, between socioeconomic disadvantage and low attainment" (p. 12). The Department for Education (1992) reinforced this concern, suggesting that the educational attainment of children in disadvantaged inner-city locations was not only lower than in more affluent areas, but was even falling. McCallum (1997) showed that children from families in which the head of the household was in partly skilled or unskilled work (a key indicator of social class) did less well than their more affluent peers in standardized tests in English, math, and science.

Similarly, there is a significant concern about levels of access and performance in education by children from minority cultural and racial groups, notably those of Afro-Caribbean and Bangladeshi heritage. Here again the evidence of underperformance is compelling. Mortimore, Sammons, Stoll, Lewis, and Ecob (1988) noted that children of Afro-Caribbean origin obtained lower scores in reading and mathematics at ages 7, 9, and 10 than did their white counterparts. Tizard (1988) highlighted one of the possible factors causing this. There was a tendency for nonwhite children to receive less positive feedback from their teachers; indeed, the research suggests that Afro-Caribbean boys in particular had far less contact (whether negative *or* positive) about their schoolwork than did white boys.

Both of these issues are central components in a second concern: The differential performance of children, outlined above, has been exposed by the publication of schools' league tables of academic performance that indicate that schools in disadvantaged urban locations perform less well than those in more affluent locations. As a result, the recent tendency has been to view some schools as "sink schools"—establishments to which parents are increasingly reluctant to send their children for education. A spiral of decline sets in: The school, with its poor reputation, fails to attract pupils from good backgrounds, becoming known locally as the place where mainly problem pupils are educated. The number of pupils gradually declines, the school receives less money, its buildings cease to be maintained, and its teaching resources fail to meet the needs of the learners. In such a situation, the teachers themselves become demoralized, and many move away. Subsequently, the school has difficulty in recruiting staff, particularly those in key curriculum areas like English, mathematics, and science.

Once again the evidence for this state of affairs is compelling and points to sharp differences in the levels to which successful and unsuccessful schools are financed. The National Commission on Education (1993), for example, was able to confirm a continuing gap between the effectiveness of schools in different locations. Those in disadvantaged urban locations tended to be represented by academic underachievement, problem behavior by pupils, high staff turnover, and low levels of parental participation. Moreover, the impact of funding cuts, as Kumar (1993) has indicated, is most felt by schools situated in disadvantaged urban locations. These are the schools

that have been most affected by the market-led education philosophy of recent Conservative governments.

Fundamental among these problems is the imbalance of resources between schools, made all the more serious by the fact that schools with higher proportions of children with learning difficulties are less well funded than others. The result has been, and still is, that "it is the least able . . . who bear the brunt of reduced or inappropriate provision" (DES, 1986). The current concern is that schools are now ranked according to the performance levels of pupils, irrespective of background factors (Sammons, Nuttall, & Cuttance, 1993), confirming the public perception that schools in disadvantaged areas are, unilaterally, less good than those elsewhere.

THE FUTURE OF SOCIETY AND SCHOOLING

In May 1997, a new Labor government was elected in England. One of the central components of its election manifesto was education. The new administration also presented a more dynamic approach to social disadvantage and inequality. Given that education and society in England are inextricably bound up with matters of social class, it would appear that a two-pronged commitment to education and social welfare in a climate of intense optimism may offer the first realistic opportunity to address the concerns outlined in this chapter.

Thus, the government has pledged itself to guaranteeing nursery education for all 4-year-olds, to cutting class sizes, to more spending on educational infrastructure (schools, curriculum materials, teachers), and to a greater devolution of power from central to local government. Above all, the new government has acknowledged a commitment to reducing the disparities that exist in educational opportunity and performance, and in the level of confrontation between central authority and local interests. Without these, it may be argued, English society, and its educational provision, will remain elitist, governed by traditional mechanisms of social class and economic wealth.

Many of these issues have reoccurred in my overview of the English system of education and the society it functions within. The question remains as to whether, in the face of the negative and deep-seated impact of almost twenty years of right-wing education and social policy, such policy reorientations are too little too late. The trial is beginning—the jury will remain out until beyond the millennium.

REFERENCES

Barber, M. (1996). *The learning game*. London: Gollancz.

Barnett, C. (1986). *The audit of war*. London: Macmillan.

Briault, E. (1976). A distributed system of educational administration: An international viewpoint, *International Review of Education, 22*, 429–439.

Darling, J. (1994). *Child-centered education and its critics*. London: Paul Chapman Publishing.

Deacon, A. (1991). The retreat from state welfare. In S. Becker (Ed.), *Windows of opportunity: Public policy and the poor*. London: CPAG.

Dearing, R. (1993). *The National Curriculum and its assessment: Final report*. London: School Curriculum and Assessment Authority.

Department for Education (DfE). (1992). *School examination survey 1990/1: Statistical bulletin 15/92*. London: HMSO.

Department for Education (DfE). (1994). *Pupils with problems: Circulars 8/94–13/94*. London: DfE.

Department of Education and Science (DES). (1986). *Report by HMI on the effects of local on education provision in England*. London: HMSO.

Department of Education and Science (DES). (1987). *The National Curriculum 5-16: A consultation document*. London: HMSO.

Frayman, H. (1991). *Breadline Britain in the 1990s*. London: Domino Films/LWT.

Gould, A. (1993). *Capitalist welfare systems*. London: Longman.

Heller, H. (1992). *Policy and power in education*. London: Routledge.

Knight, P. (1992). Secondary schools in their own words: The image in school prospectuses. *Cambridge Journal of Education, 22*, 55–67.

Kumar, V. (1993). *Poverty and inequality in the UK: The effects on children*. London: National Children's Bureau.

Lawrence, I. (1994). From 1944 to 1994: What have we learnt? In I. Lawrence (Ed.), *Education tomorrow*. London: Cassell.

Lawton, D. (1989). *Education, culture and the National Curriculum*. London: Hodder & Stoughton.

Learmonth, J. (1993). Monitoring, evaluation and development: The role of inspection in school improvement. In J. Learmonth (Ed.), *Teaching and learning in cities*. London: Whitbread.

McCallum, D. (1997, April 18). Social class linked to results. *Times Educational Supplement*.

Moore, J. (1988, October 12). Speech to Conservative Party Conference.

Mortimore, P., & Blackstone, T. (1982). *Disadvantage and education*. London: Heinemann.

Mortimore, P., Sammons, P., Stoll, L., Lewis, D., & Ecob, R. (1988). *School matters: The junior years*. Wells: Open Books.

National Commission on Education. (1993). *Success against the odds: Effective schools in disadvantaged areas*. London: Heinemann.

National Union of Teachers (NUT). (1993). *Survey of support services for special education*. London: Author.

Office for Standards in Education (OfSTED). (1995). *Framework for the inspection of schools*. London: HMSO.

Plowden Report. (1967). *Children and their primary schools*. London: Central Advisory Council for Education/HMSO.

Phillips, M. (1996, September 8) Back to school—to be de-educated. *The Observer*, pp. 14–15.

Rutherford, A. (1986). *Growing out of crime*. Harmondsworth: Penguin.

Rutter, M., & Madge, N. (1976). *Cycles of disadvantage: A review of research*. London: Heinemann.

Sammons, P., Nuttall, D., & Cuttance, P. (1993). Differential school effectiveness: Results from a reanalysis of the Inner London Education Authority's Junior School Project Data. *British Educational Research Journal, 19*, 381–406.

Tizard, B. (1988). *Young children at school in the inner city*. London: Erlbaum.

CHAPTER 7

From Theocentric to Market Paradigms in Irish Education Policy: Equality, Difference, Virtue, and Control

DENIS O'SULLIVAN

Denis O'Sullivan *is associate professor of education at University College Cork, having previously taught throughout the Irish educational system. As well as teaching qualifications, he holds a master's degree in sociology and a doctorate in education from the National University of Ireland. His research has been published in Irish and international journals. His books include* Irish Educational Policy: Process and Substance *(co-editor),* Social Commitment and Adult Education *(editor),* Commitment, Educative Action and Adults *and* Paradigms and Power: A Cultural Politics of Irish Education *(forthcoming).*

After a War of Independence against the British and a bitter civil war, what was then known as the Irish Free State gained sovereignty over all but the six northern counties of the island of Ireland and set about nation building in 1923. It wasn't surprising that it looked to the distinguishing characteristics of religion (Roman Catholic) and language (Gaelic) to cultivate a sense of uniqueness, pride, and cultural identity. A history of colonization that involved confiscation and resettlement of land, economic exploitation, religious persecution, and cultural and linguistic suppression fueled the political remembrance that constructed a nationalizing project within set boundaries of censorship, religious and cultural orthodoxy, linguistic pieties,

The research in connection with this chapter was assisted by a grant from the Arts Faculty Research Fund, University College Cork, which is gratefully acknowledged.

and economic and trade barriers. The slogan Sinn Féin (*ourselves alone*) captures the spirit of this nationalizing project. The erosion of this insulation commenced with the economic programming of the 1950s and gained momentum through social and cultural change from the 1960s.

THE SOCIAL FABRIC

Economic

Throughout the 1950s it became increasingly obvious that Ireland was in the grip of an economic crisis. A litany of economic and social ailments characterized the period, including high inflation, balance of payment crises, industrial and agricultural decline, and massive emigration. Some 400,000 persons left to seek employment elsewhere, mainly in Great Britain, during the decade (Breen, Hannan, Rottman, & Whelan, 1990).

The policy response was economic planning, orchestrated by civil servants together with academic advisors rather than politicians (Lee, 1989). The First Program for Economic Expansion in 1958 signaled a key redirection in economic development: It abandoned protection in favor of free trade and encouraged foreign-owned manufacturers with a strong export commitment to locate in Ireland. The economic prosperity that followed in the 1960s was itself followed by economic crises in the 1970s associated with rising energy costs, and in the 1980s with a spiraling national debt. However, such is the buoyancy of the current economic climate that Irish economic growth in recent years has attracted the title *Celtic Tiger*. Thus, in reference to Ireland's high economic growth rates, low interest and inflation rates, and reduced national debt, a report of the Union Bank of Switzerland painted a glowing picture of Irish economic success that it saw as "the envy of Europe" (Kirby, 1997, p. 149).

On the darker side of this economic miracle is a high unemployment problem in which the incidence of long-term unemployment is particularly distinctive. Ireland's long-term unemployment rate is higher than the overall unemployment rate in OECD countries. Poverty continues to be a significant problem and, in the context of the stubborn social class system, the term *underclass* is being used to describe sections of Irish urban society marginalized and excluded from the general rising economic tide.

Demographic

A crucial parameter within which educational policy and planning operate is demographic structure and change. The changing patterns of nuptiality, fertility, death, and migration that influence the number requiring education have been recently analyzed by Courtney (1995). The rampant population growth in the late eighteenth and early nineteenth centuries was checked dramatically in Malthusian fashion by the famines of the 1840s. Between then and 1926, the Irish population declined continuously, almost halving from just over 8 million to slightly in excess of 4 million in the total island of Ireland. After the partition of the island in 1922, the population in what is now the Irish Republic continued to decline until the 1960s, apart from a small increase between 1946 and 1951. It was not until the 1950s that the other Malthusian preventive check on population so characteristic of the Irish Republic—high permanent celibacy and late age at marriage—began to change more in line with European norms. These marriage patterns had been counterbalanced by

high levels of fertility. In the 1940s, for instance, despite late marriage, families were twice as large as in Europe's low-fertility countries.

Emigration has also been a persistent and significant influence on population change in the Irish Republic. The statistics demonstrate how it was only in the 1960s that the population of the Irish Republic began to steadily increase. Of particular interest to educational planning, however, is the similarly striking and even more substantial decline in fertility since 1981. Overall, it is estimated that there has been a decline of 55 percent in the total marital fertility rates since 1961. Various factors have been suggested as explanations—changing kinship obligations, lifestyle aspirations, labor force participation, and the liberalization of family planning legislation in the 1970s.

Religious and Linguistic

The two props of nation building—religion and language—also experienced change in recent decades. A recent study of cultural change in Irish society is particularly provocative in this regard. "Just how 'Gaelic' is the self-image of a country which, within the past decade, has had a Minister for Education who could not speak the Irish language? And just how 'Catholic' is a land which no longer produces priests in sufficient quantity to service the increasingly elderly and depopulated parishes in the major archdioceses?" (Kiberd, 1995, p. 648).

But as Nic Ghiolla Phádraig (1995) has pointed out, Ireland is the only country in the English-speaking world that has a Catholic majority, at its most recent count 93 percent of the population. Religious practice has traditionally been high and church teaching has been reflected in its constitution and laws, as, for instance, in the prohibition on abortion and divorce, the latter recently rescinded.

Secularization theory would suggest that processes of modernization such as industrialization, urbanization, and rationalization should lead to a secularization of Irish society. Hornsby-Smith (1992) found some decline in weekly mass attendance and in orthodoxy of belief, and a big decline in monthly confession as well as movement to a greater reliance on personal judgment in matters of private behavior and belief. Overall, however, he concluded that during the 1980s there was no change in the level of traditional belief and religiosity, a modest decline in confidence in the church, a significant increase in permissiveness, and a strengthening of civic morality. Moreover, European comparisons suggest that the scores of Irish respondents on religious items are well above average and that they also display lower levels of permissiveness and a slightly more absolute view of civic morality.

Gaelic (or Irish, as it is more colloquially known) occupies a special place in official national policy. Under the Constitution, Irish is the first official language, and it is only in recent decades that the ideal of revivalism was replaced by a more pragmatic bilingualism in which the objective was to maintain the language and to extend its use. The study of Irish is obligatory in primary and post-primary schools. Entrance to the constituent colleges of the National University of Ireland, though not to the newer universities, demands qualifications in Irish.

Gaeltacht areas, where Irish is the daily medium of communication, account for no more than a few percent of the population and are located in rural and more isolated regions of the country. Outside of these areas the most recent survey (Ó Riagáin & Ó Gliasáin, 1994) indicates that about three-quarters of the population do not use Irish themselves even at minimal levels; about 5 percent claim to speak Irish frequently at home or at work. There has been little change in the proportion claiming fluency in spoken Irish in the past twenty years. About half said they had little or no Irish, about 40 percent felt that they could manage a few simple sentences or parts of conversations, and just over 10 percent said that they would handle most or all conversational situations. By contrast, the ability to read Irish has risen substantially during the period.

Nationalism

Along with the revival of the Irish language, the unification of the country has been a national objective to which little more than lip service has been paid since the partition in 1922 resulted in the six northern counties remaining part of the United Kingdom. When in 1969 a civil rights movement campaigning for equal rights in voting, housing, and employment erupted into violence, the Republic was faced with a situation that forced it to rethink its position, not merely on Northern Ireland, but on its definition of Irishness and nationality. The campaign of violence that followed with its complex sectarian (Catholic/ Protestant) and political (nationalist/unionist) dimensions has only recently abated. At present, the dominant discourse is one of peace and reconciliation that recognizes different traditions and identities within Ireland and speaks only of unification as an aspiration to be achieved with the consent of all the interests involved.

Gender

As well as changes that resulted from an internal dynamic, Ireland has also been influenced by the new social movements. The agenda of the women's movement has proved to be particularly relevant to education. Employment legislation granting equal rights to women in matters of pay and the removal of discrimination was passed from the 1970s onward. The women's movement has also been involved in successfully campaigning for the legalization of contraception in the 1970s, for the removal of the constitutional ban on divorce, recently rescinded, and in the 1990s for the legalization of abortion information and the introduction of abortion in limited circumstances.

Political

The political system through which these social and cultural changes came to have a bearing on the policy process has a number of noteworthy features. For the immediate future, Irish governments seem destined to be coalitions. This is a function of the Irish electoral system of multiseat constituencies and the single transferable vote in which it is difficult for any one party to gain an overall majority. In fact, no party has gained such a majority since 1977. Catch-all parties are cultivated by this system, by the need to be sensitive to the policies of possible future partners in government, and with a view to maximizing cross-party transfers in voting. The message to interest groups was that they needed to organize and press their claims on the state rather than attempt to penetrate the ideology of any particular party. In the political configurations that emerged, the interests of the radical right and left were organized out of the political process.

SCHOOLING

Preschool

Education is compulsory in the Republic of Ireland from the age of 6. Nonetheless, Irish children routinely enter primary schools after their fourth birthday. In fact, 65 percent of all 4-year-olds and almost all 5-year-olds attend the infant classes of primary schools. Preschooling, in the strict sense of being prior to primary schooling, is multifaceted and includes playgroups, nursery schools, day-care nurseries, and so on. Traditionally, this has been unregulated by the state and it is only with the implementation of the relevant sections of the 1991 Child Care Act in 1996 that this situation changed.

Primary

At primary level there are three types of schools: ordinary primary schools, special schools, and non-aided private primary schools. Together they serve almost 500,000 children. In all, there are in excess of 3,200 primary schools, 115 special schools, and 79 private primary schools. With the exception of the latter, which receive no state funding, the current and capital costs of primary schools, including the full costs of teacher salaries, are predominantly funded by the state, supplemented by local contributions. A feature of the Irish primary school sector is the small size profile of the schools; more than 50 percent of the schools have four or fewer teachers.

The pedagogical orientation of primary education derives its ethos from the 1971 curriculum. Greatly influenced by both the content and spirit of the English Plowden Report (Great Britain: Central Advisory Council 1967), *Children and Their Primary Schools,* the 1971 curriculum was meant to facilitate greater flexibility and child-centeredness in learning and curriculum organization. The National Council for Curriculum and Assessment, on the invitation of the Minister for Education, is currently conducting a review of the primary curriculum within the context of the basic principles adopted in 1971.

There is no formal assessment of pupils at primary level; the former primary school certificate examination was abolished some twenty-five years ago. A 1992 Green Paper, however, recommended testing at the ages of 7 and 11. It argued that since there is no formal external examination until pupils have completed between nine and eleven years of formal schooling, there's a need for some objective criteria by which to measure their progress at earlier stages of their education with a view to complementing school-based tests. Expressions of concern from the teaching bodies that this could result in a reintroduction of formal testing resulted in a dilution of the proposal that stressed its diagnostic rather than its evaluative function.

Almost all primary schools are either parish schools or schools with an explicit, usually Roman Catholic, religious ethos. The Education Act currently being processed by the legislature proposes changes in the management structures of primary schools.

Secondary

The second level sector comprises secondary, vocational, community, and comprehensive schools. From a total of 775 public schools, 452 of these are secondary, 247 are vocational, and 76 are community or comprehensive. In all, about 370,000 students attend this sector.

Secondary schools have evolved from the academic grammar tradition of post-primary schooling. They educate 61 percent of second-level students and are privately owned and managed. The majority are administered by religious communities and the remainder by boards of governors or by individuals. As well as meeting almost all of the cost of teachers' salaries, the state also provides allowances and capitation grants for the 95 percent of schools that participate in the free education scheme.

Vocational schools were originally established under the Vocational Education Act (1930) to provide vocational and technical education. They continue to have a strong practical emphasis, though since the late 1960s they have expanded the academic sections of their curriculum and now prepare students for the same examinations as other post-primary schools. Vocational schools are administered by vocational education committees appointed by local government authorities. They educate 26 percent of all second-level students.

Comprehensive schools date from the 1960s and were meant to serve as a prototype for a type of school that would integrate both academic and practical dimensions of learning. They were meant to provide the full range of educational choices for all post-primary pupils in their catchment area. This idea of a unified rather than a bipartite post-primary system has been continued with community schools, the first of which was established in 1972. Community and comprehensive schools educate 13 percent of second-level students. They are administered by Boards of Management and reflect a denominational ethos, Catholic or Protestant.

Second-level education consists of a three-year junior cycle followed by a two-year senior cycle with an intervening transition year program. At Junior Certificate level, students follow a wide-ranging program including languages, mathematics, scientific and social studies, as well as religious and physical education. This culminates in the Junior Certificate examination, which is usually taken at the age of 15 or 16 years.

Education is compulsory to the age of 15 years, though the great majority now stay on until the end of post-primary schooling. It is expected that by the year 2000, nine out of ten students will complete the senior cycle. The implication of this is that there is now considerable diversity of abilities and aspirations among students in second-level schools. To cater to this diversity, three leaving certificate programs are now offered. These are the Leaving Certificate (LC), the Leaving Certificate Vocational (LCV), and the Leaving Certificate Applied (LCA). Up to recent years, the Leaving Certificate was the only mainstream program available to senior cycle students. While it is being revised at present, it remains the more academic of the three programs and is geared towards those who plan to transfer to third-level education.

Students are required to take at least five subjects, including Irish. Because of university entrance requirements, they take English, mathematics, at least one modern language, and a choice of scientific, business, or aesthetic subjects appropriate to their aspirations. The Leaving Certificate Vocational program is the regular Leaving Certificate program but with a concentration on technical subjects together with additional modules on enterprise education, preparation for work, and work experience. The Leaving Certificate Applied incorporates a cross-curricular rather than a subject-based structure. Its aim is the preparation of participants for adult and working life through a holistic program including general education, vocational education, and vocational preparation. The Leaving Certificate Applied is specifically intended to meet the needs of those students who find themselves unsuited to the other leaving certificate programs.

Post-Secondary

At the third level there are almost 90,000 students enrolled in higher education institutions. In excess of 53,000 of these are in universities, more than 35,000 are in technological colleges, and about 500 each are in teacher training colleges and non-aided private higher education colleges. There are four universities, the largest of which, the National University of Ireland, has a federal structure with colleges in Dublin, Cork, Galway, and

Maynooth. In the technological sector, the Dublin Institute of Technology has an enrollment of almost 10,000 students. A network of eleven Regional Technical Colleges throughout the country serves almost 25,000 students. These provide courses in a wide range of areas including business studies, science, technology, engineering, music, art, and design. Their degrees and diplomas are for the most part awarded by the National Council for Educational Awards.

Five specialist colleges provide for the training of primary school teachers, all of whom are now awarded a university degree. Almost three-quarters of all second-level teachers are trained in the universities. The model is typically a consecutive one with students following a professional course of formation after being awarded a primary degree.

The Higher Education Authority, established in 1971, has the responsibility for the development of higher education, coordinating state investment in the sector, and advising the minister on patterns of demand and need. A major intervention by the government in relation to student support schemes has been the recent abolition of undergraduate tuition fees in publicly funded third-level institutions.

Outside the mainstream educational system, a number of specialist programs such as the Youth Encounter Projects, Youthreach, and Community Training Workshops cater to those who cannot adapt to regular schooling; who have left full-time education without any formal qualifications; or who are at risk due to poor educational attainment, literacy, numeracy, personal difficulties, and low self-esteem.

Policies

An unprecedented process of policy making was initiated with the publication in 1992 of the consultative Green Paper, *Education for a Changing World* (Government of Ireland: Department of Education, 1992). Following the receipt of voluminous submissions, the Minister for Education organized a National Education Convention in

October 1993, in which representatives from forty-two organizations took part in structured discussion on key issues arising from the consultative process (Coolahan, 1994). In the light of this, the government published its policy intentions in the White Paper, *Charting Our Education Future* (Government of Ireland: Department of Education, 1995). In this, the government was more explicit in outlining its philosophical orientation on education, which it proclaimed to be informed by a commitment to quality, equality, pluralism, partnership, and accountability. The content of the promised Education Act (1997) at present being processed by the legislature is narrower than expected and is confined to the establishment of boards of management in individual schools and ten new regional education boards as a process of decentralizing the governance of education. Specific features and proposals from within this total policy process from consultation to legislation will be introduced as appropriate in the sections that follow.

MAJOR ISSUES, CONTROVERSIES, AND PROBLEMS

A full understanding of the controversies and issues besetting contemporary Irish education requires consideration of the comprehensive shift that has occurred in Irish educational policy paradigms in recent decades. Policy paradigms are frameworks that govern the policy process; they embody linguistic, normative, epistemological, identity, and ideological dimensions. They regulate what is to be defined as a meaningful problem, how it is to be thematized and described, who is to be recognized as a legitimate participant and with what status, and how the policy process is to be enacted, realized, and evaluated. Policy paradigms are powerful regulatory forces in the generation and enactment of policy.

From Theocentric to Market Policy Paradigms

During the past forty years Irish education has experienced a dramatic change in how the institution of education is understood. This has been particularly evident at the official level, where the theocentric paradigm, which dominated until the 1950s, was replaced by a market paradigm that continues to expand. The current problems and concerns of the system can only be understood in relation to the nature of this cultural change, the social processes by which it has been achieved, and the manner in which it has influenced other theories of what education is, what it is for, and how its character is to be determined. The theocentric and market paradigms of education can be sketched from official sources such as the reports of the Council of Education that was largely active in the 1950s and such contemporary reports as those of the National Economic and Social Council, the Industrial Policy Review Group, the Green Paper, as well as ministerial statements from the 1990s.

The Council of Education *Report on the Curriculum of the Secondary School* (Government of Ireland: Council of Education, 1962) emphasized that "The purpose of school education, then, is the organized development and equipment of all the powers of the individual person—religious, moral, intellectual, physical—so that, by making the fullest use of his talents, he may responsibly discharge his duties to God and to his fellow men in society." According to this report, the aim of the school was to prepare pupils "to be God fearing and responsible citizens" (p. 88). In stark contrast, by 1990 the major national advisory council on social and economic matters (Government of Ireland: National Economic and Social Council, 1990) was arguing that in the educational system "the principles of consumer representation, participation, and accountability should be reflected in management and decision making structures" (pp. 313–314). It criticized the absence of a formal appeal mechanism for parents at primary level, and at second level the fact that there was no formal system whereby parents can "obtain factual and evaluative data about schools, in order to make appropriate educational choices." The Council concluded that the absence of accessible data on schools of the type indicated above touches on the issue of accountability.

The Culliton Report (Government of Ireland: Industrial Policy Review Group, 1992) gave pride of place to criticisms of the educational system. It noted that "The contribution of productive enterprise to our social and economic objectives should be an issue of primary importance at all educational levels to de-emphasize the bias towards the liberal arts and traditional professions." As well, "A higher priority must be attached in the education system to the acquisition of usable and marketable skills. This is evident both from the perspective of the requirements of industrial development and for the employment prospects and self-fulfillment of young people" (p. 52).

The Green Paper (Government of Ireland: Department of Education, 1992) mirrored these sentiments, claiming that in the business world there is a wide recognition that many Irish young people tend to lack "the range of technical skills needed in today's industry; the communication and other interpersonal skills sought by employers; the critical thinking, problem-solving ability and individual initiative that an enterprise culture requires; the language skills to work and win markets across the EC, and to take part in tourism related activities" (p. 11).

While it would be wrong to assume that the details of the education system can be read off from a knowledge of the dominant policy paradigm, there is no doubt that the character of its aims, power relationships, roles, and evaluation will vary in the light of whatever policy paradigm informs educational decision making. Some of the more salient contrasts between the theocentric and market paradigms in this regard are summarized in Table 7.1.

For the theocentric paradigm, the aim of education is a settled matter, to be determined by unchanging principles based on a Christian view of human nature and destiny. In contrast to this dogmatic prescriptiveness about the purpose of education, the market paradigm adopts a populist approach, holding that what education is for is a matter for consumers of the system, such as pupils, parents, civic leaders, and business interests, to decide.

TABLE 7.1   Contrasting Manifestations of Theocentric and Market Policy Paradigms in Education

	THEOCENTRIC	MARKET
Aim	Determined by unchanging Christian principles	Determined by the consumers of the system
Ownership	Christian authorities	Individual/collective initiative
Policymaking	Expert-based	Broadly based
Role of Users	Beneficiaries	Vigilant
Role of Educators	Trustworthy professionals	Requires visibility and accountability
Schools	Solidaristic communities	Commercial
Pedagogical Relationship	Paternalistic	Contractual
Evaluation	Truncated, incomplete	Quantifiable
Role of State	Subsidiary	Facilitator

If the purpose of education is to lead people to God and to facilitate them in reaching their eternal salvation, it follows that the designated religious authorities—church, religious personnel—can claim privilege in relation to the ownership, management, and general control of schools. On the other hand, if consumers are entitled to decide what education is for, they must also have the entitlement to establish schools through individual or collective initiative according to their philosophy of life. Policy making in the theocentric paradigm is a matter for experts since the knowledge, skills, and understandings that this process of formation requires are not universally distributed and decision making needs to be in the hands of a knowledgeable few. For the market paradigm, decision making must be more widely based and facilitated by public information about the system.

In the theocentric paradigm, the complementary roles of user and educator are those of beneficiary and trustworthy professional, respectively. Clients of the system need do no more than use it in an unreflective and trusting manner to derive its benefits. Professionals are dedicated and committed to the ideals of the educational system, and they can be relied on to act in the pursuit of the interests of those who are in their charge. In the market paradigm the delivery of an educational service is seen as something approaching an amoral activity. Because trust in educators isn't sufficient to protect the users' interests, the processes and standards of education need to be visible and answerable to the public.

Where schools are founded on the pursuit of God's plan for humanity, those who participate in its activities are bound together by a sense of membership of a common community of believers. In the market paradigm, schools are to be understood and assessed according to the same commercial principles as any other organization offering a service, such as efficiency, cost effectiveness, quality control, and surplus and deficit in relation to market requirements.

At the focused level of the pedagogical relationship, the core of the educational process, the theocentric paradigm conceives of the teacher *in loco parentis,* concerned with the ultimate salvation of the pupil and empowered to act as the teacher thinks fit to further assist in that salvation. In the market paradigm, the relationship is contractual, based on increasingly circumscribed and specified responsibilities and entitlements.

Since in the theocentric paradigm, education aspires to influence one's status in the next life, evaluation of its effectiveness through worldly measures is necessarily incomplete and truncated. The market paradigm, however, asserts that the success of the educational system can be quantified by the use of pivotal indicators. Finally, the state in the theocentric paradigm is obliged to assume a subsidiary role, playing second fiddle to the church, which along with pupils, whose interests they represent, are considered to have prior rights in relation to education. While the state is also a secondary force in the market paradigm, its role is a more active one in regulating the operation of the various interests in the marketplace of education and of facilitating a level playing field in matters of regulations, subsidies, and curricular prescriptions.

The implications of these cultural changes in the aims, agents, power relationships, and truth regimes of education will now be considered in relation to the policy debates on four contemporary controversies and issues: equality, difference, virtue, and control.

Equality

Ireland, in common with most educational systems, has problems with uneven rates of participation and achievement across a range of significant categories within society. It is in relation to these disparities that the question of equality is routinely discussed. Class differences in educational opportunity have been the focus of attention since the 1960s, gender differences came to be recognized during the 1970s and particularly in the 1980s, while in recent years Irish travelers, who lead a nomadic lifestyle, have successfully claimed entitlements in education because of their distinct ethnicity.

Gender differences have seen considerable change in recent decades. While female students have traditionally had higher rates of completed post-primary schooling, in the past twenty-five years they have succeeded in progressively translating that advantage into increasing participation rates in higher education. From a representation of about a third in 1970–1971, female students are

now in the majority in Irish universities and are approaching parity throughout the third-level sector. In terms of achievement, at the critical Leaving Certificate examination level, the overall performance of women is superior. Women, however, remain significantly underrepresented in mathematical, scientific, and technical subjects at second and third level.

Travelers' participation rates in primary education have improved dramatically, moving from a situation where 114 traveler children were regularly attending primary school in 1963 to the current situation where there is almost universal participation. Participation rates in post-primary schooling are extremely low and the White Paper has set specific targets in this regard. The educational experiences of travelers, however, is more appropriately considered in terms of "difference" and how their ethnic identity is to be recognized within the educational system.

In terms of the scale of disparities in achievement and participation and the numbers affected, nothing compares with the problem of class inequalities in education. Clancy (1995) found that at the basic level of participation, one-fifth overall fail to make it to Leaving Certificate level. The retention rate varies significantly by social class. The figure for the children of unskilled manual parents is about half, while only 3 percent of the children of higher professional families fail to remain in school to sit for the terminal examination of post-primary education.

Class continues to be a force in making the transition to higher education even for those with similar levels of achievement. For those with a minimum pass level, about three-quarters of the higher professional group as opposed to less than one-quarter of the unskilled manual group transfer to higher education.

When one examines the policy issues that the principle of equality generates, one finds a basic focus on individual opportunity that in recent years has added a concern for achievement in addition to the previous concentration on access and participation. Repeatedly, equality is seen in terms of equity in the development of a pupil's abilities and is represented in a manner that is informed by the market paradigm or at least neutral toward it.

Early debate from the 1960s on equality of educational opportunity was in the context of the human capital approach to education. The tapping of unrealized talent was seen as socially beneficial, indeed even essential, if the economy and production were to be fully energized. With the growth in the economy, the demands on education are now even more comprehensive, no longer merely requiring that those with talent be recognized and developed, but that all pupils be adequately trained for the increasingly higher technological demands of modern industry.

Concern for low-achieving school leavers is repeatedly represented in terms of their experience in the labor market. One's chance of getting employment, the length of time one remains unemployed, the level of the labor force one enters, all have implications for individual status and reward. However, variations in employment rates across those with different levels of educational credentials is repeatedly treated in a manner that elides the distinction between employability and job chances.

One recent survey (McCoy & Whelan, 1996) demonstrates how the prospects of school leavers securing employment one year after leaving school improve consistently with each level of educational attainment. While less than 34 percent of school leavers without qualifications were found to be in employment, the corresponding figure for those with junior-cycle qualifications was 54 percent, and for those with senior-cycle qualifications 68 percent. Furthermore, the association between increasing educational attainment and greater labor market success has become more pronounced over the years. For instance, in 1980 the unemployment rate of those without qualifications was 14 percentage points greater than for those who had attained the Leaving Certificate. By 1995, the unemployment rate among those with a Leaving Certificate was over 40 percentage points lower than among those without qualifications.

Initiatives aimed at furthering equality of educational opportunity from the 1960s include free post-primary schooling and transport, third-level grants, and the Rutland Street preschool intervention program for disadvantaged children, one of the earliest of its kind in Europe. However, since the 1980s, efforts to combat class-related underachievement have become more specific features of educational policy. These interventions embody a number of features. The idea of preschool compensatory education has been revived to be followed by targeted allocation of resources to ensure low teacher–pupil ratios and better capitation grants in designated disadvantaged schools. Specific targets in terms of achievement and participation rates for the disadvantaged have been set throughout the educational system. For those who fall through the net, second-chance programs are available for unqualified school leavers (Youthreach) and for adult recipients of social welfare (Vocational Training Opportunities Scheme). In general, these interventions are characterized by a change of focus from inequalities in access and participation to the underdevelopment of talent and potential.

Difference

The tendency to regard Ireland as a homogeneous, integrated society was a feature of nationalist ideology, nation-building strategy, and Catholic social teaching—all of which conceived of society in terms of consensus rather than conflict. To suggest otherwise—that the nation, the people, the Irish, or Catholic Ireland might be in need of differentiation to take account of complexities of distinct identity, values, and lifestyle—was disruptive of the self-understanding of Irish culture in the manner in which it sought to assert new groupings and categories. As this pertained to education, it constituted a case study of boundary politics.

The most striking and path-breaking assertion of difference in contemporary Irish education has been the interdenominational school movement now operating under the umbrella of Educate Together. Áine Hyland, one of the founders of the movement, has traced its origins, struggles, and achievements (Hyland, 1996). She describes how she and her husband, having returned to Ireland from abroad, sought something other than the denominational school system for their children in the early 1970s. Along with other like-minded parents, they set up the Dalkey School Project in Dublin in 1975 for those committed to a multide-nominational option within the national school system. The movement faced considerable resistance, but political support eventually grew and there are now fourteen schools throughout the country affiliated to Educate Together, which is also recognized by the Department of Education as a consultative body and as such took its place at the National Education Convention in 1993. As well as the logistical problems of funding, premises, and bureaucratic regulations that assume denominational schooling, Hyland also notes the opposition of a conservative Catholic group.

One has to be struck by the unrelenting commitment of the interdenominational school movement's leaders and participants. A less visible factor in the success of the movement was the manner in which it drew on dimensions of both the theocentric and market paradigms. Merging the categories of the theocentric paradigm with the principles of the market, Educate Together effectively legitimated a new classification of the users of educational services. But it achieved this innovation through a process of diversification rather than disruption of the existing cultural categories of identity, conscience, and world view.

The reemergence of Irish-medium schools since the 1980s can also be considered in terms of the construction of difference—in this case, the classification of linguistic communities within Irish society. Whatever the motivation for the growth of Irish-medium schooling, as they evolved they drew increasingly on a minority rights discourse. Those whose preference was for the Irish language argued for their entitlement to educational as well as recreational and cultural facilities through the medium of Irish.

There were obvious benefits to be derived from adopting a minority rights argument in the context of a European Union committed to respecting cultural diversity. Once the unity of the Irish people in the designation of linguistic communities was disrupted, and language acknowledged as a matter of choice rather than ethnic ascription, it opened the way for those who felt no affinity with Irish to seek abrogation from the requirements of the state's Irish language policy. If those who wished to use Irish as a medium of communication could claim special treatment in pursuit of their cultural values, then equally those who did not include the learning and speaking of Irish in their cultural preferences could feel entitled to exemption in this regard. This argument gained sustenance from the current politico-ideological environment of rapprochement in Northern Ireland. The most public manifestation of this argument is to be found in the suggestion by the Irish National Teachers Organization that there should be schools with Irish as the medium of instruction, schools with Irish as a compulsory subject, and also a new type of school in which Irish could be an optional subject (Watson, 1996). This assertion of cultural difference is likely to be voiced even more vigorously in the future.

The most successful claim to cultural distinctiveness in Irish education has been the recognition of the ethnic identity of Ireland's nomadic people, now referred to as travelers. This has been argued on the basis of their endogamous nature, distinct language, values and lore, shared sense of a common history, and patterns of mutual identification with the settled community (Kenny, 1991; Rigal, 1989). This represents a major shift in the official definition of this group since the 1960s when the policy was one of sedenterization and settlement of traveler families and the treatment of traveler children as culturally deprived.

The acceptance of the distinct ethnic identity of travelers is reflected in the Green and White Papers, which proposed modules on traveler culture in teacher preparation courses and in the school curriculum. It would appear, however, that there are different views within the groups representing travelers as to the relative emphasis to be placed on Irish and traveler identities (Irish

National Teachers Organization, 1992). Nor is it at all clear as to what the nature of the relationship between traveler culture and the school curriculum ought to be. Is it presumed that traveler culture provides a sufficient basis for a curriculum in the knowledge, skills, and values that the pupils will need to contribute to and benefit from society? Or is it being claimed that the culture provides a medium through which the skills, knowledge, and values of mainstream culture can be as effectively communicated? Or is it intended that a spirit of multiculturalism should prevail? Or is it merely being proposed that illustrations from traveler culture be used to make an otherwise unaltered curriculum appear more immediate and in touch with the experience of traveler pupils?

Virtue

A distinguishing feature of the theocentric paradigm was the very explicit and directive manner in which it pronounced on what might be generally labeled as virtue. This covered a wide span of behaviors and dispositions including the social domain of charity and justice; personal virtues such as truthfulness, patience, and temperance; and the duties of citizenship including obedience to lawful authority, as well as more specific areas such as sexual behavior and the sanctity of the family. An uncompromising aspect of educational programs relating to these virtues that operate within the frame of the theocentric paradigm was their confident prescription of right and wrong based on church teaching derived from revelation and natural law.

As the theocentric paradigm lost its controlling power, the legitimacy of this prescriptiveness became less secure. What had been the certainties of the religion class and of the general practices and ethos of Catholic schooling became less compelling to students and even invited open challenge and dissent. A new set of values was emerging that centered itself on the individual and proclaimed the priority of personal autonomy, self-direction, and choice. Behavior, most publicly

relating to alcohol, drugs, and sex, that in the past was differentiated in terms of right and wrong, was increasingly treated as lifestyle choices. The function of educational programs was seen to be the preparation of young people for the making of these choices rather than their instruction in what constituted proper, correct, and moral behavior. The market characteristics of diversity and choice figure prominently in the justification of this approach.

The obvious tensions between the teaching of correct behavior and the facilitation of lifestyle choices came to a head in relation to a range of new programs, developed from the 1970s, variously described as social and health education, life skills, human relationships, pastoral care, and education for living. These were offered in postprimary schools in association with Youth Associations, Health Boards, and the State Health Education Bureau, and sought to expand the traditional curriculum beyond its cognitive/intellectual focus and its emphasis on examinations.

These programs were targeted by sections within the Catholic Church as a source of threat to religion and religious values. Two of the pivotal criticisms are relevant here: the wide interpretation of health education and the moral relativism and subjectivism of the courses. Critics of the programs point to components dealing with family living, morality, human growth and development, relationships and sex education, all of which should more properly feature in the Christian formation of young people. Quite simply, the domain of moral belief and principle was considered to be under invasion from a predominantly secularizing set of influences in a manner that disguised both the intrusion and the shift of ideology.

The methodology of these programs included group discussion, sociodrama, role play, and value clarification techniques and followed approaches from training manuals imported from North America. Of these, the values clarification technique has been repeatedly criticized for the manner in which it teaches that there are no absolute rights and wrongs (Family Solidarity, 1987). By far the most widely quoted and strident criticisms of the values clarification techniques are to be found in Manly (undated). She accuses the formulators of the techniques of being "total moral and philosophical relativists" and of being "subjectivists and emotivists." She sees the values clarification approach as an invitation to young people to abandon the values they were reared with and encourages them to say "I now find this value unattractive, it doesn't suit my personality or self-concept, so I'll throw it in the dustbin. It's just not my style" (pp. 55–57).

The Stay Safe Program for primary schools further generated wide-ranging and public confrontation. Conceived as a response to child abuse and bullying, the program was introduced regionally to schools in 1992. There are twelve lessons in the program, each of about 30 minutes duration, dealing with such experiences as getting lost and coming into contact with strangers, bullying, and touches that make one feel "unsafe." The most contested feature of the program was the approach to teaching children to use the distinction between yes and no feelings to discriminate between abusive and nonabusive acts. Casey (1993a, 1993b) has been a foremost critic of this emotive/affective approach to teaching children to distinguish between right and wrong.

What needs to be kept in mind is that far from being a conflict between those who propose a value-laden education and those who don't, the tension is between different sets of values and how these ought to be reflected in the classroom. On the one hand, there is the view of the Public Policy Institute of Ireland (1993), firmly grounded in the theocentric paradigm, that Irish education should be premised on "belief in the human person as possessed of an eternal destiny, as morally free but in need of formation in virtue since this is considered to be an essential element in the self-understanding of the vast majority of our people" (p. 43). On the other hand, developers of these programs adopt a set of values that are in tune with the market paradigm in that they prioritize the individual and choice and seek to promote, in the context of mutual valuing and respect, the qualities of self-actualization, personal fulfillment, and self-direction.

Control

The current controversy regarding the control and management of schooling can be traced to the nature and representation of the governance of schooling in the Irish Republic. As we saw earlier, Irish education is an aided rather than a state system with almost all primary schools and the majority of post-primary schools owned by religious authorities. While within the theocentric paradigm this would have been unremarkable and its anti-statist character totally consistent with the Roman Catholic principle of subsidiarity, it came to be repeatedly contested from the 1960s onward.

The representation of the existing system of school governance that featured in this contestation had a number of distinguishing features. Hyland (1996), in common with a number of other commentators, uses the comparative perspective to draw attention to the distinctiveness of the Irish system of school governance: "The structure of the education system in the Republic of Ireland is unique among the countries of the European Union . . . unlike other EU countries where the norm is the publicly owned and publicly controlled school, in Ireland the norm is a privately run school." Secondly, the extent of public funding to private institutions is highlighted: "The state pays over 80 percent of the capital costs of building and facilities, and over 90 percent of current expenditure if one includes teachers' salaries" (Coolahan, 1994, p. 23). Finally, there is the casting of religious ownership of schools in terms of self-appointed authority, unmandated power, and unresponsive control. The root metaphor of the market is prominent in this discourse, drawing heavily on the image of paying the piper and calling the tune, on the principle of responsiveness to the wishes of the users of the service, and on the existence of alternative mechanisms for satisfying educational needs.

In attempting to rebut these criticisms, apologists for the existing system found themselves drawn into this discourse, effectively abandoning the theocentric paradigm and seeking to compete on the basis of the logic of their opponents. Common arguments included the relative efficiency of religious schools in the use of public funding when compared with more publicly controlled schools, the extent of state control in terms of curricular content, public examination requirements, the registration and inspection of teachers, and the fact that the parents of the children who are availing of this publicly funded education have themselves contributed to it as taxpayers. The fact that these arguments appear not to have convinced is, of course, important for the current debate. What is more significant, however, is the manner in which the aided character of Irish schooling came to be thematized as self-evidently undemocratic in a manner that was derivative of the market paradigm both in its assertion and contestation.

Despite a greater assertiveness on the part of the state in seeking to direct the shaping of Irish education and the growth of boards of managements in schools since the 1970s, some (e.g., Breen et al., 1990) conclude that the state has become the main financier of the educational system while attaining very little control over it. It was in this context that the Green Paper sought to remove majority control on the boards of managements of their schools from the religious trustees and patrons. As a result of an extensive debate culminating in the National Education Convention, an accommodation seemed to emerge whereby majority control of boards of management would be conceded in return for some legal affirmation of the religious ethos of the school in a suitable deed or article of agreement.

The provisions of the Education Bill (1997) came as a shock to religious authorities. Representatives of almost every religious faith in Ireland—Roman Catholic, Anglican, Presbyterian, Methodist, Quaker, Muslim, and claiming the support of the Jewish community—gathered to oppose what they regarded as a threat to the denominational character of their schools. At the press conference, the senior education spokesman for the Anglican community referred reporters to what he described as the "brilliant analysis" of the Bill by the Roman Catholic Church's Conference of Religious. This analysis (Conference of Religious of Ireland, 1997) proposed a number of modifications to the Bill for the purpose of making the role of patron and the relationship between patrons and boards of managements more explicit. The most fundamental of these modifications, and the one from which all the others are derived, was as follows: "The patron of a school has a right to require that the school protects and promotes particular principles and core values" (p. 22).

What seems to have happened, both in the policy debate as a preamble to the Education Bill and in response to it, is that a number of distinct themes came to be fudged. There are at least four:

• The entitlement of committed agents (not necessarily religious) to establish and maintain schools in accordance with their principles, be they religious, secular, linguistic, or otherwise.

• Casting the patrons of schools established in the foregoing manner as representatives of those parents who opt to avail of their educational services.

• Facilitating the participation of groups with legitimate interests in the running of the school.

• Arranging for the financial answerability of institutions in receipt of public funding.

In the prioritizing of these themes, in their interaction, and in the manner in which they came to be built into a convincing discourse within the current culture of debate and legitimization, we can again observe the spirit of the market paradigm. While the themes of commitment and representation will be merged in the operation of a school, they remain distinct in the rights and responsibilities they confer. One's right to assembly and speech does not depend on the support of others, though a case for the public funding of whatever enterprise might follow does. Financial answerability can be adequately served by practices of accountability. But it is usually deployed in debate as a theme to boost the entitlement of clients of the educational service to participation in decision making, rather than relying on justifications in terms of democratic values, which favor participation at the most immediate level of decision making. In fact, the requirement of financial answerability continues to be prioritized as a fundamental principle.

The approach to legitimating parental rights is consistent with the market values of consumerism and monetarism. Significantly, the distinction between representative and committed agent was also fudged in the report of the National Education Convention. It recognized the mission of the patron: "The different religious authorities, and indeed other ethically and culturally motivated groups such as the multi-denominational schools or *gaelscoileanna,* who set up and operate schools do so because they wish to ensure that certain fundamental beliefs, values and culturally valuable practices are effectively taught and learned/internalized within the schools they set up." But it went on to subsume this under the representative role: "The Patron/Trustee in this sense stands for, or acts on behalf of, a body (usually organized) of people who wish their children to be educated within a particular religious, ethical or cultural tradition" (Coolahan, 1994, p. 24). Here, also, there is no awareness that the representative role of religious authorities in relation to parents is circumscribed by a particular mission in that they are only committed to representing those parents who share their religious convictions and wish to transmit them to their children. It is strongly indicative of the effective marketization of current Irish culture and consciousness that this principle has been edited out of the discourse on the control of schooling.

THE FUTURE OF SOCIETY AND SCHOOLING

The demise of the theocentric paradigm is destined to be confirmed in the educational planning of the future. Religion will remain a force in people's lives and schools will continue to serve the wishes of those who desire to have their children educated within a specific religious ethos. But the collective cultural orientation on which Irish educational ideas will draw, be it in terms of the view of the human person, individual freedom, social obligations, or personal virtue, will be derived less and less from a world view that places God and His intentions for the world and its people at its center. The most serious contender to replace the theocentric paradigm in the recolonization of the Irish conceptualization of education is the market paradigm.

Many of the features of Irish social, cultural, and political life identified earlier in this chapter support this recolonization. Processes of secularization and the erosion of the orthodoxies of Irishness from the nation-building phase have left a cultural void both in terms of self-definition and culture. Attempts to contain the Northern Ireland conflict have found the notion of Europeanization an attractive strategy for submerging disputes about territory, allegiance, and identity. The globalization of the mass media presents culture as a matter of choice and personal taste, largely irrelevant to nation and identity. The world of the Celtic Tiger is increasingly a geography of markets rather than political territories, peoples, or cultures. All of these influences have forced a disruption of cultural inheritance and contributed to identities that seek to define themselves in the first instance in a manner that asserts their distance from their past. Sources for such a definition, such as religion and nation, have been excluded and the dominant politically centrist ideology provides no inspiring visions. The private world of personal and family consumption takes precedence, with social action largely confined to essentially middle class movements such as feminism, environmentalism, animal rights, and peace. In such a cultural context, the market paradigm, in the absence of a competing grand vision, is well positioned to become the dominant force in the formation of educational policy.

One can only speculate on the fate of the issues raised in this chapter—equality, difference, virtue, and control. As presently conceived, they are largely compatible with the market paradigm.

There are obvious attractions in reducing under-achievement, recognizing distinctive identities and traditions within the school, preparing pupils for lifestyle choices, and introducing democratic structures. But these benefits may be short-term, ephemeral, and, most likely, deceptively progressive. The real consequence may be a narrowing of the imperatives of equality, a fragmentation of the basis for community, behavior bereft of a social morality, and a formalist understanding of citizenship.

Since holding out other possibilities for the interpretation of equality, difference, virtue, and control in education is the task of intellectuals, a problem exists in such a small country as Ireland where their number and range is limited and almost all are involved in some sense in the policy-making mechanisms of the state. One is forced to conclude that whatever progress is made in Irish education in the immediate future will occur in a manner that is at least culturally sympathetic to, if not culturally shaped by, the market paradigm of education.

REFERENCES

Breen, R., Hannan, D., Rottman, D., & Whelan, C. (1990). *Understanding contemporary Ireland: State, class and development in the Republic of Ireland*. London: Macmillan.

Casey, G. (1993a, June 10–11). Why I am opposed to Stay Safe. *Intercom*.

Casey, G. (1993b, 14 July). Stay Safe campaign sends wrong message. *Irish Times*.

Clancy, P. (1995). Access courses as an aid towards addressing socio-economic disparities in participation in higher education. In *Proceedings of the HEA seminar, Access Courses for Higher Education*. Dublin: Higher Education Authority.

Conference of Religious of Ireland. (1997). *Education Bill 1997*. Dublin: Author.

Coolahan, J. (Ed.). (1994). *Report on the National Education Convention*. Dublin: National Education Convention Secretariat.

Courtney, D. (1995). Demographic structure and change in the Republic of Ireland and Northern Ireland. In P. Clancy, S. Drudy, S, K. Lynch, & L. O'Dowd (Eds.), *Irish society: Sociological perspectives* (pp. 39–89). Dublin: Institute of Public Administration.

Family Solidarity. (1987). *Health education courses in post-primary schools*. Dublin: Author.

Government of Ireland: Committee on Irish Language Attitudes Research. (1975). *Report*. Dublin: Stationery Office.

Government of Ireland: Council of Education. (1962). *Report on the curriculum of the secondary school*. Dublin: Stationery Office.

Government of Ireland: Department of Education. (1992). *Green Paper on education. Education for a changing world*. Dublin: Stationery Office.

Government of Ireland: Department of Education. (1995). *White Paper on education: Charting our education future*. Dublin: Stationery Office.

Government of Ireland: Industrial Policy Review Group. (1992). *A time for change: Industrial policy for the 1990s. (Culliton Report)*. Dublin: Stationery Office.

Government of Ireland: National Economic and Social Council. (1990). *A strategy for the nineties*. Dublin: Stationery Office.

Great Britain: Central Advisory Council on Education, England. (1967). *Children and their primary schools (Plowden Report)*. London: Stationery Office.

Hornsby-Smith, M.P. (1992). Social and religious transformations in Ireland: A case of secularization. In J. H. Goldthorpe & C. T. Whelan (Eds.), *The development of industrial society in Ireland* (pp. 265–290). Oxford: Clarendon Press.

Hyland, A. (1996, June). Multi-denominational schools in the Republic of Ireland 1975–1995. Paper presented at the conference Education and Religion, Nice.

Irish National Teachers Organization. (1992). *Travelers in education*. Dublin: Author.

Kenny, M. (1991). Interculturalism and Europe's nomads. In J. Coolahan (Ed.), *Teacher education in the nineties: Towards a new coherence*. Limerick: Mary Immaculate College of Education.

Kiberd, D. (1995). *Inventing Ireland: The literature of the modern nation*. London: Jonathan Cape.

Kirby, P. (1997). *Poverty and plenty: World and Irish development reconsidered*. Dublin: Trocaire and Gill and Macmillan.

Lee, J. (1989). *Ireland 1912–1985: Politics and society.* Cambridge: Cambridge University Press.

Manly, D. (undated). *The facilitators.* Dublin: Brandsma Books.

McCoy, S., & Whelan, B.J. (1996). *The economic status of school leavers 1993–1995.* Dublin: Department of Education.

Nic Ghiolla Phádraig, M. (1995). The power of the Catholic church in the Republic of Ireland. In P. Clancy, S. Drudy, K. Lynch, & L. O'Dowd (Eds.), *Irish society: Sociological perspectives* (pp. 593–619). Dublin: Institute of Public Administration.

Ó Riagáin, P., & Ó Gliasáin, M. (1994). *National survey on languages 1993: Preliminary report.* Dublin: Institiúd Teángeolaíochta Éireann.

Public Policy Institute of Ireland. (1993). *Shaping educational change. A response to the Green Paper on Education, 1992.* Dublin: Public Policy Institute of Ireland.

Rigal, J. (1989). Some issues concerning the integration of Irish travelers. *Administration, 37,* 87–93.

Watson, I. (1996). The Irish language and television: National identity, preservation, restoration and minority rights. *British Journal of Sociology, 47,* 255–274.

CHAPTER 8

French Education at a Crossroad: The Limits of Public and Centralized Management

FRANÇOIS ORIVEL
ESTELLE ORIVEL

François Orivel is carrying out research on economics of education within IREDU (Institute for Research on the Economics of Education) and teaches the same topic at the University of Burgundy (Dijon, France). He has published many articles, reports, and books on the evaluation of educational systems and of educational policies. He works as a regular consultant for different international organizations (UNESCO, OECD, The World Bank, and UNDP). He is currently vice president of the executive committee of the Comparative Education Society in Europe (CESE).

Estelle Orivel is associate professor in the Department of Economics at the University of Burgundy (Dijon, France). She teaches statistics and microeconomics. Her main domain of research is related to the economic analysis of the social sectors, in particular education and culture. Her work is carried out within the framework of LATEC (Laboratory for the Analysis of Economic and Accounting Techniques).

THE SOCIAL FABRIC

Demography

France is one of the four western European countries that belong to the group of formerly seven, now eight, biggest economic powers (G7 and G8). Before the collapse of the communist system in Central and Eastern Europe, these four European countries (France, Germany, Italy, and the United Kingdom) were more or less equivalent in terms of demographic importance. With the reunification of both parts of Germany (the Federal Republic of Germany and the Democratic Republic of Germany), Germany has emerged as a significantly greater power.

France is one of the first countries to achieve its "demographic transition." Its fertility rate began to fall as early as the beginning of the nineteenth century, immediately after the French Revolution. After having been the most populated European nation in the seventeenth century, France was passed by Russia, Germany, and the United Kingdom. Yet during the past decades, France's fertility rate has not reached the low point of most its partners. Among the members of G8, its fertility rate is currently among the highest (1.72), and the combination of a relatively high net migration surplus during the twentieth century and a positive natural demographic growth has greatly improved prospects.

Economy

France has the fourth largest GDP in the world, after the United States, Japan, and Germany. Its GDP per capita is close to the European Union average. After a rapid increase in the thirty years that followed the Second World War, France's slow down during the past two decades was slightly more consequential than those of its partners. This last period has been strongly influenced by the objective of European integration, which has forced French authorities to adopt a more rigorous monetary policy in order to fight inflation and to reduce deficits. The reduction of the public deficit is today one of our most urgent issues. The

European Union introduced the common currency, the Euro, in 1999 and has made compulsory a target of three percent of GDP as a maximal authorized deficit.

This policy has been painful for the French population and has led to a growing unemployment rate, presently one of the highest among the G8s (about 12 percent). Many economists think that this unusual level of unemployment is linked with the employers' obligation to pay a minimum salary. The present level of this minimum salary, about $1500 per month, is viewed as too high for the maintenance of certain jobs currently offered in other countries. Jobs such as cashier assistants who fill customers' bags and employees who pump gas have disappeared from the French economy as the cost of this labor generates a price increase big enough to encourage customers to use competitors who do not provide these extra services.

The tradition of state intervention in the economy, dating back to the seventeenth century, has made the French economy less flexible than many others. This lack of flexibility, while not necessarily a big issue during periods of slow changes, is a real handicap in periods characterized by rapid technological changes. The French population looks to state authorities for protection against the undesirable effects of progress, such as adjusting to new technologies, retraining the working population for new jobs, and competing with emerging economies worldwide.

In spite of these difficulties, the French economy is progressing and has been able to maintain good indicators in several fields: The inflation rate is at a historically low level (between 1 and 2 percent per year), the value of money is stable against most major currencies (DM, U.S. dollar, and yen), the external trade balance is characterized by high surpluses, showing that the competitiveness of the economy remains good by international standards, especially in the fields of agriculture, luxury products, aircraft, and automobiles. The most important remaining problem is the lack of confidence of the French population concerning economic prospects, which leads to a tendency for households to underconsume and for entrepreneurs to underinvest.

Politics

Since the French Revolution of 1789, France has known no less than seventeen constitutions, from parliamentary republic to empire, from parliamentary monarchies to the Vichy regime. However, the dominant feature of the past two centuries is the attachment of the population to the notion of republic, the present one being the Fifth Republic, which was born in 1958 with the return of the Général de Gaulle to power. It is a bizarre mixture of a parliamentary regime in which the Prime Minister and his or her government is dependent upon the majority in a parliament elected for five years and a presidential regime in which the President, elected for seven years, derives legitimacy from the votes of citizens. When the majority in the Parliament leans to the same side as the President, no conflict occurs between legislative and executive powers. Yet, given the fact that both elections do not necessarily coincide, the President's political affiliation may be different from that of the parliamentary majority.

The Fifth Republic emerged in a context of severe political conflicts arising from the decolonization process. A civil war was taking place in Algeria where about 2 million French citizens had settled and wanted to maintain Algeria within the French republic against the wishes of indigenous movements for independence. Général de Gaulle negotiated a peace agreement in Algeria that gave independence to the country, and he organized the return to France of most French settlers from Algeria. As well, de Gaulle gave independence to former colonies located in sub-Saharan Africa.

Unlike the United Kingdom, France has maintained close ties with most of its ancient colonies. It has constantly provided financial assistance and education support, in the framework of a global "Francophone" project that aims at maintaining French as a common language for enhancing cultural, political, and economic relations. This policy has known its successes and failures, but undoubtedly the French language would have declined in importance more rapidly without this "voluntarist" policy that sometimes raises a little irony in the English-speaking world.

As mentioned earlier, state intervention is deeply rooted in the French tradition. The importance of the state is not limited to economic production, but also concerns the redistribution of wealth. The welfare state has been extensively developed and covers the whole social security system, which provides health care to everybody, family allowances to households with children, pensions to retired people, unemployment allowances, and free education for all from kindergarten to university. It also allocates subsidies to a wide range of cultural activities. The importance of the role of the state is reflected in the share of GDP captured by public taxation—as much as 45 percent. In the majority of developed countries, this share is between 30 percent and 40 percent.

The involvement of the state in socioeconomic affairs has been strongly challenged in the recent past for two reasons. The first is linked with the declining competitiveness of public management with respect to the private sector. The second is associated with the building of the European Union, which sets up new regulations to ensure fair competition within the Common Market. This movement is parallel to the worldwide tendency toward globalization and deregulation in order to enhance free initiative and improve competition. As a consequence, since 1986 France has entered a phase of privatization of public enterprises. However, due to public opinion and the resistance of trade unions, this movement is less advanced than in other countries. Moreover, frequent political changes (during the last six parliamentary elections, voters have chosen alternately the left and the right) have hampered the achievement of this privatization movement.

Religious Context

Christianity was introduced into France in the fifth century and has shaped its tradition, culture, values, and landscape. The French successfully stopped the advance of the Islamic invasion in Poitiers in the eighth century. At the time of the Lutheran reform, France remained faithful to the Catholic affiliation and to the Pope. It was then called "the elder daughter of the church." In spite of the fact that only a minority of the French population is today practicing (about 10 percent), the vast majority still claims to belong to the Catholic church.

Tolerance toward other religions has been uneven. At the time of the reform, King Henry IV introduced some openness vis-à-vis the Protestants. But later on, the latter suffered from the Catholic persecutions—assassinations and forced emigrations. Anti-semitism developed during the first decades of the twentieth century and culminated under the Vichy regime, when France was occupied by the Nazi army. The Jewish community in France is presently the largest in Europe (700,000 people). It is considered well integrated into French society. On the other hand, the integration of a growing Muslim community, mostly from North Africa, is creating problems. The present size of the Muslim community is about 4 million people, or 7 percent of the total population. The rise of the extreme right political party (Front National) led by Jean Marie Le Pen illustrates the growing intolerance toward the Muslim community. This political party bases its political influence (about 15 percent of the electorate) on xenophobic, anti-immigrant, and anti-Islamic slogans.

Cultural Context

France is proud of its cultural achievements. During the medieval period, France built thousands of churches and cathedrals. Almost all art was religious. In the eighteenth century, French artistic values were adopted in most European royal courts. While Germany was a dominant producer in the field of music, France held for a long time the lead in fine arts. In the nineteenth century, the French "salon" of fine arts was the most important event of the year for artistic life in Europe and Northern America. Most modern tendencies, from impressionism to cubism, from art nouveau to

Fauvism, were born in Paris, which attracted many artists from other countries.

For a long time, France has been considered as a welcoming country for foreigners and those persecuted in their own country. It welcomed Armenians after the Turkish genocide in 1915, the Russian aristocracy after the 1917 revolution, the Spanish republicans after the victory of Franco, and many others who have been attracted by better economic prospects (Polish, Italians, Portuguese). Since decolonization (around 1960), most new immigrants come from the south (North and sub-Saharan Africa, Asia, and in particular Vietnam, Cambodia, and China). The integration of this new wave is not progressing as smoothly as previous ones. Ethnic, cultural, and religious differences are much wider and require more time to integrate these new immigrants. If this integration is characterized more conflict than in countries such as the United Kingdom, it is due in part to the fact that France pursues an objective of full assimilation of immigrants rather than of cohabitation between different communities that maintain their own traditions. One can also illustrate the French conception by its language policy. Until the nineteenth century, French was the language of the elite, while the rest of the population practiced local dialects. The disappearance of most of these dialects in the past hundred years is the outcome of an affirmative policy to impose French in the educational system as early as preschool.

SCHOOLING

The French education system mirrors the main features of French society just described. It is centralized, state-oriented, and unified. It is free and egalitarian, which does not mean necessarily that it is equitable.

Historical Perspectives

Before the middle of the nineteenth century, the majority of schools were run by the Catholic Church. Since then, a struggle has developed between the state and the Catholic Church for the control of schools. In the early 1880s, a law made primary school compulsory, free, and secular. Another law then set up the separation of Church and state and confiscated Church properties for the benefit of the state. These two events transferred the main responsibility for providing education from the Church to elected public authorities. However, the Catholic Church has not disappeared from the educational scene. It was allowed to open its own schools for fees, an option used more often for secondary schools where the public supply was limited. The opening of Catholic primary schools was concentrated in certain regions with very strong Catholic traditions, especially in the west part of France (Brittany and Vendée).

A certain competition between the Church and the state has persisted during most of the twentieth century, with both sides showing some level of aggressiveness toward the other. Two political events have brought this fight to an end. Under Général de Gaulle's presidency, it was decided that teachers' salaries in Church schools would be paid from the state budget. In exchange, private schools had to accept the control of state authorities and follow the unified curriculum. This last condition had already applied, since the objective of Church schools was to prepare pupils for the *baccalaureate,* the final exam at the end of upper secondary education, a strong unifying goal in the French system. The change in salary structure thus has allowed Church schools to charge very low fees and to open their doors to pupils from low socioeconomic backgrounds. As a consequence, their role and image have changed. The provision of religious education has vanished and their new role is now that of giving a second chance to low achievers.

The second event took place in 1984 when Mr. Savary, the Education Minister of the socialist President, François Mitterrand, encouraged by the secular lobby, tried to restrain the public financing of private schools. This attempt became a total political failure and raised such hostility in the French population that the government withdrew its project. Analysis of public opinion at that time showed clearly that the main motivation behind this discontent was not the preservation of a Catholic system as such, but the preservation of the possibilities of a second chance and choice.

At any given time, about 20 percent of the school-age population is enrolled in private schools. However, at some point in their schooling, 37 percent of French pupils have attended a private school. At the end of the century, the competition between the two systems is reduced and the cohabitation is quite peaceful. Public opinion polls show that the French population is satisfied with present arrangements.

Structure of the System

Preschool. The availability of preschool is a well-known characteristic of the French system. Preschool is part of the primary education system; its teachers have the same training and qualifications as primary teachers and they can work alternatively in both levels.

Children enter preschool at age 2 for four years. The participation rate is 35 percent at age 2 and 99.5 percent for ages 3, 4, and 5. Preschool lasts 6 hours a day, 3 in the morning and 3 in the afternoon, and has been a powerful tool for allowing mothers to take jobs on the labor market. If necessary, children can arrive earlier and leave the school later to fit the working schedule of the parents. During these extra hours, children are not looked after by the teacher, but by a municipal employee.

Primary and Secondary Schools. The French education system has known three waves of expansion. The first one took place in the late nineteenth century when primary education became compulsory. The second one occurred between 1960 and 1970, when the first cycle of secondary education became *de facto* compulsory after de Gaulle's decree of January 1969 that declared school compulsory until age 16. The third wave took place from 1985 to 1990, under the influence of the Education Minister, Mr. Chevénement, who took the decision, not written

in the law, that 80 percent of every generation should attend the level of baccalaureate. While only 60 to 65 percent of pupils actually succeed in obtaining of the baccalaureate, this policy had an immediate impact on the expansion of higher education because, according to French law, every baccalaureate holder is entitled a university seat.

The expected number of years of schooling in 1994 was 16.2 for a child of 5 years old, slightly above the OECD average of 15.3 (OECD, 1996). Of 27 OECD countries, eight are above 16 and none is above 17. If preschool education were included in these data, France would likely rank first. There is little gender difference. The indicator is slightly superior for girls (16.4 versus 16.1 for boys); this is explained by the fact that girls tend to succeed better in secondary education, in particular in the baccalaureate. After compulsory education, the participation rate in 1994 was 92.2 percent at the age of 17, 84.1 percent at the age of 18, and 68.6 percent at the age of 19, against respectively 78.3 percent, 64.6 percent, and 47.1 percent for the OECD average (OECD, 1996).

Upper secondary education is divided into three tracks that lead to different types of baccalaureates. The largest and oldest track provides general education. It represents about 57 percent of total enrollment. It is itself divided into three categories: sciences, humanities, and social sciences. The second track leads to the technological baccalaureate and concerns 28 percent of students. It includes many types of technological specialties, which can be broken down further into industrial specialties and tertiary specialties. Finally, the third track enrolls students preparing a vocational baccalaureate and concerns 15 percent of total enrollment. This last baccalaureate, recently created, was designed for upgrading the status of vocational training.

The French baccalaureate is not very selective. On a given session, three out of four candidates pass it. Among those who repeat, another half gets it, which makes an overall passing rate of about 90 percent. With all students, including those who do not try to get the baccalaureate, in the middle of the 1990s, about 63 percent of French school leavers hold the baccalaureate, 19 percent have a diploma of professional education of lower status than the baccalaureate, and 8 percent do not have anything.

Higher Education.   Access to higher education is determined by passing the baccalaureate. The percentage entering higher education is on average high, but differs according to the type of baccalaureate. It is close to 100 percent for those who hold the general baccalaureate, but significantly lower for other types of baccalaureate, especially the vocational one. It is difficult to provide precise figures, because the situation has not yet stabilized.

The French system of higher education contains some specific features that do not exist in other systems. The most striking feature concerns the fact that the elite of secondary schools leavers do not enter university, but a network of institutions called the *Grandes Ecoles*. This network has developed in the last two centuries. There are presently 237 engineering schools and 257 business schools. Unlike the ninety universities, the Grandes Ecoles are structured hierarchically. For instance, among engineering schools, the best one is the *Ecole Polytechnique* run by the Ministry of Defense. The competition for entering the best Grandes Ecoles is intense and tough. Students prepare for the entrance exam during the two years after the baccalaureate in certain *lycées* (upper secondary schools). In the past, a competitive exam was based on cognitive competences, principally in the humanities, Latin, Greek, and philosophy). But since the 1960s, it is mainly based on mathematics and sciences, considered as a more objective tool for the identification of the most talented and promising students. About 40,000, or 5 percent of a cohort, enter the Grandes Ecoles every year.

The ninety universities enroll the majority of baccalaureate holders who want to enter higher education. They cannot select their students who are entitled by law to have a seat in one of the universities located in one of the twenty-seven *académies* of which their parents are residents.

A third group of students attends nonuniversity types of higher education institutions providing professional training for two years. These short-term professional degrees are offered by three types of institutions: IUTs (Technological University Institute) are affiliated to universities; STS (Department for Higher Technicians) are located in technological lycées; a network of specialized institutes, mostly operated by the Ministry of Health and Social Affairs, trains nurses and other paramedical specialists.

Altogether, there were 2.2 million students in higher education in 1996. The rate of increase of enrollments has been very rapid during the past decades. There were only 310,000 students in 1960, 1,175,000 in 1980, and 1,700,000 in 1990. This growth will slow down in the near future, since the rate of increase of baccalaureate holders is becoming close to zero.

Organization and Governance

Centralized France has a centralized education system. Decisions concerning any aspect such as legal framework, certification, or management, are taken by central authorities (Parliament and government). Most of the budget is also centrally determined. The recruitment of teachers and non-teaching personnel is centrally regulated and most of the personnel are civil servants. It is sometimes said that the French Ministry of Education is the biggest world employer after the Red Army. It employs more than one million people, of whom 800,000 are teachers. To facilitate the management of schools, the Ministry of Education has set up local branches, called the *Rectorats*. Each Rectorat is headed by a rector, nominated by the government, who represents the Minister of Education for a variety of decisions. Most rectors are replaced when a new political majority is elected. There are twenty-seven rectors who are responsible for a territory called an *académie*.

There are nevertheless some responsibilities given to lower levels of administration. The maintenance of primary schools (including preschools) has always been the responsibility of municipalities. When primary school became compulsory in the late nineteenth century, it was quite common, especially in rural areas, to see the schools located in the same building as the city hall and the needs of classes concerning heating, maintenance, cleaning, water supply, and so on were mixed with those of the municipality. However, the state was, and still is, responsible for recruiting and paying teachers as well as fixing regulations.

Until 1982, junior and upper secondary schools and higher education institutions were entirely managed and financed by the state budget. In 1982, a new law introduced a limited decentralization process. The *Départements* and the *Régions* have received some responsibilities in the management of respectively junior and upper secondary schools.[1] Yet this decentralization process has not given them any authority for staff management. The Minister of Education remains the only authority in charge of personnel. Basically, *Départements* and *Régions* build and maintain schools. However, it is clear that they cannot build a new lycée without the clearance of the central government, which will provide the relevant staff. The following figures give a relatively good idea of the scope and limits of the decentralization process. In 1992, the budget for secondary education represented 120 billion French francs for the Ministry of Education, 11 billion for *Départements* and *Régions* (maintenance costs), and 21 billion for capital costs. This last figure is exceptionally high due to the expansion of upper secondary education in this period (MEN, 1996).

Curricula

Curricula are determined by the Ministry of Education. At the end of primary education, pupils are supposed to master the three Rs (reading, writing, and arithmetic). Religious education is not part of the curriculum. Few changes have been made in the recent past, except for two issues concerning civic education and foreign languages. Both changes have been introduced on a pilot basis. Definitive decisions will be taken after appropriate evaluation.

The OECD (1996) published comparative data for the curriculum of junior secondary schools, which show that France stands approximately in an average position. For instance, the amount of mathematics and sciences in the curriculum, which goes from 20 percent in the Netherlands to 30 percent in New Zealand, is about 24 percent in France. Similarly, France is close to the average for the percent of reading and writing, social sciences, foreign languages, and physical education. It is slightly below the average for art and the natural sciences. It is generally considered that the French approach is a bit abstract and theoretical and relies too little on practical experience. New technologies, in particular computer science, have some difficulties entering the curriculum. The length of the school year is slightly above the OECD average (1000 hours versus 920) and is concentrated into a lower number of school days. This last feature produces a chronic debate over the issue of school rhythms.

At the upper secondary level, curricula are closely related to the objectives of the different tracks (general, technological, and vocational). In general education, it is often thought that the content of curricula is excessively large and should be lightened. This issue has never been addressed because of the pressure of different lobbies that each feel its field is so important that it could not be reduced. In the late 1980s, the government set up a high commission for the development of new curricula, but its work hasn't had any impact yet.

At the university level, France has set up a system of national diplomas. The degree obtained by students is recognized by the French government, regardless of the university in which they passed it. As a consequence, the curriculum of each university in each discipline is controlled by a national commission located within the Ministry of Education. In spite of the theoretical freedom left to universities to organize their curricula, the commission has a strong homogenizing effect.

Pedagogical Theory and Practices

As in most countries, France has evolved toward less authoritarian pedagogical practices, relying less on memorization and more on the development of critical thinking. In addition, it has adopted the theory of individualization of the learning process. Yet teachers remain entirely free to utilize any pedagogical practice and are only obliged to follow the curriculum. It is therefore difficult to ascertain the effects of modern theories of pedagogical practices.

At the higher education level, the French approach relies heavily on lectures given to large student audiences and very little on small learning groups or on the guidance of tutors. The theory of individualized learning has hardly penetrated the universities. Some pilot programs are going on, but there is clearly a financial issue for which there is no foreseeable solution.

Teaching Training

For almost a century, primary teachers (including preschool teachers) have been trained in a network of so-called Normal Schools. Trainees were recruited at the end of junior high school and made their upper secondary education in the Normal Schools where they passed their baccalaureate. After the baccalaureate, they received some professional training, which was comprised of a significant amount of practical work as teachers in close-by primary schools (application primary schools) under the supervision of experienced teachers. This system became clearly obsolete at the end of the 1970s, and several successive reforms have been implemented. The last one closed all Normal Schools and replaced them in the late 1980s by a smaller number of training institutions, called IUFMs (University Institutes for Teacher Training). These new institutions, while closely associated with universities, enjoy a relative autonomy. Two major changes have been introduced with the IUFMs. The first one is the upgrading of teacher training to the level of university training (instead of one year of training, there are five years of training after the baccalaureate, a four-year university degree and one year of professional training).

The second change is that primary and secondary teachers are now trained in the same institution, are exposed to a similar training program, and expect similar careers and compensations. Before the creation of IUFMs, there was no specific training for secondary teachers. Students with a university degree in mathematics or French could teach these specialties in any secondary school without any professional training. Yet in order to become a certified civil servant, they had to pass a competitive recruitment exam. Those who were recruited as civil servants spent their first year of work as "beginners," which meant some support in the form of in-service training.

Pupil/Teacher Ratios

For primary and secondary education, French pupil/teacher ratios are close to the developed countries' average. For primary education there are 19.3 pupils per teacher against the 17.5 average in OECD countries; for secondary education, 13.2 versus 18.8 on average. Similar and reliable comparative data for higher education does not exist (the estimate of full-time equivalent teachers is more complicated at this level). However, it is widely known that French higher education system is atypical from this point of view, in the sense that it has a larger number of students per teacher than other OECD countries.

These pupil/teacher ratios should therefore lead to a slightly lower percentage of education staff within the active population in France. Actually, this is not so—the ratio 6.1 percent in France versus 5.5 for the OECD average, because the total number of pupils and students in the total population is comparatively higher.

Evaluation

France has not developed the tradition of standardized tests for the evaluation of pupils and student performance, because it has always been skeptical about the merits of multiple-choice exams. Rather, its tradition is based on the utilization of written essays by students. Of course, it is more difficult to give objective scores to students for such exercises. However, in spite of this difficulty, French pedagogues still believe that this approach provides more information on effective capacities and competences of students (quality of expression, capacity of structuring ideas, and so on) than multiple-choice tests. Nevertheless, France has participated in several rounds designed by the IEA (International Education Achievement) group. France's performances have been uneven, but on the whole relatively good. For reading and writing, the ranking of France is in the first quarter; for mathematics, it is significantly above the average; and for sciences, it is below the average. Sciences are the weak point of the French education system, a fact that is related to the already mentioned excessively abstract approach of its curricula.

Expenditure and Unit Costs

According to UNESCO data, public education expenditures represent about 5 percent of the GDP worldwide. Within OECD countries, this percentage is slightly higher, at 5.4 percent. France is close to this last average, with a percentage of 5.6. However, unlike other countries, this percentage does not seem to be stabilized. It is growing slowly due to the ongoing expansion of access to secondary and higher education. In addition, in many developed countries, the school age population is declining due to demographic evolution. France's demographic situation is slightly different, and the decline of the school-age population is slower than in most OECD countries. Finally, French household expenditure as a percentage of GDP is smaller than elsewhere, about half the OECD average.

Unit costs usually increase with the level of education. In OECD countries, secondary education is on average 43 percent more expensive than primary education and higher education is twice as expensive as secondary education. All levels combined, the French average unit cost is relatively close to that of OECD countries. However,

the hierarchy between levels is quite different. Secondary education is more expensive than the OECD average, while higher education is significantly cheaper (50 percent less). France is the only example where higher education is cheaper than upper secondary. This is due to the poor student/ teacher ratio and more generally to relatively modest teaching and learning conditions at this level (especially in universities).

MAJOR ISSUES, CONTROVERSIES, AND PROBLEMS

Management Issues

The actual management of the teaching staff has two major important drawbacks. First, no care is taken to match teachers and positions (beginners are often assigned to the harshest positions). Second, there is no evaluation of the quality of the work done by teachers, and no system of promotion according to performances or merit exists.

The strong tradition of centralization has opened the door to the constitution of powerful teacher unions. Because more than one million teachers are employed by the Ministry of Education, they represent a decisive bargaining force. This has led to an atypical system of allocation of staff, entirely driven by a set of rules designed by the unions and among which the fundamental criterion is the desire of teachers to be assigned to certain places, in certain schools. These desires are not mainly based on income differences (salaries scales are determined for the whole country and based on seniority rather than on merit). They have other motivations that can be practical (to be closer to his or her spouse), contextual (a fancier city, a nicer climate), and educational (a better school, more rewarding pupils). Because the best assignments have more candidates than there are positions, the unions have set up a queuing system, in which one reaches the head of the queue by accumulating points. Points are reached by seniority, the length of waiting time, the distance of spouses, and so on.

The main disadvantage of the system is the fact that school authorities have nothing to say about the recruitment of a teacher, and virtually nothing to say concerning his or her departure. They cannot attract teachers with specific profiles adapted to specific and local circumstances, and they cannot reject those who do not fit these circumstances. One of the unfortunate consequences of such a system is the fact that when a position is vacant and not requested by an existing teacher, it is filled by a new teacher without experience. Vacant positions are indeed those that are considered by teachers as harsh positions—for instance, positions in difficult suburbs, in violent cities with widespread criminality problems, with large proportions of low achievers, and so on. These are hardly positions for beginners.

While it is generally recognized that the quality of the French teaching staff is good by international standards, it could be significantly improved with better staff management. Moreover, this average good quality does not exclude the presence of a significant minority of relatively ineffective teachers. Several evaluation studies on the determinants of school achievement have shown that after the personal characteristics of the student and his or her social background, the most important differentiating factor is the teacher. The teacher effect is much more important than all other input affecting the learning process (class size, textbooks, and other materials, time spent studying, school conditions, expenditure per pupil, and so on). It is clear that better pupil performances could be obtained if the selection process of teachers was improved and if the management of teaching staff was based on their performances. Decentralization is not necessarily the solution if the present centralized system is simply applied at the regional level. What is important is to give more decision power to school authorities in the selection of teachers and to let them have some influence on their careers. The issue is therefore more a question of autonomy of schools than of decentralization.

Concerning higher education professors, France has not initiated a system of evaluation of teaching capacities. Promotion is obtained after peer reviews based only on the academic research of the candidate. Moreover, students are not invited to give their opinions, as is the case in Northern America, and a bad professor can stay in a position until his or her retirement. Similarly, a good professor is not rewarded for the efforts he or she makes vis-à-vis his or her students.

There are some other minor problems concerning the management of teachers. One is the coexistence in secondary schools of two major categories of teachers. The first one, called *agrégé,* is selected on highly selective academic criteria. It has higher monthly salaries and fewer teaching hours. The second one, called *certifié,* is less severely selected, paid less, and has more teaching hours. These differences of status are not based on actual performance nor on professional competences. The higher salary offered to the *agrégés* for their entire careers is acquired before he or she has even started teaching—even if he or she happens to be a bad teacher.

Having two categories of teachers could be justified, one of them being better paid, if it allowed those belonging to the lower category to be promoted under certain conditions of retraining and evaluation of effective performance in the process of teaching. However, the French dualism does not allow for this possibility. There is no way for a *certifié* teacher to become an *agrégé* as a reward for his or her effectiveness. This lack of perspective may explain why the French teaching staff tends to be conservative in its pedagogical practices. It is not open to new technologies, and external evaluation is rarely used as a means for managing the system and improving its performance. Recent evaluation efforts made by the Ministry of Education to measure pupil performances are utilized in a very cautious way, and the Ministry is not allowed to publish comparative results between schools.

Some observers believe that the Ministry of Education tends to be a bureaucratic monster. Its total staff, 4,000, is considered as excessive. It has a reasonably good evaluation and planning department but, as part of the political sphere, it has not the necessary external view that could give the scientific objectivity that everybody could trust.

Education Policy for Low Achievers

The egalitarian tradition that resulted from the French Revolution has introduced a similar philosophy within the education system. Each French pupil is entitled to the same rights, and those who face specific obstacles do not deserve specific treatments. It is a conception of equity based on equality rather than on the unequal treatment of unequals. School careers are purely determined by merit, and low achievers are excluded from the system when they do not meet its requirements.

This approach has generated intense debates concerning the educational attainments of low achievers. A certain proportion of pupils leave the system being illiterate. This proportion varies according to the definition given to illiteracy. The most restrictive one, which is based on the capacity of writing one's name, is measured on men for the army at the age of military service. Only 1 to 2 percent of an age group are in this category, of which a significant proportion is immigrants who have not attended French schools. Larger definitions test the capacity of people to read and understand more or less difficult sentences within a given period of time. The percentage of a given age group of illiterate people according to this last definition varies between 5 and 10 percent.

Several attempts have been made to address this issue. The most known, initiated in 1982, was called the "ZEP project" (*Zone d'éducation prioritaire* or Priority Education Area). Another project aimed at helping low achievers is known under the name of GAPP (*Groups d'Actions Psycho-Pédagogiques* or teams for psycho-pedagogical intervention). Experienced psycho-pedagogues are assigned to make diagnoses concerning the difficulties faced by some pupils and to provide some assistance.

A certain number of pedagogues argue that one could get better results with low achievers if they were separated from other pupils and received special treatment within specific groups, classes,

or schools. Pilot experiments have been set up in France to test this assumption. For instance, in some schools low achievers have been exposed to a three-year program replacing the two-year regular program for other pupils at the beginning of junior high school. However, recent evaluation shows that such an approach may be wrong. It seems that low achievers tend to learn more when they are mixed with other regular pupils rather than with other low achievers.

The debate around the issue of the treatment of low achievers remains quite intense. However, it tends to ignore the fact that the variability of scores obtained at the last IEA survey on mathematics and sciences performances between French pupils is not larger in France than in other countries. On the contrary, if one takes countries with a similar average score, the dispersion of results is rather smaller in France. This outcome is probably linked with the centralized tradition of France that tends to homogenize the operation of schools.

Public Finance and Equity

The tradition of free education is deeply rooted in French society. On July 15, 1997, the leading newspaper, *Le Monde,* published an article denouncing the tendency of increasing fees in French universities. It reflected the views of several student unions as well as those of the newspaper itself and a large proportion of the French intelligentsia. Such views would appear awkward to many foreigners. The fee increases that were contested represent virtually nothing, a handful of dollars, a tiny proportion of what French students allocate to their leisure budget (the amounts implied were less than what American students pay for obtaining an application form in a university).

Undoubtedly, free access to education in France has opened the door to education for everybody, regardless of the socioeconomic status (SES) of pupils. Children from low socioeconomic background have easy access to higher education. Differences of access to higher education according to socioeconomic status have been reduced constantly during the past decades.

Nevertheless, if one puts a closer eye to equity issues within the system, it appears that the best tracks tend to be monopolized by students from high economic backgrounds. For instance, at the upper secondary level it is more likely for a pupil to enter a vocational track if he or she originates from a low SES, and more likely for a pupil from a high SES to enter general education. In order to have access to the elitist sector of higher education, one has to attend the best *lycées* and within the best *lycées,* the best classes. From this point of view, the system does not work in a fully transparent way. Only well-informed families are able to develop strategies to get access to the most promising avenues. Among these strategies are specific disciplinary options, such as a rare foreign language (Russian, Chinese) or rare combinations (Latin and mathematics). These strategies allow the possibility of concentrating able students in the same classroom and preparing them for the most difficult paths leading to the Grandes Ecoles. This concentration of the most able students is based mainly on merit. An incompetent pupil from a good SES will not be accepted in an elitist class. However, slight biases due to uneven information and lack of transparency of procedures (for example, in the way school authorities decide the allocation of pupils in different classes) lead to a significantly high concentration of high SES students in good tracks. The consequence can be clearly observed in the social origin of students having access to the best Grandes Ecoles. Unlike access to universities, there has not been an equalization of chances with respect to SES for the Grande Ecole during the past decades. On the contrary, it is likely worse. The chances for a pupil from an immigrant family to have access to the Ecole Polytechnique are likely lower today than they were twenty years ago, a de facto phenomenon of a monopolization of the access to the best Grandes Ecoles by privileged social classes.

In addition to the fact that students from high SES enter the best schools, the inequity of the system is even more clear because per student expenditure is much higher in these best schools. The best French *lycées* in Paris that enroll the children of the elite tend to have more means than less known provincial *lycées.* Comparing the two main categories of higher education institutions, the average unit cost in Grandes Ecoles is about $13,000, while it is equal to $5,000 in universities. Even comparing the same types of institution, variations can be important. Recent cost studies within French universities show that one program can cost forty times as much as another within the same institution. While some of these differences are justified according to the field of study (it may be more expensive to train a future physician than a future lawyer due to differences in equipment and pedagogical devices), this factor does not explain satisfactorily the scope of unit cost variations. Similarly, concerning per student expenditure for Grandes Ecoles, the costs variations can be huge, from about $6,000 to $100,000 per year.

While part of a high cost can be explained by bad management, some of it reflects real additional programs and a supposedly better quality of schooling. The rationality for that difference of treatment has never been politically explained. The result of this situation is that pupils of low SES or low achievers tend on average to attend schools with fewer resources per pupil than those attended by students of high SES. As a consequence, taxpayers' money is allocated more generously for privileged students than for underprivileged ones.

The democratic rules and the supposedly egalitarian treatment supporting the general organization of the system are actually strongly inequitable. This raises the question of a desirable positive discrimination in favor of underprivileged children in terms both of socioeconomic status and school achievement and of fewer public subsidies for the most privileged sectors of the education system.

Inconsistencies in the Operation of Higher Education

First, there are incoherent procedures for assigning students within subsectors of higher education. Present procedures for assigning students in the system were set up at a time at which only a small minority (less than 5 percent) of an age group attended higher education. The large majority of candidates met the minimum requirements in terms of ability. However, these procedures are much less efficient for the management of a mass higher education system. The most able students tend to be enrolled in institutions that practice *numerus clausus* (or admission quotas): the Grandes Ecoles, medical studies within universities, and short-term professional education (IUT and STS). According to the law, other tracks in universities cannot practice any selection, except for the necessity of having the baccalaureate. As a consequence, they eliminate unable candidates during the course of the studies. This explains why the internal efficiency of the university is low by international standards. Less than half of new entrants gain the equivalent of a bachelor degree. It is not unusual to have a passing rate at the end of an academic year of less than 20 percent. Moreover, in certain tracks, such as law, the passing rate for certain type of baccalaureate holders (technological or professional) is below 5 percent.

It would be more logical to assign students in the different institutions or tracks by optimizing their profiles with the characteristics of tracks. This principle would have led to enrolling students having a technological or a professional baccalaureate in the IUTs. Yet IUTs belong to the category of institutions allowed to select their intake, which they do. And they prefer to enroll the best candidates—those who hold a general baccalaureate, preferably a scientific one. When these candidates have filled up available places, there are no more seats for technological baccalaureate holders. Of course, after the end of their two-year program, IUT graduates, who belong to the group of most able students, think they should continue further higher education to reach the equivalent of a bachelor degree or more. Unfortunately, they have been poorly prepared for that second step, because the type of education provided in IUTs is more practical than theoretical

and more professionally oriented. It is sufficient for a job. Furthermore, this training is based on a pedagogy that provides a better pupil/teacher ratio, more extensive lecturing and workshop training, and less personal homework than that of the universities. Paradoxically, it fits more closely the needs of low achievers than those of the most able students of a given age group. The least able students are relegated to university tracks that have the highest pupil/teacher ratios and the lowest level of tutorial services (law, economics, and humanities). They are not prepared for such a situation and they fail.

Second, we must examine the role of universities and Grandes Ecoles in the field of research. French universities have developed the standard tradition of education and research as being a joint product of academic services and at the same time feeding each other. All university professors are supposed to be both teachers and researchers. In addition to university professors, a specific category of full-time researchers exists, managed by an independent authority, the CNRS (*Centre National de la Recherche Scientifique,* or National Center for Scientific Research). These professional researchers do not have teaching duties, but the vast majority of them are assigned within university research laboratories, jointly with professors. Their research performance is evaluated by the same criteria as for university professors. The recent evolution has reinforced the merging of CNRS activities with that of universities. A growing number of CNRS researchers are involved with teaching at post-graduate levels on a part-time basis and are active in the supervision of doctorate students. Undoubtedly, this evolution is positive for the French research sector.

The weak point of the system is the ambiguous role of Grandes Ecoles. Grandes Ecoles have not developed a strong tradition of research; most of them do not do any research at all. They are rarely involved in Ph.D. programs, a duty that is not formally included in their status. If they want to engage in Ph.D. programs in any way, they have to conclude an agreement with a university. This can be seen as a humiliating procedure (they enjoy a higher status but have to place a request). For a long time, this lack of research activities was not felt as a disadvantage by students of Grandes Ecoles. The French labor market worked in such a way that graduates from Grandes Ecoles had no problem finding well-paid and interesting jobs. The economic return of a Ph.D., which would have required three additional years of training, was very poor and unattractive.

This situation may not last forever because it is not entirely satisfactory from a socioeconomic point of view. First of all, one can regret that the most talented and able students of a generation do not engage themselves in research. The system does not encourage them to embrace such a career. Second, the labor market for high executive positions tends to favor research experience more than in the past. Grandes Ecoles graduates arrive on the labor market at a very young age (23 on average), in a period in which most other employees with a lower status arrive later than in the past. Spending three years in a research laboratory, between ages 23 and 26, could be additional valuable preparation for entering high-responsibility positions.

Unfortunately, Grandes Ecoles as they are now operating cannot enter the research market in a convincing way. They are small institutions (on average 200 students per school, almost 100 times less than an average university) and cannot afford to set up teams of full-time researchers. Their teaching staff is too small to engage in today's highly specialized research. Moreover, a significant proportion of the Grandes Ecoles' teaching staff is made of part-time professors who have full-time positions in a university. The involvement of Grandes Ecoles in research is further complicated by the fact that they are spread all over the country and cannot be easily merged for the creation of bigger units. The Ministry of Agriculture runs a network of about fifteen Grandes Ecoles and is trying to reduce this number by the setting up of new "entities" supervising different small schools. Yet the Ministry faces serious obstacles in implementing this project due to the distance separating units from each other. The

future involvement of Grandes Ecoles in research remains rather bleak.

Education and the Labor Market

Holding a diploma has always been a useful prerequisite for entering the labor market in the French context. The "sheepskin" role of education is important. It is reflected by the differences in the rates of unemployment of young French people with respect to the formal education they have received. The rate of unemployment is the lowest for Grandes Ecoles graduates, followed by that of university graduates, baccalaureate holders, professional diploma holders, and finally those who don't have any diploma at all. In the middle of the 1990s, the rate of unemployment for Grandes Ecoles graduates was below 2 percent, while that for school leavers without any diploma was around 40 percent. The French model illustrates particularly well the queuing theory developed by Thurow and Lucas (1972), according to whom the education level of an individual determines his or her position in the queue for interesting job opportunities. This phenomenon can be observed in most countries, but it is more accentuated in France. Partly because of a rising unemployment rate, more and more education is perceived as a "sesame" for entering the labor market. This may lead to unjustified education investment. One can observe in the recent years a tendency for acquiring several diplomas in the hope that it will give a better position in the queue.

The French tradition for a professional career does not rely on the idea that a new employee should begin at the bottom of the firm hierarchy with ancillary tasks and get progressively promoted. Unlike Germany and Japan where a majority of high executive positions are filled with employees who have climbed up the hierarchical ladder, most similar positions are filled in France with Grandes Ecoles or university graduates. Surprisingly, a recurrent debate concerns the capacity of the education system to prepare school leavers for entering the labor market. The education system is accused of being poorly adjusted to job market requirements. It is similarly often accused of feeding unemployment. This accusation ought to be discarded. The education system is not responsible for the dynamism or the passivity of the French economy in terms of job creation. It may be true that in certain sectors it is difficult to find some categories of manual workers, yet this has nothing to do with the operation of the education system. It is the operation of the labor market that favors white collars against blue collars and makes white-collar positions more attractive to the young generations.

It must be recognized that the lack of dialogue between the French education system and the productive world, which used to be one of the commonly denounced drawback of the French system, has been substantially reduced in the recent years. This issue can no longer be considered a major one.

Weaknesses in the Field of Pedagogical Innovations

As previously discussed, the French education system tends to be conservative regarding pedagogical innovations. While this conservatism has not strongly damaged the overall effectiveness of the system, there is a problem with the wide dissemination of new information technologies (NIT). The French schooling context is not properly adapted to this evolution.

The first attempt to introduce NITs within education was decided by Prime Minister Mr. Fabius in the mid 1980s with his famous *Plan Informatique pour Tous* (Computers for All). This project was aimed at providing 100,000 computers to primary and secondary schools within a two-year period. Yet the centralized and bureaucratic French tradition has generated the conditions for a big failure of the project. The 100,000 computers were ordered from a state company that developed a specific type of computer that was not compatible with any of those available on the market. The computers were delivered to schools after a very short training (about one week) of some teachers and without the appropriate software for the proper utilization of computers in classrooms. The life expectancy of these 100,000 computers was shown to be very short, not because of a lack of reliability, but because of premature obsolescence. Moreover, one of the objectives of the project, which was to support the state company in world competition, entirely failed, since this company has disappeared from the list of significant PC producers.

After this initiative—which ended up in disaster—the penetration of NITs in the French education system has been very slow. Only a small proportion of teachers have taken individual initiatives and no new centralized plan has been set up. The last political intervention concerning this issue was announced at the beginning of 1997 by the President during a TV interview in which he expressed his willingness to see every school connected to the Internet in the year 2000. It is interesting to notice that this initiative is not coming from the Ministry of Education itself. It may reflect once again the passivity of this institution vis-à-vis the issue.

Primary School Rhythms

It is regularly claimed in the media, as well as in some pedagogical circles or by health authorities, that French primary pupils are overloaded by an extensive curriculum that has to be absorbed in long working hours during school days, while holidays are excessively long. It is argued that six hours a day of teaching plus intensive homework is too much for a significant proportion of pupils. The reactions of the Ministry of Education in this controversy have been constantly cautious. The debate raises several issues for which there is no consensus in French society. The miracle solution has not yet been identified and most suggestions have the undesirable effect of raising costs.

An acerbic controversy opposes on one hand those who would like to set up a four-school day week and liberate Saturday mornings (Wednesdays are already off and this is not expected to change) and on the other hand those who think that it will make the school day load even more unbearable as far as the curriculum; 4.5 days would have to be covered in four days. Although the four-school day week is hardly a solution for improving school rhythms, it is often favored by parents who are seeking the possibility of enjoying full two-day weekends.

A second approach to changing school rhythms is based on the principle that cognitive activities should be concentrated in the morning and less intensive ones (arts, music, sports, discovery of the world by nature, or museum trips) would be done in the afternoon. The problems with this approach are first that present teachers are not trained for insuring certain activities and second that it requires additional budget and additional staff. According to the law, the duty of the Ministry of Education is to provide teachers. Other inputs for primary education come from the municipalities who decide how they envisage carrying out the changes. The Ministry of Education is reluctant to provide additional means from its budget and thinks it is wiser not to impose any new obligations on municipal authorities. In 1996–1997, rather surprisingly, initiatives have emerged from the Ministry of Sports and Youth Affairs. It has signed agreements with about 200 municipalities concerning the introduction of experimental new schedules. Preliminary evaluation of these initiatives shows that unit costs tend to increase by about 25 percent and that the cognitive performances of pupils remain more or less stable. Other education outputs have not been clearly identified and measured. The future of such initiatives remains uncertain. It is correct to say that the exposure of French pupils to arts or to music is not satisfactory. Many reports have pointed out the deficiencies of the French education system in these domains and have made several recommendations. The problem is in the degree of professionalism in the solutions. There is a real danger of introducing amateurish practices that could be worse than the status quo.

Educational Science Research

The fact that for more than a century primary teachers' training was not undertaken in universi-

ty institutions and secondary teachers' training had a cosmetic exposure to professional training has not helped French universities to develop education departments similar to those in other developed countries. One could have hoped that the recent creation of IUFMs would have developed stronger education departments. This hope has vanished since the decision was made to recruit the existing teaching staff of previous Normal Schools for these new IUFMs. This staff does not have any academic research experience and tradition. IUFMs have also recruited university professors in different fields (mathematics professors for the training of future secondary school mathematic teachers and so on). However, it was agreed that research activities of university professors would be performed in their university departments of origin and not within the IUFMs. As a consequence, this new context is not significantly more favorable for enhancing education research within IUFMs nor within universities.

The most important institution for carrying out research on education has traditionally been the INRP (*Institut National de la Recherche Pédagogique,* National Institute for Pedagogical Research), which used to be a department of the Ministry of Education and not an academic institution. It acted under the political authority of the Minister rather than under the scientific control of peers. This status has recently changed. It is today more academically oriented, but still employs the same staff. It is too early to evaluate the impact of this change.

This context explains why the status of academic research in the field of education has remained modest in France. Moreover, the CNRS, which covers a large variety of academic fields from physics to philosophy, has never created an education department. The lack of education research is reflected in the political and societal approaches of education. Everybody feels authorized to have a definitive opinion on the right solution concerning educational issues. Experts who speak on French television are rarely educational experts, but physics Nobel prize winners and the like who have undoubtedly some talents in physics and some talents as teachers—but these individual merits are of little use for the development of general solutions. Hundreds of books on educational issues are published every year, rarely based on recognized research, but on the personal intuition of their authors. The opinions expressed are not validated by any scientific methodology. This leads to a highly ideologically biased debate on the French scene. This context gives to every political person becoming Minister of Education the feeling that his or her political capacities qualify him or her for promoting a new education reform. Lack of time and lack of knowledge of the milieu and of the results of existing research do not allow the Minister of Education to go beyond cosmetic changes nor to change in depth the bureaucratic forces that run the system.

THE FUTURE OF SOCIETY AND SCHOOLING

It seems more and more likely that the future of French society will take place within the framework of the construction of Europe. This evolution will accelerate the decline of the state's role, give more importance to European regulations, and also very likely more responsibilities to local authorities, in particular to *Régions.* Concerning education, the extension of decentralization will raise the issue of whether to dismantle the centralized education system of staff management. Changes will be difficult to implement. Two options are open. While the first one would transfer the responsibility of staff management to *Régions,* the second would give more responsibilities to school authorities. Teacher unions are opposed to both solutions. Yet if they had to choose one of them, they would likely favor a regional management, a solution that could open the door to a new co-management role.

From an education efficiency point of view, it is clear that the other solution would be better. It would offer schools the possibility to match more appropriately teachers' profiles and schools' needs. It would also give headmasters more control concerning the motivation of the teaching staff, for they would hold some decision-making authority on recruitment and promotion, or on renewal of teacher contracts. Highly incompetent teachers would probably be forced to leave the system.

Europe will also have some homogenizing effect on the operation of educational systems. For instance, in terms of public finance, the fact that France's past atypical behavior of increasing the share of GDP allocated to public education expenditure will no longer persist due to the necessity of insuring a convergence of public finance and fiscal revenues between European countries. France belongs to the group of European countries that have the highest share of public expenditure within the GDP. This being a threat to the future competitiveness of the economy. French political authorities will have an incentive to design policies aimed at reducing this share.

If the expansion of the system cannot rely on additional public expenditure, there will be renewed attempts to charge fees for certain users (post-compulsory education, privileged tracks, and education programs that have high economic returns for users). These initiatives will raise intense fighting between lobbies. Part of the left may join part of the right to defend the status quo. Part of the modern left may converge with the liberal right in the promotion of new approaches.

The future role of new technologies of information on world education is still open. One cannot yet anticipate what will be the exact expansion of this role in terms of individualized learning outside the formal system. In any case, France is behind the most advanced countries in this respect (United States, Canada, Northern European countries). Yet France has developed outside the school system a competitive competency in the field of software development. It could use this capacity for the development of educational programs. The only problem is that of creating the right incentives for teachers. This requires legal modifications concerning the delivery of diplomas and the ways of defining teachers' duties. For the time being, their duty is only expressed in terms of hours of teaching. Other duties, such as private tutoring, distance tutoring and guidance, and education software development, are presently not accounted for properly. Pedagogical innovations are not rewarded. Moreover, certification of pupils' performances is still excessively teacher referenced and rarely done through external independent evaluation procedures. This also should change.

The French education system is close to the end of its quantitative development. It will be able to concentrate its efforts on quality improvements. Past experiences concerning measures for enhancing the quality of the system have had disappointing results and the present mood is more inclined to encourage local initiatives rather than centralized ones. The flourishing of different types of decentralized innovations should allow, after proper evaluation, the identification of the most promising innovations that could be disseminated later. For instance, there is the approach presently developed in higher education concerning the use of NITs in the framework of a project aimed at promoting "á la carte" learning in which students can select an individual menu among different methodologies of access to learning. Each student can accumulate credits acquired through different ways (residential, semi-residential, with or without computer programs, at a distance, and so on).

This new path for designing French education policies for the future is still modest but creates positive signals for a more efficient approach. Pessimistic observers may think that the process is too slow. Yet optimistic ones can argue that such a change is in itself an important revolution in the operation of the French education system.

ENDNOTES

1. The *Département* is a geographical entity created after the French Revolution, which is administratively run by a *préfet,* the main representative of the central power at this level. There are 95 *Départements.* The *Région* is a newly created geographical entity that is a set of four *Départements* on average. There are 24 *Régions.* A *Région* is very close to the concept of *académie.*

REFERENCES

Ministère de l'Education Nationale (MEN), de l'enseignement supérieur et de la recherche. (1996). *Repères et références statistiques sur les enseignements et la formation.* Paris: Direction de l'évaluation et de la prospective.

OECD. (1996). *Education at a glance.* Paris: Author.

Thurow, L.C., & Lucas, R.E.B. (1972). *The American distribution of income: A structural problem.* Washington, DC: Joint Economic Committee of the United States Congress.

CHAPTER 9

The Spanish Education System: Educational Answers to Social and Political Changes

DIEGO SEVILLA

Diego Sevilla is Associate Professor of Educational Policy at the University of Granada, Spain. He is head of the Department of Doctoral Studies of his university and is a specialist in the theory and history of higher education policies in Spain.

THE SOCIAL FABRIC

Geography and Demography

The land area of Spain (504,782 square km) makes it the second largest country in Europe after France. Together with Portugal, which is five times smaller, Spain occupies the Iberian Peninsula. Part of Spain are two archipelagoes (the Balearic Isles, off the Mediterranean coast of mainland Spain, and the Canary Island, distant from the Iberian Peninsula, in the Atlantic Ocean off the Sahara, south of Morocco). There are also two cities in North Africa—Ceuta (population 70,777) and Melilla (population 61,524). It was toward the end of the fifteenth century that all these territories were united under the Spanish monarchy after eight centuries of dynastic alliances and struggle against the Muslim invaders who first arrived in the eighth century.

It has been said that the Spaniards are a particularly individualistic people, given to holding dearly to their local peculiarities. This is in part due to the different origins of the people, the variety of climatic conditions, and the mountainous nature of much of the country, which has prevented ease of communication and encouraged cultural and linguistic diversity.

At present, the population of the country is 39,209,711 with an average density of 78 inhabitants per square km. There are large differences between different provinces. Barcelona, for example, has an average of 597 inhabitants per square km, whereas Teruel and Soria have only 10.

Economics

In 1986, Spain joined the European Economic Community, today known as the European Union. However, Spain is one of the poorest member states, with an extremely high unemployment rate (31.51 percent) and a GNP per capita of $12,359. It has just 76 percent of the average purchasing power of other European Union countries, a figure only higher than those of Portugal (67 percent) and Greece (65 percent).

Agriculture was the main activity of 47.8 percent of the total working population in 1950, 40.8 percent in 1960, and only 23.9 percent in 1970. Between 1960 and 1969, equipment in Spanish homes improved. For example, at the beginning of the decade 46 percent enjoyed running water; this increased to 80 percent over the decade. Those with cars rose from 2 percent to 27 percent, with refrigerators from 4 percent to 63 percent, and with television sets from 1 percent to 62 percent. The 6- to 13-year-old sector of the population attending school rose from around 50 percent at the beginning of the 1950s to 87 percent at the end of the 1960s.

Politics

In the eighteenth century the French Bourbon dynasty of monarchs attempted to impose a centralized, uniform state in Spain. This aim was continued by the Spanish liberals of the nineteenth century but met with fierce opposition, mainly in those populations with more distinct cultural and linguistic differences (Catalonia and the Basque country). This was to later grow into the nationalist and separatist movements of the twentieth century that the Second Republic (1931–1936) attempted to accommodate by formally recognizing them. However, during the Civil War (1936–1939) brought on by the military uprising against the Republic and the ensuing dictatorship of General Franco (1936–1975), these movements were harshly repressed. This led eventually to deeper resentment and the appearance of terrorist groups that continue to survive, even after democracy was restored. The most important is E.T.A., *Euskadi ta Askatuta*—Basque Country and Freedom.

The dictatorship imposed by the victors of the Civil War seemed to remove all hope of reform. However, Spanish society underwent a striking change in economy, social structure, and attitudes in the 1960s. It is true that such changes had slowly begun much earlier, albeit with gains and setbacks, but this decade saw the coming together of a number of circumstances that gave them greater urgency.

If we also consider the contact with other lifestyles due to emigration to Europe and the rise of tourism in Spain, we can see that the changes that took place were not only in the social and economic structure, but also in habits and attitudes. All of this goes to explain why, although the democrats were unable to consolidate the Second Republic under the threat of extremist violence in

the 1930s, when the dictator Franco died in 1975 his authoritarian regime disappeared also and the present democratic rule sprang up naturally, one might almost say.

The first democratic elections in 1977 were a clear sign of the overall desire to exclude forever attitudes that might threaten another civil war. It showed as well the will to establish a fully democratic state along European lines, without putting in danger the social and economic gains recently achieved at such great effort. The voters expressed their preference for middle-of-the-road political parties and for nationalist parties in Catalonia and the Basque country. The Constitution of 1978 was drawn up as the result of agreement, so that it should not contain anything objectionable to any political group and, simultaneously, all groups could develop their political programs without any need to alter the Constitution. It is a lengthy document since reciprocal doubts and misgivings led to its including many precautionary clauses. One of the difficulties that had to be overcome was the acceptance of nationalist aspirations without stirring up the animosity of an army trained to defend national unity. So a sort of Federal State (*Estado Autonómico*) was drawn up, with a measure of power sharing between the central state and its constituent autonomous regions (*Comunidades Autónomas*). Spain became a constitutional monarchy, consisting of seventeen autonomous regions, each with its own parliament and government. This formula, similar to federalism, allows for the political recognition of nationalist tendencies and cultural diversity. Spain is, therefore, a nation of nations.

SCHOOLING

Historical Background

The Spanish education system developed in line with the evolution of Spain into a modern state. Within the context of the evolution of Spanish society, and as a direct result of it, the Spanish education system's closest precursors are to be found in the members of the Spanish Illustration. In the second half of the eighteenth century, they produced memoirs and reports on public instruction and universities. Their intention was to excite public interest in national education and to involve the monarchy in this task. In 1812, the first of the commitments of the state toward education specified the uniform nature of education for all, as it preferred a guaranteed minimum rather than trusting to public or private initiative. However, just as a solemn declaration of this principle was made, the country was ravaged by the Peninsular War against Napoleon (1808–1814) and the public treasury was bankrupt. It is no surprise, then, that in the years immediately ensuing the proclamation of such laudable ideas, the number of children attending school was no higher than 17 percent.

It was not until 1857 that a Law of Public Instruction was passed thanks to the efforts of what was known by the peculiarly Spanish term of moderate liberalism (*liberalismo moderado*) that was a mixture of liberalism, conservative tendencies, and the interests of dominant social groups. Hence, the aim of the 1857 Public Instruction Law was neither to transform teaching nor even to extend it, but rather to give it an ordered legal basis. The manner in which it sought to do so was more in the interest of the ruling classes than in attention to the needs of the working classes, thus leading to problems of school attendance and illiteracy. In fact, with the brief exception of the Second Republic, these problems were only seriously tackled in 1970, at the end of General Franco's dictatorship, when this law was replaced by the General Law of Education (*Ley General de Educación*).

The 1857 Law maintained the principle of uniformity and declared primary education obligatory, but free only for those who certified their poverty. The onus for financing this level of education fell on the towns, but since resources were very limited, the public schools and schoolmasters were reduced to penury. Secondary education covered general studies and also those required for the industrial professions and depended on

financial provision from provincial budgets. The (Catholic) Church was authorized to teach Christian religion and morals in the public schools, and the Law made it possible for religious institutions to set up private schools.

A century later, the Minister for Education (1968–1973), Sr. Villar Palasí, undertook a searching report entitled *Education in Spain: Foundations for educational policy* (1969) in which the deficiencies of the education system were brought to light, together with its lack of adaptation to a modern, developing society. One of the main problems detected was the extremely unfair selective nature of the system. It was shown that in the 1960s, 15 percent of children of school age did not attend school. Only 30 percent attended primary school for four years to elementary *Bachillerato* level (*Bachillerato Elemental*); 15 percent continued to higher *Bachillerato* (*Bachillerato Superior*); 5 percent reached the final stage of secondary education (*Curso Preuniversitario*), and only 3 percent finally went to the university.

As a result of this report, the General Law of Education (1970) reflected technocratic ideas on education and incorporated modern advances in pedagogy and psychology. Its intention was to modernize the entire education system by introducing profound changes at all levels from primary school to university. For Spanish society of the time, perhaps its most revolutionary innovation was the enforcement of school attendance to the entire population between 6 and 14 years of age along the lines of a comprehensive education known as general basic education (*Educación General Básica*). Naturally, the application of the new law met with many difficulties. On the one hand, it was too progressive for the supporters of the dictatorship, while on the other, it was unacceptable to progressive sectors of the population since its origin was a Ministry of Franco's regime. In addition, the economic crisis of 1973 that came after a decade of impressive growth posed problems for the financing of such an ambitious project—problems that would only be overcome with the advent of democracy.

Political Influences on Education

The Spanish education system as it stands today has been to a large extent modeled by the policies of socialist governments. After the first democratic elections (1977), followed by five years of centrist government, the PSOE (*Partido Socialista Obrero Español,* Spanish Labor Party) governed the country without interruption for fourteen years (1982–1996). But rather than increasing financing for education, socialist government policy was perhaps more influential in reforming the education system by increasing the degree of participation and democratization and transforming a centralized system into one that is almost federal.

After the general elections of 1977, all political parties, trade unions, and other groups signed the Moncloa Pact (*Pactos de la Moncloa*), which implemented political consensus in the socioeconomic sphere. They accepted voluntary wage restrictions to control the rampant inflation (25 percent in 1977) in exchange for concessions such as fiscal reform, the extension of social security, and, most importantly as regards our present concern, the creation of a large number of school options to guarantee an education system in accordance with Spanish society of the last third of the twentieth century.

As regards education, the Constitution of 1978 forbids discrimination on unjust grounds, recognizes the teacher's right to independence in the classroom, establishes the powers of the central state and the autonomous regions, and dedicates Article 27 to ratifying the irrevocable standpoints of left and right wings on the education issue. Article 27 defines the concept of education: It states that education's aim is the full development of the human personality in the context of respect for democratic principles and fundamental rights and liberty. It guarantees the right of every citizen to receive education and the right of parents to provide their children with moral and religious formation according to their own convictions; it recognizes the freedom to set up centers of learning; it assumes financing of private schools, but stresses the participation of parents, teachers, and pupils in the running of all centers receiving public funds; and, finally, it recognizes the autonomy of the universities.

The most notable feature of this period was the increase in spending on education, which multiplied by 2.17 in real terms between 1980 and 1995, rising from 3.84 percent of the GNP to 5.68 percent. This allowed the system to accommodate the demand for expansion of the nonobligatory levels of education, to raise the number of teachers and their salaries, and to set up a broad policy of grants.

Private finance in education in Spain makes up about a fifth of the total, while the public sector finances private schools that sign an agreement with the administration for the obligatory levels. This agreement requires such schools to operate along lines similar to those of public schools, mainly in questions such as the participation of teachers, parents, and pupils in the running of the school, and criteria for the admission of pupils and employment of teachers. It may be that because of such agreement, private education in Spain, with the exception of university education, continues to make up a third of the total. Nonetheless, government spending on education in Spain continues to be lower than the average of the OECD nations, both in terms of GNP percentage (6.4 percent average in 1991) and as regards expenditure at any level of education, when Spaniards do not on average reach 50 percent.

Participation and Democratization

These are the two most characteristic features of the difference between left-wing and right-wing educational policy. The socialists came to power with the commitment to substitute democratic processes (rule from below) for the authoritarian structures of the education system (rule from above). Therefore, since 1985 the main governing body in each school is the School Council (*Consejo Escolar del Centro*), which is mainly made up of teachers, representatives of parents, and pupils. A member of staff is elected as Headmaster by the School Council. Unfortunately, the results of this change have not lived up to expectations. About half of the headmasters are designated by the administration because no candidates come forward and there is a very low degree of participation of pupils and parents in electing their representatives. We should also add that the socialists ceased to have much trust in the virtues of participation and came to underline the importance of evaluation and management. Accordingly, since 1995, only persons previously accredited by the administration are now eligible for the post of Headmaster.

Other Reforms of the Education System

Apart from introducing participation into the education system, the socialists wanted to reform it. Their aims were to move toward the establishment of the welfare state and a more democratic society. On another level, they wanted to modernize the organization of the educational system so as to better integrate into the European Union and find a place in an increasingly dynamic world.

Reform was first approved for the University in 1983 but postponed for other levels of education until 1990. In 1990 the LOGSE (*Ley de Ordenación General del Sistema Educativo,* Law for the General Ordering of the Education System) was passed, replacing the 1970 General Law of Education (*Ley General de Educación*).

The new law implies the complete restructuring of the Spanish education system, a process that will not be completed until the academic year 2001–2002. The justification of these changes is to be found in the deficiencies detected in the system in 1989. These were as follows: lack of regulation of the nursery school stage (0 to 6 years); the dropout rate at the end of general basic education (30 percent of pupils failed to obtain their final diploma, *Graduado Escolar,* and 14 percent abandoned formal education forever); early streaming (on finishing general basic education at fourteen years, those pupils obtaining their final diploma could continue to *Bachillerato,* whereas those who failed their final exams could only continue to Technical Education, *Formación Profe-*

sional; the high failure rate in the first years of *Bachillerato* (28 percent leaving after the first two years) and *Formación Profesional* (50 percent failing to pass the first two years); the excessively academic nature of teaching in *Bachillerato;* and the gap between *Formación Profesional* and the labor market.

It is clear that most of the problems affected the 12- to 18-year-old range; that is, secondary education (*Enseñanza Secundaria* or *Enseñanzas Medias*). However, the socialists decided not to concentrate just on this area, but to reorganize the system from top to bottom. This solution was certainly far-reaching and ambitious, but it also required great effort and expenditure. Indeed, the cost may have been excessive, because the changes began to be introduced at the beginning of the 1990s, coinciding with an economic crisis, the decline of the undisputed power of the socialists in Spain, and with the self-imposed obligation in European countries to restrict public spending.

The reforms proposed by the socialists were finally accepted by all the parliamentary groups, with the exception of the conservatives. Ironically, the latter won the general election of 1996 and, therefore, are charged with putting into effect the most difficult and controversial aspects of the reform. The Spanish education system has thus completely changed the structure of its nonuniversity levels. The 1990 system is shown in Figure 9.1, and the levels are explained below.

Pre-obligatory Education

This is from 0 to 6 years and is one of the most significant innovations. Reformers wanted to establish an educational plan for schools at this level, to extend public education throughout the population, and to combat the social and cultural deficiencies of underprivileged families. Preschool has therefore been given a specific character and is linked with the education administration. It is voluntary and the aims are more formative than instructive: physical, intellectual, affective, and moral development. The methodology is to be

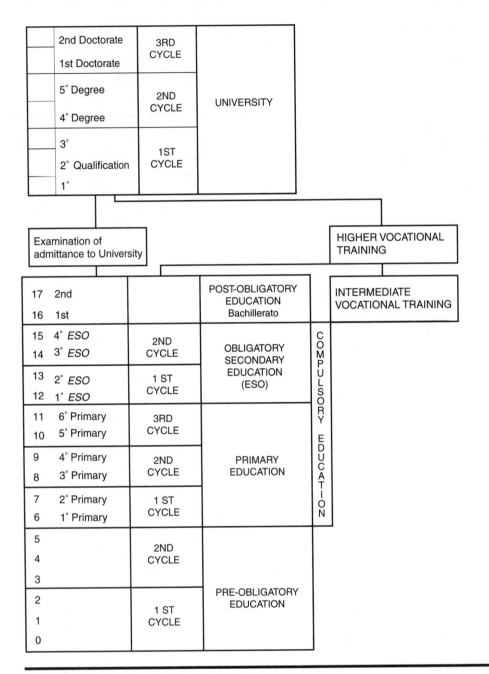

FIGURE 9.1   Spain's educational system (1990).

based on experience, activities, and games in an atmosphere of affection and trust. The system is subdivided into two cycles; the first up to the age of 3 and the second from 3 to 6 years. The whole stage is to be taught by duly specialized teachers and the schools must also have other specialists to guarantee suitable attention for the children. The maximum teacher/pupil ratios depend on the age of the children: 1 to 8, 1 to 18, and 1 to 25.

In recent years progress has been made in the attendance of children between 3 and 5 years of age, coinciding with the fall in birth rate. (Spain, together with Italy, is the country with the lowest birth rate in the world, 1.2 children per woman). Thus, between 1987 and 1995 the child population has fallen 21.8 percent while school attendance has risen. For 3-year-olds it has grown from 16.5 percent to 57.3 percent, 4-year-olds from 86.4 percent to 100 percent; and for 5-year-olds it has remained at 100 percent. Together with a small rise in the number of teaching staff for nursery and primary schools (4.9 percent), the fall in birth rate has helped to improve the teacher/pupil ratio from 1 to 25.1 to 1 to 17.9.

Obligatory Education

In the redesigned education system, the minimum period of obligatory instruction is ten years (from 6 to 16). It is to be carried out in all schools according to a comprehensive, integrated model and covers two closely linked stages: primary education (*Educación Primaria*) and obligatory secondary education (*Educación Secundaria Obligatoria* or *ESO*). Primary education covers the 6- to 12-year-old age range and includes three cycles of two school years each. The objective of this level of education is to provide all children with a unified education that will allow them to acquire basic cultural knowledge; the skills concerned in spoken expression, reading, writing, and arithmetic; as well as increasing freedom of action in their environment.

The evaluation of the learning processes of the pupils is continuous and overall. Didactic methodology is directed toward the general development of the child and must adapt to the learning rhythms

of each pupil. The maximum teacher/pupil ratio is 1 to 25 (it is, in fact, already lower). There must be at least one teacher per group. One of the outstanding novelties regarding the teaching staff is the requirement for each school to have specialists in music, physical education, and foreign languages, for it was thought that these disciplines were not receiving the attention the deserve. Each school must also have a supplementary teacher whose purpose is to make possible the adequate attention to the different needs of the individual pupils.

Obligatory secondary education (ESO) is the first stage of secondary education and forms part of the period of obligatory school attendance. It covers the 12- to 16-year-old age range and consists of two cycles of two years each. The objectives are to transmit basic cultural knowledge, to prepare children to assume responsibilities and exercise rights, and to prepare them to take part in working life or to continue to *Bachillerato* or Medium Grade Specific Technical Education.

This stage is ruled by the principles of comprehensiveness and attention to diversity. In the first two years, more emphasis should be put on the common nucleus of obligatory subjects than on optional subjects, whereas the opposite should occur in the second stage (third and fourth years). The methodology should be individual, based on autonomous learning and group work. Evaluation should be continuous and integrative. The maximum teacher/pupil ratio should be 1 to 30 (this ratio is commonly achieved as an average, but this does not mean that there are not schools who have difficulty in reaching it). Schools must also have a back-up teacher to help with comprehensiveness and diversity.

Obligatory secondary education (ESO) is a novelty in the new design of the education system and it is without doubt its greatest challenge. Some of the innovations, particularly in Spanish secondary education, are the already mentioned extension of the school-leaving age to 16; the formative nature of the system, rather than being one of preparation and selection for the next stage; and the inclusion of basic technical education in the general formation. The latter should allow the pupils to understand the practical dimensions of their knowledge and prepare them to enter the world of work. The intention is to overcome the gap between academic programs and preparation for work. These new aspects also include specific social guarantee programs that are meant for pupils who do not achieve the objectives of this stage and cannot, therefore, move on to *Bachillerato* or Medium Grade Technical Education. They should provide basic occupational formation to allow them to take part in the world of work.

From the theoretical point of view, the design of obligatory secondary education is very well thought out. However, its practical application, which is at present being implemented throughout the country, is sure to encounter endless difficulties. In the first place, problems will arise because of the stage of schooling it is intended to cover, for it is here where the seeds of failure sown in earlier years break through to the surface. In Spain, these are the last years of Obligatory General Education and the first years of the old-style *Bachillerato* and Technical Education.

Second, there is the problem of the mentality and traditional attitudes of Spanish secondary school teaching staff. In general, these are teachers who believe in the importance of the acquisition of knowledge and preparation for the university. Their professional attitudes are therefore very distant from the spirit of this new stage in which so much importance is given to comprehensiveness and adaptation to diversity. Third, there is the problem of the need to increase the finances available to implement this new stage. New schools must be built or, at least, there must be significant alterations to the existing ones. Classrooms must be prepared in which to teach the new technical education in its integrated version; more teachers are needed to attend support groups; and a new attitude must be encouraged in those responsible for integrated Technical Education and the Social Guarantee Programs for them to make contact with the world of work, and so on. Part of these difficulties are to be tackled using new methodological strategies that the teaching

staff must accept. Thus, the curriculum takes precedence over the syllabus and so we speak of curriculum design, curricular plan, curricular adjustments, and so on. Emphasis is also laid on the formative conception of evaluation rather than the merely punitive aspect. I do not deny the importance and value of these approaches, but their effectiveness will be conditioned by the opportunities of the teaching staff to spend time on them, as well as their mentality and attitude.

Post-obligatory Education

According to the 1970 General Law of Education, post-obligatory education included, on the one hand, the option for 14- to 18-year-olds to obtain the Unified Polyvalent Bachillerato (*Bachillerato Unificado y polivalente,* BUP) and the University Preparatory Year (*Curso de Orientación Universitaria,* COU), open only to those who attained the *Graduado Escolar*. On the other hand, Technical Education (*Formación Profesional*) was for 14- to 19-year-olds with or without the *Graduado Escolar*. The new structure includes *Bachillerato* or second stage of Secondary Education and Medium Grade Specific Technical Education (Figure 9.1).

The *Bachillerato* should prepare pupils to continue to higher education—Higher Grade Technical Education or university education. The *Bachillerato* has four main areas: arts, natural and health science, humanities and social science, and technology. It would seem necessary for all four areas to be taught in every school teaching *Bachillerato*. However, for budgetary reasons, only two areas will be taught in some schools. The teacher/pupil ratio may rise to 1 to 35. Basic Technical Education begun in Obligatory Secondary Education will continue in *Bachillerato*.

Technical Education

This was one of the areas of the Spanish education system most in need of reform. Technical education took on a proportionally low number of pupils in comparison with *Bachillerato* (approximately one-third of the whole school population of the same age). This is a result of the low esteem in which manual work is held by Spanish society, meaning that families prefer their children to study *Bachillerato* and then progress to university, even when they have manifestly higher capacity for the skills taught in technical education or would have better job prospects through it. The first two years of Technical Education, especially, have become a refuge for pupils that have not made satisfactory achievement in General Basic Education and cannot enter *Bachillerato*.

Another of the deficiencies most clearly manifest in technical education in Spain is that it was carried out in a much more school-like manner than work-like in the sense that both theoretical and practical classes took place in the school workshops with practically no connection with the business world. This was also influenced by the scant propensity of the staff, sometimes amounting to opposition, to relate their teaching with social needs. On top of all this, we have the fact that Spain has one of the highest unemployment rates in Europe, especially juvenile unemployment. In 1966, there were three and a half million unemployed, 22 percent of the working population. Unemployment for the 16- to 19-year-old age range was 25.5 percent and 60.7 percent for the 20- to 24-year-old age range. There was an also insufficient number of intermediate technicians and skilled labor. All of which meant that there was an urgent need for suitable technical education.

The present design takes account of these errors and requirements. It integrates Basic Technical Education (*Technological Education*) into the general formation of Obligatory Secondary Education and *Bachillerato,* thus attempting to overcome the split between academic and practical formation. It requires pupils to have succeeded academically in the previous stage and so avoid going to Technical Education simply because they cannot enter *Bachillerato* or the university. Specific Technical Education is exclusively oriented to the acquisition of particular technical skills.

It remains to be seen whether the human, technical, and financial resources required to put the scheme into effect will be provided; whether the slow rate at which the plan is being implemented (what was passed in 1990 will not be operative until 2002) is the result of caution or lack of decision and finance; and whether any errors detected will be corrected or the system will carry on with routine and inertia. Finally, we must see whether Spanish society, and most particularly young Spaniards, will perceive the advantages of these changes and make use of them, and whether businesses will find it useful to give employment to those who complete Medium or Higher Grade Technical Education.

Special Education

A new model of special education has been designed. Maximum priority is given to the principles of normalization and integration in the school life of children with special educational requirements. The basic idea is that all pupils need personal treatment and, in this sense, special education ceases to be seen as the education of a different type of pupils, to become a set of human and material resources. Authorization for attendance in centers or units of special education will only be given in extreme cases when integration in ordinary centers proves impossible.

Attention to pupils with special educational needs will extend to nursery education, primary education, and obligatory secondary education. Use will be made of psycho-pedagogical ratings and individualized curricular adjustments.

Teacher Education

The objective of the educational reform of the 1970s was to achieve 100 percent school attendance. Once this was achieved, it is clear that the objective for the 1990s is to achieve a higher quality of schooling. Therefore, since "no education system is better than its teachers," teacher training takes on particular importance.

Spanish teachers consist of *maestros,* in charge of nursery schools and primary education, and secondary teachers. The training of the former consists of a three-year course at the university, whereas the latter hold full degrees after attending the university for four or five years. They are therefore two professional bodies distinguished by their initial formation and also by having different professional attitudes.

Primary school teachers attend Teacher Training Colleges (*Escuelas de Magisterio*), institutions that were integrated into the university structure in 1972 after almost a century's existence. A striking fact is that no attention whatsoever is paid to the question of the recruitment of future primary school teachers. No consideration is made of their social, emotional, or intellectual maturity. Very often, a considerable numbers of pupils at teacher training colleges attend simply because they failed to achieve entry to other university courses. After three years (1900 class hours, of which a third are practical classes in schools but that, in general, bear little relation to the theoretical classes), they obtain their Diploma in Teaching in one of the seven existing specialties (Nursery Education, Primary Education, Special Education, Physical Education, Musical Education, Foreign Language, and Hearing and Language). Graduates are then entitled to sit for a competitive examination to obtain a post as a teacher in the public system or to seek employment in the private sector.

Secondary teachers take a university degree course, after which they must study for a teacher training certificate. There is widespread agreement as to the scant usefulness of this certificate, but it has nonetheless been maintained with only slight alterations since the 1970s.

Despite the importance the Socialist Party gives to education and the ample opportunities it has had to modify things, it has kept the same structure as before in the sphere of teacher training. Some innovatory projects were put forward that could have brought about significant changes. In some cases, there was a suggestion of overcoming the split between pedagogy and other skills or knowledge in the formation of teachers; that is, to confront the problem that up to now it has been accepted that teachers of children need a pedagogical formation, whereas teachers of adolescents have to take a degree and then acquire a

smattering of pedagogical awareness. But the politicians did not take steps to alter this state of affairs, so the model inherited from the previous political regime is still in force.

If we consider the demographic trend in Spanish society, it is clear that there is no need for a large number of new teachers. Overall, therefore, improvement in teaching staff depends more on continuous formation than on initial formation. Continuous training of teachers is undertaken by Education Science Institutes (*Institutos de Ciencias de la Educación,* ICE), which are part of the university structure. These institutes undertake training of primary and secondary teachers on a clearly hierarchical basis.

In 1984, without abolishing the ICE, Teachers Centers (*Centros de Profesores,* CEP) were set up following the British model, and at first great hope was set by them. It was thought that they would make contact with the needs and concerns of teachers, for their organization and management were assigned to members of the so-called Movements for Pedagogical Renewal (*Movimientos de Renovación Pedagógica*). These were lively dynamic groups, most active during the last years of the dictatorship and the first years of democracy in which teachers most concerned about political, trade union, and school affairs would meet. Relations between the Socialist Party and these groups were very harmonious because, in many cases, the members of the Movement were also card-carrying socialists who agreed very closely with party policy. It seemed that the CEPs would basically direct their efforts to making teachers consider their situation and their work in a positively critical manner. However, relations between the Socialist Party, trade union members, and teachers' Movements gradually worsened, especially after teachers in public education carried out a prolonged strike in 1987–1988. The CEPs then adopted much more bureaucratic and organizational attitudes.

At present, most teachers attend numerous courses and seminars. In many cases, one might say that their intention is to obtain a diploma by which to improve their professional position or place of work, rather than to improve their teaching practice. To arrest this trend, the administration has designed programs intended to improve teaching in the teaching centers. Indeed, in 1995 a law was passed with the intention of regulating the participation, evaluation, and management of schools to thus compensate for previous trends. Participation is no longer the central criterion; attention is also being paid to the need for institutional evaluation of the schools and their management. In any case, it would seem that the paucity of resources and the importance given to control of bureaucratic procedures will continue to impede improvement of the continuous training of teachers.

Toward a Federal System?

It was stated above that one of the most important events in Spain at the end of the dictatorship was its transformation from a centralist to a heavily decentralized state. Starting with a single, uniform state, simultaneously with the implantation of freedom and democracy, the demands for self-government (independence, even) from different regions had to be dealt with. The solution contained in the 1978 Constitution provided a new arrangement of territorial power. The new model, known as the State of Autonomous Regions, is more than a *regional* state but less than a *federal* state. This organization has permitted a new distribution of powers between the central state and the territorial organisms with political autonomy (Autonomous Regions, Provinces, and Boroughs). The central state now has exclusive control of those affairs in which uniformity is necessary throughout Spain; in affairs in which a minimum of homogeneity is required, the basic rules are set at the level of state and the Autonomous Regions are charged with their implementation. Affairs in which variety is possible are the exclusive competence of the Autonomous Regions.

From the start, the regions with their own languages and a strong nationalist tendencies were extremely keen to acquire maximum control of education. They naturally saw education as one of the key instruments to revitalize their culture, their language, and, on this basis, their national awareness.

The central state has reserved for itself—not without tensions arising—the overall organization of the education system, the regulation of academic and professional titles, the establishing of educational minima, and the higher inspection of the education system. The Autonomous Regions, on the other hand, are charged with the regulation and administration of teaching at all levels, degrees, and specialties.

The Autonomous Regions have set up their own education administrations and put into effect their individual educational policies. The trend has often been to emphasize idiosyncrasies and possible differences. It should be added that the basic contents of teaching minima, established by the central government, cannot occupy more than 55 percent of the timetable in Regions with a language other than Spanish, or 65 percent in the others. It is thus easy to imagine the differences between teaching programs in the different Autonomous Regions. Considerable differences can be seen in the working of the education system and the reality of school life. Curiously enough, on occasions the Autonomous Regions have repeated the centralist scheme, so that instead of having a single centralism of state government, there are now several centralisms of autonomous governments. Let's emphasize, therefore, that the decentralization of education does not simply mean changing from monocentralism to pluricentralism. We should also recognize the merits of the intermediate organisms (educational districts) of the municipalities and schools.

The commitment to maintain the balance between unity and autonomous diversity demands revitalization of the organs of coordination, cooperation, and collaboration. These consist of the *Conferencia de los Consejeros de Educación,* which is the body that brings together all the Heads of Education in the different Autonomous Regions under the presidency of the Minister for Education; the *Instituto Nacional de Calidad y Evaluación* (*INCE*—National Institute for Quality and Evaluation), whose function is to avoid discrepancies in the education system, and which could have a very important role to play, if we consider that evaluation should be based on participation with the autonomous administrations; and finally the *Consejo Escolar del Estado* (State School Council), which is the highest participative and advisory body, bringing together representatives from all the sectors involved in education, administration, and significant social sectors. The influence of the State School Council could be greater if it also coordinated the School Councils of each Autonomous Region.

University

The first Spanish universities were founded in the Middle Ages. But their main features, which persist to this day, were established in the second half of the nineteenth century. The Law of Public Instruction (*Ley de Instrucción Pública*) of 1857 copied the model of the French Napoleonic university. Spanish universities were consequently established as exclusively dependent on the state. Because the state had complete control of university education and responsibility for finance, all the universities depended on the central government and followed the model of the central university of the state capital. Staff consisted of a body of state functionaries or civil servants. Authority descended in hierarchical fashion from the Rector, who was named by the government. Hence, universities have no degree of independence whatsoever; they were completely dependent on the central Ministry of Education.

With scarcely any changes this model of the university was maintained until 1970 when the General Law of Education was passed. In practice, however, it continued until the Law of University Reform (*Ley de Reforma Universitaria—LRU*) was passed by the socialist government in 1983.

Certainly, the university began to change along with the changes in Spanish society in the 1960s. It rapidly became a mass university with very strong political movements, mostly in opposition to the ruling regime. This political awareness ebbed with the normalization of the political situ-

ation in the second half of the 1970s, but the accelerated growth that had begun in the 1960s continued. In the last forty years, the number of university students has multiplied by almost 30 (almost doubling every ten years) and the 3 percent of the 18- to 20-year-old population that entered it has now grown to over 45 percent.

At present, Spain is the second country in the European Union (the first is Holland) in the number of university students per 100 inhabitants. This rapid, uninterrupted growth is the most outstanding feature of the Spanish university in the past forty years. This is also the result of the lack of appreciation of Spanish society for technical education, the fact that all education after secondary level is channeled through the university, and the high rate of youth unemployment (the highest in the European Union). It is also because people see the university as offering a chance for economic and social improvement, though this is probably greatly exaggerated at present.

The 1983 *LRU* gave the universities considerable autonomy regarding their statutes and governing bodies, academic questions and syllabuses, administration and management of resources, choice and promotion of teaching staff, and established democratization and participation in the running of the universities. Most of the organs of university government are elected and they include representatives of teachers, students, and those involved in administration and services of the university. The drawback to this widespread democratization and participation is the slowness of administration and decision making and the lack of accountability.

Among its governing bodies, each university has a Social Council. Three-fifths of its members, including its President, must come from outside the university. Its functions are to promote the participation of society in the university, the collaboration of society in financing the university, the supervising of economic affairs, and the end results of its services. On a national level, the Universities Council (*Consejo de Universidades*) is charged with organizing, coordinating, planning, proposing, and advising on all matters related to the university. It is presided over by the Minister for Education and consists of the Heads of Education of the Autonomous Regions, the Rectors of the public Universities, and fifteen members of outstanding prestige.

There are considerable differences among the fifty-four existing universities, of which forty-four are public and ten private. The total number is still rising because of the creation of private universities and also because the autonomous regional governments are encouraging the creation of public universities, an event highly appreciated on both a political and a socioeconomic level. Almost half the universities have been established in the last ten years—fourteen public centers and all the private ones, except for four that, since they belong to the Catholic Church, were able to operate thanks to the privileged relations between Church and state. Universities are also very different in size—the ten private universities have less than 60,000 students (4 percent of the total), whereas the six largest public universities have over half a million students (one-third of the total).

There is also a significantly disproportionate distribution of students in the different areas of study: over half (53 percent) study law and social science (one in five university students studies law), 21 percent study technical subjects, 9.42 percent study humanities, 8.1 percent experimental science, and 7.68 percent health sciences. As at all levels, the teacher/pupil ratio is high (1:23).

Although over half the student population is female (51.94 percent), the proportion varies by area: 67.36 percent in humanities, 66.85 percent in health sciences, 57.33 percent in law and social science, 48.28 percent in experimental science, and only 22.66 percent in technical subjects. On the other hand, only one-third of the teaching staff are women.

The most outstanding feature of the Spanish university is its growth rate. However, alongside this positive fact, we should make some less positive observations. Finance is low (1 percent of the GNP, whereas the average of the OECD countries is almost double at 1.9 percent; expenditure per student is US$3,875, whereas the average in

OECD countries is $9,326). There is a high drop-out rate (one in seven students fails to obtain his or her degree in the stipulated time and one in five leaves university without completing studies); the high degree of job protection (nine out of ten posts available are adjudicated to members of the department advertising the post); and the excessive dependence on public finance (80 percent comes from the public budget, while 17 percent is provided by student registration fees and only 3 percent from social sources). There is a high proportion of teaching staff without tenure (44 percent), and the implementation of university autonomy and self-government has not been complemented by demands for competitiveness from the newly founded Social Councils.

In addition, after a long drawn-out elaboration of new syllabuses throughout the university and before these have been put into practice in their entirety, they are being subjected to severe criticism. They are seen to respond more to internal struggles between departments in an attempt to acquire more teaching capacity than to any scientific or pedagogical principles or a desire to respond to social needs. Even the growth in student numbers could lead to a drop in standards or, indeed, deception of those wishing to study at university, for they would basically be offered the chance to follow inexpensive courses, rather than courses leading to work opportunities.

It is therefore important that the universities should not feel flattered by the high demand and sheltered by a corporate spirit and the benevolence of their own standards. They must move forward by improving student mobility and competition between universities, open their doors to mature students who combine their professional activities with study, undertake realistic institutional evaluation and streamline their administration and management, and take advantage of all the opportunities to be obtained from modern telecommunications and computer science. Finally, they must reinterpret their own new-found independence. After a dictatorship, it is understandable that the intention was to achieve the highest possible degree of autonomy. However, it would now seem preferable to continue with the assurance of complete academic freedom in both teaching and research on the one hand, and, on the other, to link self-management, administration, and finance to the principle of accountability.

CHALLENGES AND FUTURE TRENDS

Education in Spain has undergone fundamental changes in recent decades. While the outcomes of these changes cannot be predicted with certainty into the future, it is clear that the process of change is not over. Some of the main contours of the evolution of the system into the twenty-first century include the following.

First, it is clear that the Spanish education system will continue to be affected by factors originating in society itself. The most important of these are demographic evolution, the degree of importance given to democratization and participation, and the change from a centralist state to a practically federal one. In any case, it is important that the system be open to these influences but also that its reactions to them be moderate.

Second, it is important to appreciate how ambitious and sweeping the reform that has been set in motion is. However, there is doubt as to whether it will be completed, because it depends on specific, detailed financing. Without sufficient resources, the changes will be merely cosmetic or terminological and may even be counterproductive.

Third, it is a credit to the nation that comprehensive education has been broadened and intensified. However, it seems that not enough importance has been given to social inequality and the degree to which it is present in Spanish society. Comprehensive schooling will be severely limited by this and a minimum guarantee of correct operation is only possible if schools are given more human resources and infrastructure.

Fourth, the critical issue of fiscal support needs to be squarely addressed. Overall, education in Spain is insufficiently financed. The historical backwardness of Spanish education has only been corrected regarding rates of school attendance. Financing must be increased if we are to achieve the quality of education corresponding to the rate of development of the country. Fourteen years of Socialist government failed to solve this problem, and now it seems that once again policies of reduction in social spending are coming into force. Finance in education will therefore need to be carefully studied and investment selected with care, for there will not be enough money.

Fifth, the renovation of technical education (*Formación Profesional*) is a priority. The faults common to the whole system are most noticeable here: excessively theoretical teaching, low quality through lack of finance, and scant connection with social needs. Improvement of this sector would lead to *Bachillerato* and the university being streamlined, a reduction in youth unemployment, and a solution to the traditional lack of specialized labor and medium technicians. This can only be attained by involving the relevant sectors of society, in particular the world of business.

Finally, the government and education bureaucracy must turn its attention to seriously rethinking teacher training. The initial education of teachers has not been adequately modified, and in-service training is not sufficient. However, the attitude and mentality of the teaching staff are key factors in the success of any reform and for the quality of the education system as a whole.

CHAPTER 10

Education as a Panacea: The Case of Greece

PANAYIOTIS PERSIANIS

Panayiotis Persianis studied literature and philosophy at Athens University and education at the London University Institute of Education. He is the author of Church and State in Cyprus Education (1878–1960) *and* Political and Economic Factors as Main Determinants of Educational Policy in Independent Cyprus. *He has also written, in Greek, several books and articles on education in Cyprus. He is currently an associate professor in the Department of Educational Sciences, University of Cyprus.*

The Greek culture is an ancient one. Its evolution constitutes a proud heritage that to this day is a primary force in Greek society, politics, and education. Ironically, old and strong as this heritage is, it is seen to be fragile and in need of constant nurturing and support. Today, Greece is coping with major economic, social welfare, political, and other adjustments made necessary by its participation in the European Union and its hurried progress along the path of modernization. In this era of rapid and sometimes turbulent change, education remains a crucial institution for the preservation of Greek identity and culture.

THE SOCIAL FABRIC

Demography, Religion, Politics

Greece is a small country of 131,957 square kilometers; just over 80 percent consists of mainland, the rest is a collection of islands. Nearly half the 10.2 million Greeks live in two big urban centers: Athinae and Thessalonike. Population density is 82 inhabitants per square kilometer in the conti-

nental part and 56.9 in the islands (National Statistical Service of Greece, 1995).

Over 98 percent of the population is Christian Orthodox. The remainder are mainly Muslim, most of whom live along the Turkish border in Western Thrace. As a national institution and custodian of culture, the Greek Orthodox Church is extremely important. One small but telling indication of the persuasiveness of the Church in Greek life is the fact that education comes under the Ministry of Education and Religious Affairs.

A parliamentary democracy, Greece is formally aligned with other European nations through membership in the North Atlantic Treaty Organization (NATO), the European Union (EU), the Organization for Security and Cooperation in Europe (OSCE), the West European Union (WEU), and the Council of Europe. It will also soon become a member of the Economic and Monetary Union (EMU) of the EU.

Economy

In the European community, Greece's economy is atypical in several important respects (Economou, 1993). For one thing, the per capita income in 1993 was US$6,093. This is only half the EU average. As well, the nation has a large agricultural population (about 25 percent of the total active population). This is three times higher than the EU average. Only 18 percent of the population is involved in manufacturing. Wage earners comprise only one-third of the economically active population; another one-third are self-employed, a percentage that is the highest in EU. It should also be noted that there is exceptionally wide-

163

spread multiple employment and a large shadow economy. Another important feature of Greek society is the closely knit family. This is reflected in the widespread practices of family employment and support for unemployed family members. Finally, the government and parastatal enterprises employ large percentages of the working population—one-third of the labor force in general and about half of university graduates (Lambropoulos & Psacharopoulos, 1992). This is possible because revenues amounting to 60 percent of the GNP are under public control.

Since 1990, Greece has been following a program for restructuring and stabilizing its economy. A result of this stabilization effort was the reduction of the inflation rate from about 20 percent in 1993 to about 10 percent in 1997 (Christodoulos, 1997).

Major Forces Shaping Greek Society

The most important forces shaping the social milieu are geography, history, and culture. We must also add a strong urge for modernization and the Greek Diaspora.

Perhaps geography and history have played the most important roles in shaping the nation's destiny. The great number of islands and the need to travel by sea from one part of the country to another have influenced both the economic and intellectual life of the Greek people. Coping with the risks of seafaring has forged an entrepreneurial spirit in Greeks since the ninth and eighth centuries BC, when they established colonies all over the Mediterranean. Today, Greece has a strong mercantile navy (the largest in the European Union) and a considerable percentage of its GNP comes from fishing, water transportation, trade, and tourism.

Geography also determines, to a large extent, national security. Greece's relations with its neighbors (Albania, Bulgaria, Yugoslavia, and Turkey) have, as a rule, been very strained for many centuries. This is especially true with regard to Turkey with which there is a long history of bitter and revengeful military confrontations. Greece

was occupied by the Ottomans for four centuries and was freed after a revolutionary war that last intermittently for about a century.

Present day Greco-Turkish relations are overshadowed by two recent issues: the Cyprus problem (Turkey invaded Cyprus in 1974 and has since occupied 37.6 percent of the territory) and Turkish claims for the Aegean Sea. Greece's tense relations with its neighbors have led to severe crises on several occasions and have created a feeling of insecurity within the Greek people. This has affected not only the country's foreign policy, but also its budget and education policy.

History has also provided the Greek people with a very rich culture dating back to ancient Greece and Byzantine times. The two most important elements of this culture are the language, considered to be a direct development of the Ancient Greek language, and the Orthodox religion. Language has always been cherished as the most valuable element of national identity—it has played a very important role in promoting national unity and social cohesion. In fact, for a very long time in the nineteenth century, language was used as a means to revive the ancient Greek culture.

To this effect, successive governments decreed that the language to be taught in schools would not be the popular language (*demotike*) but an artificial language known as *katharevousa,* a language "purified" of all non-Hellenic vocabulary and grammar acquired over the ages, and therefore very close to the Ancient Greek language. Until the 1960s every effort to substitute *demotike* for *katharevousa* in the teaching of language generated fierce opposition and, on some occasions, serious incidents of bloodshed (Bouzakis, 1991).

Greeks also cherish their Orthodox religion. In fact, this is the second strand of the linguistic/religious modern Greek cultural ideal known as Helleno-Christianity. Greek is the language of the *Bible,* and so it was argued that the survival of the language meant also the survival of the Orthodox religion. Furthermore, the Greek and the Christian traditions converge on certain general principles and points of view; namely, idealism, a humanistic approach, and emphasis on the moral and spiritual character of education at the expense of the scientific, practical, and technical (Kazamias, 1968).

The third major force shaping the Greek social milieu is a strong drive toward modernization. The poor natural resources of the country dictate that native intelligence must be the nation's principal resource. This attitude generates an enormous impetus for modernization (Bouzakis, 1992). Modernization is conceived as a conversion to western European forms of economic, social, and political organization. However, this should not come about through sweeping social and economic reforms but through education.

Finally, there is the great force of Greek emigrants abroad, mainly in the United States. These people assisted Greece financially in the past through remittances sent to relatives in Greece and through donations for the construction of schools, churches, and other public institutions in their native towns and villages. Today, Greek emigrants and their descendants living in the United States—among them some congressmen—constitute a strong lobby for Greek rights and interests.

Major Events That Have Shaped Greece

The first major event that shaped present conditions in Greece is the Greek civil war of 1944–1949. This confrontation pitted Greek nationalists and right-wing political elements, supported by Anglo-Americans, against Greek communists supported by the Soviet Union and neighboring communist countries. The war has left deep wounds, both in the minds of people who lost loved ones and in the political life of the country. These wounds have not yet fully healed and are at times reflected in a fanaticism, passion, and unwillingness to compromise that is often apparent in Greek politics. Indeed, present political groupings in Greece reflect, to a large extent, the political confrontations of the previous generation. As a rule, children still follow the political ideology of their fathers and grandfathers.

The restoration of democracy in 1974 after seven years of dictatorial rule by a military junta is the second major event. Its significance is that it emphasized the importance of democratic institutions and increased the sensitivity of people to their democratic rights. This has increased pressure for more democratic reforms.

However, the most important event in modern Greek history is joining the European Common Market (now European Union) in 1981. This is expected to have far-reaching consequences for the economic, political, and social life of the country. It will open up and modernize all aspects of Greek society, including social attitudes and values as well as political orientations and the functioning of government (Economou, 1993).

Unique Cultural and Social Realities

The interplay of the above forces and events has created some unique cultural, social, and political realities in Greece. These we have to keep in mind because they impact on education.

Culture is extremely important to Greeks. In particular, they take extreme pride in their language, as it is the oldest in Europe and has had a great influence on other European languages. This pride in language and culture make it difficult for Greeks to make concessions towards other cultures in the curricular content of their schools. Even more difficult is the idea of accepting multicultural education.

An equally important reality is the widespread acceptance of egalitarian ideals and practices. Unlike most other European countries, modern Greek society has never been deeply stratified. There is not a big gap between the wealthy and the poor and no deep divisions in social consciousness. These features facilitate social mobility, especially by means of education.

Advanced schooling has always had, as a rule, high economic returns and conferred high social status. This explains the century-old tradition of "overeducation"; that is, the production of more high school and university graduates than the country needs (Bouzakis, 1991). In fact, one can argue that the drive for social mobility has been the principal reason for quick educational expansion in post-war Greece.

The last unique reality is a political one. The Greek state is a very centralized and bureaucratic entity. It has used its concentrated powers and structure to forge a unitary and homogeneous state, but one that comes at the expense of regional and local institutions of self-government (Mouzelis, 1992). It also created a bloated state bureaucracy.

The unfortunate results have been an overexpanded, inefficient, and politicized civil service, and important local communities that are overly dependent upon the state. As will be shown in the next section, all this has led to dysfunctions, inefficiencies, and inertia in many sectors of society, including education (Kazamias & Kassotakis, 1995).

SCHOOLING

Organization and Structure

Education is free, a state responsibility, and compulsory until the age of 15. The Greek education system consists of six-year primary schools, three-year lower secondary schools (*gymnasia*), and three-year higher secondary schools (*lycea*). About 80 percent of the 16-to-18 age group complete the lyceum level.

Schools in Greece have always offered a uniform program. There was never a three-tier system as in other European countries or internal organization in the form of conspicuous or disguised tracks or *filières*.

Post-secondary education consists of three-year higher technological institutions (TEIs) at one level and four-year universities at the next level. About 40 percent of young adults graduate from a post-secondary institution in Greece or abroad. All post-secondary institutions are public because the 1975 Constitution prohibits the establishment of private institutions.

There is a system of *numerus clausus* (restricted admission) for entry into university. According to Psacharopoulos (1990), "Greece is the most tightly regulated country in this respect" (p. 62). Students are selected on the basis of results in pan-Hellenic competitive entrance examinations

organized by the ministry of education. There are several sets of subjects in the examinations and candidates take the set or the sets that are prescribed for the university department or departments they are competing for. Many of those failing in the competitive entrance examinations apply for places at universities abroad.

Primary and Secondary School Teachers

Secondary school teachers have traditionally been trained in universities. For primary school teachers, this has been the case only since 1988, when two-year pedagogical academies were closed down.

Primary school teachers are polyvalent; that is, they teach all subjects in the curriculum. In recent years, however, there is a tendency to appoint specialists in primary schools to teach subjects like physical education, music, and art. Secondary school teachers have always been specialists. Their professional training, however, is commonly perceived to be insufficient. In response, the ministry of education has organized special introductory pedagogical courses for newly appointed secondary school teachers. These are part of a general emphasis in-service training.

Aims and Objectives of Education

The main functions of education in modern Greece are ideological-political. As summed up in the 1975 Constitution. "Education aims at the moral, intellectual, professional, and physical training of the Greek people, the development of their national and religious conscience and their molding into free and responsible citizens." These objectives are very resilient; they have remained practically the same for almost two centuries, undergoing only some changes in the hierarchical order (Flouris, 1992).

Curriculum and Culture

The Greek state has always paid very close attention to the curriculum, which it sees as embodying national values indispensable for national identity and social cohesion. That is why the curriculum has always been prescribed by the state and is uniform across the country. Textbooks are prepared under the auspices of the state and supplied to pupils free of charge; even university students are entitled to free textbooks.

Sensitivity to the cultural transmission and preservation functions of education is also why the state reserves for itself the right of certification for all education qualifications acquired in private schools in Greece and in foreign universities. No one can be appointed to a public position unless the education qualifications are state-certified.

Greek culture has been a determining factor for the mainly humanistic content of education, the preference for literary subjects, and the emphasis on *la culture generale* in secondary education. In European countries, the preference for *la culture generale* throughout the eighteenth, nineteenth, and first half of the twentieth centuries was justified by the belief that it contributed to moral training and the shaping of character—the training of the mind—and was a unifying element for national cohesion (Vaughan & Mark-Lawson, 1986). There were two additional reasons for preferring *la culture generale* in Greece. First, it was very crucial for national identity because it embodied the teaching of Ancient Greek. Second, it was a matter of national pride. That is, if nations like France, Germany, and England taught Ancient Greek in their schools, surely it should be taught to the descendants of the ancient Greeks themselves.

Thus, Ancient Greek was compulsory even in primary schools during the nineteenth century, and in the gymnasia until the 1970s. It was taught for seven to eight periods per week, which is about 22 percent of total teaching time. Since 1976, Ancient Greek authors are taught in the gymnasia in translation, while in the lycea Ancient Greek is still compulsory (Theorakopoulos, 1976).

Another prominent subject is the Orthodox religion. It has always been compulsory and is taught two periods per week. Its traditional and current high prestige is reflected in its position in the official lists of subjects; it is always listed first in the hierarchy.

Such an emphasis on humanistic education resulted in a prejudice against and neglect of mathematics, science, and practical subjects for a long period of time. This helps explain the late development of technical and vocational education in Greece (the state established technical schools only in the early 1960s) as well as the small number of students currently enrolled in technical and vocational schools compared with the number in the general lycea.

In an effort to reduce the general prejudice against technical and vocational education, the A. Papandreou socialist administration established "multibranch lycea" in the 1980s. These were a new type of higher secondary school, one that offers a combination of general and technical subjects.

Administration

The governance of schooling has always been centralized. The state has always used legislation to establish schools; to appoint, transfer, discipline and pay teachers; and to prescribe curricula, syllabi, and textbooks. Centralized administration is justified as an effective way of achieving quick results when governments want to implement education policies, and it is preferred in many developing countries (King, 1967).

In Greece it is also justified as a means of providing equal access to schooling for all citizens, and a mechanism to reduce opportunities for patronage and appropriation of schools by interest groups. In a society characterized by "a distressing lack of trust at many levels of the system," the state has assumed the role of being not only the guarantor of education opportunity but also the guarantor of equal opportunity (OECD, 1993, par. 12, 13).

State Control, Initiatives, and Priorities

Strong public demand for education has been an important factor in increasing the state's power in education. The Greek people cherish education and always have been very strongly committed to it (OECD, 1993). This attitude can perhaps explain why education in Greece has not yet been commercialized, as is the case in some other countries. It can also explain the constant public pressure on the government, often expressed through strikes and processions, to increase its education budget.

For its part, the state has presented education as a kind of panacea. Education can shape national identity; modernize social, political, and economic institutions and practices; contribute to economic progress by training the manpower required in a new technological age; promote equity and social justice; and train the young generation in democratic thinking and practices.

It is helpful to give some examples of the mechanisms the state has used to promote these objectives. Equality of opportunity, for example, has been pursued through ensuring uniformity of curricular content across the nation, through extending free education to all levels of schooling (including free textbooks for all students), through abolishing entrance examinations for students progressing from the gymnasium to the lyceum, through allowing an unlimited number of sittings for university entrance examinations, and through dramatically increasing the number of places in higher education institutions (Lambropoulos & Psacharopoulos, 1992). Perhaps the most interesting and indicative initiative, however, came in 1983 with the establishment of "post-lyceum coaching centers." These are tutorial institutions for secondary school leavers who have failed their university entrance examinations, but are willing to try again after receiving coaching (Bouzakis, 1991).

Yet despite all these measures and initiatives, the state feels that it still does not have the full trust of its own populace. It is this eagerness to gain legitimacy that helps explain the state's very frequent recourse to education reforms and innovations, as we will see in the second part of the next section.

MAJOR ISSUES, CONTROVERSIES, AND PROBLEMS

In Society

Most of Greece's social issues, controversies, and problems are related to its accession to the EU. Most prominent are the following:

- The question of identity
- Economic changes resulting from international competition and economic globalization
- Seeking a balance between preserving the welfare state and meeting requirements for the economic convergence of EU members
- Defining the relation of the state to civil society
- A growing legitimacy crisis for the state

There is also a sixth issue, one that is not directly tied to the EU. That is the serious and volatile matter of Greece's strained relations with one of its neighbors.

Identity.   This is a very controversial subject, as it touches upon the issue of the very survival of the Greek people as a separate national entity. To keep their national identify, Greeks need to preserve their national language and culture.

Yet the Greek language, being the language of a small nation, will be in danger when it is forced to compete with the most widely used languages of EU member countries, especially English. Culture will also be in jeopardy of erosion, by both strong individual European cultures and the common European culture that is expected to emerge eventually.

Thus the Greeks are in a great dilemma. On the one hand, they consider themselves Europeans *par excellence*. That is, they believe that the roots of European civilization are mainly Greek, and they want to be considered Europeans. On the other hand, they are reluctant to let their nation integrate with other European nations because they fear multiculturalism.

The solution for Greece is either to adopt a defensive attitude by entrenching in its own system of values and developing mechanisms to keep other cultures out (Economou, 1993) or to open a dialogue with the other European cultures, a policy described by N. Mouzelis as the communicative approach (1996b). The first is advocated by the Neo-Orthodox, a group of Greek purists who consider everything western to be consumerism (Mouzelis, 1996a) and point to the danger of Greece losing its very essence, that is, its language and religion.

The second is supported by progressive people favoring the active involvement of Greece in shaping the new Europe. They justify their approach by pointing to the particular elements that Greek culture can offer to the new reality that will evolve from Europeanization. They also argue that this was exactly the way ancient Athenians dealt with foreign influences. Athenians were not xenophobic like the Spartans; they were an open society that tried to assimilate whatever was useful and productive in foreign cultures. Progressivists also point to the fact that Greece has already developed into a multicultural society by virtue of the fact that a considerable number of people of Greek origin, but hardly speaking Greek, settled in Greece from countries of the former Soviet Union (Kazamias & Kassotakis, 1995). Of course, the problem will become far more severe when the provisions of the Maastricht Agreement for free circulation of labor are fully implemented.

In the 1960s and 1970s the dilemma over Europeanization was both political and cultural. During that time, all left-wing political parties, as well as the communists, were against strong political relations with the West. They were against the policy of Greece being a member of NATO and against accession to the European Common Market. In the 1980s, however, their policy changed. The debate today is mostly about culture, although there have been examples of Euro-skeptics in all the administrations of the last twenty years.

International Competition and Economic Globalization.
The issue of international competition and economic globalization is related to the major impact deregulation and free competition will

have on the occupational and economic structures of the country. Many vested interests oppose allowing market forces to shape the Greek economy without state regulation. They argue that the Greek economy is not yet ready for this move, as high inflation, unemployment, and public debt rates indicate.

They point to the fact that the Greek economy has been greatly dependent on the West European economy ever since the establishment of the modern Greek state. This has resulted in distorted and imbalanced economic development (hypertrophy of the agriculture and services sectors at the expense of industry, parasitic economic activities, extreme dependency of rural regions on urban centers, and excessive numbers of self-employed people) and serious social dysfunctions (Bouzakis, 1992). Also put forth is the argument that rapidly changing the economy will mean a deepening of this dependency and perhaps a decrease in the nation's economic potential for quicker development. Greek industry will never manage to compete with the high technology industries of other European countries unless it is given time to change through infrastructure improvements (public transport, telecommunication, energy, banking, and especially education). With their industries at a competitive disadvantage, the Greek people will be doomed to content themselves with the role of "waiting on European tourists in Greece."

Economic unification will also, it is feared, negatively affect culture. If the logic of economics replaces the logics of culture and social solidarity in the shaping of Greek social policy, this will prove disastrous to cultural and social freedom (Mouzelis, 1996b).

Preserving the Welfare State.
Objections to the rapid mergers of the European and Greek economies are also related to the restrictions this would impose on the welfare state. Since the early 1980s the Greek economy has faced stagflation and high fiscal imbalances (Economou, 1993) as a result of public overspending and the unwillingness of administra-

tions to impose market discipline on the nation. In the early 1980s, deteriorating economic indicators forced the government to take austerity measures in an effort to restructure and stabilize the economy. These austerity measures have been continued by successive administrations, despite fierce public opposition.

Reduction of public deficits will be assured only through higher and more comprehensive taxation. This will mean a loss of many of the benefits of the welfare state that Greeks enjoy. It will also mean smaller education budgets, fewer possibilities for the improvement of education, and therefore less adequate preparation of the younger generation for international competition.

Relation of the State to Civil Society. This issue has to do with the extreme centralization of administration, the bureaucratic mentality of the civil service, and the "patronage" and "clientele" systems that the state applies. A recent report described the situation very aptly:

> *A large number of people rely directly or indirectly on the state, expecting it to intervene in their favor. The belief that personal or group welfare come from the activity of a benevolent state prevented till now the formation of a civil society that can function autonomously. . . . Social groups direct their demands mainly toward the state asking for favorable treatment or protection against other groups. (Economou, 1993, p. 282)*

The state bureaucracy is also a major obstacle to progress. It can be intentionally obstructionist, reluctant to assume responsibilities, inefficient, and distort and misinterpret the law. Struggles for power in Greece do not end with general elections; they go on in the area of autonomous public administration (Papaderos, 1986).

Legitimacy Deficit of the State. The shortcomings of a centralized and bureaucratic state become more evident as free market economies press for deregulation, flexibility, decentralized decision making, and innovation. It is now widely accepted that a state characterized by legal,

administrative, and structural rigidity and that "stifles the abilities of gifted and highly motivated people" (OECD, 1993, par. 4) is quite inappropriate. It should change in the direction of a transition from the public to the private, from protection to competition, from the group to the individual (Economou, 1993).

New conditions make it impossible for the Greek state to continue functioning as it has in the past. There is a need for radical change in political and social attitudes and values. It may now be possible to make this change because of the emergence of a small but dynamic private sector that has adopted the West European ethos and is envigored by participation in the EU. Participation has also opened up new channels of communication for Greek individuals and institutions (Economou, 1993).

Relations with Turkey

In addition to the above issues, which are all related to the European Union, there is also the major issue of Greece's strained relations with Turkey. There are many people in Greece who believe that there will be an armed conflict in the near future (Someritis, 1997). In an effort to dissuade Turkey from any thoughts of making an offensive strike, the Greek government is spending, in the words of the Prime Minister, "disproportionate" amounts of public money on armaments.

In result, it becomes more difficult daily for the Greek economy to meet the Maastricht requirements. It also means that there will be a need for severe cuts in other sectors, among them education, in order to save money for defense. Finally, these developments will certainly fan nationalism and make it more difficult for any initiatives toward multicultural education.

All these unpropitious developments and prospects have led some politicians and intellectuals (Mouzelis, 1997) to advocate abandoning the policy of a confrontational stance against Turkey. They advocate instead an alternative policy based mainly on diplomacy and on friendly relations with the EU and the United States.

In Education

There are four major issues in education: controversy over curriculum changes in secondary education; concerns over equity, quality, and quantity in higher education; debate on what should be the role of the state in education; and unimplemented reform plans. As will be shown, these four education issues are closely related to the societal issues discussed in the preceding section.

Curriculum Change in Secondary Education. Controversy over changes to the secondary school curriculum focuses on attempts to substitute modern and practical knowledge for the humanistic body of knowledge traditionally taught in secondary schools. This is not new; the issue provoked polemic debates from the late nineteenth century up to the late 1970s. Every time such a proposal was advanced, church leaders, professors at the University of Athens, and conservative intellectual and political forces rallied a strong opposition that defeated the proposed reform.

In the last twenty years, however, a profound change has taken place. Although there continue to be strong differences over other education issues, there is surprising political consensus and tacit agreement to accept this reform. The only caveat is not allowing a modernization of the secondary school curriculum to go to the extent of completely eliminating the humanities curriculum (Kazamias, 1995).

This profound change in attitude is the result of a deep concern on the part of both conservative and progressive social, intellectual, and political leaders in Greece over the impact modern technology and Greece's accession to EU will have on Greek identity and culture. It is an acknowledgment that Greece will be integrated into the EU and therefore education must somehow find a way to achieve two conflicting objectives: strengthening national ideals and Greek identity, while simultaneously facilitating the integration of Greece into the EU.

The fact that Greece has never had a tradition of multicultural education makes the problem particularly difficult. It is significant that, even though Greece has been a member of the EU since 1981, no major effort has yet been made in this direction. There is significant cultural resistance to the structuring of European space in Greece (Kassotakis, 1994).

Accordingly, the author believes that there is a need for an ideological reconceptualization in Greece. In fact, such an attempt was made back in 1958. A Committee on Education was instructed by the administration to come up with proposals for the modernization of primary, secondary, and higher education. The Committee proposed a new ideology that they labeled "broad and lofty humanism" based on "a broad and lofty conception of Greekness." The proposal was not taken up. But in present day political and educational discourse there is a renewed call for modern Greece to stand up to the challenge of taking an active role in the construction of a new Europe, thus proving that it is a worthy successor of Ancient Greece (Kassotakis, 1994, p. 27). But the call remains rhetoric.

The result is that the necessary public and political consensus to give the government a legitimate mandate to proceed in this direction does not exist. Without such support, the Greek government is reluctant to act unilaterally. Thus, measures to implement policies of multicultural education that would make Greeks fully cognizant and tolerant of other cultures while remaining sufficiently aware and committed to their cultural heritage have not materialized (OECD, 1993, par. 5).

There is also a need for more specialization in, and emphasis upon, science and technical subjects. Recently, demands for putting more emphasis on these subjects, along with abandoning traditional formal pedagogy, have greatly increased. The need for higher technical skills has increasingly been underlined by international competition, and some new community programs have opened fresh opportunities for Greek vocational and technical schools and their students (Kassotakis, 1994).

All these developments, together with an increasing heterogeneity of Greek society, a serious economic recession, and high unemployment, have resulted in a breakdown of consensus over education goals. In the minds of parents, there is a direct link between knowledge, success in university entrance examinations, and future employment. This notion of education is very different from the objectives of education expressed in the constitution, laws, and official statements. In a situation like this, the task of curriculum change becomes even more controversial.

Equity, Quality, and Quantity in Higher Education. Our second major education issue focuses on higher education. Here, the matter is complex. It really consists of six problems, all of which seem intractable at the moment. These problems are the great demand for access to higher education, the large number of Greek students abroad, equity, modalities of student selection, private coaching for university entrance exams, and status differences between the three-year technological institutions (TEIs) and four-year universities.

Demand for higher education continues unabated. Neither a great increase in the number of university places over the last twenty years nor establishment of TEIs has managed to reduce the intensity of the problem. Every year, there are still about 140,000 candidates for only 40,000 places in universities.

One reason behind this great demand for university education is an unrealistically optimistic expectation of high returns on investment in higher education. This is in spite of the fact that the actual economic return for university education had diminished from 15 percent in the 1950s and 1960s to 2 to 3 percent by the end of the 1980s as a result of too many graduates. Students and parents, however, are either not aware of, or oblivious to, this new reality (Lambropoulos & Psacharopoulos, 1992). Another reason is the high social status conferred on people with university qualifications. This has traditionally been the case, and in a society of closely knit families this parental attitude continues to be widely inculcated in the younger generation (Economou, 1993).

One result of this great demand for higher edu-

cation is the large percentage of Greek students studying in foreign universities. In this regard, Greece ranks second only to Hong Kong (Lambropoulos & Psacharopoulos, 1992). This serious drain of foreign currency reserves and education manpower to other countries is a constant concern for Greek politicians, economists, and sociologists.

The government is being pressed to cope with the problem by increasing the number of university places and by modifying the constitutional clause that prohibits private universities. There are already signs that the ministry of education is showing preference for the first solution.

The minister of education has announced plans for a yearly increase of new places by 10 percent, leading to an abolition of *numerus clausus* in the year 2000 and the establishment of an Open University (Despotopoulos, 1991). In the meantime, the government does not seem to object to some branches of foreign universities (for example, New York College, under the State University of New York) operating in Greece unconstitutionally. It is also expected that the pressure for constitutional change will increase along with Greece's continued economic integration with the EU.

The third problem in higher education, equity, is related to the fact that higher education is free in Greece. All political parties support this on the principle that it promotes a transfer of resources from the rich to the poor, thereby contributing to social equality. However, education economists (Lambropoulos & Psacharopoulos, 1992) have shown that public subsidization of higher education leads to the opposite result. This is because the rich are overrepresented in higher education. Nonetheless, all political parties have turned a deaf ear to that finding and continue to support free higher education. The conclusion of some Greek social scientists is that ideology and reality are not the same in Greece (Mouzelis, 1996b).

The problem of modalities of student selection is often a subject of debate from the viewpoint of equity and quality. It is argued that university selection criteria, which are based on written examinations, reward passive knowledge, rote memorization, and are pedagogically neither valid nor reliable. These criticisms prompted the government to come up with a proposal, in 1996, for a National Leaving Certificate (*Ethniko Apolyterio*) on the model of the French baccalaureate. The explicit aim was to enhance the quality of learning in the lyceum by encouraging individual learning, promoting critical thinking, and developing analytic and synthetic skills (Ministry of National Education and Religion, 1996). However, just a few months later, the plan was withdrawn. The reason given at the time was a need for further scientific study of the whole project. But, in view of recent plans to gradually abolish *numerus clausus,* it is safe to say that the project has been virtually abandoned.

Parapaedeia (private coaching) is viewed as one of the greatest problems in Greek education. It costs parents huge amounts of money and therefore defeats the idea of free higher education. It also suggests, since parents have to go outside it to maximize their children's learning, that the public system is inefficient and unsatisfactory. The situation is aggravated by the fact that low salaries seem to be a motive for some teachers to encourage this practice. All government efforts to cope with the situation have been in vain.

The problem inherent in a binary higher education system (that is, a system divided into three-year technological institutes and four-year universities) is again a problem of equity. In the 1970s, the state established three-year higher technological institutions (TEIs) for two main reasons: first, to increase the number of technically trained personnel; second, to accommodate the tremendous demand for higher education.

The governance and financing of these institutions are almost identical to that of universities. However, from their inception they were hierarchically distinguished from universities. They were labeled as institutions of higher education, while universities were designated institutions of highest education. In result, academic qualifications granted by TEIs have a lower social status than university degrees, and the majority of their students come from lower socioeconomic backgrounds (Psacharopoulos, 1989). TEI students

resenting this distinction have repeatedly demanded that TEIs be upgraded into universities, but the government has not yet yielded to the pressure. However, the general feeling is that the state, following the general trend in Europe, will eventually make the change.

Role of the State.   Our third major education issue is the role of the state in education. This is crucial for many aspects of education, such as equality of opportunity, diversity and flexibility, quality, and the professionalization of teachers.

Equality in Greece is identified with uniformity. People believe that diversification automatically leads to some areas, or groups, or individuals benefiting at the expense of others. The result has been strong support for centralized administrations, with authority to distribute public money and public posts equally. Importantly, distribution is based on the principle of absolute equality; further rational or empirical criteria are not invoked. How teacher appointments are made provides an illustration: The ministry drafts a waiting list of names of graduates (*epeterida*) solely on the basis of the date of graduation. Merit or suitability for a particular job are not considered.

Although there has been some movement toward decentralization, results have been very disappointing. Researchers even argue that some of the measures taken have in fact led to more centralization (OECD, 1993). Until now, the state has turned a deaf ear to calls for more local authority and school freedom "within the principle of elective public control," and for the open advertisement of teaching and professional posts coupled with measures that would "guard against clientism and patronage" (OECD, 1993, par. 28). The truth is, such calls have not come from either the general public or the people directly concerned (teachers). They come from social scientists and comparative educators concerned with the rational use of resources in education and quality in education. What matters politically is that voters are still in favor of uniformity.

It is of course true that, by contributing toward social cohesion, uniformity served the nation well in the past. In present conditions, however, it is very unproductive. It stops education from responding to student diversity, to different regional and local needs, and it obstructs efforts at quality improvement.

Reform. Our final education issue is a concern about a long series of abortive educational reforms. Some historians of education attribute the failure of reforms to the economic dependency of the country (Bouzakis, 1991). One sociologist of education explains it as a result of a complex political discontinuity (Frankoudaki, 1992). Kazamias (1995) presented it as the result of four interplaying factors, namely the nature and the role of the Greek state, the nature of Greek socioeconomic formation, the relative autonomy of schools, and the contradiction of the liberal reforms themselves. He described it as "the curse of Sisyphos."

All these theories, however, explain only why educational reforms were not implemented. They do not account for why so many administrations from different political and ideological convictions have made the design and planning of educational reforms such a priority. The author believes that a satisfactory explanation for this emphasis on planning is the need of the Greek state for compensatory legitimization.

Almost exclusively until the 1970s, the state utilized legislation and invoking the constitution as strategies to legitimate itself. Since the restoration of democracy in 1974, there has been a great increase in sensitivity to democratic rights. People question not only the authority of the state as decision maker, but also the modalities of decision making and the nature of the process itself. This has forced the Greek state to employ additional strategies—those of expertise and participation (Weiler, 1988, 1990).

One example of the strategy of expertise was the reestablishment in 1976 of the Pedagogical Institute. This scientific institution provides analyses and scientific justification for education reforms the state may wish to introduce. The socialist PASOK government of the late 1980s

and 1990s provides an interesting example of the strategy of participation. Although implemented halfheartedly and carried out with limited success, provisions for the decentralization and democratization of education were made. Various representative bodies for democratic planning were established that would participate at the national, regional, and local levels, and political parties, trade unions, rural organizations, and parent associations were to be represented. School and university students were also given a voice through participation in various representative bodies (Bouzakis, 1991; Pesmazoglu, 1994).

The above four issues give a broad account of contemporary education discourse in Greece. All four are burning issues and are closely connected to major concerns and expectations in the national, political, social, and economic life of the country. They are debated in parliament and in the media, as well as at teacher trade union assemblies and education conferences; they are the subject of empirical research at the Pedagogical Institute and in university departments of education. As the debates go on, one notices a gradual transformation of the education discourse from a mainly political tone and stance in the 1960s and 1970s, to a more scientific one as the century closes.

THE FUTURE OF SOCIETY AND SCHOOLING IN GREECE

The preceding discussions on social and educational issues can shed some light on the direction in which Greek society and schooling might evolve. At least six developments are possible:

- Family ties will loosen.
- Economic influences will have increasingly profound social implications.
- State powers will decrease as civil power increases.
- Society will become more and more multicultural.
- Education institutions will become more flexible.
- Education reforms will be implemented.

First, developments in the Greek family will affect both society and education. Loosening of family ties will mean that the evils of modern society (crime, drugs, AIDS), which until recently have been rather limited in Greece, will be aggravated. There will also be less demand for higher education as the younger generation emancipates itself from the values of the older.

The economy will most notably influence social changes through occupational restructuring. The number of self-employed and those employed in the civil sector will probably decrease. Because there will be a need for more highly trained people, education will lay more emphasis on "transferable skills" needed for employment. It will also mean that industry will probably undertake more technical training tasks.

In light of the developing social and economic situations, the federal state will not be able to maintain its power at present levels. It will have to hand over some of its powers to regional and local governments. Thus, it will have to develop alternative means of administration, beyond those defined by strict and detailed legislation. One approach may be to define objectives, and then call upon citizens to achieve them in their own individual ways (OECD, 1993). There will also be pressure to substitute meritocracy and fair play for clientism and patronage.

As for the demographic evolution of Greek society into a multicultural entity, this will mean more openness toward, and understanding of, foreign cultures. There will also be more emphasis on foreign language teaching in schools.

As these social changes continue, education will probably be pressed to become more flexible. One result will be a greater emphasis upon community-based programs. There will also be more attention paid to quality in education. In view of the fact that the public system has great difficulty in changing, this will probably mean that the private sector in education will expand. Privatization will also occur in the university sector, where the state will be forced to abolish the constitutional prohibition against private universities.

The state will continue to use education reforms for compensatory legitimization. However, these will not be *grandes reforms,* as was the case until recently. Future reforms will consist of minor changes aimed at piecemeal improvements in the quality of the public system. However, putting through even such minor reforms will not be an easy task. There will be a constant necessity to legitimate not only the content of decisions, but also the decision-making process itself. This means that the state will have to show that proposed changes have been scientifically planned and empirically evaluated before they are introduced into the system. It also means that those affected by reforms will be actively involved in all the stages of the reform; that is, study, design, planning, and implementation. All these changes mean that the state and the public education systems will have increasing difficulty acting unilaterally.

REFERENCES

Bouzakis, S. (1991). *Modern Greek education.* Athens: Gutenberg. (In Greek).

Bouzakis, S. (1992). Education reforms during the 1980s: An analytical interpretive approach of the new efforts and the new impasses. In J. Pyrgiotakis (Ed.), *World crisis in education.* Athens: Gregoris. (In Greek).

Christodoulos (Bishop of Dimitrias). (1997, 19 January). The Greek nation and Europe. *To Vima,* p. A.17. (In Greek).

Despotopoulos, K. (Minister of Education). (1991). *Education and the 1992 prospects and consequences.* Address before the Secondary School Teachers Association Conference. Athens. (In Greek).

Economou, G. (1993). Greece: Shaping factors. In A. Jacquemin & D. Wright (Eds.), *European challenges post-1992: Shaping factors, shaping actors.* Aldershot: Edward Eglar Publishing Limited.

Flouris, G. (1992). Disharmony between educational laws, school program, textbooks, and teaching practice: An aspect of crisis in Greek education. In J. Pyrgiotakis (Ed.), *World crisis in education.* Athens: Gregoris. (In Greek).

Frankoudaki, A. (1992). *Educational reform and liberal intellectuals* (7th ed.). Athens: Kedros. (In Greek).

Kassotakis, M. (1994). Greece. In C. Brock & W. Tulasiewicz (Eds.), *Education in a single Europe.* London: Routledge.

Kazamias, A. (1968). Greece: Modernizing secondary education. In T.R. Murray, S. Lester, & D. Brubaker (Eds.), *Strategies for curriculum change: Cases from thirteen nations.* Scranton, PA: International Textbook Company.

Kazamias, A. (1995). The curse of Sisyphos: The tormenting course of Greek educational reform. In A. Kazamias & M. Kassotakis (Eds.), *Greek education: Prospects of reconstruction and modernization.* Athens: Sirios. (In Greek).

Kazamias, A., & Kassotakis, M. (1995). Educational manifesto: Problematic for the restructuring and modernization of Greek education. In A. Kazamias & M. Kassotakis (Eds.), *Greek education: Prospects of reconstruction and modernization.* Athens: Sirios. (In Greek).

King, E.J. (1967). *Other schools and ours. A comparative study for today.* London: Holt, Rinehart and Winston.

Lambropoulos, H., & Psacharopoulos, G. (1992). Educational expansion and earnings differentials in Greece. *Comparative Education Review, 36,* 52–70.

Ministry of National Education and Religion. (1996). *National leaving certificate: Guarantee of knowledge, a passport for life.* Athens: Author. (In Greek).

Mouzelis, N. (1992). *Metamarxist perspectives.* Athens: Themelio. (In Greek).

Mouzelis, N. (1996a, October). *Multi-cultural Europe: Strategies of educational and cultural integration.* Paper presented at the 17th CESE Conference. (In Greek).

Mouzelis, N. (1996b, November). *The citizen of the 21st century.* Paper presented at the First Pedagogical Meeting organized by the Cyprus Education Association, Nicosia. (In Greek).

Mouzelis, N. (1997, January). What is the appropriate alternative in foreign policy? *To Vima,* p. D15. (In Greek).

National Statistical Service of Greece. (1995). *Concise statistical yearbook of Greece, 1994.* Athens: Author. (In Greek).

OECD, Organization for Economic Co-operation and Development. (1993). *Educational policy review of Greece* (Prepared by Denis Kallen, Maurice Kogan, and George Papadopoulos). Paris: OECD.

Papaderos, A. (1986). Points of attrition during implementation. In A. Kazamias & M. Kassotakis (Eds.), *Educational reforms in Greece: Efforts, impasses, prospects.* Rethymno: Crete. (In Greek).

Pesmazoglu, S. (1994). Government, ideology and university curriculum in Greece. *European Journal of Education, 29,* 291–304.

Psacharopoulos, G. (1989, 29 June). Efficiency and equity in higher education. *Financial Mail.* (In Greek).

Psacharopoulos, G. (1990). Education and the professions in Greece in the light of 1992. *European Journal of Education, 25,* 61–74.

Someritis, R. (1997, 19 January). Those in Greece who want war. *To Vima.* (In Greek).

Theorakopoulos, J. (1976, February). The importance of ancient Greek. *Kathemerine,* 8. (In Greek).

Vaughan, M., & Mark-Lawson, J. (1986). The downgrading of the humanities in French and English secondary education. *Comparative Education, 22,* 133–147.

Weiler, H. (1988). The politics of reform and nonreform in French education. *Comparative Education Review, 32,* 251–265.

Weiler, H. (1990). Curriculum reform and the legitimization of educational objectives: The case of the Federal Republic of Germany. *Oxford Review of Education, 16,* 15–27.

CHAPTER 11

Changing Contexts and Evolving Prospects: Societal and Educational Dynamics in Switzerland

PETER BONATI

Peter Bonati is a professor in the School of Education (Schulpädagogik) *and Director of Teacher Training for secondary level II at the Department for Higher Secondary Teacher Education, University of Berne, Switzerland. His publications are in the fields of German education* (Fachdidaktik Deutsch) *and school education* (Schulpädagogik)*. He is presently engaged in a study titled "Change in Maturity Schools: 1964–1994" ("Das Gymnasium in Wandel-Veräanderungen an Maturitätsschulen 1964–1994").*

For a small country, Switzerland has a great number of educational systems. Education lies essentially within the competence of the twenty-six cantons and the federal state only supports them. There is no federal ministry of education but actually twenty-six different school systems. They differ in the number of primary school years, in the structure of cantonal secondary schools, in the amount of weeks of vacation, and in the salary of the teaching staff.*

*I would like to thank Mr. Moritz Arnet, general secretary of the Swiss Conference of Cantonal Ministers of Education, Berne; his staff, Ms. Annemarie Streit and Ms. Helen Lehmann for their valuable advice and additional information; Ms. Regula Grossen for her translation of the manuscript; and Ms. Brigitte Müller and Ms. Dorothea Lanz, assistants at the Department for Higher Secondary Teacher Education at the University of Berne, for their research and critical checking of material.

THE SOCIAL FABRIC

Country

Switzerland is a small country, covering an area of 41,300 square kilometers. It is bordered in the north by Germany, in the west by France, in the south by Italy, and in the east by Austria and the principality of Liechtenstein. The three main regions are the Central Plain between Lake Constance and Lake Geneva; the Jura in the northwest; and the Alps, which stretch from the southwest to the northeast. The main rivers rise in the Alps: The river Rhine runs into the North Sea, the river Rhone into the Mediterranean, the river Inn into the Danube. Berne is the seat of the federal government, while Zurich is the biggest city and financial center. Geneva is the center of international relations.

Population and Culture

In 1996 the population of Switzerland was just over 7 million inhabitants, but it is only growing slowly. The percentage of elderly people is constantly increasing, similar to Japan and the north European states. In 1950, the age group above 65 was still 9.6 percent; by 1990, it reached 14.6 percent. The average life expectancy is 80.8 years for women and 74.1 years for men.

At the same time, the percentage of the age group 0 to 19 years has decreased from 30.6 percent to 23.4 percent (Gretler, 1995). This age structure is a burden for the social insurances (retirement insurance, health insurance) insofar as the costs rise continually and the decades-old idea of solidarity, whereby the working population pays a certain percentage of their salary toward the retirement insurance that is paid directly to the elderly people, is now being discussed openly.

Compared to the rest of Europe, the proportion of foreigners (19 percent in 1994) is relatively high, accentuating the multicultural element, which has always been historically present in Switzerland, thanks to the various languages and religious denominations. The four official languages are German, French, Italian, and Rhaeto-Romanic, which are also the mediums of instruction in school. Of the twenty-six Swiss cantons, twenty-two cantons teach in one language, three cantons in two languages (German and French), while one canton, namely Graubünden, runs schools in three languages (German, Italian, Rhaeto-Romanic). The language distribution is shown in Table 11.1.

As to religious denomination, 46.1 percent are Roman Catholics, 40 percent are Protestants, 5 percent belong to other religions, and 8.9 percent are without a professed religion (BBW/BIGA/BFS/Sekretariat EDK, 1995). Whereas at the time of the Reformation and in the middle of the nineteenth century, religious disputes often led to civil wars, nowadays the different religious denominations live alongside one another in peace. A rise in mobility of the population and the ecumenical movement, as well as an increasing religious ab-stinence, have had a calming effect. However, certain problems have arisen through the emergence of fundamentalistic movements (for example, cults in Protestantism and radically conservative movements in Catholicism) as well as the complications involved in the integration of people with non-Christian denominations.

The family structure is also changing. The divorce rate is relatively high compared to other European countries and the proportion of one-parent-families (especially with mothers) is rising. Parents and children, but also authorities and political groups, make great demands on the school system—demands that used to be met by the family and the social environment.

Political System

In 1291 three central Swiss cantons (Uri, Schwyz, Unterwalden) founded a first alliance. The collapse of the old confederation at the end of the eighteenth century, the Napoleonic wars at the beginning of the nineteenth century, and a state crisis from 1798 to 1848 made way for modern Switzerland. In 1848, the modern state with twenty-five cantons and a new federal constitution was founded. In 1978, the canton of Jura was added.

Government and administration are still at three levels: a federal level, the cantons, and the communities. At the federal level, a Federal Council governs. It consists of seven ministers who belong to the four biggest parties. Legislative power

TABLE 11.1 Language Distribution

	PERCENTAGE OF POPULATION WHO SPEAK . . .	LESSONS ARE TAUGHT IN . . .
German	63.7%	73.0%
French	19.3%	22.0%
Italian	7.6%	5.0%
Rhaeto-Romance	0.6%	0.5%
Other languages	8.9%	

Sources: BBW/BIGA/BFS/Sekretariat EDK, 1995, p. 9; OECD Indicators, 1996.

consists of two houses: a National Council (200 deputies representing ten political parties) and a Cantonal Council (46 deputies, normally two per canton).

For our purposes, there are three most important features of the political system. The first revolves around internal stability. There are certainly changes of power at elections and now and then some surprises during certain votes, but generally there is peace and quiet, a certain stalemate among the big parties, a continual slow reform of the administration, and a policy of consent between the various lobbies, parties, cantons, and regions of the country.

The second salient feature is direct democracy. The people decide by vote many questions of national importance, but above all about cantonal and communal issues. By means of initiatives and petitions for a referendum, the political parties and interested groups can additionally submit controversial issues (for example, the operation of nuclear power stations or genetic engineering) to the people.

Finally, Switzerland has the feature of open neutrality. Switzerland is neither part of the UN nor the European Union (EU), but part of many subsidiary UN organizations and of supranational organizations (for example, OSZE, OECD, Partnership for Peace). However, Swiss foreign policy is increasingly broadening its range. At the present time, there are negotiations with the EU about a bilateral agreement that should regulate the movement of people, economic exchange, traffic by land and by air, and other important issues.

While the cantons have a similar political structure to the Confederation (cantonal government, analogous structure of administration with a single-chamber system), the cantons do not have much say in foreign and security policy. However, they do have a great deal to say in the educational system. And, to create synergy and to reduce costs, most of the medium-sized and smaller cantons cooperate (for example, in the provision of hospitals, schools for further education, and the supply of energy).

The 3,029 local communities have consider-able autonomy. Every community, for example, has its own taxation rates. The differences are considerable and partially responsible for a community's attractiveness.

Economy

Switzerland developed relatively early from an agrarian to an industrial country and finally to a service-dominated economy that is still growing (banks, insurances, public services, tourism, education system). This process was accompanied by increasing urbanization. All in all, 59.8 percent of the population live in an urban environment, 40.2 percent in rural areas.

Because of a lack of natural resources, the economy strongly depends on exports, mainly of high-quality products. However, imports exceed exports slightly. From the 1950s to the middle of the 1970s, the economy developed continually. After the oil crisis and the collapse in the middle of the 1970s, it recovered quickly and there was a period of economic boom in the 1980s when the services sector, the proportion of foreign labor, the revenues from taxation, general prosperity, and individual demands were growing. There was also a strong increase in the number of women in the labor force.

Until recently, the state heavily subsidized weak sectors, most obviously agriculture, and the economy was relatively highly regulated. From the beginning of the 1990s, the policy has been one of a "social market economy." The state is reducing its interference, but supports ailing sectors so that they can survive. This deregulation is moderated by social welfare contributions that are partially made by the state (dependents' allowance, obligatory retirement insurance AHV, unemployment insurance, compensation of salary for people who do compulsory military service) and partially covered by reductions in salary as well as taxation. A part of it is also directly financed by the persons affected (retirement insurance, health and accident insurance, personal pension schemes).

Switzerland has the second highest pro rata

income ($40,600) in the world. From the beginning of the 1990s, recession has affected many parts of the Swiss economy. The rate of unemployment increased from 1.8 percent to 5.3 percent between 1991 and May, 1997, then dropped to 3.5 percent by early 1999. The Ticino and the French-speaking cantons are most affected. Even if rates are relatively low compared to other countries and the persons affected are well insured, the public is very concerned by the problem of unemployment, which constitutes a big challenge to education policy.

SCHOOLING

General Structure of Formal System of Education

Preschool.   Normally, 99 percent of all Swiss children spend one or two years in kindergarten (nursery school). Kindergartens strive for a balance between play and preparation for school. In the French-speaking part of Switzerland there is an emphasis on the latter. The classes are mixed and usually contain between twelve and twenty-five children.

Primary School.   Primary school begins mostly at the age of 7, relatively late compared to other European states. It lasts four, five, or in most cases six years, depending on the cantons. Primary school is a comprehensive school with the exception of classes for handicapped children.

The smallest schools in rural areas are made up of one single class, containing several school years, and even the biggest schools in the cities do not have more than several hundred pupils. The number of lessons per week is between twenty (class one) and thirty-six (upper classes). The school year lasts 36 to 40 weeks. The classes usually contain between fourteen and twenty-eight children.

Secondary Level 1 (ISCED 2).   Sometime between the ages of 11 and 13, pupils start their lower-secondary education, which lasts three to five years, depending on the canton. While in the last few years there has been a certain tendency toward comprehensive schools, in most cantons schools are still classified into two groups. About 60 percent of all pupils go to schools with extended requirements, and about 30 percent go to schools with basic requirements. The classes usually contain between fifteen and twenty-eight children. Both at the beginning and at the end of lower secondary education, important decisions are made about the pupils through examinations (see BBW/BIGA/BFS/Sekretariat EDK, 1995).

Secondary Level II (ISCED 3).   About 93 percent of an age cohort start an upper-secondary education; 85 percent of these students finish this education. The classes usually contain between ten and twenty-five children. What is significant in Switzerland is the internationally unique proportion of vocational training (75 percent of all students at secondary level II) (OECD Indicators, 1996). The Swiss maturity exam rate of 17.5 percent is therefore relatively low.

Vocational Training.   Similar to Germany, Austria, and Denmark, this training follows an individual system. The students serve an apprenticeship after the compulsory school years and acquire practical skills in an enterprise during three to four days a week. They receive theoretical and general instruction in a vocational school during the rest of the weekdays. In addition, the apprentices attend special courses from trade organizations, which means that the training is actually often threefold. The proportion of purely school education is low; it is mostly found in the French-speaking part of Switzerland (in training workshops and schools). About 260 jobs can be learned in this way.

Maturity Schools (Type of Grammar Schools, ISCED 3).   The traditional school type at secondary level II school is the *Gymnasium,* which offers a broad and general theoretical education. The most important criterion for the school curriculum is still good preparation for university.

The structures are not uniform. Depending on the canton, they extend from a short-term *Gymnasium,* which lasts three years after the compulsory school years, to a long-term *Gymnasium,* which starts after the completion of primary school and lasts six to seven years.

Diploma Schools (ISCED 3).   This relatively new school type prepares students for tertiary vocational training over a period of two years.

Tertiary Education (ISCED 5 and 6).   The tertiary level reflects in many ways the situation at the secondary level II. Whereas only 13 percent of the young adults enroll at a university, 27 percent enroll for extra-university vocational training. Compared to other European countries, this is a relatively high proportion.

Universities.   Switzerland has twelve universities: five cantonal universities in the German-speaking part of Switzerland (Basel, Zurich, Berne, St. Gall, and Lucerne); four in the French-speaking part (Lausanne, Geneva, Neuchâtel, and Fribourg/bilingual); and the two federal institutes of technology in Zurich and Lausanne. Very recently, a university opened also in the Italian-speaking part of Switzerland. The academic year lasts thirty weeks.

Extra-university Tertiary Training.   Apart from a small proportion of teacher training, extra-university tertiary training is mainly vocational training. After the completion of an apprenticeship, interested students can get further qualifications in two ways: either through attending an institute of higher education (*Fachhochschule*) or through attending courses organized by trade organizations that prepare them for higher professional examinations.

Further Education.   Special courses are aimed at adults. They are offered by private organizations that are sometimes ideologically based (*Volkshochschulen*), commercially based by associations, or government-based institutions (communities, universities for senior citizens).

Main Considerations

Despite the great variety of education systems seen in Switzerland, there is also a lot of common ground. Commonalities may be summarized as:

- *Education is mainly a public task.* Since the nineteenth century when school attendance became compulsory, most schools have been public. Children of all social classes should have equal opportunities, and the schools themselves are ideologically and denominationally neutral.

Maturity schools, teacher training colleges, colleges of higher education, and universities are public. There are only a few private schools, though most adult education is also private. Hence, public policy is to support a broad education rather than to promote a small elite.

- *The education system is decentralized.* Education and schools are mainly a cantonal matter and every canton organizes its schools differently. This autonomy is an important expression of political and cultural identity, claimed not only by the canton, but also by smaller units. The community looks for its own teachers, and every single school has its own financial budget. This variety, however, is expensive and makes mobility difficult.

- *Culture is democratic.* All levels in the education system have a say in the various matters. Even the teaching staff in a school will be heard before an important decision is made. The population votes on all important decisions such as opening new schools, buildings, and education laws. Given this popular vote, the change of the school system from four years primary school and five years secondary level I to the prevailing system of six years primary school and three years secondary level I was passionately discussed in the canton of Berne and finally only approved of by a narrow majority. As well, a drawback is that all these decisions take up a lot of time.

- *The schools should assist the regions with mutual agreements.* In order to secure peace and understanding between the different language speaking and cultural regions, children are taught a further official language as early as the fifth school year (French or Italian for German-speaking children, German for French-speaking and Italian-speaking children). Regionally, interlingual education is gaining more and more importance. In bilingual and transitional regions (Fribourg, Valais, Bienne, Graubünden), the same class is taught in their first language for some subjects and in their second language for others.

Syllabuses and Curricula

The cantons are responsible for curricula, which are developed by committees on which teaching staff are well represented. There is considerable freedom in teaching methodology and instruction materials for the individual teacher. New teaching methods have long been initiated by experimental groups such as the educational institutes of the universities, the teacher training institutes, and individual teams of teachers. Most of the innovations concern new methods of teaching, interdisciplinary learning, and student assessment. In more recent times, the government has also promoted methodological reform. An example of this is a project, "Enlarged Learning Forms," which started in northwestern Switzerland in 1990 (BBW/BIGA/BFS/Sekretariat EDK, 1995; OECD Indicators, 1996).

Generally speaking, primary schools, lower secondary schools, and teacher training institutes are open to reforms. Maturity schools and the universities are less so.

In terms of levels of education, syllabuses and curricula can be described by the following:

Primary Schools and Secondary Level I.   In primary schools more elementary subjects and more recently, interdisciplinary subjects, such as Man-Nature-Environment, are taught. The individual teachers are all-rounders and teach most subjects themselves. At the secondary level I, the following subjects are offered: native language, mathematics, second official language, natural sciences, geography, history/political science, arts. In schools for extended education, there are additions such as a third language, bookkeeping, and

classical languages. Teachers mostly teach two to five subjects.

Secondary Level II/Maturity Schools.   Recently, education goals and national curriculum recommendations (*Rahmenlehrpläne*) have been centrally developed. The latest reform replaces the former types of matura diploma by a uniform matura diploma with extended optional subject choices for each student. The individual teachers are free to choose whatever teaching material they think appropriate.

Vocational Training.   Here the government is responsible for the curriculum. It cooperates closely with the employers' federation and trade unions.

Teacher Training.   Teacher training is being standardized at present. The traditional teacher training colleges are making way for education at a tertiary level as we discuss in more detail below.

Universities.   The course of studies lasts from eight to ten full-time semesters for a *licentiate* (degree) or diploma; in medicine it is twelve to thirteen semesters. Normally, the licentiate is taken in one to three subjects and corresponds to a masters degree. Only a minority of students finish with a doctorate or do postgraduate studies.

The universities have provided further education for academic and nonacademic professionals for several years. However, correspondence degree courses at Swiss universities are little known.

Organization and Supervisory Structure

Areas of Competence.   The twenty-six cantons enact the laws themselves and delegate the organization of the kindergartens and of the compulsory schools to the communities. The federally determined competencies are restricted to a few important but limited areas. For example, the Confederation sees to and controls vocational education (in cooperation with the cantons) and physical education/sports. It supports the technical institutes in Zurich and Lausanne, the Swiss Institute for Vocational Education (*Schweizerisches Institut für Berufspädagogik*) and the Federal Sports School (*Eidgenössische Sportschule*). As well, access to medical studies and to the federal institutes of technology (ETH) and the recognition of maturity diplomas is ensured federally. The Confederation also finances cantonal tasks (scientific research at the cantonal universities, scholarship allowances), and the Swiss schools abroad. It controls the education and integration of handicapped children and young adults, and launches temporary education programs (for example, research programs, impulses for further education, support of young academics, European cooperation) (see BBW/BIGA/BFS/Sekretariat EDK, 1995).

Coordination.   In order to secure a certain harmony in the federalist system, the Swiss Conference of Cantonal Directors of Education (SCCDE) was founded as early as 1897. The SCCDE has a permanent secretariat and is divided into regional conferences. Their most important agreement is the Concordat on School Coordination of 1970 in which the cantons agreed on an approximate age for school beginners, the duration of the compulsory school years, the duration of education up to the maturity diploma, and the point of time when the school year begins. In addition, this Concordat is a basis for the cantons to support a legal standardization, to cooperate in reforms, to recognize diplomas in all cantons, and to finance intercantonal school and university attendance.

Supervisory Structure.   There are full-time inspectors for the compulsory schools and for vocational training in certain regions. This function is carried out mainly by school directors at the upper-secondary education level. In addition, there are supervisory committees at all levels. As a rule, the universities do their own supervision autonomously.

Quality Assessment.   In order to make economical use of the available finances, to improve teaching, and to introduce a salary scale for teachers

based on efficiency, the authorities have initiated a system of quality development and maintenance at schools. Other countries have undergone such a development for quite some time; in Switzerland, however, it has mainly been a matter of further education. The assessment is often delegated to the institutions concerned, which cooperate with the authorities and the scientific institutes.

Evaluation

The Swiss school system is regarded as selective. There is an entrance requirement or exam for each level. The first takes place between primary school and secondary level I. Decisive for promotion, depending on the cantons, are average marks, recommendation of the teacher, final or entrance exam, and further assessments.

At the end of upper secondary education (ISCED 3) there is a final examination (maturity diploma/apprenticeship certificate). A maturity diploma gives free access to all Swiss universities. At the end of all courses at universities and higher technical colleges, there is also an examination (BBW/BIGA/BFS Sekretariat EDK, 1995; Gretler, 1995; OECD Indicators, 1996).

Features of Students

Here I will pick out only two questions. The first concerns the participation of women. The second question revolves around the integration of foreign children.

Women in Switzerland attained political rights relatively late, although now equality is slowly progressing. The proportion of young women with a maturity diploma is relatively high. It has risen from 30 percent to 51.1 percent in 1996 (BFS, 1996). However, the distribution among the individual professions is far from equal. There are typical female professions (for example, social services and health, retail, administration, personal hygiene, kindergarten and primary school teaching, that is, lower and intermediate functions) and typical male professions (technical-scientific professions, management, teachers at higher education schools, that is, senior positions). According to this distribution, women choose different subjects at the maturity schools, in vocational training, and at the faculties of the universities.

The proportion of foreign children is 23.9 percent in nursery school, 20.5 percent in primary school, and 20 percent at secondary level I. In schools with basic requirements, this proportion is as high as 31.8 percent; in schools with extended requirements it is only 14.8 percent. These children, mostly sons and daughters of immigrants, receive special language schooling. At secondary level II the proportion is 17.0 percent; in maturity schools 13.4 percent, other upper secondary level, 18 percent, and at tertiary level 16.3 percent (BFS, 1996).

Teaching Staff

International comparisons show that Swiss teachers work the longest hours (on average 1085 lessons per year). The international average is 912 lessons per year. At the bottom are Greece (696), Norway (686), and Sweden (624) (OECD Analysis, 1996). However, Swiss salaries are among the highest in the world. On average, the first salary of a primary school teacher is US$44,581 per year. No fewer than 46 percent of all Swiss teachers work part-time. There are more women in the lower schools and fewer in the upper schools.

On average, kindergarten teachers get approximately the same amount of money for a lesson as their colleagues in the primary schools. Other working conditions may differ, depending on the community. The kindergarten teachers strive for equality, via uniform, cantonally regulated working conditions, and by obtaining training similar to that of the primary school teachers.

For primary school and secondary level I teachers, the working conditions are laid down by cantonal laws. At secondary level I, there are primary school teachers with additional training for schools with basic requirements, and there are teachers for special subjects (two to four subjects) for schools with extended requirements.

Secondary level II/maturity school teachers have a university licentiate (degree) and teach one or two subjects. At the tertiary level there are the classical categories of lecturers at the universities and the federal institutes of technology. In extra-university tertiary education, there are specialists from the world of commerce, professionals for the special subjects, and teachers of secondary level II for more general subjects.

Teacher Training

Teacher training is being completely reformed in many cantons, frequently triggered off by changes in the school system. Efforts are being made to balance out the differences between the cantons; to orient training to school levels and not to school types; to recognize diplomas and certificates in all the cantons; and to take some of the load off the basic training in favor of further education. Note that the bigger cantons have their own institutions for further education. Years ago, for example, a national institute for further education was established for teachers of secondary level II in Lucerne (OECD Indicators, 1996).

For kindergarten and primary school teachers, one of the main reforms is the replacement of teacher training institutions that still exist at secondary level II by a tertiary training system. At secondary level I, teachers for schools with basic requirements are usually trained by the cantons; the greater number of teachers for schools with extended requirements undergo a university education.

For secondary level II/maturity and other schools for general education, teachers are trained at the universities and the federal institutes of technology (ETH). The course of studies usually takes six full years: five years of licentiate or diploma studies (in the relevant field) and one year of educational and didactic training. The education of teachers for secondary level II/vocational training depends on the field and is either held at the Swiss Institute for Vocational Education (*Schweizerischen Institut für Berufspädagogik*), at a university, or in special courses.

Adult Education

In 1992/1993 there were almost two million adults (40 percent) who participated in at least one course for further education—a statistic that makes Switzerland one of the leading countries in this respect. Further, the Confederation launched a generously remunerated program for further education, the so-called *Weiterbildungsoffensive* in the 1990s. Lifelong learning has also crossed the border into private initiative.

Costs and Financing

Public spending on education amounted to approximately 20 billion Swiss francs in 1996. This high proportion represents 20 percent of the overall expenses of the Confederation, the cantons, and communities. Education spending represents 5.4 percent of the gross national product, which is similar to other European countries (OECD Indicators, 1996).

The Confederation, the cantons, and the communities share the financial responsibilities. On average, the communities finance kindergarten and 35 percent of compulsory education, while the cantons finance post-compulsory education, a proportion of 53 percent of vocational training, and part of the tertiary level. The confederation pays towards vocational training, the universities, and institutes of higher education (*Fachhochschulen*).

Basically, there are no fees for public school attendance. At secondary level II, students are usually required to pay a certain amount toward the cost of school books and media. (A discussion is taking place at the moment about introducing a moderate school fee.) At the tertiary level, there are relatively low fees. Public university and institute of higher education fees are between 1000 and 1500 Swiss francs per year. The costs for further and adult education are considerably higher, and a further increase in fees is planned in order to cover the costs.

The barely sufficient resources available will force the universities to cooperate in a Swiss University (*Hochschule Schweiz*). In fact, the neighboring universities of Berne, Neuchâtel, and Fribourg cooperate in many fields of studies, and places to study medicine are allocated centrally. Costs are being reduced at practically all levels. For example, the University of Lausanne has to cut its budget by 22 million Swiss francs (or 9 percent), which has triggered off rationalization measures and closer cooperation with the University of Geneva.

Research in Education

Educational research has a long-standing tradition in the French-speaking part of Switzerland; for example, Claparède, Bovet, and Piaget. In the German-speaking part of Switzerland, there was an emphasis on philosophical and normative matters until the Second World War. Research in an experimental and empirical direction was established at the end of the 1960s. The most important pillars are university institutes, bigger cantonal or regional establishments of education, and private institutions (Gretler, 1995). The Swiss Science Council (*Wissenschaftsrat*) provides new impetus, coordinates matters, and in 1971 established the Swiss Coordination Center for Research in Education in Aarau. This mediates between widespread initiatives and provides information about current projects.

International Context

Since referring to a national education policy is virtually impossible, and since one can easily get lost in the "federal nature of the problems," I would now like to include the international context more explicitly than I have done up to now in order to facilitate a better grasp of the situation in Switzerland. Recent developments and the current situation of the education system and policy in OECD countries, of which Switzerland is also part, can be used to put matters into context.

First, I will refer to common aspects of Swiss and international developments in education and then to aspects in which they differ. I have therefore chosen two problems that I will discuss further: models for the combination of education and work that are being applied in Switzerland and the plight that is created by the increasing number of students striving for higher education but frustrated by the limitations of the education system.

Education Policy of the OECD

Although there are naturally many differences, OECD countries have the following objectives:

• *Enlarged participation at secondary level II and tertiary level.* Because the basic education of the population has reached a certain level and illiteracy has been virtually extinguished, endeavors have been shifted from primary school and secondary level I to secondary level II and tertiary level. One main objective is to make an education at these levels available for "all the citizens of all age groups" (OECD Analysis, 1996, p. 7). This is the same egalitarian ideal that was expressed years ago by the motto "Science for all Americans."

• *Promotion of lifelong learning.* Whoever participates in further education is ensuring his or her chances in a labor market that is today characterized by restructuring and a high rate of unemployment.

• *More efficient use of resources.* Whatever the countries invest in education should have a double effect. First, the national debt and the economic situation forces almost all countries to cut costs and to run education on the same amount of money or less than before. Second, efforts should be efficient in the sense of preparing young people as well as possible for the adult world and the labor market.

• *Improvement of vocational training.* The transition from an education system to an employment system is probably the most critical stage of the current developments. The OECD studies assign a very important role to vocational training. The aim is to improve training in this respect so that the transition is done optimally and that young people can be spared unemployment.

Swiss Peculiarities

These OECD objectives correspond more or less to the conviction of the policymakers and to the expectations of the Swiss population. However, our country has some remarkable peculiarities. They can be verified empirically by taking into consideration the so-called "education indicators"—important measures for a quantitative registration of the education systems—that are in most cases expressed as a number or proportion that allows "an insight into the comparative functioning of the education system—reflecting both on the resources invested as well as on the returns" (OECD Indicators, 1996, p. 9).

Recent studies by the OECD refer to four such indicators: participation at secondary level II, costs for education, level of education of the population, and transition from education to the employment system. I am going to restrict myself to those indicators where Switzerland deviates from the average of the OECD countries so as to bring out those aspects that are significant for our educational system.

• *Participation at secondary level II.* In the OECD countries, the participation in education has been rising continually for several decades. At secondary level II, participation has reached an average of 80 percent; in Switzerland, it is 85 percent (OECD Analysis, 1996).

• *Costs for education.* When the costs of education in Switzerland are compared to the Gross National Product, it is seen that they are slightly below the national average. However, when the costs of education per student and year are examined, it is obvious that Switzerland is at the top of the list (OECD Analysis, 1996).

There are several reasons why the pro rata costs in Switzerland are so high. First, compared to the whole population of Switzerland, the proportion of young people (5- to 29-year-olds) is relatively low due to a high percentage of old people. Therefore, the costs are distributed to fewer people. Second, the quantitative participation in education is lower because Swiss children start school relatively late. The third and main reason is the high salaries of teachers. Not only do Swiss teachers earn a very high salary compared to their colleagues in other countries, but comparisons in

Switzerland show that they also do very well with respect to the general pro rata income. Finally, the fact that the ratio of students per teacher (15.3 students per teacher) is relatively low is an additional reason for higher costs. In this respect, Switzerland also differs from almost all other OEC countries, which follow the principle: The higher the salaries of the teachers, the less a country can afford low students/teacher ratios (OECD Analysis, 1996). The only factor that lowers the costs is the fact that Swiss teachers work relatively long hours.

• *Educational level of population.* According to different statistics, the Swiss population has reached a considerably high level of education in certain fields. The average standard of achievement of 12- to 13-year-olds in mathematics is clearly above the OECD (see OECD Analysis, 1996). On the other hand, the reading and writing skills of the population between 16 and 65 years are only mediocre. However, one should take into consideration that the proportion of foreigners in this study—the International Survey on Reading and Writing Skills of Adults (IALS, 1994, cited in OECD Analysis, 1996, pp. 30–39)—was 23 percent. Another indication of the high level of education is the above-average participation of the population in further education.

• *Transition of education to employment.* According to the OECD, the problem of young people being unemployed is especially serious (OECD Analysis, 1996). A common objective, therefore, is to improve the transition between education and employment in order to spare younger people unemployment and other forms of exclusion.

ISSUES IN SWISS EDUCATION

Models Combining Education and Employment

Although unemployment in Switzerland is not as big a problem as in most other countries, it is still worrying. The Swiss economy is in the process of restructuring and is subjected to concentration and rapid technological renewal. A stabilizing factor is the prevalence of small and medium-sized companies that, in contrast to bigger companies, still create jobs, even in recession times such as these. Note that in 1991 only seventy-three companies employed more than 1,000 people (Wettstein, 1994).

The strategy of the OECD is not to separate education and work, but to link the two together. Feasible possibilities are a suitable first education, lifelong learning, and part-time jobs for students. Switzerland has some experience in all three areas and, following an internationally acknowledged strategy, has developed models that are particularly useful at the present time of economic recession.

Vocational Training

The actual basis of vocational training in Switzerland is the *apprenticeship,* which developed from the former guilds. Vocational education as it is known today is based on a law of the federal constitution of 1930. This law charges the Swiss federal government with the regulation of practical and theoretical education and makes vocational training a public duty. Apprentices have to attend vocational schools and take final examinations (Wettstein, 1994).

Even nowadays, an apprenticeship is the predominant form of vocational training. Table 11.2 presents a survey of the professions that can be learned in an apprenticeship.

The apprentice enters a company at the age of 16 or 17, does on-the-job training, and attends a vocational school one or two days a week. Depending on the standard, an apprenticeship takes between two and four years, mostly three to four years. School attendance is free, and the companies pay the apprentice a moderate salary as a contribution to the costs of living.

There are a few full-time vocational schools, especially in the French-speaking part of Switzerland. For more practically minded young people with weaker school performance, there are the *Anlehren.* This is also a dual system, but with only one day of school per week and a shorter duration

TABLE 11.2   Areas of Vocational Training

AREA OF JURISDICTION	TYPICAL PROFESSIONS	NUMBER OF PARTICIPANTS 1992/1993
Legislation on Vocational Education	clerk, sales assistant, mechanic, electrician, draftsman, butcher, carpenter, bricklayer (about 300)	163,778
Swiss Red Cross	nurse, medical lab technician, therapist (about 10)	8,955
Agriculture	farmer and other agricultural professions	4,828
Forestry	forester	941
Other Public Professions	musician, police	2,318
Other Nonpublic Professions	medical secretary, telecom assistant, ticket conductor, infant educator, post office official	16,287

Source: Adapted from Wettstein, 1994, p. 19.

of training. This is used for 1 percent of all the apprentices.

A more demanding form of vocational schools are intermediate diploma schools (*Berufsmittelschulen*), which are open to talented and motivated apprentices who go to school half a day or one whole day. Since 1993, a new kind of diploma, a so-called *Berufsmaturität* (certificate of upper secondary vocational education) with technical, artistic, commercial, agricultural, or administrative specialization (similar to the German exam, *Fachabitur*), has been introduced. This education is very demanding. Apart from doing an apprenticeship in an enterprise, the apprentices also attend special courses on two days of the week and have to study in the evenings as well as on weekends. After completing this education, students can enter a institute of higher education without taking any further exams. The certificate of upper secondary vocational education (*Berufsmaturität*) can also be obtained after the diploma of a maturity school in addition to a one-year training in an enterprise.

Completed vocational training is a prerequisite for admission to tertiary education programs, which offer management and specialist training in technology, agriculture, administration and trade,

hotel business and tourism, communication and information, art, education, social work, and health and commerce. At the tertiary level, vocational training is mostly extra-university. Thus, at higher specialized schools, the number of engineering students is three times higher than at the two federal institutes of technology. This system has some real advantages.

The first advantage is the practical suitability of the graduates. Because the apprenticeship combines work and training and the apprentices are continually confronted with concrete tasks, it is practically oriented and suitable for practically minded young people. Those graduates who have completed an apprenticeship or a tertiary education successfully can, as a rule, be of use straightaway in a profession and do not have to undergo further training. Another advantage refers to the flexibility of the young people. The offer of positions for apprentices depends on the economic situation. At present there is a lack of such positions in commercial, technical, and artistic professions, whereas positions in agriculture, sales, catering, and the construction industry are still open. Hence, the rapid change of economical structures demands great flexibility from students who want to begin an apprenticeship. A third and major advantage of this apprenticeship system is the low cost. Because the proportion of time spent in an enterprise is high, and employers as well as trade organizations are highly committed to the education of their apprentices, the government pays considerably less for an apprentice than for a maturity student or any other kind of full-time student.

Comparisons between OECD countries show that Switzerland has so far succeeded in reducing youth unemployment, and that the system of vocational education is a prerequisite for this (OECD Analysis, 1996). Not only are young people without a qualification at secondary level II most affected by unemployment, it is also a fact that a vocational education with an apprenticeship is more protection than an education based solely on school. The OECD Analysis (1996) explicitly states that "in general, lower ratios of youth to adult unemployment are found in countries with strong apprenticeship-type systems—Denmark, Germany, and Austria—and where workplace-based vocational programs form a major part of upper secondary education, such as in the Netherlands" (p. 52). Such conditions apply to Switzerland to a great extent.

It is an open question whether the dual system is *flexible* enough to react to rapid changes in the economical structures and whether it can anticipate them. In the important field of computer studies, for example, a basic education at secondary level II has been missing for a long time and has only been established lately. The number and profiles of the professions to be learned are being checked all the time, and educational courses are being revised. In this ongoing reform, authorities, vocational schools, and trade organizations cooperate; one objective is to reduce the multitude of current professions. The disappearance of traditional professions and the rapid emergence of new ones raises the question of which are the important competences in this state of flux and what a basic education should consist of. What is clear is that this education should do justice to the changes in professional fields and professional profiles.

Adult Education and Further Education

Vocational training with an apprenticeship is an institutionalized form of combining learning and working. There are also more individual combinations to be considered in this context, namely further education and students who do part-time studies and work at the same time. Both cases are very common in Switzerland.

Swiss participation in forms of lifelong learning is relatively high compared to other countries (about 40 percent of adults). It has been pointed out that "participation in continuing education is very clearly a function of the level of basic education: the higher it is, the higher the participation rate in continuing education" (Gretler, 1995, pp. 951–952).

Further education is usually in the form of courses, of which 19 percent are offered by public educational institutes, 31 percent by employers, and 50 percent by commercial institutions (OECD Indicators, 1996). A traditional form is cooperatively administered open universities (*Volkshochschulen*) that are spread over the whole country and that offer courses held mostly in the evenings. An example from the recent past are the courses for people, preferably women, who would like to take up their profession again after an interruption due to family reasons. Another example are programs for further education and retraining of unemployed people that were introduced tentatively at the beginning of the economic recession, but that have increased in number and originality in recent times. There is much more to do in this field in future, and the financial resources for these programs are very limited compared to the costs of unemployment insurance (Wettstein, 1994).

Student Workers

The OECD Analysis (1996) draws special attention to those students, mostly at tertiary level and partially also at secondary level II, who work part-time. It is internationally seen as a growing tendency for people who finish their education between 20 and 30; that is, it is more and more common to finish one's education and to start working relatively late.

The student workers fluctuate between education and work in individual ways. Most widely spread are student workers in Australia, Canada, Denmark, and the Netherlands (OECD Analysis, 1996). Generally, students wish to become more financially independent during their long education or they may have to support themselves. But usually the studies take longer; this means greater costs and reduction of the chances of graduates when in competition with younger people. In addition to this, the quality and success rate in studies suffer, as is shown in an Australian study (Robinson & Long, 1992). On the other hand, working as well as studying enables students to be more independent and to make important connections to their future professions. Society profits from the fact that parents and the government is providers of grants are financially relieved. The working students pay taxes and are flexible employees who usually have good basic qualifications but earn lower salaries than regularly employed people.

According to a study at the university of Berne (Arber, 1991), there is also a high number of student workers in Switzerland. About 70 percent of the students at the University of Berne have part-time jobs; a considerable part of those students work not only in the holidays but also during the semester. When Arber compared the Universities of Berne and Kassel (Germany), he came to the conclusion that Bernese students received considerably less government support than the students in Kassel because they worked more (Arber, 1991).

Up to this time, tertiary education curricula have hardly taken notice of part-time students. The structure of studies and exams is geared to full-time students and there are only few attempts to make allowances for student workers. For example, at the University of Berne, students who are studying to become teachers at secondary level II (ISCED 3) can choose a one-year course for full-time students or a course that lasts several years and is meant for student workers. This innovation was intensively discussed between the cantonal department of education of Berne, the supervisory committee, and the educational institution; a large delegation of students was also heard. The two sides—namely the demand for educational coherence and the demand for a combination of this education with an education that makes further specialized studies (for example, work on a dissertation) possible with a part-time job—were weighed against each other. The result of the discussion was a compromise. A strict course of studies of one year, as well as a two or more year course with a lower time density, were introduced. The two models are largely identical and differ only in organization, not in content, methods, or requirements. According to first indications, a similar number of students opt for one or the other model. The fears that different study models would be too difficult to organize and that the coherence of the parts would suffer were without foundation.

The Demand for Higher Education

The demand for higher education is continually rising in Switzerland and has almost reached its limits. Therefore, I would like to raise the following questions: How big is the demand for higher education and what motives are behind it? According to the rising demands, how are the most recent developments of the Swiss education system to be assessed? Can the education system be balanced with respect to supply and demand?

Demand and Consequences

In this section I will deal with the traditional academic way of classification; that is, preparation for maturity schools at secondary level I (ISCED 2), maturity schools (ISCED 3), universities (ISCED 6), and the employment system. The interesting aspects of this scheme are the demand for higher education, the capacity of the system, and the quality of higher education. The important indicator for this demand is the *maturity quota,* that is, the number of maturity diplomas among the 19-year-olds. It is relatively low (17.2 percent) when compared to Germany (22.6 percent) and France (36.3 percent) (OECD Indicators, 1996).

However, the Swiss maturity quota is catching up fast, in the most recent past at a rate of 1 percent per year, although the differences between the cantons are considerable. The growth is responsible for the general pressure exerted by the students on the universities.

The reasons for the rising quota of the last few years include the fact that women have been catching up, a tendency towards nuclear families, and an urbanization of the population (Arnet, 1997). In addition, in democratic societies education is granted and not denied, if possible, and taxation measures are only considered if everything else fails. This is also true for Switzerland, whose educational tradition is explicitly liberal. Another major reason for the rising demand is that parents want to make sure that their children get the best qualifications in order to improve their social position. In order to learn an attractive profession and to reduce the risks of being unemployed, higher education is needed in these times of rapid change and threatened job situations.

The run on maturity schools causes an imbalance in the whole system because it devalues diplomas of a lower quality and because it is a serious competitor to vocational training. Maturity diplomas themselves risk losing quality and may therefore in future no longer provide access to university. According to international experience, universities respond by introducing restrictions on admission if the maturity quota exceeds 20 percent. Switzerland is approaching this critical rate, and the cantons with universities and the universities themselves have already begun to take measures by creating a legal basis for the introduction of a *numerus clausus* (restricted number of admissions). Above all, this affects medical studies because a great number of students want to study medicine. So far, it has been possible to avoid a *numerus clausus* by diverting students to neighboring universities.

THE FUTURE OF SOCIETY AND SCHOOLING

Predictions about the development of society and education systems in Switzerland are of course

subjective. As mentioned above, tasks such as the coordination of offer and demand in education or the introduction of institutes of higher education exceed the means of the cantons. However, general conceptions that have been taken up again since the middle of the 1980s aim to harmonize and rationalize education.

I am counting on an increase in coordination that will exceed joint planning and development. The periphery will have to delegate competences to central institutions, as is the case in the whole university system, which will in the end have to be taken over by the Confederation, because it consists of establishments of national importance and because of a need for national coordination. The extent and rhythm of this process will probably be determined by financial necessities.

Although centralistic tendencies with respect to structure are legitimate, they can also be problematic elsewhere. I am, for example, thinking of the teaching profession, which will be functionalized much more than it has already been done. Swiss teachers enjoy many professional liberties; they can structure syllabuses and curricula with great independence and are relatively free with respect to the organization of their working hours outside school. In the last few years, precisely these working hours have been regulated more strictly and the professional activities have been divided into quantifiable functions (for example, school lessons, administration, school development, advising of parents, and further education). Both a salary scale for teachers, based on efficiency, and at the same time a refined system of evaluation and supervision will be introduced in the foreseeable future. The intention is to strive for more efficiency in school and teaching; however, there is also a danger of attracting more teachers who only do what they have to do and no more.

Finally, I am expecting a greater amalgamation between educational theory and practice, especially between academic educational science on the one hand and school and teaching on the other. This amalgamation is necessary for teacher training. Theoretical educational disciplines will continue to focus on the standards of their science and will introduce the students to academic thinking, but they will have to become more open in their choice of content and teaching methods with respect to practical problems of the school and teaching. Only then will they succeed in imparting what they intend to, namely the knowledge that will enable the teacher trainees to understand what is going on in the schools and in teaching. Integrative teaching and learning methods are called for that can link theoretical impulses with the everyday theories of the teachers-to-be and with their first practical teaching experiences. Moreover, the didactics of special fields that are taught in an extremely practical way in the course of Swiss teacher training need a more reflective basis. Theoretical didactics will have to be developed in such a way that practical aspects will also be considered.

A further field for the amalgamation of educational theory and practice is educational research. Here a convergence can be seen, for example, in accompanying school trials or in the support of school evaluations through scientific institutes. Switzerland has a real lack of empirical data for the critical secondary level II and partially for the tertiary level. We need, for example, studies on the efficiency of selection measures, on the success and achievement of students, and on the efficiency of teaching methods.

Some trends in the near future will probably stay constant with respect to certain sociocultural values of society. An alternative to the prevailing individualism, which puts personal independence above everything else, is represented by only a few groups, and one cannot expect solidarity among the generations to increase, especially not solidarity among different social groups and among employers and employees. However, postmaterial values such as those of the younger generation (time, balance of the roles of the sexes, self-restriction, ecological lifestyle, communication) can gain importance and have an effect on society and the labor market. An example of this is the increasing demand for part-time work and the attempt to find a place in certain niches in society.

It is a completely open question how the historical consciousness and the emotional attitudes toward our own country are going to develop; the current discussion about the role and the responsibility of Switzerland in World War II is more or less pointing at a polarization, less between political conflicts but more so between a certain disinterest on the one hand, and an active debate on our own history on the other.

REFERENCES

Arber, D. (1991). *Studentenjobs: Eine repräsentative Untersuchung über die Erwerbstätigkeit von Studierenden an der Universität Bern.* Bern: Institut für Marketing und Unternehmungsführung der Universität Bern.

Arnet, M. (General secretary of the Swiss Conference of Cantonal Ministers of Education). (1977, May 14). Interview in Berne.

BBW/BIGA/BFS/Sekretariat EDK. (1995). *Strukturen der allgemeinen und beruflichen Bildung in der Schweiz.* Berne: Sekretariat EDK.

BFS. (1996). *Bildungsstatistik 1996.* Berne: Bundesamt für Statistik.

Gretler, A. (1995). Switzerland. In T.N. Postlethwaite (Ed.), *International encyclopaedia of national systems of education.* Oxford: Pergamon.

OECD Analysis (1996). *Education at a glance—analysis.* Educational Center for Educational Research and Innovation (English translation). Paris: OECD.

OECD Indicators (1996). *Education at a Glance—OECD Indicators.* Educational Center for Educational Research and Innovation (English translation). Paris: OECD.

Robinson, L., & Long, M. (1992, Spring). Student workers: New data on gender and educational differences. *Youth Studies Australia,* pp. 14–20.

Wettstein, E. (1994). *Berufliche Bildung in der Schweiz.* Hrsg. von der Deutschschweizerischen Berufsbildungsämter-Konferenz (DBK) in Zusammenarbeit mit anderen Amtsstellen und Gremien. Luzern: DBK.

_____ CHAPTER 12 _____

The Challenge to Education in an Arctic Region: Greenland

HANS JUNKER MORTENSEN
TRANSLATED BY MARIANNE RISBERG

Hans Junker Mortensen *earned his Ph.D. in international relations. Since 1993 he has been associate professor at the Department of Management and Economic, Ilisimatusarfik—University of Greenland. He has served as administrator for the U.N. in Niger and Rwanda (1975–1981), consultant for Danish trade and industry (1981–1985), and consultant for a consortium of Danish companies to the World Bank (1986–1991). Since 1991, he has also contributed as a lecturer in the Department of Political Science at the University of Copenhagen and the Department of Organization and Industrial Sociology at the Copenhagen Business School.*

Greenland is the world's largest island. It has 840,000 square miles, 85 percent of which is inland ice. Being situated in the North Atlantic, the climate is arctic, with tremendous variations from the north to the south. The mildest climate is on the southwest coast where 90 percent of the 55,732 inhabitants live. The largest city is the capital Nuuk with a population of 13,148.

Greenland achieved independence from Denmark in 1979 (home rule). One of the major themes of Greenland's development is the meeting of the traditional Greenlandic culture with modernity. The two foci of this paper are built on this theme. As leaders in development need training, we focus on higher education within the university system. But we also discuss a teacher training program designed to address more traditional cultural considerations.

THE SOCIAL FABRIC

Traditional Greenland

Traditionally, Greenland was a very isolated society of hunters. The inhabitants lived in sparsely populated settlements along the coast, and only a few towns, or colonies as they were called at that time, harbored more than 1,000 people.

The Inuit legal (social) system is an example of the influence from traditional knowledge. Europeans arriving in Greenland in the eighteenth century thought that the Greenlanders had no understanding of a legal system. In truth, they did in fact have a very splendid system, but it was based on a totally different way of thinking. Their system combined religion, law, and customs, all woven into a fine mesh that governed and sustained their type of society. Few serious crimes were ever committed because children were socialized into believing that one should conduct oneself in such a way as to avoid conflicts.

More recently, scholars have achieved greater understanding of the Inuit system, partly by reconstructing the abundant notes left by the Danish polar explorer, Knud Rasmussen. Rasmussen said he once asked an Inuit the reason for a particular set of customs. He received the very wise answer: "Too much thinking leads to disorder. We repeat the old stories as we have heard them with the words we recall. You (Europeans) always need to ascribe some meaning to supernatural events whereas we do not care about this, we are satisfied with not understanding." Rasmussen also asked the Inuits what they actually believed in, to which they responded: "What we believe in? We do not believe in anything, we merely learn." Asking about the creation myth, the answer was, "We do not know anything about that, we only know what our ancestors have told us." This demonstrates the existence of an old oral tradition, well grounded in collective consciousness, and closely tied to myths and supernatural elements.

For the Inuits, law is a natural part of the social system. There are examples where certain customs prevail in one part of the country, but not necessarily in other areas. Customs were adaptable. In the area around Thule, for example, there used to be a connection between sexual behavior and food. If food was plentiful, the attitude toward sex was more relaxed, since children being born were not likely to starve to death. During periods of food shortage, rules were introduced to prevent childbirth.

There was a very close relationship between nature and society. The Inuits also had totally different ways of diverting attention from and avoiding conflicts, such as song competitions, which were used to solve conflicts. Hence, in traditional society, law was not autonomous, it was intrinsically tied to customs, religion, and morality. Law integrated society, it was not isolated from society, as in the European approach.

In 1921, Greenland held a bicentennial celebration of the arrival of Hans Egede, the Danish missionary who, supported by the king, came to Greenland to convert the Inuits to Christianity. The years surrounding this bicentenary marked an important turning point in the history of Greenland. Changes in climate had reduced seal hunting to the extent that the population in the south was no longer able to survive on seal hunting alone. However, the milder climate meant more fish, especially cod and halibut, and fishing became the new primary industry. This change affected the entire economy. The previous self-sufficient barter economy had to be abandoned in favor of a monetary economy.

Recognizing that the Greenlanders had to be socialized into a modern society linked with the rest of the world, a new statute was introduced in 1925. This modernization process continued slowly until the Second World War, when Denmark became unable to maintain the flow of supplies. As Greenland had become dependent on supplies from the outside world, diplomatic relations were established with Canada and the United States.

Since 1941, Greenland has played a strategic role in global security, including the interplay between American, Danish, and Greenlandic interests throughout periods of changing international political constellations and conditions. Over the course of these years, American interests have dominated. This has been determined almost exclusively by military-strategic relationships with the other major powers in international politics, initially Germany and later the Soviet Union, making the international position of Greenland for the past half century intimately connected with the fight for hegemony in international politics (Petersen, 1992). This pressure from hegemonistic conflict, along with the physical presence of the American military on Greenland and the asymmetric relationship between the United States and Denmark, caused the Americans to create supply lines beginning in World War II, ensuring that Greenland received the most urgent necessities.

As a result of Greenland's increasing exposure to the outside world, the Provincial Council and the Danish government decided to attempt the modernization of the country. However, turning the island into a modern society proved considerably more complex than anticipated. In 1950, the Danish Parliament introduced new legislation that completely changed the form of rule in Greenland. The country was suddenly opened up to the rest of the world, people were allowed unrestricted travel in and out, and new goods were imported. Then, in June 1953, Denmark's constitution was changed and supplemented with a new paragraph stating that the constitution applied to all parts of the Kingdom of Denmark. Greenland ceased to be a colony, became a Danish municipality, and the Greenlanders were granted Danish citizenship. (Mortensen, 1996). But changing the constitution did not change the situation overnight. Despite Greenland's progress after World War II, it was in nearly all aspects a developing country, primarily because the former colonial policy had functioned as a straitjacket, restricting the Greenlanders financially and culturally and making progress impossible.

So the major task was for Greenlanders to achieve status on a par with Denmark—financially, politically, and culturally. One way was to abandon the Danish state's monopoly on trade and investment, allowing private capital investments and encouraging private initiative. However, toward the end of the 1950s, the Provincial Council lost patience with the slow progress toward achieving equal status with Denmark. As it had proven impossible to attract private investment capital, the government intervened and invested large sums in production equipment (Dahl, 1985). In 1955, the Construction Council was established in an attempt to satisfy the need for coordination and control. In addition, the Provincial Council submitted that the Parliament adopt a long-term policy for developing Greenland and for encouraging Danish-Greenlandic cooperation.

To set these initiatives in motion, a committee was established for the purpose of monitoring the development process. In 1964, this committee submitted its report, G60, which then constituted the foundation for the intensive industrialization of Greenland during the period from 1966 to 1975 (Lidegaard, 1973). The theory and development process underlying the G60 report entailed a series of measures, the purpose of which was to expand the population's political awareness, social development, and cultural growth and to raise standards of living by increasing material welfare and improving education. Furthermore, the aim was to widen the population's codetermination and responsibility for the country's development.

The committee worked out a ten-year plan, giving high priority to industrial development and education. This development had to be founded on the particular nature and conditions for economic development characterizing Greenlandic society. Therefore, the committee unanimously recom-

mended the establishment of the Greenland Council, the major task of which was to undertake the central planning and coordination of the development process. In 1965, the Greenland Council and its secretariat consisted of five political representatives from Greenland, five members representing the Parliament, and a chairman appointed by the Danish government. Planning was central and, once approved by the secretariat, each individual sector, such as health care, education, technical firms, housing construction, and industrial development, was overseen by the Greenland Council. However, due to a shortage of skilled Greenlandic labor, the objective of codetermination for the Greenlanders could not be satisfied, even though the Provincial Council and municipal councils were involved in the planning of investments. In effect, Danes were allocated the responsibility for many of the development tasks.

Modern Greenland

Today, Greenland is a modern society. Over the last forty years, it has been transformed from a developing to a modern country. Despite the fact that this modernity was planned and to a great extent implemented by Danes, the Greenlanders consented to the plans and participated as well. The modernization, which began in the 1950s, has had its share of mistakes and involved human and social costs. Restructuring and intensive changes were accompanied by extensive urbanization of the population, who were forced administratively to move into towns where the prospects of creating export-based fisheries were most favorable. But urbanization also led to increasing social problems. Integrating the populations of various settlements into small urban communities was difficult and led to a rise in crime and alcohol abuse.

The rapid transformation process also implied a sizable increase in the Danish population, and Danish expatriates were paid considerably higher wages than the Greenlanders, which naturally caused dissatisfaction among the latter. Wages were determined by the so-called birthplace criterion, which meant that Greenlanders only received

85 percent of the wages paid to Danes when performing identical tasks. The birthplace criterion was not abandoned until 1991. Another difficulty was that Greenlanders were subjected to requirements for learning Danish, a development that had started around the turn of the century. Consequently, the Greenlandic language came to occupy a secondary position. Mastering Danish became attractive and synonymous with a road to education, influence, and high positions. This triggered a massive influx of Danish language teachers. Over a period of five years, from 1960 to 1965, the number of Danish language teachers increased from a third to representing half of the total teaching staff.

It was impossible to educate the Greenlanders at the same speed that technical development was taking place. Therefore, as an increasing number of managerial and other important positions were filled with expatriate Danish experts who were paid higher wages than the native populations, this resulted in a growing Danish upper class and predominant underclass of Greenlanders. But not everything was rosy for the Danes, who found that they made contributions without feeling any appreciation in return.

In 1960, the number of Danish expatriates was 2,762; by 1980, the population of Danes had increased to 8,826. In consequence, development proceeded to a great extent along Danish premises. Thus, the overall object of the process, equal status and decolonization, was devoid of content, and the twenty-year transformation process rather resembled neocolonialism (Dahl, 1985).

Dissatisfaction with the transformation process spread among the Greenlanders in the 1960s. They criticized the Danish oppression of the population, as well as their influence on Greenlandic politics. This criticism was raised by the well-educated elite, primarily consisting of Greenlanders who had become increasingly politically conscious through their participation in the national debate about future development. A group of Greenlanders living in Denmark played a role in the emerging new ideas about how the future should proceed. They had more ideological inspiration than their fellow countrymen back in Greenland. Living in Denmark offered them contact with "fourth-world minorities," which was especially helpful in creating ideas about the relationship between Denmark and Greenland (Petersen, 1990).

Home Rule

Along with living in Denmark and their consequent contact with the outside world, this group of Greenlanders were exposed to the concept of the ethnic minority, which then became part of the cultural and political debate back home. As Greenlanders became aware of what it was to be an ethnic and oppressed minority, soon they began to revolt. This feeling of being an ethnic minority was further strengthened when Denmark joined the European Community in 1972.

In June 1970, a conference was held on the future of Greenland in which only Greenlanders participated. The themes discussed were language, salaries and wages (including the birthplace criterion), population density, general education, upbringing, school and education, trade conditions, alcohol problems, and the future government of Greenland (Sørensen, 1983). The results of the conference became the new guidelines for Greenland policy. That is,

- Greenlandic should be given higher priority.
- The increase in population density should be reduced or stopped.
- Greenland should move toward political independence.
- Greenlanders in Greenland should be respected as a separate people with their own language and culture. (Johansen, 1971, p. 258)

The first formal step toward Home Rule in Greenland was taken in January 1973 by establishing the Home Rule Committee that was composed exclusively of Greenlandic politicians. The Home Rule Committee was of the opinion that:

- Greenlanders represent a separate people.
- Greenland is geographically separate from Denmark.
- Greenland has its own culture and language, which it wishes to preserve.
- Colonialism and remote control have resulted in perceptions by Greenlanders that they are excluded from decision processes.
- Greenlanders wish greater autonomy.

Therefore, the committee suggested that a series of social responsibilities be transferred into the care of internal Greenlandic affairs, such as internal administration, taxes, public welfare, trade conditions, schools, culture, preservation, family and criminal law, and the rights to extract subsoil raw materials (Dahl, 1985).

With the introduction of Home Rule on May 1, 1979, it was made clear that the law regarding Home Rule was an ordinary parliamentary decision by which the Danish Parliament delegated specific legislative competence to the Greenlanders. This competence included responsibility for a number of areas previously handled in Denmark. However, certain areas, considered affairs of the state, were not included in consideration of the commonwealth. Still, eighteen years after the introduction of Home Rule, areas such as infrastructure, trade and economy, education, social health and welfare, and housing have experienced progress.

Some Aspects of the Colonial Experience

As I have pointed out, many changes have occurred in Greenland. It has moved from being a traditional, very socially closed society of hunters living in scattered communities along the coast to a sudden exposure to external influences. It has gone from a self-sufficient barter economy to a monetary system; to experiencing greater openness toward and contact with the outside world; and to the establishment of diplomatic relations, along with the introduction of Home Rule. All

these factors have resulted in the development of the region with implications for the cultural, social, educational, and business conditions throughout the Arctic economy.

Even though Greenland has taken over responsibility for various tasks of state, being inexperienced in such activities means that the country is still dependent upon Danish models. Therefore, having accepted these responsibilities, one of the major tasks of Home Rule and the politicians is to govern their domains in a Greenlandic spirit. Greenland adopted the Danish system of democracy and administrative practice, particularly when assuming control over the civil services. But it is important to infuse one's own spirit into the system over a longer period. The Greenlanders have no other option than to learn from their own mistakes in order to achieve satisfying results in the future.

SCHOOLING

In contemporary Greenland, western science is merely one type of knowledge to be considered among several. There are other types of knowledge, such as traditional knowledge, nonwestern, nonwritten, and tacit types of knowledge that attract attention. But while the typical western way of organizing educational services is the antithesis of the endemic social structure of the indigenous people, it is true that within the educational sector, Greenland is dependent upon its former colonial power, Denmark. That is, "The Western educational system has made an attempt to impose a mechanistic and linear world view into contexts previously guided by the typically cyclic world views of indigenous people" (Kawagley, 1993, pp. 116–117). The factory model of school organization found in most schools in the Arctic regions is rooted in this mechanistic and linear worldview that opposes traditional values. Whereas authority in western schools is hierarchical, or vertical, and bodies of knowledge compartmentalized, the authority of those responsible for learning in traditional indigenous societies is horizontal and communal. Indigenous societal bodies of knowledge are derived from, and are analogous to, that part of nature from which they come. Such knowledge is practical and immediately useful.

The western school model superimposed on native societies unfamiliar with, or not yet accustomed to, western culture has often been only marginally productive at best, and at times devastating. However, contemporary problems in schooling are attributable to the ways in which schools are organized and cultural differences are not unique to the Arctic regions. Since much of western society is also in transition, our difficulties may apply as much to western as to native societies. Answers to three pertinent questions may help to focus on these problems.

1. What other alternatives are there, besides either a western or a traditional native style school structure, that might better enable schools to meet the requirements of societies in transition?
2. Can formal education be organized in such a way that educational programs would be designed to fit the contemporary structure of native societies and still fulfill the broad purposes mutually agreed to by the providers of educational services and those served?
3. At what stage of societal development would certain aspects of native social structure be appropriate models for school organization, and when would western style education, or an adapted version of it, be appropriate for schools in native communities?

The School System

As mentioned, the development of the educational system in Greenland has been dependent upon the educational system in Denmark, both in terms of expertise and resources. In Denmark and Greenland elementary school education lasts ten years, nine of which are compulsory. The Advanced Leaving Examination for the elementary school comprises the subjects Greenlandic, Danish, and mathematics. The Higher Preparatory

Examination entails an additional three years of education on top of the compulsory nine years of elementary school.

Danish is a very important subject in the schools, and it is compulsory from the fourth grade on. However, it is left to the individual municipality to decide whether to introduce Danish as early as the second or the third grade.

Higher Education

For many years, Greenlanders received vocational training or higher education in Denmark, since no system for further training or higher education had been established in Greenland. For the Greenlanders, attending higher education in Denmark means being Danicized. That is, Greenlandic traditions meet Danish traditions that, due to their values, worldviews, and insights, subscribe to different philosophies of life and societal development.

One important aspect of the current transformation process is that the Greenlanders themselves are now responsible for adapting education to their social structure based on their own experiences. Responsibility now lies with the Greenlanders themselves, because there is no longer any "vicious" state to point at.

When Greenland was granted Home Rule in 1979, a series of objectives emerged for the future organization and structure of the developing society. Decisions had to be made regarding which processes were to be given priority in order to facilitate the influence of Greenlandic culture and mentality on society. Five different dimensions were prioritized:

1. The political economical dimension—conducting their own affairs, taking over various areas of responsibility from the Danish State.
2. The administrative staff dimension—educating and qualifying Greenlanders to take over positions occupied by Danes.
3. The educational political dimension—establishing a series of educational institutions in the country.

4. The cultural dimension (a)—assimilating the usage of Greenlandic into as many contexts as possible.
5. The cultural dimension (b)—preserving existing settlements, which have been decreasing at a high rate. (Grønlunds 837, 1978)

Since the 1980s, Greenlandic politicians have pointed out the necessity of having the younger generation receive training or education in order to reduce the need for foreign manpower. Due to the drastically increasing need for educated manpower as a result of intensified public development efforts in Greenland, it was commonly agreed in the early 1960s that the need for education was much greater than anticipated if Greenland is to meet modern society's demand for manpower and replace foreign manpower.

Thus, the need for higher education for Greenlanders was and is urgent if they are to acquire the competence to take over positions currently occupied by Danes. The aim is to furnish Greenlanders with education similar to the Danish but using different and longer routes than the Danish system, since the adaptation of local traditions will broaden the Greenlandic educational system.

Achieving these objectives would require that education be designed to match business development and in anticipation of the development of society and the labor market; the quality and level of education must ensure business and academic competence inside and outside Greenland; preferably, all young Greenlanders would receive some kind of education after finishing elementary or grammar school; educational policy should contain further education of skilled workers, and specialist courses for unskilled workers; and Greenland should become self-sufficient in manpower to the greatest possible extent. As well, information technology must be an integral part of learning at all levels; the educational system must be coherent; and the educational system must be adapted to the present situation, and made more efficient in order to better exploit available resources (Grønlungs, 1995).

Shortly after Home Rule was introduced, there-fore, Greenland invested considerable effort into becoming self-sufficient with regard to professional teachers for the system of higher education, resulting in the establishing of the Inuit Institute in 1981, renamed Ilisimatusarfik in 1984. Until 1987, Ilisimatusarfik was an institute for Greenlandic culture and language, offering two-year courses. In 1987, Ilisimatusarfik was turned into a university. In 1990, an institute for administration was established.

Today, Greenland has three higher educational institutions: the Institute for Administration, the Institute for Greenlandic, and the Institute for Culture and Society. Fifteen percent of all higher education activities now take place in Greenland. The basic principle of these and of Ilisimatusarfik is for the university to be a free, independent, and self-governing institution, responsible for individual employees performing critical research within all fields. At Ilisimatusarfik, the remainder of working hours spent after teaching and administration is spent conducting research.

Ilisimatusarfik is very open to international collaboration in higher education and has exchanged students and teachers with institutions in the United States, Canada, Scandinavia, and Europe. Furthermore, the university has participated in relevant conferences, symposiums, and seminars that have been sources of essential inspiration to the institution and its image. If the institution were to isolate itself, it would not achieve a fundamental quality assessment because methods, scientific language, and ways of thinking are assessed by international research standards.

Higher Education Students

A student attending higher education is defined as one who receives educational aid from Greenland's Home Rule, having fulfilled the requirements of affiliation and competence (Danielsen, 1995, p. 3). Higher education is divided into short (BA) and long education (MA). Most short education takes three years and the long from five to six years.

During the period from 1975 to January 1,

1995, 165 persons earned a degree, 96 an MA and 69 a BA. Of these 165 persons, 97 were men and 68 women. Thirteen of the 165 graduated from Ilisimatusarfik, with the remaining 152 graduating from institutions in Denmark or abroad. Ten out of the 13 persons (77 percent) graduating from Ilisimatusarfik lived in Greenland as of January 1, 1995. Of the 152 graduating from institutions in Denmark or abroad, 87 (57 percent) lived in Greenland as of January 1, 1995. Thus, of the 165 persons graduating from higher educations, 97 (59 percent) lived in Greenland as of January 1, 1995. Of those returning to Greenland after having finished their studies, 75 percent returned the very same year they graduated. Only 7 percent of those spending more than three years abroad returned to Greenland.

At Ilisimatusarfik's commemoration on February 16, 1996, 5 candidates received their MA diplomas: 3 from the Institute for Administration, 1 from the Institute for Greenlandic, and 1 from the Institute for Culture and Society. Eight received their BA diplomas: 4 from the Institute for Administration and 4 from the Institute for Culture and Society (IlisimaTusaat, 1996).

In 1975/1976, 10 students enrolled in higher education, all of them for institutes in Denmark. From 1985/1986 to 1993/1994, the number of new students had risen to between 60 and 80 annually, apart from 1990/1991 and 1992/1993. In 1990/1991, 95 new students enrolled in higher education. This year was different in that 15 persons started college education in the United States and in Canada. In 1992/1993, 112 students enrolled in higher education, of whom 25 started on a basic studies program at one of the university centers in Denmark. The unusually high number in this year reflected the solid efforts to reduce dropouts among GU-students (Greenland's high school education). It is significant, however, that only 59 enrolled in higher education in 1993/1994. In that year, 12 students started at Ilisimatusarfik, 7 of whom were in the basic studies program.

Over the years, the gender distribution has changed from being primarily men to including an equal number of males and females. In 1993/1994, 55 percent of new students attending higher education were women. The number of students in progress has grown significantly. As of December 15, 1975, the number of students in progress was 22, distributed throughout nine different institutions in Denmark. In 1993/1994, this number had grown to 346. Of these, 75 were studying at Ilisimatusarfik in Nuuk. The 346 students were distributed among 77 different programs.

Education of Teachers in Local Communities

In any society, there is always a demand for change in the educational system. But what is any given educational activity worth to Greenland, and what does it cost? By answering this question, it should be easy to assess whether to implement the given activity. If the value of education is greater than the costs, education must be implemented; otherwise, not. In that way, education is treated on a par with other investment potentials. However, calculating the value and costs of any particular educational activity is complicated because it is often difficult to assess the effect or utility of the activity.

One consideration is that local communities will always encompass a group of people who should be given the option to further their education without having to leave their community. Since many of the young people who have undergone educational training elsewhere do not return to the local community, it is important to introduce measures that ensure that the younger generation stays in the area. This is easier said than done, but improving local education opportunities are worth investing in (Mortensen, 1994).

Also, according to recent statistics, the future need of the Greenland educational system's for teachers will be greater than estimated. Current prognoses (Direktoratet for Kultur, Uddannelse og Forskning, 1994a, 1994b) estimate that the demand for teachers will have increased by 15.6 percent by the year 2000.

The teaching staff of the Greenland educational system is made up of people with very different professional backgrounds—for example, prep school teachers with a social education; subject teachers with a two-year education sometimes supplemented with various courses; and teachers educated at teachers' colleges for a varying numbers of years. Furthermore, the staff is comprised of a large number of Danish teachers educated at Danish teachers' colleges, as well as a large group of temporary Greenlandic teachers who have no particular education at all.

Changes in the educational system—for example, evaluation and integration schemes—create increasing demands on teachers, professionally as well as socially. Therefore, it has become a topic of interest to consider raising the levels of temporary teachers. A large proportion of these teachers are deeply rooted in the local communities in terms of family relations, housing, and so on. Due to this, it would be extremely costly for the individual instructor to move to the teachers' college in Ilinniarfissuaq, Nuuk. Greenland's nature, size, climate, scattered settlements, and complex and expensive communications tie the individual to his or her home. If a person wanted to attend continuous training outside of his or her community, it might only be possible to visit home towns and families during the summer holidays. One example of the difficult traveling conditions is two students from Kullorsuaq in the Upernavik municipality who attended the decentralized teacher training and had to first travel by dog sledge, then by helicopter to Ilulissat, and then by plane to Nuuk. Depending on weather conditions, this journey can take several days. In order to attract qualified temporary teachers, the Landsting introduced decentralized teacher training.

The objective of decentralized teacher training is to educate elementary school teachers. This training provides the professional and educational insight and practical skills necessary to perform the job as a teacher. The training takes into consideration just how the teachers can contribute toward student personal development.

Ilinniarfissuaq's Decentralized Teacher Training

Ilinniarfissuaq's decentralized teacher training is based on certain objectives, admission requirements, conditions for establishing training in individual towns/settlements, the structure of the training, and an evaluation process, all of which are listed below.

Admission Requirements. Admission is based on the following criteria: The applicant must be between 25 to 45 years old, have five years of occupational experience, and she or he must be a provider. Individuals who simply have theoretical knowledge with no experience are allowed to apply for admission. This implies a graduation certificate from school or other relevant types of education. The applicant must speak Greenlandic, but also be able to understand and interpret texts in Danish at a relatively high professional level. If there are more applicants for decentralized teacher training than there are placements, the headmaster of Ilinniarfissuaq is responsible for selecting among the applicants.

Conditions for Establishing Training in Individual Towns/Settlements. Decentralized teacher training can be established provided that a given town or settlement harbors qualified teachers who can function as external teachers for Ilinniarfissuaq. The location must contain suitable facilities in terms of premises, opportunities for teaching practice, and a sufficient number of qualified applicants. The local school must be able to guarantee the applicant that he or she will be able to teach relevant subjects at a rate of eight to twelve lessons per week.

Content. The decentralized teacher training is comprised of independent teaching, particularly in the subjects of Greenlandic, mathematics, and at least one practical or art subject. There is self-learning, including one annual residential course in the following compulsory subjects: education, including educational theory and practice; psychology, didactics, and course-related practice; and Greenlandic, mathematics, and integrated studies, including religion. As well, there is one year of supplementary training at Ilinniarfissuaq, comprising the following subjects: educational theory and practice; Greenlandic; one main subject specialty and optional subjects: needlework, arts, sports, music, woodwork, or domestic science (Grønlands, 1989).

Evaluation.   Training is concluded with a final examination in two of the following subjects: Greenlandic, integrated studies including religion, or mathematics. After one year's supplementary training, the fourth year is concluded with final examinations in the field of education theory and practice, Greenlandic, and the chosen main subject. The optional subjects are concluded with a mark for general proficiency. The student's independent teaching is concluded with the evaluation "approved" or "not approved." Course-related practice is concluded with the evaluation "approved" or "not approved." Students take the first examinations after three years, and the final examinations in after an additional year at Ilinniarfissuaq (Grønlands, 1989).

In 1990, the first class of 20 students started on the decentralized teacher program. Of these, 13 graduated in the summer of 1994 after their final year at Ilinniarfissuaq in Nuuk; by 1996, the remaining 25 had graduated. In the spring of 1994, 55 students were participating in decentralized teacher training. A survey conducted among a group of students showed that, prior to embarking on training, 64.7 percent worked as temporary teachers. Most of them indicated that they wanted to continue working for the schools at which they were currently teaching, while only 2 were prepared to move to other places. Since it has been very difficult to persuade teachers educated at Ilinniarfissuaq in Nuuk to move out into the small towns and settlements, decentralized training seems to be a viable policy.

Fulfillment of Admission Requirements.   The average age of trainees has been 35 years, varying

between 25 to 43. The average number of years of occupational experience is around eleven years and four months, varying from three to twenty-two years. On average, the students have 2.8 children, varying from none at all to six children.

This educational form has proven to be attractive. In the spring of 1994, 70 applied for admission, of which 15 were accepted, having fulfilled the admission requirements. However, it should be emphasized that none of these students came from East Greenland, which still has a shortage of supervisors.

As mentioned earlier, conditions for establishing decentralized teacher training require that students be guaranteed between eight and twelve lessons a week during which they can teach relevant subjects. The training location must also be able to appoint supervisors. In this context, local education authorities are responsible for ensuring the students opportunities for completing their study, since it is up to the authorities to hire students as temporary teachers for these required eight to twelve lessons a week.

School headmasters assist in selecting qualified supervisors who visit Ilinniarfissuaq twice to receive instructions and material. These supervisors are not to act as teachers. Rather, their role is to support and motivate student teachers in connection with their teaching practice and homework. The survey shows that it is primarily the student who contacts the supervisor. The distribution of student contact with the supervisor shows contact daily, 20 percent; contact every week, 73 percent; contact every month, 7 percent.

Except for a few who communicate by telephone, most students are in personal contact with their supervisors. These supervisors have found it necessary for students to go to Ilinniarfissuaq to finish their education, but only 60 percent of the students consider it necessary to go to Nuuk.

Evaluation of the Program.   The great advantage of decentralized teacher training is that the students gain vast practical experience while studying. This experience comprises teaching, contact with parents, practical arrangements, pupil-related problems, and so on. Another advantage is that, after having completed their education, most students want to continue working in their home town or settlement.

Since 64.7 percent of the students worked as temporary teachers prior to embarking on teacher training, the decentralized training has contributed significantly to raising the existing professional level, since 140 teaching jobs are handled by temporary teachers.

Comparing centralized to decentralized teacher training, centralized training includes English or physics and chemistry (Grønlands, 1989). These subjects are not included in the decentralized training, a demerit for the system. Therefore, at the professional level, the two types of training are not comparable. However, since decentralized training includes such a large number of teaching opportunities—from eight to twelve lessons a week—such a workload would be too comprehensive if it were to include the same number of subjects as the centralized training, even though decentralized training is currently one year longer than centralized training.

Since any type of higher education or vocational training requires command of Danish (the language of instruction and in the textbooks), it is evidently a handicap for those teachers who have passed decentralized training if they are not qualified to teach Danish.

Children growing up in the outlying districts and settlements, who receive inadequate instruction in Danish (or English), are faced with fewer opportunities for further education. Therefore, it is important to give serious consideration to whether Danish and English should be introduced, as well as physics/chemistry, into decentralized training. But since there is little tradition for studying English and physics/chemistry, it will probably be difficult to find qualified supervisors for these subjects. In some cases, Danish supervisors are used. The students themselves wish to include these as their remaining optional subjects, so if the decentralized training is to continue, these must be included.

Ilinniarfissuaq offers continuous training in Danish through two correspondence courses: Danish 1, comprising 105 lessons, and Danish 2, comprising 210 lessons. The latter is equivalent to Ilinniarfissuaq's main subject level. Admission requirements stipulate one restraint: The applicant must be between 25 and 45, which excludes the very young from participating, forcing them to move to Nuuk if they want to qualify as teachers. This represents a dilemma, since much is done otherwise to persuade the young to stay in the outlying districts and settlements.

It is somewhat uncertain whether decentralized training will continue. The politicians are in favor of its continuation, whereas education officials are in favor of abolishing it.

Remote Instruction

In order to reach local communities, alternatives to the present educational system are necessary. By integrating information technology into all parts of the educational system, alternative teaching forms, such as remote instruction, become possible. Such an alternative is characterized by the separation of teacher and student, unlike face-to-face teaching; the educational institution's influence; the use of technical means, usually printed, for contact between teacher and students and for communicating the content of teaching; the possibility for two-way communication, enabling the student to benefit from or initiate a dialogue; and the possibility for occasional meetings, both for didactic and social purposes (Nørreslet, 1996).

There are several models for remote instruction that could be adapted to Greenland. Three possible models for remote instruction are displaced teaching, simultaneous teaching, and private studies. The models are combinable in different ways in order to ensure the most efficient form of teaching didactically, organizationally, financially, and technically. The main purpose is to expand the supply of qualified educators.

One advantage to using remote instruction is that it facilitates equal access to education, since it would no longer be dependent on living in the immediate vicinity where the desired education takes place, and it would not be necessary to have a sufficient number of students in the same neighborhood wanting a specific education. Remote instruction would allow for flexible organization adapted to the needs of the individual student's family and working situation.

However, the question is whether the number of students is sufficient to warrant the cost of establishing a stimulating and development environment for remote instruction, taking into consideration just how expensive this would be. Nevertheless, the decentralized training of teachers (duration corresponding to BA), which started in 1990, has proven successful, and this education is much coveted by local Greenlandic communities.

THE FUTURE

In Greenland, there is a need for change and renewal within education. Renewal of both Greenlandic and western traditions will probably happen by infusing an old form of parliamentary democracy and legislation with new ideas, because this form would be applied in a different spirit, a different climate, a different tone, and with the purpose of realizing several diverse values. But in order for criticism to be constructive and visionary, it must conscientiously take into consideration the specific circumstances, while simultaneously demonstrating the stamina it takes to ensure that it will be heard and taken note of.

Within a relatively short period, Greenlandic politicians have issued 550 Home Rule orders covering industrial and nonindustrial issues pertaining to the country's major industries: fishery, trapping, and hunting. Of the 550 orders, 190 fall within this area, while another 100 concern education and culture. These figures indicate that politicians are interested in the educational sector and are aware that education plays an important role in creating an independent Greenland. In the future, it will be the task of politicians, public servants, and educational institutions to formulate proposals for the structure and contents of present and future education. This is to ensure the suitable

education of graduates to prepare them for undertaking functions in Greenland, as well as in international, private, and public organizations that require higher education.

The purpose is to formulate an overall vision for what the country wants from education and for what is to be expected of future graduates. These visions must subsequently be transformed into practical objectives for the various educations, including scale, structure, and contents. Based on an estimation of what demands future graduates will be expected to meet, and the influence and framework to which this education will be subjected, the final planning of Greenland's educational future can be made.

REFERENCES

Dahl, J. (1985). *Arktisk selvstyre*. Viborg: Denmark Akademisk Forlag.

Danielsen, M. (1995, December). *En analyse af videregående uddannelser 1975–1994*. Greenland: Grønlands Statistik.

Direktoratet for Kultur, Uddannelse og Forskning. (1994a). *Folkeskolen i Grønland*. Nuuk, Pilersuiffik Nuuk, Greenland: Author.

Direktoratet for Kultur, Uddannelse og Forskning. (1994b). *Redegørelse o læreruddannelsen, de sociale uddannelser, Ilisimatusarfik og campus*. Nuuk, Greenland: Author.

Grønlands Hjemmestyre. (1978). *Betænkning 837/1978: (Vol. 1–4)*. Copenhagen, Denmark.

Grønlands Hjemmestyre. (1989). *Landstingsforordningen nr. 1 af 16. maj 1989 om uddannelse af lærere til folkeskolen og om sociale uddannelser*. Nuuk, Greenland.

Grønlands Hjemmestyre. (1995, May). *Uddannelsespolitisk redegørelse*. Nuuk, Greenland.

IlisimaTusaat. (1996, March). *Five new candidates from Ilisimatusarfik 1995–96*. IlisimaTusaat, No. 1, Greenland.

Johansen, L.E. (1971). *Rapport fra Holsteinsborg*. Copenhagen, Denmark: Godthåb.

Kawagley, A.O. (1993). *A Yupiaq world view: Implications for culture, educational and technological adaptation in a contemporary world*. Unpublished doctoral dissertation, University of British Columbia, Canada.

Lidegaard, M. (1973). *Det gælder Grønland*. Copenhagen, Denmark: Forlaget Schultz.

Mortensen, H.J. (1994, May). *Decentralized teachers' college in Greenland*. Paper presented at Comparative Education Society in Europe, Denmark.

Mortensen, H.J. (1996). *Udviklingen inden for det videregående uddannelsessystem*. Copenhagen, Denmark: NOCIES.

Nørreslet, B. (1996, February). *Fjernundervisning, debat om IT og dens uddannelsesmæssige perspektiver*. Paper presented at Nuuk, INUTEK Conference.

Petersen, N. (1992). *Grønland i global sikkerhedspolitik*. Copenhagen, Denmark: SNU.

Petersen, R. (1990). *On the development of the Greenlandic identity*. Paper presented at the 7th Inuit Studies Conference, Alaska, USA.

Sørensen, A.K. (1983). *Grønland—Danmark i det 20. århundrede*. Copenhagen, Denmark: Nyt Nordisk Forlag.

PART III

Central and Eastern Europe: Building Democracy in a Post-Communist World

The years 1985 to 1991 witnessed social, political, and economic transformation in central and eastern Europe that constitute the beginning of a new epoch in modern world history. The unimaginable happened—the Soviet era ended.

This series of events started with Mikhail Gorbachev assuming leadership of the Soviet Union in March 1985, was propelled by the remarkable new attitude of *glastnost* (open dialogue) and policies of *perestroika* (structural reform), changed the political face of eastern Europe with the lifting of the Iron Curtain in 1989, and culminated in December 1991, with the formal dissolution of the Soviet Union itself. Contemporary events in eastern Europe are postscripts to the developments of 1985–1991; echoes, repercussions, and reactions to the tumultuous changes of that seven-year period.

Ironically, it is Russia that is reeling most from the forces she herself set into motion. Accordingly, Part III begins with a report and analysis from Russia. One cannot help but be struck by the degree of social disintegration that the nation is undergoing. Virtually every crisis imaginable—economic, political, demographic, religious, cultural, and social—continues to grip the world's largest nation, with no end in sight. Caught in the middle of this are all public institutions, and education is no exception.

As the education system attempts to literally reinvent itself, our contributing author outlines the major hurdles facing educators and the profound depth of the changes being implemented. Yet, pessimism is not the lesson drawn or conclusion reached. As Russia and her schools enter a new and unprecedented era of democratic evolution, that most characteristic and admirable of Russian traits comes through. In spite of an almost complete absence of encouraging signs, hope springs eternal and confidence in a better future remains unshaken.

Of course, the ending of the communist era in eastern Europe resulted in deep disruptions for all nations involved. A microcosm of those turbulent changes is found in Lithuania, and so we have placed that national case study as our second reading. As this small and complex nation attempts to reestablish its national and cultural identity, nurture democracy, modernize its economy while coping with financial crises, strike a balance between secular and religious forces, and accommodate demographic changes, we gain an appreciation of the hard realities facing all the eastern European nations that were once Soviet satellite states.

The themes of the first two chapters are repeated, with important different nuances and emphases, in the studies on Poland, Hungary, and Croatia. Poland's and Hungary's relative economic successes, won at the expense of comprehensive and often painful social and fiscal reforms, has perched those nations on the threshold of full integration into the European Union.

An integral component of their social and economic modernization strategies has been deep education reform, of which there has been much. As Poland and Hungary continue their rapid social changes, this penchant for education reform shown no signs of abating. In the process, remarkable progress has been made. This is reflected in a modernization of curriculum and pedagogy, changes in teacher training, increased choices in schooling options, and enhanced local autonomy. On the other hand, issues of equity, equality of opportunity, efficiency, system fragmentation, inadequate funding, and lack of financial and professional support for teachers pose constant challenges and plague the emerging education system.

The problems of Poland and Hungary, however, pale in comparison to the Croatian situation. While Croatia's initial adaptation to post-communist life was less traumatic than Poland's and Hungary's, events specific to the violent disintegration of Yugoslavia engulfed the nation. Nevertheless, education reforms continue to be implemented at a brisk pace and visible progress is in ample evidence. Indeed, if one seeks proof positive that meaningful evolution of an education system can take place even in the most trying of circumstances, few nations can provide a better case in point than Croatia.

In all five countries, the education systems both reflect ongoing national debates and problems and are looked to as a major means of implementing solutions. This role for schooling is indicative of the primary social function of education in eastern Europe, and it places great responsibilities on the education community.

CHAPTER 13

Education in Modern Russia: Is It Modern?

NIKOLAI D. NIKANDROV

*Nikolai D. Nikandrov received his Ph.D. in education from Leningrad University (USSR) in 1973. He worked as a professor in education first in Leningrad (later St. Petersburg), then Moscow, before moving to the USSR Academy of Educational Sciences (now the Russian Academy of Education) in 1983. In October 1997, he was elected president of the Academy. His research interests are in the fields of comparative education, the methodology of educational research, and methods of teaching and learning. He is author of about 200 publications on these subjects, among them several books (*Programmed Learning and the Ideas of Cybernetics, 1970;* Pedagogics of Higher Education, 1974;* Higher Education Abroad, 1978;* Creativity in Teaching, 1990;* Values Education: The Case of Russia, 1996;* Russia: Values in Society at the Threshold of the 21st Century, 1997; and others).*

Education in modern Russia means education and educational development since 1991 (the year of the disintegration of the USSR). Gorbachev's era of *perestroika* (restructuring) was too brief to change much. Although democratic changes and pluralistic models in education originated in that time, the economic decline that followed left few resources to make real structural changes. Still, some meaningful changes in education have been accomplished. Perhaps the three most important are the new choices in types of schooling available, the independence of schools and teachers, and the substantial changes in the content of education at all levels, from preschool to tertiary education. However, many ideas that are now in vogue date back to the beginning of the century; that is, to Russia before the October 1917 revolution.

THE SOCIAL FABRIC

Political, Economic, and Social Transformation

In June 1991, Boris Yeltsin became the first democratically elected Russian president; in August a coup d'etat against him failed; in December a tiny place in Byelorussia made history by witnessing the abolition of the Soviet Union and the formation of the Community of Independent States (CIS). Dramatic as these events were, they do not constitute the starting points of modern reforms in Russia.

In fact, the reforms began in 1985 with the coming to power of Mikhail Gorbachev, who assumed the then most important post of authority in the nation—Secretary General of the USSR Communist Party (later, he also took the position of President of the USSR). However, in spite of Gorbachev's position of power, it must be kept in mind that, whatever his motivation for pursuing reforms, his actions posed a tremendous personal risk for him. The Old Guard (the hard-line Communist Party and Soviet functionaries) could have possibly demoted him or even put him on trial for high treason. Soon afterward, Yeltsin's situation was much less precarious. He criticized Gorbachev, the Communist Party, and Soviet traditions only when he was personally hurt by unjust criticism from Gorbachev, but never before. And there was no serious risk for Yelstin, for almost all the hard work of putting the old guard out of power had been done by Gorbachev.

At the height of his power, admired by so many in Russia and indeed the whole world, Gorbachev set into motion the processes that would transform Russia. A decade later, in the presidential election of 1996, Gorbachev was able to convince only about one percent of the electorate to endorse him. The explanation for this remarkably miserable showing is the failure of Gorbachev's reforms in the economic field. And failure it was, without any doubt.

Today, not quite a decade and a half since Gorbachev came to power, the country is in deep crisis. A good question here might be, though—which country? It is not the former Soviet Union; it is Russia as the largest country of the disbanded Union. It must be appreciated that Russia's ties with the other republics were not solely the product of seventy-odd years of Soviet power; they had been built over hundreds of years, over the whole history of the Russian empire. The significant economic interdependence of the republics, based on a division of productive powers, was a Soviet innovation. With the disintegration of the Union, these symbiotic production and trade relations were interrupted, and this caused immediate economic problems.

The abolition of the Union was accomplished in December 1991, in Belovezhskaya Pushcha (Byelorussia). Many of the ties binding the USSR were severed overnight and almost all the others followed suit with little delay. During the 1991 Russian presidential election campaign, Boris Yeltsin's most important slogan was "Take as much sovereignty (independence) as you can swallow." It was swallowed in very large lumps. As time passed, what was clear to many at that time became manifest to all: Market reforms, coupled with the severing of economic, cultural, and political ties could not but result in a drastic production slump.

To appreciate why production fell into chaos, one must understand the degree to which much of the manufacturing in individual Soviet Republics was intimately tied into production in other republics. For example, in the USSR a truck manufactured in Byelorussia would be assembled with parts manufactured in virtually all the other republics, depending on where raw materials and

energy were least expensive. This is not to say that such a division was always reasonable or based on effective economic criteria, but there it was. Today, these production sites are located in independent countries, are under different forms of ownership and management, subject to different regulations, and so on. This fragmentation has destroyed what was once a unified, integrated, economic infrastructure.

Various estimates put the drop in production at about 50 percent by 1997, with raw materials suffering the least, heavy industry and consumer goods the most. To understand the staggering proportions of this drop in production, we might compare it to the losses suffered in the war of 1941–1945. These amounted to about 17 percent (of course, the loss of over 20 million people was much more important in human terms). The obvious and immediate economic and consequences of the dissolution of the Soviet Union were a drop in the standard of living and quality of life.

Demography

The demographic situation is also serious. In the Soviet era, the birthrate was barely sufficient for population-level maintenance. However, this is a deceiving statistic, for it represents an average for the entire Soviet Union and the birthrate in the southern republics had always been greater than in Russia. Now, with the republics gone and Russia standing alone, the population is noticeably diminishing.

It is interesting to note that, at the tide of perestroika (1986-1987) the birthrate in Russia rose slightly—perhaps a reflection of hopes for fast economic progress. Such hopes vanished swiftly after 1991 and the birthrate is now the lowest in many years. Many parents just do not feel secure with the thought of having children in light of the ongoing economic instability. So the population of about 148 million people is diminishing, even though immigration of Russians from troubled areas in the Caucasus, and especially from Middle Asia, helps to mitigate this trend. But the positive aspects of immigration also have a reverse side.

Most immigrants are people who do not have roots in Russia, there is public resentment against their presence, as it is popularly believed that they are the source of problems in housing, employment, and so on.

Religion

As far as religion is concerned, Russia has experienced profound changes—some decidedly for the better. Before 1917, Russian Christian Orthodoxy was the state religion and the people who abided by it had clear privileges over atheists and exponents of other religions. For example, most Jews practicing Judaism were not allowed to live in large cities, they were allowed to enter universities only under special provisions, and they had no right to inherit real estate (Calendar, 1902).

After 1917 the country's communist leadership did all it could to convert all people to atheism. In a sense, the majority of people did accept the new way of life; however, many did so out fear of persecution, others out of career considerations. Where people did feel more free to honestly express their religious orientations was in anonymous public opinion polls. In the 1980s, the percentage of religious believers was estimated at about 30 to 35 percent. Now, with state pressure to profess atheism gone, recent data reveal that over 50 percent of the population claims to hold some form of religious belief. Interestingly, young people (aged 16 to 19) are most prominent in the group (Statistics, 1996). The same research also claims that the Russian Christian Orthodox possesses much greater moral authority than the president or the government.

The problem is that Christianity is only one of many religions in Russia. While it is the dominant religion statistically, there are also Judaists, Hindus, followers of Islam, pagans, and new-religion followers scattered over the vast territory of Russia. This religious diversity has social and political consequences. While there is certainly not conflict between followers of the various religions on the scale found in early Russian history, some of the problems of independence and sovereignty in Russia can well be traced to different religions or have a religious overtone. To use schooling as an example, we find today that, although officially all state-run education is secular and the church is separated from the state, educators are increasingly feeling pressure to cater to pupils of various religions in the same class or school.

Culture

Russia has always been a country with a significant cultural history. Russian architecture, music, literature, dance, and so on, are well known all over the world. In the Soviet times it was the professed goal of the leadership to encourage patriotism as expressed in love of classical Russian high culture. Western high culture was encouraged also. However, pop culture was frowned upon and was only partially and unwillingly admitted into the country. The screening out of pop culture was fairly easy because of the ideological iron curtain that remained intact until the Gorbachev era. However, with the fall of the curtain, a massive influx of western pop culture ensued and changed the orientations of the Soviet era. Westernization is clearly seen now in almost all fields of culture, with the classical western and Russian heritages having fewer and fewer opportunities to be viewed, heard, and appreciated.

The situation is not simple or one-sided. It must be emphasized that the positive result of perestroika is still here, in the sense that today no ideological barriers stand in the way of those who want to read, see, or hear whatever they choose. But on the negative side the reality is that low-level pop culture, with erotic undertones bordering on pornography, is overriding everything else. Expectedly and understandably, this has an undesirable influence on the young.

The solution to the problem is not simple either. First, there are large profits (from shows, videos, audio cassettes and CDs, printed matter, and so on) to be made by the promoters of pop culture. Second, it is understandable that a substantial proportion of the young, in reaction to a former society characterized by direct suppression, should eagerly embrace the forms of expression and rebellion embodied in much of pop culture. Third, the Russian constitution contains direct provisions for freedom of information and against censorship. So, while the difficulties for worried parents, educators, and others, are clear, the solutions are not near at hand.

The above arenas—politics, economics, social structures and relations, demography, religion, and culture—are but some of the major locations of the profound changes taking place in post-Soviet Russia. The changes taking place are ubiquitous; they permeate all aspects of society, including formal education.

SCHOOLING

Historical Roots

In Soviet times (1917–1991) there were many educational reforms in Russia—though not everyone is willing to call them reforms. The Russian Minister of Education from 1990–1992 put it in this way: There are reforms, counterreforms, and pseudoreforms—that is, would-be reforms (Dneprov, 1994, 1997). The implication is, of course, that the changes he tried to initiate were genuine reforms, while the immediately preceding changes were merely pseudoreforms. There is no doubt, however, that what was done by Gorbachev in a wider context (particularly politics and economics) were very serious changes that unquestionably constitute genuine reform.

Russia was then part of the Soviet Union, which was autocratically ruled by several top people in the hierarchy of the Communist Party. Sometimes stronger words, like dictatorship and totalitarianism, are used to describe the situation. I will not start another debate on semantics, but there certainly was no single dictator at the time Gorbachev came to power. A direct comparison of the latest years of Soviet power with fascist regimes would also be far-fetched.

But more interesting is the fact that the contents of the changes to education that were initiated in the Gorbachev era can well be traced to much earlier times. In Russia at the end of the nineteenth century, there were about 200 educational journals and magazines in publication—a number never since surpassed. Even a superficial analysis of these publications shows that all the principal ideas for reforming education were already there. There was a demand for democratization, including equal opportunities for all and greater access to advanced levels of education. No limitations should be on the basis of sex, nationality, material well-being, religion, or social status. The general public (parents, teachers, all interested people) were urged to take part in controlling education; the state should not be the omnipotent and sole administrator. Local authorities should also have more power, while schools themselves should be autonomous. Private initiative in education (including setting up private schools) should be encouraged. A unified system of education, with interconnected levels for greater student mobility, should be set up. Education should be separated from the church. Special provision should be made for the education of mentally or physically handicapped children. Elementary education should be free and coeducation should be general practice. Teaching should be free (have academic autonomy) and the contents of education should be radically changed to provide for the changing needs of children. Finally, in many of the publications, social change (abolition of the czarist state) was also propagated.

Looking at these demands of educators at the end of the nineteenth century, one is struck by how they parallel the slogans of today. Indeed, they are too ambitious and modern for the beginning of the twentieth century; they are the language and ideas we are taking into the third millennium. Perhaps the only thing that seems to be missing, if these demands are to be applied to contemporary thinking about education, is continuing or life-long education. At that time pressure for continuing education was not yet felt, though some educationists—such as Nikolai Rubakin—did raise the idea of continuing education.

Many of these educational demands were incorporated into the "Statute of the Unified Labor-

Oriented School," instituted by A. Lunacharsky, the first national Commissar (or Minister) of Education after the revolution of October 1917. The Statute also included abolition of all exams, punishment, and homework assignments. It provided for school councils to act as bodies of school self-government, allowed a variety of school books to be used, and encouraged teachers to be creative.

Because of these changes to schooling initiated by Lunacharsky, some historians of Russian and Soviet education refer to the 1920s as the "golden age" of Russian education. Those education ideas and practices, however, ceased to be implemented at the end of the 1920s when the strict political control of the Communist Party penetrated into all spheres of life, including education. Variety and creativity gave way to centralization and uniformity and after about 1930 very little, if anything, was left over from the "golden age."

Thus we recognize that the reformers of Russian education from 1985 onwards picked up many ideas that date back to the first quarter of the twentieth century. Indeed, even before Yeltsin came to power, these ideas had been passionately discussed by teachers, parents, and grandparents. The Soviet system of education was being criticized as authoritarian and obsolete and innovative teachers summoned huge audiences by demonstrating more humane and cooperative teaching. When change finally came, the euphoria over the changes in education was as strong as the euphoria over Gorbachev's perestroika as a whole.

Recent Legislation

As was emphasized above, some of the important provisions for recent educational reform in Russia are echoes from at least the beginning of the century. But the latest and most important document that provides an insight into Russian education is The Law on Education adopted in 1992 and amended in 1996 (The Law, 1992). Article 2 states the principles of education policy of the country while proclaiming the humanistic nature of education; priority of general human values, human life, health, and free personal development; edu-

cation of love for one's country and civil maturity; unity of educational space in the country; protection by education of national cultures and regional tradition under the conditions of multiculturalism in the country; free access to education for all; adaptivity of the education system to students' abilities and development; secular education in state-run and municipal institutions of education; freedom and pluralism in education; democratic state- and society-oriented administration of education; and autonomy of educational institutions. Again, similarity of these principles to many of those in existence at the beginning of the century is quite evident.

Among other important provisions of the Law of 1992 worth noting is the requirement that no less than 10 percent of national income (gross domestic product) is to be allocated to education. There is also a provision allowing school choice for parents and students, including private education. Finally, there is a provision for the introduction of education standards.

Goals and Objectives

While legislation articulates general principles of education policy and proclaims the priority of certain general values, it is important to remember that there are no precisely formulated and clear, specific, national goals or objectives of education in Russia today. In contrast to earlier times, specific goals have been replaced by very general ones—a reaction to the rigidity of schooling in the former Soviet era. However, we can identify an overriding, transcending goal of education that is so broad that it encompasses even the general goals and the objectives outlined above.

For many years now, Russian educators have been committed to the ideal of all-round development of a student's personality. This is not a post-Soviet innovation; it was deduced from Marxist theory and taken up by Vladimir Lenin when the communists came to power. Accordingly, some educationists in Russia argue that this is a Marxist idea and therefore it should be done away with. This is a dubious presumption; the roots of the orientation date back much farther, into ancient times. The Greek *kalokagathia* (teaching about the beautiful and the good) was the ideal of the ancients and was adhered to by many later educationists. Perhaps more importantly for modern schooling is the fact that in the Universal Declaration of Human Rights, adopted by the United Nations in 1948, article 26 articulates practically the same general goal.

This idea of all-sidedness, all-round development, is certainly there in Russian education, and I would say that this is a good principle for the most general orientation of education. However, this concept is another example of how what is considered by some to be a new characteristic of modern education is in fact not so modern at all—it goes back well before its communist interpretation. Historians of education will certainly remind us that well before 1917 many prominent Russian educationists and philosophers stressed the concept of development. Today, few people would deny development as the key word in the present-day philosophy of education in Russia.[1] The chief proponent of so-called development education is Vassily Davydov (Davydov, 1996), who in turn draws on the educational philosophy of the eminent Russian psychologist Lev Vygotsky.

It must be appreciated that the idea of development education in Russia is not be interpreted to be the polar opposite of a purely cognitive approach. The Russian notion of development is tempered with a cognitive element; a balance of knowledge and development is often stressed. This is a legacy from Soviet times when the cognitive approach was considered to be extremely important and the quality of education was primarily measured by the quantity of knowledge acquired by students.

Finally, it must be recognized that the very definition of what constitutes "all-around development of student personality" is really dependent upon social ideas of the time. And, of course, what is practical and possible to accomplish depends on the education system, on finance, on traditions, and so on.

Research in Education

For many years the most important method of research in education in the Soviet Union was what was called "generalization of the experience of education." It meant that researchers drew heavily on the experience of successful teachers, trying to confirm by experimentation what was found to be good in practice. The good practice was then carefully worked out in minute detail and the result usually was a collection of instructions on the methodology of teaching.

Many teachers liked the approach because it provided them with an instrument at hand to use in class. It was also convenient because of the frequent and rather strict checkups that the education inspectorate organized in schools. There were teachers who tried to think of something new and succeeded splendidly in communicating their ideas. Some were well known not only in education circles but became public cult figures and were as well recognized as pop stars. These innovators contributed solutions to the problems of school reform while adding ideas of democratic school administration, cooperative climate, and development to Soviet schools. While the influence of individual innovators may have been short lived, the cumulative effect of the dialogue they generated among educators and in society lingers. Today, acceptance of innovation and development is very much in vogue at all levels of school administration.

This new atmosphere has some very desirable outcomes. For one thing, now teachers who want to experiment may, in most cases, do so without fear. Pluralism in education is a reality in contemporary Russia; it is there in law and in practice. Innovations in methods of teaching are another

---

[1]In Russia—as in the Soviet Union before—the term "educational philosophy" was and is hardly used. Rather, the most general problems of education are discussed under the heading of "methodology of education," which does not mean "methods of teaching." Books specially devoted to philosophy of education are rare exceptions and the very different choice of topics shows that there is no common understanding of what it is.

positive development. However, curriculum is one area where diversity and innovation have yet to make inroads.

The Structure of the Education System

The Russian educational system is based on eleven years of general education in the sense that eleven school years spent studying relatively common subjects is a prerequisite to enter universities and institutes (university-level specialized institutions). Nowadays, American-type bachelors and masters programs are also available, the principal idea being to enhance academic mobility of students. Post-university education includes candidate of science and doctor of science degree programs. Both require a demanding series of papers and examinations and a public defense of a thesis (dissertation).

The route of eleven years of general education followed by entry into a university or institute is not for all students. After nine years of basic education, children may enter two- or three-year vocational schools that train skilled workers, or so-called special secondary education institutions that train technicians, secretaries, computer operators, and so on. (The former name of technical-professional school is hardly ever used, having given way to more appealing names like lyceum and college. Also included here are the so-called innovative schools.)

It is not mandatory for students to go beyond basic education. According to article 43 of the Russian Constitution, children are allowed to leave after nine years of schooling. Clearly this is a step backward from the requirement of eleven years of compulsory schooling that existed in the USSR before 1992. The matter of compulsory school ages is not straightforward in Russia. A presidential decree has now raised the requirement back to the old level, but there are more than a million children of school age out of school. To appreciate why, it must be remembered that the Constitution is the supreme law of the country. So, if one wants to ignore the presidential decree on the upwardly revised age for school leaving,

the Constitution provides a legal basis for doing so.

Russia has 66,600 preschool institutions (nursery schools and kindergartens) that 5.6 million children attend. Preschool education is not compulsory. Compulsory schooling begins at the age of 6 or 7, depending on the parents' wishes, and less than half of preschool children go to crèches (nursery schools) and kindergartens. It is worth noting that the statistics on preschool have changed the most drastically of all education statistics since the end of the Soviet era. The preschool system had about 9 million children in 1990; almost double the current enrollment. Today only a small proportion of parents wish their very young children be educated out of home. This large decline is partly explained by the growing number of unemployed parents, and thus the expense that many families cannot cope with. A final factor is the increasing number of private preschool institutions. But here the statistics are unreliable, for many private kindergartens consist of very small groups of children not registered anywhere.

There are over 70,000 schools of general education teaching over 21 million pupils. Going further up the education ladder, some 4,200 vocational institutions (in Russia this level of education is called basic professional education with the objective of training skilled workers) and 2,640 secondary professional institutions (colleges) exist to meet the needs of 1,923,300 students. Finally, 2,642,000 students are found in 566 state-run institutions of higher education.

Standards and Evaluation

Perhaps the most important recent curricular innovation is a proposed introduction of state education standards. This was not an issue during the days of the USSR, with its unified system of education allowing little autonomy for teachers and little differentiation for the interests and abilities of students. With the change of government came pluralism in education, academic freedom, and vast regional differences in education content.

Accordingly, a call emerged for state education standards to guarantee that students at all levels receive the programs that they are supposed to get. The Law on Education even provides for lawsuits against poor-quality education; however, not a single case of the sort is known to me.

State standards for basic education are to be introduced as a law by the Federal Assembly (the Russian Parliament), while the standards for vocational and university education are adopted by government decrees. Public debate about whether to employ uniform educational standards and what these should be is raging unabated in educational circles. My hope is that the idea of state standards will triumph, for there are numerous cases where teachers and schools are abusing their newly won freedom by providing very poor-quality education.

Soviet education was notorious for a lot of examinations beginning with the fourth grade. As time passed, examinations were gradually abolished except after basic school and full secondary education. Now each school has the right to introduce exams it deems necessary and some schools do use the right to the full. Sometimes testing similar to U.S. patterns is used. Educational standards are supposed to be accompanied by a system of tests to measure achievement, but this is still in the preliminary stage.

Administration

In the USSR, the Ministries of Education (the central USSR Ministry and the ministries of the republics) had very firm control over the day-to-day running of education, although overall control lay with the upper echelons of the Communist Party because almost all General Secretaries deemed it necessary to exert some personal influence on education. Since then, the changes that have taken place in the administration of education are tremendous. It is now an important part of educational policy to devolve power to lower echelons of administration. For example, just over 30 percent of education content as expressed in the standards discussed above is prescribed from the center (the so-called federal component). All the rest (the regional and the school components) lies with regional departments and the schools themselves. The same is true about financing education. Now less than 10 percent of money comes from the center; the rest comes from local authorities.

At the beginning of the 1990s many school directors were elected, some of them from people with no expertise in teaching but with progressive (reformist) ideas. This vogue has now peacefully passed away (although the possibility of electing directors is still in the Law on Education). In most cases directors are appointed by city (district) departments of education. Directors have overall control of a school system and are responsible for personnel and finance. They are helped in their duties by deputies who are responsible for running the education process. School psychologists also work in many schools to address special student problems. Their duties are similar to work in the counseling and/or guidance services.

Teacher Education

Teachers are trained in universities and pedagogical universities. The latter, formerly called pedagogical institutes, changed their name for prestige purposes (though in many cases with little change in substance). The term of study at any university-type institution is five years or more. Teachers are usually trained to teach one or two subjects. However, with unemployment problems now pressing, some institutions train rural school teachers who can (and very often do) teach three to five subjects. Typical combinations are mathematics/physics/astronomy; biology/geography; literature/language; or literature/history/civics. Sports is very often added as another element to these combinations.

Nonformal Education

In the USSR there was a well developed system of nonformal education. All schools (exceptions were practically nonexistent) had at least sports and artistic circles to cater to children with such interests. There were also many forms of nonformal education taking place in the so-called Palaces and Houses of the Young Pioneers and in other public institutions. Practically all sports facilities were also free. At present, however, almost all services take fees and, because of the economic situation, participation is quite low.

School Discipline

A consistent observation about Soviet schools made by people coming from abroad is that students were very well-behaved and disciplined. With perestroika and especially later events, people in general have become more independent-minded, and this has been paralleled by a slackening of discipline in the schools. I think some time must pass until a reasonable balance is struck between responsibility and freedom—in both the wider social context and in the classroom. Today Russian students (school pupils as well as university students) are certainly more relaxed, more demanding of their teachers, and many of them are more responsible than in Soviet times. But crime has also grown substantially; juvenile delinquency is growing at a rate several times faster than adult crime. Russian education is now beset with troubles such as early pregnancy, prostitution, drug abuse, and all sorts of violence; all these were rare exceptions only a dozen years ago.

SOCIAL AND EDUCATION ISSUES

Finances

Some people say that the market economy, in spite of being the official objective of economic development in Russia, is not functioning at all. My understanding is that it is functioning, but in a very peculiar way.

In Soviet times there was a joke that under capitalism wealth is unevenly distributed; under socialism, poverty is evenly distributed. Perhaps it was not exactly that way, but it is true that there really were no striking differences in life standards among people during the Soviet regime.

True, the party and Soviet elite had greater opportunities and there certainly existed rich people in the shadow economy. But nobody could really flaunt his or her wealth for fear of persecution for economic crimes. Even petty trading, like buying something in a shop and selling it for a profit outside, was illegal (though widespread because fashionable goods were scarce).

Then, almost overnight, such restraints were removed. By special decree, Yeltsin proclaimed a radical liberalization of trade that was almost without restrictions (although such blanket freedom was tempered several years later). Shadow businesspeople openly used their money to accumulate capital and buy privatized enterprises. Liberalization of prices resulted in skyrocketing inflation that practically annihilated savings collected by people over many years. A contemporary joke ironically sums up this sad situation. A dying grandmother tells the grandfather sitting by the bedside, "I have been saving money to buy a car; give it to our grandson, let him buy an ice cream."

In the short span of two or three years, a differentiation in income emerged that left the vast majority of people poor, a few well off, and a very few rich and super rich. Again, statistics are not very reliable, but the general estimate is that the income ratio of the richest 10 percent to the poorest 10 percent is 1 to 15. In contrast to earlier times, there is now no talk about equality of opportunity; differentiation is not only admitted but encouraged. The latest published state report on the situation of children in the Russian Federation emphasizes the "prolonged poverty" of many families and gives vivid examples of hunger, child mortality, early pregnancies, social diseases, and so on that I will not dwell upon (The State, 1996).

All this has consequences for education. True, education in the Soviet Union was never financed too generously. Still, in the 1950s it was about 10 percent of gross domestic product; a very respectable percentage. But from the end of the 1960s that percentage began to decrease gradually. In 1970 it was 7 percent, by 1994–1996 less than 4 percent. Put into broader contexts, we can compare this with Great Britain or France where the figures are relatively stable over the years, varying between 5.3 percent and 5.5 percent. From a global perspective, we note that the average world figure is about 5.5. However, the actual state of Soviet and Russian education financing must also include a consideration of per capita production, which was and is low. Therefore, the above percentages do not translate into as much actual cash for the education system as might be thought at first glance. The net conclusion is that education in Russia has been underfinanced in the past and today is drastically underfinanced (Nelassov, 1997).

There is another important aspect to education financing, one which is quite new for Russia. Formerly almost all funding came from the central authorities. True, this was distributed by the local authorities but no administrator at the local level would ever think of channeling even a fraction of the money allocated for schooling to anything other than education. Now most funding comes from local budgets. The result is, of course, gross differences between various regions in terms of percentages and real money. And because Russia is in a prolonged economic crisis, federal authorities are unable to mitigate these regional differences, leaving some regions locked into a terrible situation of underfinancing.

What is the net result of these financial concerns? First, we recall that the Law on Education adopted in 1992 requires that education be financed to an amount of no less than 10 percent of the national income. Furthermore, according to the Law on Higher Education adopted later, higher education should get no less than 3 percent of the federal budget. Sorting out the different terms (federal budget, national income, gross domestic product, consolidated budget, and so on) is no easy matter. However, combining the available different approaches and statistics, one comes to the conclusion that in 1997 the adopted budget provides about one-third of the minimally necessary finance of education. It leaves the system in a situation where it can barely survive, let alone develop.

This overall conclusion can be better understood with a few additional comments on important points and some illustrations of the drastic effects underfinancing has had. First, it is recognized that since 1992 a trend of steady lowering expenditures on education has become firmly established. This is perhaps the thing that saddens us most of all. Very few people expected that after the dissolution of the USSR economic revival would immediately follow. But, with much talk about imminent stabilization, hopes were raised. Yet there is no sign of an end to what has become a series of economic crises. Education, along with other institutions, continues to suffer from a lack of adequate resources.

Students clearly feel the consequences of this new era of underfunding of education as less and less money and resources are spent per student. For example, student scholarships in tertiary (post-secondary) education are not even sufficient for survival. They do not cover food costs, let alone other expenses. Or, if a student buys a monthly public transport ticket to get about in the city, this will leave nothing at all from his or her scholarship.

Educators are affected just as harshly. According to the Law, teachers should get a salary equal to the average in industry; university professors should get double the amount. In fact, teachers and professors barely get half of what they should. In addition, salaries are often two to five months in arrears, so there is a shortage of teachers in many places (Webber, 1996). Researchers find themselves in similarly dire straits. Education (especially higher education) is closely linked with research, but this is also grossly underfinanced. In 1996 the USA spent $130 billion on research, South Korea $10 billion, Russia $1.2 billion. University professors are now almost deprived of research funds.

Other problems abound. Over a third of school buildings are decrepit. The school year of 1996/1997 began with one textbook for two school pupils (it must be noted, however, that the federal standard schoolbooks are free of charge). Schoolchildren's health is appalling: only for about 10 percent of pupils can it be considered normal. Many children are hungry all the time. The adolescent crime rate is growing fifteen times faster than the adult rate. We are also experiencing troubles that were barely felt ten years ago: early pregnancy, child abuse and prostitution, drug abuse. All this can be put right with a massive influx of money. But, with production falling and a lot of money and raw materials exported abroad, I am not optimistic that the money can be found by the present authorities.

Inequality of Access and Opportunity

Differentiation in income and economic decline could not but be followed by differentiation in education. One natural consequence is a growing number of non-state-run schools and post-school institutions. This is a very important change in comparison with the USSR, where private education was not allowed at all. In principle, this is a positive development. Since about 10 percent of the people in Russia are quite well off, why not let them spend their money on the education of their children? But, emotionally, many accustomed to the relative equality of the former Soviet state are not at ease with the perspective.

There are about 1,000 schools of general education (including 300 in Moscow) that are not state run. They cater to about 1 percent of the total student population—a low percentage that is explained by the relatively heavy fees demanded by most of these institutions. There are also 193 non-state-run higher education institutions with 136,000 students. Most private higher schools are small and tuition fees are high.

Interestingly, limited career opportunities because of the economic situation have not drastically affected demands for post-secondary education. Since under present conditions good education is in most cases little rewarded in money or position, it is reasonable to expect that there is little incentive for getting it. To some degree, this attitude exists and is partly reflected in the large number of out-of-school youth. Nevertheless, there continues to be a strong demand for

higher education. True, the competition is nothing like it was fifteen to twenty years ago with five to twenty-five applicants for each vacancy; now it is about two to three on the average and over ten or more for the humanities, law, and finance.

However, once students gain access to an institution of higher learning, their circumstances are not ideal. Most students now have to work. If they are lucky, they are able to work in their special field of interest, such as future teachers working as private tutors, but most have to take anything that is available. Some are able to work abroad for a period of time to save money. There is also the temptation to raise funds illegally as through prostitution, racketeering, and so on, which raises serious moral issues.

This is a new circumstance. In the Soviet era, students who really wanted to learn full-time had the opportunity to do so. Scholarships were very low but they were sufficient for survival and students could apply all their time and energy to their studies. Now scholarships are not sufficient; students either have to work or get money from parents. When one takes into account the number of class hours in Russian higher education institutions (greater than in other nations), the necessity to work almost certainly means less time, effort, and energy for learning, and the quality of education suffers.

Ideological Change

What is called in Russia *monoideology* (the political ideology of Marxism-Leninism that pervaded all teaching at all levels) has been done away with. That ideology left little space for personal choice and development, it was based on totalitarian ideas, and little criticism of those in power was allowed. Still, it did have some positive effects. For example, even though it was only half-heartedly shared in the last period of the USSR, it did unite the people, especially at times of crisis (like the war of 1941–1945). Now, with the abolition of that ideology, an ideological vacuum has emerged in Russia.

In result, the value system of Russian society

has become extremely loose. While the personal value systems of very many people have generally become void of cultural and spiritual content, replaced by the omnipotence of money (Nikandrov, 1996), some would say that this is not bad because it provides for choice and personal interests. Put into the context of education, it is true that people can, at least in theory, choose their schools, teachers, books, ideas, and ways of life freely.

But why is the caveat phrase "at least in theory" needed? Again we must return to the reality of severe economic constraints. Yes, we can choose schools and teachers. But some schools are overcrowded and very high fees in many of the better schools restrict our options. Yes, we can choose textbooks. But in many places there are just not enough textbooks for each child to have one. Yes, we can go anywhere to spend a weekend or a holiday and rich people do go to Rome, Paris, or the Canary Islands. But most Russians today have difficulty in just going forty to fifty miles away from where they live, let alone traveling to the south—the Black Sea coast that was generally accessible and very popular a decade ago. Still the freedom of choice in education should not be underestimated. Even with the abovementioned limitations, it is now in principle greater than at any other time in our history.

For example, some time ago there were only "unified labor-oriented polytechnic schools" in this country—that was the official name of schools. Unified meant uniformity in the curriculum, which was strictly controlled by the state. Now, about 70 percent of schools try to use innovative approaches to teaching. With few exceptions this is encouraged at all levels—from the center (the Ministry) down to the school itself. There are now over 3,000 schools with names that were not used a few years ago: lyceums, gymnasiums, colleges, education complexes.

As for resources, while there is a shortage of textbooks, it is also true that better schools use the possibility of choice and provide various textbooks for their students that they think are more suitable for this or that reason. And school subjects, especially social subjects and the humanities, are concerned to give a more balanced approach and sometimes a revaluation of many facts in history, politics, and many other fields of human endeavor.

All this was conditioned by the change of values after the dissolution of the USSR. But the change was not all for the better.

Crime, Morality, and Values

Almost everyone in Russia will now agree that moral standards have become very loose and the morality of the people has fallen. Greater political and moral freedom, more independence in forming one's own views, and initiative in the choice of one's own way in life are now accompanied by an upsurge of criminality, especially among younger people. Some developments hardly heard of before are now in prominence, such as violence, prostitution, child abuse, drug addiction, bribery, vote rigging, and so on.

Teachers try to cope with all this with varying (mostly little) degrees of success by teaching or clarifying values. Values education poses problems everywhere, but in Russia this is particularly acute (Nikandrov, 1992). In education the problems may be stated as: What are appropriate values? Do teachers have to take responsibility for teaching values?

In the USSR, neither problem seemed to exist. The first one was solved when the 22nd Communist Party Congress adopted the Program of the Party with the *Moral Code of the Builder of Communism* as its integral part. It had general human values, but the principal goal for everyone was building communism in the country and in the world. As for the second question, there was no controversy in the USSR about whether teachers had to take responsibility for teaching values; they did. However, at the very beginning of independent Russia many thought they did not. Now, with morality falling, most people agree teachers should be teaching values. What are the values, though? Because there is a moral vacuum in the nation, schools do not have a clear set of values to teach. And these values will certainly not be found inside the education system itself.

In response to this dilemma, President Boris Yeltsin, in January 1996, mentioned the necessity of formulating a national ideology ("the national idea"). I am not sure that this can be done to order. A national ideology should ripen in the society itself and Russian society is now very much divided.

Workload and Standards

The Soviet school was always criticized for overloading students with work. Both the quantity of curricular content (too much) and the quality of teaching (presenting material in too difficult a manner) were blamed. The situation has now changed, but it has hardly become better. For most school students, overload does not exist: They are sure that they will be given school certificates no matter how poor their results are. Most schools issue certificates to all school leavers and give them better marks than they deserve.

But for the approximately 20 percent of school leavers who plan to continue their education in university-level institutions, overload is very much a reality. Universities, especially the more prestigious ones, arrange entrance examinations at a much higher level of difficulty than ordinary school-leavers can cope with. So, parents who can afford to provide their children with additional lessons at school, paying fees and hiring teachers for lessons at home. All this makes for a working day of ten or more hours, which (together with poor food and environment and little exercise) leads to poor health. By the time students leave school, nearly 90 percent have health problems.

Organization and Administration of Education

For a long time there were two different ministries of education in Russia; one for general education and the education of teachers, another for higher education. In 1996, a new Ministry of General and Professional Education incorporating both was established. This change in administrative structure has significant consequences.

When educational reform began in 1990, the two ministries of education were headed by individuals who had very different ideas about education in the previous Soviet regime. Edward Dneprov, a very talented historian of education who had never had experience in teaching or management, was Minister of (General) Education. He had a very low opinion of Soviet education and thought it necessary to destroy the system and put another in place (Dneprov, 1994). Vladimir Kinelev was Minister for Higher Education and he had always had high respect for the quality of education in the USSR, though he admitted the necessity for reforms (Kinelev, 1995). So, although university-level institutions developed innovative approaches in the curriculum field, there was no talk about destruction. The result of the different orientations and approaches to reform of the two ministers was that general and higher education set out in different directions and the two systems no longer functioned in an integrated, complementary manner. This poses problems now that the two ministries are united. One consequence is that all Russian higher-education institutions are autonomous in their curricula and admittance procedures.

But the issue of whether education should be administered by one or two ministries is not the only problem. As debate continues on whether it would be desirable to divide the ministry again, more important is the question of the distribution of power within the system. While the centralization tradition has been destroyed, the practice of decentralized government is quite new and difficulties are common. Unfortunately, students are the ones who suffer most. For example, when a school gives instruction of poor quality and when some subjects are not available for study, there is little accountability. The reason is that there are no clear and consistent educational standards.

Education and Employment

Before 1990, a job was guaranteed to all graduates of higher education institutions through a system called "distribution." This meant that, a few months before graduation, a specially appointed committee determined where each graduate had to work for at least three years. Only students with serious family or health problems could seek exemption. The virtue of this system was that students had a real guarantee of finding employment in a job that reflected the specialty of each student. Now this is all in the past. Though registered unemployment is under 3 percent, in practice it is above 10 percent. In some areas and in some population groups it is substantially higher. For example, among registered unemployed people 62 percent are women and 39 percent are young people under the age of 30 (Ivashchenko, 1997).

THE FUTURE OF SOCIETY AND SCHOOLING

Though the picture I have painted above may seem gloomy, in fact I feel slightly optimistic about the long term (although not about the near future). The present authorities are too much preoccupied with economic and social problems they themselves have created to give enough attention to education. In a curious way, they are supported by public opinion. True, almost everybody understands the importance of education and almost all people are directly or indirectly connected with the system through being a student, a parent, a grandparent, or a teacher. But there are pressing problems in almost each family, like food, clothing, housing, personal security, environment, health, and so on. So, in public opinion polls, education usually places tenth or eleventh as a priority issue.

This cannot last forever. The problems will, for all their acuteness, somehow be solved either by the present authorities or by the authorities of tomorrow when solving the problems of education will again become a real priority. When future governments turn to solutions, I emphasize again that one of the major sources for ideas will be the education concepts that originated about a hundred years ago. Educational experience abroad is also a resource that might be used, perhaps sparingly. And the Russian tradition of great respect

for education—maintained through the Soviet period and not destroyed in the turmoil of reforms after 1990—will help people to overcome the seeming chaos of the present day. So, appending no timetable, I believe Russian society will eventually solve its education problems.

One important element will be consensus on a basic set of values for all children as citizens of a free society. In this agreement, a reasonable balance between national and general human values will be found. As a positive current step in this direction, it seems that President Yeltsin's plea for intellectuals to work out "the Russian national idea" is being taken seriously. I personally wonder if something like a national idea can be made to order. But it is felt in all quarters that if some consensus on basic values is not found, Russian society will in fact be torn to pieces. The task is not easy. While there are comparatively few people who would really wish a complete roundabout turn to communist ideology (though many feel nostalgia for the social security of that era) many are apprehensive of the uncertain future that seems to await society in the post-USSR era. Still, striking a balance between extremes is now more probable than some time ago.

Eventually, the state will put more money into education, making it a priority in deed, not just in words. Currently the government is completing work on a document titled *The Concept of the New Stage of Reforming Education*. Though some fear it is specifically aimed at cutting education budgets at all levels, such a perspective is too gloomy to be taken seriously. Rather the reverse may be true.

Soon, eleven years of full secondary education will again be the rule. And, in a few years time it will be twelve years. In fact, one of the research programs of the Russian Academy of Education is aimed at preparing the methodology and contents for a twelve-year full secondary education (and the abovementioned government document is supposed to include the provision).

Although the debate about national educational standards will not cease, general agreement on standards to legally provide a reasonable minimum of education for all students will be achieved. A practicable division of administrative power and financial authority will be achieved between the various echelons of educational administration. Currently, the accent is on more power and money for the regions rather than for the center. This, however, is a precarious matter and the issue of distribution of power and financial control is far from resolved.

Finally, a gradually rising standard of living and financial well-being of the population will make choice in education not only legally, but also practically, possible for all children and young people. However, it remains to be seen if such a dramatic rise in material social well being in the foreseeable future is not wishful thinking.

REFERENCES

Calendar, *The motherland for 1902* (1902). St. Petersburg: Publishing House A. Caspari.

Davydov, V. (1966). *The theory of developing education*. Moscow: INTOR. (In Russian)

Dneprov, E. (1994). *The fourth school reform in Russia*. Moscow: Interprax. (In Russian)

Dneprov, E. (1997). *The present education reform and the development of education in Russia*. Moscow: MARIOS-press. (In Russian)

Ivashchenko, I. (1997). The new cannibals. *Tverskaya, 13,* 12.

Kinelev, V. (1995). *The objective necessity. The history, problems and prospects of reforming higher education in Russia*. Moscow: Respublika. (In Russian)

(The) Law of the Russian Federation on Education. (1992, August 4). *Uchitelskaya Gazeta,* N2. (In Russian)

Nelassov, N. (1997). The situation with educational finance is catastrophic. *Pedagogichesky Kaleidoskop, 3.* (In Russian).

Nikandrov, N. (1992). Values education in Russian schools today. *New Education* (Australia), *14,* 3–9.

Nikandrov, N. (1996). *Values education: The case of Russia*. Moscow: Magistr. (In Russian)

(The) state report on the situation of children in the Russian Federation 1995. (1996). Moscow: Sinergia. (In Russian)

(The) statistics prove that the young are looking for a way to the church. (1996). *Pedagogichesky Kaleidoskop, 14.* (In Russian)

Webber, L. (1996) Demand and supply: Meeting the need for teachers in the "new" Russian school. *Journal of Education for Teaching, 22,* 9–26.

CHAPTER 14

Between Past and Future: The Dilemmatic Context of Schooling in Lithuania

ZIBARTAS JACKŪNAS

Zibartas Jackūnas *is currently a member of the Lithuanian Parliament and Chairman of the Committee for Education, Science, and Culture. From 1992 to 1996 he was director of the Institute of Pedagogics, Vilnius. His research interests lie in the areas of aesthetics, the philosophy of culture, and pedagogy. His work in these areas contributed to the elaboration of the theoretical foundations for current educational reforms in Lithuania.*

Since the restoration of independence in 1990, the development of Lithuania has been marked by political, social, economic, and cultural changes that are characteristic of the transitional processes taking place in many countries of central and eastern Europe. The efforts of Lithuanian society are directed toward strengthening the independent state; creating a modern, open, pluralistic society of free citizens; developing a sustainable economic life based on market principles; and fostering the national and cultural identity of the country. This provides a unique opportunity for Lithuania to join the community of democratic European nations.

THE SOCIAL FABRIC

Lithuania, with an area of 65,300 square kilometers, is a part of the geopolitical region known as the Baltic states. In 1996, the population was 3.7 million persons with a density of 57 inhabitants per square kilometer. About 67.8 percent of inhabitants live in urban areas; 32.2 percent in the rural ones.

Lithuanian independence ended in 1939 with the signing of the Molotov-Ribentrop pact between Hitler and Stalin. Many decades of hard sovietization (1940–1990) followed. Yet, the nation never lost its identity and a second chance for autonomy came with *perestroika* at the end of 1980s. The steps started by the Lithuanian Reform Movement (*Sàjûdis*) in 1988 led to a proclamation of independence on March 11, 1990.

Demography

Radical changes in the ethnic composition of Lithuania were brought about during the Second World War. Lithuania lost about one million of its inhabitants: 300,000 were deported and 210,000 were murdered by the Nazis, among them 135,000 Jews. Today Lithuania's ethnic composition is relatively homogeneous with more than 81 percent Lithuanians, 8 percent Russians, and 7 percent Poles. The remainder is composed of Belarussians and people from other parts of the former Soviet Union.

Beginning in 1990, the population growth rate began to slow down; since 1992, population size has started to decrease. This was partly a consequence of the reemigration of part of the population to the former Soviet Union republics, and partly because the mortality rate exceeded the fertility rate. At the same time, the average life expectancy dropped until it is now below 70 years of age. The difference between male and female life expectancy is increasing, and in 1996 this gap was 11.6 years.

The official language of the country is Lithuanian. Many people speak one or more foreign languages, most commonly Russian and one western European language. Lithuanian, together with Latvian and Prussian (now a dead language), belongs to the Baltic language group, which is a branch of Indo-European language. Lithuanian is considered to be the oldest of the living Indo-European languages. The nation is predominantly Roman Catholic. Other religions include Evangelical Lutheran, Evangelical Reformer, Orthodox Church, Judaism, Church of Old Rite, and Baptist.

Economy

Main industrial fields include electrical engineering (with the largest nuclear power plant in Europe), petroleum, machinery, chemical plants, forestry, paper and pulp manufacturing, and food production. In the midst of the 1990s Lithuania's economy was categorized by UNESCO as upper middle-income. In 1996, the per capita Gross Domestic Product (GDP) was US$2,100. The total labor force was 47 percent of the resident population. In the wake of the communist withdrawal, the role of private enterprises substantially increased: The percentage of the total labor force working in private businesses rose from 22 percent in 1990 to 67 percent in 1996.

In 1996, 22.4 percent of the labor force was employed in agriculture, 18 percent in manufacturing industry, and 14 percent in trade and services. At the beginning of 1997, officially registered unemployment slightly exceeded 6 percent. The number of unemployed with professions that are not in demand by the labor market has increased. Opportunities for new professions, especially those with higher qualifications, has been increasing. The demand for professionals—physicians, lawyers, teachers of foreign languages—is still great. In contrast, the demand for unskilled labor is steadily decreasing. At the end of 1996 a majority (73.4 percent) of the unemployed consisted of people who have secondary or lower education. Only 7.6 percent of the unemployed were people with higher education. The average monthly salary was equal to 810 litas (US$202) in the public sector and to 714 litas (US$179) in the private sector.

Politics

Lithuania is a parliamentary republic governed by a democratically elected parliament, the *Seimas*. Fifty percent of Seimas seats are directly elected and 50 percent are elected on a proportional system. During the last elections (October 1996) a majority of seats (50 percent) in the Seimas was won by the party of Homeland Union (Lithuanian Conservatives), which formed a coalition with Lithuanian Christian democrats. The coalition represents the right wing in the spectrum of the political forces in Lithuania and has approximately 61 percent of the seats. The other major political parties represented in the Seimas are the Lithuanian Labor Democratic Party, Lithuanian Social Democrats, and the Party of the Center.

Policy of the ruling coalition is based on a range of principles. These include respect for private property, fostering a market economy, strengthening national independence, preserving national identity, promoting humanistic values characteristic of the European cultural legacy, and developing an open and democratic civil society.

The government is headed by a prime minister who is usually the leader of the political party in power. Government jurisdiction is divided between federal and municipal governments. The main efforts of central authorities are directed toward overcoming the social and economic tendencies that prevailed during the rule of the previous government the Lithuanian Labor Democratic Party. In particular, special attention is being given to the processes of privatization assistance to small and middle enterprises, halting impoverishment, encouraging foreign investments, and reducing the foreign debt (which amounts to approximately US$1.2 billion). Another serious concern for the new government is the high level of crime and the necessity to strengthen the judicial system of the country.

SCHOOLING

After 1940, when Lithuania was occupied and annexed by the Soviet Union, education was restructured along the lines of the Soviet education system. Since the beginning of the movement for the restoration of independence (1988), the Lithuanian education system has been involved in the processes of reform.

The main sources that have exerted a significant impact upon the current development of education in Lithuania are: a critical approach to Soviet education; national traditions of education; ideals of national liberation; general principles of a democratic, open society; modern pedagogical ideas and practices of foreign, especially Western, countries; and some trends of contemporary educational thought—humanistic psychology and pedagogy, cultural and holistic education, to mention but the most important ones. These ideological sources correlate with the following main principles of Lithuanian education and its reform; namely, humanism, democracy, renewal, and a commitment to Lithuanian culture and the preservation of its identity and historic continuity.

Goals and Aims of Education

The goals and principles of reformed secondary education, as well as the strategic lines of its development, reflect common aspirations in Lithuanian society to raise the quality of education and culture in general and to strengthen its role in shaping democratic institutions and the way of life in the country. These goals and principles are accepted by the education community, a large majority of the population and the government.

The main goals of Lithuania's education were formulated in the Law of Education of the Republic of Lithuania, 1991. Therein, education is identified as a priority and an instrument of national development. Education must contribute to the nation's cultural, social, and economic progress and strengthen people's solidarity, tolerance, and cooperation. It is stressed that the main tasks of the education system of Lithuania are to enhance the power of the individual, lay a firm foundation for morality and a healthy lifestyle, and to stimulate the intellect by creating conditions for the development of individuality. Other tasks are to afford the young generation an opportunity to acquire both a general and professional education in science and culture, develop a sense of civic duty and understanding of personal rights and obligations to the family, nation, society, and the state of Lithuania, and stimulate participation in the cultural, public, economic, and political life of the Republic. It is assumed that education must help an individual discover universal human values and base his or her life upon them. Education should encourage a person who is able to think critically, make responsible decisions, and act independently. It should prepare a person for professional activities and develop his or her ability to adapt to ever-changing social and economic conditions.

The above goals and aims underlie education's structure, curriculum, management and preservice and inservice teacher training.

Enrollments

Enrollments in Lithuanian education show much change. From 1990 until 1994, for example, there was a decline. This was an effect of sociocultural processes in the transitional period: unfavorable demographical trends (in 1994 the natural increase rate of the population became negative), the emigration of approximately 100,000 Russian speaking people between 1990 and 1995, the decreasing prestige of education, economic recession, impoverishment of a considerable part of the population, and legal nihilism. As well, a considerable number of pupils were not attending school, in spite of the fact that they had not reached 16 years of age. In the 1994/1995 school year the decline of enrollments in secondary education was reversed. The prestige of schooling, especially of secondary and higher education, has regained anew its merited attention and importance. By 1986, age cohort participation was 96.7 percent for primary schools, 90.9 percent for basic schools, 81.2 percent for secondary schools, and 25.9 percent for higher education institutions.

Governance

Education institutions are under the supervision of several levels of administrative structures. The Seimas is responsible for establishing the legal groundwork for the education system, determining strategic educational development directions, and allocating money to various education sectors. The Ministry of Education and Science is responsible for forming and implementing education policies, preparing curricula and programs, setting and enforcing education standards, working out criteria and methods for financing education, organizing inspections, encouraging pedagogical research, teacher training, and certification. Some responsibilities are also held by the Ministry of Agriculture, such as administrative and pedagogical supervision of agricultural vocational schools. The Ministry of Social Security and Labor is responsible for labor market education institutions.

Regional education departments in districts and municipalities are responsible for developing and implementing regional education programs, organizing inspections, creating opportunities for teacher qualification improvement, and teachers' working conditions. Education institutions are responsible for meeting state education standards, creating optimal learning conditions, constantly revising content and methods, organizing cultural programs, encouraging teacher creativity, and qualification improvement.

Preschool Education

The formal education of children begins in crèches and kindergartens. There were 741 preschool education institutions attended by 90,300 pupils in 1995. A new type of mixed educational institution,

school-kindergarten, was recently created. There are 141 institutions of this type now.

The number of preschool education establishments and pupils attending them has significantly decreased in recent years. Presently only about 30 percent of pupils aged 1 to 6 are in preschool education. An especially big decline in enrollments has been observed in the rural areas. This unhealthy tendency was caused by the transition of the country to a market economy, the vicious processes of privatization, and the decay of collective farms (which were then unable to maintain their own preschool institutions). This process of decline has now been stopped and reversed.

Some 11,800 teachers worked in preschool education establishments in 1995. Of these, 45 percent have higher-education qualifications and 49 percent college-level education. A large majority of teachers have acquired special training as teachers for preschool education institutions. The education of pupils in kindergartens follows a new curriculum. Today, modern, alternative methods of education (including Montessori and Waldorf) are increasingly used in the kindergartens.

General Education

The current system of primary and secondary general education covers a number of different branches: primary schools (grades 1 to 4), basic schools (grades 1 to 10), full secondary schools of general education (grades 1 to 12, of which grades 11 and 12 are considered upper secondary education), and four-year gymnasiums (corresponding to grades 9 to 12 of the full secondary school). There are also special education institutions for children with special needs, youth schools offering basic education (presently several of them provide upper secondary education, too), two programs in vocational education providing a possibility to complete both basic and secondary education adult education (including centers, adult education divisions in schools of general education), and programs of secondary education still preserved in a number of colleges.

Since the restoration of independence, a number of changes have been made in the system of general education. The duration of compulsory education (previously it extended to grade 12) was changed. It now lasts until the age of 16. All teaching materials used in primary and secondary education were revised, taking into account new social, economic, and political conditions and the aspirations of Lithuanian society.

Primary school is already working on the basis of a new curriculum and textbooks. At the secondary levels, reform efforts have had a strong impact on the development of secondary education and on the restoration of gymnasiums. Today there are fifty gymnasiums as well as thirty gymnasium classes in ordinary secondary schools. As well, upper secondary education is gradually being differentiated. There are two main streams—humanitarian and real. Each stream can have a narrower profile; for example, modern languages, classics, arts, and so on, in the humanitarian stream and sciences and maths in the real stream.

A new type of general education, the so-called youth schools, has also been created. Recently, nineteen youth schools have been established. Youth schools are an alternative to the ordinary basic school of general education. They are attended by pupils who lack motivation and/or have difficulty adapting themselves to the learning conditions of comprehensive schools.

Considerable shifts in the sphere of the education of pupils with special needs deserve particular mention. Noticeable results in integrated education for pupils with special needs have been achieved. The number of pupils with disabilities being educated at special schools has decreased from 11,800 in 1989 to 7,400 in the 1994/1995 school year. The large majority of pupils who have left special schools are now enrolled in the ordinary schools of general education.

Ethnic minority children, belonging mainly to the Polish and Russian population, have approximately the same conditions of education as all children in Lithuanian schools. At the present time, there are secondary schools where the language of instruction is Russian, Polish, Yiddish, German, or Belarussian. Ethnic minority groups are also in vocational schools, colleges, and higher education institutions. In the 1994/1995 school year, 85.4 percent of pupils attended Lithuanian schools of general education, 11.3 percent attended Russian schools, and 3.3 percent attended Polish schools.

Lithuania rejects a unified, strongly centralized curriculum of general education in favor of a more flexible, school-based curriculum. Recent new curriculum guidelines for primary and secondary education put a special emphasis on fostering human and Christian values, responsible citizenship, aptitude for communication and cooperation, entrepreneurial skills, harmonious personal development through ethics, an independent view of the world, ecological awareness, a many-sided education, cultural awareness, and lifelong education. The new curriculum is meant to help develop the individual's basic knowledge, skills, and values; provide general practical knowledge and the skills necessary for everyday life; convey to the young generation the national and European cultural heritage; foster humanistic values; promote solidarity with others; develop a vision of a common future; foster awareness of the urgent needs of Lithuanian society and culture; educate people to meet these needs with due responsibility and competence; and promote the all-round personal development of pupils.

State education standards are prepared on the basis of these new curriculum guidelines. The core curriculum of grades 5 to 10 of the basic school consists of fifteen compulsory subjects—ethics or religious education, native language, foreign languages I and II, mathematics, nature, biology, physics, chemistry, history, geography, arts, music, crafts, and physical education.

Vocational schools (numbering 107 in the 1994/1995 school year) are administered by both the Ministry of Education and Science (63 schools) and the Ministry of Agriculture (41 schools). Three vocational schools are private. Vocational schools were attended by 45,100 pupils in 1994/1995. The duration of studies varies from two to four years. Only students who have reached the age of 14 years are admitted.

Five types of courses are offered to students in vocational schools. Two are for pupils who have not completed basic education. The first is for those who want to acquire only vocational education; the second is for pupils who want a vocational education as well as a basic general education. Another two types of courses are devoted to students having completed basic education. One is for those who are interested only in a vocational education, the other is for pupils who want to acquire a secondary general education in addition to vocational training. Still another category of courses is offered for those students who have completed secondary education and want to obtain vocational education.

Higher Education

In 1996/1997 there were fifteen state higher education institutions in Lithuania: six universities, seven academies, and two institutes. About 10,000 to 12,000 secondary school graduates are admitted annually; this comprises about 40 to 45 percent of the total graduates from secondary level schools. In the 1996/1997 school year there was a total of 58,800 students. The number of students has increased in the last two years.

Studies in higher education institutions consist of more than 200 programs. These are usually conducted in the Lithuanian language, but in a number of higher education institutions some study programs are conducted in foreign languages (English, Russian, Polish, and others). Higher education may be pursued at the basic and specialized professional or master's degree levels. Upon completion of basic studies (duration four to five years) a bachelor's degree, an equivalent academic degree, or a professional qualification is awarded. Beyond this there are specialized professional and master's degrees. The Seimas approves the sum total of all allocations for research and higher education. In 1995 these comprised 6.96 percent of the state budget, or 1.18

percent of the gross domestic product (GDP). Higher education institutions receive about 75 percent of this.

Adult Education

Adults (persons over 18) are trained in schools of general education for adults or in centers of vocational education for adults. As well, there is a considerable number (about 300) of nonformal education institutions (most of which are non-state-owned) providing education services for persons of different age groups, including adults.

The number of general education schools for adults and students in them has steadily decreased in the last years—from 59 schools with 12,000 students in 1990 to 28 schools with almost 7,000 students in 1995. On the other hand, the number of centers for vocational training and retraining of adults, especially of the unemployed, is increasing. This is caused by growing rates of unemployment and a fast-changing situation in the labor market. The Ministry of Social Security and Labor has created thirteen labor market training centers, which were attended by more than 29,000 people in 1995.

Teacher Training

Teachers may be initially trained in pedagogical colleges and universities, or by appropriate faculties of other universities. College graduates are entitled to work as preschool, primary, and basic school teachers, and in some cases as upper secondary school teachers. Second level (bachelors) graduates have the right to work in general education secondary schools. Students with masters degrees are oriented to work in gymnasiums and colleges.

The teacher training curriculum is the subject of considerable reform. Contrary to previous practices, teachers are now trained to teach not one, but mostly two or three, subjects. New qualification requirements for teacher training were recently approved by the Ministry of Education and Science. These specify the knowledge and skills that are essential for the professional competence of a teacher. They cover three main spheres: general humanitarian and social education, psychological and pedagogical education, and subject(s) related to education.

In-service training is undertaken by the Lithuanian Teachers' In-Service Training Institute. About 20,000 teachers participate every year. There are in-service teacher training centers in different regions of the country, as well as in-service teacher training faculties or centers housed in universities. Only those qualification and retraining programs that are approved by Ministry of Education and Science are financed from the state budget.

Teachers

In 1996, 49,400 teachers worked in schools of general education, including 4,800 in vocational schools, 4,000 in colleges, and 9,100 in all the combined higher education institutions. Of teachers in the schools of general education, 86 percent are females. A large majority (85.5 percent) of teachers have college diplomas in higher education. However, a considerable proportion of teachers (18 percent) is engaged in teaching activities that do not correspond to their academic training and professional qualifications. An especially unsatisfactory situation is found in the field of teaching foreign languages, where 28 percent of teachers who teach English are not trained as English language teachers.

A teacher's level of professional preparation is indicated by a qualification category granted through certification. There are four main qualification categories: teacher, senior teacher, teacher-methodologist, and teacher-expert. Every five years a teacher must go through recertification in order to confirm his or her qualification category acquired earlier, or to receive a higher category.

Financing of Education

Education institutions are financed by the state and municipal budgets. Teachers' salaries are low in Lithuania. Average monthly income was approximately US$150 at the end of 1996. Thus, teachers' salaries were lower than the average salary in the public sector (US$203). This difference remains and is the reason why some teachers leave their profession for the private sector of the economy.

MAJOR ISSUES, CONTROVERSIES, AND PROBLEMS

The current education scene in Lithuania is marked by changes, debates, tensions, and controversial developments. There are competing ideological orientations toward schooling, debates over the best structure for the education system, conflicting approaches to the improvement of the content and methods of education, arguments over what is the most appropriate system of evaluation, and uncertainty over needed changes in administration.

Education Reform

Lithuania, like many other post-Communist countries, manifests an ambiguous attitude toward the influence of modern European and world culture. One can observe some tension between those who are inclined toward an open, friendly, acceptance of external culture and those who more or less want to preserve the ethnic identity of the country and its endogenous culture. This discrepancy in attitudes becomes apparent in education, too. Advocates for democratic, modern schools that are open to external cultural influences are sometimes violently attacked by those who emphasize national character and the traditions of education. A shift to the nationalistic, patriotic, and civic dimension in education is especially apparent in the activities of the Ministry of Education and Science since the national election in October 1996. However, the dominant position remains a balanced one that stresses both attitudes; the view that it is necessary to preserve the ethnic foundations of the Lithuanian school while modernizing and democratizing it.

A careful look at the context of ideological debates that are taking place in Lithuania enables us to discern two conflicting perspectives. There are people, including education scientists, parliamentarians, functionaries in the Ministry of Education and Science, teachers, and principals, who are inclined to orient schools increasingly toward Christian values. Many cherish a hope that a Christian education will be able to improve the moral climate of society. In contrast, advocates of a more liberal, secular, and democratic approach to education believe that parents and pupils have the right to choose between religious and secular courses of moral education.

Courses in both religious and secular moral education are offered in schools. In the 1995/1996 school year 69 percent of students took religious education and 31 percent studied (secular) ethics. Of these, 96.4 percent were Roman Catholic and only 3 percent Orthodox Church. The 1996 election of a conservative majority in the Seimas was followed by a noticeable increase in attention to the religious traditions of education. But religion is only one problem for the reformers and managers of Lithuanian education. There are also numerous unresolved structural problems in the education system.

Rural Schools

Lithuania has a relatively dense school network. However, many schools, especially in the rural areas, are small and their maintenance is very expensive. There have been periodic attempts to close small rural schools; however, these efforts were usually unsuccessful because of strong opposition from local communities. They stress the role of a school as the local hearth of culture and the difficulties pupils would have finding transportation to centralized schools. These constant tensions result from efforts to restructure the existing school network.

Minority Populations and Enrollment Regrouping

Due to the emigration of the Russian-speaking population after the restoration of independence,

Lithuania's Russian schools have lost a significant number of students, especially in the towns. One consequence is an underuse of school buildings. At the same time, many Lithuanian schools are overcrowded and obliged to work in two shifts. These circumstances initiated a regrouping of urban school enrollments. This, however, is not an easy task. Local communities strongly oppose attempts to carry out regrouping. Education authorities are often accused of violating the rights of national minorities and worsening their learning conditions. Hence, the problem of student regrouping is still not solved and is a source of great tension.

Changes in the orientations of ethnic minorities, especially those living in the Eastern part of Lithuania, are also related to a need for structural reshaping of the country's schools. Children from Russian- and Polish-speaking families are increasingly inclined to choose schools with Lithuanian as the language of instruction for their children. A study undertaken by a joint Lithuanian-Polish team of researchers in 1994 showed that 52.2 percent of Poles living the eastern part of Lithuania wanted their children to attend Lithuanian schools. Parents hope that attending Lithuanian schools will help their children integrate more easily into Lithuanian society and will enhance their career possibilities. Unfortunately, the whole process of ethnic readjustment and the establishment of Lithuanian schools in the abovementioned region is difficult.

Structural Reform

In the 1998/1999 school year, Lithuania adopted a new structural scheme (4+6+2) for general education schools. This prolonged basic education by one year; it now lasts ten years. As this change continues toward full implementation, small secondary schools in the countryside certainly will be transformed into basic schools. Therefore, the total number of secondary schools will noticeably decrease.

This process of transformation will be hard to realize. Some opponents argue that two years of upper secondary education is too short to guarantee due preparation for the *matura* examination and entrance to higher education. In addition, some partisans of the old structural scheme have the opinion that schools in the countryside are providing a qualitatively lower education and therefore the prolongation of the basic school and will bring about a decrease in the quality of general education.

These arguments are counterbalanced by advocates who argue that the ten-year basic school will contribute to an increase in general standards of education in the country will create favorable conditions for children (especially those in rural areas who will be able to attend the schools closer to their homes) and will contribute to the retaining of more pupils for a longer time in the system of general education. Anyway, because these plans for structural changes in the system of general education are supported by the Ministry of Education and Science, they will certainly be put into effect without serious delay.

Equity and Comprehensive Schools

Lithuanian education reformers face significant difficulties in their attempts to create a fully differentiated system of general education. The general attitude adopted by reformers is that it is desirable to avoid early specialization. Today, differentiation increases gradually with an increasing level of education. A common grade 1 to 8 curriculum allows relatively few possibilities for differentiation. This situation changes radically after the eighth grade, when schooling splits into three main branches: four-year gymnasium (corresponding to grades 9 to 12 of a secondary school), continuation of basic school (covering grades 5 to 10) and vocational education.

These separate structural components are further marked by internal differentiation. For example, the gymnasiums split into two main profiles—humanitarian and real. Each covers several different types of gymnasiums: humanitarian (classics, modern languages, social sciences, arts) and real (sciences, economical-commercial). Within the

area of initial vocational education, five different programs are offered. A similar tendency toward increasing differentiation is also found in preschool education, special education, adult education, and complementary education.

The main problem that emerges is the practical one of how to create syllabuses and education standards for these different streams. The intention is to have two or three different courses, constituting different varieties of the same subject, with corresponding standards for each course. However, the design of such courses and standards involves serious theoretical and practical difficulties. For example, some see the common basis of variants of the same course in the skills and abilities that are to be developed by students. Others put the emphasis upon the volume of content to be mastered by pupils. Others are inclined to combine the two above positions.

Efforts aiming at reshaping post-secondary education are also concerned with structural changes. Lithuania is striving to harmonize its education system with the main principles and developmental links of European education. Problems about the role and status of college-level institutions (formerly called *technikums* in the Soviet era) emerge in this context. Created as intermediate institutions between secondary and higher education, they are now striving to become full-fledged higher-education establishments. These efforts of colleges to evolve toward the status of tertiary education institutions are resisted by some institutions of higher education, which see them as a danger to their hegemony in the sphere of higher education. The final result will probably be that some *technikums* will evolve into institutions of tertiary education while others will become ordinary vocational schools. These two lines of development are being encouraged by the Ministry of Education and Science.

Curriculum and Content

The ongoing process of education change is marked by some problematic issues related to the content of education. Efforts are now focused on strengthening the ethnic/national dimension of education content, reintroducing the traditional values of the European cultural legacy, making schooling more relevant for students and responsive to the realities of modern society, developing students' academic and vocational competencies, devising differentiated curricula and standards for the many streams of schooling, and achieving curriculum integration based on interdisciplinary and thematic models of integration. All these initiatives pose tremendous theoretical and methodical difficulties and sometimes embody conflicting approaches. That is why progress in the sphere of content renovation is slower than it was expected to be. Much remains to be done and many fundamental issues need to be resolved.

The process of reform in the sphere of teaching methods is also marked by controversy and tension. An absence of active pedagogical strategies, ones that involve and engage students in the process of learning, is seen as a shortcoming of current education practice in Lithuania. Methods of teaching based on the principles of lecture still prevail in the schools, including higher education institutions. This situation has stimulated the appearance of different education projects that aim at the development of teachers' skills in active methods of teaching and learning. Some researchers emphasize modern methods of education that require the teacher to interpret and actualize teaching materials in the context of the urgent interests and needs of pupils, local communities, society, and the international community. Encouraging these changes in pedagogy is a major priority of school reformers.

Special Education

An equivocal attitude toward the integrated education of disabled students is manifested on the part of teachers. Most teachers are inclined to favor the idea of integrated education. However, a significant number of teachers argue against it. They stress the necessity to provide qualified assistance for disabled students and feel that such assistance cannot be provided in the ordinary schools. Thus, they favor the preservation of special education institutions for all disabled students. Despite this controversy, the implementation of integrated education is progressing and the number of the disabled persons in the ordinary school system is gradually increasing.

Information Technology

Only slow progress in the computerization of the teaching and learning processes is being made. This is one of the shortcomings of education reform in Lithuania. A special program was launched recently by the government in order to speed up the process. The plan is to ensure that each comprehensive school will have at its disposal at least one modern computer. This will enable schools enhance their ability to communicate with each other and with schools outside of the country and to have access to the Internet.

Evaluation

A very important issue concerns the process of evaluation in education. The problem is crucial because it is related to many other aspects of education such as teacher effectiveness, the learning process, professional qualifications of teachers, and measuring the quality of education. At present Lithuania does not have evaluation tools for all these aspects of education. However, a number of steps toward their development have been taken.

The Lithuanian Center for Quality Assessment in Higher Education was recently established, and a National Examination Center has been founded. The latter is charged with preparing maturity examinations and developing tools for different kinds of assessments. Both centers were developed with the assistance of international organizations.

Developing evaluation procedures and tools is a major element in establishing an education monitoring system. It will provide the necessary information for effective management of schooling and for comparing Lithuania's schools in an international context. With these aims in view, the elaboration of a national system of education indicators, based on those the OECD uses, has been started.

The development of a large system of education assessment is, of course, a very complicated and difficult task to accomplish. It goes without saying that there are many difficulties and controversies. Currently, Lithuanian educators are discussing many issues related to evaluation procedures. These include the nature and kind of different courses in the upper levels of secondary education, administration and evaluation of the leaving examinations taken by students at the different levels, coordination of final examinations and higher education entrance requirements, and interpretation of the relatively poor results achieved by Lithuanian students who took part in the Third International Mathematics and Science Study.

Centralization and Decentralization

Contradictory tendencies also mark the progress of Lithuania's schools toward a democratic system of governance. The underlying principle here is supposed to be increased local autonomy and power for the local authorities (schools as well as various bodies of civil self-governance). Unfortunately, this process is not progressing very smoothly. A contrary tendency, leading to the centralization of management, appeared with the creation of a new administrative unit—the district.

Ten districts were established, and many education supervision functions that were previously performed by municipal authorities were transferred to these districts. Accordingly, the role of municipal authorities in the administration of education and the promotion of education reform was significantly limited. The active involvement of local communities, school principals, teachers, and social partners in the reform processes in evidence during the initial stage of educational reform became increasingly weaker. In its place, an emphasis upon top-down administrative measures emerged. This has been steadily strengthen-

ing and is today the dominant tendency. Thus, the progress of education reform in Lithuania has encountered a very major obstacle. This circumstance is stressed by some reformers and educational researchers and must be corrected without delay.

There are, of course, many other problems that merit discussion. Special attention should be paid to the problems of democracy in education, the appearance of selective and elitist tendencies in the sphere of schooling, the quality of education services, and so on. An intelligent education policy that will meet these challenges is always the goal of educators.

THE FUTURE OF SOCIETY AND SCHOOLING

Lithuania has chosen to create a democratic and open civil society. The fostering of a democratic personality, one capable of meeting with competence and self-confidence emerging challenges and able to adapt to a rapidly changing social, economic, professional, and cultural environment, is the main mission of its education system.

However, there is resistance from some sectors of Lithuanian society and the education establishment. Many still hold a one-sided, reductionistic, instrumental, and functional concept of human personality development and an equally one-sided view of the school as a social institution that is instrumental, formal, and reactive. These attitudes must gradually be replaced by a vision that emphasizes the active, reconstructive, interpretative, interactive, and dynamic nature of the education processes. The school must become an interpretative cultural community, taking an active part in the processes of renewal and progress. The policy of survivalism that still manifests itself in many schools must give way to a policy of empowerment. The progress of education must be founded on the principles of cooperation and development between the education communities and local community life. This is the right course toward to the gradual establishment of a democratic and participatory society and schools.

These are, of course, ideals that are hard to realize. However, they can be achieved through balanced steps that simultaneously combine both evolutionary and revolutionary measures.

Indeed, as has been shown in this chapter, Lithuania has already addressed many of the largest problems and can reasonably expect to achieve significant successes in the coming years. In closing, we may recount some of these and project into the future.

The reshaping of the school system will continue and soon a new structure of general education (4+6+2) will emerge. This will serve as a catalyst for an essential reshaping of the whole system of secondary education. An important element will be the thorough differentiation of upper secondary education with respect to different profiles, programs, and levels of courses. While this continues to remain a task so far unresolved, it will be realized in the very near future. The role and place of various types of institutions, in particular gymnasiums and ordinary secondary and basic schools, also will be reconsidered in the context of the new system of general education. An important complementary question is the territorial distribution of education institutions. As we have seen, there is a considerable number of small schools, whose maintenance is very expensive.

It is also important to make education available for more age groups. Lithuania lacks a well-established adult education system, and this is an area in need of expansion. A similar problem is faced by the vocational education system, which at present doesn't encourage pupils to obtain basic or secondary education. This is one of the weakest points of the whole system and the capability of vocational education to enlarge the opportunities for secondary education will be strengthened in the future. Currently, there are plans to establish technical and commercial lycea within the system of vocational education.

An essential renewal of the curriculum is another priority. The key point in this respect is to achieve a radical enrichment of the curriculum through national and European cultural traditions and values. These must permeate all curricular components: guidelines, standards, individual programs, textbooks, exercise books, teachers' books, and so on. Local, national, regional, European, and international perspectives must be taken into account. To succeed in this task, a holistic, cross-curricular approach is required. The curriculum's potential to foster students' personalities, skills, and value systems must be raised significantly.

To measure success, a monitoring system able to afford exhaustive and reliable information about the functioning of the education system and the quality of provided services is a priority and is being developed. Once in place, this system must guarantee quality control of education and serve as a diagnostic tool for corrective measures. One aspect of this is the establishment of fair and objective conditions for admission to higher education. Therefore, the creation of a well-grounded system of school-leaving examinations and testing centers should be realized without delay.

There are other important challenges to be met. Making teachers competent in modern alternative teaching methods (based, in particular, on cooperative learning), computer literacy and using technology information in schools, and international recognition of Lithuania's school-leaving certificates come to mind. The list is long but everything points to one realization. Teachers must increase the scope of their professional competencies and must actively participate in education reform. A large involvement of Lithuanian teachers in cooperation with their colleagues abroad would contribute significantly to that. That is why in-service teacher training and retraining now become tasks of paramount importance.

SELECTED BIBLIOGRAPHY

Evaluation of research in Lithuania. Vol. 1. *General observations and recommendations prepared by the Advisory Board, and summaries of the Panel Reports.* (1996). Oslo: RCN.

General concept of education in Lithuania. (1994). Vilnius.

Law of education of the Republic of Lithuania. (1991). Vilnius.

Law on research and higher education. (1991). Vilnius.

L'éducation: Un tresor est cache dedans. (1966). Paris: UNESCO.

Lietuvoje, L. & Lenkijoje, L. (1995). *Poles in Lithuania—Lithuanians in Poland.* Vilnius: Varðuva.

Lietuvos bendrojo lavinimo mokyklos bendrosios programos. Projektas. Vilnius. (General programs for general education in Lithuania). (1994). Draft.

Lietuvos statistikos metraðtis. (Lithuania's Statistics Yearbook). (1996). Vilnius.

Lietuvos studentija ir moksleivija. (Lithuania's students and pupils). (1995). Vilnius.

Lietuvos valstybinës mokslo ir studijø institucijos. (State Higher Education and Research Institutions in Lithuania). (1994). Vilnius.

Luksienë, M., & Jackûnas, Z. (1994). Lithuania: System of education. In *The International Encyclopedia of Education* (Vol. 6) (2nd ed., pp. 3484–3491).

Svietimas. (Educations). (1997). Vilnius.

Symposium sur "Competences cles pour l'Europe." (1996, 27–30 March). Rapport general par M.Walo Hutmacher (pp. 51, 52). Berne: CDCC.

Vaiku ir jaunuoliø ugdymas ðvietimo ástaigose. (Children and youth in the education establishments). (1996). Vilnius.

Zibartas, J. (1995, 4–7 October). Reformes de l'enseignement secondaire en Europe de l'Est: Lituanie/Symposium sur les reformes educatives en Europe centrale et orientale: bilan et processus. Prague.

CHAPTER 15

A Society and Education System in Transition: Poland

CZESLAW MAJOREK

Czeslaw Majorek is a Professor in the History of Education, nominated by the President of the Republic of Poland, at Krakow Pedagogical University (Wyzsza Szkola Pedagogiczna). He has written extensively on education in the eighteenth and nineteenth centuries in Poland, and his research interests also include recent educational changes in Poland and the other central eastern European nations. He has published six books and over seventy articles in Polish, English, Russian, German, Serbian, Hungarian, and Catalan. Twice he has served on the Executive Committee of the International Standing Conference for the History of Education (1985–1988, 1991–1993), and he has been a visiting fellow at Churchill College (Cambridge, UK), Northern Illinois University (DeKalb, Illinois, USA), and the University of Lethbridge (Lethbridge, Canada). He is Chair of the Commission for the Science of Education at the Krakow Branch of the Polish Academy of Sciences.

Since the late 1980s, Poland has been going through a difficult, but very promising, era of extensive economic and political change. That process has moved the country rapidly toward becoming a fully democratic society, with social structures and political institutions that reflect a democratic value system in form, content, and function. One of the main vehicles for Poland's ongoing transformation is education reform.

THE SOCIAL FABRIC

The Polish education system shares many of the features and concerns of education systems in the other former iron curtain countries. However, the country's geography, sociopolitical framework, and history have generated some unique educational structures, issues, and problems.

Geography

Basically a plain, Poland is located between the Baltic Sea to its north and the Carpathian Mountains to its south. It is bordered by Germany on the west, Russia and Lithuania on the northeast, Belarus and Ukraine on the east, Slovak Republic and Czech Republic on the south.

Poland's total area of 312,680 square km is varied as a result of the belt arrangement of natural geographic regions. Lowlands stretch along the Baltic seashore, the vast northern area is a lake district, the lowlands of central Poland form the main agricultural region and also have vast virgin forests. The uplands are highlighted by an ancient mountain range, and last, high mountains cover the south.

Political History

World War II was one of the most tragic events in Polish history. A staggering 22 percent of the total Polish population (over half a million fighting men and women, and 6 million civilians) died. About 50 percent of these were Polish Christians, and 50 percent were Polish Jews. Approximately 5,384,000, or 89.9 percent, of Polish war losses were victims of prisons, death camps, raids, executions, annihilations of ghettos, epidemics, starvation, excessive work, and ill treatment. One million war orphans and over half a million invalids

239

were created. The country lost 38 percent of its national assets (in comparison, Britain lost 0.8 percent and France 1.5 percent) (Kasprzyk, 1996).

After the War ended, Poland found itself in the Soviet orbit of interests, its politics and economy dependent upon its big neighbor. However, increasingly frequent protests and growing social tensions eventually forced the imposed communist government to make concessions. On June 4, 1989, the first elections were conducted in which noncommunists could run for Parliament. This sparked a series of events constituting Poland's peaceful transition to democracy and a market economy. The first noncommunist government behind the iron curtain was appointed, and some rather chaotic economic reforms were implemented. At the same time, Poland identified membership in NATO and the European Union (EU) as its main strategic goal. In February 1994, Poland became associated with the European Union; two months later Warsaw submitted an application for EU membership.

Demography

In terms of population, Poland is a relatively young country. One-third of Poles are under the age of 20. Furthermore, for every 100 people in their working years, 74 are of retirement age. Over the next few years there will be an increasing proportion of people in the latter category (Glowny Urzad Statystyczny, 1992).

At the end of 1995, the population of Poland was 38,792,442, with a growth rate of 0.36 percent and birthrate of 13.34 per 1000, which is fairly stable. Life expectancy at birth is 73.13 years overall; 69.15 for males and 77.33 for females. It is also a fairly densely populated country (124 habitants per square km), and almost 62 percent of the population lives in 883 towns (Glowny Urzad Statystyczny, 1996).

In terms of ethnic and religious composition, Poland is a homogenous society. The population is: Polish, 97.6 percent; German, 1.3 percent; Ukrainian, 0.6 percent; Belarussian, 0.5 percent; Roman Catholic, 95 percent (about 75 percent

practicing); Eastern Orthodox, Protestant, and other, 5 percent. Poland is also a culturally developed society. The literacy rate for those aged 15 and over is 99 percent (Glowny Urzad Statystyczny, 1993).

Structural Changes and Social Consequences Under Communism

There is no doubt that structural reforms initiated under communist domination generated revolutionary social and economic changes. Increased and widespread industrialization and urbanization greatly reduced economic disparities between regions and increased horizontal social mobility. The effects of an expanded and accessible educational system and higher standards of living for rural populations reduced differences between town and village and brought about an increasingly uniform social structure. However, new social differences emerged as a result of the governing party's nepotistic practices, such as providing an elite few easier access to coveted goods.

Public Attitudes in the Communist Era

Communism also generated a new social consciousness. In the time of so-called "real socialism" the general social orientation was one of equal social security for every group and every citizen. The system guaranteed full employment; free health care; free schooling at all levels of the education system; and free or very inexpensive access to cultural goods, such as literature, theater, movies, sports, recreation services, and so on (Topolski, 1992).

However, on the negative side, the dictatorial communist political establishment kept individuals from developing a sense of individual responsibility. A feeling of dependency was nurtured and reinforced by state paternalism. It suggested that the "ideal citizen" always conforms to the official stance in every respect, identifying obediently with that standpoint without criticism. The state tried to instill faith that all tensions and troubles would safely be solved or removed by those in authority (Morody, 1993).

The Transformation to a Free Market Economy

In the communist era, Poland was an industrial agricultural country. It was also successful; economic progress fared favorably in comparison to the average of developed countries. However, after the communist withdrawal in 1989, a radical reform of the economic system was launched. A policy of "shock therapy"—decontrolling prices, slashing subsidies, and drastically reducing import barriers—was implemented.

Almost immediately, this led to a recession, a steep decline in production characteristic of transitions from centrally run to market-based economies. The Gross Domestic Product decreased quite dramatically, unemployment skyrocketed, and inflation reached an incredible peak of 50 percent monthly in late 1989. In spite of these hardships, the short-term goal of largely stabilizing the economy was achieved rather quickly.

From a relative perspective, the costs incurred by Polish society in making the transition to a market economy have not been too great. However, despite unquestionable economic achievements to date, Poland's road to a developed market economy is still long. Market structures and efficient techniques need time to be put in place and to function properly. A better life has now begun for satisfied minorities, such as young educated people, new entrepreneurs, and successful businessmen living in big cities. But, for the larger sections of the population, daily life has become more difficult than it was during the last years of communist rule, and it is becoming miserable for a growing number of people now hit by unemployment and poverty.

SCHOOLING

Historical Background

The system of education now existing in Poland was formed and developed in difficult post-war conditions. As a result of World War II, Poland's infrastructure and economy were virtually destroyed. The country was also left with almost 3 million illiterate people and a devastated school network. Over 60 percent of pre-war education buildings were in ruins, most education equipment was missing, and almost 95 percent of school library books perished. Therefore, rebuilding and development became the task of first importance.

Success in the restoration and development of schooling facilities made it possible to launch a general attack on illiteracy. The operation against illiteracy was carried out in the years 1949–1951. Illiterate people beyond the age of 50 were taught in courses organized in school buildings, educational centers, their places of work, and individually. Of the total 700,000 persons qualifying for literacy courses, 618,000 completed them successfully.

The next stage was to raise the general level of education up to at least grade 7. Because of the massive rebuilding effort, the whole country was already covered with a network of elementary schools, so primary education was rapidly achieved for nearly 100 percent of children. In result, secondary schools and higher learning institutions became accessible to young people from all social strata. Furthermore, schooling at all levels became tuition-free, students from rural communities were ensured accommodation in boarding houses and campuses, and those with limited resources received scholarships. Thus, the school system offered a wide range of educational possibilities to children, young people, and adults, especially from the lower social strata.

In the course of this rapid expansion, ideological control of the schools was firm. The communist political establishment believed that forming a new society was the task of the state, and a cornerstone of the new social order was egalitarianism. Accordingly, efforts to counterbalance the effects of being economically, socially, and culturally underprivileged were a priority. It became the central concern of schools and teachers to bring their underprivileged students up to the level of the others and to fill in gaps in their education.

There were even special compensatory courses for working-class children before they started school, and various supportive courses, special instruction classes, and smaller groups organized for them during their school years.

However, these efforts did not achieve the hoped-for results. By the late 1970s and early 1980s it became apparent that the elimination of social inequalities could not be achieved by schools. Studies showed that schools had a selective effect, despite all efforts to achieve the opposite. Politicians and education leaders had to face the fact that, by the time children got to school, they showed great differences in achievement and development levels. Moreover, the differences identified at the beginning of schooling became permanent and were in very close correlation with performance in later years. Finally, it was evident that the hierarchical school system was further increasing inequality of opportunity among the various social strata (Kozakiewicz, 1990).

Thus, the communist education system was unable to achieve its most cherished ideological goal, creating the conditions for egalitarianism. This coincided with another problem. Schools under communism were more or less restricted to transmitting knowledge, but that knowledge was insufficiently relevant to real-life problems. Students were not expected to question and check what was taught, or to develop competence and sound judgment by discovering things for themselves.

The result was that, from the early 1980s onwards, young people started publicly criticizing schools, often from the perspective of the Roman Catholic Church. In particular, attention was drawn to education's insufficient support for creative personality development; lack of a relationship between school curricula and students' real-life experiences; absence of connections between subject matter knowledge taught and the worlds of emotion, imagination, and human ethics in general; the Communist party's monopoly on the ideological and/or religious education of young people; and the state's refusal to find compromises between conflicting individual and group interests (Kwiecinski, 1995).

The Structure of Schooling

While the ideological, curricular, and pedagogical objectives and foci of schools in Poland changed as a result of the above criticisms and the fall of communism, the actual structure of the education system (see Figure 15.1) has not changed significantly since 1961 (Ustawa z 15 lipca, 1961; Ustawa z 7 wrzesnia, 1991). However, since 1991 schools and other education centers are divided into public and nonpublic institutions. Public schools are those established, conducted, and supported by the Minister of National Education or other organs of the government administration, communities, or community associations. Nonpublic schools are those established and conducted by other legal and private persons, parents, public associations, religious associations, and so on. Public schools provide free education, within general educational programs. They enroll pupils according to the principle of general accessibility; employ teachers who possess specified qualifications; implement the minimum curriculum in compulsory subjects and the general education program designated for this type of school; and implement principles of evaluation, classification, and promotion of pupils set by the Minister of National Education.

A nonpublic school may obtain public school rights, particularly the ability to bestow national certificates or diplomas, if it implements the minimum curriculum program, applies official principles of classification and promotion of pupils, and employs fully certified teachers. Such nonpublic schools and education centers receive financial subsidies from the local or national budget. The amount of the subsidy is 50 percent of the current expenses carried by public schools or education centers of the same type, allocated on a per pupil basis. In 1994, there were 20,840 public and 338 nonpublic preschools in Poland (Glowny Urzad Statystyczny, 1995).

The major structural components of the Polish school system are as follows.

Preschool.   Preschool education takes place in nursery schools and in nursery sections of prima-

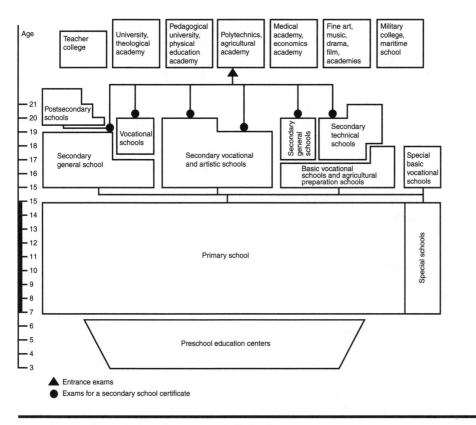

FIGURE 15.1   Formal education system in Poland.

ry schools. Children aged 3 to 6 may attend. But, at 6, children have a legal right to a year of preparation before attending primary schools. Local councils are responsible for providing preschool facilities. Preschool education covers all forms of organized and sustained school-based and center-based activities designed to foster learning and emotional and social development in children.

A sharp decrease in the number of children attending preschool institutions occurred during the period of political transformation. Beginning in 1990, these institutions were taken over local councils and preschools run by factories and industries were closed down, fees rose, and a decrease in the birthrate meant there were fewer young children (Karwowska-Struczyk, 1996). The decrease in the number of preschools is also a result of economic factors. Unemployment has reduced demands for the formal education of young children. On the supply side, there is the fact that many of these institutions were closed down after they were taken over by local governments. When central finances and a guaranteed supply of able teachers and other professionals disappeared, many local governments were unable to keep their preschool institutions open. Finally, a rise in tuition fees also reduced demand.

Primary Schools.   Primary school provides a basic education for students aged 7 to 17. In principle, primary school should be "preparatory," that is preparing students for upper (secondary) education, and not "terminal," preparing students for entry into the working environment. The eight grades of primary school are compulsory; schooling must start in the beginning of the school year in the calendar year during which the child becomes 7 years of age and lasts until the completion of primary school (but not longer than until the end of the school year in the calendar year during which the pupil turns 17). Upon application from parents, a schoolmaster may allow the education of a child to take place outside school—for example, for health reasons. In special cases, individualized programs may be set up.

About 96 percent of primary school graduates go on to continue their education. Of these, about 28 percent enter general secondary schools, 28.3 percent go to full secondary vocational or technical schools, and 39.5 percent to basic vocational schools.

Recently, there has been a growth of elementary schools offering alternative education programs. These are invariably exclusive schools located in large towns and catering to well-off families seeking educational advantages for their children. This is a new phenomenon in a country which, for half a century, experienced uniform schooling. It poses a fundamental challenge to the public school system's ideal of providing equality of educational opportunity for all children.

Secondary Schooling. Secondary education may be either terminal, preparing students for direct entry into the workplace, or preparatory, a stepping stone to tertiary education. Both public and private secondary schools are divided into three main types: basic vocational schools, secondary vocational and artistic schools, and general secondary schools.

Basic secondary schooling usually lasts three years, and its main purpose is to prepare qualified workers for different branches of the national economy.

The certificate of completion given at the end of the program is not considered a secondary school certificate (matura) and does not qualify for university entrance. These schools constitute the most diversified vocational education component of the school system and are differentiated by

vocational profiles and how they organize their work experience programs.

The certificate of completion given out by basic secondary schools confirms the recipient is a qualified worker in a specific job or category of jobs. It also gives the holder the right to apply for admission to a full secondary school with a general or vocational program; however, few graduates continue their education.

Full secondary vocational and artistic schools prepare a qualified labor force with relatively comprehensive credentials. They also provide a secondary general education. Studies in vocational secondary schools last four or five years, depending on specialization. The goals of these schools are twofold: to train skilled work persons and to make it possible for young people to obtain a full secondary education.

Upon completing courses at a vocational secondary school, students may write a matriculation exam or receive a certificate of completion from their school. A certificate of completion attests the holder possesses technical qualifications relevant for a specific trade and in addition has successfully completed general secondary schooling. A matriculation certificate allows the holder to write entrance exams for entry into higher studies institutions. So far, however, graduates of these schools rarely apply for university (Kaczor, 1989).

General secondary schools lead toward a matriculation certificate and prepare students for higher education. Acceptance is on the basis of an entrance exam completed upon graduation from primary school. Subject matter is differentiated into categories such as mathematics, classics, and so on, and education programs may also be differentiated through widening the scope of teaching in some subjects. In many schools, there are school-specific options. Recently, general secondary schools have grown dramatically; their numbers increased from 1,164 in 1991 to 1,688 in 1995. Of these, 225 are private institutions.

Studies generally take up to four years and graduates who pass the matriculation exam become eligible to write entrance exams for institutions of higher education. General secondary school graduates who pass their matriculation exam but do not seek (or fail to gain) entrance into higher education schools, did not take the matriculation exam, or do not wish to enter the labor force immediately may continue their education in post-secondary schools.

Post-Secondary Vocational Schools   These one- and two-year schools prepare candidates for particular occupations as skilled manual workers or specialized white-collar employees. The location of these schools, the specific programs offered, and the scale of admissions depend on the particular needs of the national and local economy at any given time. The core of a post-secondary vocational school's curriculum is a set of general vocational subjects, usually connected with one group of occupations. In addition, a large number of special courses of varying lengths provide more focused vocational preparation. Finally, some general education subjects, designed to give students a larger outlook on their future work, are included. Graduates of these schools obtain a certificate confirming that the holder possesses skills relevant for a particular trade. In the case of those who graduate from two-year studies for white-collar workers, their certificate confers the rank of "technician" or some other occupational title.

Higher Education.   There are several different kinds of higher education institutions in Poland. This is a legacy of the communist era, when various faculties were separated from universities in order to create new institutions. Some institutions, like universities, pedagogical universities, institutions of higher technical education, economics academies, agricultural academies, and theological academies, were put under the control of by the Ministry of National Education. Others, such as medical academies, music academies, fine art, drama, film schools, physical education academies, military, and maritime academies, come under other ministries. Hence, the system of higher education is very fragmented. Importantly, since 1990 it has been legal to open private institutions of higher education. By the end of 1993, 36 such

institutions had been founded; by 1995 there were 80, with 89,399 students enrolled (Glowny Urzad Statystyczny, 1996).

Decisions on setting up, closing down, or amalgamating state institutions of higher education require legislative approval. The 99 state institutions include, among others: 11 universities, 18 institutions of higher technical education, 9 agricultural academies, 5 economics academies, 9 pedagogical universities, 11 medical academies, 17 art and music schools, 6 academies of physical education, 2 maritime academies, and 2 theological academies.

The Ministry of National Education regulates overall enrollment in both state and private higher-education institutions according to labor market demands and the general process of the country's economic transformation. At the transition period, a goal to significantly increase the number of students in higher education was set. At present, about 16 percent of the 19-to-24 age group are enrolled in higher education institutions. In 1995 there were 179 tertiary education institutions, with 794,000 students enrolled. However, when compared with developed countries, the percentage of students in tertiary education in Poland is considered to be very low (OECD, 1996).

It is worth noting that the higher education system, representing only 4 percent of total school enrollment, absorbs 18 percent of total expenditures on education. Primary education, accounting for 58 percent of total school enrollment, receives only 54 percent of total expenditures. Equally unbalanced proportions can be perceived in the case of vocational and general secondary education (Dietl, 1994).

Adult Education

Educators and economists realize that adult and nonformal education has an increasingly important role to play in economic and cultural development (Bogard, 1992). New socioeconomic circumstances in Poland underline the significance of adult education as an important element of employment programs. Traditionally, adult education is administered within the formal education system and embraces all levels and types of education: primary, secondary, and higher. There are extramural courses that can take the form of day schooling, evening classes, correspondence courses, and university extension. Candidates must be over 17 years of age.

In recent years, nongovernmental organizations, community groups, teachers' organizations, cultural and artistic organizations, and youth organizations have initiated adult education projects. Such groups are also often involved in programs run by government agencies. New open and distance education programs are also being implemented. These include any form of learning not under the persistent or direct observation of teachers or instructors, but that nevertheless benefits from the planning and delivery of a tutorial organization. These modes include a large element of autonomous learning and hence are greatly dependent on the instructional arrangement of materials.

All these initiatives demonstrate the growing roles and different forms of contemporary adult education, training, and retraining. They are also responses to the increasing demand for education in Poland. These are radical changes in the structure and delivery of education.

Teacher Training

Since 1989, much attention has been paid to reshaping initial and in-service teacher training programs. However, fundamental or revolutionary changes have not resulted; only some innovations in content and methods have been made. In Poland, there are three approaches to teacher education, and they are implemented in three types of teacher training institutions. Universities provide academically oriented programs; teacher training colleges focus on practically oriented programs; pedagogical universities offer combined programs.

Over the last few decades, there has been an increasing trend to assimilate teaching training into universities. Under "universities" we include both universities and higher-education teacher training

institutes attached to polytechnics, economics academies, agricultural academies, medical academies, and academies of music, fine arts, and physical education. To a certain degree, pedagogical universities (founded after World War II) and a new form of three-year teacher training colleges (established in the early 1990s) can be included in this sector as well (Ministerstwo Edukacji Narodowej, 1994). Interestingly, these diverse teacher training institutions seem to be increasingly embracing and copying the orientations of universities. As a result, the "university model" dominates the country's teacher training programs.

Eleven Polish universities train teachers for all subjects in the eight grades of the general elementary school curriculum and offer courses for secondary school teaching candidates in over twenty disciplines. Teacher preparation programs for kindergartens and the first three grades of primary schools have also appeared in universities. University programs provide five-year, full-time MA or MSc courses in particular disciplines, usually combined with some education training. Students graduate with degrees that provide them with advance disciplinary knowledge in school-related subjects such as history, mathematics, philology, geography, biology, and so on. Concurrently, they obtain teaching qualifications for both elementary and secondary school levels.

This approach to teacher training is currently under attack. A recent Ministry of Education report points out that "The role of universities in training fully qualified teachers is declining . . . as some of them completely abandon pedagogical training and others reduce the amount of time spent on it. They no longer comply with the specified minimum hours for teacher training subjects" (Republic, 1992, p. 57). To understand why this is the case, it must be appreciated that in the Polish academic tradition the accent is on subject expertise. Therefore, students, including teachers in training, are required to take just one discipline over five years of university studies. However, while the university contributes to this specialized scholarly development, it tends to neglect the professional preparation of teachers in training. This model therefore leads to a one-sided education of future teachers.

In response, at the beginning of the 1990s, three-year teacher training colleges were established to promote a skill-based and more practically directed approach to teacher education. One of the core innovations in the college arrangement is the emphasis placed on practical training. This includes lesson preparation, questioning, interpersonal communication, classroom management, and evaluation skills. It is argued that carefully planned, arranged, and supervised teaching practice is the most fundamental qualification of a fully prepared teacher. These institutions are still a novelty in the system, though in recent years they are coming to be regarded as the best models for training elementary school teachers, especially those in the early grades.

The third form of teacher education is offered by nine state-maintained pedagogical universities, established in the last fifty years. As time went on these institutions, called *higher pedagogical schools,* became more and more similar to universities. They obtained full academic rights and, like universities, offered undergraduate, graduate, and postgraduate courses. They run five-year courses in both single subject areas and in groups of disciplines associated with broader education studies.

However, in contrast to universities, pedagogical universities have harmonized education studies with academic subject areas. In consequence, there is a balance between professional training and single subject academic knowledge. Pedagogical universities organize practical experiences for prospective teachers in the regular classrooms of public schools and, at the same time, strong support and guidance exists within the program. However, in spite of intentions, this combination of theoretical studies and practical training often lacks coherent and well-thought-through education objectives and is inclined to emphasize and accredit narrow teaching competencies. Ultimately, such a narrow professional focus is inconsistent with the wider roles teachers and schools are

called upon to play in Poland's rapidly changing society.

SOCIAL AND EDUCATION ISSUES

Education Reforms and Social Transformation

Education reform, in the shape of important changes in education policies, objectives, and structures, is an internal part of social transformation. It has repercussions beyond the educational system itself; it is linked to broader social change. In other words, the idea of education reform tends to be linked to broader ideas of societal change.

The changing education system in Poland is part of a more complex and long-term transition in politics, economy, and culture, as well as in social structure and public attitudes. The withdrawal of the socialist system cannot be considered as "a simple transition" but rather as "an inversion of the whole system: from a totalitarian, self-referential society to a democratic and open society providing the widest political, economic, and social freedom for all individuals" (Wichmann, 1996, p. 1).

Two elements have particularly important roles in the transformation of an education system: redefining education objectives and creating new education policies and administrative structures to implement the new objectives.

Redefining Education Objectives. Today, school objectives focus on shaping virtues such as initiative, the ability to take risk and responsibility, creativity, imagination, self-sufficiency, and so on. During the communist era, the centralized school system hardly reacted to new situations and challenges created by scientific, technological, and economic changes. An old-fashioned concept prevailed in the post-war period; the ideal of political leaders and of the factory managers was the "obedient" and "faithful" worker.

Another fundamental change in education objectives after the communist withdrawal was a shift in emphasis that involved accepting the principle of individualization; a recognition of differences in students' personal, intellectual, emotional, and practical skills according to their physical and psychological development. The previous dogmatic collectivism, ready to sacrifice the unfolding of the individual in the name of an abstract "common personality," was rejected.

Yet another major change is rejection of the ideological uniformity and official indoctrination that had been imposed on schools during the communist period. This is expressed in the idea that public schools ought to be neutral or "objective" in matters concerning ideology and attitudes. However, in Poland this principle remains unrealized. Since the communist withdrawal, public schools have become an arena of religious inculcation. As early as 1990, the government introduced religion classes in all elementary and secondary schools. Thus (although the rights of religious minorities were legally protected), public education became *de facto* denominational with the granting of special status to Roman Catholicism.

Following the official sanction of religion classes in public schools, the Roman Catholic Church has become more active in debates on education philosophy. Officially, Catholics (strongly supported by the Church) call for "critical independent thinking and free choice," an "active involvement in a democratically reformed Poland which promotes responsible social participation by the individual," and "an education system founded on philosophy which advances individualism, self-education, and continuing education" (Nowak-Fabrykowski & Sosnowski, 1995, p. 57). In reality, however, they represent conservative and dogmatic modes of reasoning on education matters and tend to dominate the whole system.

Another recent main development is the efforts directed toward rebuilding national autonomy and national identity. The education system is viewed as an important instrument in preserving the nation's cultural unity. In official education documents, it is clearly advocated that the provision of knowledge and skills in schools, as well as the development of students' intellectual abilities, emotional responsiveness, and ethical civic values, should be based on national values.

Finally, tolerance is advocated. While internationalism, equity among individuals, and solidarity with oppressed people and those fighting for their freedom were ideological cornerstones of education in the former socialist model of education, in fact, racial, religious, national, and ethnic biases and prejudices did not diminish. On the contrary; they remained sharp. Today, as the economic conditions of the country deteriorate, these biases and prejudices are becoming accentuated.

Creating New Education Policies and Administrative Structures. With the fall of communism, the Polish state's monopoly on establishing and running schools was broken. Nonstate schools were opened at various levels of the system and with various specializations. At the end of 1980s, there were only 10 nonpublic (that is, not run by the state) schools, compared to 25,000 public schools. In 1995 the number of nonpublic schools reached 1,300 (OECD, 1995). There are now community schools, founded by parents who cover most of the expenses to maintain them and private schools, which are profit-making enterprises attended by children of wealthy families.

Unfortunately, available data do not permit indepth analyses of the development of the nonpublic sector of the country's formal education system. Nevertheless, as a hypothesis, it may be postulated that the education provided by state schools is increasingly acquiring the characteristics of mass education, while nonpublic education is increasingly elitist.

With regard to the management and administration of education, post-communist governments pursue a policy of decentralization. For almost half a century, the system of education in Poland was strongly centralized. The decision-making center, moreover, was placed outside the Ministry of National Education; that is, in the Central Committee of the governing communist party. The Ministry, as well as lower divisions of the education administration, was only expected to implement directives coming from that center. At the local levels of the formal education structure, there were almost no decisions made on school management or curricula. The result was curricular stagnation. Extreme uniformity killed teachers' curricular and methodological initiatives and at the same time lowered the quality of education.

Thus, elimination of excessive administrative control and supervision became an essential task. Hierarchical management structures were abandoned in favor of horizontal ones. All schools of a given type are no longer required to apply precisely the same curriculum, work in exactly the same organizational conditions, and use only one textbook. This means fewer directives from above and more cooperation at the grassroots level. Most decision making has been delegated to education councils (school, local, and national), which are composed of representatives of teachers, parents, students, and local communities. In 1996 the responsibility for running preprimary, primary, and certain secondary schools was transferred from the government administration to local self-governments. At the same time, higher education institutions were granted extensive autonomy with regard to both curricular and organizational arrangements.

However, these changes must not be interpreted as a full, radical decentralization of schooling in Poland. The new education regulations also established a new hierarchy of decision making and responsibility. The Ministry of National Education coordinates and implements state education policy, supervises local education superintendents, and decides on every regional education program. This power is exercised through control of the purse strings—local initiatives are financed at the discretion of the Ministry. Thus, the system of educational management remains centralized, but allows some modifications to reward and encourage local participation.

When we turn to reforms that have been centrally initiated, we find changes in methods, means, and organization of education. However, the most important change has been an attitudinal one. In sharp contrast to the orientation of the communist era, central and local educational authorities, as well as educational researchers, are in agreement that the schools should provide students with an education corresponding as much as possible to their individual abilities and interests.

Teaching Democracy and Teaching About Democracy

Developing democratic competencies and democratic behavior is considered an indispensable primary task of contemporary Polish formal education. The phrase "teaching democracy" is frequently understood as providing opportunities for self-education during which students can develop and organize their personal experiences, acquire specific competencies, and gain knowledge about the possible implementation of democratic procedures in future professional activities. The emphasis placed on the development of these competencies is a result of the view that democracy is a dynamic process and thus a democratic society is process oriented. Social, institutional, and government changes occur in democratic societies faster than in other societies. Accordingly, it is not the task of schools to inculcate students with static prescriptions for behavior. Rather, it is to help them learn how to cope with change and to develop adaptive strategies.

Curricular Innovation

Two major, but antithetical, perspectives underlie recent moves to elaborate new curricula for both the elementary and secondary schools. The first emphasizes an unlimited autonomy for teachers and school administrators; the second advocates a precise specification of subject matter and lessons in every subject and period of teaching. These two opposing perspectives can be found in all debates on education policy in post-communist countries (Szebenyi, 1992).

As early as 1990, alternative teaching programs, consistent with the state core curriculum, became permitted. That was a prologue to major changes in the whole education system. Under the former overly centralized decision-making system, the teacher's task was content transmission. The curriculum drawn up at the central level was the same for the entire country. With the successive introduction of alternative teaching programs by post-communist governments, a systemic school reform has been initiated.

However, with diversity it then became necessary to devise mechanisms for ensuring equivalency in the new curricula. Such a guarantee is contained in the core curriculum, established centrally by the Ministry of Education. This takes the form of curriculum guidelines, which serve as education canons in general education. In other words, the Ministry rejected a detailed central curriculum, but at the same time deemed the core curriculum indispensable.

Curriculum reforms introduced into at the school level have also resulted in curricular changes in teacher education. Curriculum studies have recently become a very substantial part of teacher training programs. Teacher education programs now emphasize how to teach teachers in training on "a free choice of subject matter," in "a specification and understanding of instructional objectives," on "reflecting the growing diversity in the background and ability of students originating from different social strata," and so on (Slawinski, 1994).

These positive curricular innovations do not eliminate the incoherence that appears within the school education in Poland. While a wide area of freedom for various actors in the education system has been opened, what have not been defined are the quality of education to be provided by schools and the specific competencies required of pupils. As a result, there are no mechanisms for the evaluation of the effectiveness of education at the school and classroom levels and, on a nationwide scale, there is no comparability of school certificates and diplomas.

Gender, Schooling, and Jobs

In the last few decades, lower vocational schools and technical secondary schools have been rapidly expanded. However, the student population is predominantly male because of the historically deeply rooted social convention that technical or artisan occupations are appropriate for boys, while girls are better served by studies for clerical, medical (nursing), teaching, commercial, and similar professions. The ironic side effect of that assumption is a considerable increase in higher education opportunities for females. While males numerically dominate lower vocational schools and technical secondary schools, females constitute the vast majority of the general secondary school population.

That social phenomenon was not predicted by policy makers; they had unconsciously created a condition for overcoming schooling gender discrimination resulting from traditional sex role stereotyping in Polish society. Recent figures show that women are beginning to surpass men, at least at the level of attaining a university education. But, this is not reflected in terms of jobs. Entrance to higher positions is still much more difficult for women than for men. Thus, there is a pressing need for action (including legislation) that will diminish discrimination against women in the workplace and in vocational training at secondary and higher education levels.

The Market Economy and Vocational and Higher Education

The objectives of vocational training clearly represent a shift from serving the requirements of a centrally planned economy to serving a market economy. Secondary vocational schools are now viewed as instruments for implementing professional training that emphasizes an ability to transfer core skills to new situations, an ability to adjust to a rapidly changing occupational environment, competence in occupational skills, and habits that complement work, community expectations, and adult life. Thus, there is a visible tendency to form a bridge between general and vocational education.

To achieve these aims, some innovative initiatives have been undertaken. These include the establishment of so-called polyvocational classes, implementation of broad-profiled training, creation of curricula in new occupations and specializations, establishment of general secondary schools attached to vocational schools, encouraging teachers to develop curricula, and, finally, improving practical training and school workshop activities.

The focus of these innovations is modernization rather than radical structural reform. At the moment, the idea of a fundamental reform of the structure of the education system cannot be put into effect due to inadequate funding for education and the current economic crisis. Still, many organizational and curricular innovations are being introduced throughout the structure of secondary education as a new correspondence between schools and society has been established (Caillods, Atchoarena, & Bertrand, 1995). Thus, a basis for building a competitive national economy and developing a high standard of production technologies and expert services is being put in place. In terms of both national business development and international economic relations, it is only logical that attention is being focused on preparing highly skilled and professional technical managerial staff.

THE FUTURE OF SOCIETY AND SCHOOLING

The "Strategy for Poland"

As a consequence of introducing comprehensive and socially painful reforms, in recent years Poland has become the fastest growing major economy in Europe, recording an annual growth of 7 percent. The country's return to the international market has been widely acknowledged. Its accession to membership in the OECD underlines is success in reforming the national economy. The evidence to date clearly demonstrates that Poland has undergone a major transformation, both politically and economically.

A new program, titled *Strategy for Poland: Package 2000,* has been launched to nurture favorable trends in the Polish economy and to allow the country to meet Maastricht Treaty requirements for full membership in the EU. The program establishes sound prospects for both the present and future growth of the national economy, and constitutes a framework for a positive climate in the country's social and political development (Strategia, 1996).

Education Priorities in the Future

The *Strategy* articulates the need to invest in "human capital" and affirms education as a key factor in the country's economic and political development. It maintains that expenditures on science, education, culture, health, and environmental protection should be regarded as investments. Indeed, the government is considering increased expenditures on education and research in the form of education subsidies, research grants, and student financial assistance.

However, the reality is that, over the last ten years, expenditure on education and training averaged only 4 percent of Gross National Product and shows a downward trend. From 1993 onward it has been below 3.5 percent. In the other OECD member countries, with much higher GNPs per capita, the range is 4 to 7 percent.

The prevalent opinion is that within the next decade it will be necessary to raise education's share of the GNP to 5 percent and, at the same time, undertake far-reaching reforms that will allow for a more effective use of allocations for education and training. In particular, schools at all levels need to sufficiently equipped with modern teaching aids. The present inadequate supply of computers, electronic books, journals, and so on, must be overcome. Special emphasis should be placed on preparing the young for the information society, new technologies, and a scientific environment.

Education policymakers also seem to recognize that, as schools enter the twenty-first century, there needs to be a focus on teaching students effective work habits and self-discipline, developing international awareness and understanding, nurturing intellectual curiosity and a desire for lifelong learning and, finally, developing students' ability to think and evaluate critically, constructively, and creatively (Ministerstwo Edukacji Narodowej, 1996).

As a result, at the beginning of the next century Poland should be a country that has unleashed its indigenous intellectual potential, successfully promoted the development of high-tech industries and services, and become an information society. It should also be a nation whose economic development complements the social needs of its population. Today, perhaps for the first time in the modern history of Poland, neither a strong sense of national identity nor a pervasive ideology/ religion are being emphasized in official state documents on education. Hence, it can be said cautiously that recent education guidelines are free of overt ideological content. However, as emphasized earlier, it must be remembered that Catholic fundamentalism continues to play a very significant role in the country's education system.

Polish educators and education policymakers and planners recognize that Poland is a rapidly changing society and that education reforms have serious social implications for the future. Yet, as OECD inspectors advise, "A reformed educational system will form the surest base on which the new Polish social order may be built" (OECD, 1996, p. 2).

REFERENCES

Bogard, G. (1992). *For a socializing type of adult education: Report*. Strasbourg: Council for Cultural Cooperation.

Caillods, F., Atchoarena, D., & Bertrand, O. (1995). Trends and challenges in eastern Europe. *IIEP Newsletter, XIII* (1), 1–3.

Dietl, J. (1994). *Economic expansion and educational reform: Closing the gap*. In internet: http://april. ibpm.serpukhov.su/friends/education/audem 93/dietl2. html - size 80K - 2 Nov 94.

Glowny Urzad Statystyczny. (1992). *Rocznik statystyczny GUS* (Polish statistical yearbook). LII. Warszawa: Author.

Glowny Urzad Statystyczny. (1993). *Rocznik statysty-czny GUS* (Polish statistical yearbook). LIII. Warszawa: Author.

Glowny Urzad Statystyczny. (1995). *Rocznik statystyczny GUS* (Polish statistical yearbook). LV. Warszawa: Author.

Glowny Urzad Statystyczny. (1996). *Rocznik statystyczny GUS* (Polish statistical yearbook). LVI. Warszawa: Author.

Kaczor, S. (1989). *Stan i perspektywy szkolnictwa zawodowego w Polsce* (Condition and perspective of vocational schooling development in Poland). Warszawa: PWN.

Karwowska-Struczyk, M. (1996). *Who is caring for young children in Poland?* In Internet: http://biz.map.com/polfined.html - size 102K - 24 Jun 96.

Kasprzyk, M. (1996). *The history of Poland*. In Internet: http://www.kasprzyk.demon. co.uk/www/History-Polska.html.

Kozakiewicz, M. (1990). Educational research and Polish perestroika. *Prospects, XX,* 41–48.

Kwiecinski, Z. (1995). *The sociopathology of education*. Torun: Edytor.

Ministerstwo Edukacji Narodowej. (1994). *Glowne kierunki doskonalenia systemu edukacji w Polsce* (Main directions of Polish education system improvement). Warszawa: Author.

Ministerstwo Edukacji Narodowej. (1996). *Zalozenia dlugofalowej polityki edukacyjnej panstwa ze szczegolnym uwzglednieniem programu rozwoju ksztalcenia na poziomie wyzszym* (Assumptions for a long-term state education policy with special focus on the program of higher education development). Warszawa: Author. (Manuscript in author's collection)

Morody, M. (1993). *Spoleczenstwo polskie w procesie przemian* (Polish society in the process of transformation). In M. Grabowska & A. Sutek (Eds.), *Polska 1989–1992. Fragmenty pejzazu* (Poland in 1989–1992. Fragments of the Social and Political Landscape). Warszawa: IFiS PAN.

Nowak-Fabrykowski, K., & Sosnowski, A. (1995). Education in transition: Changes in the Polish school system. *Canadian and International Education, 24,* 55–64.

OECD, Organization for Economic Cooperation and Development. (1995). *Raport na temat polityki edukacyjnej w Polsce. Raport i pytania wizytatorow* (Report on education policy in Poland.

Report and questions of the OECD examiners). Warszawa. (Manuscript in the author's collection)

OECD, Organization for Economic Cooperation and Development. (1996). *Review of education policy in Poland: Examiners' report and questions.* Paris. (Manuscript in the author's collection)

Republic of Poland Ministry of National Education. (1992). *The development of education in Poland in 1990–1991.* Warsaw: MEN.

Slawinski, M.S. (1994). Les reformes en Pologne. In Conseil de l'Europe. Conference permanente des pouvoirs locaux et regionaux de l'Europe. *Le partage des responsibilites et des competences en matiere d'education.* Strasbourg: Conseil de l'Europe, pp. 2–4. (Manuscript in the author's collection)

Strategia dla Polski. Pakiet 2000 (1996). (Strategy for Poland. Package 2000). In Internet: http:// 158.66.233.27/programy/pakiet1.html.

Szebenyi, P. (1992). Change in the systems of public education in east central Europe. *Comparative Education, 28,* 19–31.

Topolski, J. (1992). *Historia Polski* (History of Poland). Warszawa-Krakow: Poloczek.

Ustawa z 15 lipca 1961 o rozwoju systemu oswiaty i wychowania (Act of July 15, 1961, on the development of the system of education. *Dziennik Ustaw Polskiej Rzeczypospolitej Ludowej, 32.*

Ustawa z 7 wrzesnia 1991 o systemie oswiaty (Act of the Education System of September 7, 1991. *Dziennik Ustaw Rzeczypospolitej Polskiej, 95,* point 425.

Wichmann, J. (1996, October). *The transformation of educational systems in central and eastern Europe: Prospects and problems.* Paper presented at the 17th CESE Conference, Athens.

CHAPTER 16

Traditions in Transition: Schooling and Society in Hungary

MÁRIA NAGY

Mária Nagy is a senior researcher at the National Institute of Public Education, Budapest, Hungary. Her main fields of interest include: educational policy making, educational administration, comparative education, and teacher policies. Recent publications include: Tanári szakma és professzionalizálódás (Teachers and Professionalization), *Budapest: Keraban, 1994; "Hungary" in Sjoerd Karsten and Dominique Majoor (Eds.),* Education in East Central Europe: Educational Changes after the Fall of Communism, *New York: Münster, 1994; with Peter Darvas, "Teachers and Politics in Central Eastern Europe" in Mark B. Ginsburg (Ed.),* The Politics of Educators' Work and Life, *New York, London: Garland, 1995. She sits on the editorial board of* Curriculum Studies.

THE SOCIAL FABRIC

The Hungarian Republic is a central European country with a population of 10,212,000.[1] Its territory is 93,000 square kilometers, about one percent of Europe's area. Of the population, 62.6 percent live in urban areas, 18 percent in the capital of Budapest.

From an ethnic point of view, Hungary is a rather homogeneous country. About 96 percent of the population is Hungarian and speaks Hungarian (a unique language in the area, belonging to the Finno-Ugrian language group). The main national minorities are of German, Slovak, Serb, Croat, Romanian, and Slovene origin. Gypsies constitute a major ethnic minority group, numbering about 500,000. The Hungarian diaspora is estimated to be about 5 million, of which about 2.5 million live as national minorities in the neighboring countries, most of them in Romania and Slovakia, while the others live scattered all around the world.

Religious life has been reviving since the fall of the Soviet-type political system at the end of the 1980s, but it is still difficult to estimate accurately the number of religious people. According to recent opinion polls, about 14 percent of the population declare themselves to be actively religious, while about 30 percent identify themselves as nonreligious. It is estimated that about two-thirds of religious people are Roman Catholic, while Protestants constitute the second biggest group. Traditional churches are not as popular among young people as they are with the elderly. However, youth tend to be more religious than the middle generation.

Hungary is an aging society; the population has been declining since the early 1980s. In 1995, the natural decrease rate was 3.3 per thousand of the population. The aging index (the proportion of the age group above 60/the proportion of the age group under 15) has grown from 54.3 to 108.1 between 1960 and 1996. In 1960, about one-fourth of the population (25.4 percent) was under 15, and only 13.8 percent of the population was 60 or more; in 1996, old people outnumbered the youngest generation (their rates were 19.4 percent and 18.0 percent, respectively). This worrisome tendency can be explained by two parallel unfavorable social indicators: a falling birthrate and deteriorating life expectancy indicators. Life

---

[1]The majority of statistical data of this section of the study is taken from the *Statistical Yearbook of Hungary, 1995* (1996).

expectancy at birth in Hungary has declined in the last few decades, at least among men, while it has only slightly increased among women. Today the life expectancy for newborn boys is 65.25 years, and for girls it is 74.50 years, the worst in Europe (*Statistical Yearbook of Hungary, 1995*, 1996).

Such unfavorable demographic and health indicators can be explained partly by the rapid social, political, and economic changes that the country has been undergoing not only in recent years, but also in its twentieth-century history. The country began the twentieth century as a minor partner in a medium-sized European state (that of the Austro-Hungarian monarchy), then underwent two world wars, lost about two-thirds of its territories and population, and survived eight major political system changes. Though the most recent change (from a monolithic to a democratic political system and from a centrally planned to a market economy system) is considered by outside reviewers as favorable in the long run (and this consideration is basically shared by the Hungarian public as well), everyday life during this transitional period seems to be rather difficult and tiresome for most of the population. This is perhaps the main reason why the people of this country are so often described as being very pessimistic. In the following, I try to introduce some of the main economic, social, and political changes.

Political and Economic System

After the Second World War, Hungary became part of the eastern bloc, a member of the Warsaw Military Pact, and the economic group Comecon. Since the collapse of the Soviet-type political, economic, and military system after 1989 (hereafter referred to as the political system change), Hungary, just like other post-communist countries, has been experiencing rapid political, social, and economic restructuring. Today Hungary is a parliamentary democracy with a one-chamber parliament. After the first free election in 1990, the country had a conservative-liberal-Christian government, while the 1994 election was won by socialist and liberal political parties. Six major parties are represented in Parliament and the polit-

ical party system can be considered rather stable. According to opinion polls, however, public support of the political parties is declining.

As defined in the Constitution, the political power of the head of the state (the President) is weak. The Constitutional Court (established in 1990) plays an important role among checks and balances in the system. The system of public administration is fairly decentralized. Local self-governments play crucial roles, including in the area of education. The country is a member of the European Council and of the OECD.

In response to a national debt that had been growing since the early 1970s, Hungary had to begin restructuring (or reforming) its economic system somewhat earlier than most other formerly socialist countries. However, even early interventions could not prevent the country from experiencing a serious economic decline after the fall of communism. The loss of most of its previous markets (the ex-Comecon countries) and the need for a new and challenging economic orientation was accompanied by growing foreign as well as domestic debt, growing inflation, and unemployment. The gross domestic product (GDP) decreased dramatically between 1989 and 1993. A slight increase and stagnation has been the characteristic trend since then. The per capita GDP was US$4,273 in 1995.

Labor participation rates have also changed since the late 1980s. In 1989, the unemployment ratio was 0.3 percent; by 1993 it was 12.6 percent, and then it began to show a slight decrease—in 1995 it was 10.9 percent. Unemployment is highest among young people (29.5 percent among the 15-to-19 age group and 12.9 percent among the 20-to-24 age group). There is also a growing rate of so-called passive unemployment. The dependency ratio (the number of inactive persons per the number of economically active population) has dramatically increased from 89 to 150 between 1989 and 1995. Employment by industries has also changed considerably. In 1994, 9 percent of the employed labor force worked in agriculture, 32.4 percent worked in industry, and 58.6 percent were employed in the service sector (Lannert, 1997).

A painful consequence of the restructuring of

the economic system is the growth of social differences. The speed at which differentiation occurred is remarkably rapid. While, for example, in 1992 the per capita income of the top 10 percent of the population was 6.678 times greater than that of the lowest 10 percent; by 1995 this rate was 7.261.

While social differentiation in the post-communist market economy is not an unexpected phenomenon, some characteristics of this process cause public concern. One is the shrinking size of the middle classes and the ever-growing lower social strata. Another is the growing regional differences, especially the growing impoverishment of certain regions and certain types of settlements, particularly villages. A further striking feature is that families with children are becoming the most disadvantaged group of the population. The proportions of poor families (those receiving less than half of the average monthly income) has changed between 1990 and 1995 in different parts of the country and in different families. While the total rate of poor families has slightly increased (from 9.3 percent to 10.9 percent), it has almost doubled among families with children (from 12.7 percent to 21.6 percent). Poverty is especially great among village people with children and Romany families are overrepresented among them (*Statistical Yearbook of Hungary, 1995,* 1996).

The deteriorating social data and rather unfavorable and only slowly improving economic indicators contrast with some educational and cultural indicators and also with the cultural traditions and ambitions of the population. Some people even speak about "overconsumption" in education (e.g., Horváth, 1992). But some other educational indicators, such as school enrollment data on each school level or pupil achievement in different subjects, are fairly favorable in a European comparison.

SCHOOLING

Historical precedents

The origins of public education in Hungary go back to the late eighteenth century. However, the first Education Act on public education was enacted only in 1868 by the independent Hungarian Ministry of Religion and Public Education of the Austro-Hungarian monarchy. The act introduced compulsory education for children between the ages of 6 to 12 and obliged municipalities to set up public schools where the churches had not set up any. Kindergarten as an education provision was also made a public duty at that time.

Until the Second World War, the development of education in Hungary—as in other countries of the Central European region—was much influenced by the German-speaking countries. Some characteristics of this development—for example, teacher- or subject-centered educational methodology and philosophy in education, the high academic quality of general secondary schooling (*gimnázium*) ending with maturity examinations, and the traditional links of professional or apprenticeship education with the world of work—were more or less preserved after 1945, even though the country fell under Soviet political and economic influence (Nagy, 1994). The most significant changes after 1945 were the unification of the school system and the monopolization of governance and decision making for schooling by the ruling Communist Party.

Unification of the school system was rapidly carried out in 1945. All the previous types of schools (the traditional eight-year *gimnázium* among them) were abolished and replaced with an eight-year long compulsory General School for the 6- to 14-year-old age group, four-year general and vocational secondary schools, and two- or three-year vocational (apprenticeship) schools. This 8+4/3 school structure remained basically unchanged until the late 1980s.

Unification was further affected through a total centralization of curricula and textbook publishing and strict and highly ideological and political supervision of classroom practice. This type of unification and centralization was substantially loosened by the end of the 1980s. Education, especially in the 1950s, served ideological and political objectives (indoctrinating socialist materialistic and internationalist thinking). The objective was the production of the "socialist type of human being." Education was also meant to be a major device in manpower planning: Its main task was to fulfill the labor force demands of the economy. The objectives of personal human development and individual ambitions did not appear among the official objectives of schooling.

Besides unification, schooling after 1945 was characterized by rapid expansion. The school-leaving age was raised to 16 in 1961. By the 1980s, more than 95 percent of children finished the eight-year general school by the designated age.

Educational Objectives in the 1990s

With the birth of different political parties and public declarations of different political ideologies, conflicting educational philosophies and objectives have appeared both in educational debates and in policies. In contrast with previous policies, a main objective of successive educational governments since 1990 is that education should be responsive to the individual needs of students and also supportive in preparing them for future life. As for what the best preparation should be, however, opinions differ considerably. Due to decentralization and the abolishment of the state monopoly in education in 1990, the development of education has been much more influenced by local and institutional needs and ambitions in recent years than by government educational policies.

Changes in public opinion about the objectives of education point to expectations that have increased in connection with the development of cognitive skills (mother tongue and foreign language teaching included) on the one hand, and with the tasks of schools in preserving and supporting the physical conditions of their students (catering and sports) on the other. It is also interesting to note how much expectations on schools to develop cooperative attitudes in students have increased, in view of the growing individualism in economic and social processes mentioned above.

Changes in pedagogical theory and practice reflect public expectations and policy objectives. In recent years there has been a revival of child-centered pedagogy. Both in initial and in in-service teacher training, new courses of so-called alternative pedagogy (Montessori, Freinet, Waldorf, and so on) have been introduced, and communicative and cooperating skills have been strengthened.

Education Legislation and Policies

Public life in Hungary during the last decade of the twentieth century is characterized by intensive legislative processes in every field. Almost every aspect of education has been reregulated in recent years, sometimes as part of the broader public sphere. Some major pieces of legislation are introduced below.

Before 1990, schools were under state ownership. Even before the first free election, the *1990 Amendment of the 1985 Education Act* abolished the state's monopoly in founding and maintaining schools. This made the founding of denominational and private schools possible. By 1996, 5.4 percent of schools were private or run by churches; 4 percent of pupils attended these schools. These rates were much higher at the secondary level, where 13.8 percent of schools are private or denominational and 8.2 percent of pupils attend these schools (Lannert, 1997; Sugár, 1997).

The reform of public financing had also preceded the political system change of 1990. In 1989 the *System of Financing Public Education* replaced the central planning system, which had been much influenced by informal negotiations and the lobbying of different interest groups and individuals with funding principles based on per capita grants. The *1990 Local Government Act* made school provision a local government duty. This Act also abolished regional governments, so today there is a two-tiered government system in Hungary in which the local governments enjoy great autonomy.

Education is only one—though usually the most substantial—duty of local governments (beside health, roads and transport, water supply, and so on). Schools receive about 60 percent of their revenues from state grants (education per capita grants included), and they are free to decide on spending. This freedom, however, is limited by several factors. In 1992, for example, the *Act on Public Employment* introduced a central salary scale for public employees, teachers among them. With a central salary scale, with the employment system of teachers (the school director being their employer), with falling student numbers (and, consequently, decreasing per capita grants), and with growing social problems, local governments face difficulties in planning local budgets.

In 1993, three *Education Acts* (one on public, one on higher, and one on vocational education) were passed by Parliament. Substantial amendments to the first two acts were made later in 1996. The main points of these new laws in the field of public education can be summarized as follows. The freedom of schooling (the rights of opening and running educational institutions, freedom of conscience, and the rights of children in schooling) was declared. A new system of shared responsibility was introduced in which central governments, local governments, and schools are the main actors. A new system for curriculum policy was established with the approval of a New Core Curriculum by Parliament and with the enactment of the duty of individual schools to elaborate or adopt their new programs and local curricula by the beginning of the 1998/1999 school year. This new system of curricula is supplemented by a gradual introduction of a new system of evaluation and assessment. Changes in school structure have been accepted.

Organization and Governance of Schooling

Responsibility for schooling is shared by several agencies. On the national level, different ministries take responsibility for public education. The Ministry of Education and Culture is responsible for education on the whole; however, it shares responsibility for vocational schooling with several other ministries, primarily with the Ministry of Labor. The Ministry of Finance has the basic role of controlling the financing of public services, education included. The Ministry of Interior supervises local public administration, educational administration included.

The main responsibilities of the Ministry of Culture and Education are to provide national guidelines for curriculum development, to exercise professional control in textbook publishing, to define the requirements of national examinations, to provide professional support for schools, to collect and publish information on schooling, to elaborate plans on educational development, and to support educational research. The work of the minister is supported by two main advisory bodies representing the main stockholders in public education (teacher unions and associations, local governments, churches, professionals in higher education, parents, and students).

In the school year 1996/1997, 94 percent of schools were run by about 2,300 local governments. Though the decentralization of school governance is seen as a major democratic development in public education, the high number of local education authorities is also causing considerable public concern because of the lack of sufficient financial resources and administrative expertise in most of the smaller municipalities. It is the duty of local governments to establish, reorganize, and close schools; to provide the budgets of schools; to exercise financial and legal control on local schooling; to employ school directors; to approve the pedagogical programs of schools; and to evaluate the work of schools with the help of experts. However, according to a 1995 survey, local governments differ greatly in their ability to fulfill these tasks. While all the big cities and more than half of towns had a special department dealing with education in the local government office, only 9 percent of villages did so. In about 60 percent of villages there was not even a single person whose sole duty was to deal with education (Halász & Lannert, 1996).

Schools enjoy considerable autonomy in resource management, in curriculum and textbook choice, and in pupil enrollment. Teachers are employed by school directors, though within the budgetary framework provided by the local government. Most decisions are legally delegated to the teaching staff. However, the autonomy of the school is basically limited by the financial resources provided by the local budgets and may be influenced by school-level governing bodies representing teachers, parents, and local government. As noted in the preceding section, this was instituted by the 1985 Education Act, made compulsory by the 1993 Act, and made voluntary again by the 1996 Amendment. In the period since the political system change, schools have played a major part in school innovations.

School Structure

School attendance is compulsory for 6- to 16-year-olds (since 1961), although the 1985 Education Act made the starting age rather flexible. Due to the latter regulation, and because of the wishes of some parents, in the school year 1996/1997, 2 percent of those enrolled were under 6, 13.6 percent were 7 or more, and only 80.6 percent were 6 years old. There is a tendency to send children to school at a later age (preferably at age 7). This is partly to prolong their childhood, and partly to postpone their entrance into the world of work (or into youth unemployment?).

As mentioned above, the post-war 8+4/3 school structure has seen changes since the late eighties. First, the 1985 Education Act reintroduced the old eight-year-long secondary grammar schools (*gimnázium*) and initiated the new (modern West-European) six-year long secondary general schools. The 1990 *Local Government Act* made it the right and duty of local governments to decide on the structure of the local school system, and the 1993 *Education Act* declared all kinds of secondary schools (four-, six-, and eight-year-long secondary schools) legal. It means that Hungarian children today can decide to enter secondary education at the age of 10, 12, or 14. This makes the Hungarian school structure (see Figure 16.1) a rather mixed one.

Preschool education in Hungary has a long tradition and is considered to be rather efficient in comparison to other European countries. Preschool education is voluntary, but because of the high rate of female employment, attendance is high. In 1996/1997, 87.5 percent of 3- to 6-year-old children attended kindergartens. The 1993 Education Act made one year of preschool education compulsory so that no child can enter school without previous experience in kindergarten education.

General schools are still the most numerous type of schools in the Hungarian educational system, though the number of pupils has steadily declined since the late 1980s. In the school year of 1996/1997, 94.7 percent of these schools had eight grades, 5.3 percent fewer than eight grades (half of these had four grades). These smaller schools can be found in little villages, and they are often ungraded. The eight-year general school is divided into two levels (see Figure 16.1). The lower four grades are characterized by class teaching; on the upper level, subject teaching is provided. In an international context, this level can be considered as lower secondary schooling. Teachers for the two levels are trained in different types of institutions named, respectively, *tanító* and *tanár*.

While lower-level general school education is considered rather efficient and innovative, there are a lot of problems with the upper level. Some of these problems stem from its origins. The introduction of eight-year long unified primary schooling after 1945 was rapidly implemented, imposed from above, and was not based on social, political, or professional consensus. The unification of curricula and textbooks further deepened the basic controversy over this type of school; that is, all schools had to lead pupils on the very same road to three different targets: to general secondary schools (and so to higher education); to vocational secondary schools (offering both maturity examinations and vocational skills); and to vocational training of two to three years in length. The attendant introduction of teacher training institutions to prepare teachers for these tasks created further problems and controversies. Teacher training institutions have been continuously blamed both for their graduates' low level of subject knowledge (compared to university level, secondary teacher training programs) and for their inefficiency in transferring practical teaching skills.

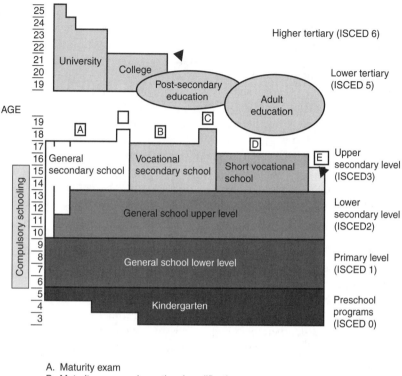

A. Maturity exam
B. Maturity exam and vocational qualification
C. Technician certificate
D. Skilled worker qualification
E. Lower level vocational qualification given by special short vocational school

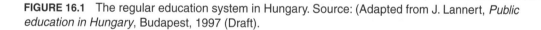

FIGURE 16.1 The regular education system in Hungary. Source: (Adapted from J. Lannert, *Public education in Hungary*, Budapest, 1997 (Draft).

Some of the problems of the general schools of today, however, come from more recent changes in the school system. The introduction of eight- and six-year-long secondary general schooling means that secondary schools "cap" the most able students of general schools (in 1996, 3.2 percent of the pupils in grades 5 to 7, and 7.7 percent of pupils in grades 7 to 8 learned in secondary schools). It means that the second level of general schools has been gradually becoming the schools of "the rest." This way, subject teachers in general schools are threatened with losing their jobs because they are losing a considerable number of pupils. They are also disturbed in their professional identity as they are losing their most able

pupils. On the whole, teachers are not prepared to fulfill their changing tasks. They lack the methods, and sometimes the willingness, too, to teach "the rest."

In the school year of 1995/1996, 96.8 percent of pupils finished eight-grade general schools by the age of 16. This was made easier for low achievers by the introduction of special grades 9 to 10 in general schools in the beginning of the 1990s. After finishing general schools, pupils can chose among four different types of further education. In the school year of 1996/1997, 27.3 percent of pupils entered general secondary schools, 33.7 percent entered secondary vocational schools, 34.2 percent went to three-year-long vocational training schools (providing no full secondary education), and 4.3 percent entered two-year-long or even shorter training leading to no qualifications.

Secondary level schooling has been characterized by rapid expansion in recent years in schools providing full secondary education (especially so in secondary vocational schools), while the number of pupils in vocational training has been steadily declining since the early 1990s. The latter is mainly due to economic factors: Until the system change, this type of schooling was connected to big state firms, most of which have gone bankrupt since then. However, it is a thrust of the government to increase the rate of secondary-level vocational training. The 1993 *Act on Vocational Education* postponed the beginning of vocational training after the school leaving age, and declared ten years of general education desirable for the whole population in the long run.

An important tendency in secondary schooling is the growing convergence of general and vocational schooling. With declining enrollment, most secondary schools try to attract new groups of pupils. Secondary grammar schools open classes for 10- and/or 12-year-old pupils; less academic secondary grammar schools offer new secondary vocational classes; secondary vocational schools open general school classes and/or offer shorter vocational training for the local school population. Some new forms of secondary schools have also been introduced since the late 1980s: bilingual secondary general schools of five grades (in the first grade students are taught only the foreign language in which they are going to study some of their subjects the next four years); or secondary vocational schools of five grades, where some kind of tertiary education is offered in the last year.

In secondary general schools the dropout rate is the lowest (10.4 percent in school year 1993/1994); it is 16.7 percent in secondary vocational schools and 21.1 percent in vocational schools. In 1996, 44.5 percent of the age group took the maturity examination, and 52.3 percent of them continued their studies in higher educa-tion. In the school year of 1996, 16.17 percent of the age group was enrolled in higher education.

Curriculum

Before turning to curricular changes, it is important to note that it is the role and regulative function of curriculum that has changed most since the political system change in Hungary. The centralized and unified system of the post-war period was a basically a top-down system, where curricular change was centrally mandated and resulted in curricular reforms at the national level. However, the last major curricular reform of this kind (in 1978) introduced some optional subjects, and in certain subjects a "second" textbook, too, thus offering some choice in curricula. This "softening" of curriculum control was reinforced by the 1985 Education Act (well before the political system change) that made school-level innovations possible (with ministerial control, of course). The idea of changing the regulative function of curriculum and the move toward even greater local input and autonomy was initiated by a group of curriculum experts in 1990. So, a new system of incremental curriculum changes (with a Central Core Curriculum and several local curricula) gradually took root and is basically accepted by all political as well as professional actors.

However, in contrast to the rather easily reached consensus on the new functions and forms of curriculum, debates centered on the changing contents of curricula have been more acrimonious. Heated political debates characterized the early 1990s (especially about history curricula, and a proposed new National Core Curriculum). At the close of the decade, the debates now focus on the implementation and local adaptation of the new National Core Curriculum, adopted in 1995.

The National Core Curriculum defines the basic requirements for the period of compulsory schooling (grades 1 to 10) and at the end of grades 4, 6, 8 and 10 in ten areas of culture (see Table 16.1). It also defines the basic knowledge to be taught, the skills and competencies to be developed, and the minimum requirements for continu-

TABLE 16.1   Subject Areas of the National Core Curriculum and the Distribution of Teaching Time Among Them (%)

SUBJECT AREA	GRADES 1–4	GRADES 5–6	GRADES 7–8	GRADES 9–10
Mother tongue and literature	32–40	16–20	11–13	11–13
Foreign language	—	11–15	9–12	9–13
Mathematics	19–23	16–20	10–14	10–14
Man and society	4–7	5–9	10–14	10–14
Man and nature	5–9	8–12	16–22	15–20
Earth and environment	—	—	4–7	4–7
Arts	12–16	12–16	9–12	9–12
Informatics	—	2–4	4–7	4–7
Home and practical knowledge	4–7	5–9	6–10	5–9
Physical education and sports	10–14	9–13	6–10	6–10

Source: Adapted from Halász (1996).

ing studies in the next stage. The National Core Curriculum also encourages teaching cross-cultural studies like communication, health education, environment protection, and life skills.

Within the framework of the National Core Curriculum, schools are free to decide which subjects, and in how many lessons, they will offer both compulsory and optional subjects; the forms and procedures of pupil evaluation; and the special provisions for ethnic and national minorities. Schools are obliged by law to elaborate their programs and their local curricula by the beginning of the school year 1998/1999. Their work is helped by a large professional support system.

Changes in curricula can be highlighted by the fast development of the textbook market. Textbook publishing has become a big business since the end of the state monopoly. By 1995, general schools could choose, on average, from six to twelve textbooks available for each subject. The increase in textbook options for foreign language teaching is even more remarkable. While English teachers in 1989/1990 could choose from only six textbooks, by 1994/1995, the choice grew to 214.

Evaluation

Pupil assessment is the responsibility of individual teachers. Hungarian schools use a 5-point mark-ing system (5 being the highest score) to evaluate pupils. At the end of the two school semesters (in February and in June) pupils get a report in which they are evaluated in each subject. Until recently, there was only one examination (the maturity examination at the age of 18), but the evaluation of pupils could be different from school to school and from teacher to teacher. This is why higher education institutions used their own entrance examinations and did not wholly accept the results of the maturity examinations. Since the mid-1980s, however, standardized written examinations have been introduced. This now means "common" maturity and higher education entrance examinations for students that choose this kind of examination. Those who do not can take their "home" maturity examinations, as before.

Testing and other forms of pupil assessment, however, are rapidly spreading within the schools themselves. Competing for pupils, most schools have introduced new curricular offerings, such as extra foreign language teaching, computer skills, and so on. With no inspection in the system, schools that want to measure their achievements, and also local governments that want to evaluate their schools seek the help of evaluation experts. In this way a kind of test market is fast evolving (Vári, 1997).

Teacher Training

Teacher training in Hungary is based on four main and different types of institutions for the four major groups of teachers (Nagy, 1997). Kindergarten teachers (*óvodapedagógus*) are trained at the college level in special institutions in four-year courses. Until the end of the 1980s, there were also kindergarten teacher training secondary schools, but the 1993 *Educational Act* abolished training at the secondary school level and now a college diploma is required of kindergarten teachers.

Teachers for the first stage of basic schools (*tanító*) are trained in another type of four-year college. They learn general subjects, but they can specialize in some subjects (arts, PE, language, and so on). Teachers for the second stage of basic schools (*általános iskolai tanár*) have their own four-year training institutions where they specialize in two subjects. Teachers for secondary schools (*középiskolai tanár*) are trained at university level in five-year courses. They specialize in two subjects (although in recent years one-subject specialization has become a possibility).

Teachers for special education (*gyógypedagógus*) are trained in a special college (Bárczy Gusztáv College for Special Education) in four-year courses. Teachers of special subjects in secondary technical and vocational schools are trained in other higher education institutions (technical, agricultural, arts, or other universities), where teaching qualifications can be obtained during or after initial studies. Due to the shortage of foreign language teachers, three-year, one-subject specialist training for language teachers was introduced in the early 1990s. In the school year 1993/1994, teachers in the four main categories of training made up 86 percent of the teaching force, while 14 percent fell into five other teacher categories (of which teachers having been trained in special education teacher training are the most numerous).

School practice is part of all teacher training programs. It is usually carried out in practice schools that have a special status in the public education system. The teaching hours of the schoolteachers that participate in training student teachers are lower than their colleagues' and they have special tasks to help students in preparing for the profession. The efficiency of these practices is often in doubt, though. There is a general impression that young teachers are better prepared in their subjects than in teaching them, especially in training for higher levels of schooling (the second stage of basic schools and secondary schools).

Because of the growing autonomy of teacher training institutions, it is difficult to collect information on recent changes in teacher training. At the institutional level, several innovations related to integration of training for different levels of schooling have been introduced since the end of the 1980s. Integration (or at least cooperation) among institutions is encouraged by the latest legislation. According to policy plans, it is very likely that colleges training teachers for the second stage of basic education will be merged with the pedagogical departments of universities and will become the basis of a new system of teacher training. Structural changes in public education have also influenced changes in teacher training (colleges for the first stage of basic education, for example, began preparing teachers to teach in the fifth and sixth grades, too).

As for changes in the content of training, the number of innovations in the field of pedagogy is rather substantial—especially in introducing child-centered pedagogy (so-called alternative pedagogies), new communication skills, curriculum development, and pupil assessment. There are several innovations in the field of subject teaching as well (introducing new subjects, like home economics, environmental studies, visual arts, and so on). No information about the quality of changes is available, although the accreditation of higher education programs (teacher training included) has begun.

Until recently, enrollment in teacher training was substantially increasing. This was part of a general increase of enrollment in higher education. Between 1987 and 1994 the number of students in higher education increased about 75 percent; the increase of students in teacher training was smaller, about 60 percent. The growth of the enrollment rate in teacher education programs stopped for the first time in 1996, which was the year a stricter employment policy in education was experienced. Relatively high enrollment, however, is likely due to continue as a result of the expansive policies of teacher training institutions and to a great social demand for higher education (limited formerly by stricter central manpower planning) than to the manpower market considerations of participants. Expansion is partly supported by government policies that aim at increasing enrollment at this level. Teacher training—one of the least costly forms of higher education—can easily profit from these ambitions.

It should also be mentioned that two denominational universities (one Catholic and one Protestant) and one denominational college (Catholic) were training teachers for the second stage of basic education. Four denominational colleges (two Catholic and two Protestant) were training teachers for the first stage of basic schools, and an independent higher education institution training teachers for the second stage of basic education also offered initial training for teachers. There is also an independent special institution (Pető Institute for the Education of Disabled Children) that, besides educating disabled children, trains teachers (*conductors*) for this special purpose (conductive education).

The bulk of in-service teacher training is provided in twenty regional (county) pedagogical institutions originally set up at the end of the 1960s. These teacher centers underwent substantial changes in the late 1980s, and they were experimenting with a new type of service function even at that time. Though during recent years (since 1990) they have had to face both political aversion and financial stringency, most of them were able to renew their activities and even expand their services. Universities and other teacher training institutions have also expanded their in-service activities in recent years. Professional associations, private entrepreneurs, and foreign institutions have also appeared with their in-service offerings. The Protestant Church has also founded a pedagogical institute of its own, and the Catholic Church is planning to open one, too.

This expansion is no doubt fueled by the large number of changes taking place in the public education system that makes both the education establishment and individual teachers aware of the need for retraining and continuing training. The introduction of the new National Core Curriculum, local implementation options, and the need for curricular as well as methodological innovations serve as main forces for expansion on both the demand and the supply sides. It is a major policy aim of the government to encourage teachers to participate in continuing education and to establish a system of rewards and career progress incentives based on the in-service activities of teachers.

The 1996 Amendment of the 1993 Act on Public Education introduced compulsory in-service training within ten years of service for new entrants. The aim of this provision is to make special examinations a condition of teachers keeping their jobs. To achieve a higher level of integration, with the help of Austrian, German, and Swiss experts, in 1996 a new in-service center was founded with the function of coordinating the activities of different actors and disseminating information. A new Committee of Accreditation of in-service [INSET] courses has also been set up to ensure quality control in INSET.

According to the initial data of a 1996 survey on the life and working conditions of teachers, about 60 percent of teachers have participated in INSET activities during the past five years (almost half of them more than once). This is almost the same number who had taken courses in INSET before that time and those who intend to participate in INSET courses in the near future. The great majority of these courses were rather short (more than 70 percent were less than 60 hours) and most (about 70 percent) offered training in subject methodology. New types of courses (like psychological-communicative or training in school evaluation) were also attended by about 6 to 7 percent of teachers. Almost 60 percent of courses were provided by pedagogical institutions, and about 20 percent by teacher training higher education institutions. It is interesting to note that private enterprises and foreign institutions have already entered the market with about 2 to 4 percent of the offerings. About 10 percent of teachers paid for INSET themselves, although the majority of courses were financed either by the school and the educational authority, or from mixed resources. When asked how satisfied participants were with the courses, on a scale of 1 to 5, courses received a grade of 4 as a mean.

On the national level, two institutions attached to the Ministry of Culture and Education provide service for the school system. The *National Institute of Public Education* supports curriculum development, carries out school evaluation, and conducts macro-research in education. It is also the task of this institute to publish a report on public education every two years. The *Hungarian Institute of Educational Research* carries out empirical research on public as well as higher education. The *National Institute on Vocational Training,* an institute of the Ministry of Labor, carries out research and provides curriculum development support in vocational training.

Adult Education

In recent years adult education, especially at the secondary level, has become a major device of social correction of the school system. For those who have dropped out of the system, and also for those who have qualified in shorter vocational training (that is, who had not had full secondary education), adult education serves as a kind of "second chance" education. Between 1989 and 1994, 12 to 15 percent of the age group finished secondary schools in adult education (Lannert, 1997). As well, adult education also serves as a "parking place" for young people who otherwise would face unemployment. According to surveys in urban areas, 20 to 50 percent of young people finishing three-year vocational training in formal education continue their studies in adult education, either for a second vocational qualification or for full secondary education.

There are several forms of adult education: complementary two-year secondary schools for adults; three- or four-year secondary vocational

schooling for those with shorter vocational training; two-year vocational classes for adults with only general school education; short courses leading to second vocational qualifications; and two-year vocational training for those with secondary general education. Adult education is provided either in public schools in evening classes, or in special evening schools for adults. It is expected that the role of this kind of supplementary education will increase in the near future. On the one hand, with a growing number of people with full secondary education, it is becoming inevitable for everyone seeking jobs to have secondary level qualifications. On the other hand, the role of adult education in maintaining the most up-to-date qualifications needed by the fast changing economy is becoming more and more crucial.

In contrast to its growing importance, adult education has serious organizational, educational, and financial problems. While the need for special methodological and subject knowledge is urgent, well-equipped schools are rare and there is a shortage of good teachers on this level. It must also be noted that adult education is a rapidly expanding sphere of education that is also fueled by economic interests on the supply side. Because of this, there is a remarkable spread of enterprises offering all kinds of supplementary education for adults.

MAJOR ISSUES AND CONTROVERSIES, FUTURE PERSPECTIVES

The majority of problems stem from outside the educational system itself. First of all, demographic determinants, from both an educational and economic point of view, seem rather unfavorable for the near future. Low birthrates and deteriorating life expectancy do not indicate happy prospects for future development. Slightly improving home economic indicators and improving international perspectives (a vision of a common Europe in which both the luckier and the less lucky nations could live peacefully together), however, might result in better chances and decreasing pessimism for the Hungarian people in the near future.

At present, however, falling student numbers

also mean growing per pupil costs. It is strange that, with fewer students in the school system, the number of schools and teachers has increased in the 1990s. This can be explained by the growing autonomy of schools, the decentralization of the system, and by the democratization of education policy. All this resulted in founding new schools (new private and denominational schools, new schools in small villages with new democratically elected leaders), even if there are fewer children. This expansion is justified on the secondary level, where new clients have appeared (pupils of social background that had previously left school earlier, or had not entered full secondary education), but it is very difficult to accept and finance expansion on the general school level. Due to this expansion, Hungarian teachers today may be characterized as having rather favorable teaching hours and teaching loads in international comparison, but very unfavorable and fast deteriorating pay conditions.

The number of teaching hours per year at the primary level, for example, is about the average of the OECD countries (which was 869 in 1996). While the "most overloaded" teachers (in Switzerland and in the Netherlands) have 1085 and 1000 lessons a year, respectively, Hungarian teachers work 798 lessons (somewhat more than their colleagues in Germany, 760). This is considerably more than how much the least overloaded teachers in Norway or in Sweden (686 and 624 respectively) have to teach (OECD, 1996). Even more favorable is the teacher/pupil ratio in Hungary. On the primary level, the number of pupils per teacher was 11.2 in 1996. This indicator is lower only in Denmark and in Italy (11.2 and 9.9, respectively), while this number varies between 11.8 (in Austria) and 27.6 (in Turkey).

Nevertheless, Hungarian teachers are worse paid than any other teachers in the OECD countries. The salary of a primary school teacher with fifteen years of practice, as compared to per capita GDP of the country, varies between 1.027 in Norway and 1.724 in Switzerland, while this rate is only 0.68 for Hungarian teachers (Szép, 1997). Moreover, teachers' pay conditions have steadily decreased since the early 1990s, parallel with the fall in student numbers. Teachers' pay is considered low not only in international comparison, but also within the Hungarian salary system. It is well known that teacher salaries (as well as those of other people employed in the state sector) are lower than of those employed in the business sector everywhere in the world. The usual rate of difference is about 10 to 15 percent. In 1990, it was the same in Hungary, too, but by 1996, the difference has grown to 41.9 percent, while state expenditure on education had even slightly increased.

While it is obvious that there is overemployment in the school system, especially on the general school level, it is not easy to solve this problem. After forty years of full employment in the central planning system (which, however was accompanied by low economic achievement and low salaries), it is difficult both for the central and local governments to initiate and/or implement the reduction of teachers, and also for teachers to accept the situation. The first democratic government after 1990 even chose to reduce the number of teaching hours to avoid reduction. However, this was not accompanied by a substantial increase in state expenditure, so local governments had to spend most of their educational expenditure on teachers' salaries whether they wanted to do so or not. It caused a lot of tension between central and local governments and could not satisfy teachers either, who experienced a relative decrease in their salary.

Financial crises forced the central government to introduce a restrictive budgetary policy in 1995. The teaching hours were raised and local governments were urged to "rationalize" local budgets. Several local governments introduced early retirement schemes in schools and several teachers were dismissed, too. By 1996, 3.5 percent of teachers were unemployed, and that rate is expected to grow. Unemployment is the highest among kindergarten teachers, teachers in general schools, and among those in vocational training. Though teacher unemployment is much lower than unemployment in the whole population (where it is 10.8 percent), it is somewhat higher than among those with higher education (3.4 percent).

The reduction of jobs also means narrowing possibilities for young teachers to enter the schools, which again, from an educationalist point of view, is an unfavorable development. The role of young teachers in representing new ideas in education, initiating more innovation, having more informal contacts with pupils and making a kind of "bridge" between pupils and the older generations of teachers, is crucial.

Growing social differentiation also has effects on schooling. As mentioned before, this differentiation is even greater among the school population because the rate of poor people is higher and fastest growing among those with children of school age. Lots of teachers now have to experience the impoverishment of many of their pupils, their parents losing their jobs, growing health problems, and so on. However, the social experiences of teachers themselves have become very different. Empirical data show that in most places where a growing differentiation of the school system is experienced, social segregation in schools has been growing (Halász, 1997). Though teachers as state employees have a common salary scale and their teaching conditions are regulated by state laws, they differ very much in their circumstances as regards the social background of their pupils. The latter is much influenced by the economic prospects of each area. In recent years, there is a growing differentiation among different regions of the country as well. In the eastern regions, unemployment is higher and the rate of production is lower than in the capital city or some western parts of the country.

For many teachers, it is difficult to face these new conditions. It is especially so at the secondary level where new groups of pupils with more disadvantaged social backgrounds have appeared in great numbers. Expansion on this level would require new teaching methods as well as new attitudes of teachers. New regulations allow for these differences and even urge schools and teachers to elaborate their own school ethos, their own curricula and their own teaching methods. But this work has only been started. And this leads us to the core educational problems of present day Hungarian

schooling. These problems, which could be summarized under the three main headings of equity, efficiency, and quality, however, are experienced more or less in school systems all around the world today.

It has already been mentioned that the decentralization of school governance can be considered as a device of democratization of policy making in education, but it also means a loss in the integration of the system. Schooling in Hungary in recent years has been basically determined by local decisions of individual schools and local government bodies. It is equally true for decisions made about curricula and teaching methods and decisions about school structure and pupil enrollment. It is guaranteed by law that each pupil of school age should receive some kind of education, but the contest for the best places has not usually been regulated and its rules made clear for local people in general. More affluent and more informed parents could profit from this deregulation, while no schemes of equal chances have been elaborated in most of the cases.

Equity problems have also arisen from the differences of the local governments. No real supplementary system on the central government level has yet been elaborated to eliminate or at least to decrease the basic financial differences of local governments. Several ear-marked budgetary resources have been introduced into the system, but the future schooling prospects of individual pupils are still basically determined by the place and the family individuals are born into. Unfavorable demographic tendencies, however, in this respect, are enhancing their chances, as schools are striving for all kinds of pupils, and try to improve their offer to keep as many pupils as they can and make their schools attractive for new clients as well. Demographic decline makes schools more competitive and this is a basic guarantee for improvement. System-level integration, however, is still wanting.

This leads to several problems of efficiency. It is very frequent that parallel offers within a local system prevail, each attracting a very small number of pupils, while a reasonable integration would make the system work at a lower cost with the same (or even better) results. It would, however, need a more determined and better trained local educational administration. Though their expertise has developed remarkably through experience since the political system change, a systematic training of the administration staff is still missing. (This is less true for head teachers; management training has been developing quickly.)

The low level of system integration leads to quality problems, too. While competition among schools guarantees growing standards, system-level evaluation is still underdeveloped. Monitoring pupils' achievements on a national level in 1995 showed decreases in almost all subjects since 1991 and 1993 respectively. This general decrease, however, covers a growing differentiation of results; that is, much improvement in the achievement of the best and considerably great deterioration among the worst. Empirical studies make it probable that it is because schools try to adopt to local needs, and this means a growing differentiation of school tasks as well. Schools with more disadvantaged social backgrounds have to strengthen the social integration function of education, while elite schools can concentrate more on developing the cognitive skills of their pupils. While it is a natural consequence of growing school autonomy and decentralization, this would require more integration on national as well as regional level. Minimum requirements of the National Core Curriculum, however, are not ensured and controlled by national examinations yet, and it requires some time to make the whole system of a core curriculum, local curricula, and standardized national school evaluation work. Meanwhile, there is a danger that schooling itself helps growing social differentiation instead of playing a corrective role in social processes.

It should be remarked, though, that these problems are conceptualized and much discussed in public. Most stakeholders in Hungarian education today are well aware of the present difficulties, and there is a basic consensus that schooling is (as it has always been) a major device in the development of the nation. If nothing else, this makes future perspectives promising.

REFERENCES

Halász, G. (1996). *Major trends and actors of educational policy and reform in Hungary.* Budapest: National Institute of Public Education. Draft.

Halász, G., & Lannert, J. (Eds.). (1996). *Jelentés a magyar közoktatásról, 1995* (Report on the Hungarian Public Education, 1995). Budapest, 1996.

Halász, G. (Ed.). (1997). *Az oktatás minősége és az önkormányzati oktatásirányítás* (The Quality of Education and the Governance of Schools by Local Authorities). Budapest: Okker Kiadó.

Horváth, T.D. (1992). *Transition of education and the economy in Hungary in the early 1990s.* Paris: OECD.

Lannert, J. (1997). *Public education in Hungary.* Budapest: National Institute of Public Education. Draft.

Nagy, M. (1994). Hungary. In S. Karsten & D. Majoor (Eds.), *Education in East Central Europe* (pp. 29–75). New York: Munster.

Nagy, M. (1997). *Teacher training in Hungary, Poland, the Czech Republic and the Slovak Republic.* Budapest: National Institute of Public Education.

OECD. (1996). *Education at a glance.* Paris: Author.

Statistical yearbook of Hungary, 1995. (1996). (Magyar Statisztikai Evkonyv, 1995). Budapest: KSH.

Sugár, A. (1997). *A közoktatási rendszer szerkezeti változásai* (Structural changes in public education). Budapest: National Institute of Public Education. Draft.

Szép, Z. (1997). *A pedagógusok munkaerőpiaci helyzete és kereseti viszonyai* (Manpower market position of teachers and their payment). Budapest: National Institute of Public Education. Draft.

Vári, P. (Ed.). (1997). *Monitor '95. A tanulók tudásának felmérése* (Monitor '95. Assessing Pupils' Achievements). Budapest: National Institute of Public Education.

CHAPTER 17

Clear Needs, Uncertain Responses: Change in Croatia's Education System

ZLATA GODLER
VLATKA DOMOVIC

Zlata Godler *holds a Diploma, 1959, and a B.A., 1965, from the University of Zagreb, Croatia. Her M.A. is from McGill University, Montreal, Canada, 1973, and her Ph.D. is from the University of Toronto, Canada, 1981. From 1959 to 1974 she was engaged in social work in Croatia, and in Canada and from 1974 to 1979 she was a R and D assistant at the Ontario Institute for Studies in Education, Toronto. Since 1979 she has been professor of pedagogy in the Faculty of Philosophy, University of Zagreb. Her research orientations in comparative education include multicultural/intercultural education, teacher training, educational policy, educational organization and administration, human rights education, and civic education. She serves on the Executive Board of CESE and holds memberships in C.I.E.S; SIETAR Europa, SIETAR International, and I.A.I.E. She is also president of the nongovernmental Croatian citizens' association Interkultura.*

Vlatka Domovic *received her B.A. in Pedagogy in 1986 and her M.A. in Adult Pedagogy in 1991 from the University of Zagreb, Croatia. Since 1991, she has been working as a teaching assistant in Pedagogical Sciences in the Faculty of Philosophy at the University of Zagreb. The projects she has participated in include "Improvement of Educational Activities of Employers," "Education as Factor of the Quality of Life," and "Genealogy and Transfer of Models of Interculturalism." The research project she is presently involved in is "School Curriculum and Characteristics of Croatian National Culture." Vlatka Domovic is a member of Croatian Academy of Educational Sciences, the nongovernment citizens' association Interkultura, SIETAR Europa, and I.A.I.E.*

In many ways, Croatia is typical of all so-called post-communist countries, particularly in the suffering of the political and economic disintegration that took place in the 1990s. It is also unique. Most significantly, it has endured the destruction of a recent war. In both material and human terms, Croatia will take a long time to recover from the ravages of war. The country is also atypical in that it had a much softer version of communism than other iron curtain countries. This should have made the introduction of a market (capitalist) economy and democratic political and social institutions easier.

A change from communism to capitalism is a fundamental and dramatic change for any society to undergo. In order for a whole society to change with a minimum of traumatic effects, it is desirable, in theory, for political, ideological, cultural, economic, and educational changes to be simultaneous and synchronized. However, this is more easily stated than achieved. Even when desired changes are clearly envisioned and are explicitly articulated in the form of goals and objectives, unforeseen and uncontrollable factors can intervene and can become decisive variables. This is very much in evidence in Croatia.

THE SOCIAL FABRIC

History

Situated on the Adriatic coast, Croatia's varied geography has continuously influenced its histor-

271

ical, political, economic, and cultural development. From its beginnings in the seventh century, Croatia encompassed many islands, the mountainous Karst region of the interior, and the fertile Pannonian Plains of the north. However, this natural geographic division had a less natural political manifestation. The land was separated into distinct political units and each was governed, at different times, by different foreign rulers. It was not until 925 A.D. that Croats established their first unified kingdom (at the same time as they embraced Roman Catholicism). However, they lost their independence in 1102 when they entered into a crown union with Hungary (*Pacta conventa*). Although formally united, the northern and the southern Croatian lands were to follow different historical paths, changing hands many times and sharing in the fate of those who ruled them well into the twentieth century.

An overwhelming desire of Croats for many centuries, therefore, has been for the unification of their lands and their people under their own rule and for the development of a unified national culture. It seems that the northern parts had been somewhat luckier in achieving at least a partial cultural autonomy during the late nineteenth century, while the southern parts had to wait until the beginning of the twentieth century for similar concessions. However, this does not necessarily mean that a national culture (particularly as expressed in the literary and visual arts) did not develop. On the contrary. In the sixteenth, seventeenth, and eighteenth centuries the arts and sciences were flourishing, especially in the southern parts where Dubrovnik (Ragusa) is found.

In the nineteenth century several national movements for political and cultural independence were nurtured by the Croatian nobility and intellectuals. Of particular significance was the Illyrian National Movement of the 1830s. A second important movement occurred in the 1870s. The aim of this movement was primarily the revival of elements of Croatian national life and culture; the foci were the national language and the establishment of national cultural institutions. The third important movement occurred in response to the forced Mag-

yarization that was taking place in northern Croatia during the Khuen-Herdervary regime. The Hungarian nobility of that period reasserted itself, imposing upon liberated peasants a system of servitude similar to what had existed under serfdom, which had been abolished. Although they made up close to 75 percent of the population, Croatian peasants had not yet gained the right to vote, and they had no leaders who would take up their cause. However, because they were isolated from the urban population and nobility, they were able to preserve elements of Croatian national culture. A Progressive Youth group led by intellectuals, with the aim of building a link between intellectuals and peasants, emerged.

The transition years between the nineteenth and twentieth centuries were marked by notions of preservation and enhancement of Croatian national culture and life and with notions of entering into political union with other South Slavs. The latter proved to be the future of Croatia. A pistol shot, fired by a young Bosnian Serb revolutionary on June 28, 1914, killed Archduke Ferdinand of Austria and brought internal political rivalries and long-seething international tensions to a climax. The First World War had begun.

After the war, a union of South Slavs was created in the form of the Kingdom of Serbs, Croats, and Slovenes. This union, which was never happy, turned into a nightmare for Croats. Their representative in Parliament, Stjepan Radic, was assassinated at a Parliamentary session in 1928 by a Serb. The king, threatened by political turmoils and other unfavorable circumstances, dissolved Parliament and proclaimed a new Constitution that vested all powers in himself in 1929. From then on, Croats were certain that their ideals for the union would not be realized. In the meantime, the Second World War was on the horizon and a new world order was emerging in which Croatia had its special place.

In 1941 Croatia became an independent state. Albeit, it was a state in name only as its new regime was an extension of Mussolini's and Hitler's expansions and its borders were diminished as, for example, Italy annexed the whole of

Dalmatia and the Istria Peninsula. While for many Croats this is an unpleasant part of their history, for others it represents the time when Croatia was, after a long time, able to have its own national state. Despite the official policies of that state during the 1941–1945 period, the antifascist partisan movement gained impetus in Croatia. Croatian people, in general, greeted and welcomed the liberation of their country and looked to the future with great expectations. Unfortunately, they found themselves once again in an unfavorable union. Five republics (Bosnia-Herzegovina, Macedonia, Montenegro, Serbia, and Slovenia) formed the Federal Republic of Yugoslavia, with a communist regime at its helm.

The Yugoslav leader, Josip Broz Tito, soon quarreled with big brother (the Soviet Union) and Yugoslavia was subsequently expelled from the Cominform. Western powers stepped into the breach with economic help and an economic and political era unique in the communist bloc began. However, in spite of all the measures that were introduced to democratize Yugoslavia and to facilitate its economic progress, the internal struggles between the federal units and the central government continued. In particular, Slovenes and Croats clamored for the right to control their own regions and to have a greater influence in federal government policies. While President Tito was alive, problems had been kept somewhat under control. After his death, differences could no longer be patched up. The dissolution of Yugoslavia was inevitable.

Unfortunately, unlike the processes that took place in some other post-communist countries, the dissolution of Yugoslavia turned into a blood bath. Nevertheless, the tragedy rallied Croatian people from all walks of life; first in their anguish and anger, later in their rightful demands for justice and for full acceptance of Croatia as an independent and free state and nation. This spirit, despite Croatians' awareness of irregularities in their country's political and economic affairs, their disenchantment with social policies, and their drastically diminished standard of living, still persists. The sentiments of the populist, collectivistic,

ideals expressed in the form of Croatian nationalism are especially to be found among refugees from those parts of the country that were occupied by Serb insurgents during the war, or still remain occupied. They are also embraced by the less educated rural population, which today constitutes about one quarter of the total population, as well as by staunch leading party supporters.

From Communism to Capitalism

In the case of Croatia, designs for massive social changes, specifically in the realms of economic reform and political and ideological transformation, were drawn up and implementation has started. The country has a blueprint for making the transition from communism to capitalism, and progress is being made.

A major component of the reforms is economic, focusing on state or public ownership being gradually replaced by private ownership. This economic aspect of the transition seems to be somewhat less painful in Croatia than in some other former Soviet-bloc countries. In the former Socialist Federal Republic of Yugoslavia, Croatia was (along with Slovenia) economically the most developed and advanced region. Furthermore, a particular, unique brand of communism in Yugoslavia allowed several types of private ownership as well as the self-management of workers. The population in general was at least aware of a market economy; indeed, a large number of people in fact embraced the system of capitalist values. This was partly due to the fact that many people from Croatia had lived and worked in western European countries for a number of years as guest-workers and as immigrants in overseas countries. Croatians abroad were thus exposed to different democratic institutions within multiparty systems and developed a taste for different ideological and cultural orientations that they shared on visits or through correspondence with those who had remained in Croatia.

Furthermore, the introduction of changes at the structural level of politics was rather painless. The single-party system was quickly replaced by a multiparty system. By all appearances, the political transformation of the nation was being smoothly and rapidly effected. However, a multiparty framework did not successfully translate into a genuine sharing of political power or the enfranchisement of all groups. The overwhelming victory of a single large party (the Croatian Democratic Union) over several smaller ones soon evolved into a situation that resembled politics under the old single-party system. The most recent elections (held in April 1997) further underscored this point. As formerly under the communist regime, the social structure is bipolar. The majority of the population is economically and politically marginalized, while the minority is privileged, either through its economic, party-political, or state-bureaucratic positions. The middle class is undeveloped; however, there are emerging *nouveau riche*.

The interests of various social groups, therefore, are not really adequately represented in the corridors of political power. Indeed, political debate does not revolve around the needs and aspirations of diverse social groups. Almost equally, all political parties appeal to the electorate on the basis of general cultural values rather than individual or group interests. Thus, a collectivist and populist orientation is more prevalent then a democratic liberal one. This is partly due to the influence of the recent past, where the collectivism embodied in the values of the communist party, the state, and the working class was the dominant orthodoxy. Today, this preference for collectivism is no longer expressed in communist values but takes the form of national and religious ideologies that put aside, at least for the time being, the individual and group interests that form the basis of politics in liberal democracies.

Another source of the populist collectivistic orientation is to be found in the response to aggression. Croatians have united in a common front in the face of external threats confronting their nation. As long as external threats remain a reality, they will serve as a unifying agent for all segments of the population. The political consequence is that internal differences of opinion and debates between diverse elements of the population will remain secondary considerations in the national political arena.

Furthermore, the history of Croatia, as a land, nation, society, and culture, has a great bearing on the present situation. Croatia is not by any means just a newly carved out geographic and political entity. For many people, the contemporary Croatian state represents a resurrected national and cultural reality that has been denied its people for many centuries.

Nevertheless, transition Croatia has undertaken in its evolution from communism to capitalism, and liberal democracy is not as painless and smooth as theory may suggest. First of all, the representatives of the present political order, those in the ruling party as well as those in the opposition, either grew out of the ranks of the communists formerly in power or consolidated themselves from the ranks of the former political dissidents, many of whom had been imprisoned under the previous regime. In either case, many of them are now high officials, belonging to the party that has won election. As this party has political supremacy, the total social system, including education, resembles more the old uniparty system than a genuinely democratic order. This has great consequences for the transformation of schooling. In a highly centralized system it is very difficult to even expect, let alone realize, the democratic changes that are necessary for the educational system to start functioning as a promulgator of democratic ideas and practices.

Shaping the Future

Croatia has the will to become a democratic society. This is prominently evidenced in the economic transformations that are modernizing the country. Croatia has embraced the idea of Europeanization; its vision of the future includes full acceptance into the European Community and membership in major world organizations. A commitment to democracy is also demonstrated in the legal rights that have been afforded minorities and ethnic groups and communities. Today Croatia, covering an area of 56,538 square kilometers and having a population of 4,800,000, represents a truly multicultural society. Her inhabitants, according to the last census taken in 1991, are 77.9 percent Croat, 12.2 percent Serb, 1 percent Muslim, and 9.8 percent other minorities (Hungarians, Slovenes, Italians, Roma, and so on). This fact is very important, particularly in the context of furthering the process of democratization. The multicultural reality of Croatia will have to be reflected in overall national policy development and will have to be carefully considered in the formulation of national educational policies.

Historical Background

Various church orders were responsible for the establishment of the first schools in Croatia. These schools were essentially appendices to their churches and monasteries. The first secular school was opened in 1480 in northern Croatia (*Vara`dinske toplice*). The first School Law was passed in 1874; it legislated four years of free and compulsory education for all children. From that time until the dissolution of the Hapsburg monarchy in 1918, the nature of the school system in Croatia was dictated by the monarchy.

From 1918 until the Second World War, the educational system in Croatia more or less followed the legal arrangements, first, of the Kingdom of Serbs, Croats, and Slovenes, and then of the Kingdom of Yugoslavia. However, even though the ideal of compulsory education by then had been legally enshrined for half a century, in practice it did not reach all children. For example, between the two world wars elementary education served only about 55 percent of the population. The result was that a significant number of people were illiterate. After the Second World War, the school network, particularly of elementary schools, was expanded and the duration of elementary schooling was extended to seven years. It was further extended to eight years in 1953, where it remains today.

One of the more significant recent changes is the secondary school reform that occurred in the Socialist Federal Republic of Yugoslavia in the 1970s. This divided secondary education into two parts. The first two years of secondary education were assigned a general common curriculum; the subsequent years became streams into various professional programs. The two most noted problems in that period were the large number of dropouts during the first two years and the unemployability of graduates who had elected to enter the academic streams. One such academic stream was for so-called teacher's assistants. However, graduates were, in reality, not adequately professionally prepared; they would have to continue their education at higher levels to have hope of finding jobs in schools. On the positive side, it must be said that a democratization of education was taking place. This was especially the case during the period of 1960 to 1970—a time of major reforms to universities. The changes enabled many more people to further their education either in university programs or in two-year higher schools that provided additional professional education in various branches.

For a brief period of time after the dissolution of the Socialist Federal Republic of Yugoslavia in 1990, Croatia's educational system retained intact the institutions it inherited from the previous regime. However, a succession of new Laws was soon passed (for example, Law on Elementary School, Law on Secondary School, Law on Social Care for Preschool Children, Higher Education Act, and Law on Scientific Research Activities). The organization of school management was also changed. At the present time, the educational system encompasses elementary, secondary, and higher education, as well as parts of adult education and preschool education.

Preschool Education

Even though preschool education is not compulsory, it is fully under the control of the Ministry of Education and Sports. All preschool organizations, whether public or private, must comply with the pedagogical standards and program orientations set up by the Ministry. Preschool education consists of various types of full- and part-time child-care programs, including nurseries and kindergartens. Also included are a variety of additional special programs in music, sports, language learning, and so on. Preschool organizations can be founded by district authorities, work organizations, private institutions (mainly religious and humanitarian), professional associations (such as Montessori and Waldorf), or private citizens with adequate qualifications and premises.

The updated Law on Social Care for Preschool Children stipulates that preschool organizations may start providing child-care for children at the age of six months. Children can stay in nursery programs until they reach the age of 3. After that, children are divided into educational groups by age so that they attend kindergarten programs in groups of 3- to 4-, 4- to 5-, and 5- to 6-year-old children. Upon reaching the age of 6, they enter elementary schools. However, not all children attend nursery and kindergarten programs. Those who have not attended kindergarten must stay for one year in a pre-elementary school program popularly known as Little School.

Financing of preschool programs is somewhat complicated because there is a division between publicly and privately funded programs. Privately owned organizations are funded directly by parents, sometimes with accompanying fund-raising drives. Publicly owned organizations' so-called "basic activities" are covered by district budgets and by direct financial contributions from parents, which are calculated on the basis of family income. Additional funding, such as for the accommodation of ethnic language programs and programs for children with special needs, is provided by the federal government. All educational programs and activities beyond the basic ones (foreign languages, sports, drama, music, and so on) are paid for by parents directly. The one elective program for which parents do not pay is religion. Based in Roman Catholicism, and technically an elective, it is in fact aimed at all children regardless of whether their parents profess the Roman Catholic faith or not.

It is a well-known fact that private preschool organizations, even though they are required to comply with Ministry directives, enjoy greater autonomy than their public counterparts. For example, staffing can include not only qualified preschool teachers, but also additional experts in the arts, sports, languages, and so on. The exception is in the care and education of children with special needs. Whether in segregated or integrated settings, preschool organizations must ensure an adequately qualified staff of special education professionals, psychologists, and preschool pedagogues.

Elementary Education

Elementary education is provided through public schools and by a few newly established private elementary schools. Educating children from the age of 6 or 7 until the age 15, the elementary system is compulsory, uniform, and free of charge. Whether public or private, schools are uniform in their aims, objectives, programs, textbooks, organizational structure, pedagogical standards, and staff qualification requirements. Varying in size and enrollment, there are 752 elementary schools in Croatia.

Elementary school is divided into two parts: primary school includes grades 1 to 4 and upper primary grades 5 to 8. Larger schools located in cities and towns may include grades 1 to 8, while rural schools typically consist of only grades 1 to 4. After the completion of grade 4 in such smaller units, students continue in grades 5 to 8 at the nearest large school. In most cases, busing service is provided. Schools with all grades (1–8) are supposed to work in shifts; that is, children attend school for half a day, mornings or afternoons, alternating shifts every week. For children in grades 1 and 2 in both towns and cities, after-school care is provided. Children usually attend morning classes and remain in aftercare during the afternoons until their parents return from work and collect them.

Grades 1 to 4 are taught by primary school teachers. In principle, primary school teachers teach a cohort of students through all four grades. However, students can have access to specialist teachers. For example, learning a foreign language becomes mandatory in grade 4 (and there are some programs in early foreign language acquisition that start in grade 1). There are also specialized extracurricular activities in some schools. If the class teacher does not have enough expertise in such areas, specialists may be hired. Grades 5 to 8 are taught by individual subject teachers, but each class has its own classmaster or mistress serving as a sort of teacher coordinator. In addition to teachers, elementary schools have on staff a headmaster (principal) who directs and manages school affairs; support personnel such as psychologists, special education teachers, pedagogues (personnel specifically trained in teaching skills and in solving students' problems); and, in some schools, school librarians.

Elementary schooling is coeducational and begins with the student entering grade 1 at the age of 6 (if the child is 6 years old by the April 1 of the current year). As already noted above, elementary schooling is compulsory and the grade 1–4 program is almost fully uniform and prescribed. A significant exception is that all students may choose an additional subject to study. It is noteworthy that, at the present time, that subject is usually instruction in the Roman Catholic religion. However, and importantly, once selected, the subject ceases to be an elective for the student—it becomes a compulsory part of his or her program of studies.

With the exception of children with learning disabilities or with special needs, children may remain in elementary school until the age of 16. Those who turn 16 without obtaining a graduation certificate may complete their elementary education in adult education institutions.

Very recent changes to the structure and curricula of elementary schooling have been minimal. Some worth mentioning include a reduction in the hours of instruction allocated to the teaching of music and the visual arts in grades 5 and 6. Today, only one hour of instruction per week is offered in each subject. History, and language and literature, are two other subjects that have been affected. Both have undergone revisions expanding the amount of content dealing specifically with Croa-

tia. Finally, for the first time alternative textbooks are permitted, but only on an experimental basis.

Secondary Education

The biggest recent changes to schooling in Croatia, particularly in terms of structural reforms, were aimed at secondary education and have occurred in the last five years. The reforms have two major characteristics. First, they are marked by an increased diversity in schooling options at the secondary level. Second, the reforms are not an innovation based on future-oriented changes. Rather, the reforms are rooted in tradition in that they are a reinstitutionalization of the secondary school system as it existed in the 1960s. The reformation of secondary schooling started in 1990, and the most obvious manifestation is the division of secondary schooling into three parallel streams: academic high schools, art schools, and trade schools.

Academic high schools lead to further education on all levels—most significantly, entry into university and college programs. Four years of study culminate with students writing the *matura*. These are graduation examinations in four subjects: mother tongue, a foreign language, and two subjects of choice.

Art schools allow students to pursue specific programs of study and training in ballet, music, design, and the visual arts. These programs are also four years in duration. Students attending art schools enter their programs with prior formal training received instruction through educational programs available in the elementary schools they attended (in addition, of course, to completing the regular elementary school curriculum).

Trade school programs are the most complex of the three types of high schools. First, there are two types of trade schools: A schools offering four years of courses in technical training (including medicine and economics) and B schools specializing in industrial-vocational training that lasts three years. Within the four-year technical schools there are three separate streams, leading to different types of professional competencies. The A-1 stream is for technicians wishing to develop general knowledge of a specific technical field. Graduates may continue on to higher levels of education at colleges and faculties, or they may directly enter into employment. The A-2 stream is aimed at producing graduates who are technicians with specific competencies and deeper technical knowledge in a particular field. However, graduates normally enter the workforce because this stream offers fewer possibilities for continuation into higher education. The A-3 stream focuses on the development of even more specific technical knowledge and competencies directly relevant for the world of work, and graduates will not continue into higher formal education.

To earn a graduation diploma, students in all three streams are obliged to pass a written three-part graduation examination. This consists of an essay providing a technological solution for a particular problem, a written examination in Croatian language and literature, and an examination in one subject relevant for the student's particular profession. These written examinations are followed by oral ones in each of these areas. It is also interesting to note that students in the medical services, administration, food services, and tourism programs alternate school attendance and practical work each week; 50 percent of their program consists of gaining practical experience in the workplace.

The B schools are three-year vocational/industrial trade schools providing a combination of general courses, professional studies, and electives. The newest feature of these schools is the requirement for students, as part of their program of study, to enter into a contract with a master tradesman who is obliged to provide practical work experience for his or her students. After the completion of their training, students must pass final examinations in the theoretical knowledge relevant for their chosen trade, as well as being able to demonstrate their mastery of the practical skills that trade requires. Graduates can then work for a year and later enter into the fourth year of a program in a technical school to become technicians, or they can enter into a master tradesman pro-

gram and eventually become master tradesmen themselves. Within the B schools there are some additional provisions made for the training of semiskilled personnel. These are one- or two-year programs targeted at adults without skills and students who have failed in their regular programs in vocational/industrial schools.

Higher Education

There have not been any significant changes implemented in the area of higher education in recent years. Studies continue to be organized by teaching subjects, and examinations must be passed in order to be promoted to the next year of study. On the whole, programs are structured in such a way that there are very limited possibilities for elective subjects within any particular faculty, and even fewer for interfaculty or interdisciplinary study. There are four large university centers located in Zagreb, Split (Zadar), Rijeka, and Osijek. In addition, there are satellite units of these respective universities delivering elements of their programs. The university system provides studies at specific faculties, academies, and schools of higher education leading to bachelors, masters, and doctoral degrees, as well as a variety of diplomas and specialization certificates.

In principle, entry into higher education institutions is restricted by three factors. First there are quotas; second, students face rather severe entrance examinations; third, low cumulative and individual subject marks from secondary school eliminate some students. Despite this, it is estimated that within the last eight years the number of students in Croatia has increased by about 20 percent (Kalogjera-Brkic, 1997a).

Teacher Education

Preschool teachers are graduates of two-year postsecondary preschool teacher training programs. These are usually attached to Pedagogical Faculties or to the Pedagogical Sciences Divisions of Faculties of Philosophy (as is the case at the University of Zagreb). These programs also provide upgrading for preschool teachers who have only completed four years of secondary training but have found employment as teachers. These teachers must take an additional two years of course work on a part-time basis.

Primary school teachers, those teaching children in grades 1 to 4, are also trained in Pedagogical Faculties or in Pedagogical Sciences Divisions of Faculties of Philosophy. However, their training requires four years of study. This is a rather new feature; until recently primary school teachers, like preschool teachers, required only two years of study. One result of the new four-year training requirement for primary school teachers is that admissions standards have improved; two-year programs have lower requirements than four-year ones. At the time of writing, the first of the new teachers with four years of training are graduating. As in the past, the majority of preschool and primary school teachers are female.

Today, elementary and secondary teachers are trained in the same programs at respective faculties belonging to the four universities. Upper primary and secondary teachers are subject specialists and, in most cases, their studies are the combination of two subjects (however, there are also the single subject studies). The majority of students attend Faculties of Philosophy and Faculties of Natural Sciences, although in Osijek and Rijeka they study at Pedagogical Faculties. There are also subject teacher training programs at the Academy of Arts and at the Academy of Music. These four-year programs give students, upon graduation, the title of professor and qualify them to apply for subject teaching jobs. However, in their first year of teaching their work must be monitored by appointed mentors, and at the end of that period they must pass special qualification examinations.

It must be stressed that at all levels of teacher training, pedagogical training is not consecutive but concurrent. All future teachers take theoretical pedagogical subjects and practical courses in teaching methods in parallel. Those who will be subject specialists (upper primary and secondary teachers) also concurrently take courses in their subject major.

There are, however, a number of teachers in Croatia's schools, particularly in technical and vocational secondary schools, who do not have pedagogical training. This is because they were hired for their particular professional expertise in an area where there exists a shortage of trained teachers. These individuals are expected to complete pedagogical training quickly, usually within one year of being hired. To that end they attend specially devised courses in psychology, pedagogy, didactics, and, wherever possible and available, courses in teaching methods for their subject specialization. This type of additional pedagogical training is expected to go on for an extended period of time because there will always be a need for skilled professionals, whose training does not involve pedagogical training, to teach.

Adult Education

Adult education assumes many and varied forms. Both in-service teacher training and part-time studies undertaken by preschool teachers who have taken their training in secondary school can be considered part of adult education. Job-oriented skill-upgrading courses of a technical or economic variety organized by firms and other work organizations are also included under adult education. Furthermore, all types of formal education at both the elementary and secondary and secondary levels that are targeted at adults are also part of adult education, as is education for upgrading or retraining. In addition, a wide variety of private schools also offer adult education in various forms. This includes a great diversity of subjects and content such as language learning, sports, aerobics, yoga, ballet, dance, computer use, marketing consultancy, and art appreciation.

A special and newly instituted form of adult education is provided by a division of the Open University called the "Third Age University." This was started in Zagreb in 1992 for retired citizens.

Average enrollment is about 150 students in a variety of programs such as health seminars, foreign languages, art seminars, and field-based activities such as exhibitions and outings.

Organization, Management, and Financing

A major difference exists in these areas between public and private education. The private sector of education has some room for flexibility despite its obligations to comply with the regulations of one or more ministries. The public sector, on the other hand, follows rather rigid organizational rules that are clearly delineated and are enforced. A hierarchical order is firmly established and administration is highly centralized. In matters affecting elementary and secondary schools, the Ministry of Education and Sports is the center of power. The Ministry has close contacts with district educational administrations and with school directors, whom it in fact appoints. There is also an Office of the Inspectorate, which is charged with ensuring compliance of regulations at the district levels. In the case of higher education, final decisions ultimately lie with the Ministry of Sciences.

The financing of education varies with the level of schooling. Preschool education is paid for through a sharing system that involves parents, district authorities, and the government. The actual financing depends on many variables, such as the costs of financing special programs that may be required for ethnic groups, minorities, and children with special needs. Elementary schooling is compulsory and is provided free of charge. Also provided free of charge are textbooks. These are given to the child for use over the school year and then the student is obliged to return them to the school. Secondary education, although not compulsory, is also free and financed by the Ministry of Education. However, textbooks must be purchased. Higher education is financed by the Ministry of Sciences and by fee-paying students. Although the government supports some programs (for example, the training and retraining of war veterans and invalids), adult education is primarily financed through a great variety of private sources.

Although there are private preschool institutions, elementary and secondary schools, and adult education organizations, private institutions of higher education do not exist yet. Indeed, the exception to this rule, the previously private Theological Faculty, is now part of the regular university establishment and is today governed, managed, and financed along the same lines as all the other institutions of higher learning.

SOCIAL AND EDUCATIONAL ISSUES

One of the most interesting features of the Croatian educational system is the virtually complete lack of involvement of parents in the school environment, both in educational policymaking and in the actual running of schools. The internal organization of the school system is rather rigid, not allowing for the empowerment of either teachers or parents, or indeed of other interested citizens, and changes are difficult to implement from outside the bureaucracy. The governing of schools, the programming of courses, and the control of outcomes are all in the hands of appointed government officials.

However, many and diverse community organizations are deeply involved in education. These groups are not under the authority of the Ministry of Education and Sports; they mostly fall under the auspices of the Ministry of Culture. Many of these community organizations are vestiges of institutions and organizations that flourished under the communist regime and have been reorganized to suit the new social and political realities of Croatia. Among them are various cultural centers, sport organizations, libraries, children's and youth choirs, and technical associations. These groups offer a variety of good-quality nonformal educational programs and services to children, youth, and adults. For example, very popular among parents whose children do not attend kindergarten are play groups offered by libraries that provide young children with educationally enriching activities and the opportunity to interact with other young children.

In terms of internal organization, teaching

(except for the primary level) is divided into distinct subjects and clearly delineated school levels. The result is a division of teachers into distinct communities of interest based on the subjects they teach their level of school level. Significant cooperation within a broader community of teachers is therefore reduced, team teaching (except in some integrated programs for children with special needs) is rare, alternative teaching methods are more difficult to explore, and the prevailing pedagogical strategies continue to be lecture-styled and teacher-centered.

Teachers are also a disgruntled professional group. One major cause of this discontent is very low salaries; many teachers have to moonlight simply in order to survive. Many leave teaching as soon as the opportunity presents itself, dissatisfied both with their salaries and large workloads. For example, in secondary schools teachers teach 18 to 20 hours per week and still deal with their other duties. Remedies are difficult to effect because teachers are members of different unions, divided by school levels and by specializations within these levels. Furthermore, teachers' unions are mostly interested in the salaries and the social security and standards of living of their members. Issues of professional development and of individual professional advancement are not receiving priority.

As far as general research into educational matters is concerned, apart from some studies commissioned by the Ministry of Education and Sports for special purposes, educational research is compartmentalized, carried out in isolation, and narrowly focused on particular and specific issues. Interdisciplinary research is uncommon as researchers work in isolation, not in expert teams. Research projects in education must usually be approved by the Ministry of Science. Approval depends upon the reputation and expertise of the individual researcher who will carry out the task and the significance of the research project as judged in the context of national development or the development of the sciences.

A major external influence is the acceptance of Croatia into the European and international communities. This has raised new and significant social and educational issues. Of particular and immediate importance here is the need for Croatia to apply the concepts, laws, and regulations of organizations such as The Council of Europe and UNESCO in areas such as human rights, children's rights, and protection of the environment. This, combined with the new influence and presence of external nongovernmental agencies and organizations (for example, SOROS—Open Society—and Amnesty International), has resulted in new orientations in areas such as civic education, education for human rights, education for tolerance and peace, and conflict resolution. These have yet to be incorporated into educational research, policies, and practices.

A more immediate problem is how to comply with recent changes in the Law on Social Care for Preschool children. Revisions lowered the age of entry into preschool from one year to six months. Such young children require additional space, as well as additional care for their nutrition and hygienic needs. This, in turn, requires more personnel and resources. However, additional resources to handle the increased number of children are not materializing. According to the complaints of parents whose children attend public preschool educational institutions, the major problems are lack of space, lack of proper facilities, and, above all, lack of staff. This results in rather large groups of children in the care of just one person with almost no opportunities for individualization and program differentiation. These problems are acutely felt by parents who must send their children to public preschool educational institutions because they cannot afford private care.

On the other hand, private preschool organizations, unlike public ones, must strictly comply with regulations governing the number of children in each group, the adequacy of the premises, and staffing. This leads to certain elitism and inequality in child care. Those who can afford the more expensive private nursery and kindergarten facilities for their children are securing much better services for their children than those who are forced by economic circumstances to rely upon public preschool educational institutions.

Interestingly, revisions to the Law on Social Care for Preschool children were not brought about as a result of requests from parents. Rather, they are connected to new restrictions on working mothers' rights to maternity leave. Until recently, a working mother could stay, on full pay, with her child until the child's first birthday. Now she is entitled to full pay only for the first six months of her leave, which gives her two options. She can return to work when her child becomes six months old, making either private arrangements for the child's care or putting the child into the care of an early nursery program. Or she can stay home with her child until he or she is one year old, but with drastically reduced financial support. At the present moment, the reduced financial support amounts to the equivalent of only about 400 German marks per month. However, all mothers are equally entitled to this reduced support; even some mothers who have never been employed. In the case of mothers who are not employed, support will be provided only for the third and subsequent children. The intention of the law is to provide an incentive for families to produce more children. This is all part of the drive for demographic revitalization of the Croatian nation, whose present rate of reproductivity is only 0.8.

Turning to elementary education, perhaps the major issue is the organization of school work into shifts. This is particularly inadequate for children in the primary grades (1–4), because only a limited number of them are in before- and afterschool care programs. Such programs are provided only for children in the first two grades. Children in grades 1 and 2 who are not in these programs, and their older colleagues, are known as children with "keys hung about their necks" while their parents are at work, they must care for themselves alone. For the time being there is not a Child Protection Law that would remedy this situation.

In secondary education, the reemergence of the general academic program has resulted in a serious problem for some graduates. While most secondary school graduates of four- or three-year programs can directly enter into employment upon graduation, those who have completed a general academic program have not learned any professional skills during their studies. The only thing they are qualified for is further study, but some may not be able to continue. Major reasons include financial limitations, limits on the number of student places in particular programs of studies (*numerus clausus*), and low marks in high school. These individuals become virtually unemployable except in the lowest level jobs.

However, there are also difficulties in technical/vocational programs. There is a great shortage of some types of textbooks for use in technical schools, particularly in vocational/industrial schools. The number of students who would use any particular text is very limited, and there is a large variety of specific courses. The publishing costs of producing a great variety of specific technical texts for small audiences are rather prohibitive. Moreover, there is little interest on the part of potential textbook authors to write such textbooks, as limited demand means little financial reimbursement for authors.

At the post-secondary level, pedagogy is one of the main problems. For the most part, teaching at higher educational institutions is lecture based, focuses on the cognitive, and rewards the mechanical acquisition of knowledge. The structure of higher education is hierarchical, and teacher–student distance is great. The latter is often the result of very large groups of students attending lectures and an undeveloped system of tutorials, discussion groups, seminars, and workshops.

Completion times and rates constitute another problem. The majority of students at all faculties take longer than expected to complete their studies. There is also a high percentage of dropouts, especially in the first and the second years of study. It is estimated that only about 30 percent of enrolled students complete their studies.

Another concern is the significant disproportion between the number of students entering natural sciences and technology and those entering the social sciences, humanities, law, and economics. It must be pointed out that students who enter faculties such as medicine, law, economics, social work, and so on, are not required to take those studies at graduate levels, that is, following pre-requisite undergraduate courses. Rather, they enter these faculties directly after completion of secondary education.

The difficulties of those who are successful in entering the higher educational system and going on to complete their studies do not end upon graduation. Many graduates cannot find employment in the specific fields they are trained in. In result they are forced to take up other jobs or, as is often the case with very successful students, to leave the country to seek work abroad.

Some of the above problems may be addressed in new proposals, which are now under discussion, for the reform of tertiary education. One element being considered is a further diversification of post-secondary education. New and different institutions of higher education, not intended to become a part of the current university system, are being considered. In particular, the creation of institutions that would provide only specialized courses leading to specialist diplomas and higher degrees is being considered. Unlike traditional universities, these new institutions would not offer programs of study leading to higher degrees such as the M.A and Ph.D. The proposed reforms of higher education will also affect teacher training. Teacher training programs are likely to be taken out of the present system and put into a new system consisting solely of teacher training institutions.

Worth noting here is an issue related to the training of preschool teachers. Until just recently, that training was considered to be too short and serious consideration was given to extending it from two years to three. At this point, however, it is unlikely such an extension will be mandated, and this brings about another problem. After the completion of their training, preschool teachers do not have access to continuing higher-level studies. The only thing they can do is start a new area of study from the beginning. There is no provision made for academic advancement within their particular field (except in cases of promotion to the position of mentor to students in training at their place of work). The same problems of academic advancement face primary school teachers. As a

new and different division of elementary school is being proposed (in which the primary level would last three years instead of four, and the upper primary an additional three years), there is a question as to whether current primary school teachers will be considered qualified to teach in the new division. Will they be allowed to teach only in the first three years of the proposed primary level, or will they be allowed also to teach at the upper level? If the latter is proposed, it is certain these teachers would be required to take additional training as, at the upper level, some subject teaching will be taking place. In the present proposals, none of these questions are being openly answered.

In addition, it must be pointed out that there is a continuing shortage of teachers in some subject areas at both the upper elementary and secondary levels. There always was a shortage of teachers of mathematics and physics. but lately schools are also experiencing a shortage of trained language teachers. It has recently been reported that there is a shortfall of 3500 teachers of various subjects (Kalogjera-Brkic, 1997b).

Many of the concerns associated with the shortage of subject teachers can be traced back to problems in the way teachers are selected and trained. For one thing, many university students who end up in teacher training programs are not really interested at all in studying education and becoming teachers are in teacher education programs by default. That is, the spaces available in the so-called scientific university programs are very limited. Students who are not able to secure one of those spaces are automatically assigned to the teacher education programs. Understandably, upon graduation those whose inclinations lay elsewhere find employment outside of the schools.

Furthermore, some subject teachers consider themselves poorly trained for teaching. In teacher education programs, students have very limited experience in practice teaching and therefore are ill-prepared for the realities of teaching in schools. In addition, there is inadequate opportunity for students to integrate practice teaching with their introductory courses in psychology, pedagogy, and didactics because of the scheduling of these courses in the program of studies. There is also the problem of relevant pedagogical content not being covered simply because the total hours reserved for the material are very limited. Some faculties consider them only an additional and unnecessary burden for students and have taken measures to reduce them to a critically low minimum number of hours per week. For example, at the Faculty of Philosophy at the University of Zagreb, teaching hours in the pedagogical subjects have been so drastically reduced so that they are now taught only two hours per week during only one semester.

As for adult education, at the moment it is at its lowest ebb. Work organizations either have insufficient money to provide training for their workers, or cannot see their business future clearly and therefore cannot plan with confidence. Public institutions such as Open Universities, which previously have been rather popular both in their general appeal to the adult population and their very low cost, have been in decline for the past five years. The dilemma for public adult education institutions is that they are caught in the harsh realities of a market economy. In order to survive, they will have to charge high fees. This they cannot do because the population is, in general, impoverished. On the other hand, private educational organizations that offer courses to adults are oriented towards profit making and attract a limited clientele that can afford high fees. They have therefore become elitist both in clientele and in selection of programs.

CROATIA'S EDUCATIONAL FUTURE

The above brief outline of major issues, problems, and controversies was offered to provide some insights into the nature of schooling in contemporary Croatia. If time and space permitted a more detailed scrutiny of the educational system, a severe lack of clarity in Croatian educational planning would be revealed. One consequence is that making predictions about what the future of education and the system of schooling is going to be is very difficult. At this point what seems certain is that the future of education will continue to depend primarily on political and economic developments. Whether the educational system is going to become less centralized, thereby leaving more room for innovation, freedom, and participation in decision making, depends on the process of democratization.

If Croatia becomes a full-fledged member of bigger and stronger European institutions, this will influence the organization, content, and ideological orientation of public schooling in the direction of democracy. The introduction of civic education, education for human rights, and intercultural education would be some immediate curricular manifestations; pedagogical innovations would complement these curricular innovations. At the same time, if Croatia is considering becoming fully market-oriented, it must also seriously contemplate its technological development. For such a purpose, a whole new system of education, one with clearly stated aims and objectives for the training of a new type of professional, would have to be introduced. This would be a mammoth task.

In light of the above, about the only thing that can be stated with confidence at this time is that that the future development of education in Croatia is totally clouded in uncertainty.

REFERENCES

Kalogjera-Brkic, J. (1997a, April 25). Brucose ceka 25,500 mjesta. (For freshmen there are 25,500 places). *Vecernji list,* Zagreb, p. 3.

Kalogjera-Brkic, J. (1997b, March 23). Nedostaje 3,500 naaastavnika, a 10,000 ih ceka mirovinu. (3,500 teachers are lacking, and 10,000 are ready for retirement). *Vecernji list.* Zagreb, p.5.

PART IV

The Middle East and Africa: Progress in the Face of Unresolved Struggles

At least some of the nations included in this section will seem familiar to you. Most of these countries are prominent in the media; the events taking place within their borders have ongoing repercussions in international relations and diplomacy.

We predict, however, that you will be surprised when you compare the ideas you developed from media accounts with your reading of these chapters. This is because, to borrow a phrase from the Palestine chapter, these are "reflections from the inside." Contributors will draw you inside the social realities of each nation to let you experience those realities articulated in their own cultural voices and from their perspectives. Once you have this "inside reflection," things will look different; your perceptions will have been challenged.

In our reflections on this section, we are struck by how all five societies are constantly in a state of becoming; a state of transition and evolution toward sometimes remarkably clear, other times somewhat opaque, but always unwavering goals. That evolution is both a very long and extremely traumatic historical process. Tension, conflict, unresolved antagonisms from the past—these are very serious problems that all five societies continue to address and seek frustratingly elusive solutions for. These are nations in turmoil and, always, political imperatives overshadow all else.

We begin with Israel and Palestine, the two chapters forming an instructive juxtaposition. Both entities continue to be shaped in the cauldron of Arab-Israeli conflict. That conflict has had a profound impact on virtually all aspects of Palestinian and Israeli daily life. The depth and significance of that conflict, and the unresolved degree of mutual antagonisms, cannot be overstated. As you read these two chapters, you will gain a deeper appreciation of the differences that have divided these two peoples for so long—and continue to do so with profound international ramifications. You will find both sides of the story told.

Yet, divided as Israel and Palestine are, there are remarkably similar issues and problems that both societies are independently facing and struggling with. For example, both Palestine and Israel seek to bring their dispersed people home into one geographic area and under one cultural and national identity. Even though Israel has had a homeland since

1948, the process of the "return to Israel" is ongoing. For Palestinians that process is a profoundly frustrating one, as the primary goal of a fixed, final, and independent homeland has not been realized.

Who are these peoples? Clearly, neither Palestine nor Israel are internally homogenous entities. Both are politically, religiously, and ethnically diverse societies. Tensions between religious factions and between religious and secular elements are facts of life, ones that necessarily spill over into the political arena because there is not a clear separation between religion and the state. This lack of separation means that education, culture, religion, and politics become fused, and the objectives, contents, and delivery modes of schooling are directly molded and shaped by those elements.

That is why education is so dearly valued by both; the highly schooled societies of Israel and Palestine recognize the power and potential of education in the ongoing forging of their cultural and national identities. Education is also recognized by both as a tool in the struggles for economic, technological, and even physical survival in times when national security is a constant issue. Both societies and their citizens are under relentless stress; neither education nor any other social institution can escape its urgent duty to serve the public interest and advance the national agenda.

As we turn to Turkey, we find that this "bridge" between East and West continues to be caught in the dilemmas and contradictions that its historical role makes inevitable. As Turkey increasingly moves in the direction of full economic integration with Europe, its education system is a primary vehicle for the transformation of the country from a traditional society to a modern nation state. However, there are political, cultural, and other social ramifications. In particular, the search for a national identity in times of rapid and destabilizing change and the central place of religion as a constituent of that identity have become thorny and unresolved issues.

The themes of national identity and the role of religion are emphatically accentuated in the next national case study, Pakistan. A state forged in the heat of a religious and cultural quest for autonomy, Pakistan recognizes that an Islamic state cannot be separated from an Islamic-based education system. On that basis, economic modernization can be effected without undermining the very social fabric and cultural cohesion of the nation. Pakistan's struggles in that direction, in the face of formidable obstacles such as low literacy rates and financial crises in the education sector, are illustrative of both the challenges and accomplishments found in many Muslim nations around the globe (some of which, like Indonesia and Malaysia, are found in the next section of this book).

The section ends with an examination of a nation whose race policies have been a focus of world attention for half a century. A new, post-apartheid South Africa has shown the world how dramatically a nation can change politically. Now, it is time to build upon that political change to create a new social and economic order. In that cause, education is a key instrument. Just as a segregated school system was one of the most stark manifestations of apartheid, a newly integrated system is the vanguard for transforming the political and social consciousness of South Africa. Although completely different in content and character, the ongoing transformation of South Africa is no less revolutionary, fundamental, and internationally significant than the social, political, and economic transformation of eastern Europe, the subject of our last section.

CHAPTER 18

Educational Dynamics in Israel: Retrospective and Future-Oriented Philosophies, Pedagogical and Interactive Processes

YAACOV RAND
MATI RONEN
RIVCA REICHENBERG

Yaacov Rand was born in Rumania, survived the Holocaust, emigrated to Israel after the war, and served as a captain in the Israeli Defense Forces. His academic studies were undertaken at the Hebrew University (Jerusalem) and the Sorbonne (Paris). He is a professor of special education and has served as dean of both the School of Education and the Faculty of Social Sciences at Bar-Ilan University, Israel. He is co-director and senior researcher at the Hadassa-Wizo-Canada Research Institute and the International Center for Enhancement of Learning Potential (Jerusalem), a member of the Israeli National Council for Higher Education, and holds the Kunin-Lunenfeld Chair for Research of the Special Child at Bar-Ilan University. He is also currently rector of Talpioth Teacher College (Tel Aviv) and Touro College (Jerusalem). His books and scientific articles have been published in a variety of educational and interventional areas.

Mati Ronen received his doctoral degree in sociology from the Hebrew University of Jerusalem in 1985. Since then, he has served as a lecturer in the School of Education at Bar-Ilan University in Ramat Gan, Israel. His research interests are medical sociology, gerontology, community schools, parental involvement in schooling, and methodologies of the social sciences.

Rivca Reichenberg was born in Israel, served in the Israeli Defense Forces as a teacher of new immigrant children, and received her academic degrees at Bar-Ilan University, Israel. She has been head of the Branch for Special Education at Schein Teachers College and is currently working and lecturing at the Teacher Training Department of Beith Berl College, Israel. She is head of the Branch for Prospective Teacher and In-Service Training at the Institute for Development and Research (Mofet) of the Ministry of Education. Her scientific publications are in the areas of education of the gifted, special education, resource room teaching, and teacher training.

THE SOCIAL FABRIC

Some five and half million people live in Israel today. A majority are native-born, popularly called *Sabras* (the Hebrew name for cactus fruits). The rest come from every country in the world, comprising a complex mosaic of people from varied religious and cultural backgrounds. Currently, the Jewish population stands at four and a half million. The million non-Jewish peoples are comprised mostly of Arabs, including the Druze and Bedouin segments of the Israeli population. The Arab population increased significantly after the six-days-war, which integrated Israeli Arabs and Arabs living in the various West Bank agglomerations.

Complementing this cultural and ethnic variety is a diversity in general lifestyles. This ranges from modern, through traditional, to ultrareligious, from urban to rural, and from individual to group-oriented ways of life. Israeli society is relatively young, with a median age of 25.6 years. More than 85 percent of Israelis are city dwellers. About 10 percent of the population lives in rural areas. The majority of the rural population is settled in two unique cooperative frameworks: the kibbutz and the moshav, both of which developed in Israel at the beginning of the twentieth century.

Many modern urban centers, integrating the old and the new, are built on sites known since antiquity, such as Jerusalem, Safad, Beer Sheva, Tiberias, Nazareth, and Akko. Others, such as Rishon Le'Zion, Hadera, and Petach-Tikva, began as agricultural villages in the prestate era and gradually evolved into towns and cities.

In the early years of the state of Israel, developmental towns were built in order to accommodate the needs of the accelerated population growth generated by mass immigration. The intention was to disperse the population throughout the country and to promote a closely interlocked rural and urban economy by drawing industry, commerce, and social services to previously unpopulated areas. Towns founded upon this rather pragmatic basis include Arad, Karmiel, Kyriath-Gat, and Beith-Shemesh.

Currently, nearly 3 percent of the Israeli population lives in about 270 kibbutzim. Traditionally, they were considered the agricultural backbone of Israel. However, in the last three decades, considerable efforts and financial resources have been directed toward development of industry. A more recent trend is the emphasis on tourism, including organization of musical festivals and other cultural events. Today, a large proportion of kibbutzim income derives from these branches.

The moshav is an agricultural village in which each family maintains its own farm and household, while cooperation extends to purchasing, marketing, and the provision of community services. Most of the 450 moshavim were founded and developed by immigrants coming after the establishment of the state of Israel. On average, each moshav is composed of about sixty families; together moshavs represent about 3.5 percent of the country's population. The moshavim supply a large portion of Israel's agricultural products and are intensively involved in exporting agricultural products all over the world.

Villages of various sizes are inhabited by Arabs, Bedouins, and Druzes. These compose about 25 percent of the Israeli rural population. Land and houses are privately owned and farmers cultivate and market their crops on an individual basis. Most Bedouins (who number about 110,000 in total) are no longer nomads. Nevertheless, some 40 percent of the Bedouin population still follow their ancient traditional ways of life, tending flocks of sheep and goats in the not-yet-cultivated regions of Israel.

Political Aspects

Israel is a parliamentary democracy consisting of relatively independent legislative, executive, and juridical institutions. The basic institutions are the presidency of the state, the legislative parliament (Knesset), the government, and the juridical system. Following the fundamentals of classical democratic regimes, these institutions are based upon the principle of separation of powers, with checks and balances, in which the executive branch is subject to the confidence of the legislature, and the independence of the judicial system is guaranteed by law.

Currently, elections for the Knesset and of the Prime Minister are held at the same time, in intervals of four years. The entire country constitutes a single electoral constituency, and all citizens are eligible to vote from the age of 18 years.

Having equality before the law, the Arab population is represented in the Knesset, either through its own parties or integrated within the existent Jewish political frameworks. The same is true for the central Union organization (Histadrut), as well as for other national and local sociopolitical institutions.

Economic Background

Although basic networks of highways, transportation means, postal and telephone facilities, as well as water, electricity, and communication systems existed already in 1948, they were totally inadequate for the development of a modern economy. To meet the necessary requirements for economic growth, the infrastructure had to be extensively expanded and upgraded. This included also a total reorganization and enlargement of the public services necessary to ensure the population's well-being.

Today, Israel's per capita Gross Domestic Product (GDP) places it among the twenty most developed countries in the world. Albeit a very small country, Israel's international position in some areas of industrial and agricultural production capacity, as well as its export to foreign countries in these domains, is remarkable. Israel has developed intensive commercial relationships with a great number of countries over five continents. Special ties were established with the European Union and the European Free Trade Association, as well as with the United States. Israel's active involvement in international business enterprises contributed meaningfully to the country's accelerated growth in the last two decades.

Israel's most striking economic achievement is perhaps the fact that its high developmental rate was attained while simultaneously coping with a number of highly expensive national challenges. Foremost among these, as noted below, are ensuring national security and coping with large-scale immigration. However, in the last decade the financial situation of the country has often required significant budget reductions.

National Security

Since its establishment as an independent state (and for many decades before), Israel's very existence has been threatened daily. This requires huge investments in purchasing and producing arms and ammunition, as well as in maintaining active security forces ready to intervene as promptly as possible in order to ensure the lives of its citizens. Israel's balance of payments, as well as its inflation rate, are significantly affected by the demands of the security forces. Technological developments also have an impact on the econom-

ic difficulties due to the high prices of high-tech arms and security devices.

On the other hand, the Arab-Israeli conflict has had a positive impact upon the Israeli economy. The tremendous and continuously demanding security needs led to the concentration of national efforts and financial resources in a lengthy and complex process of industrial and technological development. We may suppose that until peace is reached, national security, and its inherent social difficulties, will remain a most powerful determining factor of the country's economic development for many years to come.

Immigration

The *in-gathering of the exiles* is perhaps the major *raison d'etre* of the state of Israel. Established about three years after the Second World War, and the horrible holocaust of the Jewish people in Europe and North Africa, Israel became the land in which the survivors hoped to find peace and freedom from persecution. Since 1948, Israel has absorbed more than two and a half million people from about 150 countries of the globe, that is, more than four times its population at the beginning of the state. Moreover, in its first four years (1948–1952), Israel's population more than doubled, as about 700,000 immigrants, mostly from the refugee camps in Europe and the Arab states, poured into the country.

This tremendous growth in population has imposed severe strains upon Israel's economic and social system. Housing, the creation of working places, the development of the educational system, and so forth, made absorption a highly costly endeavor. Although the newcomers were largely in their productive years, their transition from immigrants to productive citizens took many years and was dependent to a great extent upon heavy governmental assistance.

This process continues even now; each year Israel absorbs on the average around 100,000 newcomers coming from the free occidental countries as well as from various areas of distress. The most recent waves of mass immigration comprises people from the large Jewish community of the former Soviet Union, which struggled for decades for the right to emigrate to Israel. While some 100,000 managed to overcome all difficulties in the 1970s and early 1980s, since 1989, over 700,000 have succeeded in coming and settling in the country. Among the latter, there are many highly educated professionals, well-known scientists, and acclaimed artists and musicians, whose expertise and talents are significantly contributing to Israel's economic, scientific, academic, and cultural life.

Cultural Aspects

Israel is an old-new country, small in size, but with an active and a widely varied human landscape. Its five and a half million population is culturally heterogeneous, and it enjoys a highly active and most differentiated cultural life. It is a place where the oriental cultures confront the occidental ones, where the past touches significantly the present and expand together into the future. Ancient, as well as modern ideologies mold a variety of lifestyles, as expressed in daily interpersonal relations and social activities.

About 4000 years of Jewish heritage, more than a century of Zionism, and about five decades of modern statehood have contributed to the development of a culture that has already created an identity of its own, while preserving to a great extent the uniqueness of each contributing community. Emerging from the encounter between the individual and various social backgrounds, it blends tradition with innovation, steers a course between Israeli particularities and universal orientations, and grows from a conflict between artistic freedom and the need to cater to public tastes.

Israel is a culture of integration. The social, ethnic and cultural diversity created by the Jewish dispersion all over the world over millennia, and the national aspiration to "bring the Jews home" and to ensure their physical and cultural existence, yielded a strong need for such integration. During the lengthy time of living within other nations, the Jews found many ways to both preserve their own

heritage and to integrate within their daily life many foreign cultural components of the various cultures that hosted them.

The revival of the Hebrew language is doubtless one of the most important cultural events of our era. Rooted in the ancient Biblical and Talmudic texts, and "irrigated" by a strong aspiration of cultural revival, Hebrew became again a spoken language, continuously growing, in order to cover the needs of a highly developed technological society. The encounter between Western modern cultures and the Jewish historical and religious traditions, as well as the transition from a "dead" language to a living one, are of paramount importance to the Israeli cultural life.

Israel has a strong Arab minority. Although history has shown that integration between Jewish and Muslim cultures is possible, and interchange was intensive in many Arab countries in which Jews lived for generations, this does not happen in Israel. The impact of Arab culture upon Israel's cultural life is rather limited, and this reduced influence is mostly linked to music, as well as to folklorist cultural expressions, imported by the newcomers from many Arab countries, and in particular those from North Africa and Yemen.

Due to the Arab-Israeli conflict, and to the general aspiration of the Arab minority to preserve its own culture, the impact of the Israeli culture upon this minority is also reduced, although relatively stronger than in the opposite direction. National as well as potent religious factors play a determinant role in the tendency of both Jews and Arabs to maintain cultural separation.

Religious Aspects

Current Jewish society in Israel is composed of observant and nonobservant subgroups, running from ultra-orthodox to nonobservant Jews who regard themselves as secular persons. About 20 percent of the Israeli Jewish population consider themselves as religious, affirming full adherence to religious laws and practices. About 60 percent view themselves as traditional, following some combination of these laws, according to personal choice and preference, often colored by ethnic and family traditions. Only about 20 percent can be considered as essentially nonobservant. Being conceived as a Jewish state, Israel's official institutions and public life observe Shabat (Saturday) as a day of rest, as well as all other Jewish religious holidays.

It is safe to assume that about 30 percent of the Jewish population is basically of religious orientation, and the great majority of people are significantly rooted in Jewish tradition for national reasons or in order to maintain family and ethnic traditions. The declaration of the establishment of the state of Israel (1948) guarantees freedom of religion to the entire population. Each religious community is free, both by law and practice, to exercise its faith, to observe its holidays and rituals, to keep its weekly day of rest, and to manage its internal affairs. Each religion is entitled to have its own religious council and courts. These are recognized by law, having jurisdiction over all religious affairs and matters of personal status, such as marriage and divorce.

As there is no clear separation between religion and state, a central social-political controversial issue has always been the extent to which Israel should manifest its Jewish religion in both juridical laws and procedures, as well as in daily public life. The orthodox establishment seeks to enlarge religious legislation beyond the area of personal status, over which it has exclusive jurisdiction. However, the nonorthodox segment of the Israeli population regards such legislation as religious coercion and an infringement on the democratic character of the state. Until an overall solution is found, authority lies in an unwritten agreement, reached on the eve of Israel's independence, known as the "Status Quo." It stipulates that no fundamental changes would be made as to the status of religion in both jurisdiction and public life.

Minority Communities

Over one million people, comprising close to 19 percent of the Israeli population, are non-Jews, usually defined as the Arab citizens of Israel.

While almost all are Arab-speaking, this segment comprises a number of different ethnic constituencies with distinct cultural characteristics.

Muslim Arabs.   This group is composed of about 780,000 people; most are Sunni-Muslims. They constitute more than 75 percent of the Israeli non-Jewish population. They reside in small towns and villages, over half of them in the northern part of the country. According to the law in vigor, they are considered Israeli citizens with all rights and obligations, except for serving in the army, from which they are exempted, for obvious reasons. Most of this population lives in monolithic regions and communities. Some of the Israeli cities, such as Jerusalem, Jaffa, Haifa, and Akko are mixed. Arabs and Jews live together and are governed by the same municipal authorities.

Christian Arabs.   This is the second largest minority group, comprising around 150,000 people. They live mainly in urban areas. They are a heterogeneous population in terms of their Christian definition. The majority of them (42 percent) are affiliated with the Greek Catholic Church. About 32 percent of the Christian population is Greek Orthodox; only 16 percent define themselves as Roman Catholic.

Bedouin Arabs.   This segment comprises about 10 percent of the Israeli Arab population. They live in separated communities and belong to more than thirty distinct tribes. Most of them are scattered over a wide area in the south of the country. Formerly nomadic shepherds, the Bedouins are currently in a transitory stage, from a tribal kind of social framework to a stable-settled society. The Bedouins are gradually entering the general Israeli labor force, especially in agriculture. They serve in the Army, mostly as ground scouts, due to their way of life and profound knowledge of the desert.

Druze Arabs.   The Druze community includes about 80,000 Arab-speaking people. They are scattered over twenty-two villages, mostly in the northern regions of the country. They constitute a separate cultural, social, and religious community. While the Druze religion is not accessible to outsiders and is only orally transmitted from generation to generation, one principle of its philosophy is well-known, namely the concept of *Tagiyya*. It calls for complete loyalty of its adherents to the government of the country in which they reside. Based upon this principle, young Druze regularly serve in the Israeli army, reaching high levels in the hierarchy of the IDF.

SCHOOLING

In essence, Israel can be considered as an old-new state with strong links between its ancient educational philosophy and modern-oriented ideological perspectives. This mixture is profoundly anchored in Jewish history. It is also a most powerful determinant of social attitudes: to some extent, these philosophies are determined by realities, and to some extent they are powerful determinants of the readiness to cope with newly emerging, and/or long-lasting, socio-educational issues. The democratic nature of the Israeli society is an additional determinant of its Israeli educational philosophy, leading towards social liberalism, multicultural orientations, and social integration trends. These latter elements also corroborate with the well-known Jewish aspiration for progress and high intellectual achievement.

Since the establishment of the state about fifty years ago, the Israeli legislative authorities have had a most liberal approach to education. They advocate the democratization of the school system and a broad enlargement of the pupils' possibilities to progress and optimally materialize their capacities. There is a high level of congruency between the legislative orientations and the ethos (*Zeitgeist*) of the Israeli society.

Recent Israeli legislation in the field of education, as well as in other areas of social activities, can be considered as highly progressive, liberal, and profoundly committed towards creating adequate and varied possibilities to promote and develop a generation of productive and self-fulfilling citizens.

Structure of the Education System

The school system is organized according to following four major divisions. These are General State Education (GSA), Religious State Education (RE), Independent Religious Education (IRE), and the Arabic Section (ASE). The first three divisions serve solely the Israeli Jewish population. All subject matter is taught in the Hebrew language, except for second languages, which are an integral part of the curriculum. In most schools, English is the prevalent second language and often the only one offered to the students. In some schools, Arabic, French, and even Yiddish are also made available to the students, contingent upon the expressed desire of the parents.

General State Education. The Israeli law of education, promoted in the early 1950s, as well as the later amendments adopted by the Knesset, ensures mandatory and free-of-charge education to all children between age 5 (kindergarten) and 16 (10th grade), residing in Israel. The total number of students enrolled in the Israeli educational system is close to 1,500,000. It should be noted that this figure does not include children attending ultra-orthodox or private institutions that are not under the control of the Ministry of Education.

The national investment in education, as reflected by governmental budget allocations, shows that education is the second highest budget item, following security. Moreover, it is continuously increasing, indicating the paramount importance attributed to education by the Israeli society. The percentage of budget allocations for higher education is also increasing. This is due to the continuous general growth of the population, as well as in the number of students reaching the age to be admitted to higher academic institutions. It can also be ascribed to the development of additional higher education institutions, such as regional, professional, and teacher training colleges, which were established in order to cope with the growing needs imposed by a highly developed technological society.

About 40 to 45 percent of students finish their

high school studies with a Matriculation Degree (*Bagruth*). This diploma is of high importance because it is an absolute necessary condition for admission to the universities or levels of the military.

The current general educational system of Israel is based upon a 6x3x3 model of schooling. Primary public schools (PPS) include the first six grades, and most of the children pass into the junior high school (JHS), which is composed of three classes (7–9), leading towards high school (HS), also composed of three classes (10–12). At the stage of JHS, the students have to decide as to the general orientation of their high school studies, such as letters, natural sciences, technical professions, computers, arts, and so forth.

About 62 percent of high school students continue their education in one or another post-secondary academic institution. More than 60 percent of them are studying towards an academic university degree, whereas about 17 percent are involved in advanced studies leading to a MA or a Ph.D. degree. These latter represent about 28 percent of the total BA student population. These proportions are relatively high, even when compared with those reported from a variety of other western highly developed countries.

Religious State Education/Independent Religious Education.

Three school divisions (GSE, RSE, ISE) serve the Jewish student population.

Primary education of the General State Education (GSE) dropped significantly across the last fifteen years (1980–1995), to the benefit of both religious divisions (RSE, IRE). On the other hand, enrollment went up in the secondary schools, albeit not to the same extent (– 5.8 versus + 2.4). The picture for the Religious State Education (RSE) is in the opposite direction. Enrollment went up slightly in the primary schooling frameworks, but lost much more in the secondary ones (+1.2 versus – 4.5). Independent Religious Education, that is, the most orthodox division, shows a consistent trend of increase in both primary and secondary education (+4.6 and + 2.1 respectively).

These data reflect a general trend of the Israeli population that is characterized by a process of enhancement of religious rather than secular orientation. The increase in the percentages of the religious educational frameworks may also be attributed to a higher birth rate of the religious population as compared with that of the nonreligious one.

Also, Oriental Jews—those coming from Asian and African countries—differ sharply from the Jews of European and American origin in their socioeconomic levels and educational backgrounds. Most of the Oriental Jews came to Israel after the state was already established and were settled according to the government's policy in towns, communities, or neighborhoods that were homogeneous by country of origin. Most of them were practicing religious people in their home countries so that their children were more likely than those of European and American origin to be absorbed by the state religious educational frameworks.

Arabic Section.

The Arabic division of the schooling system (ASE) includes subdivisions of the Druze and Bedouin ethnic groups. According to official figures, this section represented in 1980 about 16.4 percent (176,000) and in 1995 17.4 percent (260,000) of the total Israeli student population. These figures reflect kindergarten, primary, and secondary schools.

The figures show a considerable increase in absolute numbers, but remain highly constant in terms of percentages of the total Israeli student population. We may assume that the generally higher birth rate of the Arab population, as compared with the Jewish one, is outweighed by the immigration of Jews from other countries, in particular from Ethiopia and the former USSR.

Subject matter in the ASE educational frameworks is mostly taught in the Arabic language. There are certain exceptions to this, as determined by the specific nature of the subject matter, such as Bible or Hebrew literature, which are taught in Hebrew. There are also some Arab schools within which the Hebrew language is much more prevalent and most of the curriculum is taught in Hebrew.

These differences depend to a great extent upon basic orientations of the local authorities. The current prevailing regulations of the Israeli school system allow for such differences. It should be remembered that they permit a meaningful impact of parents upon the school curriculum.

Higher Education

Higher education in Israel is controlled by the Council for Higher Education (CHE). This is a public independent institution established by law, having all the liberties and power to orient all academic institutions in the country, as well as to act according to the policies established by the council. The law ensures its independence, as well as its powers of control. All new academic programs have to be submitted to the CHE and cannot legally be activated without its prior official approval. The same applies to the opening of any new academic institution in the country.

One of the major institutions of the CHE is the Committee for Planning and Budgeting (CPB), which is responsible (and the only channel) for the distribution of the national funding to the higher academic institutions and their respective budgets. Thus, the CHE has a strong impact upon the development of the academic institutions in the country, as well as upon the future planning and implementation of the national academic life.

Within this framework, all higher education institutions have full academic freedom as to content, organization, ways of teaching, and so forth. Thus, high-level academic programs are ensured and multidirectional research is promoted and reinforced.

The higher academic institutions can be divided into the following major categories: universities; regional colleges; teacher colleges; technical, arts, and professional colleges; branches of foreign academic institutions; and private academic institutions. Only the first three will be overviewed herein.

Universities.   Higher education in Israel is mostly entrusted to its seven universities. Five of them (Jerusalem, Tel-Aviv, Bar-Ilan, Haifa, and Ben-Gurion) are multivaried academic institutions covering a great variety of academic disciplines including medical sciences and law. All of them offer academic programs leading towards the three conventional academic degrees: Bachelor of Arts (BA), Master of Arts (MA), and doctorates (Ph.D.). Additional diplomas are offered within the framework of in-service training in various fields of activity.

The other two higher academic institutions are of more specific nature, concentrating around more specific academic and professional disciplines. The Weizman Institute in Rehovoth is mostly research-oriented and gives only MA and Ph.D. degrees in the areas of the exact sciences. The Technion in Haifa offers all the three conventional academic degrees, but solely in the areas of technology, electronics, engineering, and so on.

Schools of Education are an integral part of the major universities, acting as any scientific department and according to the same academic and research requirements. In addition to the regular academic degrees (BA, MA, Ph.D.), they are also accredited to issue Teachers Licenses for all disciplines taught in the junior and secondary high school.

Regional Colleges.   In addition to the above-mentioned institutions, there are currently twelve regional colleges in Israel. These are spread over the country with the aim to offer possibilities to enter higher education for population segments living in localities that are remote from the metropolitan areas in the center of the country. Most of these institutions are connected to one or another accredited university, which ensures academic responsibilities and appropriate level of studies.

In the last few years, four of those institutions reached the necessary academic level for independent accreditation, and they were authorized by the Council for Higher Education to offer BA degrees in a number of academic disciplines. Some others are acting intensively to reach this required academic level. None of these institutions are accredited for advanced degrees.

The regional colleges fulfill additional cultural

functions of a more general nature by organizing and offering nonacademic activities in various fields. Thus, they became community-oriented cultural centers, fulfilling an essential role in diffusing general knowledge in various fields, including arts and folklorist activities.

Teacher Colleges.   There are more than forty teacher colleges in Israel. They are spread all over the country and fulfill an essential role in preparing new teachers, as well as in offering in-service training for educators and teachers in a wide spectrum of pedagogical and didactic areas of activity. They are an integral part of the Educational Divisions (NSE, RSE, ISE, ASE) and provide for most of their needs in terms of new teachers. They prepare annually more than 1,000 new teachers.

About a third of these educational institutions are accredited to issue Bachelor of Education (B.Ed.) degrees in a number of teaching and educational areas. This adds considerably to the general educational level of the teachers in Israel, as well as to their social status.

Educational Objectives

As can be seen from the above, the major educational objectives of the current Israeli educational system are manifold. Briefly stated, they can be summarized as follows:

• Maintaining roots with the Jewish history across millennia, which impregnated so deeply Jewish society over the world.

• Maintaining and continuing the Jewish rich culture and traditions. This latter objective bears significantly upon the existent and future links of the Jews living in the Diaspora and those who returned to Israel, and their feelings of identity and belonging to the same nation.

• Preparing the new generation to actively integrate within both a multicultural and a modern society. This objective requires increased attention to the development of individuals within the technological professions. But it also implies the need to accentuate moral and ethical education in order

to avoid misuse which may have various negative outcomes.

• Preparing the new generation for the twenty-first century and the dynamic course of life that can be predicted from the continuously growing and changing society and life conditions that characterize our current life.

• Considering the strong internal and external tensions and conflicts featured in Israeli society, emphasis is placed upon educating the young generation toward mutual tolerance and acceptance of the different. This element is crucial for national survival, both from internal and external perspectives.

• Due to the development of modern educational sciences, as well as emphasis on the varied needs and of the multiple areas of educational activities, an eclectic pedagogical approach is most desirable and also frequently practiced.

• As to the general theoretical orientations prevalent in Israeli education, we consider two basic theories as predominant:

(a) The Piagetian theory. For more than four decades, this theory served as an explanatory paradigm for a variety of educational phenomena and as a theoretical framework for many applied programs, mostly in the area of regular education. Piagetian theory revealed itself as most heuristic, having a potent impact upon teaching and education.

(b) The Feuerstein Structural Cognitive Modifiability theory. Since the early 1970s this theory, as well as its major Mediated Learning Experience (MLE) concept, impregnated to a great extent educational thought and practice in the Israeli educational system. The applied methods developed within this theoretical framework, such as the Instrumental Enrichment (IE) program and the Dynamic Assessment procedures (LPAD), are nowadays practiced in Israel on a relatively wide scale due to their positive impact upon wide segments of children and youngsters having educational and scholastic difficulties.

Guiding Educational Philosophies and Practice

As the objectives show, the Israeli school system is multivaried in terms of its basic philosophical approaches. This is related to a number of historical facts and developments that are specific to the Jewish culture in general and to the Israeli realities in particular.

Since ancient biblical times, cultural transmission is one of the elementary imperatives in Jewish life, and in many ways modern Israelis' education is anchored in Jewish ancient sources. For example, it is expressed in a biblical religious commandment as:

> *And thou shalt teach them diligently unto thy*
> *   children,*
> *and shalt talk of them (the Lord's commandments),*
> *when thou sittest in thine home,*
> *and when thou walkest by the way,*
> *and when thou liest down,*
> *and when thou risest up. (Deuteronomy 6:7)*

The holistic and unconditional nature of this commandment places full responsibility for the children's education upon every father. It has to be performed at all times of the day and everywhere. Although this commandment is directed to the individual and not to society, it became a general characteristic of Jewish life across history and was intensively practiced under all life circumstances.

In the Babylonian Talmud, we find the following instructive texts:

> *At the beginning . . . they were introduced (into the*
> *school) at the age of 16 to 17, and when the master*
> *was angry, he was kicked out, until Joshua Ben*
> *Gamla made a regulation that teachers shall be*
> *posted in each region and each town, and they*
> *should be enrolled at the age of 6 to 7.*
> *When you punish a child do it only with your shoe-*
> *laces. Whoever reads—let him read. Who does not—*
> *let him be a team with his friend (who reads).*
> *(Baba-Batra 21:a)*

The basic educational ideas revealed in these texts have been, and are, characteristic of Jewish education. That is, education as a social responsi-

bility and not only a parental obligation, the creation of an adequate learning atmosphere using mild disciplinarian means, and the integration of weak students with those of higher capacities.

Further, commitment to education and innovation are important. Hence, after the Roman victory over Judea, and following the exile from the Holy Land (around 70 A.D.), the Jews were dispersed over many countries, mostly in Europe and North Africa. They never forgot their culture and, despite most adverse life conditions, continued to transmit their national and religious legacy. Thus, culture and education became of paramount importance as tools to maintain the unity of the nation, despite the complete loss of all national symbols, such as a territory, a common language, a national flag, an anthem, an army, and so forth. These latter had to be replaced in order to avoid a cultural vacuum that inherently leads to national annihilation. Thus, the idea of education for everybody was fully practiced even in times and places where the surrounding and predominant society remained "elitist" and was far from fostering general education practices.

The predominant pedagogical practices governing current Israeli education are characterized by an openness to innovation. New programs linked to both curricular subject matters and ethical-social education are continuously developed, practically implemented, and tested in the field. Short- and long-term research is activated by both the universities and the office of the Head Scientist of the Ministry of Education. Programs showing high efficiency in reaching their respective goals are frequently adopted and integrated in the regular scholastic activities.

SOCIAL AND EDUCATIONAL ISSUES

The tension between the religious and secular segments of the population is an issue of paramount importance to both the current life and the future development of the Israeli society. While the cultural-oriented conflicts between the eastern and western Jews are decreasing, the religion-oriented ones are becoming more and more prevalent.

Some sociologists claim that the fact that there are separate school systems for the religious and non-religious plays a determining role in the development and preservation of those tensions.

To some extent, the separation of the school settings and programs on the secular-religious dimension precluded education from becoming a unifying element in national unity. This situation presents a most significant dilemma for the educational system, which was originally conceived as one of the essential tools for national integration and the development of a common culture anchored in both historical ancient roots and contemporary modern vision.

Independent Schools

In the last few years, a considerable number of independent unique public schools were established in various places of the country by initiatives of the respective municipalities, and/or parental organizations and educators. These schools are elitist, mostly rooted in the fact that the national school system, based upon the principle of equal educational input for all children, failed to answer the needs of children with superior capacities and scholastic achievement.

Another major reason for the emergence of these schools is the incapacity of the actual centralized school system to cope with the cultural pluralism that characterizes Israeli society. The uniform and rather conservative nature of the school system did not allow for innovative approaches and practices, although increasingly parents showed interest in preserving their own cultural background and transmitting it to their offspring.

The early currents were an outcome of the country's needs to cultivate excellence, rather than social equality, for the sake of its future development. However, in the last two decades the educational policy adopted emphasizes the importance of parental influence in shaping the school programs and basic orientations. Yet we may speculate that the combination of national needs with potent social and cultural determinants may increasingly become a source for both development and social conflicts.

Immigration, Diversity, and Integration

Massive immigration has brought to Israel large groups of individuals and families with various special social and educational needs. The latter were always, and continue to be, a heavy burden upon the Israeli economy. Inherently, they are also a permanent source for social stress and conflicts.

Diversity is doubtless one of the most striking features of Israeli society. The usual classical distinction between the *Ashkenaz* (European) and *Sepharad* (Oriental) segments of the Israeli population is basically artificial. Language and cultural diversity within those large groups is not less, and sometimes even more, prevalent than the differences between the above mentioned large segments.

Furthermore, social stratification is notably visible in the still high correspondence between non-European provenance and relatively low socioeconomic status. However, the wide range of national educational programs, including enriched curricula and efforts, at both primary and secondary level, represents a determined effort to break this correlation. The continuous development of high technological industry, as well as the needs for educated manpower in a wide array of social and public services, significantly promote an integration process of qualified non-European members of the Israeli society. This process also fosters the need for achievement and social mobility. The relatively lengthy period of army service and the common experiences for the struggle for survival create most optimal conditions for socio-ethnic integration. In the last three decades, inter-ethnic marriages are most frequent, and members of the non-European groups hold high-prestige political, social, and military positions. Still, some groups feel that, according to their numbers, they are politically and socially underrepresented.

Sociocultural integration is perhaps the major internal problem because it is crucial not only to the daily course of life but also essential to the nation's future. The process of transforming discrete and most varied segments of the population into one nation is a task for generations. But it will ultimately determine if the "Return to Zion" will be a durable and long-lasting episode in Jewish history.

The idea of integration (socioeconomic, ethnic, and levels of scholastic achievement) is pivotal to the Israeli educational system. It started with socioeconomic integration during the prestate era, in which social norms were not money- or possession-oriented, but rather of a socialist nature. School integration was a genuine expression of a *Zeitgeist,* which characterized the great majority of those who came into the country in order to build a new society.

The egalitarian kibbutz movement, which yielded a great number of settlements, was one of the most salient expressions of this trend. Essentially, a kibbutz is a social and economic unit in which almost no private property exists. Decisions are made by majority votes of the general assembly of its members or by democratically elected committees that are responsible for specific areas of activity of the kibbutz. Property and means of production are owned by the community. Meals are prepared by a central kitchen and served in a communal dining hall. Clothing and linens are washed, mended, ironed, and distributed by central laundry services. Members of the kibbutz work in the various sections of its economy. Dining hall, kitchen services, and other central duties are fulfilled on a rotation basis. No payment is received for work done but members' needs are provided for by the kibbutz.

The kibbutz movement also represents an educational current. Because the kibbutz promotes a social and economic life based upon values such as equality, social integration, and honesty, education is considered to be of paramount importance. Children grow up together in a children's community, living, eating, and studying together. In some kibbutzim, children are to be found sleeping in the Children's Home from very early ages, although in the last two decades the general tendency of the Kibbutz movement is that children should live together with their parents until adolescence.

At a later stage, after waves of immigrants from all the four corners of the world immigrated into the new established state, socioeconomic integration became interwoven with ethnic integration. Due to the population dispersion policy, as well as for other practical reasons, people from the same cultural background were settled together in various areas of the country. This fact lead to a most negative homogeneity. Geographically deprived regions, mostly of oriental ethnicity, were generated, with low socioeconomic levels. Division on such dimensions was a real danger to the new society and became a major issue of the educational philosophy and practice. Ultimately, these phenomena led toward adoption of a law by the Knesset tending to activate an integration process by imposing adequate administrational procedures and developing educational and teaching programs deemed to foster integration and national unity.

Yet there is social integration between all ethnic and cultural diverse groups. It is based upon feelings of belonging to the same people, having a common history across millennia, and sharing the same hardships and daily struggles for survival. Group differences become less salient within the new generations. Children frequent the same schools and are taught similar contents with identical language. A common culture rooted in both ancient traditions and modern perspectives is generated and fostered. Full integration is still far from being reality, but it is continuously progressing despite all the ups and downs that characterize the Israeli dynamic society. The fact that an integrated Israeli society has been created within a remarkably short time from an enormous array of social, cultural, and linguistic diversity is a most unique phenomenon of modern history.

Special Education

As we mentioned, the Talmud speaks to low-functioning children not as a reason for exclusion but rather for the mobilization of common efforts, including peers, who may become a most powerful component of social and educational integration. Today, the general trend toward integration has developed a new outlook concerning children with handicaps and functional difficulties. Children of different levels of functioning share the same class, while being divided into two or three levels for specific subject matters, such as foreign language or mathematics. This grouping system (*Hakbatza*) significantly minimizes exclusion of culturally deprived children from the regular classes and their transfer into special education frameworks. It contributes also to maintaining the low-functioning students' social relationships with their peers. In many cases, it has a positive impact upon the students' self-image.

In the last two decades, inclusion policy became an official and strongly supported trend of Israeli education. Nowadays, many handicapped children—including those with hearing or visual problems, the emotionally disturbed, or those with otherwise inadequate functioning—have the possibility and the privilege to benefit from regular education and to remain an integral and contributing part of society. Special funds are allocated by the state to support these trends in terms of assisting manpower and elaboration of special teaching and educational programs. Particular efforts are directed to provide special education components to the programs of training prospective teachers as well as in-service training activities. For students enrolled within the framework of special education, free education is provided up to the age of 20 years.

Parents have meaningful rights to determine their children's school setting and, to some extent, even the program and curricula of their class. Special placement committees have been established by law in which representatives of parental organizations are full-rights members. The parents of the respective child have also the right to appear before these committees and to affect their decisions.

Teacher Training

Teacher training programs are undergoing significant changes. These are mostly determined by the current well-accepted educational and social ideologies that aspire to include within the regular frameworks as many children as possible deviating from the wide range of normal functioning. Assuming that within the framework of such a general approach every teacher will have to cope with issues and problems of handicapped children, a reorientation is now in action, preparing prospective teachers to handle efficiently special education children from both teaching and interaction components of their daily work.

THE FUTURE OF SOCIETY AND SCHOOLING

It is hard to predict future developments in general, and in particular as far as it concerns Israeli society. This comment is based upon the fact that Israel is perhaps on the top list of changing societies. This dynamic outlook is determined not only by its high technological development but also by the dangers it incurs daily and by a struggle for survival that has characterized its daily life for about five decades. On a speculative note, we may mention the following points:

• As far as one can forecast into the future, security tensions will continue to preoccupy Israeli society. Even if optimistic hopes become reality and peace treaties are signed with all of its Arab neighbors, it will take generations until real, long-lasting, and well-accepted peace will reign over the Middle East.

Hence, technological development will remain pivotal to the nation's existence. Israel will have to do much more than it does today to detect and cultivate its "brain treasury" in order to be able to maintain its technological and military superiority.

• These basic needs are somewhat antagonistic to the social-oriented equalitarian ideologies that affected tremendously the prestate society, as well as the social orientations of Israel across its existence. The state will have to find highly efficient ways to cultivate excellence while ensuring basic education and socioeconomic possibilities for progress to all of its members.

• Due to the dynamic changes intervening so rapidly in modern life, much more attention will have to be accorded to professional reorientation of the adult population. In the twenty-first century, professions acquired in young ages will become inefficient within relatively short periods. Without providing ample and most varied possibilities for professional reorientation, broad segments of the population will become marginal to society, and their contribution to the well-being of society will be minimal. We may also predict that the state will have to invest meaningful resources for the materialization of such widespread education.

• Teaching will have to rely much more upon preorganized data banks, providing information via electronic means of communication, rather than upon class-oriented information transmission. This will surely affect the nature of teacher/student relationships during as well as after classes. Computerized teaching may become a kind of an informal, noninstitutionalized communication that will reinforce a more equalitarian kind of social relationship based less upon hierarchy and more upon mutual respect.

• Teacher training will become central to all future educational development. Similar to the fact that current teacher training is less and less oriented towards segregation and more towards integration, future teacher training will have to emphasize modifiability rather than stability. The relative elimination of hierarchical teacher/student relationships mentioned above, and the increasing needs for a most knowledgeable and flexible teacher, will require us to channel the best and most intellectual citizens toward education. Society will have to invest efforts and finances to raise the status of education in general, and the teacher in particular, in order to render education most attractive for bright university and college students. Steps will have to be undertaken at the high school level to increase the "youngsters'" motivation toward education as a life career.

As stated at the beginning of this section, these are speculations and only time will teach us to what measure did we really succeed to look into the future and to predict its developments.

CONCLUDING COMMENTS

Israel is doubtless a most fascinating society, characterized by vehement inner and outer conflicts and struggles. It is unique both in the variance of its problems and their intensity, as well the nature and quality of its efforts to resolve even partially its conflicts. These efforts create unique opportunities to the majority of its population.

The dispersion of the Jewish people all over the world, since they lost their national independence, created strong needs to combine together a wide spectrum of cultural differences. An old people had to be reborn, and diversity has led to harmony and coexistence. Israel is currently characterized by a full-fledged and highly complex cultural process, by which diversity is maintained and feelings of belonging to the same culture are promoted and reinforced. In order to create optimal conditions to develop a new and unified people out of individuals with most diverse cultural attitudes and conducts, a monumental effort is required, a process that will continue for many decades to come.

Israeli society and immigration are closely linked to each other. Israel differs from other immigrant societies, such as the United States, by the fact that almost all of them share a common feature, belonging to the same national-religious entity, for many generations before immigration. To be reunified as a people on their own land was the predominant aspiration of the great majority of the newcomers. This is a most powerful "rope" that keeps together the entire Jewish population despite its high diversity.

CHAPTER 19

Reflections from the Inside: The Struggle of the Palestinian Education System

SAMIR J. DUKMAK

Samir Jabra Dukmak is a member of the Central National Committee for Rehabilitation in Palestine and a member of the International Association of Special Education. He is employed as Children Services and Community Projects Coordinator by the British agency Action Around Bethlehem Children With Disability. He is also a consultant for, and representative of, the agency at the Bethlehem Arab Society for Rehabilitation (BASR) in Bethlehem. A graduate of the University of Bethlehem, he served as a social worker before going to England in 1986 for further studies under the sponsorship of Christian Aid. There, he completed an Advance Diploma in Community-Based Rehabilitation at the Institute of Child Health at London University, and a Master's degree in Special Education at the University of Manchester. Currently, he is enrolled in a doctoral program at the University of Manchester.

Education cannot be understood in isolation from the background of the people it serves. Brief historical, political, sociocultural, and demographic background information is needed to provide a general perspective on the people's education in Palestine. The education system in any region of Palestine has essentially operated within a fragmented sociocultural and psychological situation.[1]

---

[1]The words *Palestine* or *Palestinian society* have been used interchangeably all the way through this chapter to indicate either Palestinian society as a whole (the West Bank, Gaza Strip, and East Jerusalem) as well as to indicate only to the West Bank and Gaza Strip. The term *Arab Israelis* is used for Palestinians who are Israeli citizens and live among Israelis.

THE SOCIAL FABRIC

Palestine is a small country in the Middle East. Its boundaries are Lebanon and Syria to the north, Jordan to the east, the Mediterranean Sea to the west, and the Red Sea to the south. Major areas are the West Bank and Gaza Strip, under Palestinian Authority, and East Jerusalem, where Arab Israelis who are citizens of Israel live.

According to the Palestinian Central Bureau of Statistics (1996), the estimated population of the West Bank and Gaza Strip is 2,534,598 distributed as 1,571,572 and 963,026 respectively. The number of the Palestinians who live with the Israelis in their areas is more than 600,000. The above figures are estimated and as a result of the natural growth and the peace treaty that encouraged many Palestinian immigrants to come back home, it is expected that the current population of Palestine is about 4 million.

More than half of the Palestinians in the West Bank and Gaza Strip live in refugee camps and villages, which means that they are experiencing the worst living conditions and deprivation. The economy of the West Bank and Gaza Strip is dependent upon income from small shop and factory owners, small farmers, and others involved in agriculture. Many work as laborers in the Israeli areas.

There are two religions in the country—Islam and Christianity; the majority of Palestinians are Moslems. Due to the holy nature of the country, most Palestinians are religious. Generosity, friendliness, courtesy, and love of the land are the most common features characterizing the Palestinian people.

Historical Developments

Palestine was under Turkish rule for four centuries (1517–1917). Immediately after World War I and as a consequence of it, Palestine, along with other Arab countries, was subjected to the British mandate, which in Palestine lasted for three decades. In 1948 Israel was established as a Jewish state in the major portion of Palestine. The remainder belonged to Egypt (Gaza Strip) and to Jordan (the West Bank).

Arabs were the majority in Palestine until 1948 when they suddenly became the dominated minority in their land. Until that time, Arabs and Jews in Palestine were involved in a continuous war that started on a semi-organized basis in the 1920s and has escalated since then. The most noticeable fighting periods were the late 1930s and the late 1940s before the establishment of the state of Israel. In fact, Arab-Jewish relationships in Palestine so far can best be characterized as a continuous bloody conflict. In times of relative quiet, both sides prepared for the next round. An atmosphere of suspicion and overwhelming mistrust has dominated the relationship for many decades.

The Period After 1948

In May 1948, the British evacuated Palestine; on the same day, Israel was declared a Jewish state. About 156,000 Arabs remained within the boundaries of the newly created state (Israeli Arab part). Although war had ended, or at least seemed to have ended, mutual mistrust continued. One of the consequences of Jewish mistrust was the subjection of the Arab minority to military administration, which lasted until 1966. Military administration meant, among other things, curfews and special permits for most Arabs to be able to leave their villages and towns to look for jobs, and restrictions in education and trade (Mar'i, 1978). However, I believe that Palestinians experienced the worst of the various

forms of violence of the Israeli occupation in the two wars—that is, 1948 and 1967.

Throughout, however, the Palestinians lived through fighting and confrontations with the Israeli army. Many Palestinian youths were killed, injured, or detained as a result. The conflict in those years was up and down. The situation remained as such until 1987 when the *Intifada* (uprising) started. After this, the Palestinians suffered more than seven years of severe conflicts, confrontations, and torture that again led many Palestinians to be detained, injured, disabled, or killed.

From the writer's point of view, the Oslo Agreement in 1994 showed that the Palestinian people wanted to be part of the solution to their problems. They accepted the Oslo agreement, although it favored the Israelis much more than the Palestinians, hoping to spell the end of their suffering. Unfortunately, this was not to be; many people started to experience a different suffering—that of being locked up in their cities (self-ruled areas) and not being able to move freely. On many occasions, Palestinians have not been allowed to move from one city to another, even among those cities ruled by the Palestinian Authority. All Palestinian people who live outside Jerusalem are not allowed to go to Jerusalem or any other place ruled by the Israelis unless they have a special permit from the Israeli authorities. Getting such a permit is a miracle, and the vast majority of Palestinians (more than 95 percent) cannot get one.

Hunger due to unemployment and the inability to move freely between the cities are two of the most common sufferings experienced by the Palestinians not only during the Israeli occupation but also during the self-rule period in the last three years. Unemployment is a major problem caused by the permanent closing of certain areas. Many Palestinians work as laborers/workers in the Israeli-ruled areas. As a result of closing Jerusalem, the vast majority of workers cannot go to their work any longer and this has led to unemployment. Due to the prevailing financial circumstances of the people in general and the workers in particular, some workers take a risk and sneak to the Jerusalem or Tel Aviv areas to their work. A few of them continue to work peacefully, but many are caught, jailed for months, and forced to pay hundreds of dollars as fines for their actions.

Confiscating Palestinian land to build new settlements and/or to enlarge the old ones in order to accommodate the Israeli immigrants, as well as confiscating lands to build huge roads, has remained a problem after the peace treaty. This is serious, especially for those whose land is considered their only source of income or for those who wish to settle and reside on their own land.

SCHOOLING

The education system in Palestine has very recently been transferred to Palestinian authority, after being affiliated with the Jordanian education system while Palestine was still under the Israeli authorities. The Palestinian educational system has been affected greatly by the negative practices and dominating forces that have been carried out by the Israelis (Dukmak & Kanawati, 1995).

Structure of Schooling

Before the scholastic year 1991/1992, there were three stages of general education: primary level, preparatory level, and secondary level. At the beginning of the 1991/1992 scholastic year, general education in the West Bank was divided into two stages: basic level (10 years) and secondary level (2 years). At the beginning of the 1994/1995 scholastic year, the Ministry of Education and Higher Education decided to divide general education in the Gaza Strip into basic and secondary education, the same as in the West Bank (Abu-Libdeh, 1995). Higher education is divided into intermediate higher education (community colleges) that extends over two years, and university education, which extends over a four- or a five-year period.

There are three types of mainstream schools in the country. These are private, public/government, and UNRWA schools (United Nations Relief and Works Agency) (Abu-Libdeh, 1995; Kamal & Zughby, 1996). According to the Palestinian Central Bureau of Statistics (1996), the number of students attending schools (basic and secondary) in the West Bank and Gaza Strip, including East Jerusalem, in the year 1995/1996 was 662,427 (340,390 males and 322,035 females). The number of teachers in the same year was 21,563 (11,641 male teachers and 9,922 female teachers).

In terms of university education, the West Bank, Gaza Strip, and East Jerusalem have twelve universities. The number of students at these universities for the year 1995/1996 was 37,094 (21,190 males and 15,904 females). The number of graduates in the same year was 3,032. The number of teachers also in the same year was 1,369 (Palestinian Central Bureau of Statistics, 1996).

In addition to public education, Abu-Libdeh (1995) lists other types of education:

• *Illiteracy and adult education* is provided for those who are above 15 years old and who have never attended school, those who have received education only for a short period, or those who have lost the skills they acquired over time.

• *Private education* is provided for talented children or any other special needs student. Other types of private schools—Christian and Moslem—have existed in all Arab countries for many years. These schools also exist in Palestine at present, especially in the West Bank and Gaza Strip; there are no Moslem schools operating in the Israeli part of Palestine.

Christian schools sponsored by western European religious organizations existed before and after the creation of the Israeli state in Palestine. Because these schools were nongovernmental, they enjoyed an increasingly high status, especially after the creation of the Israeli state. This is due to the fact that Palestinian people refused to send their children to the government schools, and Christian schools were almost completely independent from the influence of the Israeli educational authorities. Christian schools were occasionally refused by the Moslems in rural areas because Islam was not taught as a religion. However, there was a common traditionalism between the Christians and the Moslems related to the high emphasis on the value of physical punishment in education and the separation between males and females in schools. This bond made them forget about religion sometimes.

- *Irregular education* is comprised of short courses in computer, languages, secretarial work, and the like.
- *Vocational training centers* are centers used to graduate technical workers over a period of one or two years.

Governance

Administratively, the current directorates of education are divided into two types: governmental and UNRWA directorates. The main task of the UNRWA directorates of education is to supervise UNRWA schools directly. According to Abu-Libdeh (1995), the governmental directorate supervises directly the government schools in the West Bank and Gaza Strip and follows up private education. For example, they issue the permission needed for the inauguration of private kindergartens and schools. They also control the curriculum and the extent to which they meet the required conditions and circumstances of the educational process. In Jerusalem there is only one directorate belonging to the Jordanian Ministry of Waqf to supervise the Waqf and private schools in East Jerusalem.

School numbers in Palestine differ from one place to another. For example, the total number of schools in the rural West Bank and Gaza Strip in 1993/1994 was 1,357. Of these, 992 were governmental schools, 111 were private, and 254 were UNRWA schools. The number of schools in the Gaza Strip for the same year was 300, of which 140 were governmental schools, 6 were private, and 154 were UNRWA schools. On the other hand, the number of schools in East Jerusalem in the year 1985/1986 was 91. These schools were governmental, private, and UNRWA distributed at 30, 48, and 13 respectively (Abu-Libdeh, 1995).

Legislation and Policies

Before moving on to discuss the current legislation and policies in education (which are not many), it is very important to give a clear historical description of the legislation and policies that were carried out by various occupying powers in the country in the last few decades.

Early Period. Ibrahim Basha (a Palestinian leader) led an educational policy in Palestine that included the widespread development of education with new styles of schools and resources. This was, however, a long time before the British mandate.

British Mandate. When Palestine was occupied by the British in 1917, the educational movement that had been started was greatly affected. The establishment of new schools in Palestinian villages was forbidden and, in many instances, schools were closed because they did not cooperate with the British authorities. As a result, education became the central point in Palestinian thought and behavior and led the Palestinians to establish their own schools and provide them with teachers. The number of schools in the period between 1941 and 1945 reached 558,236. Most were private. Some were partially supported by the British government; 322 were supported totally by the government.

The attitude toward education in Palestinian society was the most positive one among Arabs in the Arab world. For example, in 1945/1946, 10 percent of the Palestinian people attended schools, while only 3.4 percent, 5 percent, and 2.4 percent from the general population of Iraq, Syria, and Jordan respectively, attended schools in that year. In 1946/1947 the percentage of those who attended schools in the Palestinian society grew to 15.7 percent. This was the highest percentage in the Arab world after Lebanon (Al-Nimer, 1993).

Post-1948.   After the Israeli occupation of the larger part of Palestine in 1948, education became more and more important for the Palestinians, especially those who became refugees. The living conditions of the Palestinians were characterized by the loss of means of production, an increasing number of authorities that supervised the education of the people, an increase in the countries and cultures from which many Palestinians received their higher education, and the handing of Palestinian educational responsibility to various bodies such as the United Nations Relief and Work Agencies (UNRWA; considered as an international relief agency by face and an American agency by heart). These differences fragmented the Palestinian people and led many Palestinians to leave the country searching for jobs in other countries. In Saudi Arabia alone, educated Palestinians formed 90 percent of teachers in Saudi schools (Al-Nimer, 1993).

The Israelis tried hard to create certain educational policies (or lack of policies) for the Palestinians in order to control them easily in certain ways. In fact, the lack of policy on education in the Palestinian schools in the whole country in general, and in the Israeli part in particular, became a policy in itself. The best the Israeli authorities could do was not to form a clear policy (Mar'i, 1978).

First, they neglected education among the Palestinians according to a plan that aimed at converting the greater number of Palestinian students to ignorant people so as to decrease consciousness among them. They did not emphasize the basics of primary education for Palestinians in order to keep them at an elementary stage with a minimum of education; at the same time, primary education was strongly emphasized for Israeli students.

The Israeli occupation policies greatly affected the curriculum used in the country and made it a lot worse. For example, the curriculum that was used in the West Bank was introduced during the Jordanian rule of the country before 1967. The Israelis refused to carry out any modifications on the curriculum, although this curriculum had been reviewed, modified, and changed many times in Jordan since 1967. This also happened to the curriculum in the Gaza Strip, which was affiliated with Egypt.

The curriculum at the Israeli schools included very important subjects—Hebrew to the mastery level, the Bible, old Israeli history, modern Israeli history, general history, Israeli geography, general geography, and arithmetic. On the other hand, the curriculum used in the Arab schools in particular and in the West Bank and Gaza Strip in general never emphasized the elements that dealt with the land of Palestine, the history of Palestine, the Palestinian personality, and the like. The Israelis used to impose the content of the curriculum on Palestinian teachers and they were forced to implement it, otherwise they would have been jailed or forced to leave work or both. As a result, their families would have been exposed to a life full of joylessness and deprivation. If any of these teachers left work, they would have been replaced by unqualified teachers (Al-Nimer, 1993).

As an example, the goals for teaching history were consistent with, and an extension of, the general statement of goals for the education of Israelis. The goals of Jewish education emphasized the inculcation of Jewish consciousness and identity, while the goals for Arab education tended to ignore Arab consciousness and identity (Mar'i, 1978). There was weak, if any, emphasis on Arab nationality and culture. In fact, in various lessons concerning Moslems and their times, this curriculum gave two contradictory pictures to the Palestinian students at the same time. One was the picture of the Arab past that was full of disputes and problems over the decades; the other, a picture of Israelis who contributed to the development of Islamic culture.

The geography curriculum was also designed in a way to give a very bad picture of the people of the Arab countries, including Palestinians. For example, the curriculum books said that the majority of people in the Arab nation were farmers, many of whom were poor and lived difficult lives. They started working in their fields very early in the morning and worked until evening. The houses in the villages were simple and built from dried mud. The streets in these villages were so small that cars could not move in the streets freely. Bedouins still lived in tents under poor conditions and suffered from hunger.

Let us now look at the books used in the Arab schools in the Israeli areas. As the Israelis changed the names of almost all areas, villages, and cities in Palestinian society, they even omitted the name of Palestine in all the books used (Al-Nimer, 1993).

The Israelis neglected maintenance of the physical structure of schools. The bad conditions of Palestinian schools were emphasized by Israeli newspapers. For example, on May 29, 1955, *Al-Hamishmar Newspaper* published an investigative report about the education of Palestinians. It noted that "The situation of Palestinian schools is very bad in terms of physical structure and furniture; and most of these schools are similar to caves, have no seats and pupils sit on the floors on dirty and torn rugs." On September 5, 1971, the *Davar Newspaper* described the bad conditions of Palestinian schools in terms of curriculum, teachers, and the schools' physical structures by saying that

> *Until the fifties there was not available in Palestinian schools any single good book and the Israeli Ministry of Education was never interested in producing school's books at the same standard of those for Jewish schools, teachers are not qualified . . . employing teachers is not according to their professional abilities because tens of teachers who are qualified and have a long time of teaching experience have been fired out of their work because of their political views.*

The natural result of this policy was to reduce the number of students at the Palestinian schools year after year and to reduce the degree of success in the general examinations among remaining students (Al-Nimer, 1993).

As a result of the 1967 war, the number of students in the secondary education stage in the West Bank and Gaza Strip of Palestine decreased by half, due to many factors. For example, many families left the country for fear of the Israelis. Many young Palestinians were arrested by the Israelis, and many left school in order to work with the Palestinian resistance movement. Others were encouraged to leave school and work in jobs such as fruit picking, where they received good salaries for their work. Too, many countries like the United States and the Gulf, with the support and help of UNRWA, opened their doors for the immigration for Palestinians. Palestinian students also suffered from educational problems such as long absences from school, avoiding registration for the elementary stage, and truancy. Obstacles were put in front of those students intending to pass the general examination.

Another factor was those parents who were not convinced of the benefits of education for their children. For example, the study of religion, Arabic literature, and the history of Islam were not particularly stressed (Mar'i, 1978). Further, some parents believed that what their children learned was against their beliefs. They realized that education in the Palestinian schools had "a Palestinian face and a Jewish blood and soul." The aims of education were in conflict with Palestinian heritage. Therefore, the Palestinian students lived in multiple cultures represented by a clear contradiction between what the student believed in, his or her parents' aims, and what the Zionist movement planned for that student.

Palestinians place a high value on formal educational attainment, which provides them with a passport to greater economic security and enhanced life chances (Badran, 1979; Mar'i, 1978). Higher education became the major outlet for coping with the lack of statehood in terms of a political entity, the deep social structure transformation, the lack of dependence of education on internal economic structures, and the like (Mar'i, 1978). Because the Israelis know this, it is the reason behind their closing of educational institutions as a collective punishment for the Palestinians.

Since the beginning of the Israeli occupation of Palestine, schools, colleges, and universities have been the places where demonstrations, protests, strikes, and confrontations with the Israelis have taken place. As a result, these academic institutions have been closed for different periods of times and many teachers and students have been harassed. For example, each time a confrontation started, students blocked the road, set fire to tires, and threw stones at the advancing soldiers who usually responded by shooting tear gas and rubber and live bullets at the students. After that, school would be interrupted by closing it through a military order until further notice. Later, the *Intifada* (uprising) in 1987 was used as an excuse by the Israeli authorities to close schools and universities for a few years. At one stage in the Intifada and as a result of closure of academic institutions, the popular neighborhood committees organized alternative educational classes that were held in private homes.

Palestinian Authority. Since the Palestinian authority only recently took over the responsibility for education in the West Bank and Gaza Strip, not much legislation and policies have yet been established. The Palestinian authority is about to set up a compulsory education policy, supportive education programs for children with low achievement in schools, and an inclusive education program to include children with disabilities in the mainstream system of education. This will change the curriculum, increase the number of schools, upgrade the skills of existing teachers, and create more newly qualified ones.

Structure of Schooling

Preschool Education. Preschool education (kindergarten) is popular in Palestinian society. The kindergartens in the West Bank and Gaza Strip are distributed between two supervisory authorities, private and UNRWA. Most kindergartens belong to the private sector, and the number of pupils in private kindergarten is much higher than the number in UNRWA's, about 97 percent of the total.

Basic Education. The legal attendance age (attending first elementary class) is the same in all Palestinian schools; the child's age must be 6

years at the beginning of September (Abu-Libdeh, 1995).

Students' fees depend on the type of school the student attends. For example, in government schools (before the Israelis handed over the West Bank and Gaza Strip to the Palestinians) the Israeli Civil Administration was responsible for covering expenses, and students only paid small fees to cover the cost of materials and equipment. In UNRWA schools, students do not pay fees at all. In private schools, some schools charge students relatively high fees, but some other charge little or no fees. This depends on whether these schools are aiming at financial profit or if schools are organized by charitable societies or foreign and local organizations (Abu-Libdeh, 1995).

Special Education. Special education services for school-aged children with special needs in the country are not much developed due to the fact that there are very few qualified persons in this field. There are, however, a good number of institutions and programs that provide rehabilitation services. In 1993 there were sixty-two centers, forty-six of which are in the West Bank and sixteen in the Gaza Strip. Among these centers, ten were providing services for people with physical handicaps, fifteen for people with visual impairments, eight for people with hearing impairment, fifteen for people with mental handicaps, and seven for persons with drug addiction. In addition, there were seven advisory centers (Abu-Libdeh, 1995). From the writer's point of view, the number of institutions and programs that provide rehabilitation services for people with special needs are actually more than the cited numbers, and those that provide effective special education services are very few (not exceeding four or five institutions and/or programs).

There are various factors that impede the rapid and efficient development of special education provision in the West Bank and Gaza Strip. These include the absence of a well-developed national education system as well as a national curriculum, lack of policy for a whole school approach to special needs, financial constraints, limited resources and teaching materials, attitudes of parents as well as the attitudes of staff and administrators, lack of advisory and support services, and a lack of well-qualified professionals.

Curriculum

The Palestinian educational system does not have a national curriculum. Since 1967, Palestinians in the West Bank have been using the Jordanian curriculum, which is too long and does not allow the teacher to move freely and create various activities outside it. The only concern of the teacher is to complete this curriculum in the year; otherwise, he or she would be severely criticized. The curriculum used in the Arab schools in the Israeli part is an Israeli designed one that emphasizes the interests of the Israeli people and ignores the interests of Palestinians. Many subjects such as history, geography, religion, and languages contain many wrong facts. The facts show the Israelis as a civilized nation with a bright future of which each Israeli individual can be proud. These facts also show the Palestinians as an uncivilized nation that has a dim future, and with little of which to be proud. Hence, the Israeli policy, as it is reflected in the curriculum designed for Palestinians living in the Israeli side, is to create an uneducated Palestinian people who will not be able to recognize their nation's characteristics and many other important facts.

The teaching methods used in the majority of schools in the West Bank and Gaza Strip are fairly traditional, although there have been some attempts to carry out changes. Traditional methods are based on rote learning and on practices such as sitting down calmly and not talking to other students, paying attention to the teacher's speech, not talking unless the teacher allows you to do so, not asking many questions, doing class work alone, and so on. The teacher adopts the "chalk and talk" approach and the student adopts the "paper and pencil" approach. The child sits at his or her desk the whole day long listening to the teacher. No small group activities are used and not many creative activities are used, such as playing with sand and water. Science experiments are often used by teachers but the students only watch. Outside curriculum activities are forbidden, parents are not involved much in the educational process of their children, and not much emphasis is placed on music or the arts.

There is an important emphasis on subject exams, which are considered the only method of assessing student's progress and understanding of the subject. Since the Palestinian authority took over the education system in the country (except in Jerusalem and other Israeli Arab areas), it has been hoped that various measures would take place to implement modern pedagogical theories and practices in the field of education. Indeed, a few modifications have been carried out on the curriculum and currently there is a special committee consisting of many experts in the field trying to replace the existing curriculum with a pure Palestinian one.

Student Characteristics

Palestinian students are aware of the political, economical, and social situations in their country as well as the need for many educated people. As a result, the percentage of educated people in Palestine exceeds the percentages of educated people in other Arab countries, and there are comparatively high levels of education among the Palestinian population. Studies show that the educational attainment of the refugee camp population is higher than the educational attainments of the population of the cities. One 1993 study (cited in Abu-Libdeh, 1995) showed that 21 percent of the camps' population in the West Bank and Gaza Strip, excluding old people, had gained an education higher than the General Secondary Certificate Examination in comparison with 9 percent in the rural West Bank and 7 percent in East Jerusalem. As well, 45 percent of the refugees in the West Bank and Gaza Strip completed at least ten years of education in comparison with 36 percent of the rural West Bank and Gaza Strip population. There was also an increase in the number of those who completed nine to twelve scholastic years in different years. The number of students who completed these scholastic years in 1985 was 30 percent; this number increased to 41 percent in 1993.

A few studies show that the level of education attainment among Palestinian males is higher than among females for all age groups. The rate of males who completed thirteen scholastic years in 1993, for example, was 13 percent while for females it was 6 percent. The rate of males who completed nine to twelve scholastic years reached 45 percent, while the rate of females reached 37 percent. The percents of those males and females who never attended schools in 1993 were 9 percent and 25 percent respectively (Abu-Libdeh, 1995).

Various studies show that the illiteracy percentage among both males and females has been reduced with the passing years. The level of illiteracy among females in the Gaza Strip decreased from 75.6 percent in 1970 to 31.7 percent in 1990; in the rural West Bank from 84 percent in 1970 to 31.7 percent in 1990. The rate of the population who can hardly write in all areas is higher among males than females. The rates among males were 72 percent, 77 percent, and 78 percent in the Gaza Strip, rural West Bank, and East Jerusalem respectively; the rates among females were 69 percent, 57 percent, and 75 percent.

Note that in the Palestinian schools, however, the Intifada Palestinian uprising, which started in 1987 and lasted for seven years, had a major impact on Palestinian children and created a generation of students characterized by stubbornness, aggression, violence, and school and authority rejection. Many of these students left school; others still struggle with the school's requirements and show an inability to cope. The number of pupils experiencing learning problems that are not actually detected has been constantly increasing, especially in the last decade as a result of the constant curfews and closure of schools during the uprising that have led to the deterioration of educational levels. Pupils' acquisition of basic acade-

mic skills in Arabic language and math have been greatly affected.

Keep in mind that teachers, too, are under considerable stress. There are several factors that may add stress to the regular class teacher. These include the overall number of pupils in the regular classroom, the number of pupils with learning problems therein, particularly those with behavioral problems, the confined timetable, and the restricted period of time in which the curriculum must be covered. Furthermore, some teachers lack the knowledge and experience needed to cope socially and academically with pupils with learning problems. In general, schools in Palestinian society place great emphasis on competition and academic achievement. Hence, most teachers are intent on the inculcation of academic knowledge and skills, and pupils are constantly under pressure to achieve academic success at school.

Higher Education

The socioeconomic and political transformations seen in Palestine are of special significance to the topic of higher education. One reason is that the socioeconomic and political dynamics usually recognized in developing (and to some extent in developed) countries as selection or screening processes do not operate as such within Palestinian society. Employment opportunities and economic rewards are not dependent upon social class affiliations but on merit (Mar'i, 1978).

The deprivation of Palestinians of a nation-state has helped facilitate higher education because the lack of politically determined selection processes has helped many who would have been otherwise deprived achieve higher education. The Palestinian experience of uprooting and dispersion has helped weaken the traditional social structures that usually are responsible for depriving the majority of a traditional society from achieving education, particularly higher education. Neither is the Palestinian society a self-contained economic entity, nor does it have an independent economic structure, which would have been selective as in most other human societies. Efforts to identify a pattern of correlation between opportunities for higher education and social class are in vain; instead, university students in villages and towns in the West Bank are distributed almost proportionately among the different socioeconomic classes (Mar'i, 1978).

Teacher Training

There are two types of academic institutions that give training for school teachers in the country—the teacher training colleges and the universities. The former award undergraduate diplomas that qualify participants to be teachers; the second award diplomas and bachelor degrees in education in various areas. Postgraduate courses in the field of education, postgraduate diplomas, and masters degrees are also offered by some universities in the country. The high colleges and universities require students to successfully complete the General Secondary Certificate Examination (*Tawjihi*)[2] in order to apply for admission at these universities. The majority of these universities are modeled on the North American system of course credits that require students to earn a certain number of credit hours obtained from a range of course credits in order to graduate.

Many years ago, employment opportunities in the field of education were only available for men. Palestinian women only started working as teachers a few decades ago, and this was at the Palestinian schools in the Israeli parts of the country. They started as teachers in the kindergartens or in the lower grades of the elementary schools (Mar'i, 1978).

Currently, many women work as teachers in the Palestinian schools that exist either in the Israeli parts or in the West Bank and Gaza Strip in all grades. This encourages many parents to send their daughters to school.

[2]This is a general examination held at the end of the secondary stage. One examination is held for all twelfth class students in the West Bank and another for Gaza Strip students. Successful students get the General Secondary Certificate.

MAJOR ISSUES, CONTROVERSIES, AND PROBLEMS

In Society

Palestinian society has been exposed to various major issues, controversies, and problems. We can date these to the beginning of the Turkish occupation many centuries ago, followed by the British mandate, and then by the Israeli occupation of the country in two stages—the 1948 war that was ended by occupying two-thirds of Palestine and the 1967 war that ended by occupying the remaining one-third of Palestinian land. Both prior to 1948 and afterwards, Palestinians have encountered a series of traumatic experiences.

Therefore, one could safely observe that while Palestinian society has not disintegrated, it has, as a result of such encounters, undergone drastic socioeconomic and political transformation. Many Palestinians have become refugees and have helped transform the former social structure into a new one easily characterized by the relative lack of the farmer class. When much of the cultivable land was lost to Israel, new living resources emerged, especially in the area of labor. The traditional political leadership has vanished, and a new, nontraditional leadership has emerged, both at the local and the national levels. The occupation adversely affected the economics of the country through controlling employment opportunities, which led people to be exposed to poor and limited medical and health services. It created different social classes that made the vast majority of people belong to the lower class with a minority distributed among the middle and higher classes. This has negatively affected the relationships between people. As a result, Palestinian people have become divided into almost ten conflicting political groups.

In Education

The occupation had a great impact on the education system in the country in terms of curriculum, student characteristics, teacher training, and the like. During the Israeli occupation, political and colonization practices were reflected mainly in curriculum and on the level of schooling in general in the West Bank and Gaza Strip. The effect of the Israeli occupation on Arab schools in the Israeli part was also very bad because the Israelis imposed a curriculum that went with their occupation plan and refused to give the Palestinians an autonomous educational system. Although there is an autonomous educational system in Israel, there is also a pattern for heteronomy imposed on the minority by the majority's institutional structure (that is, the Department for Arab Education), which controls and intervenes in the lives of the Arabs. Due to the continuous conflict in the Middle East, the Israelis thought that giving the Palestinians who lived in their parts autonomy in education would lead to a demand for political autonomy.

Curriculum

The gap is too big between the curriculum used in Palestinian society and what a good curriculum is supposed to be. The curriculum for young children should consider children's knowledge and skills in all of the developmental areas such as physical, social, emotional, and intellectual. Such a curriculum teaches children how to develop strategies for learning as well as developing their self-esteem, sense of competence, and positive feelings toward learning. Children move at their own pace in acquiring important skills in writing, reading, spelling, math, social studies, science, art, music, health, and physical activities (Bredekamp, 1993).

The curriculum used in Palestinian society is far from the one explained above. It is mainly limited to six major subjects including reading, writing, math, science, history, and geography. Art and sport are two subjects that are not emphasized in the curriculum. The older generation, for example, usually denies the value of art in school because they think that people cannot make a living from that. Their emphasis is on the subjects that help children in their daily lives such as Arabic studies, math, reading, and writing. The older generation

sees modern schools in the country as institutions in which time is wasted and students are corrupted due to their alienation from tradition as a result of lack of emphasis on religious studies and the absence of physical punishment. As well, the younger generation of Arab Israelis sees the main function of the school as the development and consolidation of pupils' cultural and national Arab identity. Thus the weak, if any, emphasis on Arab nationality and culture constitutes a denial and deprivation of relevant curricula for Arab students.

Teaching Practices

The curriculum is usually reflected by the teaching strategies used in the schools. With appropriate practices, the curriculum is integrated so that learning occurs primarily through projects, learning centers, and playful activities that reflect the current interests of children. Teachers prepare the environment so children can learn through active involvement with each other, adults, and older children. Teachers encourage children to evaluate their own work and to determine where improvement is needed; errors are viewed as a natural and necessary part of learning. Peer tutoring as well as learning from others through conversation while at work or play occurs on a daily basis. Appropriate teaching emphasizes the use of concrete and real materials and the use of activities which are relevant to children's lives (Bredekamp, 1993).

In contrast, teaching strategies and practices in the existing schools in Palestine are inappropriate. These strategies are traditional and based on teacher-directed activities that take up most of every morning. The teacher every morning starts lecturing for the whole group, emphasizing total class discussion and paper-and-pencil practice exercises or asking pupils to complete worksheets silently and individually at desks. Other activities such as projects, learning centers, play, and other outdoor activities are allowed if time permits or are used as a reward. Teachers spend most of their time correcting worksheets and other in-seat work. Little time is offered on preparing enriching activities. Children in class work individually and they are not allowed to talk; if they do so, they get punished. No one can participate in a playful activity unless all the work is finished.

Class Size

Concerning the average number of students in classes, the size of classroom groups and the ratio of teachers to children should be carefully regulated in order to allow the active involvement of students. This is not the situation at preschools or schools in Palestine. The average number of students in private kindergartens is less than the average in UNRWA kindergartens. In 1993/1994, the average in the rural West Bank ranged from between 26 to 32 pupils for each class; it was 24 to 27 for the Gaza Strip private kindergartens and 31 to 42 for each class in UNRWA kindergartens. In schools, the average number of pupils in classes was the highest in UNRWA schools and lowest in private schools; in government schools it was close to the general average. The general average of pupils in each class in the government schools was 34 students in 1993/1994 (Abu-Libdeh, 1995). Al-Nimer (1993) argues that the number of students in classes in government schools may reach 40 or 45; 30 to 35 in private schools. Only one teacher is only assigned to each class with this large number of students.

Teachers' Issues

Ideally, teachers at schools should work in partnership with parents, communicating regularly to build mutual understanding and greater consistency for children. Decisions that have a major impact on children such as enrollment, retention, assignment to remedial classes, and the like are based primarily on information obtained from observations by teachers and parents, not on the basis of a single test score (Bredekamp, 1993).

In Palestinian society, the teacher-parent relationship follows the traditional way. Parents view teachers as experts and they contact them only when problems or conflicts arise. Decisions con-

cerning retaining a child, placing him or her in a remedial classroom, or entry into any other program are based on psychometric tests.

The qualifications of teachers is another important factor that should be taken into consideration when talking about schooling and the school system. Many teachers in the Palestinian schools have few or no qualifications at all. During the Israeli occupation of the West Bank and Gaza Strip, the Israeli authorities implemented a policy of forcing qualified teachers to leave their work and replaced them with unqualified persons. The Israelis claimed that these teachers were intervening with politics. The real reason was that the Israelis did not want well educated people to fight them back through education.

The availability of science labs at schools is an important indication of the level and teaching standard of science in the schools. In one study (Kamal & Zughby, 1996) it was found that one-third of the schools studied do not have science labs. The situation is much worse in terms of teachers' qualifications to teach science, and science lab shortages in the West Bank and Gaza Strip schools, mainly in the government schools.

Special Education

Integration for school-age children with disabilities into mainstream schools has been given much attention by many nongovernmental organizations, especially before the Palestinian authority took over the education responsibility in the country. Although such integration programs were never implemented during the Israeli control of the educational system, the attitudes of many school directors were positive toward this issue. A recent study by Dukmak (1991) carried out in twenty-seven schools in greater Bethlehem suggests that the majority of school administrators who participated in the study (89 percent) foster positive attitudes toward mainstream education. These schools, which include public, private, and UNRWA schools from different cities, villages, and refugee camps, comprise 85 percent of all schools in greater Bethlehem. Thus, these findings can be generalized with respect to attitudes toward special education provision for special needs students.

An inclusive education program has been adopted by the Palestinian Ministry of Education and will be carried out soon as a pilot project in a few government schools in different regions of the West Bank. Inclusive education program is a program that emphasizes education for school-age children with disabilities together with normal students in mainstream schools. Of course, such a program cannot be implemented without carrying out major modifications to the current educational system in terms of curriculum, classroom size, and teacher training. The Ministry of Education is currently carrying out a training program for thirty teachers to implement this pilot project in a few government schools.

Currently, there is a pilot project serving pupils with low educational achievement in three private schools in the Bethlehem region, implemented by a nongovernmental organization located at Bethlehem, the Bethlehem Arab Society for Rehabilitation (see Dukmak, 1994). Such services have been provided through special classes that have been established in each school. Pupils with learning problems receive specialized individual instruction in certain areas of the curriculum with which they are having difficulties. This program has been adopted by the Palestinian Ministry of Education and will be implemented as a pilot project in the government schools soon. This program, called a "Supportive Education Program," will serve pupils who have mild learning problems in one or more areas of the curriculum and who can be served after schooling hours. Currently, the Ministry of Education is carrying out training for forty teachers to implement this pilot project.

THE FUTURE OF SOCIETY AND SCHOOLING

According to Kamal and Zughby (1996), the major problems in East Jerusalem schools, which can also be considered the major problems for

schools in the West Bank and Gaza Strip, are as follows: shortages of classrooms, halls, labs, and the like; shortages of suitable squares and playgrounds; lack of school hours due to strikes and security checkpoints; neglecting school duties by students; lack of cooperation between parents, teachers, and the administration; lack of teaching facilities and equipment; and low salaries that sometimes are not paid on time.

The following needs have been also identified—rich educational resources such as developed curricula, effective learning materials, libraries, modern scientific labs and the like; suitable school environments such as good buildings and suitable playgrounds; qualified and enthusiastic teachers who are satisfied with their profession and situations; and effective educational leadership such as general supervisory body, good educational guides, and experienced directors.

Joining the above are other strategic problems in education. These may be summarized as:

• *Supervision.* We suffer from the existence of many supervisory bodies over schools in the Palestinian society—that is, the Israeli authorities for twenty-seven years, together with UNRWA and private organizations. These contributed to cutting the body of Palestinian society into parts and preventing it from facing the difficult challenges. With the existence of the Palestinian authority as a result of the peace treaty, the Israeli authorities do not have control of any type over Palestinian schools in the West Bank and Gaza Strip. Jerusalem currently is still under the control of the Israeli authorities and the educational system is greatly affected by the Israeli occupation.

• *Leadership.* There is an absence of high level educational leadership for all the private schools in Palestinian society.

• *Collaboration.* There is a lack of cooperation between schools and the community in general and between schools and parents in particular. This can be due to lack of people's confidence in the existing schools because of the administrative and financial problems that these schools suffer from; a high frustration level that Palestinian society has suffered since before the peace treaty. Jerusalem nowadays still suffers from this frustration as a result of worsening economic, demographic, and security aspects. Too, the poor financial situation makes parents work very hard for long hours with no time remaining to follow up on their children's progress in school.

• *Procedural problems.* As mentioned, there is a weak school infrastructure that may include the lack of classrooms, activity halls, labs, playgrounds, and the like; a lack of qualified school teachers and directors; a lack of support activity in the learning process, including equipment, aids, and material needed for the learning process such as videos, TVs, computers, photocopiers, and the like; a lack of student support services such as health, psychology, social, counseling, and vocational services; and a lack of noncurriculum activities such as cultural, art, and other important activities (Kamal & Zughby, 1996).

Solutions to Palestine's educational problems stretch far wider than just the schools. However, educational solutions—as opposed to political and social ones—include the following:

• To provide enough and ongoing financial support to academic institutions in order to give effective educational services. Financial support is also needed to establish new academic institutions and develop the old ones.

• To strengthen the existing Palestinian educational system that recently took over the educational aspects in the West Bank and Gaza Strip.

• To work on changing the curriculum to a purely Palestinian curriculum that emphasizes modern educational aspects.

•. To create coordination and cooperation among all private schools in the society and among all schools (government, private, and UNRWA schools).

REFERENCES

Abu-Libdeh, H. (1995). *Education statistics in the West Bank and Gaza Strip.* Ramallah, West Bank, Palestine: Palestinian Central Bureau of Statistics, Current Status Report Series (No. 5).

Al-Nimer, K. (1993). *The ordeal of the education in Palestine.* Saudi Arabia: Dar Al-Mujtama' for Publication and Distribution. (Arabic version)

Badran, N.S.A. (1979). *Education and modernization in the Palestinian Arab Society* (2nd ed.). Beirut: Palestine Liberation Organization. (Arabic version)

Bredekamp, S. (1993) (Ed.). *Developmentally appropriate practice in early childhood programs serving children from birth through age 8.* (Expanded Ed.). Tenth printing. Washington, DC: National Association for the Education of Young Children.

Dukmak, S.J. (1991). *Integration in education for school age children with disabilities in the West Bank.* Paper presented at the Second Biennial Conference of the International Association in Special Education, Milwaukee, WI.

Dukmak, S.J. (1994). The West Bank and Gaza Strip. In K. Mazurek & M.A. Winzer (Eds.), *Comparative studies in special education.* Washington, DC: Gallaudet University Press.

Dukmak, S., & Kanawati, R. (1995). Special education provision: Establishing a special class for low achievers in three mainstream schools in Greater Bethlehem area. Project proposal, Bethlehem Arab Society For Rehabilitation, Bethlehem, Palestine.

Kamal, S., & Zughby, S. (1996). *The needs of Jerusalem in the year 2000 in the field of education and teaching.* Jerusalem: Arab Studies Society. (Arabic version)

Mar'i, S.K. (1978). *Arab education in Israel.* Syracuse, NY: Syracuse University Press.

Palestinian Central Bureau of Statistics (1996). *Palestinian Territories—Statistical brief.* Pamphlet: Issue No. 1. Ramallah, West Bank, Palestine: Author.

CHAPTER 20

Transition and Education: A Case Study of the Process of Change in Turkey

FÜSUN AKARSU

Füsun Akarsu received her BA, MA, and Ph.D. from the Hacettepe University in Ankara. She taught at the Middle East Technical University (METU) and the Hacettepe University. She is presently an associate professor of education at the Bosphorus University in Istanbul. She coordinated the foundation activities of a gifted school in Istanbul, and she has also been involved in setting up new schools and centers for MOE, the World Bank, and for private firms and charity foundations.

Turkey is sited between the East and West and has been a bridge between them for centuries. This is true not only geographically, but also historically and culturally—a fact that is important because it sheds light on some of the issues to be discussed in this chapter. The focu of this chapter is the rapid and difficult educational and social transition presently taking place in Turkey.

THE SOCIAL FABRIC

Location and Status

Turkey is a country with a portion of its land (Thrace) in Europe, and a larger part (Anatolia–Asia Minor) in Asia, more specifically in the Middle East. Turkey neighbors several Eastern European countries: Russia, some former Soviet republics, and a few Middle-East lands in what was once a "fertile crescent" of the Mediterranean. Within this space, various climatic zones, cultural patterns, and constantly evolving social and historical realities have been shaping and reshaping societies and civilizations for more than 5000 years. The process continues today.

The modern Republic of Turkey was founded under the leadership of Kemal Atatürk in 1923, after a war of independence that followed the collapse of the Ottoman Empire. The capital of this new Republic was placed in Ankara, a town in the middle of the Anatolia, rather than in Istanbul (or the former Constantinopolis, which had served as a capital of several major empires for centuries). Kemal Atatürk chose a new capital city to reinforce the concept of a new beginning. In the twentieth century, Turkey wanted to be seen as an independent, modern state and an active participant in the development of contemporary Western civilization. It became a member of NATO and the OECD (Organization for Economic Cooperation and Development) and has recently been accepted as a partial member of the European Union.

The population of Turkey is about 60 million. Ninety-five percent of the population is Muslim. However, Turkey is one of the four countries in the region where sharia'h laws, the "laws of God" are not practiced. The state is secular, or as it is commonly called, *laique,* with the civil code being an adapted form of the Swiss model. This situation constitutes a major shift in the history of the Turks, since the Caliphate of the Islamic state was for more than five centuries the system of governance in the Ottoman Empire. The tensions resulting from this historically new and dramatic imposition of a secular state and civil laws upon a culture long shaped by religious customs constitute a dilemma the country is still trying to resolve. In addition to being secular, the state is also described in the Constitution as democratic and egalitarian. This has also resulted in ongoing debates over issues like the role of the government in economic and social life, human rights, freedom of thought and speech, and the role of education in promoting social change.

History

During the Turkish Revolution, which took place in the 1920s, a number of major changes followed the abolition of the Sultanate and the religious leadership of the Caliphate. For one thing, Kemal Atatürk introduced the Latin alphabet as a replacement for Arabic script. With minor adaptations, it became a phonetically efficient alphabet in the sense that each sound in Turkish has a corresponding letter. It proved very suitable for the Turkish language, was easy to learn, and in only a few years the literate population had started using the new Turkish alphabet. The price for this dramatic change, however, was the severing of cultural links with the past that had used an Arabic, Persian, or Ottoman script. The consequence was that new generations had to learn these as foreign languages in order to understand their own history and culture.

Other reforms included Western dress, giving equal rights for women, and a nationwide unification of basic educational structures and practices. A Unification of Education Act, passed by Parliament in 1924, has since become a source of conflict between the pro-Western Atatürk generation and the more conservative and fundamentalist Islamic segment of the population. The current crises Turkey finds itself in, not only in education but also in political, economic, cultural and religious arenas, are centered around this legislation.

For more than four centuries, there were basically only two kinds of schools in the Ottoman Empire. The first was the palace school (*enderun*) and its preparatory schools in three cities. Therein, young pages recruited from all over the Empire were trained to become *janissary* soldiers or high-level government officials like *vezirs* and *pashas*. There were also religious schools (*medreses*) that were attached to mosques and functioned as health, education, and culture centers. Medrese

education was based on the interpretation of the holy book of Islam, the *Kuran,* and the applications of the sharia'h laws. There were also some children's schools (*sibyans*) and some Kuranic courses that were financed by foundations. The aim of the more informally organized and individually taught Kuran courses was to teach the Kuran and to initiate young children in Islamic codes of conduct. Most of these courses took place in small rooms attached to mosques or medreses. Approximately one-quarter of all children had access to the abovementioned type of the programs; the others had no formal training at all.

In the late nineteenth century, when the Empire was in decay and pro-Western "Young Turks" were influential in the political arena, some secular elementary and secondary schools were opened. These were characterized by their greater emphasis on Turkish, mathematics, and the sciences. There were also military schools and a few institutions of higher education that were based on the French model. For almost a century, these secular Western types of schools coexisted with the traditional religious schools. However, this dual education system was ended in 1924 with the above noted Unification of Education Act, which mandated a single-track, five-year, compulsory program controlled by the National Ministry of Education.

Demography

Modern Turkey has witnessed a continuous migration from rural areas to urban areas and from the east to the west of the country over the last decades. Recent data indicate that in the mid-1990s 59 percent of the population lives in cities, compared to 43.9 percent in 1980. This demographic movement, coupled with a high annual birth rate (2.17 percent), has had and is having tremendous consequences on education and on equality of educational opportunity in Turkey.

The literacy rate is 88.8 percent for males and 72 percent for females, with an overall rate of 80.5 percent. The high rate of illiteracy, especially among women, has consequences in the high rate of infant mortality (0.53 percent) and low life expectancy (UNDP, 1996). Turkey also has a young population. The proportion of the population with educational needs (from 5 to 24 years of age) is 42.2 percent. This large segment of the population does not contribute actively to the economy, but does require investments whose returns are not likely to be realized for at least fifteen more years. Furthermore, rapid population growth can be expected as these large numbers of children enter young adulthood.

The educational profile of the workforce presents another important aspect of the situation. According to the 1990 census, only 5.2 percent of the active workforce had higher education; 9.7 percent were graduates of high schools or their equivalent, and 7 percent had graduated from middle schools. The rest, 79.1 percent, had only a five-year elementary school education or received no schooling at all.

When the workforce is analyzed in terms of levels of education and sectors of employment, it is revealed that 90 percent of the workers in agriculture are illiterates, whereas 87 percent of the graduates of higher education work in the services sector. The average years of completed education were 3.3 in agriculture, 6.2 in industry, and 7.6 in the service industries. The 1990 census also indicates that 43.8 percent of the population is economically active. The ratio is 56.2 percent for males and 31.1 percent for females.

The overall picture emerging from these statistics is of a country in which the majority of people work in agriculture, where the level of education is low, and the educational needs of both the working populations and their children are immense. Low economic productivity and efficiency in all sectors, inadequate utilization of technology, and limited ability to compete in a free global market underline the urgent need to improve educational services both quantitatively and qualitatively for all segments of the society.

Economy

However, in spite of the above concerns, the Turkish economy is not insignificant when measured on an international scale. In spite of some occasional contractions, the Turkish economy has been one of the most dynamic anywhere. While the GNP per capita is still only around US$2,600, the growth rate in recent years is almost 8 percent, which compares favorably with a world average of 5.6 percent. This is a result of Turkey's economy not being dependent upon a single commodity and the existence of thousands of small firms functioning in a broad range of economic areas. A young population, which in general has an entrepreneurial spirit, heralds a promising future. But there are some serious obstacles, both internal and external, to be faced.

The first of three major internal difficulties is a widespread misconception in the nation about the nature of capitalism. Capitalism's long-term focus on increased production and improvement of product quality (thereby ultimately generating more profit) is often disregarded. Instead, various levels of government take an oversimplified, short-term attitude to the manner in which capitalism generates wealth and revert to populist approaches in their policies, such as the redirection of scarce resources away from skilled businessmen into politically popular programs aimed at potential voters and the placation of powerful interest groups.

A second obstacle is a lack of proper record keeping, filing, and organizing of information for the improvement of business. The lack of reliable statistics and information relevant for business frustrates able young businessmen because it hampers their ability to make decisions based on sound data. There also exists a large underground, unrecorded economy that has consequences ranging from the government's being deprived of revenues to the facilitation of illegal fund transfers to criminal terrorist groups.

A third difficulty is the ineffectiveness of the educational system in training properly qualified manpower. Rather than giving priority to teaching practical skills in vocational and technical training, education at the secondary and higher levels focuses on academic, theoretical, and scholastic programs. The result is the graduation of millions of young graduates who are unable to perform in the practical areas required by business.

The above internal difficulties are compounded by external problems. Various powerful states in the world have different expectations of, and visions for, Turkey. Those that are geographically and historically distant, like the United States, Canada, and Japan, do not see Turkey's economic development as a threat to their interests. However, many European countries do not wish to see a fast-growing rival economy developing in the region. Also, there are countries that had been under Turkish rule or dominance for centuries and so have historical reasons for not wanting to help Turkey increase its share of the world market or its influence in international relations.

If Turkey can manage to resolve, or at least control, its internal problems, an improvement in education can be facilitated. Otherwise, Turkey will have to live with these internal and external difficulties for a long time.

Politics

Following its foundation in 1923, and in the years up to 1950 when its first free political election was held, the young Republic of Turkey was run by a single party on the principles of republicanism, populism, secularism (*laicism*), nationalism, and revolutionism. During that period, Turkey also avoided entering the Second World War, which dramatically reshaped the map and the relationships of the world.

However, in 1950 a shift in political power took place to a more conservative and anti-republican party. The government initiated a series of changes, the result of which was an internal political power struggle that still dominates the political scene. In 1960, 1972, and 1980 the military intervened, claiming that the country was being diverted from the basic foundation principles and Atatürk reforms. The last two coup d'etats were intended to crush the left-wing parties and illegal organizations at times when the struggles between socialist/communist and extreme nationalistic fronts were bringing the country to

civil war. Although no significant leftist influence has been observed since 1980, the turmoil taking place now seems to be between the secular pro-Western majority and the Islamic fundamentalist segments. The latter wish to restore the old traditions of sharia'h law and Islamic order.

The most recent elections in 1996 brought to power a coalition of a pro-Islamic party with one of the more liberal conservative parties. Since then, the Constitution of the Republic has been safeguarded by a military-dominated Security Council. The Security Council has recently demanded that the present government extend compulsory education to eight years and preserve the integrity of the principles enshrined the 1924 Unification of Education Act.

SCHOOLING

Educational Philosophies

Since the foundation of the Turkish Republic, the major aim of education has been to transform society from its traditional and conservative religious outlook to that of a contemporary modern state that is a part of Western civilization. Education was clearly defined as the key agent in implementing the Turkish cultural revolution by the leader of the Reform. After the War of Independence, Atatürk compared teachers to soldiers in a cultural war against ignorance and conservatism, and he gave the responsibility for carrying out these reforms to the youth of the country.

In consequence, at all levels of schooling the first aim of education is "training children to become good citizens and helping to develop their country along the lines of Atatürk's principles and reforms." In the 1990s, this first aim has been rephrased as "training children to become good citizens by providing them with basic knowledge, skills, behaviors, and habits in line with national ethics and morals" (MOE, 1997, p. 8). The second aim is to help children develop according to their abilities and interests and to prepare them for a higher level of education (MOE, 1995). This dual purpose—that is, the training of young minds to serve their nation, and its traditions, mores, and morals (religion), and at the same time to help them become individuals by developing their own abilities and interests—encapsulates the dilemma that the country has been trying to resolve for the last seventy years.

Structure

The Turkish educational system is divided into two main sections: formal and nonformal. Formal education includes preschool, primary, secondary, and higher education. Preschools are still optional and can either be independent public or private schools or annexed to a primary school. Only 7.3 percent of eligible children attend preschool (MOE, 1995).

According to the Turkish Republic's constitution, elementary education is compulsory for the first five years and is free of charge in public schools. It is seen as a constitutional right of citizens. This five-year primary and compulsory education period is soon to be extended to eight years by joining it with the following three years of middle school training. Secondary education encompasses general, vocational, and technical educational institutions. After three years of middle school, which presently are a part of secondary education, students have three options. They can enter general university preparatory lycées, technical lycées that prepare students for various skilled professions with a four-year program, or three-year vocational lycées that prepare them for the work world. The graduates of all these lycées may take the university entrance examinations and continue their higher education if successful.

Tertiary education includes all higher education institutions that offer two or more years of training. Since 1981, all higher education institutions—universities, institutes, colleges, and prelicense programs—function under a higher education law (Law No. 2547) and are coordinated and controlled by a board called the Higher Education Council. In state universities, education is free of charge, and scholarships are provided to the needy. There are now seven private universities, five of

which were opened in 1996. Students pay fees to enter there, whereas tuition is more or less free in the forty-three public universities scattered around the country. Some of the best and most crowded (20,000 to 40,000 students) universities are in the three major cities: Istanbul, Ankara, and Izmir. There are a number of small and underqualified universities in Anatolia, all of which have been opened in the last ten years. There is also an open university that provides various courses and programs through correspondence and in which 14.2 percent of the total student population is enrolled. The overall quality of education is quite low.

Nonformal education includes literary courses; vocational and technical programs for youth as well as for adults; and programs for apprentices, assistant artisans, and masters.

Governance

All educational activities in the country, private or public, are under the supervision of the Ministry of Education (MOE). It is the second largest such institution (after the Japanese) in the world with 14 million students and half a million teachers under a central authority. The structure of the MOE, with its monopoly of educational matters, is highly centralized and hierarchical.

The Ministry consists of two major parts—the central administrative section in Ankara and the provincial branches. The latter are basically responsible for implementing instructions given by the center and supervising all rules and regulations related to schooling. Local governments, civil municipalities, and other regional organizations have no influence on curricula, teaching-learning activities, evaluation, or the allocation of resources or opportunities. Until 1996 even the appointment of each individual teacher was made by a central authority in Ankara.

The MOE is run by a minister who is a member of the cabinet and therefore a politician. The minister is assisted by an undersecretary and several deputy undersecretaries. This is the top level of educational management and decisions made here may well account for some of the achievements and failures of the system. Another body, the Higher Council of Education and Training, is in theory responsible for all the pedagogical aspects of the system; that is, curricula, textbooks, evaluation, weekly and yearly schedules, rules and regulations regarding vertical mobility, transfers, and equivalences, and the introduction of changes and innovations into the system. However, since this board is subordinate to the minister, and members are appointed by the minister, the real power lies with the minister.

There are sixteen general directorates responsible for various aspects of education, ranging from primary education to tourism and commercial education. Each has a separate director, budget, location, and area of activity; there is seldom any cooperation or coordination between these directorates. There are also advisory and supervisory units, as well as support units like in-service training, investment and installation, and research and development, all within the central MOE organization. A Higher Council of Education, an advisory group that represents the nation at large and meets every few years, may have opinions and suggestions to offer, but the MOE is free to implement or reject them.

Financing

Public education is almost entirely financed by the MOE. All levels of education, including higher education, are basically free in public schools and universities. In the public universities, students may be asked to pay some fees, but these are small. Scholarships are available for those who need them. The result is that only 1.4 percent of primary and secondary school students attend private schools. The total contribution of the private sector, foundations, charity organizations, and donors in 1993 was only 5.4 percent of the MOE budget. The MOE budget for 1996 was US$240 million. The MOE's share of the nation's consolidated budget of 1997 is 12.14 percent; its share of the GNP is 2.01 percent for the same year. The share of the higher education budget in GNP

terms was 0.77 percent for 1997 (MOE, 1997). The share of the higher education budget in the consolidated budget for 1995 was 9.9 percent (MOE, 1995).

Curricular and Pedagogic Practices

Turkey has been implementing a rigid and uniform national curriculum at all levels of education. However, the implementation has not been wholly successful. In secondary schools, in spite of the uniformity imposed by the national curriculum, there are over 100 different programs being carried out in schools. Differentiation between these programs takes the form of some courses being taught in foreign languages, some schools serving as private institutions, some schools accepting students on a more selective basis (like certain select Anatolian lycées and super lycées), and some schools electing to provide a vocational-technical rather than academic focus. Further differentiations take place within the category of technical schools where many programs are designed to bypass the rigidity of the uniform curriculum.

Thus, in practice the national curriculum is often regarded as a hindrance to better learning, development, and progress, rather than an instrument facilitating learning and a means of offering equality of educational opportunity. Because the national curriculum is unable to accommodate more than one program in a school, and because it cannot accommodate differentiating courses and experiences prepared according to the needs and interests of learners, its implementation has become ineffective and inefficient.

In terms of pedagogical practices, everyday reality in the classroom is basically a knowledge-level acquisition of facts. Teachers lecture; students are passive listeners in crowded classrooms. There is little learning taking place in forums such as laboratories, workshops, libraries, and other practical areas. The student-teacher ratio is 30.5:1 in primary schools, 49.7:1 in secondary schools, and 45:1 in universities. In city schools, where the average number of students may exceed 60 to 65 per class and practical areas are rare, it is difficult to apply any teaching methods other than lecturing. There are only a few equipped and qualified schools in the country for the practice of activity-based pedagogy.

Grading System and Examinations

The grading system measuring student achievement was on a 5-point scale in the elementary schools and a 10-point scale at secondary schools until 1995. Students whose total points for written and oral examinations were below 3 or 5 points respectively had to repeat the entire year. Changing pedagogical ideas in line with a more child-centered developmental approach and cognizance of the costs of retention have resulted in the abandonment of this approach. Today, regardless of their levels of achievement, students will not be asked to repeat a year until the end of the eleventh grade. Student performance is basically measured by written, essay-type examinations, multiple-choice tests, oral examinations, and sometimes by homework or project reports.

There are entrance examinations for students who wish to continue their education at the most prestigious public or private secondary schools. Such students have to take an external, competitive, entrance examination at the age of 11 or 12, while still in the fifth grade. Every year several thousand school children take these centrally prepared and proctored examinations, and only a few hundred win admission to the schools of their choice.

The major event in the life of every secondary school graduate is the University Entrance Examinations prepared by a special testing center. In 1996, 1.4 million youngsters took the two-tier examinations, and only one out of ten was placed in one of twenty-four academic options. Those who are unsuccessful either try it again, often more than once, or stop their education at this point; 12.5 percent of the potentially eligible population is enrolled in formal higher educational institutions.

Complicated formulas are used in ranking the scores students attain in these examinations. Factors such as grade point average, the lycée attended, the type of program followed, and so on, are taken into consideration. The perceived objectivity and relative fairness of the system has led to its remaining in use for more than thirty years.

Teacher Training

One of the unique features of the early Republic's educational vision for the country was the opening of "village institutes" for the training of elementary school teachers. Starting in the 1930s and supported by a group of progressive educators in the MOE, these institutes were built and managed in cooperation with selected bright village children, with teachers, and with the villagers living nearby. A practical hands-on approach, collective management of the schools, and local participation in the educational decision-making process made these schools different.

However, conservative segments of society caused the MOE to close these schools in the 1950s. Later, higher training institutes, or faculties of education, became the schools for preparing teachers. Presently, all teachers must be university graduates, preferably of faculties of education, but may obtain a teaching certificate if they are graduates of some other four-year programs.

SOCIAL AND EDUCATIONAL ISSUES

Declared a primary agent of change at the beginning of the Republican era, education in Turkey seems to have failed in its mission. There are significant developments, measured in the sheer number of students, teachers, and schools (in line with the demographic and economic growth taking place in the last seventy years) in the country. However, the failure to accommodate significant social change and to move markedly in the direction of reaching the levels of western societies generally is apparent in both quantitative and qualitative terms. The major element of this failure can be analyzed in terms of the historical, social, and economic factors influencing the society and its educational endeavors.

In Search of Identity

Having roots that go back hundreds of years, with the founding of an empire and the governing of a multiplicity of diverse ethnic groups, cultures, and religions, modern Turkey faces serious problems in trying to transform itself into a modern nation state. Consensus on fundamental issues is lacking. Turkey's cultural heritage—including some basic assumptions about life, human beings, and the nature of learning, as well as some underlying values guiding individuals' relationships with their environment, with themselves, and with others— needs to be changed and reshaped in the light of modern realities.

For example, the idea of democracy, which is one of the leading concepts in nationwide usage, has been understood, actualized, and idealized from the widest possible range of differing viewpoints. On the one hand, Turkey has a constitution based on democratic principles, free elections are taking place, governments are being formed and run according to the rule of law, free market economic conditions are gradually emerging, and so on. On the other hand, three military interventions have taken place, an undeclared war between the military and an ethnic militant group continues to take place within the boundaries of the country, and international pressure groups are forcing the issue of human rights in the land. All these are indicators of some painful aspects of the process of democratization.

The dilemma between the past and the future, between East and West, between traditional values and rapidly changing living conditions and the demands of a competitive industrial world are making it difficult for Turks to develop a national identity. A movement calling for a Turkish-Islamic synthesis is trying to bridge the gap by bringing together stronger nationalistic feelings with a less radical interpretation of Islam. Fundamentalist Muslim groups are trying to restore sharia'h law

and form an Islamic Republic that will find its place not in the West but among the other Middle-Eastern Islamic nations. The once-strong political left and the socialists have lost power and influence after recent military interventions. Some liberal and moderately conservative groups, advocating a free economy and integration with global markets, have become prominent but have been weakened by disorganization and corruption.

The result is an ambiguity of identity and an unclear focus regarding the future of the country. Not unexpectedly, this is reflected in the educational system's lack of coherent aims and goals. A recent publication of the MOE, *Our Goals in National Education* (MOE, 1997) has tried to pave the way for a broader consensus to determine the educational direction the system needs to take. But the history of education has seen a series of sharp and contrasting turns between forms of progressive education and conservative orientations.

Religion, Politics, and Education

One major arena of social change and controversy is that of religion. One the one hand, it is clear from a recent study (Esmer, 1997) that religion is becoming a more significant factor in Turkish life. The percentage of people who said that religion is important has increased from 63 percent in 1991 to 83 percent in 1997. In the context of education, the issue of religious schools almost brought the country to the edge of another military intervention recently. Designed basically as vocational secondary schools preparing religious teachers, religious schools have been increasing in number and their graduates have begun taking critical positions in the public sector. This has contributed to a power struggle between secular republicans and fundamentalist Islamists.

Religious schools fall within the category of vocational-technical schools. More than one-quarter of all middle school students in Turkey now attend religious vocational schools. At the lycée level, the ratio is 8.7 percent. These religious *imam hatip* schools also have separate schools for girls, even though they may not practice their vocation according to Islamic tradition. The country may not need and certainly cannot employ so many religious professionals. The unstated aim is to bypass the Unification of Education Act and return to a dual track pattern dividing basic education into religious and secular components.

Coping with Numbers

The population of Turkey has increased tenfold in sixty years. The sheer number of school-age children is more than the populations of several European countries put together—about 20 million, although all are not in school. The resources and the efforts of the MOE have not yet been able to include all school-age children, despite the legal obligation to do so.

The sudden and massive migrations from rural areas to urban districts, from east to west, and from less developed regions to more industrialized areas have made it even more difficult for the MOE to plan its educational facilities. Some village schools have been closed because there are no students left; in others more than 80 to 100 students have to be trained in integrated classrooms, with three or five grade levels sharing one room and a single teacher. Most of the public schools in big cities now have double shifts or even triple shifts, with an average of 60 to 65 students in each classroom.

Financial Difficulties

Turkey is one of the few countries that allocate a minimum of its financial resources to education. The leaders of the country do not give priority to education; being a long-term investment with delayed returns, education has not attracted the "get rich quick" politicians in the government who are instrumental in determining and implementing policies. The general populace does not feel particularly responsible for the development and training of young people, either. The general social expectation is that education-related policies, decisions, and activities, as well as financing, should all be the responsibility of the government. Only recently have a few foundations in the private sector started investing in education by opening schools and providing scholarships and accommodation to students. Nongovernmental organizations, local organizations, and municipalities do not take part in educational activities.

Furthermore, only 1.4 percent of elementary and secondary schools are private (MOE, 1995). Unwilling to earn less income in the short term and lacking incentive to invest in long-term outcomes, private school owners have failed to contribute to any improvement in education. Parents seeking better opportunities for their children consequently have no choice but to send them abroad to Western countries or to take the great risk of competing for places in a few foreign schools that admit only the very "cream of the cream" by means of external entrance examinations.

There is no proper research showing the actual costs of inefficiency in the educational system. However, inferences can be made. For example, according to a study conducted for the United Nations Development Program (UNDP), the total amount of money spent by parents to compensate for the low quality of education in secondary schools and to prepare their children for the university entrance examinations is almost equal to the total amount spent by the MOE for the same level of schooling (Akarsu, 1990). However, rather than forming pressure groups to force the MOE to improve its standards and to become more accountable, parents have preferred to find individual solutions and avoid further damage to their children by an ineffective and inefficient system.

Educational Policies and the Polarization of Education

Rather than extending elementary education, and thereby assisting children during the critical years of early development, Turkey has chosen to give priority to an elitist and academic secondary education program. Neglecting considerable segments of the population by not helping them become literate, and failing to provide vocational-technical training for the intermediate manpower demands of industry, Turkey has so far failed to use education and training as a means for development. Table 20.1 indicates the lack of trained human resources; an issue that is becoming increasingly critical for the survival of the economy in a competitive world market.

The relationship between economic development and the quality of education being reciprocal, the financing, organization, and diversification of education and training suffers equally from shortcomings in policy decisions. An economy based on the transfer of technology, on a low level of production for a domestic market, and on a deficiency in trade balances between imports and exports finds its reflection in an undifferentiated and scholastic education.

Politicization

The politicization of a MOE holding a monopoly in education is inevitable, as long as the Minister is a politician representing the governing party. Priority will be given to party programs over long-term educational policies. Furthermore, pressure will always be exerted by voters for favors, such as appointing new recruits from the ranks of party faithfuls or giving preferential treatment to some teachers in requests for transfers to new schools. The average tenure of a minister in the MOE is 1.5 years. With each change, the undersecretaries and the top-level bureaucrats also change; few people stay in their positions long enough to see the effects of changes they have initiated.

The Structure and Process of Education

In addition to the pressures exerted on education from the social milieu in which the schooling system must operate, there are also a number of problems inherent in the system itself. Some of these may be summarized as follows:

Centralization.   The highly structured organization of education leads to decisions being made at the top and imposed upon the participating groups below. This top-down nature of most major changes and reform attempts is one of the main causes for their rejection by different groups with widely different needs and expectations. Uniform and rigid curricula (even at the university level), centrally prepared and proctored external examinations, no suitable mechanisms of feedback for refining the workings of the system, and defining equality of educational opportunity as the provision of the same pedagogy, content, evaluation, and so on (without regard for individual differences and local needs) are some problems arising from this centralized structure.

Organization and Administration.   A lack of organizational and administrative skills on the part of local authorities and school principals is also a consequence of centralization. Almost all school-level decisions regarding planning, budgeting, appointment of teachers, in-service training, weekly and yearly schedules, and so on, are made by the central MOE directorates. Functioning as implementation agencies of these higher authorities, local school administrators do not feel responsible for the decisions made or accountable to parents or students in their local communities.

Split Reality Syndrome.   Considering the large number of students and schools in Turkey, its different climates and cultures, and the widely varying learning needs and interests of its population, this formal and imposed chain of command has generated its own resistance. Informal local realities exert their own practical influence, impeding the implementation of central directives. This schizoid structure, where lip service is paid to central directives as they are being adapted, undermined, or even ignored at the local level, has

TABLE 20.1 Educational Profile of Population (6 years of age and above)

Illiterate	19.5 percent
Primary schooling	46.1 percent
Middle schooling	7.6 percent
Lycées	7.8 percent
Higher education	3.0 percent

Source: SPO (1996), p. 20.

become one of the major dysfunctional aspects of national education.

Teacher Training.   One of the best indicators of the value attached to education is the regard in which teachers are held in a society. On this measure, teachers in Turkey have lost much of their prestige and relatively respectable salaries in the last thirty years. Faculties of education rank among the least preferred by those who take university entrance examinations. The average annual wage of a beginning teacher is currently about US$3,700.

Teacher training models are also changed frequently, another of the shortcomings of the overall system wherein need analyses are not undertaken and rationales for changes are not carefully thought through. There is no pilot implementation, there is no collection of information for feedback, and therefore, no revisions to refine the system. Usually, before a complete implementation of a new teacher training model has been achieved and its effects assessed, a new model is introduced from the top down.

In-service training programs suffer from the same causes. The actual needs of teachers are seldom met by formal programs planned by the directorate of in-service training for teachers. Teachers cannot influence the situation because they are government employees and therefore are not legally allowed to form syndicates or professional organizations. A lack of legal and academic support from colleagues, an absence of obligation and accountability, and no responsibility for professional malpractices, leaves little room for the work ethic to flourish.

Learning by Rote, Not by Doing.   The most crucial aspect of education, the interaction between the learner and his or her environment, is not in great evidence in the Turkish system. The limited space and time provided for students and the lack of facilities such as libraries, laboratories, sports complexes, art studios, workshops, and practice areas makes participatory schooling difficult. A cultural tradition of preaching, lecturing, and telling, and an underlying belief in conveyed truth, also support a scholastic theoretical education and undermine pragmatic and progressive dimensions.

Learning a Foreign Language or Learning in a Foreign Language.   When the young Turkish Republic was establishing itself, a number of agreements with the French, Italian, German, British, and Americans were reached to allow their schools to continue. There were seventeen such schools, in addition to another forty-one minority schools where Armenian, Greek, and Jewish students were educated in their own languages and cultures.

Some of these foreign schools, especially the ones located in Istanbul and Izmir, have become the best secondary schools in the country. The medium of instruction in math and science courses, in some electives, and in extracurricular activities, is English, French, German, or Italian. Graduates speak these foreign languages fluently and are exposed to a Western culture that later makes them more eligible for top jobs in both the domestic and international marketplace.

Some Anatolian lycées exist as selective public schools and are modeled on the foreign schools, with a second language being the medium of instruction. In the past few years, there has been discussion on whether teaching students in a language other than their own is correct politically or pedagogically. It has also become difficult to find qualified teachers who can adequately teach in a second language. As a result, all instruction in these Anatolian lycées will henceforth be carried out in Turkish. The foreign schools, however, and many of the private schools modeled after them, will continue their current practices. The dominant language in such schools is English, which is also the medium of instruction in two of the most prestigious universities, one in Ankara, The Middle East Technical University (METU) and the other in Istanbul, The Bosphorus University.

The decision to abolish the teaching in English in Anatolian lycées, as well as an earlier decision to make learning a foreign language no longer compulsory, have been taken by the MOE under the influence of political pressure groups without consulting teachers, parents, or job market representatives. Such decisions become effective the day they are published in the formal newsletter of the MOE, and thus become law.

Schools, like all institutions in Turkey, embody the above contradictions and dilemmas because opposing forces are at work in Turkey. One major social thrust is for integration with the world; the other movement is a search for identity nurtured from the roots of historical past glory and religious unity.

THE FUTURE OF SOCIETY AND SCHOOLING

Turkey is a rapidly changing country, and it is very difficult to make predictions with confidence about the near future. Not only do the internal dynamics of the country play a role, but international factors and forces also constitute significant influences. Some of the major current and evolving changes in society and schooling revolve around the following.

Secular or Religious Schooling?

There are certain expectations about the future that are commonly agreed upon—primary schooling should be universal and at least eight years, plus one year of preschooling, in duration. The disagreement is in how this goal should be implemented. In terms of structure, 1+8 years, 1+5+3, and 1+5+3+1 are models being discussed. However, the key question is not a structural one; it is one centered on content. The issue is whether to start religious education as early as possible, or to postpone it as long as possible? This has resulted in a heated, polarized debate in the country; the debate is the issue on which the shape of the government will be determined in the near future. Currently, this is the major political, social, and pedagogical issue in Turkey.

Improving the Quality of Education

Academicians at all levels of schooling, the MOE, nongovernmental organizations, parents, and rep-

resentatives of the private sector are all demanding immediate improvements in the educational process. Developments in pedagogical practices will influence these efforts and will lead to more funds being freed for education and training. There is already a significant trend in the form of ambitious private schools being established by leading industrial companies and foundations. The government is prepared to support these private educational experiments; the seventh Five-Year Plan calls for government incentives to be provided to entrepreneurs investing in education. The result may well be that the MOE monopoly may give way to more privatization of educational services.

It is also possible that an increase in the length of primary education may eliminate the need for secondary school entrance examinations at the age of 12. The private courses and preparatory institutions that currently exist especially for the sole purpose of preparing students for these examinations might then divert their activities to improving and enriching the learning environment for more practical skills.

The uniformity and rigidity so obviously seen in the curricula today will have to be changed in the direction of common core courses enriched by more electives. This will lead to differentiated and diversified learning. A broad-based demand for greater adaptability to change will be reflected in more flexible programs and schedules; this will happen sooner rather than later.

Education and Work

Information technology will continue to impose its modes of producing and using information, forcing the rapid development of related skills. This will be complemented by an increasing importance of the idea of life-long learning, which has so far been an alien concept in Turkey.

Any improvements in education, whether qualitative or quantitative, will result in greater economic productivity, better quality goods and services, and improvement in the overall efficiency of the economic system. The influence of all this on the larger social system, however, can only take place through improving the overall quality of human resources. A growing public awareness of the critical importance of education in all aspects of life has already started to push educational issues to the top of the national agenda. This trend will continue and, if channeled properly, will soon begin to change all aspects of the country.

Modern Turkey's failure to employ education as the major agent in promoting social change may yet be reversed. The urgent necessity is to try again, but this time learning from the lessons of the recent past. In the coming millennium, learning and living will be one and the same; there is little time left for Turkey to make this happen.

REFERENCES

Akarsu, F. (1990). Report on Turkish education. Unpublished report prepared for the UNDP, Ankara.

Esmer, Y. (1997). Toplumsal Deðerlerimiz. Unpublished research paper. Ankara.

Ministry of Education (MOE). (1995). *Grand National Assembly: 1995 Budget Report*. Ankara: Author.

Ministry of Education (MOE). (1997). *Grand National Assembly: 1997 Budget Report*. Ankara: Author.

United Nations Development Project (UNDP). (1996). *Human Development Report*. Ankara: Author.

CHAPTER 21

Education Systems in an Ideological State: Major Issues and Concerns in Pakistan

MAH NAZIR RIAZ

Mah Nazir Riaz is Professor and Chairperson of the Department of Psychology, University of Peshawar, NWFP, Pakistan. Active in numerous academic and professional organizations, her scholarly, teaching, and service contributions have been recognized through awards and distinctions such as the Star Woman International Award.

THE SOCIAL FABRIC

Pakistan emerged on the world map on August 14, 1947, as a result of the partition of the subcontinent of India. Its creation was the culmination of the struggle by Muslims of the South Asian subcontinent for a separate homeland. The areas that comprised Pakistan initially constituted East Pakistan and West Pakistan, separated from each other by 1600 km of Indian territory. In 1971 East Pakistan separated and formed the independent country of Bangladesh.

Demographic Profile

Pakistan has a population of more than 119 million people; 97 percent are Muslims. The national language is Urdu, the historical language of South Asian Muslims, which is widely understood throughout the country. Some other local languages are sanctioned as a medium of instruction in primary schools. English is the official language of the federal government and the medium of instruction in universities and colleges. English-medium schools also have a network throughout the country.

The society is agriculturally based; around 70 percent of the population lives in rural areas. The economic pattern and standards of living in the rural areas are markedly different from the cities. Villages are highly underdeveloped. Most villages are without electricity, telephone, clean drinking water, proper sanitation, and even a proper link of roads to the cities. In a predominantly agricultural society like Pakistan, ownership of the land is a key issue in development. Despite the government's efforts to introduce land reforms in the country from time to time, landlords, tribal chiefs, and feudal and religious figures still control much of the law and many cultivators are merely sharecroppers.

Pakistani society is inegalitarian in numerous ways, with income and assets unevenly distributed between different areas, sectors, and classes. A small minority enjoys immense wealth while the great majority lives in poverty. This income distribution is directly related to education. Those who have most of the wealth are a small minority and place little demand on the education system. Those who are in need of education services have very little wealth. Education, more than any other area of public policy, is an exercise in income redistribution. But the use of education facilities is inversely related to income. Children of upper-income families are overrepresented among college graduates as compared to lower-income families.

Economic Structure

Raw and processed agricultural products (especially cotton, cotton products, and rice) form the major exports of the country. Carpets and sports goods are also exported. Labor migration to the Middle East since the late 1970s has also been an important source of foreign earnings. The Pakistani economy is dominated by the service sector, which constitutes about half of GDP; agriculture contributes about a quarter, and manufacturing about a fifth. The Pakistani economy had, for a long time, been growing faster than those of its South Asian neighbors including Bangladesh, Sri Lanka, and India. However, the country now has a heavy burden of debt servicing and is vulnerable to serious consequences unless some revolutionary economic reforms are implemented.

Political System

Under the 1973 Constitution of Pakistan, direct elections for 207 ordinary seats and 10 religious minority seats in the National Assembly must be held every five years. The Senate (upper house) consists of 87 indirectly elected members. The National Assembly and the Senate participate in the legislative process of the country. Both houses jointly elect a President as head of the State and the leader of the National Assembly becomes Prime Minister and forms a cabinet. In February, 1997, the Pakistan Muslim League won a general election with a large majority and its leader, Mian Muhammad Nawaz Sharif, became Prime Minister for the second time.

Each of the four provinces has a directly elected Provincial Assembly with a Chief Minister and Provincial Government under the overall authority of a Governor appointed by the President of Pakistan. Provincial governments are responsible for the social development of the provinces, especially education, health, agriculture, water supply, and sanitation.

The Family as a Socioeconomic Unit

The traditional family in Pakistan is an extended family. Most households consist of kinship groups of two or more generations. Children are brought up in families where parents, grandparents, uncles and aunts, and their respective families are also living and sharing the physical as well as the economic resources of the family.

The traditional family adheres to the norms of society, emphasizing sex role differentiation. Women are considered as homemakers, whereas men are the breadwinners and represent the family to the outside world. Children are socialized according to gender from a very early age, with girls helping their mothers, staying at home, and being taught to be submissive. Boys are allowed to play more, to roam freely, and to display self-confidence and aggression. However, despite this division of labor, women play a major role in the economic life of the family. In rural areas, women often work longer hours than men in rearing livestock and in almost all farm activities other than plowing and irrigation. Most urban women contribute toward family income by seeking employment or by pursuing self-employment projects.

However, whether women are homemakers or professionals, the authority of men over women, and elders over youngers, is strongly displayed in the traditional family. The eldest man in the family makes decisions in all important family matters, including marriage.

Urbanization, industrialization, western-style education, and the mass media have all had their effects on the traditional family system. Migration is scattering families. A large proportion of households, especially in towns, are composed of nuclear families, that is, a married couple and children only. Education for girls is becoming more popular and an increasing number of occupations are gradually being considered possible for women.

SCHOOLING

Education is a process involving three references: the individual, the society, and the whole content of curricula, both material and spiritual. Although a large number of Eastern and Western educators agree that education is a continuous process necessary for the full and balanced development of individuals, the interpretations of secularists,

Marxists, and religious thinkers vary. It is this variation that is creating conflicts in the modern world.

When the Muslim world started modernizing itself, it was invaded by "liberal" and "Marxist" concepts. From the doctrinal point of view, it has been easier for Muslims to resist Marxist concepts because they are totally different from our philosophy of education. But it has been really difficult to resist Western "liberalism" because all branches of knowledge have been seriously affected by it and Muslim scholars had not formulated Islamic concepts as substitutes for liberal concepts. The critics of "liberal education" believe that it has created a bewildering variety of ideas and thoughts, but does not guarantee in any way the survival of past values.

Islamic Philosophy of Education

Education should aim at the balanced growth of personality through training of spirit, intellect, the rational self, feelings, and bodily senses. Education must aim at growth in all aspects; that is, spiritual, intellectual, imaginative, physical, scientific, and linguistic. Both individually and collectively it must motivate all these aspects toward goodness and the attainment of perfection. Hence, Islamic philosophy embodies a value system that applies to all spheres of human life.

Islamic education aims at training pupils in such a manner that in their attitudes to life, their actions, decisions, and approaches to all kinds of knowledge they are governed by the spiritual and ethical values of Islam. A student who receives an Islamic education grows up peace loving, harmonious, equable, and righteous, with faith and trust in God. He or she believes that all human beings are gifted with inestimable power to control and govern the universe under the authority of God. Their lives will extend beyond this world, and they will be rewarded or punished for all their deeds and actions on the Day of Judgment.

Modern Western education places an exaggerated emphasis upon reason and rationality and encourages scientific inquiry at the expense of

faith. Muslim educators unanimously agree that the purpose of education is not to cram pupils' minds with facts but to prepare them for a life of purity and sincerity. This total commitment to character building based on the ideals of Islamic ethics is the highest goal of Islamic education.

The sources of knowledge, according to Islamic concepts, fall into two categories. First is divine revelation where Allah teaches that human beings cannot, by themselves, be rightfully guided to the Divine truth and that life cannot be regulated in the proper manner in the absence of stable and unchangeable injunctions inspired by Allah, the Wise and the All-knowing, whose knowledge encompasses all. Second, the human intellect and its tools are in constant interaction with the physical universe on the level of observation, contemplation, experimentation, and application. People are free to do as they please, subject to the condition that they remain fully committed to the Quran and the Sunnah.

Western educators have a different view, and this has invaded the Muslim world. Our academically outstanding intellectuals now prefer being educated in the West. Those who pursue higher education abroad constantly get brainwashed during their stay in the Western countries. After spending a few years there, they return to their own country filled with ideas in conflict with their traditional assumptions. Secular education and secular thinking generated by a modern scientific approach have made people empirical in attitude and doubtful about the need to think in terms of religion. Religious education in schools does not provide a deterrent, because all other books are pervaded by secularist ideas emphasizing material progress.

Efforts directed towards achievement of economic modernization through industrialization are gradually transforming our traditional agrarian society into a modern, intellectual, technological society. In our traditional education system, knowledge and virtue go hand in hand. Students acquire worldly knowledge while being faithful to their religion. Muslim scholars and scientists believed that by acquiring knowledge about the phenomenal world they were only strengthening their belief in the greatness and power of the Creator. Western scientific assumptions and sociological analyses of life are directly contradictory to our traditional religious assumptions. Consequently, "hypocrisy" has become a public style and anxiety is increasing.

Though religious education is compulsory in our schools, there has been no serious attempt to teach literature, fine arts, social sciences, and natural sciences from the Islamic point of view. As a result, what children have been learning from religion has been contradicted by what they are learning from textbooks. Such an education obviously leads to conflicts, anxieties, and tensions. There is a strong need to Islamicize the humanities and social and natural sciences by producing basic concepts and by changing the methodology of introducing and teaching them in order to create a new generation of young men and women intellectually capable of resisting the undesirable effects of secularist teaching.

The Western models of secular education that are presently dominant in our education institutions follow an anthropocentric approach. They assign a central place to humanity, its needs, its wants, its likes and dislikes, and proceed to adjust their education programs accordingly. The Islamic approach, on the other hand, is theocentric. That is, God and His will, His law, His pleasure and displeasure are the sole norms to be followed in devising and formulating education policies and programs aimed at development of an integrated personality in a harmonious manner. Such an education system encompasses the study of the Holy Quran as the fountainhead of all knowledge.

The activity and precepts of the Holy Prophet Muhammad (peace be upon Him), that is, the *Sunnah, Fiqha,* and the spiritual disciplines and the transmission of such accumulated knowledge to guide humanity toward self-perfection and self-realization, are basic. Furthermore, education in Islam emphasizes that for comprehension of principles, articles of faith, and their implicit meanings, it is imperative that knowledge of other sciences should be acquired and applied to development strategies by scientific and technological expertise (Quddus, 1990).

To conclude, we can state that the Islamic aim of education is twofold. First, there is one ultimate aim—that is, to seek the pleasure of God in achieving a state of righteousness and in acting according to the principles of Islamic justice. Second, there are immediate aims that are not fixed but are constantly changing as a result of concrete, changing situations. Islam has set an ideal in its ultimate aim of education. It is incumbent on all Muslims to achieve the best and most noble within one's capacity. Islam lays utmost emphasis on *ama'* or deed, putting into action what we learn. In other words, Islam accedes to the practical ends of education. Everything learned has to be acted upon, has to be translated into action. (For further information see Al-Attas, 1979; Al-Faroogi, n.d.; Kalim, 1993; Rizvi, 1986.)

The Holy Quran, time and again, calls upon people to use their reason and tells us that those who have no knowledge cannot be at par with those who possess it. The only quality of Adam, which made him superior to the angels, is that he possessed knowledge.

Tradition and Change

The education system of Pakistan has its roots in the education history of the subcontinent. Indigenous schools called *maktabs* and *madrasas* existed in India before the British Rule (1857–1947). Islam lays great emphasis on acquiring knowledge. Muslims, therefore, paid great attention to learning, both worldly and spiritual. However, under the British this tradition suffered serious setbacks. The British rulers introduced their own education system with English as the medium of instruction. To paraphrase the words of Lord Macaulay, they undertook to create a class of people Indian in blood and color but English in tastes, in opinions, in morals, and in intellect.

While their traditional system of education was destroyed, Muslims did not try to adjust to the new system of education. The *maktabs* and *madrasas* that had managed to survive remained exclusively devoted to religious education. Muslims believed the western education system was inconsistent with their norms and values and was an implicit threat to their cultural identity.

However, during the later half of the nineteenth century some Muslim leaders of the subcontinent began actively to create a synthesis of the two systems. Syed Ahmad Khan worked out an education plan based on the study of modern arts and sciences along with religious education. He established a school at Aligarh that soon became a college and later developed into the well-known Muslim University Aligarh. Some Muslims and *Ulema* (religious leaders) opposed Syed Ahmad's education plans and approved only the traditional education system. A large majority, representing the middle-class, responded favorably to Syed Ahmad's education programs. Numerous education institutions based on similar lines were opened in the subcontinent and became the primary centers for the education of Muslims. A majority of leaders who struggled hard for the creation of a Muslim homeland were the graduates of these education institutions.

Thus, Pakistan inherited both the traditional and the western educational systems. The former was aimed at imparting mostly religious education, whereas the western system aimed at education in modern arts and sciences. Several Commissions on Education have devoted considerable efforts to the integration of the two systems.

The traditional education system consists of an extensive network of *maktabs* and *madrasas* attached to mosques, both in towns and villages. These institutions are devoted to the study of the Holy Quran. At the more advanced level, these institutions are called *Dar-ul-ulum* (home of knowledge) where higher education is imparted by religious scholars in *Tafsir* (Commentary of the Holy Quran), *Hadis* (Sayings and traditions of the Holy Prophet Muhammad peace be upon Him), *Fiqah* (jurisprudence), *Mantaq* (logic and philosophy), and languages (that is, Arabic, Persian, and Urdu). Graduates of these institutions are called *Alim* or *Fazil,* depending on the field of their specialization. Their diplomas and degrees have been given equivalence with university degrees/diplomas.

The education system of Pakistan has undergone many changes and has greatly improved with the inception of integrated planning in the country through five-year plans. The first two plans (1955–1960 and 1960–1965) primarily aimed at bringing about a reorganization of the education system on a pattern suited to the essential needs and requirements of the country. The third five-year plan (1965–1970) envisaged a relatively larger and more broad-based education development program. The educational policies and five-year plans of the last few decades emphasize human resource development and Universalization of Primary Education (UPE) at the earliest possible date, improving the relevance of curricula, reforming the examination system, expanding technical and higher education, promoting research (particularly in science and technology at the universities) and enhancing the quality of education in general.

However, despite substantial growth in the number of education institutions, these goals could only be partially achieved due to rapid population growth and resource constraint. Due to ever-increasing demands for quantitative expansion of education facilities, adequate resources could not be allocated for qualitative improvement. Education institutions lack proper infrastructure, the curricula lack relevance, and the methodology of instruction and examination are far from being satisfactory. There are gender and rural-urban imbalances both in availability and quality of educational facilities. The dropout and failure rates continue to be high. The management and financing of the existing education system is highly centralized and lacks an effective system of accountability.

Structure

The education system is three-tiered: primary, secondary, and university. The primary level comprises classes 1 through 8; secondary, 9 through 12; and the first university degree (bachelor's) requires two or more years.

All schools run by the government are single-sex schools, whereas some of the schools in the private sector have a co-education system. In the rural areas, most of the schools are single-teacher schools, especially girls' schools. In the urban areas, schools are overcrowded and the teacher-student ratio is far from being satisfactory. Most schools do not have adequate teaching materials. They have ill-equipped laboratories and are lacking in proper facilities for drinking water and playgrounds.

Pakistan has not been able to develop an education system that can measure up to the challenges faced by our nation. With a literacy rate of 36.8 percent, Pakistan still stands far behind other nations in this field. In 1993–1994 the number of primary schools, including mosque schools, is 156,450 with a total enrollment of 15.5 million. There are 780 colleges and 24 universities in the country. High dropout rates, inadequate facilities in rural areas, population expansion, and limited financial resources are major constraints on achieving universal primary education and a higher literacy rate (Government of Pakistan, 1994).

Primary Education. Compulsory subjects in the first five years of the primary level include Urdu, Islamiyat, social studies, arithmetic, and science. The first years are marked by an integrated approach where two or three subjects are combined into one course. While officially the medium of instruction is supposed to be Urdu in all schools, many private institutions use English as the primary medium. Curriculum is officially standardized throughout the country, although some local variations are permissible if the school has adequate resources. As a result of a growing demand for learning English as the language of science and technology, business and commerce, and international communication, English has been recently introduced at the primary level and adopted as one of the mediums of instruction. This phenomenon is much more prevalent at the secondary and higher levels, especially in the teaching of science subjects.

In state-funded schools the types of courses and their content, as well as teaching methods and preparation of textbooks, are largely regulated by government policies. Efforts to expand the quantity and enhance the quality of education has led to a bureaucratic and centralized educational system. Private schools, on the other hand, are free to decide their own curriculum and medium of instruction, which is generally English. The quality of education in private schools is on the whole substantially better than in government schools, which accounts for their popularity.

Establishment and management of primary schools is carried out by provincial governments, whereas curriculum is developed by the federal government in consultation with the provinces. A separate Directorate of Primary Education is established in each province. The medium of instruction in primary schools is either the national language (Urdu), the provincial language, or English. Primary education is almost free. However, Pakistan has a very low level of primary education, ranking 78th out of 87 developing countries. Low enrollment of girls is a major determinant of lower enrollment and higher illiteracy rates (see Table 21.1).

Several primary education projects have now been revitalized to promote basic education facilities in the country. New projects have been initiated to serve as major catalysts for the improvement of quality of instruction along with a quantitative expansion of primary education. Since 1990, incentives for the private sector to open education institutions have revived the involvement of the community, mostly in urban areas. Presently, pri-

TABLE 21.1 Primary School Enrollment Rates (percentage)

	RURAL	URBAN	TOTAL
Boys	77.2	85.7	79.5
Girls	37.2	68.3	45.7
Total	58.2	77.4	63.5

Source: *Seventh Plan*, Vol. I, p. 183.

vate schools account for about 14 percent of total primary enrollment and 30 percent of all urban primary enrollments.

Secondary and Higher Education.   At the higher secondary school level (classes 11 and 12) students have an opportunity to opt for science or arts subjects. Those students who are preparing for medicine at the degree level (premedical group) have to study physics, chemistry, and biology. The preengineering group studies physics, chemistry, and mathematics. Students in the arts/humanities group have a broader range of choice of subjects. However, all students have to study the compulsory subjects of English, Urdu, Islamiyat, and Pakistan Studies.

At the end of classes 11 and 12, Boards of Intermediate and Secondary Education hold examinations. Each student has to write exams in three compulsory and three elective subjects. However, the courses of Islamiyat and Pakistan Studies are bifurcated for the two classes. Students of class 11 appear in Islamiyat and those of 12 appear in Pakistan Studies. Non-Muslim students can opt for civics instead of Islamiyat.

At the higher secondary school level students can opt for English or Urdu as the medium of instruction. However, this practice is prevalent mostly in government-run schools and colleges; in private institutions, English is the medium of instruction. This emphasis on Urdu as the medium of instruction certainly has adverse effects on the academic achievement of students who reach the university level. Their lack of proficiency in English makes them poorly equipped for continuing education at the higher level.

The curricula in science, mathematics, and agrotechnical and vocational subjects at different levels were reviewed and modified during 1992–1994. Now concepts in science are being related to the everyday observations of the learner, making them more relevant and meaningful. However, the government believes that the quality of the curricula and textbooks is far from satisfactory. Thus, the Eighth Five-Year Plan (1993–1998) proposed a new curriculum development cycle aimed at

encouraging creativity, inquiry, and analytical thinking through project-oriented and problem-solving approaches in teaching. The curricula of technical and vocational institutions will be related to the employment market and self-employment. New concepts of immediate importance such as environment, education, health education, and population education are being integrated into the school curricula. Textbooks have been revised and updated to incorporate new knowledge using graded vocabulary and a pedagogical approach compatible to the age level of the student.

Teacher Training

It is universally recognized that the quality of education depends to a large extent on quality of teaching. To improve the quality of education, policymakers have repeatedly emphasized the need for better preservice and in-service training of teachers. At present the quality of preservice training in most of teacher training institutions is outmoded and of low quality when compared to international standards. There is an urgent need to update the knowledge and skills of master trainers engaged in teachers' training.

Currently, there are proposed reforms in curricula and training methodology at teachers' training institutions at all levels. It is recommended that teacher training programs must emphasize the acquisition of practical skills that can be applied in actual classroom situations instead of the current emphasis on theory. To achieve these objectives, eight existing colleges of elementary school teachers are being upgraded as model institutions that will offer and disseminate modern teacher training curricula and techniques. In addition, 66 teacher training centers will be established on the premises of existing higher secondary schools for girls in rural areas to extend teacher training facilities to women in rural areas.

At present there are 110 institutions for the training of primary school teachers and 11 colleges for training of secondary school teachers. All these institutions provide preservice training and the following certification.

- PTC (Primary Teaching Certificate) is given to teachers seeking training after completion of ten years schooling and obtaining a Secondary School Certificate (SSC).
- CT (Certificate in Teaching) is awarded to an individual who undergoes a preservice teaching course of one year after obtaining a Higher Secondary School Certificate (HSSC). CT teachers are eligible for teaching at the middle stage grades.
- B.Ed. (Bachelor of Education) is a one-year degree course in pedagogy. The minimum qualification to seek admission is a First Degree in Arts or Science (B.A./B.Sc). B.Ed. teachers are eligible to teach at the secondary school level.
- M.Ed. (Master of Education) is the highest degree in teaching and requires a one-year degree course after B.Ed.

B.Ed. and M.Ed. classes are run by Institutes of Education and Research based in universities. PTC and CT courses are offered in Elementary Colleges of Education. Existing teacher training institutions cannot meet demand. Consequently, numerous teachers enter service either without training, or they get teacher training as private candidates. Many of these men and women are trained by Allama Iqbal Open University (Islamabad) through distance learning.

The Eighth Five-Year Plan has recommended a variety of approaches to improve the quality of existing teachers through in-service training. Proposed strategies include distance learning through nonformal education, mobile teacher training programs (particularly for female teachers in rural areas), and on-the-job training through learning coordinators. Innovative programs of teacher training, such as the modular approach and audio/video cassettes containing lessons, are also being used. A system of incentives, in the form of awards and linking the careers of teachers with in-service training and efficiency, has also been introduced.

School Administration

The federal government is responsible for policy, planning, and provision of education facilities. Provinces are responsible for policy implementation, organization, administration, and the management of public school systems. The federal government plans curricula, sets education standards, and controls a very sizable development budget. Project implementation, recruitment, supervision of personnel, and day-to-day operating budgets are the responsibility of the provinces. The federal government has financial control of the university system through the agency of the University Grants Commission. Textbooks are produced by the provincial governments in accordance with the guidelines set by the federal Ministry of Education. The Ministry of Education consists of the following major wings: Administration, Planning and Development, Primary and Nonformal Education, Secondary and Technical Education, Federal Institution, International Cooperation, Higher Education and Research, Sports Welfare and Learned Bodies, and Curriculum.

Provincial education departments are headed by education ministers, who are political appointees, and senior executive civil servants, who are called Provincial Education Secretaries. Provinces are divided into regions for administrative purposes and the head is a Director. These regions are further divided into districts, which are headed by District Education Officers (DEOs). In many cases, there are separate male and female DEOs. A district can cover a population from one half to two million people. As can readily be seen, the system is hierarchical and all decision making and control is from the top.

Evaluation

Student evaluation in Pakistan usually focuses on academic achievement. Tests and grades are used to evaluate students' learning. Teachers use the results to see whether their instruction is effective and to identify students who have difficulties in learning and are in need of additional help. Parents need this evaluation to know how their children are doing in schools, and students can use the results to see whether their studying strategies are paying off. Progress reports also serve as a consistent mode of communication between school and home. Students have to repeat a class if they fail to earn the minimum pass marks in aggregate and compulsory subjects.

A formal examination system is prevalent in Pakistan. Examinations are generally held annually and are used to promote students to higher classes. All students who get a minimum of 40 percent in aggregate marks and at least 33 percent in compulsory subjects are promoted to the next higher class (80 percent and above = A+; 70–79 percent = A; 60–69 percent = B; 50–59 percent = C; 40–49 percent = D; 33–39 percent = E; and below 33 percent = Fail). In the primary classes, examinations are conducted by the schools. However, at the end of fifth year of the primary stage, a public examination is held by the Education Department for the award of merit scholarships, and the most competent students compete. Similarly, there is a public examination at the end of the eighth class held by the Education Department for the award of scholarships. Public examinations are held by the respective regions at the end of classes 10 and 12. These examinations are conducted by Boards of Intermediate and Secondary Education; universities conduct examinations for degree classes for all institutions affiliated with them. If a student fails in one or more subjects in any one of the public examinations, he or she must rewrite and pass in order to obtain the degree/diploma/certificate.

The present system of examinations has been severely criticized for a long time. The present examination system is mostly essay type in nature, which requires subjective assessment. A comprehensive and scientific evaluation system would make the teaching-learning process more rational and efficient. The current education policy advocates the abolition of annual examinations and their substitution by a system of continuous evaluation. However, this policy recommendation can-

not be implemented unless teachers are properly trained to assess student academic achievement by an objective and unbiased method of evaluation.

Some efforts have been made to establish a National Education Testing Service (NETS) on a sound footing, preferably through the private sector or nongovernment organizations. Tests will be developed by NETS in collaboration with agencies and individual experts within and outside Pakistan. Gradually, admission to higher education institutions will be made on the basis of performance on education tests developed and standardized by the NETS.

Curriculum Reforms

The government is also fully sensitive to the need to reform the primary education curriculum. Based on baseline data, improved curriculum and instructional materials for grades 1 to 3 have already been introduced, evaluated, and refined in some districts. The development of local expertise and making the curriculum, textbooks, and learning material more relevant to the student and to the community constitute salient features of the program. Qualitative improvement of school textbooks is also receiving serious attention. Revised versions of various textbooks prepared by provincial agencies have already been reviewed, refined, and approved. The process continues as a regular exercise.

Taking cognizance of emerging realities, new global perspectives, and contemporary issues, Pakistan's education programs at other levels are also being changed. Curricula are being revised, new textbooks written, and teacher training programs redesigned to gear the education system to new challenges and new opportunities. This not only means imparting the latest knowledge and introducing the latest disciplines, but also involves preparing teachers and students to become more responsible members of their society at home and the international community at large. New programs such as *Population Education* (to increase awareness of the alarming implications of unchecked population growth), *Drug Educa-tion* (to motivate students to fight the menace of narcotics), and *Environmental Studies* (to awaken people to the devastating effects of environmental pollution) have been initiated. A new subject, "Teacher, School, and Society," has been added to teacher training programs to equip teachers with knowledge and methodology in the area of inter-national education.

Developmental Strategies for Achieving Universal Primary

Pakistan has undergone serious political instabili-ty during the last four decades. Lack of a stable and persistent political structure has adversely affected the development of social and economic institutions in the country. However, past and pre-sent political leaders are aware of the significance of education for the progress of the nation. Soon after Pakistan came into being, in his inaugural address the Education Minister emphasized the need for universal, compulsory, and free education for children. All successive governments have also made education declarations and formulated polices, but achievement of full literacy and uni-versal education remains as elusive as ever.

Starting in 1956, a succession of five-year developmental plans were implemented with only partial success. At this date, it is not yet possible to fully analyze the success of the last Five-Year Plan (1993–1998). However, a mid-plan review (Gov-ernment of Pakistan, 1995) showed that an addi-tional 10,477 primary and 1,860 mosque schools had been established in the public sector. Some 6,656 shelterless primary schools were construct-ed; 3,353 mosque schools were converted into pri-mary schools; and 8,638 new classrooms were added in overcrowded primary schools during the first three years (1993–1996). However, only 39 percent of the Plan target of an additional 3.3 mil-lion enrollment over the first three years was achieved. It was expected that by the end of the Eighth Plan, the enrollment targets would be achieved only by 65 to 70 percent. As well, a pro-ject for 10,000 basic education centers/schools

was launched through reputed NGO/community involvement. During 1995–1996, more than 1,100 such schools/centers were established. By and large, the performance of primary education (except increases in enrollment) was satisfactory during the 1993–1998 Five-Year Plan.

Beyond the five-year plans, there is one addi-tional government developmental strategy that warrants particular mention. The *National Educa-tion Policy, 1993–2002* (Government of Pakistan, 1992). Like the earlier policies, it reiterates the government's firm determination to reinvigorate its struggle for universalization of primary educa-tion by the end of the decade. As well, special measures will be taken to improve the quality of education. Primary education in the private sector will not only be encouraged by the government but will be properly regulated through stringent controls to discourage commercialization. For this purpose, education foundations will be estab-lished in each province and at the federal level.

The *National Education Policy, 1992–2000* and the Eighth Five-Year Plan (1993–1998) are complementary to each other as both give the highest priority and urgency to the achievement of universal primary education by the year 2002. Both also strongly advocate and suggest concrete steps to remove the widening gender gaps and urban-rural disparities in the provision of basic education facilities. Improvement in the quality of primary education is also strongly advocated.

Literacy Programs

Provincial governments are working vigorously to tackle the problem of illiteracy, as is the federal government. Efforts are underway for legislation to increase expenditure on education to 3 percent of GDP by the year 2003. (The figure was 2.5 per-cent of GDP in 1995–1996.) Simultaneously with trying to universalize primary education, the gov-ernment has been endeavoring to increase the lit-eracy rate through direct methods. A recent project entitled *Eradication of Illiteracy from Selected Areas of Pakistan* has been launched to make 268,600 persons literate. For this purpose,

2,097 centers have been established with an enrollment of over 35,000. A ten-year National Literacy Plan has also been prepared by federal and provincial agencies to double the literacy rate from 35 percent to 70 percent by making 24 million illiterate persons of age group 10 plus literate by the year 2003. The Plan will be carried out in two phases of five years, each relating to the country's national five-year development plans (Government of Pakistan, 1995).

Universalization of primary education both for boys and girls over a minimum period of time has been adopted by the government as the main instrument for achieving mass literacy in the long run. The distribution of illiteracy is quite uneven (see Table 21.2). The lowest illiteracy rate is in urban males and the highest is in rural females.

THE FUTURE OF SOCIETY AND SCHOOLING

Besides being an indispensable ingredient of national socioeconomic development, education is a fundamental right of every individual. In the development of Pakistan since independence there has been a substantial expansion of education facilities, but the goals set for primary education have only been partially achieved. Some of the factors that continue to be particularly great obstacles include:

• Rapid population growth (3.1 percent per annum) and resource constraint. Due to ever-increasing demands for quantitative expansion of education facilities, adequate resources could not

be spared for qualitative improvement. Almost half of girls and one-fifth of boys of the relevant age group (5 to 9) are not enrolled in primary school. The adult literacy rate is still barely 35 percent, which is far below other South Asian countries with similar levels of economic development.

• Severe gender and urban/rural imbalances both in the availability and quality of education.

• The lack of essential facilities such as teaching aids, potable water, and latrines in a large number of schools. About 35,000 primary schools are without any shelter. Besides, a large number of primary schools are run in a single classroom, adding the problem of multigrade teaching by poorly trained teachers.

• Overcentralization and noninvolvement of school teachers in policy and planning.

• Poor quality of instruction, lack of relevance in the curriculum, ill-trained teachers, and an outmoded teaching and examination system.

• Lack of a stimulating school environment, high dropout rates, and negative attitudes among parents towards education.

The government is fully aware of the problems and is determined to enable people to improve the quality of their lives by providing basic education in accordance with everyone's learning needs. Efforts are directed to reach the following four specific targets by the time we enter twenty-first century: equal opportunities in education for all; a 70 percent literacy rate, with a special focus on the

TABLE 21.2   Literacy Rate, Percent by 1981, 1990, 2000

	TOTAL			URBAN			RURAL		
	Both Sexes	*Male*	*Female*	*Both Sexes*	*Male*	*Female*	*Both Sexes*	*Male*	*Female*
1981	26.2	35.1	16.1	47.1	55.3	37.3	17.3	26.2	7.3
1990	31.6	40.6	22.1	53.5	61.3	45.1	20.9	30.4	11.3
2000	38.1	47.1	30.5	60.8	68.1	54.8	25.2	35.3	17.5

Note: 1981 figures are taken from census; 1990 and 2000 figures are projections.

female population; provision of early childhood care; and expansion of basic skills, training, and programs for out-of-school youth and adults.

A mid-plan review of the Eighth Five-Year Plan (1993–1998) shows that the following steps are being taken (Government of Pakistan, 1995):

• *Decentralization of the education system.* To achieve this objective, Directors of Public Instruction and the Director of Education are now appointed from their respective jurisdictions. Separate directorates of elementary education have also been established in all four provinces of Pakistan.

• *Public/private partnerships.* This is the hallmark of the education policy under the eighth plan. Substantial incentives are available to private sector investors in education. Under this scheme an entrepreneur who invests in the education sector can get a grant from the government equal to his or her investment in improving an institution. Development grants to private entrepreneurs are also provided by the provincial education foundations after assessment of each case.

• *Self-financing scheme.* To increase finances, a self-financing scheme has been introduced in fifteen universities and colleges. At present, 10 to 20 percent of the seats are filled under this scheme, which ultimately will rise to 25 percent. Various institutions have established linkages between industry and education.

• *Vocational and technical education.* It is anticipated that 38 percent of students will be redirected to technical and vocational streams. A large-scale expansion of vocational training and a strengthening of facilities of technical, engineering, and professional education are underway to achieve the plan targets.

A vocational education project, which envisages the establishment of seventy model vocational schools and the creation of training facilities in thirteen different trades has also been approved. The project on the one hand extends vocational education facilities to people in the farthest corners of the country and, on the other, will reduce unemployment.

The above are concrete steps that are designed to produce concrete results. In spite of continuing and difficult obstacles, Pakistan is making progress.

REFERENCES

Al-Attas, S.N. (1979). *Aims and objectives of Islamic education.* Jaddah: Hodder & Stroght.

Al-Farooqi, I.R. (International Institute of Islamic Thought, USA). (n.d.). *Islamization of knowledge: General principles and work plan.* Brentwood: International Graphic Printing server.

Government of Pakistan. (n.d.). *Five-year plans* (I, II, III, IV, V, VI, VII, VIII), Islamabad: Planning Commission.

Government of Pakistan. (1992). *National Education Policy, 1992–2000.* Islamabad: Planning Commission.

Government of Pakistan. (1994). *Economic Survey, 1993–94.* Islamabad: Author.

Government of Pakistan. (1995). *Mid-plan review of eighth five-year plan of the government of Pakistan.* Islamabad: Planning Commission.

Kalim, M.S. (1993). *Studies in education.* Islamabad: National Book Foundation.

Quddus, N.J. (1990). *Problems of education in Pakistan.* Karachi: Royal Book Company.

Rizvi, S.S. (1986). *Islamic philosophy of education.* Lahore: Institute of Islamic Culture.

CHAPTER 22

Post-Apartheid Policy and Practice: Educational Reform in South Africa

DAVID GILMOUR
CRAIN SOUDIEN
DAVID DONALD

David Gilmour *teaches in the School of Education at the University of Cape Town. He began his career in the Department of Public Administration at UCT and has taught in a variety of institutions since then, including the University of Fort Hare and Rhodes University. Since joining the School of Education in 1987, he has developed interests in policy and planning in education, the sociology of education, and the evaluation of educational projects. He has worked on a number of national commissions in the reconstruction of education in South Africa and is currently working with the Canada–South Africa Education Management Development Program for the National Task Team on Education Management Development.*

Crain Soudien *teaches in the area of Educational Foundations and Policy of Education at the School of Education at the University of Cape Town. He completed his Ph.D. at the State University of New York at Buffalo. He has published extensively in the areas of race, culture and education, school reform, and the urban history of Cape Town. He is very involved in community projects.*

David Donald *is professor of Educational Psychology at the University of Cape Town. He has taught in schools; has practiced as an educational psychologist; and has been involved in training teachers, special educationists, and educational psychologists in South Africa over a number of years. As the author of several books, chapters in books, and a range of articles, his research and publications have focused extensively, although not only, on issues affecting the delivery of education support services in developing contexts, especially in southern Africa.*

When the *apartheid* government came into power in 1948, it saw the schooling system as the major vehicle for the propagation of its beliefs. For the period of its duration, schools were one of the system's most stark symbols. Today, as a new and democratic government seeks to repair and reconstruct the fabric of South Africa's ravaged past, it is to the schooling system that much of its attention has turned.

THE SOCIAL FABRIC

In May 1994, after almost fifty years of *apartheid*, South Africa became a formal democracy. Nelson Mandela became the first freely elected president of the country and the African National Congress (ANC), which was banned in 1962, assumed the reins of power in the new Government of National Unity (GNU). The heritage that confronted this new government was complex. As a result of history, South Africa was (and still remains) a country in which the divisions of race, class, culture, and religion were deeply inscribed.

Apartheid

A central tenet of the National Party government was that the South African population consisted of discrete groups that were racially and culturally distinct. Based on this philosophy, four identifiable groups were defined: whites, Africans, Indians, and coloreds. Their places in society, according to *apartheid,* were unique and demanded political, social, and cultural arrangements that would enable them to fulfill their distinct destinies. It was therefore necessary, went the argument, that they lived in their own separate social and political spheres. African people, and indeed other people of color, had no rights or entitlements in the world of white people. Rigid and impermeable barriers were thus created between people presumed to be of different racial backgrounds.

Overlaying these boundaries were (and still are) boundaries of class that have served to separate the majority of the working and nonworking poor, which consists largely of people of color, from a relatively small middle class, which is largely white.

As part of its policy of *apartheid,* the National Party government attempted to resettle African people in ethnically distinct homelands out of the major urban areas. The homelands were human dumping grounds where people were literally forcibly resettled from "white" areas. They were generally located in the most desolate and under-provided parts of the country that offered their inhabitants little prospect of development. As is well known, these policies bred a spirit of defiance and resistance among people of color and produced what came to be known as *the struggle* for equal rights and democracy.

Economy

As a result of a combination of international sanctions against South Africa and poor management of the economy, the country spun into a reverse growth phase in the mid-1980s. By the time the new government assumed power in 1994, the capacity of the economy to support the new democracy had been severely cut back. Equally, the country is characterized by uneven growth, with much of the development occurring in the dense urban areas, especially the Witwatersrand, Durban, and Cape Town. This is significant in that 72 percent of all schools are classified as nonurban and much of the resourcing has clearly not flowed into these areas.

Demography and Diversity

In 1994, when Mandela came into office, the country had a population of 40,648,574 of whom, in *apartheid*'s terms, 30,944,267 were classified African, 1,038,851 Asian, 3,472,960 colored, and 5,192,498 white (South African Institute of Race Relations, 1996). The nation has substantial Jewish, Muslim, and Hindu communities, each with its own unique cultural visions, although the majority of its people belong to a variety of Christian denominations (Moosa, 1997). Significantly, in 1993 37.3 percent of this population was in the 0-to-14 age group category. The pressures to be placed on the education system are clear.

It was into this diverse and fractured socioeconomic and cultural space that the new government moved in 1994. Among its first steps were to introduce a slate of legislative reforms. Key among these were proposals for the restructuring of education.

SCHOOLING

Education Under Apartheid

The structure for education was marked by the central principle of *apartheid,* namely separate schooling infrastructures for separate groups. In terms of the *apartheid* principle, nineteen education departments were established. Each designated ethnic group had its own education infrastructure. Theoretically, and to some degree in practice, there was a central coordinating department called the Department of National Education. The Department of Education and Training (DET) administered education for African people outside of the homelands. Each of the homelands, ten in number, had its own separate and "autonomous" education department. Out of the House of Assembly came the Department of Education and Culture for whites with four provincial departments. The House of Representatives for coloreds and the House of Delegates for Asians likewise had their own Departments of Education and Culture.

When the new government came into power in 1994, one of its first acts was to dissolve the nineteen education departments and to bring them under a centrally constituted Department of Education. This national department was given the responsibility for formulating national policy. The nine new provinces, which came into being as a result of the new dispensation, were each entrusted with the responsibility of administering the new system. The new provinces are Eastern Cape, Free State, Gauteng, KwaZulu Natal, Mpumalanga, Northern Cape, Northern Province, North West Province, and Western Cape.

The Structure of Schooling

The South African schooling system is essentially organized into two major sectors, primary and secondary. At the primary level, African schools tended to be organized into junior and higher primary schools. Where schools are organized into junior and higher primary subdivisions, the former takes students up to the third grade, and the latter span grades 4 to 7. The division in the rest of the system was simply between that of primary and secondary, where the terminal grade for the primary school phase was the equivalent of the 7th grade. These arrangements continue to operate under the new government. Primary schooling thus consists of seven years. Secondary schooling begins at the 8th grade and is made up of five years, of which the last three constitute preparation for the end of school matriculation examinations. On completion of twelve years of schooling, eligible students enter tertiary and continuing education tracks.

In 1994 there were 7,971,770 primary pupils and 3,523,594 secondary pupils (total: 11,495,364); 209,959 primary teachers and 131,944 secondary teachers (total: 341,903); 17,993 primary schools, 3,873 secondary schools and 3,298 combined primary/secondary schools (total: 25,164 schools). Of significance here is the fact that 46 percent of African teachers, 29 percent of colored teachers, 7 percent of Indian teachers, and only 1 percent of white were un(der)qualified in 1994 (less than matriculation plus three years training) (Arnott & Chabane, 1995). This has implications for the abil-

ities of teachers to carry out the complicated curricula reforms that have been mooted and also impacts on resources for retraining. Similarly, with 72 percent of all schools being classified as nonurban (Arnott & Chabane, 1995) and an urban bias in the distribution of resources, this creates considerable difficulties in the equalization of resources.

The higher education sector consists of twenty-one universities, fifteen *technikons* (a South African variant of polytechnics), and 140 single-discipline vocational colleges (education, nursing, and agriculture). All were previously divided along racial lines. As with schooling there were/are vast disparities in terms of funding, participation rates, staff/student ratios, completion rates, and quality (National Commission on Higher Education, 1996). Entrance to these institutions proceeds immediately after completion of the matriculation phase of schooling and leads to a variety of certificates, diplomas, and degrees. Articulation between these different institutions under the *apartheid* system was weak. New proposals envisage opportunities for considerably more movement between different kinds of institutions.

Curriculum

Curriculum development in South African education during the period of *apartheid* was controlled tightly from the center. While, theoretically at least, each separate department had its own curriculum development mechanisms and protocols, in reality curriculum formation in South Africa was dominated by committees attached to the white House of Assembly. These committees invariably determined the core content of what was taught in all the other departments (see National Education Policy Investigation, 1992, p. 104). So prescriptive was this system, abetted on the one hand by a network of inspectors and subject advisors and on the other by several generations of poorly qualified teachers, that authoritarianism, rote learning, and corporal punishment were the rule. These conditions were exacerbated in the impoverished environments of schools for children of color. Examinations were profoundly important in entrenching these conservative peda-gogical approaches. Examination criteria and pro-cedures were instrumental in promoting the political perspectives of those in power and allowed teachers very little latitude to determine standards or to interpret the work of their students.

This approach was authorized as the official philosophy of the South African education system. It brought to education deeply authoritarian and intolerant values and practices. Other approaches, furthermore, were declared unscientific and invalid. The consequence of this was that the curriculum was perceived, particularly by the disenfranchised, as being oppressive and exclusionary. It came to be seen as the transmission belt for the system's hidden and explicit racism.

The South African curriculum is presently organized in such a way that students entering the final matriculation phase are required to select particular configurations of subjects that are dif-ferentiated essentially, but not only, into higher grade and standard grade divisions. Among these configurations, for example, are science, commer-cial, vocational, and human sciences tracks. Par-ticular combinations of subjects (at least five) in particular higher and standard grade arrangements determine whether students complete their school-ing with either what is called a school leaving cer-tificate or a matriculation exemption certificate. The latter is the minimum requirement for entry into university.

Governance and Financing

Under *apartheid* the system was structured so that control of the most important administrative and pedagogical tasks lay in the hands of the govern-ment. The state determined at the central level what salaries were to be paid, the guidelines for appointments that individual departments were expected to implement, and the norms and stan-dards for syllabus and curriculum development.

This state of affairs, particularly in embattled black schools, was fiercely resisted. Sweeping changes have been initiated by the new govern-ment to deal with these difficulties. It is important

to spell out the more formative steps taken. One major achievement of the process of reform has been the establishment of a single ministry of edu-cation. Another was the passing of the South African Schools Act (Department of Education, 1996b). This Act established the right of every person to basic education and equal access; the right to be instructed in a language of choice (where practicable); the right to the freedoms of conscience, belief, expression, and association; and the right to establish education institutions based on a common language, culture, and reli-gion. With respect to funding, the Act permitted schools to levy school fees but simultaneously prohibited schools from denying entry to individ-uals who were unable to pay such fees.

Other developments in process include the redesigning of the curriculum, the rationalization of a complex of different types of schools into two forms only (from eight different categories of pub-lic school), state and private schools, and the introduction of strong parental participation in school governance.

The impact of these developments has had far-reaching implications for teachers and is being felt differently in the diverse schools of the country. Having consolidated the fractured education sys-tem, the first challenge that confronted the author-ities was that of equalizing per capita expenditure and resource commitment within it.

One measure that the state adopted was that of diverting emergency funds to schools for physical upgrading. Schools in bad repair in the black town-ships were given awards of sums of money for the restoration of their structural fabric. Another mea-sure, much more controversial, was to address the differences in teacher/pupil ratios between, partic-ularly, white schools and African schools. This represents not only a pedagogical redistribution but of course a financial one. Ratios as low as 1:20 had been achieved in the former, while in the latter they had escalated to highs of 1:80. To bring uni-formity, two standards were developed for the entire system; for high schools a ratio of 1:35, while primary schools were set a target of 1:40. The immediate consequence of the measure was to initiate the process of redistributing funding from schools that were highly subsidized to those that were poorly subsidized. Of course, schools that were perceived to be overendowed were required to reduce their expenditure on staff. These measures, as we indicate below, have not been without their own disabling difficulties.

MAJOR ISSUES, CONTROVERSIES, AND PROBLEMS

Prior to the democratic elections of 1994, the ANC had already clarified its education priorities and reform agenda. The key policy initiatives for the next five years were to be the following: reconstruction of the bureaucracy, governance, and management; integration of education and training; restructuring of the format of school education; changing the curriculum; paying attention to early childhood care, adult basic education, and special education; changes in the preparation of teachers; restructuring higher education; and restoring buildings and physical resources (African National Congress, 1994).

From the above, three key issues are discussed in this section. The first area of focus is the curriculum. The second issue of discussion is inclusive education and the problem of special needs. The final section reviews the efforts by the state to deal with inequalities in the school.

Curriculum Reform

Curriculum change in the new era began almost as soon as the new education minister took office. Within months of the historic elections of 1994, an announcement was made by the Department of Education that it was undertaking a process of purging the *apartheid* syllabi of their more offensive content. An elaborate series of committees was appointed with the mandate to review texts and curricula materials.

This development took place while other curriculum debates were taking place elsewhere. A particularly important debate had begun in the early 1990s in which business, government, trade unions,

educationists, and a variety of other groups participated. The interests that were brought to this debate were varied, ranging from concerns with a curriculum that would prepare a productive labor force, to concerns about a curriculum that promotes quality in learning, to concerns about the curriculum having as its *raison d'être* the development of equity and equality. Joined in a common purpose were business leaders, educationists, and political groups. Business people were dissatisfied with the previous curriculum, which they described as irrelevant and inadequate in terms of providing young people with the knowledge and the skills to make productive contributions in a modern economy. Educationists and political groups, for their part, were unhappy about the *apartheid* bias of the curriculum.

Through several years of discussion that involved consultations with experts in countries such as the United Kingdom and New Zealand, agreement was reached around the development of a National Qualifications Framework (NQF) as the rubric within which the new curriculum could be structured. Central to these agreements was the idea of developing a learning environment and framework that would promote lifelong learning, integrate education and training, recognize learning gained outside of formal institutions and allow for flexible, portable credits and qualifications.

For grades 1 to 8, nationally agreed-upon outcomes are in the process of being formulated, together with assessment criteria that are expected to assist the educator in determining whether the outcomes have been achieved. From grade 9 on, however, outcomes are intended to be formulated in terms of nationally agreed upon standards that will be taken up in the form of unit standards. A learner is expected to demonstrate, through both understanding and application, a capacity to meet specified outcomes.

The curriculum itself is organized around eight Learning Areas: language, literacy, and communication; mathematical literacy, mathematics, and mathematical sciences; human and social sciences; natural sciences; technology; arts and culture; economic and management sciences; and life orientation. Learning Area Committees are presently developing detailed rationale, foci, outcomes, cross-curricular relations, and assessment criteria for the Learning Areas.

The significance of this curriculum development has been great, but it has not, as might be expected, been received without criticism. While the development has been welcomed as a step forward from the authoritarian and content-based curricula of *apartheid*, anxieties have been expressed about the speed of the implementation of the innovation and the underrepresentation of important stakeholders in both the conception and implementation phases of the initiative. Most importantly, there is heated debate over whether the new curriculum model is conceptually flawed.

At the heart of this debate is the accusation that the new curriculum model is a mixture of antithetical orientations that, in the final analysis, do not make it viable. The issue can be posed in equality versus equity terms. Can a competency model (which stresses the maximization of potential and can therefore be regarded as an equality model) live alongside a performance model (which seeks to maximize individual skill value in a competitive and ever-changing labor market)? (Muller, 1996).

Alongside these conceptual difficulties lie the practical problems that will be engendered in both writing and delivering the new curriculum. Teachers already stressed by the myriad of changes they face (in staff restructuring, governance, and financial reorganization) will now be tasked with implementing a new curriculum, the details and purposes of which are relatively unclear. How they respond will clearly be critical for the success or otherwise of the reform. Unfortunately, the retraining needed to move away from the old pedagogical modes will be largely unavailable.

The Challenge of Inclusive Education in South Africa

With the adoption of the new Constitution and Bill of Rights in 1996, South Africa committed itself to a policy of inclusive education. In essence, this involves a commitment to creating access to, and provision of, a process of education that is appropriate to the needs of all children, whatever their origin, background, circumstances, or abilities (Department of Education, 1996a). Thus, the emphasis falls on the system meeting the needs of the child as inclusively as possible, rather than the child having to be separated or excluded to suit the needs of the system.

While the relevant clauses in the Constitution are designed to meet the needs of all children, a particular challenge arises in relation to those with special educational needs. Inclusion may involve different ways of meeting special needs, but it does imply that, wherever possible and practicable, a child's special needs will be met in the normal, mainstream school, classroom, and curriculum.

A primary assumption in this is that the mainstream itself is sufficiently resourced and is constituted as an optimally facilitative environment for meeting the developmental needs—special or not—of all children. In South Africa this is still far from the reality.

Equity in Education

One of the key focus areas of reform since 1994 has been the linked issues of equity, equality, and redress. Given the disparities created by the previous regime, these issues not only have educational but also political significance as the new government attempts to generate visible signs of change. Space permits only a brief discussion of equity in this chapter. However, the noted overlap of equity, equality, and redress means that light will also be shed on the latter two.

While the issue of equity is multifaceted, we will limit ourselves to discussion of two main mechanisms that have been employed to achieve it. Both illustrate well the complexities involved. The first relates to input-based fiscal reallocations to provinces based on the pupil:teacher ratios (PTRs) referred to earlier (40:1 in the primary school and 35:1 in the secondary school). In this plan, equal spending between provinces on a pupil per capita basis is to be phased in by the year

2000. Given the consequences for staffing levels in "overstocked" provinces, the process is also referred to as a form of "right-sizing" or "rationalization" (*Cape Argus,* 12 June 1996, p. 25).

We may illustrate the process with the example of the first round of fiscal reallocations for 1995/1996 grants to the provinces. A scenario emerged where two provinces were to receive substantial cutbacks in expenditure. In the Western Cape the projected decrease from 1994/1995 to 1995/1996 was 4.2 percent, and in Gauteng the decrease was 1.8 percent. This was in the face of an overall budgetary increase of 7.76 percent (Provincial Budget Guidelines: 1994/95-1995/96.) In human terms this means that the Western Cape was scheduled to shed 6,000 teachers in 1996 and a further 6,000 in 1997 (35 percent of total establishment), while Gauteng was to shed 6,800 by 1997 (14.2 percent of total establishment) (*Edusource,* 1996b).

The second mechanism for achieving equity is the school-by-school "right-sizing" that is to occur within *all* provinces irrespective of the total allocation to the province. This is also referred to as "redeployment," an attempt to ameliorate "right-sizing." An exemplar of this is KwaZulu Natal where, although there is an overall shortage of 2,200 teachers, some 3,000 have to be redeployed to understaffed schools (presumably in either rural or less desirable areas) (*Edusource,* 1996b). At this level, principals are to guide the process through rationalization or right-sizing committees.

In respect of this mechanism, the policy means that not only is the burden of responsibility for deciding who should go and who should stay placed on individuals/schools, but that even in schools where there was/is disadvantage, educators there too are eligible for voluntary severance/retrenchment packages. This latter anomaly derives from teacher union pressure to apply rationalization to all schools on grounds of fairness.

Other important aspects of the rationalization process are that a condition of taking the severance package is that those leaving are not permitted to reenter the school system, and, as indicated,

it is hoped that those who are in danger of being retrenched will voluntarily "redeploy" themselves in provinces or regions where there are teacher shortages. In this way it was hoped that an equitable distribution of teachers would occur without having to retrench people. Such a mechanism obviously relies on the willingness and ability to move on the part of teachers. Thus, for this plan to be feasible, accurate information about teacher numbers and their teaching subjects, pupil distribution data, reasonably accurate demographic forecasting counts, as well as the release of posts in provinces where there were shortages is needed. Few of these conditions were/are present.

Finally, the policy also requires changes in the nature of the supply of teachers from teacher training institutions. The 1994 stock of teachers was 341,903, of whom 61 percent were primary and 39 percent secondary teachers. If the aimed-for PTRs are achieved by 2000, the National Teacher Audit estimated that there would be a decline of ± 6,000 primary school teachers (2.8 percent), and an increase of ± 49,500 secondary teachers (38 percent) by 2004 (Hofmeyr & Hall, 1996). This would seem to indicate a shift in provision from the colleges, which produce mainly nongraduate primary school teachers and which account for ± 80 percent of trainee teacher enrollments, to universities and technikons, which produce mainly secondary school teachers.

The consequences of these approaches soon became obvious. First, the process of retrenchment divided schools, generated pupil protests, created a political furore, and placed intolerable burdens on principals who have to oversee the process (in the Western Cape 25 percent of principals themselves took the packages [*Cape Argus,* September, 1996]). The effect on teacher morale and the ability of schools to take up the challenges of reconstruction cannot be underestimated.

Second, with some 12,000 teachers having taken the voluntary severance packages (*Mail & Guardian,* January 10–16, 1997) there is a stripping of expertise from the system both at the managerial level and at the level of classroom specialization. This was because there is no restriction on the eligibility of those who may wish to leave. A further irony is that the Minister is now contemplating hiring Cuban teachers in areas of skills shortage, namely mathematics and science (*Mail & Guardian,* March 7–13, 1997), at the same time as volunteer teachers from Ghana, Sri Lanka, and India in these subjects are being expelled from rural Eastern Cape schools (*Weekend Argus,* 1/2 March, 1997).

Although the Department is unclear as to which subject areas have been affected by the retrenchments, the impact on quality must be severe and is reflected (albeit by proxy) in the final year matriculation examination results. While there were provincial variations, the pass rates showed an overall decline from 58 percent in 1994 (Strauss, Plekker, Strauss, & van der Linde, 1994) to 55 percent in 1995. Significantly, "the pass rate among candidates writing examinations administered by the former Department of Education and Training (mainly Africans) decreased from 49 percent to 43 percent" (*Edusource,* 1996a). Similarly, the total numbers of those eligible for university entrance fell overall from 17.8 percent in 1994 to 15.6 percent in 1995 (Strauss et al., 1994). Obviously, the equity measures are falling on the wrong constituency.

Third, and compounding the above, has been the financial crises in the provinces caused by implementation. The first difficulty in terms of funding the retrenchments has been that funds for this were only allocated to the provinces designated as "overfunded" (Northern Cape and Free State were added to Western Cape and Gauteng), while, as indicated, all teachers could apply for the package. Second, with the reorganization of the various departments, funds that could previously have been squeezed from other departments (such as Public Works), now have to be found within Education budgets. This has meant an immediate shortfall in moneys available for capital expenditure. Third, and equally seriously, the spending excesses in the last days of *apartheid* have left several new provinces, particularly those that took over the former homelands, with deficit budgets to begin with (particularly Mpumalanga and East-

ern Cape). The overall consequence is that all provinces face immediate deficit budgets.

The response of provinces has been predictable. In almost all cases nonteaching professional services (such as counseling and special education) have been cut; building maintenance has declined; and textbook ordering has been reduced as provinces seek to cut in "soft" areas. While this is partly due to administrative chaos, it is also a consequence of deficit budgeting.

Other targets for cuts have been in teacher colleges and teacher training. Currently the funding of colleges of education is a provincial affair without any restriction on where the graduates have to teach. This obviously means that some provinces subsidize others in terms of providing teachers. In a situation of tight fiscal constraint, these institutions now respond to provincial rather than national demand for teachers, and this has meant the closure of colleges in at least two provinces (Western Cape and Northern Province). At the same time, bursary offers to teaching students have been dropped in these provinces. These short-term measures, combined with a general uncertainty about the profession, have resulted in declining education student enrollments, particularly at university levels where considerable training of secondary teachers and in-service work takes place.

The public and media reaction to and political fallout from such a situation is predictable. Indeed, the acting secretary-general of the ANC, in an unprecedented action in January 1997, issued a "friendly word of criticism" to the Minister about the unintended consequences of the policy (*Eastern Province Herald,* January, 1997). In February it was revealed that the Western Cape, having traumatically shed 6,000 teachers, would need to hire ± 3,000 teachers to meet shortfalls due to miscounts and an influx of pupils from other provinces (*Cape Times,* 1997). By the end of the first week of February, the Minister called for a "thorough rethink of the structure, specifically of the severance packages" (*Mail & Guardian,* 31 January–6 February, p. 8). The ANC-aligned teacher union, the South African Democratic

Teachers' Union (SADTU), having originally supported the changes, now blamed the National Teacher Audit for having produced inaccurate figures about teacher-pupil ratios and demanded a rethink on the ratios. This has led to renegotiation with the Education Labor Relations Council, and the whole redeployment program has now been halted pending the outcome of negotiations.

THE FUTURE OF SOCIETY AND SCHOOLING

The future of schooling in South Africa is clearly indistinguishable from the larger social, political, and economic circumstances that are playing themselves out. As indicated above, there are historical roots and tensions that perhaps have tended to compromise the reforms of the state. While these may partly relate to the exigencies of power, the compromises also reflect the scope of reform and the lack of conceptual clarity attendant upon (an understandable) haste.

The Minister's response to this situation is illuminating and indicates just how far conceptions of equity and equality have shifted and how far the process of compromise has reached. In a full-length interview on March 8 (*Weekend Argus,* March 8/9, 1997), the Minister stated that: "Equity was not related to affirmative action. . . . All that equity says is that we reduce the budgets of the provinces that were funded above average and increase the budgets of those that were funded below average" (p. 22). He further explained that *redress* is perceived of as the "redeployment" of teachers to understaffed schools, and that *affirmative action* is the promotion of African teachers. (The unwillingness of non-African teachers to shift to the "African" schools and take demotion is perceived as racism). These are very different conceptions from the original ideals, and the question is, how are these shifts to be interpreted and what influence will they have on the shape of education?

While the first steps to equity may lie through equality and consequent input-related measures, equity really relies on attention to the processes and outputs of education. This recognition distinguished the early democratic movement discourse from that of the *apartheid* state and now has seemingly been lost. The problem for the state now is how to recapture these aims within the context of its own policy-practice imperative.

REFERENCES

African National Congress. (1994). *A policy framework for education and training.* Praetoria: Braamfontein.

Arnott, A., & Chabane, S. (1995). *Teacher demand, supply, utilisation and costs: Report for the National Teacher Education Audit.* Craighall: Edusource.

Cape Argus. (1996, 12 June). Right-sizing of education. Message from Professor Sibusiso Bengu, Minister of Education, p. 25.

Cape Argus. (1996, 9 September). 1 in 4 School Heads to Quit, p. 1.

Cape Times. (1997, 14 February). Teacher shortage after cuts bungle, p. 1.

Department of Education (1996a). *National Education Policy Act, No 27 of 1996.* Pretoria: Government Printer.

Department of Education (1996b). *South African Schools Act, No 84 of 1996.* Pretoria: Government Printer.

Eastern Province Herald. (1997, 24 January). ANC slams education plan, p. 4.

Edusource Data News. (1996a, April). A brief overview of education 1995, No 12.

Edusource Data News. (1996b, December). Provincialisation of education: A review. June–October, 1996, No 15.

Hofmeyr, J., & Hall, J. (1996). *The National Teacher Education Audit. Synthesis Report.* Johannesburg: Center for Education Policy Development, Edupol (NBI),

Mail & Guardian. (1997, January 10–16). Officials and unions urge rethink over redundancies, p. 10.

Mail & Guardian. (1997, January 31–6 February). Rethink on teacher severance, p. 8.

Mail & Guardian. (1997, March 7–13). SA's plan to hire Cuban teachers, p. 4.

Moosa, E. (1997, March). *Tensions in legal and religious values in the 1996 South African constitution.* Paper presented at the Cultural Transformations Conference in Africa, University of Cape Town.

Muller, J. (1996, October). *A harmonized qualifications framework and the well-tempered learner: Pedagogic models, teacher education and the NQF.* Paper presented at the conference "Lev Vygotsky, 1896–1996: A Cultural Historical Approach: Progress in Human Sciences and Education." Moscow, Russia.

National Commission on Higher Education. (1996) *A framework for transformation.* Pretoria: Government Printer.

National Education Policy Investigation. (1992). *Support services.* Cape Town: Oxford University Press/NECC.

Provincial Budget Guidelines: 1994/95–1995/96 Budget Comparisons. (1996). Parliamentary briefing paper for the Education Standing Committee, Provincial Legislature (Western Province).

South African Institute of Race Relations. (1996). *Race relations survey, 1995/1996.* Johannesburg: South African Institute of Race Relations.

Strauss, J.P., Plekker, S.J., Strauss, J.W.W., & van der Linde, H.J. (1994). *Education and manpower development 1994, No 15.* Bloemfontein: Research Institute for Education Planning, University of the Orange Free State.

Weekend Argus. (1997, 12 March). Gestapo-style crackdown on expat teachers. p. 8.

Weekend Argus. (1997, 8/9 March). Bengu blames Olckers for teacher crisis, p. 22.

PART V

The Pacific Rim: A Landscape of Diversity

For most of the last quarter of the twentieth century, the world watched in awe as the "Asian miracle" redefined international economics. Then, as the century closed, the "Asian flu" threatened to spread economic catastrophe across the globe. A new force had been unleashed in the western Pacific Rim; the world stage has some significant new players.

Without question the giant here is the People's Republic of China (PRC). The world's most populous nation is, however, no longer a sleeping giant. The common wisdom is that the twenty-first century will be the century of China. Clearly becoming less isolationist and more internationalist, inheriting from Russia the mantle of leading the communist movement, and having made remarkable progress in solving internal problems that a generation ago seemed hopeless, the PRC is a nation whose time has come and whose significance cannot be exaggerated.

However, to much of the world the PRC continues to remain a deep mystery. Accordingly, this section begins with this fascinating and important society and its education system. Remarkably steadfast in a world rapidly changing around it, the PRC skillfully employs schooling, simultaneously and explicitly, for ideological and economic purposes. The inculcation of communist social, political, and economic doctrines takes place hand in hand with producing a highly skilled labor force to speed along economic modernization. To say that the PRC is steadfast in its sociopolitical orientation is not, however, to imply that it is static. Quite the opposite. The PRC is a remarkably complex and adaptive society that has demonstrated its ability to undergo significant transformations without disintegrating or losing sight of its socialist goals.

The PRC's transformations were and are accomplished through national economic and social reforms carried out on a scale so massive and intricate that it boggles uncomprehending foreigners. The result of these social revolutions is that today the nation is many often seemingly contradictory things. It is a remarkable and curious selective combination of Marxist-Leninist political economy (interpreted from a uniquely Chinese perspective) and state capitalism. It is a powerful, centralized bureaucracy firmly in the ideological grip of the Communist Party of China, which somehow tolerates economic decentralization, a private sector, and market mechanisms. It is a fiercely egalitarian society that nevertheless allows accumulation of private wealth and the existence of private schools, even as it witnesses the emergence of serious problems in equity and accessibility. It purges the ideas of the past, yet consciously resurrects traditional Chinese values.

To help stabilize these contradictions and to ensure that reforms do not unleash social forces that assume a momentum of their own and go off in unpredictable directions (one need look no further than the catastrophic unfolding of events in the USSR under the reforms initiated by Gorbachev to appreciate the possibility of this), the education system plays a key role. However, schools are enjoying only partial success in this key responsibility. Yet, as the PRC deals with these contradictions, continues to grapple with huge internal problems, responds to the emerging socio-political-economic realities of the twenty-first century, and reappraises its role in the world community of nations, success is likely to follow and the PRC's international prominence and significance will only increase.

In turning to Japan, we are offered a striking lesson in how profoundly the world has become a more open community. In spite of Japan's homogenous culture, strong sense of tradition, and ability to absorb outside influences by adapting them to the dominant culture, the country may have reached a point where its national culture is becoming overwhelmed.

Our contributing author argues that we are seeing the emergence of a new Japanese culture. Overwhelming outside forces in the form of modernization, internationalization, and globalization have combined with powerful internal demographic, political, economic, and other changes to undermine traditional culture. The result is a "melting society" in which the old and the new clash and the outlines of a new culture are slowly emerging. In the process some things are gained, but much is lost. In a society where the socialization and cultural transmission roles of schooling are important, the consequences for education are enormous. Indeed, it is in the education arena that the culture clash characterizing the "melting society" is starkly evident.

Forces for change—multiracial/cultural, religious, linguistic, and economic—are also causing dramatic changes in Malaysia. Cast by its history into the form of a pluralistic society, Malaysia is using its highly centralized education system to try to achieve the political objective of national unity. However, because of continuing problems with equity and unequal access opportunities, the goals of national integration and unity remain elusive. This is especially the case now that the education system is being increasingly called upon to be a mechanism for human resource development.

Indonesia, on the other hand, has settled on a clear course of action in its ongoing struggle to forge national unity in a diverse society. The binding cement is religion, and the education system is clear about the Islamic pillars it is built upon and the socialization functions of schooling. (In this respect, similarities with Pakistan are striking.) From this reference point, the forces of globalization, modernization, economic transformation, and demographic change are addressed from a consistent interpretive framework. The process is not unproblematic, however. Aspects such as the cultural and linguistic diversity of the nation, serious economic problems, and a socially disruptive transition to a modern economy, among others, continue to make the achievement of national unity and social stability based on consensus elusive goals.

However, in the case of Papua New Guinea the above cannot even be considered realistic goals. Our text ends with an overview and analysis of a nation marked by deep economic crises, a government barely able to maintain law and order, political divisiveness, major disparities and inequalities, and chronic social problems. An ineffective, inequitable, and socially divisive education system is not succeeding in ameliorating the situation. As we finish reading about Papua New Guinea, it is sobering to reflect on how challenging and frustrating it is, in all too many parts of the world, to be an educator.

CHAPTER 23

Schooling and Social Change: The People's Republic of China

WING-WAH LAW

Wing-Wah Law is an assistant professor on the Faculty of Education, The University of Hong Kong. His research interests include comparative education, higher education in the People's Republic of China, higher education in Taiwan, higher education in Hong Kong, education and development, and citizenship education.

In 1949 the Communist Party of China (CPC) assumed leadership in China, transforming it into a socialist country, the People's Republic of China (PRC). More than a quarter of a century later, after developing diplomatic and economic ties with western countries like the United States in the late 1970s, the PRC's economic system changed from socialist to state-capitalist. Under the guidance and regulation of the state, market mechanisms were institutionalized in the state sector and a private sector was created. However, the political system of the PRC has remained unchanged since its founding in 1949. The purpose of this chapter is to examine the impacts of this partial social transformation on education.

THE SOCIAL FABRIC

Socialism and Social Diversity

Demographically, the PRC is a multiethnic society with a population of 1.2 billion people, the largest in the world. Of these, 92 percent are Han Chinese; the rest comprise 55 officially recognized ethnic minority groups. Although many of the latter have their own languages, the official languages are Putonghua (based on Beijing pronunciation) and Han Chinese. Less than 30 percent of the population live in urban areas; over 70 percent in rural, mountainous, or remote areas.

Since its founding in 1949, the PRC has been under the control of the CPC. Ignoring several millennia of Chinese cultural traditions (particularly Confucianism), the PRC officially adopted Chinese socialism as its national value system. Chinese socialism is a set of economic and sociopolitical values that were modified from Marxism and Leninism and interpreted differently by PRC leaders in specific periods: Mao Zedong from the 1950s to the 1970s, Deng Xiaoping in the 1980s, and Jiang Zemin in the 1990s (Dreyer, 1993).

Communist Party of China

For administrative purposes, the PRC is divided into thirty-one regions: twenty-seven provinces and four municipalities administered directly by the State Council (Beijing, Chongqing, Shanghai, and Tianjian). In spite of being hailed as masters of the nation, workers, peasants, and soldiers were chess pieces in many mass mobilizations with economic and political agendas determined by CPC leaders (Dreyer, 1993; Liu, 1996; White, 1989). An example was the Great Leap Forward Movement in the 1950s. People's communes and factory brigades were quickly developed and were urged to hasten economic production, for example, so as to overtake Britain in steel production. Another example was the Cultural Revolution (1966–1976) in which the CPC leaders mobilized the masses to purge their enemies from political leadership and foreign and decadent Chinese traditional influences.

Moreover, the CPC controls the agenda and membership of the National People's Congress and regional and local people's congresses through which people are supposed to exercise state power (National People's Congress, 1987, Article 2). For example, 67 percent of representatives in the 7th National People's Congress (1988–1993) were CPC members and the rest were carefully screened by the CPC (Xie, 1996). The CPC also controls the power of appointment of heads in the national government (comprising the State Council, Military Commission, Procurator Council, and Supreme Court) and governments at other levels.

Economic Restructuring

Unlike the political structure, the economic system of the PRC was restructured twice. In the 1950s the CPC under the leadership of Mao imported the socialist economic model from the former Soviet Union. All means of production were exclusively owned by the state on behalf of the people. As a result, all private factories and commercial enterprises were nationalized through the transference of their ownership and management power into the state. National and regional economic developments were centrally planned and controlled.

After opening up to western countries in the late 1970s, the PRC state under Deng reformed the socialist economy by the incorporation of market forces. This not only helped the PRC increase its gross national product (GNP) by over elevenfold within fifteen years (State Statistical Bureau, 1995), but also gave impetus to the restructuring of the economic relations between the state and the people.

The first feature of economic restructuring was the broadening of ownership of means of production to include individuals and private entities at home or abroad. The 1980s witnessed the withering of state-owned enterprises, the growth of collective and private enterprises at the levels of township and village, and the influx of foreign-invested corporations particularly based in Hong

Kong (at that time a British colony), Taiwan, and western countries (Yabuki, 1995).

Another characteristic of economic restructuring was decentralization of power and financial responsibility. To reduce financial burden and improve institutional efficiency, the PRC state shifted the financial responsibility to lower units of governance. Power over fiscal and administration affairs was devolved from the central government to provincial and local governments, which in turn devolved power to institutions and individuals (Chung, 1995).

However, the PRC state created a new legal framework, as the third mark of economic restructuring, to regulate market forces and the activities of newly emerged economic actors. Between 1978 and 1996, the National People's Congress passed over 300 laws and related policies covering the economy, state institutions, administration, and civic affairs. This was done with a view toward protecting the income of governments at various levels and regulating the distribution of wealth.

The fourth result of economic reform was a pair of identity crises: a national identity crisis of the PRC as a socialist country, and a party identity crisis of the CPC as the ruling party and principal definer of the socialist national identity. First, the CPC's insistence on keeping the socialist system exclusive was challenged from abroad and at home. The downfall of socialism in the former socialist bloc in eastern and central Europe in the early 1990s heralded the end of the global ideological battle between socialism and capitalism and signified that socialism had ceased to be a viable form of ideology for development in the international community (Bromke, 1993). This posed an external threat to the CPC. At home, the introduction of market forces to revive the socialist economy further discredited the CPC's claim that only socialism could save China from economic backwardness.

Emerging Ideological Tensions

The ideological battle between socialism and capitalism in the PRC intensified, particularly at the national political level. In the life of party cadres, officials, and ordinary citizens, orthodox socialist values were losing ground whereas market-oriented values were strengthening. First, the widespread acceptance of materialistic values constituted a challenge to the image and identity of the CPC. In public discourses such as leaders' speeches and policy statements, the CPC seriously condemned some materialistic values (including competition for one's own interests with little regards for others and money-worship) and the new consumption behaviors of the newly rich (like extravagance). The CPC kept on extolling socialist values such as the importance of public ownership, the primacy of planning over the market, the final goal of co-prosperity among people, and the priority of the state over individuals (Bernstein, 1993).

Second, the role of the PRC state as a macroregulator was weakened by market forces. This was indicated by the widening of, rather than reduction in, economic disparities between regions and between subregions. Income disparity also occurred between urban and rural populations. On average, in 1995 the per capita income in urban areas was more than double that in rural areas. Furthermore, most of the people below the poverty line live in mountainous and remote rural areas in central and western regions.

Third, the authority of the CPC as the ruling party was challenged by increasing conflicts between state and nonstate actors. The most representative challenge was the pro-democracy movement in 1989. It began with a series of activities organized by college students in Beijing. The students urged the PRC state to rectify corruption problems within government officials, lift the ban on presses run by the people, increase education expenditures, and enhance the status of intellectuals. These students' activities later evolved into large-scale demonstrations supported by workers and other citizens who were dissatisfied with the performance of the PRC state. Hundreds of thousands of government officials also publicly participated in these demonstrations. However, the movement was condemned by the PRC state as counterrevolutionary and ended with the military

crackdown in Tiananmen Square. That suppression marked the limits of the CPC's tolerance of challenges to its leadership from below.

At the parliamentary level, stances of public expression that deviated from the party line were heard in the National People's Congress. Hitherto, this body was often criticized as a rubber stamp agency. Now, unlike practice before the 1990s, not all government reports, including those by the Premier, got full endorsement from the Congress.

In the economic sector, conflicts were expressed in the form of lawsuits against local governments and social protests. The causes were complicated and intertwined. They included citizens' dissatisfactions with high inflation rates and demands for higher income to catch up with inflation, local actors' disappointments with the policies set by party cadres and entrepreneurs within their territories, increased demands by locals for institutional changes and participation in local affairs, and perceptual charges of workers and peasants about the reversion of their socioeconomic rank from masters of the nation to servants of entrepreneurs and newly rich people (Li & O'Brien, 1996; Liu, 1996; Walder, 1993).

To safeguard its own political leadership, the CPC took two preventive measures. First, in 1993 it modified the constitution to endorse the continuation of its political dominance in the PRC for a "long period" and rejected any introduction of direct national elections similar to those in western countries. Second, in 1996 the Secretary-General of the CPC revitalized a nationwide discussion labeled "talking politics." To improve the image of CPC and to tighten its control of the behaviors of party cadres, the Central Committee in April 1997 issued *The Rules on Disciplinary Punishment*. The *Rules* lists mistakes that would invite punishment by the CPC. Political mistakes leading to the removal of party membership include participation in anti-partyline meetings, persistence in capitalist liberalization, public oral or written expression against party policies, and organization of protests and demonstrations. Economic mistakes leading to administrative discipline include bribery and trafficking.

Whether these preventive measures can help the CPC to stay in power and maintain its own version of socialism remains to be seen. However, the four dimensions of economic restructuring discussed above have had an impact and can be identified in the school system as discussed below.

SCHOOLING

Since 1949 the guiding education philosophies of the PRC have been heavily loaded with the sociopolitical values prescribed by CPC leaders. They include the use of Marxism, Leninism, and Chinese socialism as guiding principles; the use of education to serve socialist modernization; and the integration of production with labor (National People's Congress, 1995). Emphasis is also put on the physical, intellectual, and moral development of students.

The Structure of Education

The education structure in the PRC comprises four major levels: primary, junior secondary, senior secondary, and higher education. In 1986, the PRC state introduced a policy of nine years of compulsory basic education to cover the first two levels for children aged 6 to 15. Within basic education, four major tracks can be identified. The less common tracks are the 5+3 (five years of primary education and three years of junior secondary education) track and the nine-year complete track. The more common tracks are 6+3 and 5+4. The percentages of entrants and graduates in the 6+3 track were, respectively, 61.4 percent and 59.8 percent in 1995–1996 (State Education Commission, 1996).

Post-compulsory education comprises senior secondary and higher education. The senior secondary sector includes general senior secondary schools to prepare students for higher education, senior vocational schools, specialized secondary schools, and skilled worker schools to train different types of middle-level technicians and management personnel. Of the total student enrollment (17.8 million) in 1996, these four types of schools

took, respectively, 43.2 percent, 23.8 percent, 22.2 percent, and 10.8 percent (State Education Commission, 1997).

Higher education offers both degree and subdegree courses with approximately the same enrollment sizes. Vigorous competition occurs within post-compulsory education as is reflected in the number of entrants, student enrollment, and graduates (Figure 23.1). In 1996, the transition rates of primary and junior secondary graduates to the next education levels were 92.6 percent and 49.8 percent respectively (State Education Commission, 1997). About 6 to 8 percent of the cohort accessed higher education. The flow of students is regulated mainly by two public examinations: local senior secondary school entrance examination and national joint college entrance examinations. In poor areas where basic education has not been universalized, public examinations are also used to select primary graduates for junior secondary schools.

Economic and Political Functions

Despite different emphases in different periods, education has consistently been given two important nation-building tasks: economic and political. The first task is to train people with basic and professional knowledge and skills for economic modernization. Schools are expected to help eliminate illiteracy and enhance the technical and professional levels of the labor force across the nation. The second task is to promote among citizens the socialist national identity defined by the CPC. Specific sets of economic and sociopolitical values are selected in the constitution for transmission to students or rejection (National People's Congress, 1987, Articles 19, 23, 24). Promoted values include the "five loves" (love of the motherland, of the people, of labor, of science, and of socialism) and the "five -isms" (patriotism, collectivism, internationalism, communism, and dialectical and historical materialism). Rejected values include "capitalist, feudal, and other decadent ideas." In other words, graduates are expected to have certain levels of vocational competency and political reliability.

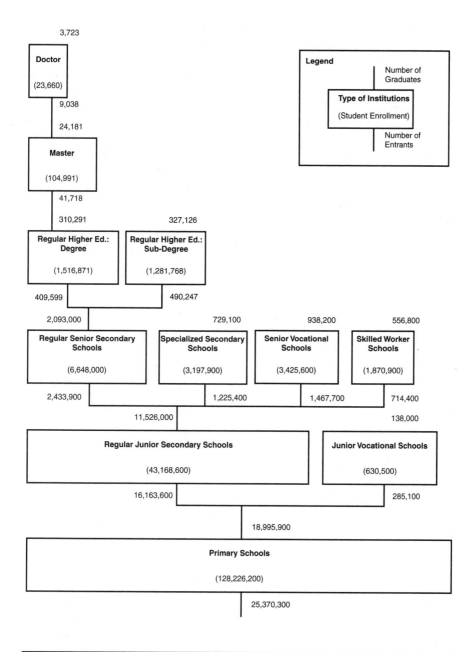

FIGURE 23.1 Education structures with enrollment sizes and numbers of entrants as well as graduates at various levels in the PRC, 1995–1996. Source: Figures taken from State Education Commission (1996), pp. 5, 58–59, 68–69.

The two nation-building tasks of education are reflected in the school curriculum suggested by the State Education Commission in the late 1980s and early 1990s. The 6+3 track of basic education may be taken as an illustration. School subjects can be broadly divided into three major groups (Table 23.1). Group I subjects cover Chinese, foreign language, mathematics, and science. Group II includes political courses and humanity subjects such as history and geography. Group III subjects, including music and physical education, focus on the cultural and physical development of students. The economic task is strongly reflected in Group I subjects, which are intended to train pupils with basic working skills including literacy, numeracy, and science knowledge. Over 60 percent of class time is allocated to these subjects.

The political task of education is mainly taken up by Group II subjects. These subjects form an important curriculum arena for the CPC to transmit its set of sociopolitical values and offer its versions and interpretation of historical, social, and international events. The class time for Group II subjects increases from about 11 percent at the primary level to 24 percent at the junior secondary level. Textbooks are filled with the political claims and positions of the CPC, such as the domination and supremacy of socialism over capitalism and the importance of the leadership of the CPC to the survival of China. Subjects in the other two groups are also used to spread political messages and achieve political purposes, such as the promotion of patriotic education (Beijing Eastern District Education Department, 1993).

It is also worth noting that, after splitting with the former Soviet Union in the 1960s and opening up to western countries in the late 1970s, the PRC state emphasized English as an important medium

TABLE 23.1   Time Allocation Suggested by the State Education Commission, 1988

TASK	SUBJECTS	NUMBER OF CLASS HOURS (%)	
		Primary Schools	*Junior Secondary Schools*
Group I	Chinese	1,717/1,734 (34.9)	566 (18.35)
	Foreign Language		400 (12.97)
	Mathematics	986 (19.9)	500 (16.21)
	Nature	272 (5.4)	
	Physics		132 (4.28)
	Chemistry		96 (3.11)
	Physiology		170 (5.51)
	Ideology & Moral Character	204 (4.1)	
	Politics		200 (6.48)
	Social Studies	204 (4.1)	
Group II	History		200 (6.48)
	Geography		153 (4.96)
	Labor	136 (2.7)	
	Labor and Skills		200 (6.48)
Group III	Physical Education	544 (11.1)	268 (8.69)
	Music	476 (9.6)	100 (3.24)
	Fine Arts	408 (8.2)	100 (3.24)
Total		4,964 (100)	3,085 (100)

Source: Rearranged for the purposes of discussion in this chapter by the writer from Liu (1993; vol. 1), pp. 365–366.

of communication for the PRC in the development of economic relations with western countries and access to their science and technology. As a result, English has replaced Russian as the most popular foreign language in schools and higher education institutions. For example, 98.7 percent of 429,521 foreign language teachers in the general secondary sector in 1995 taught English, 0.9 percent Russian, and 0.4 percent Japanese (State Education Commission, 1996).

Administration

To monitor the economic and political tasks of education, the PRC state has established a school administration system marked by the integration of political and administrative powers. In general, every school is subordinate to its local education bureau and, at the same time, local party unit. The internal administration system is supposed to be led by the principal, while party organizations on campus are to be led by the school party secretary or CPC-appointed representative. However, such a division of labor was not clear before the 1980s. Most administrative powers were in the hands of the school party secretaries or representatives, and many principals served as rubber stamps of the party's education policy. In the 1980s, party control at the school level was loosened up a bit and principals briefly enjoyed more autonomy.

However, after the Tiananmen Square incident in 1989 and the global decline of socialism in the early 1990s, the CPC began to tighten its political control over school administration and to revitalize the power of political organs in schools and particularly in tertiary institutions. The Central Committee of the CPC and the State Council reasserted the status of party organizations as the "political core" in school. They also cautiously specified the divisions of power between the school party secretary and the principal over different school affairs, and their mutual accountability was spelled out (Beijing Eastern District Education Department, 1993).

When this division of power is translated into a standard secondary school, these two school executives coadminister the school. The principal is in charge of academic and general affairs departments, but needs to consult the school party secretary on important decisions. The school party secretary is responsible for political and ideological work among staff and students at various levels, whereas the principal can advise on such work. On staff recruitment, appraisal, and promotion, the principal can make proposals to higher units of governance, which are helped by the school party secretary in monitoring and reviewing these decisions.

SOCIAL AND EDUCATION ISSUES
Change in the PRC Since the 1980s

In response to social transformations since the 1980s, the PRC state modified its strategies of manpower planning and funding. The modification initiated complicated education issues that reflect the complexity of social transformation and national identity transition. To illustrate this, six education aspects are selected: popularization of basic education, vocationalization of education, diversification of education financing, intensification of resource driven conflicts, reemergence of private education, and consolidation of political and ideological education. The first five aspects are mainly related to the economic tasks of education, and the last to the political.

Efficiency and Quality in Basic Education. The workforce of the PRC is massive, but weak in both basic and vocational skills. Of the population aged 6 and above, about 18 percent (205 million) were classified in the 1990 census as illiterate or semi-illiterate (State Statistical Bureau, 1990, 1995). Illiterates were defined as those who know less than 500 commonly used words; semi-illiterates less than 1,500 words in rural areas and 2,000 in urban areas. Over 80 percent of illiterates lived in rural areas. Moreover, the labor force (aged 15 to 59) in 1990 was 730 million and was expected to increase at a rate of about 27 million a year in the 1990s (Tan, 1997). In the mid-1990s, nearly 40 percent of the labor force was untrained.

In order to improve the quality of this massive labor force, the PRC adjusted its manpower planning by popularizing basic education and vocationalizing secondary education. The achievements in promoting basic education were remarkable. The illiteracy rate among people aged above 15 was reduced to 12 percent in 1996 (Zhu, 1997). The official net enrollment rate of cohorts aged 6 to 15 increased from 93 percent in 1980 to 98.4 percent in 1994 (State Education Commission, 1996). However, these figures mask a problem: that of student dropouts, particularly in rural areas. In 1990, 32.9 million children who should have been receiving compulsory education were not in school. Although the PRC reduced the school dropout rate among children aged 6 to 14 from 18.6 percent in 1990 to 8.8 percent in 1996, the figure is still high.

Vocationalization of Education. In addition to the strategic plan to improve basic skills, the PRC state had a parallel plan to enhance the vocational skills of the labor force. Secondary education was rapidly revocationalized by increasing the percentage of student enrollment in vocational and technical education.

In the 1980s, the PRC state began to revocationalize secondary education. Student enrollment was enlarged in the vocational track but contracted correspondingly in the academic stream. As a result, student enrollment in the vocational track increased from 18.9 percent in 1980 to 56.8 percent in 1996 (Ministry of Education, 1985; State Education Commission, 1997). By 2000, it is expected to be 60 percent as a national average, and 70 percent in cities.

In the early 1980s provincial or municipal governments also began to establish short-cycle vocational colleges to train graduates from general secondary schools. These colleges offer specializations such as secretary training, tourism, and foreign language that are specific to local economies; courses last for two or three years. A vocational curriculum was also extended to junior secondary schools while separate junior vocational schools began to emerge in the 1980s. Their enrollment

remains very small—1.5 percent (State Education Commission, 1997). More conspicuous vocationalization occurred in the internal curricular streaming in ordinary junior secondary schools. This was a phenomenon mainly in rural areas where nine-year compulsory education had not been achieved. Depending on the financial ability of local economies and school conditions, there were three major forms of internal streaming: division into academic and vocational curricula only at the third (and last) year, an additional year of vocational training for junior secondary graduates who failed to promote to senior secondary education, and the introduction of vocational curriculum across all four years of schooling.

To achieve rapid vocationalization, particularly at the senior secondary level, the PRC adopted three major strategies. First, hundreds of general senior secondary schools were converted into vocational ones and many of their teachers were redeployed to teach vocational subjects. Another strategy was the introduction of positive discrimination in employment in 1981. Employers are asked to give preference to those who have certificates of relevant vocational training. This is expected to fight against social prejudices favoring the academic curriculum and to enhance the social image of vocational and technical education. Related to image enhancement, the third and the most important strategy of rapid vocationalization was to consolidate the legal status of vocational training in the whole education system through the Vocational Education Law (National People's Congress, 1996).

However, success was limited because of insufficient financial and other resource support. A majority of converted vocational schools were not reequipped with facilities to fit the new purposes. Many teachers in the original general senior secondary schools who were redeployed to teach vocational subjects lacked adequate vocational knowledge and skills (Lewin, Little, Xu, & Zheng, 1994). The policy of positive discrimination for vocational certificates in staff recruitment also resulted in problems. Education resources were wasted as a result of a mismatch between students' training and needs of the labor market. After failing to access higher education, many graduates of general senior secondary schools simply applied for retraining for another two or three years in short-cycle vocational colleges or specialized secondary and skilled worker schools (which were originally intended to cater to junior secondary graduates).

The policy of positive vocational discrimination also created identity confusion for both students and specialized schools. This was a result of pressure on students to pursue a tertiary diploma on top of a senior secondary diploma. The double diploma phenomenon is a result of is a fundamental problem concerning diploma inflation. The market value of specialized school diplomas was suddenly magnified in the 1980s but began to depreciate when more people obtained such diplomas, or even higher ones, in the 1990s. Diploma inflation is expected to continue in the next millennium and therefore the identity crises of specialized schools and their students may be worsened (and extended to other sectors, such as general senior secondary schools).

Diversification of Education Financing. To support the popularization of basic education and vocationalization of secondary education quickly on a national scale, the PRC state decentralized financing responsibility to lower units of governance and end users of education services including students, parents, and employers. The decentralization of financing responsibility was manifested in two forms.

The first was the devolution of financial responsibility for education from the central government to regional and local governments. For example, the share of central government in the public budgetary expenditure on education decreased from 13.8 percent in 1990 to 11.7 percent in 1995 (Shanghai Institute, 1994; State Education Commission, 1996). Another form was the diversification of financial resources to include nonstate sources such as taxpayers, end users, and social communities at home or abroad. This represented a change in the definition of education

from a social welfare totally financed by the state to a public service for which end users had to pay part of the cost. The average share of nongovernment sources in education expenditure increased from 39.2 percent in 1993 to 45.2 percent in 1995 (Shanghai Institute, 1994; State Education Commission and SIDRI, 1996).

Despite the diversification of funding sources, the increase in education investment in the PRC still cannot catch up with national economic growth. GNP increased almost elevenfold between 1980 and 1994. The percentage of expenditure by the central and regional governments on education also increased from 8.92 percent in 1980 to 16.05 percent in 1995. However, the percentage of GNP on education continuously decreased from 3.1 percent in 1990 to 2.44 percent in 1996 (State Education Commission and SIDRI, 1996, Zhu, 1997). PRC authorities admitted that public funding for education was still lower than the world average (5.1 percent in 1992) and the average of developing countries (4.1 percent) and pledged to increase educational funding up to 4 percent of GNP by 2000.

Intensification of Resource-Driven Conflicts. Under this tight financial constraint, the policy of decentralizing financial responsibility in the PRC was a two-edged sword. On the one hand, local incentives were enhanced and lower units of governance had more say on financial and administrative affairs within their jurisdiction. On the other hand, the policy created competition over limited resources. The contenders were both beneficiaries and victims of the policy. To illustrate this among different contenders, three cases are selected: the withholding of teachers' salaries, the abuse of fee charging, and admission of unqualified students in state schools.

Many local governments abused their power by extracting and delaying teachers' salaries. This is illegal; it is also the law that teachers' salaries should be similar to that of civil servants. In reality, teachers' pay is very low and ranks third from the bottom in the public payroll. In 1996, the average monthly wage of a teacher (very approximately US$48) was about 73 percent of the wage of an average factory worker (Sharma, 1997). In many provinces teachers' salaries were also top-sliced by local governments. Even worse, teachers' pay was delayed for months by a number of local governments. The problem, as pointed out by Vice-Premier Li Lanqing (1996), was more serious in the economically developed regions on the east coast than in the less developed regions of the inland. The governments of the former diverted teachers' salaries to economic construction and the building of their own offices.

Teachers who were victims of local governments in turn shifted the financial responsibility to students and parents. According to national regulations, schools can only charge students very small amounts of miscellaneous fees in both basic and senior secondary education, and fee standards need to be approved by regional and local governments. However, many schools ignored these regulations and generated additional income by creating their own charging items such as school maintenance, supplementary classes, use of classroom equipment like fans, subsidies to teachers, coordination of student activities, and guaranteed deposits for promotion to next level of education.

The decentralization of financial responsibility in the school system also resulted in another nation wide phenomenon: the admission of unqualified students with better socioeconomic or political backgrounds to state schools. These students are called "school selectors" because they can choose schools at will. The phenomenon began in the late 1980s. At the level of basic education, many primary and junior secondary schools, particularly in large cities, began violating national policy by admitting students outside their school districts and charging them high fees. At the senior secondary level, many schools also admitted students who did not meet academic requirements but were able to pay high fees. In addition, some party cadres and government officials made use of their positions to reserve places for their children.

The growth of the school selector phenomenon can be attributed to four related factors. First, the education structure is pyramidal; the higher the level, the lower the percentage of admission. Sec-

ond, there are disparities in social status and quality of education services between prestigious and academically "weak" schools. Third, schools need additional income to supplement limited state funding. Compared with other ways for generating school income such as running school factories, "selling" school places is an extremely low-cost and high-reward proposition. Fourth, students and parents have strong aspirations for schools with better education services and higher promotion rates. If they can financially afford such schools, they are willing to pay. The cost depends on the supply of and demand upon places in such schools.

Four common threads link the above three nationwide conflicts over limited educational resources (holding up teachers' salaries, abuse of fee charges, and the problem of school selectors). First, all are examples of public defiance of national education laws. Second, these problems reflect the inability of the PRC state, despite its attempts to the contrary, to cope with deviant cases because it is no longer the principal sponsor of education. Third, effective mechanisms to hold lower units of governance accountable for power devolution are lacking in the school system. Fourth, the principle of fairness is challenged and redefined in the redistribution of power in the socialist market economy. Teachers are not rewarded for their efforts or time, students pay more than they are legally required, and students from socioeconomically privileged families can get a school place without earning it. All these cases illustrate a classic example of exploitation of the have-nots by the haves.

Reemergence of Private Education. In the 1990s, the PRC state reinstated the official status of private schools, schools financed and operated mainly on their own funds outside the state budget. This was a fundamental change as, formerly, the concept of private schools had been rejected. Private schools were perceived ideologically as a characteristic of education in capitalist societies and were therefore unacceptable in the socialist PRC. Too, education was perceived as part of national sovereignty and schools should not be controlled by non-PRC citizens.

Between 1950 and 1956, over 12,000 private schools and universities were dissolved or nationalized. About 85 percent of these private institutions had been sponsored by local organizations or communities, the rest by foreign churches. However, the reality is that private schools did not disappear after the nationalization movement. Rather, they continued to exist in another form, *minban* (community-sponsored or people-run) schools. This is because, in order to popularize primary education, the PRC regime not only sponsored state schools but also encouraged factories, mines, enterprises, and agricultural cooperatives to sponsor and run *minban* schools with their own funds. As a result, a large number of *minban* schools were established. Over 40 percent of primary students were enrolled in these schools in 1965 (Zhou, 1990). Many minban teachers were peasants with low education credentials and no formal teacher training.

Despite different sources of funding, the curriculum and management in both *minban* and state schools were under strict government control. In 1979, the PRC government began turning *minban* primary and secondary schools into state schools. Yet, many *minban* teachers in state schools are still not on the government payroll until their conversion of status is approved by the state. This depends on the acceptance of their teaching qualifications and the quotas set by regional and local governments.

After the institutionalization of market mechanisms, private schools began to reemerge publicly in 1982. The schools are prevalent particularly in economically developed areas such as Guangzhou and Shanghai in the 1990s (Zhu & Zhu, 1996). Unlike state schools and former *minban* schools, private schools enjoy relatively high autonomy in recruitment and management of teachers and students, determining tuition fees and teachers' salaries, and design of curriculum. Although estimates vary, in 1995 as many as .5 percent of all students may have been enrolled in 3,159 primary and secondary schools and 672 vocational schools

registered with governments at various levels. If this is the case, the proportion is similar to that of private schools in Japan (Ministry of Education, Science, Sports and Culture, 1996).

Private schools, however, remain very much under government control as they operate under major restrictions. First, they need to register with local governments and they must satisfy minimum requirements for school buildings, facilities, boards of trustees, and teacher qualifications. Certificates awarded by illegal private schools are not recognized by the state. Finally, there is a nationality requirement imposed on both private and state schools. School principals are not allowed to hold foreign passports and must be PRC residents (National People's Congress, 1995).

In terms of financing and ownership, private schools fall into three categories. The first and least prevalent type is totally private schools, which are sponsored and owned completely by private organizations or individuals. Many have their own buildings and campuses. However, a majority of private schools found they could not run without state support and thus community sponsored but state assisted (CSSA) schools, and state sponsored but community assisted (SSCA) schools emerged (Yang, 1997).

In CSSA schools individuals, enterprises or community groups are responsible for the whole or a majority of initial costs, whereas the state subsidizes them in the form of renting public school buildings and facilities without charge or at a comparatively low price. In SSCA schools, the state contracts out existing or new state schools to individuals or community groups and allows them to run them on the terms of *minban* schools. This can be regarded as a form of privatization of state schools.

In terms of tuition fees and quality of services, there are three types of private schools: elitist, ordinary, and illegal. A minority of private schools can be described as elitist. Despite extraordinary high fees, the demand of students from socioeconomically advantaged groups for places in elitist private schools has increased. However, these elitist schools were criticized by the PRC authorities as "aristocratic" and for making large margins of profit (Wang & Zhang, 1994, p. 70). In other words, they were politically inconsistent with the values promoted by the CPC.

It is interesting to note that, in addition to state-sanctioned private schools, there are also illegal private schools. Some of these schools do not even apply for registration, others continue to operate even though their applications had been turned down by local governments. Illegal private schools flourish because they serve the needs of families whose children cannot enter state schools through official channels because of residence restrictions. This is particularly an issue in economically developed cities such as Guangzhou, Shanghai, and Shenzhen. These cities attract a large number of illegal migrants from other less developed provinces or areas within the same provinces. For example, Shenzhen has about 2.2 million immigrants and over thirty illegal private schools (Wei, 1996). These schools are constantly under threat of closure by the government and cannot award officially recognized qualifications. Many of them also recruit unqualified teachers and operate in very substandard buildings.

Overall, the greater significance of private schools is that they are indicative of how, as part of economic restructuring, market mechanisms have been incorporated into the PRC school system. This represents a shift of responsibilities in education provision from the state to the nonstate sector and a successful institutionalization of market values in the school sector. Private schools also test the limits of PRC state tolerance in its ideological shift to capitalist modes of sponsorship and operation in education.

As economic restructuring had political impacts on the ruling party, ideological conflicts, as discussed next, also occurred in the political dimensions of the school system.

Consolidation of Political and Ideological Education.
The status of political and ideological education in the PRC has been frequently challenged from within and without since the 1980s. The first challenge came from the negative

sociopolitical impacts of market forces on people's lives. One impact was the spreading of values such as extravagance, materialism, and extreme individualism, which were deemed by the CPC to be contradictory to values, such as frugality and self-sacrifice for the nation, promoted in political textbooks (Huang, 1995). Corruption among government officials further challenged the credibility of the CPC, which was portrayed in classes and school assemblies as the defender, not exploiter or suppresser, of the people. The second challenge was the global collapse of socialism in the early 1990s. The CPC has persistently claimed in public discourse and political textbooks that only socialism can save China. Now that ideology was heading against an opposing one.

The third challenge arose from within political and ideological education. Many pupils found that what they were required to learn in these courses was what they and adults (including their parents, teachers, and party cadres) often failed to do outside school. In some surveys of schools and tertiary institutions, many students expressed the view that the contents of political courses were irrelevant to their daily lives and even depicted falsehoods (Geng, 1995; Zhao, 1993). Political teachers also faced a status crisis as their courses were not highly valued by students and school authorities.

To cope with these challenges, the PRC state introduced three new measures to reinforce the status of political and ideological education. The first measure was to strengthen the legal status of political and ideological education and the dominance of the CPC's values over others. In 1994, the Central Committee of the CPC formulated national Guidelines on the Implementation of Patriotic Education that reemphasize the importance of political work. For example, the transmission of the central value system prescribed by the CPC is stipulated in the 1993 Teacher Law as a compulsory duty of all teachers (National People's Congress, 1993).

Another measure was to strengthen the curricular framework of political and ideological education. The framework covers goals, contents, methods, and assessment. The major political aim is to produce politically reliable citizens to support and extend the leadership of the CPC. The target groups are clearly spelled out to include students from kindergarten to tertiary education (Central Committee, 1994). The contents are deliberately selected to make moral, civic, and political education inseparable, in the sense that each shares or serves the functions of the other two.

Teachers are encouraged to diversify teaching methods to include lectures, discussion, games, social visits, and community services. In addition to regular extracurricular activities coordinated by Young Pioneers Units, schools also organize extra activities in response to the CPC's call. For example, a movement in patriotic education began to sweep across the country in 1994. In many primary and secondary schools, students were taught 100 patriotic songs in school assemblies or music lessons and encouraged to read 100 patriotic books. Some schools also organized students to watch movies that glorified patriotic figures and themes in cinemas.

More importantly, the performance of students in public written examinations on political and ideological education is retained as a criterion for their promotion to the next level of education. Students have to give answers acceptable to the CPC in order to score enough marks to pass these examinations. They may not believe what they write, but they are not willing to risk their admission chances for the sake of demonstrating their skills in critical thinking.

As is the case with students, the performance of teachers and principals in political work on campus is also assessed and included as part of their appraisal. For example, the Guangzhou Education Commission (1996) has designed evaluation forms to assess the performance of both class and subject teachers in the promotion and implementation of politicized moral education among students. The assessment is linked to promotions and subsidies. The political appraisal of school principals serves similar functions. Of the potential 100 marks in a sample appraisal form for principals, six concern political qualities such as persistence in upholding Chinese socialism and the leadership of the CPC (Zhang & Jiang, 1996). Another eight marks focus on the development of political and ideological work, including recruitment of students into the CPC and monitoring staff performance in promoting such work.

The third measure to consolidate the status of political and ideological education is the incorporation of traditional Confucian values to act as a buffer between the clash between socialist and market values. Formerly, Confucian values were perceived as feudal and were rejected, particularly in the Cultural Revolution. However, since the economic reforms of the 1980s, the transmission and development of Chinese cultural traditions is regarded as an important educational task (National People's Congress, 1995).

THE FUTURE OF SOCIETY AND SCHOOLING

The 1980s and 1990s witnessed how economic restructuring under the leadership of Deng Xiaoping affected the school system in the PRC. The change in the economic system characterized by the adoption of market mechanisms affected both the economic and political tasks of education in the process of nation building.

The interaction between the decentralization of financial responsibility and the incorporation of market mechanisms produced three impacts on the school system. First, it created opportunities for lower units of governance and nonstate actors to create their own agendas and to play an important decision-making role in affairs at lower levels. Second, conflicts among these actors over limited resources were intensified and represented public challenges to the authority of the PRC state. Third, the ability of the PRC state in regulating regional disparities and solving these conflicts was weakened. School funding increasingly depended on the financial capacity of local economies, the commitment and ability of regional and local governments and other nonstate actors, and the use of market mechanisms to generate income. In other words, the decentralization of financial responsibility by the PRC state resulted not just in a devolution of power but also a self-imposition of constraints on its ability to regulate regional and local affairs.

The demise of Deng Xiaoping in 1997 formally sealed the era of the dominance of the founding revolutionaries in politics. However, the new leadership in the post-Deng era is likely to face four contentious issues inherited from its predecessors. The first issue may be how to maintain a balance between economic constraints and quality in education. The PRC state has attempted to upgrade teachers' qualifications at various levels and to improve teaching and learning environments in schools through investment in hardware (Jiang, 1996). But, the rate of improvement has lagged far behind the growing needs of a drastically expanding student enrollment because of low levels of investment in education.

A second related issue for the post-Deng leadership is the regulation of education disparities between schools and among the thirty-one provinces and municipalities. Resource-driven conflicts are expected to be intensified further, and vicious cycles of education disparities are expected to be exacerbated. Ironically, a new initiative to improve the quality of schooling in the PRC may reinforce further the vicious cycle of disparities at both the regional and school levels. The PRC state expects to develop a limited number of model schools meeting high national and even international standards at the beginning of the twenty-first century. Projected is a total of about 1,000 general senior secondary schools, 2,000 vocational schools, and 100 universities; each figure constitutes about 1 percent of the total number of institutions at that level. In consequence, academically weak schools may receive even less attention on the national agenda of the PRC state. Weak schools require resources as much as quality schools and poor regions as much as rich ones if education disparities are to be reduced. This cannot be achieved without the intervention of the PRC state, acting as a fair redistributor channeling education resources (and wealth) from the haves to the have-nots.

A third issue that may confront the post-Deng leadership is the development of a culture of the rule of law in education. In the course of almost two decades, the National People's Congress has promulgated six national education laws. This is expected to help cushion education from the effects of changes in leadership and changes in policy. These laws are also supposed to form a legal framework binding upon all involved parties. However, widespread irregularities such as fee abuses, admission policy violations, and delaying teachers' salaries obviously constitute a nationwide public defiance of the authority of law by a minority of government officials, school authorities, teachers, parents, and students. This points to an even more deep-seated problem and more pressing issue. It is necessary for the PRC state not only to strengthen and reinforce education laws, but also to foster a spirit and culture of upholding and obeying laws.

The fourth possible contentious issue concerns the core status of socialist values in the political and ideological curriculum in the post-Deng era. The selective accommodation of market values and Chinese traditional values into the curriculum has already signaled that the ideology of socialism does not exclusively define contemporary culture in the PRC and is insufficient to address people's needs arising from new economic contexts. The commodification or marketization of education, as demonstrated earlier, suggests that the PRC is as capitalist or even more capitalist than other societies such as the United States and Hong Kong. To minimize ideological disillusion and schizophrenia in its people's national and political identities, the post-Deng leadership may need to relocate the relative positions of socialism, capitalism, and endogenous Chinese traditional and contemporary values in the national value system.

One option would be to treat each as being of equal importance. This would help produce a political and ideological curriculum of political and cultural pluralism. As one of the few remaining socialist countries, and a user of capitalist means to revive its socialist economy, the PRC state should foster within students a spirit of accommodation, rather than exclusion, of political differences. The political task of education is to promote living, rather than dying or dead, traditions. National identity is in search of a balance between the contemporary needs of students and the state.

These are some of the education issues that the post-Deng leadership may need to tackle. However, they cannot be solved within a short period. The arrival of the twenty-first century may become an impetus for the PRC state to evaluate its achievements and educational strategies since the economic reforms of the 1980s and to formulate a new blueprint for preparing its citizens to meet the internal and external economic and political challenges of the next millennium.

REFERENCES

Beijing Eastern District Education Department. (1993). *Zhongxue geke zhongde aiguozhuyi jiaoyu* (Patriotic education in all subjects in secondary schools). Beijing: Beijing Education Press.

Bernstein, T.P. (1993). Ideology and rural reform: The paradox of contingent stability. In A.L. Rosenbaum (Ed.), *State and society in China: The consequences of reform* (pp. 143–165). Boulder, CO: Westview.

Bromke, A. (1993). Post-communist countries: Challenges and problems. In R.C. Karp (Ed.), *Central and Eastern Europe: The challenge of transition* (pp. 17–44). Oxford: Oxford University Press.

Central Committee of the Communist Party of China. (1994, September 6). Aiguo zhuyi jiaoyu shishi gangyao (Guidelines on the implementation of education of patriotism). *Zhongguo Jiaoyubao* (*China Education Daily*), p. 1.

Chung, J.H. (1995). Studies of central-provincial relations in the People's Republic of China: An appraisal. *China Quarterly, 142,* 487–508.

Dreyer, J.T. (1993). *China's political system: Modernization and tradition.* Basingstoke, Hampshire: Macmillan.

Geng, H. (1995, October). Political classes—most Important, most disliked. *Inside China Mainland,* pp. 61–65.

Guangzhou Education Commission. (1996). *Guang-zhoushi xuexiao deyu xitong sheji fangan* (*guidelines on the design of moral education system for schools in Guangzhou*). Guangzhou: Guangzhou Higher Education Press.

Huang, Z. (1995). Shichang jingji yu xuexiao deyu guangli (Market economy and management of moral education in schools). In Huang Zhaolong (Ed.), *Xiandai xuexiao deyu guanlixue* (Management of moral education in contemporary schools) (pp. 1–13). Beijing: Zhongguo Jingji Press.

Jiang, H. (1996). *Education sector in transitional economies: China case study report (revised version).* Manila: Asian Development Bank.

Lewin, K.M., Little, A.W., Xu, H., & Zheng, J. (1994). *Educational innovation in China: Tracing the impact of the 1985 reforms.* Essex: Longman.

Li, L. (1996, October 19). Youxian banhao shifan jiaoyu (To develop teacher education well as top priority). *Zhongguo Jiaoyubao* (*China Education Daily*), pp. 1, 2

Li, L., & O'Brien, K.J. (1996). Villagers and popular resistance in contemporary China. *Modern China, 22,* 28–61.

Liu, A.P.L. (1996). *Mass politics in the People's Republic: State and society in contemporary China.* Boulder, CO: Westview.

Ministry of Education. (1985). *Achievement of education in China, 1949–1983.* Beijing: People's Education Press.

Ministry of Education, Science, Sports and Culture, Japan. (1996). *Monbusho.* Tokyo: MESSC.

National People's Congress. (1987). *Constitution of the People's Republic of China.* Beijing: Foreign Languages Press.

National People's Congress. (1993). Zhonghua renmin gongheguo jiaoshifa (The teacher law of the People's Republic of China). In State Education Commission (Ed.) (1995), *Zhonghua renmin gongheguo jiaoyufa shiyong daquan* (A complete handbook on the Education law of the People's Republic of China) (pp. 437–441). Guangdong: Guangdong Education Press.

National People's Congress. (1995). Zhonghua renmin gongheguo jiaoyufa (The education law of the People's Republic of China). In State Education Commission (Ed.), *Zhonghua renmin gongheguo jiaoyufa shiyong daquan* (A complete handbook on the education law of the People's Republic of China) (pp. 25–35). Guangdong: Guangdong Education Press.

National People's Congress. (1996, May 18). Zhonghua renmin gongheguo zhiye jiaoyufa (Vocational education law of the People's Republic of China). *Zhongguo Jiaoyubao (China Education Daily)*, p. 1.

Shanghai Institute of Human Resource Development, Research Team. (1994). *Fund-using efficiency of primary school education in rural China: Research study based on case studies.* Shanghai: SIHRD.

Sharma, Y. (1997, February 28). Housing offered to stem mass exodus. *Times Educational Supplement.*

State Education Commission. (1996). *Comprehensive statistical yearbook of Chinese education, 1995.* Beijing: Higher Education Press.

State Education Commission. (1997, April 14). 1996 nian guanguo jiaoyu shiye fazhan tongji gongbao (Statistical report on educational achievements and developments in China in 1996). *Zhongguo Jiaoyubao (China Education Daily)*, p. 2.

State Education Commission, and Shanghai Intelligence Development Research Institute. (1996). 1995 nian quanguo jiaoyu jifei tongji kuaibao (Brief statistical report on 1995 education investment in China). *Jiaoyu Fazhan Yu Gaige Xinxi* (Information on educational development and reform; writer's translation), *7*, 1–8.

State Statistical Bureau. (1990). *China population statistics yearbook, 1990.* Beijing: Science and Technology Press.

State Statistical Bureau. (1995). *China statistical yearbook, 1995.* Beijing: China Statistical Publishing House.

Tan, S. (1997, January 13). Zhongguo zhiye jiaoyu fazhan de qushi (Trends of vocational education in China). *Zhongguo Jiaoyubao (China Education Daily)*, p. 2.

Walder, A.G. (1993). Urban industrial workers: Some observations on the 1980s. In A.L. Rosenbaum (Ed.), *State and society in China: The consequences of reform* (pp. 103–120). Boulder, CO: Westview.

Wang, Z., & Zhang, X. (1994). *Duoyuanhua banxue moshi tansuo (*Exploration into the diversification of sponsoring schools*).* Chengdu: Sichuan Education Press.

Wei, H. (1996). Minban jiaoyu de xiankuang he fazhan (The present situations and development of community-sponsored education). *Jiaoyu Cankao* (Education Reference, author's translation), *14*, 12–14.

White, L.T. (1989). *Policies of chaos: The organizational causes of violence in China's Cultural Revolution.* Princeton, NJ: Princeton University Press.

Xie, Q. (1996). *Dangdai zhongguo zhengfu (The contemporary government of the People's Republic of China)* (2nd ed.). Shengyang, Liaoning: Liaoning People's Press.

Yabuki, S. (1995). *China's new political economy: The giant awakes.* (Translated by Stephen M. Harner). Boulder, CO: Westview.

Yang, X. (1997). Zhongguo minban jiaoyu moshi, tezheng ji qi xingcheng yuanyin de fenxi (Analysis of the mode, characteristics, and causes of formation of community-sponsored education in China). In R. Hu (Ed.), *Zhongguo jichu jiaoyu fazhan yanjiu* (A research study on the developments of basic education in China) (pp. 234–248). Shanghai: Shanghai Education Press.

Zhang, Y., & Jiang, C. (1996). Xiandai xuexiao guanli shiwu guanshu (A practical handbook of modern school management). Beijing: Qiye Guanli Press.

Zhao, R. (1993). *Jiaohao sixiang zhengzhi ke* (To teach ideological and political course well). Beijing: Beijing Educational Press.

Zhou, Y. (Ed.). (1990). *Education in contemporary China.* Hunan: Hunan Education Press.

Zhu, K. (1997, January 21). Zai 1997 nian quanguo jiaoyu gongzuo huiyishang de jianghua (A speech by the State Education Commissioner in the National Education Conference in 1997). *Zhongguo Jiaoyubao (China Education Daily)*, pp. 1, 2.

Zhu, S., & Zhu, Y. (1996). (Eds.). *Shanghai shi minban zhongxiaoxue jiaoyu xintan* (New exploration into community-sponsored primary and secondary schools in Shanghai). Shanghai: Baijia Press.

CHAPTER 24

Education in the "Melting Society": New Challenges Facing Japanese Schools and Society

MASAKO KAMIJO

Masako Kamijo received her doctorate from the Department of Comparative Education, Institute of Education, London University and is currently a professor in the Faculty of Foreign Languages at Kanagawa University, Yokohama, Japan. Her research and teaching interests focus on the theory and practice of intercultural communication, sociocultural aspects of Japanese society, and comparative studies of Japanese and English society.

THE SOCIAL FABRIC

Japan is an island country consisting of four main islands and more than 6,800 small islands. The total surface area of Japan accounts for less than 0.3 percent of the world. Arable and habitable areas total a little over one-fourth of the nation's land.

Demographic

In 1995, the population (126 million) ranked eighth in the world and was about 2.2 percent of the world's population. The population density was the fourth in the world. The population was 125,570,000 (124,428,000 Japanese) in 1997. The population is projected to increase moderately, reaching a peak of 130 million in 2011, after which it is expected to decrease. Population growth is caused mainly by natural increase as net international migration is negligible.

In 1994, the birth rate was 10.0, the total fertility rate was 1.50, and the death rate was 7.1 per 1,000 population. The life expectancy in 1995 was 82.98 years for females and 76.57 years for males, which was at the topmost level in the world (Statistical Bureau, 1997). The aging of the population is progressing at a remarkable speed. On the other hand, the proportion of children has been declining since 1975. The average size of a household declined to 2.95 persons in 1994 because of the sharp decrease in the birth rate, together with an increase in nuclear households and one-person households. It is predicted to be 2.55 persons by 2010.

In 1994, the marriage rate fell to 6.3 and the divorce rate rose to 1.57 per 1,000 population due to an increase in women's work outside the home. The average age of people marrying was 28.5 years for males and 26.2 years for females in 1994, which was the highest since 1945. Even with the rapid increase in nonarranged "love marriages," the traditional arranged marriage is still popular.

Economy

The Japanese economy, severely damaged and disorganized at the end of World War II, recovered by the mid-1950s to nearly its pre-war level in respect to national products and peacetime levels of consumption. In the 1960s, the economy achieved high growth rates due to technological innovation and policies that gave priority to heavy and chemical industries. Japan maintained its high growth rates, and since 1967 its GDP has ranked second among the OECD member countries. Since 1989, the Japanese economy has been characterized by greater industrial and lifestyle sophistication. However, the economy has been in a severe slump since the 1991 collapse of the "bubble economy" caused by overspeculation in land and stocks.

The increasing number of international transactions involving people, goods, and capital has generated increasing economic interdependence and has pushed the Japanese economy toward a borderless operation. Japanese people travelling overseas increased to 15.3 million in 1995. Imports of consumer goods increased 2.5-fold between 1986 and 1988, but Japanese exports have grown so fast that this incites trade friction. Japan's total net foreign assets in 1988 were number one worldwide. There was a striking growth in direct investment from Japan as a result of the move by Japanese companies to establish factories and offices overseas (Tanaka, 1994).

With the growth in the service sector industries, employment in the tertiary sector accounted for 58.5 percent in 1988 (Tanaka, 1994). Employment in the secondary sector as well as the primary sector has dropped in consequence.

Japan's primary energy resources have to be supplied almost entirely by imports. In 1994, the supply of primary energy resources included coal (16.4%, 15.6% imported), petroleum (57.4%, 57.3% imported), natural gas and LNG (10.8%), hydropower (2.9%), nuclear (11.3%), geothermal (0.1%) and new energy (1.1%) (Statistical Bureau, 1996). As the use of energy resources is being diversified, efforts continue to study and develop new technologies such as solar energy and wind power.

The lifetime employment system in Japan has been decreasing since 1986. This has created more employment opportunities and encouraged job hopping, especially among young people. Unemployment rates increased to 3.2 percent in 1995 (Statistical Bureau, 1996). Women are discriminated against in employment in spite of the pressure to end this discrimination by women's groups

and the Equal Employment Opportunity Law of 1986. Nevertheless, the number of women career executives is increasing (Tanaka, 1994).

In 1996, 38.4 million males and 26.1 million females were employed (Nakayama, 1997). The average number of hours worked per person (1909 in 1995) is still ranked the highest among industrialized countries. The number of Japanese companies adopting the "2 days off a week" was still low, at 52.9 percent in 1994. The average Japanese worker took just over a half of his or her entitlement—16.1 paid vacation days per year in 1994. The average annual income increased to 7 million yen in 1995. Nearly 86 percent of Japanese private companies adopted an official retirement age of 60 in 1995.

The Japanese standard of living exceeds Western standards in terms of high average household income. It is one of the safest places to live in the world. Yet the average home has less space than in industrial countries. The high savings rate of the Japanese people is attributed to the extremely high cost of owning one's own home and the need to save because of inadequate welfare provisions for the aged.

Politics

The 1947 Constitution of Japan is the basic framework of government. It is characterized by respect for basic human rights, the sovereign right of the people, and renunciation of war. The Emperor, the symbol of the state and the unity of the people, has no powers related to the government. The government system is based on the separation of powers in three branches—legislative, executive, and judicial. All Japanese are eligible to vote from 20 years of age.

Bureaucrats who have passed the qualifying examinations for high-level posts in central government offices have considerable authority in drafting policy. They enjoyed the trust of the private sector, and they were given the credit for Japan's prosperity and miraculous economic growth. But from 1990, the bureaucracy came in for heavy criticism in connection with the bankruptcy of the housing loan corporations, HIV-infected blood products, and abuses of regulatory authority (Nakayama, 1997).

Characteristics of Japanese Culture

Japanese culture is made up of many layers—old and new, foreign and native. For example, food, clothing, and housing are blends of Japanese and Western elements. One of the reasons is that the Japanese people welcomed and adopted elements of foreign cultures out of curiosity without discarding their indigenous customs and traditions in the historic process of assimilation. The Japanese have been very adept at making foreign elements their own in order to create something that is uniquely Japanese. For example, Japanese *kana* characters were created out of the more complex Chinese characters. Buddhism arises from the Kamakura Buddhism that was introduced to Japan in the sixth century.

Japanese culture is also homogeneous. This is due to Japanese society's uniformity nationwide that developed under centralized governments. Too, primary importance is placed on the group rather than on the individual. The Japanese are highly pragmatic, emphasizing specific circumstances more than universal truths. It is this trait that made it possible to create Japan's worldly Buddhism. Even in modern science, the Japanese show more aptitude for scientific applications than for basic research (Tanaka, 1994).

The sense of oneness with nature underlies the Japanese ethos, its philosophy, thought, religion, agriculture, arts, customs, and the traditional martial arts. The sense of oneness with nature derived from the Japanese temperate climate with four clear seasons as well as the life cycles of the agricultural people of old Japan. As these people closely followed the natural rhythm of the land, they were at one with nature, and their very souls were a part of the spirit of nature.

The Japanese sensitivity to seasonal changes gave rise to a wide variety of arts and customs embodying this sensitivity such as *sansuiga* landscape painting, *waka* and *haiku* poetry, the tea ceremony, the Japanese garden, flower arrangements, and even the traditional martial arts such as kendo and judo. The identification with nature has spawned a preference to flow with the tide. It also refers to resignation—to the way things are and the lack of interest in religious promises of other worldly rewards (Tanaka, 1994).

Changing Japanese Culture

Japanese culture is melting. This is due, at least partly, to an inflow of multinationalities, international marriages, and so on. Hence, we now have the possibility to express a new Japanese culture. After the traditional *shaking society,* the present Japanese society is expressed as the *melting society* in terms of the value of time, the myth of oneself, the order of space, sex differences, truth, life and death, and the new culture.

To provide some examples: The Japanese sense of seasonal modern time is changing to that of a different sense of time where the past and future are melting, particularly through the fever of diversification and electronics. The human voice is linking people in various public and private spaces through mobile telephones (2,000 million used in 1998), which is distorting and melting the order of space. What is truth is uncertain in a society where the whole value system is changing. Since the 1980s, views on the value of life and death have also been changing. They are being dealt with lightly, and the borderline between life and death is vague among youth.

Religion

Japanese beliefs are complicated because of our openness to all religions, as exemplified in various customs or rituals, purification rites, and petitions for worldly benefits. Many Japanese visit Shinto shrines at New Year's and have both Shinto and Buddhist altars at home. They also feel a close affinity to Inari, an all-purpose god, and to the *dosojin* found on the edge of villages to protect villagers. Weddings may well be Buddhist, Shinto, Christian, or secular, whereas funerals are most often Buddhist. A Shinto priest performs purification rites for a new house and various other opening ceremonies.

The Japanese tend to avoid identifying with any single religious doctrine. Japanese beliefs have an inherent reverence for all things, which stems from their strongly rooted, nearly mystical affinity with nature, and their quest for worldly rewards. In Japan, religion is now a tool for petitioning for business profits, the safety of the household, success on school entrance exams, and numerous other concrete rewards (Tanaka, 1994).

SCHOOLING

Education played a key role in Japan's emergence as an industrial nation during the late nineteenth century. In recent years it has been a central factor in establishing and maintaining Japan as one of the world's most technologically advanced societies. The Japanese educational system underwent major reforms after World War II based on the American model. Since then, minor changes have taken place in order to cope with social changes and educational problems.

Legislation and Policies

The Constitution of Japan states the basic educational principles as democracy, peace, and welfare. The basic rights and duty of the people to receive education are stated as,

> People shall have the right to receive an equal education correspondent to their abilities, as provided for by law. The people shall be obligated to have all boys and girls under their protection receive ordinary education as provided for by law. Such compulsory education shall be free. (Article 26)

The Fundamental Law of Education states that the educational aim as to achieve

> the full development of personality, striving for the rearing of people, sound in mind and body, who shall love truth and justice, esteem the value of the individual, respect labor and have a deep sense of responsibility, and be imbued with an independent

> spirit, as builders of a peaceful state and society. (Article 1)

In order to achieve these aims, schooling encompasses equal opportunity, nine-year free compulsory education, co-education, school education, social education, prohibition against partisan political education, prohibition of religious education in the public schools, and prohibition of the improper control of education (Education Law, Articles 2–11). A series of educational statutes, the School Education Law, deal with specific provisions relating to the schools' system and organization in addition to management, financial support, and so on. The Social Education Law regulates the activities of social education.

Governance of schooling is carried out by the Ministry of Education, which gives guidance, advice, and assistance to local educational boards, social education, international exchange, and private bodies. It also approves the establishment of local, public, and private higher educational institutions (Ministry of Education, 1994).

The enrollment ratio in compulsory education is nearly 100 percent. For upper secondary education it is 98 percent, and for higher education, 38 percent.

Structure of Schooling

Preschool.   Kindergartens are noncompulsory schools for children from the ages of 3 to 6.

Elementary School.   It is compulsory to attend elementary and lower secondary school or a special education school for a period of nine years, from the ages of 6 to 15.

Secondary Schools.   In upper secondary schools, there are full-day (3 years), evening, and correspondence (3 years or more) schools for general and vocational courses. A minimum of 80 credits is required for graduation. The credit system was adopted in 1988 to award qualification for graduation by the total number of credits earned by the students of evening and correspondence school.

Higher Education.   Universities offer four-year courses (six-year courses for medicine, dentistry, and veterinary medicine). More than half of the universities have set up graduate schools: a two-year MA course and a five-year Ph.D. course (four years for medicine, dentistry, and veterinary medicine). Junior colleges offer two- or three-year courses. Five-year colleges of technology (three-year upper secondary education and two-year college) aim at training practical engineers. In 1996, there were 576 universities, 598 junior colleges, and 62 colleges of technology. The BA degree university of the air was introduced in 1985.

Nonformal Schooling.   Special training colleges (one year or more after 18 years of age) and miscellaneous schools (three months or more after 15 years of age) aim at developing the abilities required for working or practical life. The former offer fairly specialized courses for dentistry, medicine, welfare, business, foreign languages, and technology. The latter offers courses for nursing, dressmaking, cooking, accounting, and so on.

These schools are increasingly popular among students and adults. Life-long education is offered in private business schools, communities, and universities and is popular with the aged. Numerous cram schools (*juku*) exist for children to prepare for entrance examinations. Extra lessons and classes for music, sports, and so on, are popular among school children.

Curricula

The national curriculum consists of all basic subjects, moral education, and special activities (classroom activities, student council, club activities, and school events). Authorized textbooks by the Ministry of Education are distributed to all children of public and private schools free of charge.

The courses of study, curriculum, and standards from kindergartens to high schools, both public and private, are prescribed in the Courses of Study issued by the Ministry of Education. The Courses of Study provide the basic framework for curricula and the aim of each subject and the aims and content of teaching at each grade. Each school is allowed to organize its own curriculum on the basis of the Courses of Study, although in reality there is little room for it.

The Courses of Study are revised often to cope with changes in society. For example, a revision was issued in 1989 in order to cope with the present educational problems, internationalization, and globalization. Features common to all levels of schools in the revised Courses of Study emphasize creativity and individuality of children and environment.

Evaluation

In elementary schools and lower and upper secondary schools, children's attainment is evaluated by the class teacher and teachers specialized in their subjects at the teacher's discretion and at the end of each term in the year. The evaluation results by general performance and tests are written into the children's school records.

Children in elementary schools graduate regardless of their performance as long as they attended the required days in the school. They are transferred automatically to the lower secondary school. An upper secondary school admits entrants based on students' credentials from the lower secondary school, scholastic test records, and other factors. In local public upper secondary schools, scholastic tests are administered by prefectural or municipal boards of education, but the selection of entrants itself is conducted by each school. National and private upper secondary schools conduct their own entrance examinations. As for colleges of technology, the eligibility for entrance is similar to that of upper secondary schools.

Each university and junior college selects its entrants according to its own admission procedures using the applicant's upper secondary school credentials, scholastic tests, or special means. In addition to this, the NCUEE (National

Center for University Entrance Examination) is required for national and public universities.

Teacher Training

There are teacher certificates for kindergartens, elementary and secondary schools, and special education schools that are awarded by prefectural boards of education. These certificates can be regular, special, or temporary. Teacher training for regular teacher certificates is provided at universities and other institutions of higher education. To obtain the general certificate valid for life in all prefectures, students are required to have a first degree, over 18 credits of teaching, and over 41 credits in the specialized subject. Special certificates are awarded to those who have specialized knowledge or skills and are valid for not more than ten years within the prefecture that awarded them. Temporary certificates are issued for assistant teachers and are valid for three years within the issuing prefecture.

Student Characteristics

The lifestyle of children in schools is largely determined by their academic aspirations. The education system concentrates on preparing them for entrance examinations in the milieu of society and families. In order to prepare for entrance examinations, children must work hard at school and outside of school.

Educational advancement to a good school is the number one topic in families with school-age children. A good school means one with a high percentage of children who go on to a university, especially to prestigious schools. As a result, about 70 percent of school children are very busy studying for entrance examinations. They have little time, tend to be too competitive with each other, and are placed under extreme pressure. In addition to formal schools, they go to cram schools (*juku*) after school and on weekends and holidays. In addition, half of all elementary school children are taking some kind of extracurricular lessons, including *soroban,* Japanese abacus,

swimming, piano, and so on. The school year begins in April. Vacations are only about 40 days in summer and 10 days each for spring and New Year's holidays. Homework is common even during vacations and the holidays have various lessons. Children are therefore made to study hard in formal schools and in cram schools.

After the competitive pressure to get into a university, once there students have the freest four years of their lives. They get involved in clubs and part-time work, making trips inland and abroad, and seeking a job in the final year. In relation to the above and the increase in the quantity of student enrollment, the quality of students has declined. Still, the majority of students graduate and are employed.

Academic aspirations, hard work, competition, and the pressure of school children are a reflection of the academic society, the employment system, and the pressure from families. The freer life of university students reflects freedom from the pressure, the lifetime employment system, and the seniority-based rewards as students are expected to work hard once they are employed. It reflects also the expansion of the economic structure, which offers them more job opportunities in full- and part-time jobs. Hence, the students' job-hopping is a reflection of increasing job opportunities as well as a change in their uniform and dependent characters. The decrease in the quality of university students reflected the increase of population until recently.

MAJOR ISSUES, CONTROVERSIES, AND PROBLEMS

From the 1970s, the major issues in education have been numerous and serious, related to broad issues in present Japanese society. These include modernization, internationalization, and globalization, among which new values and attitudes are creating the melting down of the two conflicting traditional and modern features, the "melting culture or society."

Some serious problems for children are violence in the schools, bullying, committing suicide, injury or death by corporal punishment, refusal to attend school, and a rise in dropouts. Minority children such as the Ainu (the original inhabitants in Hokkaido), Japanese children who have returned from long stays abroad, children of Korean or Chinese born in Japan, and children of refugees or foreign manual workers have been discriminated against and bullied in schools for their differences in terms of languages, attitudes, and appearances. Other issues include assessment and entrance examinations, competition by ability for academic qualification, *juku,* uniform and academic-oriented education, strict school rules, teachers and corporal punishment, lack of instruction of guiding philosophies, and lack of respect for human rights.

Culture

The changing culture is an issue as well as a problem. The melding culture or melting of the traditional culture and a new culture is having a great impact upon the social fabric of Japan at large and seems to affect the young in particular.

The homogeneity of Japanese culture is an issue in terms of its closed nature as contrasted to a need for the internationalization of Japan. Recently, internationalization has advanced through many foreigners coming to Japan as well as some active Japanese abroad. There is an increase of international marriages. Too, some cities have admitted foreigners to work as officials by amending the Nationality Provision. These cases are melding the homogeneous culture and opening the possibility of creating a new Japanese culture.

Politics

Political issues include amending the Constitution, redefining Japan–United States security relationships, and reforming the administrative structure (Tanaka, 1994).

Amendment of the Constitution. The major issue in society in large has been interpreting the Constitution in terms of respect for basic human rights, the sovereign right of the people, and the renunciation of war. These issues are related especially to problems in employment, to the case of Okinawa, and to education.

In the case of education, two problems have been argued. One is how to interpret and realize the following statement: "All people shall have the . . . right to receive . . . an equal education . . . correspondent to their abilities" (Article 26, the Constitution and Article 3, the Fundamental Law of Education). Second is whether children's rights are being protected.

From 1947, the phrase "correspondent to children's abilities" was an important principle to anyone who advocated educational reform. However, the Japan Teachers Union did not uphold this principle. It criticized the fact that education from 1945 on was spoiled by uniform equalism without applying the principle of "correspondent to children's abilities" and stressed the need for diversification of education. The union further argued about how to interpret "an equal education" that would be "correspondent to their abilities." It interpreted it to admit the principle of ability and meritocracy or the principle to a secure education according to development and needs but also in view of human rights (Horio, 1997).

Redefining U.S. Security: The Case of Okinawa. The issue of Okinawa has been controversial in view of the Japan–United States Security Treaty. It became more serious when the time came to renew the use of 70 percent of the land for the U.S. air bases. Many outrages to Japanese girls and women by American soldiers were cited so that the Special Measure Law for U.S. Forces to use the land was adopted in April, 1997.

A majority of people strongly criticized the government for this law, which was passed after only nine days of deliberation in the Diet. The major controversy was focused firstly on the interpretation of the Japanese Constitution. Secondly, criticisms were made about the Japan–United States Security Treaty itself. The government did not even discuss measures to reduce the unbearable suffering of the people of Okinawa and their problems. The governor of Okinawa and many others felt that the law sacrificed Okinawa for Japan.

Reform of Administrative Structures. This includes all fields—politics/political parties, deregulation, privatization, economics, deregulation, destructuring, education system, teacher training, university, society, welfare, and tax. A major reason for reform is that the majority of Japanese people criticized the political parties and the bureaucracy for widespread corruption, the imposition and the rise of a consumption tax, unsatisfactory administrative reforms, problems of HIV, Okinawa, and so on. The government was heavily criticized for corruption such as the Recruit scandal of 1988 in which top leaders of the ministries of labor and education and others were indicted for taking bribes. A firestorm of opposition from citizens and nongovernment parties was sparked by the introduction of a new consumption tax of 3 percent in 1989 and its raise to 5 percent in 1997. The government argued that it was a necessary measure for national finance and the aging society. The opposite side complained of the unfair tax collection system and doubted whether this tax would be really used for the claimed purposes.

These reforms of the administrative structures in all fields have had a great impact upon the people. The government introduced 91 bills to the Diet in 1997, among which 53 bills were passed by both Houses. Among 38 bills, 22 bills were passed by the Lower House by May, 1997, including the revision bill for medical insurance, the bill for the aged care insurance (which starts from 2000), and the revision bill for the Employment Opportunity Law for Men and Women. A revision to the Civil Law (to admit different last names for husband and wife) did not pass this time.

In the 1990s, bureaucratic regulation was widely criticized because new industries could not emerge due to its stifling entrepreneurship. The main achievement of deregulation has been in the areas of transport, telecommunications, electrical power, distribution, and finance. Privatization began in the 1980s with three major government corporations: NTT, JNR, and the Tobacco and Salt. Yet many people complain that Japanese deregulation has been either too little or too late.

Demographic Changes

Measures to cope with the problem of the aging population have been discussed at great length on official and private levels. The discussion includes the need for provisions to keep older people gainfully employed; the need to raise the age at which a person becomes eligible for old-age benefits in order to reduce the burden on the working-age population; and the need to ensure that there will be sufficient affordable care providers for health and nursing care of people 75 or older, whose number will double by 2020 (Nakayama, 1997). One solution was the consumption tax that was raised to 5 percent to support the aged. As well, life-long education for aging people has been promoted and the number in life-long education has increased.

On the opposite side of aging is the lower birth rate due to the increasing number of women with no children, people marrying at a later age, or women who do not get married at all in view of the inequality of women at home and at work. In order to raise the birth rate, Japan needs urgent measures to treat women as equals at home and at work. Equality includes husbands who can take leave to help with children's care or the provision of baby sitting in working places.

Economy

There have been a number of criticisms of the Japanese system—for example, its closed nature, lifetime employment, working conditions, and female employment. While these issues are improving, the Japanese economy must achieve the twin goals of sustained, domestic-oriented growth and a qualitative rise in living standards. From here three major long-term issues emerge. First is the need for the Japanese economy to grow in harmony with globalization. Second is the need to reform Japan's traditional economic structure and system, beginning with a review of employment practices. The third issue is the importance of enhancing the long-term growth productivity of the Japanese economy (Statistical Bureau, 1996).

As the globalization of the economy (people, goods, finance) created disindustrialization, it is argued that we need a better process in terms of opening up the Japanese economy, although this must be balanced against fewer employment opportunities and production at home, which would inevitably be a threat to Japan's survival in the future. We have already seen that with changes in the economic structure since 1985, the restructuring and diversification of the economy caused serious problems to employees who were discharged, forced to retire, or transferred to other sections and areas. There have been many discussions on how to restructure, but still help such people.

As well, the collapse of the bubble economy of 1991 showed serious problems of political corruption and brought distrust of the bureaucrats involved in the incestuous relationship between bureaucracy and business. There were fiery arguments among the political parties themselves and specialists on how to cope with these problems. In particular, whether the enormous debt made by businesses should be shared with the government or not. The government decided to share it; the people showed their anger.

In more personal terms, the Japanese system has been changing. Stress in the workplace and death from overwork caused by long working hours and overtime work, as well as the issue of life after retirement, have been serious problems. Over 50 percent of all working people are said to be under stress and about 10 percent have serious stress symptoms and difficulties with personal relationships due to the demand in quantity and quality of work (Akasaka, 1996).

These problems have been discussed in relation to reducing working days, taking more holidays, and postponing the retirement age. Jobs today are chosen more according to one's ability or interest; this is impacting upon family life and upon people who are starting to enjoy their lives. Death from overwork and the stress of working people is gradually being coped with through improvements in working conditions. The government is considering postponing the start of public retirement pensions payments until age 65, which would suggest the retirement age may be raised again to 65.

Internationalization

The modernization of Japan began from 1868 when Japan began to promote industry with western systems, ideas, or techniques and sought western information and western models for establishing and developing modern systems in all fields. Japan was modernized, but the modern citizen has been an issue—trying to educate the modern citizen has accompanied the process of the modernization of Japan.

Together with modernization, the internationalization of Japan has been the major issue since the 1970s. By internationalization, I mean a process of opening all the systems of Japan to other countries. The issue stems from economic friction along with the cultural friction that arose when foreign people in business or life confronted the closed Japanese systems and Japanese people.

An associated issue is globalization, which to Japan means that people, goods, capital, information, knowledge, and technology are borderless. Globalization has been an issue from the 1990s, as the country has inevitably been involved in global problems such as environment, energy, human rights, basic needs for life and education, and so on. The recognition of globalization and global problems has only just began among the Japanese people.

Since the 1970s, the uniform formal schooling of Japan has failed to cope with the changing society. Serious educational problems occurred from the 1980s on. Society required "modern citizens," "international citizens," and "global citizens"; however, such citizens could not be educated under the educational system as it is practiced. In order to cope with these problems, educating the Japanese as "international citizens" has been promoted. Requirements for an international citizen are communicational ability in foreign languages, understanding foreign cultures, and open attitudes (Kamijo, 1989).

Debates on how to educate international citizens have focused on creating ideal international citizens and educating school children to be such citizens by promoting international understanding in the curriculum. The educational policy, *International Exchange in Education, Culture, and Science,* was proposed in 1976. However, to teach international understanding in the curriculum to students born and bred in Japan is difficult for teachers. The majority of teachers and students have no experience abroad.

Human Rights

Universal human rights of children, women, and minorities have not been well protected by the Japanese Constitution. The problems and controversies on human rights and the rights of women have been affecting children's rights to receive appropriate education, including minorities.

Japan is still a male-dominated society. Sexual discrimination remains for women in cases such as the recruitment of university graduates, status, working conditions and payment, sexual harassment, taking the husband's surname at marriage, and also a woman's role as housewife and child rearer (Kamijo, 1994a). According to an investigation by the UN Development Planning, the entry of Japanese women into society is behind, ranked twenty-seventh in the world. In spite of the enactment of the Equality Employment Law for men and women of 1986, for example, there are no women members in the Diet and only 0.8 percent women are in leading positions in the central government.

On a more private level, the mass media and women have protested against women's inequality. For example, a women's group carried out a protest and refused to work in offices or homes for part of the day on Girl's Day, March 3, 1997. They wanted an assessment on the great amount of women's work at home.

Ainu, Koreans, Chinese born in Japan, and other foreigners, especially manual workers, are discriminated against at work and in the community. They are discriminated against in the community when seeking residences because of their differences in languages, customs, and appearances. Foreigners in general cannot be employed under local government laws. Accordingly, foreign workers are employed mostly for manual work in construction, factories, or as drivers (Kamijo, 1994b).

The mass media, women's groups, and specialists, as well as citizens, have appealed and protested against this problem. Yet both government and society are slow to cope both in theory and practice. Note that recently some foreigners were employed as government officers in Kawasaki and Yokohama by a new official regulation, but limited to general work.

In 1990, Japan signed the Treaty of Children's Rights, which was adopted by UN in 1989. The report of the Japanese government on measures taken and its progress was presented to the UN Children's Rights Commission. This report was criticized by many groups such as the NGO on Children's Rights and the Japan Lawyers' Association for its insufficiency. The government report did not contain full statistics and relevant cases. For example, it did not state the number of children who committed suicide or refused to go to school. Inaccurate figures of corporal punishment and the problems concerning minorities were presented. A specialist on the Constitution and education proposed that the government should clarify factors, that the people should present concrete proposals, and that Japan should continue constructive discussion on children's rights.

Young Japanese returning from abroad were expected to be the ideal future international citizens. Yet, these children faced multiple and contradictory problems in adapting themselves in school because they had difficulties with the Japanese language, customs, and behavior. They also faced difficulties in entrance examinations for high schools and universities. Accordingly they had difficulties in employment. They also became targets of bullying due to their difference in language or behavior. Some refused schooling.

The policy of International Exchange for Education, Culture, and Science of 1976 emphasized coping with the problems of Japanese children who returned from abroad and other minority children. To successfully receive Japanese children in the public schools and universities, special measures were promoted. Specialized teachers to work with these children were placed in some public schools. Other solutions include the acceptance of special children or those with special needs, special schools in the school district, free schools for children refusing to attend schools, special schools or classes for young Japanese overseas returnees, special teachers for counseling children with problems, and a reform of entrance examinations.

According to the Ministry of Education, in 1996 over 60,000 children from 6 to 18 years old were bullied in the public schools. The number of cases of violence among children at school (8,000) drove some children to commit suicide (6); others ran away from home. For example, an elementary school boy committed suicide after he was bullied by his classmates. The final action that drove him to commit suicide was a funeral play in which his classmates pretended that he was dead and signed their names on the paper for his funeral. Surprisingly, his class teacher had also signed his name on it. Strict school rules killed a girl student; she rushed through iron gates just in time for school but was crushed because the gates had to be closed by the teachers at a certain time. A Brazilian junior high school student was bullied for his different appearance and driven to quit schooling. Children who are bullied or receive corporal punishments often refuse to attend school. The number of children who refused to attend school or dropped out of schooling was 82,000 in 1996. Sadly, it is said that the number of all the above cases is only the tip of the iceberg.

Evaluation

Children are under stress from the academic-oriented study needed for entrance examinations and academic qualifications. They study hard at school and *juku*. In this process the majority of children become either too competitive toward each other or they lose interest in study, feel tired, and become bored.

The Special Council for Educational Reforms of 1986 proposed the liberalization of education, creativity, and respect for individuals. In accordance with the policy recommendation, the Courses of Study were revised. In this relation, the school week was shortened and the entrance examination system for high schools and universities was altered, the number of entrance examination subjects reduced from five to three for high schools. Other requirements were left to the discretion of each university, although the Center Test was changed from five to six subjects (a common test basically for public universities). However, various kinds of other entrance examination measures were adopted in universities, such as accepting applicants by recommendations based on school records, special abilities, or social activities.

Curriculum

Uniform and simultaneous teaching, strict assessment, competition by ability for academic qualifications, and a uniform and academically oriented education still continues. On the whole, the educational policies and practice have not alleviated children's problems.

In this respect, a new policy expected to be realized beginning in 2003 is underway, as discussed in the previous section. This program was criticized by the LDP and the Japan Teachers Union due to its lack of clear ideas and measures. Economic circles were also not satisfied with the program. The Japan Economic Association proposed including areas to help students with the ability to think subjectively, find problems, and solve them. The Economic Doyu Association proposed "a reform of social conscience." It wanted measures to correct the competition of entrance examinations. It criticized the new 6-6-4 structure, which could increase elite schools and the educational burdens for parents.

School Choice

The freedom to choose a school is being promoted. A system of "specially recognized schools" was introduced and enforced from 1996 in special cases such as for geographical and physical reasons. There are eighteen such schools in Hokkaido in northern Japan and one in suburban Tokyo.

Free schools have been provided on the private level and parents of children who refuse schooling often send them to such schools, although at present these schools are not recognized by the Ministry of Education.

Teacher Training

Teacher training reflects Japanese culture. All teachers are trained with a uniform curriculum and tend to teach with uniform methods and pragmatic ideas. In addition, the teacher's certificate is a reflection of the expansion of the industrial structure; it is used in many cases when one cannot find a business job. Yet this tendency of "would be a teacher" has been changing to "would like to be a teacher," which reflects the decrease of the population and the government policy to reduce teachers.

Restructuring has meant a reduction of teachers in schools and universities in Japan. The retirement age also affects teachers, and the lower birth rate means a decrease in the enrollment ratio in schools and universities.

Higher Education

Higher education has changed. There are now new courses on media, new technology, or advanced information. Higher education promotes mature students, life-long education, and graduate courses.

THE FUTURE OF SOCIETY AND SCHOOLING

An investigation of Japanese society as related to these issues, controversies, and problems in education reveals that the present society is shaky and under various changes. Society faces crises in energy, environment, and population; restructuring problems in economy, politics, and education; value changes in the culture; and controversial issues on Constitutional amendments that affect, for example, the legal base of the society and Japan–U.S. relations. The numerous problems in the educational system already described and discussed are directly connected to parents, employers, or political and economic circles; that is, the whole society of Japan, the academic-oriented society, and the "Japan Company." Parents push children to be in the social stream. Employers reeducate graduates of formal and nonformal schools to meet the demand of political and economic circles.

Society may evolve as follows. With a decrease of population and an increase of the aged, older people will have difficulty in supporting themselves. Whether environmental problems will decrease is uncertain; however, government, industry, and citizens are increasingly trying to reduce problems. Unequal treatment of women and minorities in employment and daily life will be alleviated, in theory at least, with forthcoming changes in the relevant labor laws and local government regulations regarding employment of foreigners. Yet discrimination may still continue in practice, since human rights concerns are deeply rooted in the consciousness of the Japanese due to the background of the culture and to economic structure.

Restructuring, diversification, disindustrialization, and the market competition in the economy will advance. With a change of the relevant regulations, the Japanese system will change a little. Employment and working conditions will change slowly; the retirement age will be postponed to 65. Death by overwork will decrease with the change of working conditions, traditional culture, and values.

Schooling in Japan will evolve toward diversification, in terms of the aims of education, school organization, entrance examinations, and curricula, to a certain extent. This is projected from some changes in educational practice, from the pressure from society, and from the new educational policy now in process.

In conclusion, Japanese society and schooling will evolve toward diversification and people will face new problems with increasing multinational races, different values, new technology, and advanced information. Japan, scarce in natural resources, will increase international cooperation so as to cope with environmental and other problems. The internationalization or globalization in the economy will be advanced, but not rapidly in education because the educational system and practice do not reflect the needs of the economy or society. As a result, educating modern or international citizens will be slow to progress.

REFERENCES

Akasaka, S. (Ed). (1996). *Imidas*. Tokyo: Shueisha.

Horio, T. (Ed.). (1997). *Fifty years of schools in Japan*. Tokyo: Kashiwa Shobo.

Kamijo, M. (1989). *A study on internationalization of education in Japan: Norm and practice in Japanese society*. Tokyo: Taga Publishing.

Kamijo, M. (1994a). Comparative study of national policies for the education of girls and women: The situation of Japan. In M.B. Sutherland & C. Baudoux (Eds.), *Femmes et education: Politiques nationales et variations internationales*. Canada: Les Press de Universite Laval.

Kamijo, M. (1994b). Educational problems of foreign workers' children in Japan: Individuality, living and growing together. *The Journal of Psychology and Education* (No. 13). The Study Group of the Teacher Training Course, Kanagawa University.

Ministry of Education. (1994). *Education in Japan, 1994: A graphic presentation*. Tokyo: Gyosei.

Nakayama, S. (Ed.). (1997). *Japan as it is*. Tokyo: Gakken.

Statistical Bureau, Management and Coordination Agency. (1996). *Statistical handbook of Japan, 1995*. Tokyo: Japan Statistical Association.

Statistical Bureau, Management and Coordination Agency. (1997). *Statistics of Japan*. Japan: Printing Bureau of the Ministry of Finance.

Tanaka, Y. (Ed.). (1994). *Japan as it is*. Tokyo: Gakken.

CHAPTER 25

From National Interests to Globalization: The Education System of Malaysia

MAHESWARI KANDASAMY
R. SANTHIRAM

Maheswari Kandasamy currently holds the position of head, Department of Consultancies and Research in Education at the National Institute of Educational Management and Leadership, Malaysia. She is involved in developing courses for professionals in education, such as education systems managers, managers of educational institutions, educational planners, developers and evaluators, as well as educational trainers and supporting staff of education systems at all levels in Malaysia. Dr. Kandasamy has also conducted programs for ASEAN and the Pacific regions, Sri Lanka, Maldives, and Pakistan. She is currently the UNESCO Consultant for capacity building in Cambodia. Her teaching and research interests are in the areas of comparative education, history of education, educational planning, and human resource development.

R. Santhiram is a senior lecturer in the School of Educational Studies, University of Science Malaysia, Penang, Malaysia. He has been a secondary school teacher and a Research Officer with a primary school research project funded by IDRC (Canada). He teaches courses in Historical Methodology and Educational Development in Malaysia. His principal research interest is in the area of education for ethnic minorities.

THE SOCIAL FABRIC

Malaysia, a federation of thirteen states and a federal territory, straddles the equator. It is situated between one degree north to 7 degrees north latitude and 100 degrees east to 120 degrees east lat-itude. The total land area is 329,758 square kilometers. The states of Sabah and Sarawak on the northwest of Borneo island are separated from the peninsula by the South China Sea.

Malaya obtained independence from the British in 1957. Sabah and Sarawak gained their independence through a federation with peninsular Malaya in 1963, and the entire area collectively became known as the Federation of Malaysia. In the years since federation, Malaysia has faced and addressed a variety of racial, religious, and language issues that have shaped national development as a whole and the education system in particular. The Malaysian *weltanschauung* regarding the social, spiritual, economic, and political development has changed dramatically.

Economically, from the time of independence to the 1990s, the country has moved from a largely agricultural nation to import substitution industrialization, to export-oriented industrialization, to emergence as a newly industrialized country emphasizing heavy industry and sophisticated high technology. The nation has steered steadily through the New Economic Policy in the 1970s aimed at promoting national unity, restructuring society, and creating a stable climate for economic development and investment growth. Socially and politically, Malaysia has addressed issues such as national unity, the secession of Singapore from Malaysia in 1965, the racial riots of 1969, and the National Language issue.

Historical Development

The population of Malaysia is heterogeneous. Of the total population of 20,096,007, Malays constitute 9.7 million, Chinese 5.2 million, and Indians 1.5 million (Malaysia, 1997). In the states of Sabah and Sarawak the ethnic composition is more diverse. Apart from the three main races, stated above, there are several indigenous communities.

While significantly large-scale immigration of Chinese and Indians is a very recent phenomena that began in the late nineteenth and early twentieth centuries, small communities of Chinese and Indians had existed in the country for a long time; contacts have been recorded from the fifth and sixth centuries A.D. They not only acted as vehicles of cultural transmission but also tended to adopt the local way of life. These two Malaysianized communities are known as the *Malacca Babas* and the *Malacca Chetties*.

The major immigration of the Chinese and Indians accompanied the development of the extractive industries that, together with the need for raw materials by the British colonial rulers, precipitated a demand for labor that was not readily available in peninsular Malaysia. The Malay population was too small and too scattered to meet the needs of the colonial economy. Because the production of tin and rubber was extremely labor intensive, labor was indentured from China and India to work in the tin mines and rubber estates. Invariably, occupational specialization along communal lines was thus created, whereby employment in tin mining, rubber plantations, extractive enterprises, and commerce was taken over by non-Malay immigrants while the Malays tended to agricultural pursuits and fishing.

A picture thus emerges of a multiracial population with the identification of racial groups with major industries and occupations, leading to racial-occupational and racial-geographical area stereotyping. The various communities were not only confined to particular occupations but were also encouraged to preserve their own religions, languages, and social customs.

A colonial education system evolved in direct response to the economic and political demands of the colonial administration. There were two influences at work in the British policy toward education for the Malays. One was the paternal intention of English humanitarianism; the second was the concept of a "safe" education. That is, a Malay primary education kept within the confines of the nineteenth-century Malay village economy ensured the prolongation of British colonial rule (Loh Fook Seng, 1975). However, there was also a Malay elite drawn from the ranks of the nobility and the royalty that was trained to serve in the government bureaucracy through an English medium of instruction. This education was free for this group. For the immigrant populations, the colonial power tolerated an ethnically inspired and financed vernacular education for the Chinese and an employer-initiated Tamil vernacular primary education for the Indians.

This British colonial policy of separate schools prolonged the ethnic, cultural, and economic differences among the people of peninsular Malaysia. Communalism has been and still remains a thorny issue in the economic, social, and political milieu of Malaysia.

SCHOOLING

Schooling in Malaysia passed through different stages, although influenced heavily by the British in the period before independence.

British Rule

The practice of communalism led to serious forms of polarization that manifested itself in different residential, social, economic, and educational patterns. The communal groups were being educated in isolation; only in the English-medium system that developed in the urban areas was there any interaction among the different ethnic groups. However, the Malays who enjoyed the benefit of an English education were the traditional Malay aristocracy who were sent to the specially created Eton of Malaya, the Malay College, which was established in 1905. On leaving the college, the students almost entirely comprised the second echelon of the Malay Administrative Service (Puthucheary, 1978) and emerged as a distinctly affluent and socially upper-crust group, isolated from the working class and rural peasants.

Because those educated in the vernacular school system grew up in ethnic and economic isolation, the vernacular school system had a divisive influence on society and tended to perpetuate its ethnic, plural character (Ness, 1967). These schools used the mother tongue as the medium of instruction, and the content was ethnically biased, borrowed from China or India (Loh Fook Seng, 1975). The schools were isolated from one another and the uniracial composition of the enrollment encapsulated the pupils in a social environment away from cross-cultural interaction (Chai Hon-Chan, 1977).

Post-War Period

Educational policy in West Malaysia after the Second World War made no provisions for integration among children of the different races. In addition, proposals for an extension of the vernacular primary education to the secondary level tended to accentuate communal differences and undermine the creation of a united Federation of Malaya.

Some semblance of a national system of education was seen in 1951 when a special committee advocated a national school system to replace the colonial educational structure of four separate but parallel systems of education catering for the Malays, Chinese, Indians, and urban residents. Proposed was the use of English and Malay as the medium of instruction (Federation of Malaya, 1951a). The non-Malays, especially the Chinese, were galvanized to fight against this proposal because they saw it as an attempt to undermine the Chinese language. To allay their fears, the British government appointed another committee in 1951 to study Chinese education. This committee proposed a system that promoted unity in diversity (Federation of Malaya, 1951b).

The recommendations of both these committees represented divergent views of nation building—

one, the assimilation of the various ethnic groups and the inculcation of common ideals through a bilingual system of education; the other, cultural and linguistic pluralism. As a compromise formula, the government brought out the Education Ordinance of 1952, which called for the abolition of separate vernacular schools and the creation of an integrated system of national schools where only the Malay and the English language would be used as mediums of instruction. The minority languages of Chinese and Tamil would be taught at the request of a prescribed number of parents. The Education Ordinance was, however, shelved for a time. Not only was there opposition by both Malays and Chinese, but the government faced other pressing issues such as the Communist insurgency and discussions for winding up the affairs of the colonial government in West Malaysia.

Independence

Just before independence in 1957, the stage was set for the evolution of a national system of education. The recommendation was for the unification of all the four mediums of instruction in primary schools by using common content syllabuses in all these schools (Federation of Malaya, 1956). Malay and English were introduced as compulsory subjects in all primary and secondary schools. At the secondary level, three language mediums schools were allowed: Malay, Chinese, and English. A centralized teacher training program under the Ministry of Education was also proposed so that teacher education would no longer be an ad hoc and sporadic process.

The Education Ordinance of 1957 thus became the basis for the national education policy of independent Malaya. It took an accommodative stance and assured that particular ethnic groups' interests would be taken into consideration within the larger framework of a national policy. The crucial requirement of the education policy was to reorient all schools to a Malaysian outlook; this was an essential element in the development of a united Malayan nation. In keeping with the recommendations of the 1957 Ordinance that its role was to plan for the immediate future, a Review Committee was set up in 1960 to review the implementation of the 1957 Ordinance and to "consider the national and financial implications of this policy, including the introduction of free primary education, and to make recommendations" (Federation of Malaya, 1961, para 1).

The resultant Education Act of 1961 made two epoch-making changes. One was the provision of primary education irrespective of medium of instruction; the other raised the school-leaving age to 15. The Act of 1961 also introduced changes at the secondary level that strengthened the principle of a unified Malay language government-aided education system. Because the Malay language should assume a dominant position, after 1967 Malay should be the main medium of instruction at the secondary level, with provisions for teaching other languages as subjects.

Government assistance to Chinese secondary schools was to be withdrawn. As a first step, these schools had to convert to the English medium to be eligible for government grants. This change was implemented to slowly wean the Chinese vernacular secondary schools to the English medium, which was viewed as a neutral language, before making the next switch to the national medium of instruction.

In order to cope with the expected flood of pupils into the secondary school system, a comprehensive curriculum was introduced in 1965 that emphasized the development of human resources to meet the economic development and modernization needs of the country. At the end of the third year of secondary school a public examination, the Lower Certificate of Education Examination, determined students' school careers either in the academic, technical, or vocational schools. At the end of another two years of upper secondary school classes, the pupils had to sit for the School Certificate of Education Examination.

National Language

Another important development that had a bearing on education policy was the passing of the National Language Act of 1967. A national language was regarded as synonymous with the development of nationhood. But the government sought a gradualist approach as years of effort by the ethnic groups in providing education for their own children could not be undone through legislation without causing anxiety and unrest. The run up to the Bill saw a build-up of tensions and anxieties within the Malay and Chinese political parties as to how the role of their languages would be compromised (Roff, 1967). The Malays were not willing to accept Chinese economic domination any longer, while the Chinese were unwilling to accept Malay cultural domination through the Malay language. The Chinese also resented the special privileges of the Malays, which were intended to bring about greater economic equality. Any attempt to integrate Chinese schools into the national system of education was considered by them as an attack on Chinese culture.

The language issue became a focal point for long-standing communal tensions between the Malays and non-Malays and the accommodative policy failed to satisfy the expectations of the ethnic groups. Controversy arose over the role and position of the national language and other languages in the education system of the country. The Malay communal spokesmen felt that the Malay language and its position in the national education system was not given its due recognition and status (Means, 1970); the Chinese objected to the ultimate objective of making the national language the main medium of instruction in schools, and some sections of the Chinese demanded that all four languages be treated equally.

A lot of compromises were built into the first Act. It established Malay as the sole national language of the country, but permitted the continued use of the English language for official purposes as deemed fit. However, the ambivalence of the 1967 National Language Act was put to rest by the events that followed in the aftermath of the traumatic race riots of 1969. It put an end to the government's liberal policy of deliberate gradualism in its national language policy in education. The riots of 1969 showed clearly that the development programs until the late 1960s had failed to meet the challenges of national integration and unity. It exposed the very dismal participation of Malays in the modern sector of the Malaysian economy and in tertiary education (Malaysia, 1976; Snodgrass, 1980).

Interracial economic disparity was pointed out as the major source of interracial conflict. For example, on ownership of wealth, the Malays owned only 2.4 percent of equity capital, whereas the Chinese share was 27.2 percent, and the Indians' share was 1.1 percent (Malaysia, 1976, p. 6). Malay participation in tertiary education was also wanting. They constituted only 20.6 percent of the student population in Malaysia's only university in 1963–1964 (Snodgrass, 1980).

National unity was targeted as the overriding objective of the country. As the government blamed the disparities in wealth and status between the immigrant communities and the Malays for the 1969 violence, it was obvious that national unity and integration could not be created in a society where one or more social groups felt extremely disadvantaged in relation to other groups, the emphasis was to be on social integration and a more equitable distribution of income and opportunities (Malaysia, 1971).

These aims of the New Economic Policy recognized education as the principal agent for upward social mobility of the Malays; education was to play a central role in an affirmative action plan for unity, and the period after 1969, often referred to as the "era of new realism" (Mauzy, 1985) saw a fundamental change in Malaysian education. The program of action in respect to integration and national unity was the implementation in stages of Bahasa Malay as the main medium of instruction in schools with a clear course of progression for Bahasa Malay to be ultimately used as a medium of instruction right up to the university level by 1983. Chinese- and Tamil-medium primary schools were allowed to operate. It was only in the secondary, post-secondary, and tertiary levels of education that the Malay medium of instruction was to take effect.

The 1990s

A National Education Philosophy was formally documented in 1988. It focused on the integration of knowledge with values and skills, and referred to a balance between spiritual, intellectual, and physical components of the human personality. The Education Bill of 1995 superseded the 1961 Education Act and reaffirmed state control of the entire education system by bringing into its ambit preschool education, primary, secondary, post-secondary, and higher education. Until this legislation, preschools had been left to function without any form of direct control. This Act brought about some form of uniformity in the running of kindergartens that have mushroomed all over the country to accommodate working mothers in the job market. Curriculum guidelines had to be approved by the Minister of Education. The position of the vernacular languages in the school system and as a medium of instruction in the primary schools was further guaranteed by removing the power of the Minister of Education to convert the vernacular schools to the national medium. This is a very welcome signal for the nonindigenous communities who had always feared an erosion of their status because of this power of the Minister of Education.

Curriculum

The school curriculum has undergone many changes to accommodate the new challenges, aspirations, and values of a growing nation like Malaysia. The present curriculum, both for primary and secondary education, is the result of recommendations in 1979. Basically a new orientation has been given to the school curriculum to realize the spirit and goal of the National Education Philosophy and the manpower needs of the country.

The New Primary School Curriculum (NPSC), which gives emphasis to basic skills in reading, writing, and arithmetic (3Rs), was implemented (in stages) in 1983. By 1988, the NPSC was fully implemented in all classes at the primary school level (see Table 25.1).

TABLE 25.1   The Structure of the New Primary Curriculum (NPSC)

AREAS OF STUDY	COMPONENTS	SUBJECTS	
		phase I	*phase II*
COMMUNICATION	Basic Skills	Malay Language English Language Chinese Language Tamil Language	Malay Language English Language Chinese Language Tamil Language
		Mathematics	Mathematics
MAN AND ENVIRONMENT	Spiritual, Values, and Attitudes	Islamic Religious Education Moral Education	Islamic Religious Education Moral Education
	Humanities and Environment	—	Science
			Local Studies
SELF-DEVELOPMENT	Living Skills	—	Living Skills
		Music Education	Music Education
		Art Education	Art Education
	Arts and Recreation	Health and Physical Education	Health and Physical Education
	Co-Curriculum		

The NPSC is organized into two phases:
   Phase I: Year 1 to Year 3
   Phase II: Year 4 to Year 6

Source: Ministry of Education, Malaysia (1993), p. 27.

The Integrated Secondary School Curriculum (ISSC) adheres to the following basic principles: continuity in terms of educational philosophy framework; providing coherent principles, concepts, curricular content, and teaching-learning strategies; providing general education to all students; utilization of knowledge acquired through the various disciplines; emphasis on aesthetic and moral values; upgrading proficiency in and usage of Malay; and developing a strong foundation of life-long education.

A culture of excellence and positive work ethics has also permeated the education system. In 1980 a campaign to promote an excellent work culture was launched for the public services. The focus was on the quality of work and increased productivity through the incorporation of values and work culture. In line with these trends, the Ministry of Education has responded with the introduction of quality symbols such as the "Master Teacher," "Super Principal," and "Model Schools."

Structure of Schooling

The Malaysian education system serves about 4.8 million school children and over 200,000 students at tertiary levels, both internally and overseas. There are thirty-one teachers' colleges, seven polytechnics, and nine universities. There is at the same time an increased demand for places in local institutions of higher learning. The general, over-all structure of schooling in Malaysia is shown in Figure 25.1.

Preschool Education

Preschool education has gained currency since the 1960s. The private sector was more active in the foundation of preschool centers because they were regarded as profitable undertakings. Since most preschool centers were concentrated in the urban centers, the economically disadvantaged groups were unable to gain a headstart in education, thus creating further disparities between the urban and rural groups. The Education Act of 1996 took note of this disparity and recommended that greater efforts be undertaken to provide such opportunities for the rural areas. The Ministry now scrutinizes the curriculum of preschools, sets minimum qualifications, and provides teacher training for preschool teachers. The Association of Preschool Education has undertaken to improve the quality of education and teachers through a series of seminars (Ministry of Education and UNICEF, 1984). Efforts by both the private and public sectors, including nongovernmental agencies (NGOs), increased the preschool population from 328,000 in 1990 to 420,600 in 1995.

Primary and Secondary School

With the introduction of a new primary school curriculum it was hoped that a new generation of literate and educated Malaysians would be fostered. Despite this, the number of students who drop out of the government and government-aided schools is considerable. In 1995, 2.5 million children were enrolled in primary schools; of this cohort about 4 percent did not complete their primary education (Malaysia, 1996a). At the lower secondary level, the enrollment increased by 19.2 percent with the transition rate from primary to lower secondary level from 83 percent in 1990 to 84.5 percent in 1995. The transition from lower secondary level improved from 68 percent in 1990 to 83 percent in 1995, while the upper secondary

enrollment numbers increased from 50.4 percent in 1990 to 63.7 percent in 1995 (Malaysia, 1996a).

Various attempts have been made by the government to provide a more conducive learning environment, particularly in underenrolled schools where there are less than 150 pupils. This includes the building of new classrooms, better library facilities, and posting better qualified teachers. For rural children, hostel facilities are provided so that these children will be able to access education. When children complete primary education, they are given opportunities to pursue their education in fully residential schools in the urban areas. Provisions are also made in the form of financial assistance, textbook loan schemes, and a supplementary food program to increase the retention levels of schools.

The provision of education for aborigine children has been under the control of the Ministry of Education since 1995. With this move it is hoped that aborigine children will have greater access to education. Special education programs have been implemented in twenty-six special schools for the disabled; inclusive education programs have been initiated for children with slight disabilities in 139 regular schools.

Vocational Schools

Besides academic schools, there are nine secondary technical schools and sixty-nine vocational schools. Attempts are being made to increase the supply of students with a strong foundation in mathematics, science, and technically related subjects. Twenty of the existing vocational schools are being converted to become technical institutes as students from the vocational schools are mainly absorbed into the labor market, while technical institute students usually continue their studies in various science- and technology-related areas at diploma level and on to tertiary levels.

Teacher Training

About thirty-one teacher training colleges in Malaysia have trained a total of 48,090 nongradu-

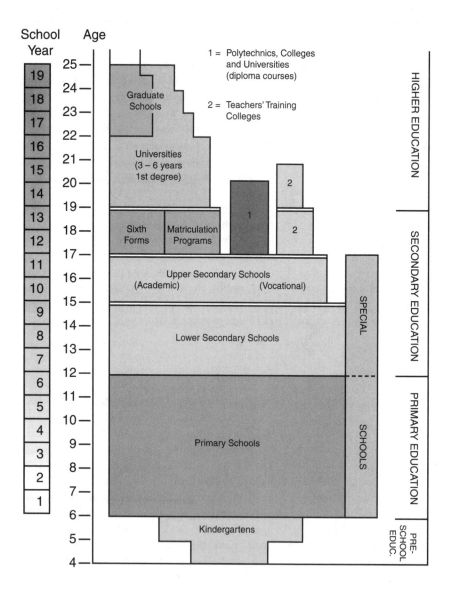

FIGURE 25.1   Structure of the education system in Malaysia. Source: Ministry of Education, Malaysia (1993), p. 11.

ate teachers for the primary and lower secondary schools. Another 22,770 graduate teachers have been trained both by the colleges and the local universities over the last few years. In spite of these numbers, both the primary and secondary schools still face a shortage of trained personnel. In 1995 there were 9,780 positions vacant for trained primary school teachers and about 4,600 positions in the secondary schools. Temporary untrained teachers have been recruited as a short-term measure to overcome the problem of vacancies.

There are plans to ensure that only graduate teachers teach in the secondary schools. In 1990, 36 percent of secondary school teachers were graduates; this figure rose to 58 percent in 1995. To operationalize this, twenty teacher education colleges have reformulated their regular programs to conduct postgraduate teacher education programs leading to Diplomas in Education. Seven other colleges are offering twinning programs with local universities so that serving teachers can obtain graduate qualifications. To encourage teachers to remain in the profession until the mandatory retirement age of 55, promotional opportunities are offered in the form of Master Teacher posts, which were implemented in 1995.

MAJOR ISSUES, CONTROVERSIES, AND PROBLEMS

In the early years of independence, educational issues revolved around issues linked to race, language, and the equitable distribution of economic wealth. Later the issues changed to promoting economic growth and industrialization. In the 1990s issues of globalization and maintaining the competitive edge are the focus for educational planners.

Equity in a Plural Society

As we discussed earlier, Malaysia started off as a classic case of a plural society (Furnivall, 1948). As this was, and is, critical for Malaysian educa-

tion, we begin this section with a review and analysis of the educational developments discussed previously.

In the early years, Malaysia's racial divisions tended to coincide with linguistic, religious, and economic divisions. At the early stages of her independence, educational issues were interwoven with communal considerations. The plural population had to be molded into a new cohesive society. Issues of economic inequalities took a very ethnic spread. There was substantial imbalance of wealth between the communities, especially between the Malays and non-Malays (Malaysia, 1971). This was tied to the weakness within the education system—an English-medium for the few but the majority receiving primary education in the vernacular with few opportunities to transfer to the English-medium secondary schools that offered social mobility through secondary school, university, and beyond.

Because of this major concern with national integration and unity, Malaysia sought to develop a national language as a way to create a national identity and mold its heterogeneous society into a unified group. The National Language Act itself reaffirmed Malay as the sole national and official language of the country as of September 1967. Malay replaced English as the language of administration and education except in the primary schools. The unassailability of the Malay language was guaranteed by the Constitutional Amendment of 1971.

This shift in the education policy had important implications for the nation. Firstly, it established Bahasa Malay as the main medium of instruction and broke down the segregation of schools so that they assumed a national character by becoming noncommunal. Second, it made it possible for an unprecedented number of Malays from the rural areas to move up the educational ladder and thereby participate in the modern sectors of the economy. This was possible through a policy of affirmative action and preferential treatment for the Malays at the tertiary level of education (Selvaratnam, 1988). Third, the new emphasis raised the aspirations and expectations of Malay youth, who perceived the educational system as their chief instrument of social mobility.

There was a new Education Bill in 1995. The mid-1990s also saw efforts to revive the position of English as an important second language. Why? Because the 1990s were a period of rapid economic development and transformation. Economic reforms emphasized economic growth, modernization, and industrialization and have put Malaysia within striking distance of becoming an industrialized nation. Malaysia's efforts at industrialization and globalization could very well be aided by having a workforce competent in the English language.

In December 1993 the government announced its intention to permit the use of English in Malaysian universities to teach subjects in science, technology, and medicine (*New Straits Times,* 28 December 1993). At the same time, foreign universities were allowed to set up branch campuses in Malaysia. This would mean that Malaysia could accommodate the increase in foreign students and at the same time reverse the annual RM 2 billion foreign currency outflow from about 50,000 Malaysians studying abroad.

Higher Education

Private sector initiative in the provision of education has always been present in the Malaysian education system. For example, there are about 53 Chinese independent secondary schools, 118 private secondary schools, and 20 international schools (catering to expatriate workers) in the country (Ministry of Education, 1993). As the demand for tertiary education outstripped the government's ability to provide places in the local institutions of higher learning, thousands of Malaysians started going overseas in pursuit of higher education. In the late 1980s there was a proliferation of English-medium private colleges preparing students for entrance examinations to foreign universities. Twinning arrangements between these institutions and foreign universities under which the first few years of a university course could be taken locally at a much lower cost were gaining popularity.

In line with this thinking, the Private Higher Educational Institutions Bill of 1996 (Malaysia, 1996c) empowered the Minister of Education to grant permission for courses to be taught in the English language by private colleges. It also provided a set of guidelines on the establishment and conduct of private higher education institutions so as to regulate the play of the private sector in higher education. The government thus encouraged the private sector to play a complementary role in the provision of higher education. Private individuals and corporate bodies were encouraged to set up private institutes and colleges. Preparatory courses and twinning programs for foreign universities formed an important aspect in the expansion of places at the tertiary level. Educational opportunities are also available at state as well as sponsored educational institutions such as the Malaysian Institute of Management, Petronas, and Shell. Two recently privatized public utility bodies (the Telecommunications Office and the National Electricity Board) were recently invited by the Minister of Education to set up universities locally. There are about 293 private colleges offering a range of academic, professional, technical, and managerial courses.

It must be emphasized that the government is not privatizing higher education. It is only streamlining and regularizing the private sector input in higher education. At the same time there is a move to corporatize the public universities. The Universities and University Colleges (Amendment) Act gives flesh to the call for corporatization of universities. This is an attempt to introduce the work culture of corporate bodies, bring about accountability, link grants and funds to performance and generate income so as to lessen the universities' dependence on the government for funds. Another act, called The National Council on Higher Education Act 1996 (Malaysia, 1996b), reflects the government's intention for a single governing body to oversee the public and private higher educational institutions in the country.

THE FUTURE OF SOCIETY AND SCHOOLING

The next twenty years or so are crucial in the realization of the Malaysian vision. The Ministry of Education has formulated its own vision for education. Progress highlights the following areas, which need the attention of the nation: national unity; self-reliance; performance of excellence; and a democratic, religious, well-behaved, tolerant, and caring, as well as a scientific and progressive society. The main ideas in the vision for education are promotion of a knowledge culture, a culture of excellence, a caring culture, empowerment, national unity, collaboration, monitoring, management style, and zero defects. This vision has been operationalized at community, institutional, and classroom levels so that continuous measures are undertaken to review the teaching/learning processes to attain credibility. The Ministry of Education is also to ensure the creation of a national system of education that produces individuals and a society that are knowledgeable, pious, and virtuous with faith and belief in God. This means that there must be attempts to improve spiritual, moral, ethical, and character development of the child through curriculum change and teaching approaches based on an integration of the above aspects. At the same time, the system needs to ensure that education becomes an effective mechanism to foster patriotism and unity among the citizens to create a Malaysian nation as well as achieve a fully industrialized nation status.

It is hoped that the ethnic and language issues that have plagued the system for the past forty years will be fully resolved. Critical targets have been formulated by the Ministry of Education. Quality education has to be maintained in the preschool, primary, secondary, and tertiary education sectors. These institutions need to be innovative, creative, and positive so as to ensure universal enrollment at primary level, near universal enrollment at the lower secondary and upper secondary level, and 50 percent enrollment at the tertiary level by the year 2020.

In order to achieve a world-class status, the education system needs the highest standards of technical excellence and professionalism in order to be proactive to changing conditions and situations. It has been stated that the number of school hours needs to be increased, which inevitably requires single-session schools. The formal curriculum needs to be enriched, focusing on reading, writing, mathematics, communication, and manipulative skills. Computer literacy has to be stressed, especially in the light of advanced technological status of the country. This would require at least one personal computer for every thirteen students by the year 2020. To meet the sophisticated, high technology manpower needs of the country, secondary school students are being encouraged to enter the science streams. Currently, 60 percent of the students apply for the arts stream and 40 percent for the science stream in grade 10. It is hoped that there would be a reversal of this trend. Special education has already been addressed by the Education Act of 1996, and now there is a move to look into the education of the elite (gifted). Special programs are being tried to help these high flyers complete their primary schooling within five years instead of the normal six years.

Democratization of education needs to be further strengthened to ensure that every child of school age receives quality education for at least eleven years, regardless of socioeconomic status or ethnicity. This also means that continuing educational opportunities must be available for all citizens. Concerted efforts are needed to improve the school curriculum, teacher education curriculum, the learning environment, and the management of educational institutions.

The government believes that Malaysia's progress towards full economic development requires mastery of English as an international language. This requires the commitment and dedication of the teaching force. Teachers in Malaysia are disgruntled about the conditions of service in the teaching profession, and this needs to be addressed urgently. The status of the teaching profession has to be restored so as to make it competitive enough to attract the best in the profession. Nonteaching administrative duties have burdened the teachers, and this has to be looked into so that they can focus on core teaching duties. Training, education, and development programs need to be accelerated if the Ministry of Education hopes to recruit only graduates into the profession. Continuous assessment of their core teaching competencies needs to be done to ensure that only the best teachers are retained in the system.

CONCLUSION

The Malaysian education system has come full circle. The education system has met head on the challenges that faced the nation since its inception. In the early stages of independence, education issues were interwoven with communal considerations. Language and education were not simply cultural issues but were linked to the economic dimension. Economic inequalities between the indigenous Malays and nonindigenous groups were attributed to the medium of instruction. After 1970, the switch to the National Language medium benefited the Malays and propelled them to the modern sector of the economy. The late 1980s and 1990s saw a shift in the education policy. Reforms in education were basically carried out to help in the transition from import-substitution strategies to export-oriented industrialization and the emergence as a newly industrialized country. A more liberal stand toward education is noticeable. There is a rehabilitation of the English language in post-secondary and tertiary education. This has an ulterior motive. Malaysia's efforts at globalization and its vision of becoming a center of academic excellence has to be seen against a backdrop of high English language competence. While private involvement in education is making an impact on the education system, the very foundation of education is still very much the province of the government sector.

REFERENCES

Chai Hon-Chan. (1977). *Education and nation-building in plural societies: The West Malaysian experience*. Canberra: Development Studies Center Monograph No. 6.

Federation of Malaya. (1951a). *Report of the Committee on Malay education*. Kuala Lumpur: Government Press.

Federation of Malaya. (1951b). *Report of the Committee on Chinese education*. Kuala Lumpur: Government Press.

Federation of Malaya. (1956). *Report of the Education Committee 1956*. Kuala Lumpur: Government Printers.

Federation of Malaya. (1961). *Report of the Education Review Committee*. Kuala Lumpur: Government Press.

Furnivall, J.S. (1948). *Colonial policy and practice: A comparative study of Burma and the Netherlands*. Cambridge: Cambridge University Press

Loh Fook Seng. (1975). *Seeds of separatism: Education policy in Malaya 1874–1940*. Kuala Lumpur: Oxford University Press.

Malaysia. (1971). *Second Malaysia Plan 1971–1975*. Kuala Lumpur: Government Press.

Malaysia. (1976). *Third Malaysia Plan 1976–1980*. Kuala Lumpur: Government Press.

Malaysia. (1996a). *Seventh Malaysia Plan 1996–2000*. Kuala Lumpur: Percetakan Nasional Malaysia Berhad.

Malaysia. (1996b) *National Council on Higher Education Bill 1996*. Dewan Rakyat 1/96.

Malaysia. (1996c) *Private Higher Educational Institutions Bill 1996*. Dewan Rakyat 2/96.

Malaysia. (1997). *Perangkaan Penting Malaysia*. Kuala Lumpur: Jabatan Perangkaan Malaysia.

Mauzy, D.K. (1985). Language and language policy in Malaysia. In W.R. Beer & J.E. Jacob (Eds.), *Language policy and national unity*. Totowa, NJ: Rowman and Allenheld Publishers.

Means, G. (1970) *Malaysian politics*. London: London University Press.

Ministry of Education and UNICEF. (1984). *Report on the seminar for national preschool*. Sponsored by the Educational Planning and Research Department.

Ministry of Education, Malaysia. (1993). *Educational statistics of Malaysia, 1993*. Kuala Lumpur: Bahagian Perancangan dan Penyelidikan, Kementerian Pendidikan Malaysia.

Ness, G.D. (1967). *Bureaucracy and rural development in Malaysia*. Los Angeles: University of California Press.

New Straits Times, 28 December, 1993.

Puthucheary, M. (1978). *The politics of administration.* Kuala Lumpur: Oxford University Press.

Roff, M. (1967). The politics of language in Malaya. *Asian Survey, 7*(5).

Selvaratnam, V. (1988). Ethnicity, inequality and higher education in Malaysia. *Comparative Education Review, 32.*

Snodgrass, D. (1980). *Inequality and economic development in Malaysia*. Kuala Lumpur: Oxford University Press.

CHAPTER 26

The Dynamics of an Education System of a Developing Country: The Case of Indonesia

CONNY R. SEMIAWAN
ROCHMAN NATAWIDJAJA

Conny Semiawan *is chairperson of the Indonesian National Consortium on Educational Sciences, directorate general of Higher Education for the Ministry of Education and Culture, and professor at the State Graduate Program, University of Indonesia and at the Institute for Teacher Training and Educational Science, Jakarta.*

Rochman Natawidjaja *is a professor at the Institute of Teacher Training and Educational Sciences, Bandung, Indonesia. He is a member of the Indonesian National Consortium on Educational Sciences and serves as domestic consultant in research and development for the PST Development Project.*

THE SOCIAL FABRIC

Demographic Background

Indonesia, an archipelago of more than 17,000 islands, has a land area of 2.02 million square kilometers. Indonesia lies across a region of various volcano activities; there are 400 volcanoes, at least 70 of them still active.

Of the population of about 197 million people, about half of the Indonesian people live on the fertile island of Java; most of the other islands are almost underpopulated. The island of Kalimantan, for instance, is, according to Jones (1973) "as big as Texas," but very sparsely populated (p. 4). A person could travel for weeks and months in the Kalimantan jungles and see no sign of habitation. Sumatra, four times the size of Java, is a very rich island, largely unexploited and not yet fully explored. While the climate differs from region to region, generally there are only two seasons (the rainy season and the dry season). However, Irian Jaya's mountains, only 4 degrees south of the equator, are permanently snow-capped.

The Religious Aspect

Between 1,000 and 1,500 years before Christ, India brought Hinduism to Indonesia; this remained until the arrival of Buddhism, also from India. Buddhism then dominated Java and Sumatra from the fifth century to the fourteenth A.D.; Islam then took over as the major religion (Jones, 1973). Christianity came when Indonesia was forced to submit to alien rule by the Dutch government, which arrived in the fifteenth century. Today, the majority of the Indonesian people embrace Islam with its one God and its direct personal relationship between God and man (Jones, 1973). With Islam, there are also Christianity, Hinduism, and Buddhism.

History, Politics, and Culture

Indonesia had already developed a distinct diversified culture of its own long before it was exposed to other cultural influences, such as Indian and Chinese. For example, originally, there were about 300 local languages.

The independence of Indonesia came in 1945. However, in the forty years before independence,

Indonesian national leaders planned to build an Indonesian society based on prosperity and justice. One official national language, *Bahasa Indonesia,* was developed. Since 1945 this has been recognized as the official national language. However, the local languages still exist and Indonesia can be considered as a pluralistic society because of the diversity of languages, lifestyles, attitudes, and customs that are rooted in several ancient subcultures.

The Financial Aspect

Indonesia has made great progress during the fifty years of its independence, especially in the educational sector, which will be elaborated later in the chapter. However, in aggregate terms, the development of Indonesia as a nation, especially in the economic sector, has to catch up with other neighboring countries.

Figures from the latest available national and multilateral sources show that Indonesia's GDP (Gross Domestic Product) and PPP (Purchasing Power Parity) per capita ranked twenty-seventh among forty-six countries in the world. GDP is the value of all goods and services produced in one year, while PPP, based on World Bank ratios, takes into account price differences among national wealth (N.N., 1996, p. 53). In recent months, the statistics have changed, and it should be noted that after more than fifty years of independence as a developing country, Indonesia's economy is still at risk.

SCHOOLING

Philosophy and Goals

Because Indonesia's motto of life is "Unity in Diversity," there is a strong awareness of togetherness and connectedness. The beauty of this philosophy is based on a deep sense of social responsibility because the individual self is essentially a social being. Hence, the stated aims for Indonesia constitute a goal toward which the country's educational efforts are directed; that is, the realization of an Indonesian "developed" person (*manusia pembangunan*). In the derivation of Indonesia's national educational objectives, there are two different spheres of existence comprising the developed person—a wholeness in his or her being (*manusia seutuhnya*) considered as the individual aspect, and the social aspect representing unity and social responsibility. That means that on one hand education aims to achieve an independent human being who should be able to develop and stand on his or her own, while on the other hand there is a demand for participation in the development of society, which is considered the responsibility of each citizen (Semiawan & Munandar, 1993). Education should let students manage their minds to place them in the situation of growing, achieving, and surviving. In spite of the fact that their personhood is grounded in society, they cannot be considered as reeds bending to every social breeze. Though their personal development to achieve optimal actualization is bound to others—an essential to their psychological existence—their active involvement in the development of their society is very much demanded.

These educational aims are based on five precepts of Indonesia's philosophy, *Pancasila,* which refers to the five integrated principles of Indonesian people's life—the five pillars of the state. The principles are: belief in the One and only God, just and civilized humanity, the unity of Indonesia, democracy led by the wisdom of deliberations among representatives, and social justice for the whole of the people of Indonesia.

Pancasila as a national and state philosophy has successfully maintained the unity of the Indonesian nation, which is really pluralistic in nature. As we mentioned, Indonesia is an archipelago with 17,000 islands inhabited by more than 350 ethnic groups speaking about 300 local languages and embracing various religions and beliefs in God Almighty. Because of the powerful spirit of *Pancasila* uniting the nation, Indonesia's national motto reads as "Unity in Diversity," or as expressed in genuine Sanskrit, *Bhineka Tunggal Ika.*

Pancasila, with its complete and indivisible five principles, convinces the Indonesian people and the nation that there will be happiness if life is based on harmony and balance in the life of a person as an individual, in his or her relations with society, in his or her relations with nature, in relations between one and other nations, in relations between man and God Almighty, and between efforts toward material progress and mental happiness (BP-7, 1991). Humans are placed in their nobility and dignity as creatures of God Almighty, aware of God's gift of being individuals as well as social creatures. Because *Pancasila* is the spiritual source of the society and the Republic of Indonesia, every Indonesian therefore considers its truthful implementation as his or her primary struggle in social and political life (BP-7, 1992a).

The various cardinal values that have been developed from the five principles of *Pancasila* have also become the basic values underlying Indonesia's educational concepts, policies, systems, aims, goals, and actions. Referring to these principles, values, and codes of conduct, the government of Indonesia defines education as having the function of developing the people's capabilities, increasing the quality of their lives and dignity aimed at the attainment and actualization of Indonesia's national goals (that is, a just and prosperous society), and maintaining the world's peace and harmony.

Hence, Indonesia's national education is aimed at developing the intellectual life of the nation and developing a holistically integrated person who is steadfastly devotes him- or herself to the One and only God. The person has a noble character, has knowledge and skills, is physically and mentally healthy, has a performing stable and independent personality, and has strong social and national responsibilities. In turn, this general goal of national education becomes a basic reference in formulating institutional, curricular, and instructional objectives, and also in selecting and developing instructional materials at all levels of education.

Underlying Pedagogical Theory and Practice

The underlying pedagogical theory of Indonesia's education is very much influenced by the history

of the nation. Today's great nation of Indonesia is a nation built on the heroic struggle of the Indonesian people against centuries of outsiders' oppression and subjugation. The long painful experience of the Indonesian people has resulted in a strong and powerful nation with its own political, social, and cultural concepts and principles that in turn influence the main ideas in science and scientific development and their application in the lives of the Indonesian people, including those related to the science of education.

Consequently, the main concepts and principles underlying today's system and praxis of Indonesian's education were developed under the influences of at least three important ideas. These are the national intellectuals' own ideas, developed since the pre-independence period of the country, which are consistent with the principles of *Pancasila;* the ideas enforced by the colonial intellectuals and scholars during their occupation of Indonesia; and the ideas of international intellectuals, scholars, and scientists adopted or adapted by Indonesian intellectuals, scholars, scientists, experts, and professionals.

The most popular and influential original concept in Indonesian's education is the one originated and developed by Ki Hajar Dewantara during the colonial period after 1928. Although his ideas were developed in the period before the birth of *Pancasila,* the ideas are congruent. In Dewantara's works on education, we can smell the nuances of heroism, patriotism, nationalism, and concerns for freedom and independence, all colored solidly by Javanese culture.

Ki Hajar Dewantara defined education simply: "Education is guidance of children's life and development" (Taman Siswa, 1962, p. 20). It means that education is an effort to guide children in developing their own natural potentialities as individuals and as members of a society so that they can achieve their maximum security and happiness. It is aimed mainly at developing children's character, their intellectual potentialities, and physical health and strength. But education is only an effort to guide the life and development of children; in reality the children's life and development is beyond the educator's capacity or expectation because children live and develop in accordance with their own natures. Education means giving children good exemplary behaviors and conduct, motivating them to develop their own positive intentions, and guiding them from behind.

Those ideas, concepts, and system introduced and developed by Ki Hajar Dewantara later became a powerful filter for ideas coming from outside cultures. Such ideas were brought on one hand by foreign experts invited by the government to help further the development of the theory, system, and the praxis of education in Indonesia and, on the other hand, by young Indonesian scholars studying in certain countries such as the United States, United Kingdom, Canada, Australia, and other Asian, African, and European countries.

Curriculum Development and Implementation

The curricula of programs at all levels of education—including preschool, primary, middle and high school, and higher education levels—are basically developed at the national level, called national curricula or core curricula. This strategy is applied to maintain a similar level of quality of education at all regions. To maintain regional needs and interest and to adjust the programs to institutional interests and capabilities, regional and institutional agencies are allowed to develop additional programs or instructional materials, but they should include all of the programs and materials of the national curricula. The additional programs and materials are all together called local contents of the whole related curriculum.

There are several criteria to be applied in the development of both national curricula and local contents. The criteria require that the contents, media, and teaching procedures applied should be:

- Consistent with the principles of *Pancasila* and the 1945 Constitution of the country
- Consistent with the general aims and goals of national education system

- Consistent with the goals and objectives of national development programs, that is, toward a just and prosperous society and maintaining world peace and harmony
- In accordance with the needs, capabilities, and level of development of the related students
- Relevant to the needs and concerns of society, including the minimum competencies required by the users of the graduates, such as industries and other employing office or agencies
- Oriented to the progress and development of science, technology, and arts
- Designed with the wise consideration and anticipation of global development of the country

Legislation of Main Educational Policies

The main policies of Indonesia's educational system and praxis have been legislated in various forms of legal documents, starting with the inclusion of related policies in the country's Constitution. There are also laws, government policy regulations, presidential decrees, ministerial decrees, and decrees issued by the related director generals and directors.

The fundamental policies of education and culture in Indonesia are stipulated in the 1945 Constitution of the Republic of Indonesia (BP-7, 1992b). Article 31 of the Constitution reads: "Every citizen shall have the right to obtain an education, and the Government shall establish and conduct a national educational system which shall be regulated by statute." Article 32 reads: "The Government shall advance the national culture of Indonesia." To fulfill what is required in subsection (2) Article 31 of the 1945 Constitution, the government adopted the Republic's Law No. 2, 1989, on the National Educational System stipulating the main policy for the whole system of national education. For the implementation of Law No. 2, a number of government regulations have been adopted (Departemen Pendidikan dan

Kebudayaan, 1989, 1990a, 1990b, 1990c, 1990d, 1992). Several Education and Culture ministerial decrees have also been adopted to regulate a more operational praxis of education referring to Law No. 2 (1989) and the related government regulations. These include those regulating the implementation of curricula and other educational and instructional praxis.

The implementation of the whole education system in Indonesia is guided by four basic references: equity of educational access for all Indonesians; quality education in terms of program, process, and product of education programs; relevance of education programs to the needs of the whole national development program in the effort of attaining national goals—namely a just and prosperous society and maintaining world peace and harmony; and effective and efficient educational management in relation to the fulfillment of the first three basic references.

Indonesia's national educational system is implemented through two main streams of programs—formal and nonformal education. Formal education is conducted in a school system, while nonformal education is conducted in an out-of-school education system, which includes family education and training programs with no specific structure of grades and continuity (Departemen Pendidikan dan Kebudayaan, 1989).

Formal Education

The school system is conducted through the specification of types and levels of education programs. In terms of type specification, the programs are classified into general education, vocational education, special education for handicapped and gifted children, specific occupation-oriented education, religious education, academic education, and professional education. In terms of level of education, the programs are categorized into basic education, secondary education, and higher education. Beyond those three levels, there is also a preschool education level, including kindergarten, nursery school, and play group activities. This preschool education level is not a required prerequisite for basic education programs; in other words, basic education is not a continuation of the preschool education level.

Beside these two categories—types and levels—there are also recognized units of education that refer to certain types and levels of education, such as primary school, middle school, high school, college, university, and institute. Basic education consists of primary school and middle school. Secondary education consists of general and vocational high schools, while higher education comprises junior and senior colleges, institutes, and university.

Schooling starts at 7 years of age in primary school. The length of schooling is as follows: six years for primary school, three years for middle school, three years for high school, three years for junior college, four years for senior college, four years for undergraduate programs at an institute or university, two years for graduate/masters programs at an institute or university, and three years for doctor program at an institute or university. In other words, it would take twenty-one years of schooling for a student to complete the whole continuous and uninterrupted schooling program from primary school up to a doctoral program. The structure of the school system is shown in Figure 26.1.

Law No. 2 (1989) indicates that the implementation of education is the responsibility of the government, society, and students' parents; the government should provide the opportunity for all citizens to obtain education or schooling. The students' parents are also required, up to their capabilities, to support the implementation of the government's education programs, both in terms of financial and nonfinancial supports.

Private sectors are allowed to conduct education programs as long as they are consistent with the government's main policies on education, the national philosophy, and the state ideology. There are hundreds of private foundations that have established private schooling services, right from preschool up to higher education levels. Actually,

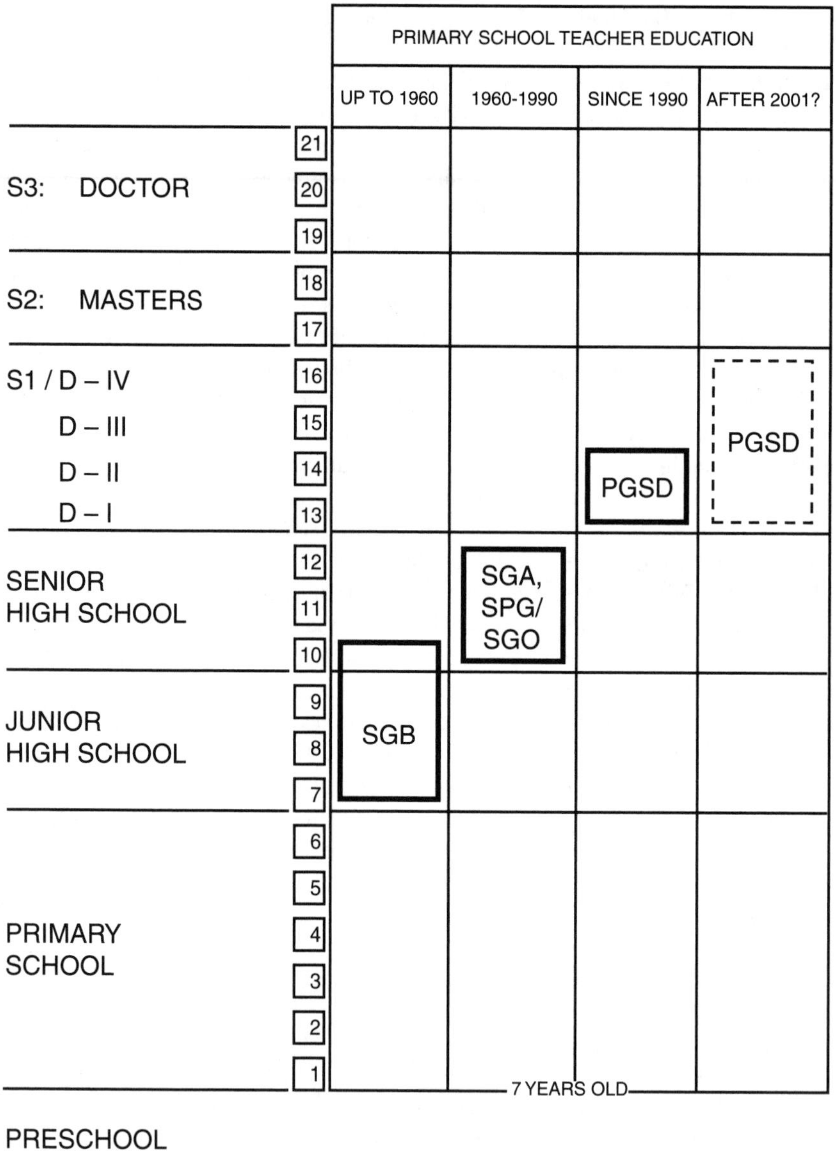

		PRIMARY SCHOOL TEACHER EDUCATION			
		UP TO 1960	1960-1990	SINCE 1990	AFTER 2001?
	21				
S3: DOCTOR	20				
	19				
S2: MASTERS	18				
	17				
S1 / D – IV	16				
D – III	15				PGSD
D – II	14			PGSD	PGSD
D – I	13				
SENIOR HIGH SCHOOL	12		SGA, SPG/ SGO		
	11				
	10				
JUNIOR HIGH SCHOOL	9	SGB			
	8				
	7				
PRIMARY SCHOOL	6				
	5				
	4				
	3				
	2				
	1		7 YEARS OLD		

PRESCHOOL

NOTES

SGB   : Sekolah Guru B (Teacher Training School, 4 years after primary school)
SGA   : Sekolah Guru A (Teaching School, 3 years after middle school)
SPG   : Sekolah Pendidikan Guru (Teacher Education School, 3 years after middle school)
SGO   : Sekolah Guru Olahraga (Sport Teacher Training School, 3 years after middle school)
PGSD : Pendidikan Guru Sekolah Dasar (Primary School Teacher Education, 2 years after high school)

FIGURE 26.1 Structure of schooling.

almost all of the preschool education institutions are owned by private foundations; very few are organized by the government. The number of private middle and high schools is much larger than public schools. This is also true at the higher education level, particularly the number of colleges, institutes, and universities.

In 1994, the government adopted nine years of compulsory education (previously it was only six years). The nine years include six years at primary school plus three years at middle school. The government plans to fully implement the nine-year compulsory education program within a decade. This nine-year compulsory education policy is mandated in an effort to fulfill the policy of equity of educational access for all Indonesians and to increase the quality of Indonesian people.

Teacher Training

Teachers from the preschool level up to high school are provided with three kinds of teacher training institutions, namely the institute of teacher training and educational sciences (*institut keguruan dan ilmu pendidikan,* IKIP), the college of teacher training and educational sciences (*sekolah tinggi keguruan dan ilmu pendidikan,* STKIP), and the faculty of teacher training and educational sciences (*fakultas keguruan dan ilmu pendidikan,* FKIP).

The institutes and colleges are independent institutions, while the faculty is a part of a university. Teachers graduated from the three institutions have the same qualifications and the same rights to be employed in both the public and private schools. The qualification of middle and high school teachers is an undergraduate certificate. This training comprises a four-year training period after high school. For a primary school, students need diploma II, which is about two years after high school.

The three kinds of teacher training institutions adopt a concurrent system of training where the students are trained as prospective teachers right from the beginning with an integrated curriculum offering both content subject matter and peda-gogy. At the end of the training program, students are required to have teaching practice through a specific direct field experience program.

The curriculum of teacher training programs consists of three components—general education, subject matter education, and pedagogy, including practice teaching. The whole program is aimed at preparing teachers with adequate professional, personal, and social competencies that include the competency of teaching performance supported by competencies of subject mastery, mastery of teaching, program development and implementation, applying appropriate procedures of teaching and evaluation, adjustment to the classroom and school situations, and competency for personality development.

A student active learning strategy is adopted at all levels, up to higher education. The strategy is applied with the intention of developing not only student academic capability but also other personal capabilities, including student creativity, proactivity, cooperation, and so on.

Norm- and criterion-referenced evaluation approaches are applied in the evaluation of student achievement. The evaluation is conducted in at least at four stages—at the subject stage intended for both formative and summative evaluation, at the semester stage, at the grade stage, and at the end of the whole program as the last summative assessment.

MAIN ISSUES IN EDUCATION

Many issues must be addressed in contemporary Indonesian education. The major issues, however, are discussed below.

Primary Schooling

The expansion of primary schooling throughout Indonesia's twenty-seven provinces has been impressive. However, it is now confronted with expanding compulsory primary education from six to nine years, and this process poses numerous challenges. On the one hand, the government has to consolidate past gains while continuing to expand access to education, which means additional facilities, teachers, laboratories, books, and equipment (Djojonegoro, 1996). A part of this issue is the financial aspect.

The bleak general economic picture impacts on the educational sector. Educational facilities for Indonesia are very limited in comparison with other Asian countries. For instance, educational expenditures are only 1.5 percent of GNP, while for India they account for 4 percent of GNP, and in the People's Republic of China, they account for 5 percent of GNP. Educational expenditures per capita per year for Singapore are US$322, for Korea US$223, for Malaysia US$126, for Thailand US$54, and for Indonesia US$4 (BPPN, 1995).

Demographic Changes

Four other major variables are detected as influencing this issue. That is, "demographic change, change in primary school intakes, changes in primary school competition rate and changes in primary to junior school transition rate" (Boediono & Dhanani, 1996, p. 1).

Except for the demographic variable, all these variables are in turn determined by a combination of social and economic factors. Social factors include, among others, the level of education obtained by the parents, government and community efforts to persuade the parents to send their children to school, efforts to overcome the traditional attitude towards girls' education, and the distance the children have to go to school. Economic factors include, among others, school fees, transport costs, and household income (Boediono & Dhanani, 1996).

Indonesia is in the midst of a major demographic transition. Family planning efforts are likely to have facilitated these changes, but significant factors such as overpopulation in Java compared with underpopulated provinces of most of Sumatra, Kalimantan, Sulawesi, and other eastern islands, as well as the relative higher infant mortality rates in a number of provinces outside Java, contribute to pronounced changes in the primary

and secondary school-age population (Boediono & Dhanani, 1996).

Changes in primary school intakes are caused by the demographic changes and the changing economic circumstances fluctuating in the 1980s. The age-specific enrollment rate of children aged 7 to 12, whether enrolled in primary or junior secondary schools, increased from 96 percent to 98 percent between 1990–1991 and 1994–1995 for the country as a whole, while the repeater rate was the most important indicator of the dropout rate (Boediono & Dhanani, 1996).

Though there are year-to-year fluctuations, the evolution in the transition rate from primary school to the secondary school can be divided into three periods. First, a rapid increase from 55 percent to 75 percent in the 1970s, followed by a period of decline from 75 percent to 60 percent in the 1980s, and finally a period of recovery from 60 percent to 67 percent by 1994–1995, especially rapid in the last two years (Boediono & Dhanani, 1996).

Poverty

One of the variables considered as a major profound source of constraint in the implementation of enhancing quality in education is poverty. Children who belong to very poor households or who are located in geographically isolated pockets are not in the school system. "This indication is provided by the number of 'least developed villages' or *Inpres Desa Tertinggal* (IDT) without a primary school, which numbered over 3,300 or 17 percent of all. 20,000 IDT villages in 1993" (CBS, 1994, in Boediono & Dhanani, 1996, p. 8). In the last decade, however, considerable efforts have been made to fight this condition. According to Boediono and Dhanani (1996) "economic growth is projected to continue to grow at the rapid rate of 7 percent to 8 percent per annum in the next fifteen years and population growth has slowed down markedly in many parts of the country. The average rate per capita income will continue to grow at 5 percent to 6 percent p.a., and likely influence the educational attainment" (p. 40).

Interwoven with household income is the educational attainment of the population, which is also influenced by the trend of globalization itself and characterized by pragmatic, interpenetrating, and competitive tendencies. These tendencies have an enormous impact on the way of life of the people. The problems in developing countries like Indonesia differ from earlier encounters in modernization. A part of the society still lives in rural areas but is also a part of an urban labor market. In the rural area, time and punctuality are not so important, while the urban population is already in the era of industry and information. So the lives of individuals of these societies, we can say, have shifted from being isolated farmers to organizational employees.

An anecdote can illustrate this issue. One of the policies of the Ministry of Education and Culture in keeping up with modern demands was five-day schooling, which was tried out for six months in 1996 in the whole country. Some of the schools in the villages in Bali as well as many other schools in other villages had a two-shift school (7:30 to 12:30 and 14:00 to 19:00) because of the limitations of buildings in those villages. Students in those villages came individually by bus, but the bus service to the villages ran only until 17:00, so many students could not go to school or had to walk long distances. This made it difficult for the children to have normal schooling and was one of the many reasons why, after a trial of six months, five-day schooling was abandoned.

Equity

Equity issues in education linked with quality imply that efforts to improve quality will be directed on a priority base. What are the components of "quality" if we relate it to the new skills and knowledge needed to meet the challenge of surviving in the twenty-first century?

Besides understanding the political environment, equity requires engagements in a dynamic process of change. Do schools in general, specifically schools in Indonesia, perform in ways that enhance the necessary competencies for life in a global era? According to Levinger (1996), "Schools often perform in ways that defeat the

development of necessary cognitive competencies for life in a global era. The disjuncture between real life in and out of school diminishes the transferability of knowledge across environments, settings and contexts. Yet, such transferability is critical in an era of rapid change" (p.12).

Transfer means generalization of identical components of an "old situation" to a "new situation" preceded by observation comparison, classification, interpretations, and prediction. These cognitive tools should include as well as the competencies to adapt oneself to specific situations through sensitivity toward real-life problems. That sensitivity will arouse meaningfulness and create the context of specific situations.

The way to think, or to learn how to learn globally but act locally, needs to be addressed with students at school as early as possible. This attitude will enhance self-adequacy and in turn promote self-confidence and self-realization in different situations and settings of life. The constellation of those skills and outlook corresponds with adaptability, knowledge transfer, and problem-solving prowess (Levinger, 1996), which are needed to meet the challenges of the twenty-first century as well as to cope with the demands of the future.

A minimum standard for instructional materials and resources should be available that accompanies articulated, comprehensive training for teachers, so that they become able to access the degree to which a school is sufficiently prepared to meet the needs of the children they serve, based on a set of "readiness" criteria (Levinger, 1996, p.12) that constitute guidelines to develop a keener awareness and reflection to facilitate their own learning as well.

REFERENCES

Boediono & Dhanani, S. (1996). *Demand for junior secondary education in Indonesia.* Jakarta: Directorate of General Secondary Education, Ministry Education and Culture, RI.

BP-7. (1991). *Pancasila: The state foundation and ideology of the Republic of Indonesia.* BP-7 Pusat. Jakarta: Government Document.

BP-7. (1992a). *Decree of the Majelis Permusyawaratan*

Rakyat of the Republic of Indonesia No. II/MPR/1978 on the psycho-motoric perception and truthful implementation of Pancasila (Ekaprasetya Pancakarsa). BP-7 Pusat. Jakarta: Government Document.

BP-7. (1992b). *UUD-1945: The 1945 Constitution of the Republic of Indonesia.* BP-7 Pusat. Jakarta: Government Document.

BPPN, Badan Pertimbangan Pendidikan Nasional. Advisory Council for National Education. (1995). *Sumber dana untuk pendidikan nasional* (Source of finance for national education). Jakarta: Government Document.

Departemen Pendidikan dan Kebudayaan. (1989). *Undang-undang Republik Indonesia nomor 2 tahun 1989 tentang Sistem Pendidikan Nasional beserta penjelasannya* (Law No. 2 on National Education System). Jakarta: Balai Pustaka.

Departemen Pendidikan dan Kebudayaan. (1990a). *Peraturan pemerintah Republik Indonesia no. 27 tahun 1990 tentang pendidikan prasekolah.* Jakarta: Author.

Departemen Pendidikan dan Kebudayaan. (1990b). *Peraturan pemerintah Republik Indonesia no. 28 tahun 1990 tentang pendidikan dasar.* Jakarta: Author.

Departemen Pendidikan dan Kebudayaan. (1990c). *Peraturan pemerintah Republik Indonesia no. 29 tahun 1990 tentang pendidikan menengah.* Jakarta: Author.

Departemen Pendidikan dan Kebudayaan. (1990d). *Peraturan pemerintah Republik Indonesia no. 30 tahun 1990 tentang pendidikan tinggi.* Jakarta: Author.

Departemen Pendidikan dan Kebudayaan (1992). *Himpunan peraturan perundang-undangan Republik Indonesia bidang pendidikan dan kebudayaan.* Jakarta: Author.

Djojonegoro, W. (1996). Giftedness: A gift and a challenge. In U. Munandar & Semiawan C. (Eds.), *Optimising excellence in human resource development. Proceeding of the Fourth Asia Pacific Conference on the Gifted and Talented.* Jakarta: Gifted and Talented Conference.

Jones, H.A.P. (1973). *Indonesia, the possible dream* (2nd ed.). Singapore: Toppan Printing Co. (s) Ptd Ltd; Mas Ayu (s) Ptd Ltd.

Levinger, B. (1996). *Critical transitions: Human capacity development across the life span.* New York: United Nations Development Program Education Development Centre.

N.N. (1996, July 22). *Asiaweek Magazine,* No. 28, p. 53.

Semiawan, C., & Munandar, U. (1993). Perspectives on the disadvantaged gifted, the Indonesian case. In W. Bell & H.B. Adams (Eds.), *Worldwide perception on the gifted disadvantaged.* London: AB Academic Publishers.

Taman Siswa. (1962). *Karya ki hajar dewantara.* Yogyakarta: Majelis Luhur Persatuan Taman Siswa.

CHAPTER 27

Education, Inequality, and Development:
Schooling in Papua New Guinea

BAREND VLAARDINGERBROEK

Barend Vlaardingerbroek B.Sc., Auckland, B.Ed.St., B.A., Queensland, M.App.Sc., Curtin, Ph.D., Otago, is at the Goroka Campus of the University of Papua New Guinea. His principal current research interests are associated with the external efficiency of formal education in agrarian developing countries. He is founding Chief Editor of the Papua New Guinea Journal of Teacher Education.

THE SOCIAL FABRIC

Geography and Demography

Papua New Guinea (PNG) occupies the eastern half of New Guinea, which lies north of Australia across the narrow Torres Strait. The nation encompasses a number of offshore islands, including New Britain and Bougainville. The interior of the mainland is mountainous and features some of the most difficult topography on the planet. There is no national road network, but a comprehensive and reliable air transport system exists. Vast, relatively unspoiled wetlands are found in western coastal areas. Most of the country is covered by lowland rainforest and montane forest, the former in particular harboring a wealth of tropical hardwood species. The nation is well endowed with mineral resources, particularly copper, gold, and oil. It is also a seismically and volcanically active region.

Human habitation in PNG began at least 40,000 years ago. Various influxes have occurred since, including a relatively recent Polynesian incursion along the south coast. Isolation, however, has tended to be the overriding influence on cultural evolution, as is evidenced by the phrase "Land of a thousand tongues" from a popular song—which contains only the merest poetic license, given that some 800 culture/language groups are now known to make up the PNG human kaleidoscope of just 4 million people. With the exception of some Papuan peoples, the unifying tongue is Tok Pisin, a *lingua franca* based on the seafarers' Pidgin English of yesteryear. Tok Pisin is converging with English, especially in the urban areas, to form a distinct PNG English.

Virtually all Papua New Guineans are of ethnic Melanesian stock. The development of a *colon* social entity is conspicuously absent from the annals of PNG history, with the exception of very small numbers of principally German and Australian colonists who settled and intermarried with local tribes in the colonial era. A very small number of Chinese settled in pockets throughout the colonial era, but most left at independence. Following the government's "Look North" policy of 1992, however, Asian influence has been steadily growing in the commercial sector.

Social development indicators tend to be uninspiring. Life expectancy is in the mid-50s, infant and maternal mortality rates are among the highest in the world, and adult literacy hovers around 50 percent. The country rates poorly on the UN's Human Development Index. The natural rate of population increase is ostensibly 2.3 percent per annum, but doubts abound given the backdrop of frequent rural nonregistration of births; the true current population growth rate is probably well over 3 percent per annum.

More than 80 percent of Papua New Guineans live in traditional rural societies and are primarily engaged in subsistence agriculture, although sales of surplus produce are often important sources of village income and some areas are involved in intensive cash cropping. Proximity to urban centers and roads is economically advantageous to villagers, and rural people are well known for their prodigious saving capacity toward desired goals, such as the ubiquitous village truck. Absolute poverty is rare.

Other than some matrilineal southern coastal and island peoples, traditional society tends to be strongly patriarchal and male dominated. Virtually all Papua New Guineans are nominally Christians, but traditional beliefs are firmly entrenched even among the educated. The conceptual ecology tends to exhibit a mosaic of traditional and exogenous paradigms.

Colonial History

Sections of New Guinea were claimed at various times by three European powers. The western half of the island was incorporated into the Dutch East Indies and is now the Indonesian province of Irian-Jaya. In the northeast, German influence was established during the mid-1800s, particularly in New Britain; British influence was pronounced in the southeast. Both Deutsch Neu-Guinea and British New Guinea (renamed British Papua in 1905) were proclaimed in 1884, in Rabaul and Port Moresby respectively. British enthusiasm about the new acquisition was short lived, Papua being ceded to Australia in 1906. With the outbreak of World War I, Australia annexed German New Guinea. The colony was mandated to Australia as a Trust Territory by the League of Nations after the war.

The mountainous interior of the mainland remained *terra incognita* until the 1930s, with some parts of the highlands remaining closed areas outside the scope of colonial administrative control until 1974—the year before national independence. The discovery of gold at Bulolo in the 1920s stimulated an intensive gold rush, a remarkable feature of which was the largest airlift of equipment ever carried out to that time, mainly by Junkers aircraft. The rapid depletion of the precious metal acted as a spur for the exploration of the highlands, which began in 1930 with the Leahy expeditions.

The Japanese incursion of 1942 constituted the only interruption to Australian colonial rule. In some parts, Japanese landing troops were welcomed by local people; the Australians had ruled the ex-German colony harshly at times, including provisions for the whipping of plantation workers at the behest of their employers. The subsequent Kokoda Trail counteroffensive was one of the significant turning points of the Pacific War.

The colonial experience of PNG was generally a positive one. There were no native wars or mass land dispossession of indigenous peoples. The Territories of Papua and New Guinea were administratively united at self-government in 1972, and the sovereign state of Papua New Guinea was proclaimed on 16 September 1975. Australian budgetary support for the new state was impressive, enabling the continuation of a legacy of heavy government spending, particularly on health and education.

Government

Papua New Guinea is a constitutional parliamentary democracy within the Commonwealth of Nations governed by a 109-member unicameral National Parliament. From 1977, various administrative functions were devolved to nineteen provincial governments. The provincial parliamentary government system was abolished in June 1995, in favor of provincial governors as a consequence of the acute fiscal crisis that developed in August 1994.

PNG is a vibrant democracy, as indicated by its favorable rating by the UN Human Freedom Index. However, many rural people have few notions of nationhood or democratic processes at this time, tribalism and regionalism being pronounced. The most serious threat to PNG's national integrity has been the secessionist rebellion in

Bougainville that flared up in 1989. There have been intermittent secessionist threats from other New Guinea Islands provinces.

Economy

In GNP terms, PNG is low-middle income. PNG's economy is characterized by an atypically large import and export volume for its size. The chief commodity exports are gold, copper, coffee, cocoa, copra, and timber, with the recent addition of oil. Manufactured goods and machinery, petroleum products, and, paradoxically, food items make up the main imports—including what are for many Papua New Guineans the principal starch and protein staples, namely rice and canned fish. The subsistence-based agricultural sector is characterized by low productivity, while cash crops are vulnerable to external commodity price fluctuations. A considerable but gradually reducing proportion of government revenues comes from direct Australian budgetary assistance.

The secessionist rebellion in Bougainville that saw the closure of the giant Panguna copper mine in 1989—previously the source of 20 percent of government revenue—precipitated a mild economic downturn that highlighted the unsustainable government expenditure regime the nation had inherited at independence. The following year saw the imposition of fiscal measures, including the significant reduction of the burgeoning public sector. The country entered a phase of profound fiscal crisis in 1994 when the national government effectively declared itself bankrupt, creating havoc in the education and health sectors. The public sector is now largely dependent on World Bank loans contingent to structural adjustments being undertaken.

A Society in Change

The rate of change in PNG over the past few decades has been breathtaking. The dissemination of the steel axe throughout remote parts of the highlands during the 1950s significantly changed many peoples' lifestyles; the coffee revolution of the 1970s and 1980s brought many of the people in the region into the world monetary economy. Development has occurred and has been impressive, with regard to both quantity and quality. But it has not been an equitable process: While the minerals boom has benefited those in the urban centers and in its proximity, some areas remain chronically underdeveloped. At societal level, a process of socioeconomic polarization has arisen featuring the development of affluent indigenous urban enclaves separated from the masses of have-nots outside by barbed wire fences, guard dogs, and the services of the booming private security industry.

Naturally, the development process has been accompanied by escalating expectations. People desperate to cash in on the bonanza have recently been involved in acts of sabotage against mining concerns, while some traditional landowner compensation claims have reached the pinnacle of absurdity. Tribalism and regionalism continue to be major forces in local politics. The Papua Besena movement seeking political autonomy for the Papuan region continues to periodically raise its head, although it has been eclipsed by the persistent secessionist rumblings emanating from the New Guinea Islands region, including the festering sore of Bougainville.

Apart from the ailing economy, the main cause of concern among Papua New Guineans is the chronic lawlessness that characterizes PNG life. The activities of highway bandits are more reminiscent of the American Wild West than of a rapidly modernizing state; rioting, looting, and pillaging are entrenched local customs for dealing with grievances against the authorities, especially in the highlands. Endemic alcohol abuse compounds the public and domestic violence that form a sadly common part of ordinary people's lives. The death penalty was reintroduced in 1994, although it seems unlikely that this penalty will be applied, particularly given the incumbent Prime Minister's opposition to it.

"Landless youth" refers principally to the emergence of an underclass of traditionally unthinkable landless people who inhabit the squatter settlements that have grown like metastatic cancers around the urban centers. Second generation urban migrants, often the offspring of unsanctioned intertribal liaisons and the products of the thriving sex industry, rely solely on a cash income for the necessities of life. In the absence of formal employment, the source of these funds is often illicit. Population control has been listed as an area of priority by several overseas agencies. The cultural values militating against the success of any such program are, however, considerable.

SCHOOLING

Historical Overview

Educational activities in Papua New Guinea were initiated by Christian missions in the late nineteenth century and focused on literacy, numeracy, woodworking for boys, and clothes making for girls. The German colonial power established a school for New Guinea boys in Rabaul in 1907. A Department of Education was established in Port Moresby in 1946, and the 1952 *Education Ordinance* established state control over curricula.

By the mid-1950s, a small number of Papua New Guineans were attending secondary school in Australia; there were seven high schools in the PNG Territories by 1960. Universal Primary Education (UPE), first mooted by colonial administrators in 1955, was set to be achieved by 1975. This goal was abandoned in favor of further secondary expansion and the establishment of a tertiary education sector following a 1966 UN Visiting Mission that emphasized the need for educated manpower provision.

The imminence of independence and its associated requirement for post-primary educated indigenous personnel acted as the stimulus for the proliferation of the high school system in the late 1960s, which mushroomed into the mid-1980s. This growth was helped by the abandonment of the colonially introduced system whereunder the academically weakest 40 percent of students were dismissed at the end of grade 8. The end of this policy was forced on Provincial Education Divisions by mounting social demand for education.

Government and most church agency schools were integrated into the National Education System by the 1970 *Education Act*. During the crucial 1970 to 1978 period, official concern with perceived manpower needs steadily focused on the post-primary levels at the expense of UPE. The 1976 *Education Plan,* the culmination of several unsuccessful forerunners that had attempted to radically change the macrostructure of the education system, was a relatively sober document that aimed at a moderate increase in primary enrollments over the next five years and the continuing expansion of the secondary school system. Then a 1977 plan, calling for a greater link between schooling and rural development, was rejected. A revised 1978 version was yet another conservative document, with a further increased emphasis on post-secondary skilled manpower provision. While the PNG *Education II* project included funding for raising provincial governments' planning capabilities, by the mid-1980s provincial planning generally had fallen into disarray. Prevailing policy had been to restrict entry to the secondary level as determined by defined manpower needs, but social demand created irresistible political pressures to the contrary. Hence, the National Planning Office put out a National Manpower Assessment in 1981, which was revised in 1984 and was instrumental in determining the post-primary oriented PNG *Education III* project.

Part of the ambitious rural development scheme that was fashionable in the mid-1970s was to turn primary schools into community schools, theoretically open to both adults and children, with curricula focusing on skills relevant to rural living. However, in reality and in spite of the name change, they have remained primary schools in the sense of being the first rung on the ladder leading to salaried jobs.

Thus, PNG developed a hierarchical education system in which each level acted principally as a stepping stone to the next, with little perceived relevance of its own. Until 1992, the system changed little in principle or practice. It muddled through the best part of two decades following independence. Then came the mooted upheavals of 1992.

Macrostructure of Schooling: Prereform

The primary cycle is six years, followed by a four-year lower secondary cycle, and a two-year upper secondary cycle. About three-quarters of children begin community school, but almost half drop out before completing grade 6. The transition rate from primary to lower secondary school is currently about 34 percent, based on performance in the externally administered grade 6 examinations. School fees at the lower secondary level are high—US$300+ *per annum* for boarding students (which is most students).

External examinations are conducted by the Department of Education and results are combined with internal school assessments to produce final grades. Grade 10 results are used to select students for the four grade 11 to 12 national high schools (to which fewer than 1 percent of the cohort progress), and for other post-school institutions such as technical colleges, community teachers colleges, and colleges of nursing. Prior to 1990, the two universities (University of Papua New Guinea and Papua New Guinea University of Technology) accepted grade 10 leavers for entry to preliminary year courses. However, since that time matriculation (*viz.,* grade 12 from a national high school, regional university center, or other approved outlet such as a Permitted School or seminary) has been stipulated.

Nearly all community school teachers are Papua New Guineans trained and certificated by the seven community teachers colleges (six of which are run by church agencies). Most lower secondary teachers are now Papua New Guinea nationals, mostly diplomates of the University of Papua New Guinea's Goroka Teachers College (Goroka Campus since 1993). However, expatriates remain influential in the lower secondary system, mainly as volunteers and members of religious orders.

MAJOR ISSUES, CONTROVERSIES, AND PROBLEMS

Most, if not all, debate about the role of education in PNG at public, political, and academic levels may be encapsulated in one word: *relevance*. The relevance controversy has a long history and varied current manifestations.

Historical Background

The German tradition of schooling a small number of New Guinea boys with a view to their taking up lower level clerical positions was continued after the transfer of the territory to Australia in 1921. The 1922 *Education Ordinance* sought "to train a certain number of natives in such a way as would enable them to take positions in the lower grades of the Government service" through English-language primary schooling. Thus, the synonymizing of a formal, academic education with formal employment dates back to those early years. It was through monetary returns readily translatable into better living standards that education became functional for Papua New Guineans, and people's attitude towards schooling rapidly shifted from apathy to high social demand in the years that followed.

However, the functions of traditional childhood education in PNG were to teach essential life skills such as gardening and hunting, and to inculcate conformity to social institutions and values conducive to social harmony. In both the developing and current system, "The tendency has been to divorce the schools from native life and thus to bring about a division of interests and outlook between the educated few and their village confreres" (Groves, 1936, pp. 75–76).

In the past, and up till today, PNG teachers tend to be authoritarian and rigid in their approach and regard students as empty vessels to be passively "filled" with knowledge. Schools in PNG often tend to be intellectually sterile environments where student life is dominated by lessons, sport, and Work Parade. Students generally function in a nebulous world of partial understanding in which survival is largely dependent on memorizing stock responses to hide noncomprehension. The effectiveness of the learning that takes place in high schools with regard to genuine comprehension translating into effective behavioral changes is arguable. Students seem ever willing to soak up masses of rote information in order to pass examinations and receive a piece of paper, but this is mere assimilation of knowledge. It does not result in a behavioral change in the pupil from a traditional cultural mode of thinking to one that will fit that person to live in the modern world (see Maddock, 1980).

An attempted compromise, adopted in 1935 and reaffirmed in 1955, was the "blending of cultures" approach involving the selective retention of traditional cultural facets and their amalgamation with selected aspects of Western culture, specifically Christianity, English, and agriculture. The policy was abandoned in 1968 due to ethical questions raised about its validity and the growing emphasis on manpower requirements for the growing economy.

Social and Cultural Impacts of Education

As indicated above, cultural alienation as well as socioeconomic stratification has understandably been a by-product of education in PNG. Schooling, especially at the post-primary level, is a form of alternative enculturation: Even the four-year exposure to facilities such as electricity while at high school condition young people away from traditional lifestyles. Secondary schooling changes young Papua New Guineans' values, bringing about greater egocentrism. Traditional religious values and beliefs are undermined. Above all, education instills a feeling of alienation from villagers' constructs of reality greater than may in fact be the case. English language acquisition reinforces the higher status and aloofness of the educated in the eyes of village people. Draper's (1974) observations regarding the outcomes of cultural dissonance when educated and unedu-

cated subsequently reunite in the village, although dated, are informative with regard to today's elite:

After years in an . . . educational environment, the younger [person] tends to regard the villager as absurdly primitive and ignorant; the elders in turn feel so ill at ease and inadequate to cope with the young sophisticate that they in turn maintain their sense of dignity by barring him from village debates and councils. (p. 12)

Paradoxically, this alienation tends to be anticipated by many parents, who expect schools to "sort and allocate children into different occupations and socio-economic statuses" (Francis, 1978, p. 54). It is hardly surprising, then, that many secondary school students display anxiety and depression symptoms, given the immense pressure to succeed.

The transfer of the traditional meritocratic paradigm to the acquisition of schooling and access to material benefits brought about the formation of an advantaged indigenous socioeconomic stratum. Therefore, far from the "spirit of solidarity" education was expected to instill,

Schooling in Papua New Guinea has created an atmosphere of conflict and misunderstanding in the minds of many traditional practitioners and leaders . . . The problems of unemployment for school leavers and of unequal distribution of educational opportunities are good examples of how the gap between the educated elites and the uneducated grassroots is further widened. (Apelis, 1980, p. 3)

Given the high correlation between educational attainment and both status and income, it is scarcely surprising that people adopt a mercenary attitude to schooling. Educational inflation has inevitably raised its head; given the maximum ability of the economy to absorb about 15 percent of all school leavers in formal sector employment in the foreseeable future, entry requirements to jobs have been steadily rising, accompanied by increasing credentialism. Ironically, the demise of primary schooling as a job ticket has promoted gender equity in terms of enrollments at that level.

The assumed transition to the formal employment sector raises one of the most serious negative effects of schooling in PNG—the creation of the status of unemployment. Unemployment was a status that very few people assigned to themselves in 1980; when asked what their occupations were as part of the 1980 National Population Census, only 2.5 percent categorized themselves as unemployed, a large 14 percent of people not engaged in subsistence farming eventually were classified under other activities, with an additional 6 percent claiming to be in nonsubsistence nonwage employment. Since then, educated youths not in formal employment have been told repeatedly by politicians and social commentators that they *are* unemployed. A perennial hobbyhorse of editorialists at the end of each year is the same topic, embellished with platitudes to the effect that schooling is failing the young people of PNG.

Finally, the indigenous elite in general appear to have long lost faith in their own education system. Many prefer local international schools or Australian boarding schools for their own offspring.

Vocationalization

Papua New Guinea, akin to many countries of similar development status over the past four decades, experimented with curricular vocationalization as a means of making formal schooling more relevant to the rural masses.

Ignoring early missionary education, vocationalization attempts may be dated back to the 1952 Vunamami School, which attempted to base its academic courses around the school's agricultural program until parental complaints about the time wasted on gardening forced the school authorities to academize the curriculum. Although technical schools emphasizing village life and self-employment skills were established in 1959, they similarly became academic institutions due to public pressure. In 1973, the Community Education Project (CEP, *Skulanka*) was introduced as a grade 7 and 8 vocational alternative for students likely to fail at the end of grade 8. It collapsed

within two years due to the animosity shown towards it by parents and students. A similar scheme initiated in 1974 that attempted a compromise between academic subjects and community-based vocational education at grades 7 and 8 level was abandoned in 1977. The disdain people showed for vocational centers was directed initially at the fledgling technical college system as well, although the ready nexus between postsecondary technical schooling and formal employment soon became apparent and the *Techs* are now oversubscribed.

The most ambitious vocationalization attempt in PNG was the *Secondary schools community extension project* (SSCEP) devised in 1977 and piloted over the period 1978 to 1982. Many of the aims of SSCEP were virtual rehashes of the Tanzanian *Education for self-reliance* (ESR) scheme—including the provision of relevant education for rural communities, breaking with elitist concepts of schooling, and encouraging favorable attitudes to manual work, with the ultimate aims of improving rural living and reducing urban drift. SSCEP was introduced at grades 9 and 10 level.

Naturally, the authors of SSCEP were well aware of the predominant reasons for the failure of vocational education programs in other developing countries. All grade 8 students at the pilot schools were promoted to a unitary grade 9, thus avoiding a dualistic system. The scheme was sold to parents as way of bolstering grade 10 examination performance, the assumption being that this procedure would develop an intrinsic satisfaction in the application of academic skills to the solution of practical rural problems that eventually would see those grade 10 graduates not advancing to higher study or able to find salaried employment *want* to stay in the village and continue to apply those SSCEP skills. At the curriculum level, SSCEP sought to implement "a behavioral objectives approach to syllabus analysis [involving] program teaching methods stressing integrated curricula and activity methods" (Vulliamy, 1983, p. 13). Specifically, core academic subjects—particularly mathematics and science—and noncore subjects—agriculture and practical skills—were to be applied to local community projects by both regular teachers and specialist staff, including local people.

Although SSCEP expanded to encompass fifteen schools over the five years following 1978, many problems emerged during its evaluation in the pilot schools. Teachers were found generally to be incapable of adapting courses to real-life situations and core subject applications generally were abandoned at an early stage. SSCEP headquarters stopped asking schools to submit modified syllabi by 1982. Technical and agricultural extension projects fared better, but the quality of teaching and assessing by the specialist staff were unimpressive. The whole area of assessment was especially problematical. SSCEP work was supposed to count for up to 40 percent of students' scores in core subjects, but many teachers were found to have difficulties applying weightings to marks. Many resisted the notion of assessing noncognitive skills. Students did not generally display positive attitudes to manual work, seeing project work as robbing them of class time for "the important [that is examinable] subjects" (Vulliamy, 1983, p. 19). Students sometimes expressed fears of falling victim to local sorcerers should they interfere with established practices. Staff at SSCEP schools were demoralized and complained of having more work for no extra reward, and many transferred out. At the same time, *academic* standards in the five pilot schools did indeed rise.

Following the trial period, the special funding and logistical support invariably associated with pilot schemes ran out. In the ten years that followed the pilot scheme, SSCEP programs generally diluted themselves out of existence by becoming increasingly academic and less vocational in orientation, and the number of schools classifying themselves as SSCEP schools by 1990 had fallen to two (now zero).

Although a large part of the failure of SSCEP is attributable to the lack of adequate and appropriate teacher training and in-service preparation of teachers involved, there was also an epistemolog-ical fallacy at work. Crossley (1984) pointed out the "naive instrumentalist approach" inherent in SSCEP and similar schemes that presupposes a transfer of classroom skills to everyday life (p. 122). Ultimately, the fundamental reason for SSCEP's downfall was "the strength of traditional conceptions of the schooling process," especially students' unfailing assumption that *academic* schooling was in their best interests "as giving the most *vocational* access to better jobs" (Vulliamy, 1987, pp. 57, 54; emphasis added).

The "Crisis of Objectives"

From an analysis of secondary education needs, one of Bacchus's (1984) two "production goals" for the PNG education system was a highly skilled minority trained to administer the country and run the economy. But in spite of all the attention that manpower needs and education have received, a poorer fit between supply and demand has been difficult to find. For example, 1975 found an oversupply of grade 10 leavers that could be absorbed neither by post-secondary institutions nor by the economy. At the same time, little has been done to alleviate long-standing skill shortages. There are serious shortfalls in the supply of indigenous accountants, managers, pilots, engineers, and technicians; skilled manual occupations remain chronically understaffed. Falling academic standards with increasing intakes at post-primary level have not helped (see Vlaardingerbroek & Ros, 1990). A high-level manpower approach to post-primary education provision has been advocated by a number of commentators for many years, but it has also long been recognized that the costs of a required high-quality system aiming at this would prohibit universality of access, wherein lies the political/economic dilemma.

The "crisis of objectives" facing secondary education was well summarized by Bacchus, Eri, and McNamara (1985):

> *In implementing the curriculum of the Provincial High Schools efforts seem to be directed less at the general all round education of the pupils and more*

towards trying to ensure their "successful" performance in the centrally set examinations for grade 10. . . . This largely results from the belief, which is shared by many, that the chief purpose of the Provincial High Schools is to prepare students for further education. . . . The counterview is that the purpose of the Provincial High Schools is to prepare their total student body for enhanced community living . . . by providing them with the most relevant knowledge, experiences, skills and attitudes for this purpose. (p. 23)

Recent Developments

By the beginning of this decade, it was clear that a radical reappraisal of the education sector was urgently required.

The Matane Report (1986) initiated a concerted push for educational reform by drawing attention to the lack of congruence between the constitutionally defined educational goal of integral human development and the outcomes of education. These findings were reinforced by the National Executive Council's report five years later (Ministry of Education, 1991) that attempted to define a blueprint of objectives for the education system as PNG approached the twenty-first century. The education system must provide relevant education for the approximately 85 percent of the population who will remain in their rural and semirural communities. The major source of employment for these citizens will be their own subsistence and small-scale community-based commercial enterprises. It must accommodate the approximately 15 percent of the population who will find paid employment, the small number of our children who have the ability to perform at top international standards, and the small but growing number of landless youth who have no villages to return to.

Major structural reforms have now been initiated: a three-year elementary cycle (preschool to grade 2) with vernaculars as the medium of instruction is being introduced, with teachers drawn from the community; grades 7 and 8 are to be transferred to the primary tier; grades 11 and 12 are to be added to the secondary schools. Uni-

versal access to grade 8 is envisaged by the year 2004, with a transition rate of 50 percent to grade 9, and of 15 percent to grade 12. A number of top-up primary schools at the provincial level and high schools at the regional level are now in operation as pilot institutions. The students of two of the latter performed comparatively well in the 1994 grade 12 examinations, although this observation must be tempered by the halo effect surrounding every well-resourced pilot scheme.

THE FUTURE OF SCHOOLING

At the time of this writing, fiscal constraints have slowed down the educational reform process. At the same time, some of the problems associated with the reforms are coming to light. For example, the inevitable pressure of numbers has forced at least one high school to return to a grade 8 dismissal procedure to make room for grade 8 graduates feeding in from local top up schools. A strong feeling of *déja vu* will undoubtedly have struck parents.

The implications of the intended reforms for educational quality are far from reassuring, and the quality issue is likely to become a focus for debate in the near future. Most primary teachers cannot hope to cope with grades 7 and 8 specialist subject teaching, particularly in mathematics and science (see, e.g., Zepp, Matang, & Sapau, 1994). The community teachers' colleges are embarking on a three-year diploma program, but little, if any, of the additional time will be devoted to academic content areas. Goroka Campus has upgraded its programs to degree level (the four-year Bachelor of Education). Hopefully, the reform at the higher end will keep pace with the supply of degree graduate teachers able to teach the upper secondary grades. This consideration is especially acute from the perspective of the production of high-level manpower, particularly in the science and technology domain, in which PNG continues to portray a heavy reliance on expensive expatriate know-how. However, the pressure of numbers has already brought about a commitment to a soft science option for top-up secondary schools.

A role for vocational centers in future high schooling was announced, although this has not been elaborated to date. Vocational centers were initially introduced to cope with the backwash from the grade 6 and grade 8 attritions and are administered by Provincial Education Divisions. To bring these ill-funded institutions, using as they do unqualified teachers (mostly tradespeople) and operating outside the parameters of the formal certification system, into the mainstream structure will be an onerous exercise. However, three Catholic schools featuring a compromise between conventional and vocational education are now in operation: Students study the core subjects and sit the national examinations, while spending noncore subject time on vocational subjects. The Ministry of Education has awarded these schools Permitted status.

Another controversy is the proposed strengthening of Christian education to address the problems of private and public lawlessness and soaring crime. While perfectly compatible with the Constitution, which defines PNG as "a Christian country," grave concerns about the wisdom of tying ethics to a specific religious viewpoint are being expressed.

The time that these words are being penned possibly represents a turning point for PNG society and education's place in it, and any attempted predictions are purely conjectural. The attempt to forge a closer nexus between schooling and rural development is admirable, but it will undoubtedly run into the attitudinal hex that sabotaged the blending of cultures approach and the SSCEP.

There are indications that PNG may be the process of developing a two-tier educational structure that, while making education more accessible, will only entrench the socioeconomic polarization that is already in place. The prestige system will consist of the better urban schools and the national high schools; the mass system will consist of rural and some urban schools offering watered-down programs that instill in graduates the same expectations as their more advantaged counterparts, but without the same outcomes being feasible. Events are unfolding and only time will reveal the outcomes.

REFERENCES

Apelis, E.T. (1980). Anthropology and education in Papua New Guinea. *Papua New Guinea Journal of Education, 16,* 1–11.

Bacchus, M.K. (1984). *A review and analysis of educational "needs" at the secondary level in Papua New Guinea.* Port Moresby: University of Papua New Guinea Education Research Unit Report No. 48.

Bacchus, M.K., Eri, V., & McNamara, V. (1985). *Report on upper secondary education in Papua New Guinea.* Port Moresby: Papua New Guinea Ministry of Education.

Crossley, M. (1984). Education and productive work: A comment on recent additions to the literature. *Papua New Guinea Journal of Education, 20,* 117–127.

Draper, S. (1974). Adult literacy for the Papua New Guinea villager. *Papua New Guinea Journal of Education, 10,* 12–17.

Francis, R. (1978). Paradise lost and regained: Education policy in Melanesia. *Comparative Education, 14,* 49–65.

Groves, W.C. (1936). *Native education and culture-contact in New Guinea.* Melbourne: Melbourne University Press.

Maddock, M.N. (1980). Cultural alienation and attitudes to natural phenomena. *Papua New Guinea Journal of Education, 16,* 19–51.

Matane Report (1986). *A philosophy of education for Papua New Guinea.* Port Moresby: Papua New Guinea Ministry of Education.

Ministry of Education. (1991). *A review of the education system and proposals for reform.* Port Moresby: Papua New Guinea Ministry of Education.

Vlaardingerbroek, B., & Ros, L. (1990). Educational transition rates and upper secondary students' arithmetical ability in 5 developing countries. *Educational Studies in Mathematics, 21,* 451–460.

Vulliamy, G. (1983). Core subject–core project integration in SSCEP: Practice and possibilities. *Papua New Guinea Journal of Education, 19,* 13–34.

Vulliamy, G. (1987). Assessment of the "vocational school fallacy" in Papua New Guinea. *International Journal of Educational Development, 7,* 49.

Zepp. R., Matang, R., & Sapau, M. (1994). Mathematics content knowledge of community school "top-up" teachers. *Papua New Guinea Journal of Teacher Education, 1,* 25–27.